D1201488

INDELIBLE
TRACINGS

INDELIBLE TRACINGS

The Story of the 1961 U.S. World Figure Skating Team

PATRICIA SHELLEY BUSHMAN

STEWART
&GRAY

© 2010 by Patricia Shelley Bushman

All rights reserved. No part of this book may be reproduced in any form without written permission of the copyright owner.

Library of Congress Cataloging-in-Publication Data
Bushman, Patricia Shelley
Indelible Tracings: the story of the 1961 U.S. world figure skating team.
Includes glossary and index.

ISBN 978-0-9846-0270-4 (hardcover)
1. Figure Skating—History   I. Title

2010908977

Stewart & Gray Publishing
Overland Park, Kansas

Visit us at www.1961team.com.

Printed in the United States of America by
The Covington Group, Kansas City, Missouri

Indelible–that which cannot be removed, washed away, or erased; lasting, unforgettable.

———————◦———————

Tracings–something that is traced as (1) a figure eight that is traced; (2) a mark left on the ice when ice dancing or in a freestyle session.

———————◦———————

Indelible Tracings–the legacy of the thirty-four-member 1961 U.S. World Figure Skating Team, "a personal loss which will never be erased from our consciousness."

To R. Gene Shelley,
the ideal skating parent

CONTENTS

FOREWORD

Finally we have the complete story of the 1961 U.S. World Figure Skating Team and the terrible plane crash in Brussels, Belgium, that took them too soon. *Indelible Tracings* describes the coaches, dedicated USFSA officials, family members, and of course the eighteen-member figure skating team who were set to participate in the 1961 World Figure Skating Championships in Prague, Czechoslovakia.

Author Patty Shelley (as I knew her when she was my young student) was a successful competitive figure skater herself. She has used her own experiences and many contacts in the figure skating world to write this fascinating and detailed description of all those impacted by the crash. She brings to life the thirty-four member delegation, whose tragic death left a void in our support.

As she describes the aftermath of this tragedy, we must all be amazed at the rapid resurgence of U.S. Figure Skating. A mere seven years later, 1968 U.S. ladies champion Peggy Fleming won the Olympic gold in Grenoble, France. Ever since, American figure skaters have regularly ascended the podium at World and Olympic competitions. This success resulted partially from the creation of the Memorial Fund, established in honor of the 1961 Team. This book reinforces the importance of the Memorial Fund, for what it has done, and will do, to support U.S. competitive figure skaters.

Those who have a true love for the sport of figure skating will enjoy this book for its detail and accuracy. They will also gain a personal appreciation for the skill, determination, energy, and dedication of this remarkable group of people.

John Nicks

PREFACE

I have known about the tragedy of the 1961 U.S. World Figure Skating Team for what seems like my entire life. I was four years old when it happened. I began skating at age five with the Arctic Blades Figure Skating Club at the Iceland rink in Paramount, California. Five members of our club were on the plane and a beautiful plaque at our rink listed the names of all thirty-four individuals who made up the skating delegation. I saw this plaque practically every day for the next ten years. The names became familiar to me, and I was aware of the famous picture taken by AP photographer Matty Zimmerman, but I knew relatively little about the skaters themselves.

During my skating career I trained at and visited the home rinks of many of the 1961 World Team members. I spent three summers training at the Broadmoor World Arena in Colorado Springs and every day saw the iconic skating memorial bench, which listed the eight names of the Broadmoor team members. In 1971 I won the Pacific Coast Junior Ladies silver medal at the Seattle Civic Center, where three team members had trained. In 1972 I won the Pacific Coast Senior Ladies title at the Berkeley Iceland rink, where five team members had trained. Years later I lived in New England and skated at The Skating Club of Boston, where seven team members had trained.

My interest in the 1961 World Team was fueled by an opportunity I had in 1986 to be involved in an event called "Celebration . . . America on Ice!" The show was held in Indianapolis—the home of three team members. I wrote the narration, which celebrated both the sixty-fifth anniversary of the United States Figure Skating Association (USFSA) and the twenty-fifth anniversary of the 1961 World Team Memorial Fund. For the first time, I saw footage of the 1961 U.S. Championships. Seeing these skaters come to life increased my curiosity.

Sixteen years later, I decided to learn more about the people who were on the plane. My goal was to chronicle and celebrate the lives of each of the thirty-four people in the skating delegation. I combed dozens of libraries across the country and conducted hundreds of interviews to get first-hand remembrances from friends, colleagues, and family members.

This book would never have happened without the generosity of so many people who graciously agreed to be interviewed. Family members, who were key players in telling the story of team members, trusted me with their memories. I express heartfelt gratitude to Susan Richards Abbe,

Christine Davies, Joseph Dineen, Wilhelmina Kipp Gozzard, Lewis Hadley, Gail Hartshorne Haggard, Ruth Scholdan Harle, Lavon Hart, Dan Hartshorne, Daryl Hartshorne, Harold Hartshorne, Tom Hartshorne, Hank Hickox, Nancy Hickox Hileick, Dorinda LeMaire Howard, Stephen Kelley, Ruth Ann Kipp, Bruce Lord, Frank Muckian, Wayne ("Mike") Michelson, Sheryl Ryan Nolan, Joan Sherbloom Peterson, Russ Pierce, Cathy Ramsay, Diane Yeomans Robins, Richard Rosborough, Roberta Jenks Scholdan, Diana LeMaire Squibb, Cathy Stevenson, James Stropp, Bill Swallender, Erik Swallender, Rose Anne Ryan Wager, Otto Westerfeld Jr., and Dixie Lee Burns Wilson.

I appreciate members of the 1961 Canadian World Team and their coaches, and other American and international skaters who were eyewitnesses at that year's North American and World Championships, and helped recreate a timeline of events. Thanks to Wendy Griner Ballantyne, Bradley Black, Virginia Thompson Brookshill, Peter Burrows, Geraldine Fenton Crispo, Doreen Denny-Routon, Karol Divin, Christa Von Kuczkowski Fassi, Bruce Hyland, Donald Jackson, Maria Jelinek, Karen Howland Jones, Shirra Kenworthy, Maurice Lafrance, Frances Gold Lind, Bill McLachlan, Marie Vichova Millikan, J.D. Mitchell, Ken Ormsby, Paulette Doan Ormsby, Bob Pearce, Marie Pearce, Gerty Desjardins Verbiwski, Ron Vincent, Jean Westwood, Debbi Wilkes, and Donna Lee Mitchell Zaleski.

The community of skaters could not have been more supportive. They shared stories and provided names of friends to call. It was pure joy to reminisce with them and hear their touching, funny, and loving accounts. I extend a big thank you to Linda Charbonneau Agneta, Fran Haigler Ainsworth, Scott Ethan Allen, Tommy Weinreich Allen, Aileen Kahre Arenson, Sidney Foster Arnold, Walter ("Red") Bainbridge, Donna Abbott Baldwin, Claralynn Lewis Barnes, Ann Seror Barr, Julie Marcus Barrett, Don Bartleson, Skippy Baxter, Carole MacSween Beazer, J.J. Bejshak, Roger Berry, Peter Betts, E. Newbold Black IV, Roy Blakey, Marianne Beeler Bourke, Lucy Joyce Curley Brennan, Harold Brown, Janet Harley Browning, Jim Browning, Ann Pellegrino Bullock, Joyce Burden, Frances Dorsey Burke, Joan Brader Burns, Elizabeth George Busconi, Mary Lou Butler-Mitchell, Dick Button, Slavka Kohout Button, Phil Cagnoni, Richard Callaghan, Jeanne O'Brien Callahan, Marshall Campbell, Janet Gerhauser Carpenter, Frank Carroll, Kathy Casey, Margie Jurmo Caton, Joan Tozzer Cave, Billy Chapel, Raymond Chenson, Fred Chescheir, Arvilla Kauffman Christensen, Myrna Bodek Clancey, Gary Clark, Mary Clarke, Ted Clarke, Roy Cofer, Roger Collard, Lorraine Hanlon Comanor, Sherry Dorsey Cook, Howard Deardorff, Bob Deuter, Vonie Marsh Dondero, Peter Dunfield, Sonya

Klopfer Dunfield, Richard Dwyer, Julie Graham Eavzan, Joanne Scotvold Emanuelson, Sarasue Gleis Essenprice, Brenda Farmer Farkas, Patti Gustafson Feeney, Charles Fetter, Chuck Foster, Jerry Fotheringill, Karl Freed, Ann-Margreth Frei-Hall, Judianne Fotheringill Fuller, Dr. Jessica Gaynor, Allana Mittun Genchel, Anne Gram Gerli, Leslie Gianelli, Darlene Streich Gilbert, Ronna Goldblatt Gladstone, Lee Carroll Galloway Goldrod, Sandy Carson Gollihugh, Beth Sundene Graham, Hugh C. Graham Jr., Nancy Rouillard Ludington Graham, Heather Rae Brown Grant, Catherine Machado Gray, Robin Greiner, Carolyn Welch Grimditch, Joan Heiser Gruber, Marilyn Grace Guilfoyle, Wanda Guntert, Jennie Walsh Guzman, Dottie Otto Halama, Ardith Paul Hamilton, Pat Firth Hansen, Charlene Sharlock Hasha, Bruce Heiss, Barbara Drake Holland, Marigold Crowley Holland, Austin Holt, Margaret Ann Graham Holt, Eileen Seigh Honnen, Margaret Hosford, Greg Hoyt, Wes Hoyt, Walter Hypes, Carol Heiss Jenkins, David Jenkins, Hayes Alan Jenkins, Peggy Fleming Jenkins, Margie Ackles Jones, Nancy Heiss Jones, Ron Joseph, Ron Kauffman, Andra McLaughlin Kelly, Peter Kennedy, Barbara Babcock Kirby, Iain Kite, Sally Haas Knoll, Virginia Bucher Kocher, Pieter Kollen, Joyce Komperda, Sondra Holmes Kovacovsky, Christy Haigler Krall, Evelyn Mueller Kramer, Ann Kamsley Kurtz, Sandy Schwomeyer Lamb, Linda Landin, Don Laws, Sundae Bafo Lebel, Nancy Madden Leamy, Micki Asher Leiter, Lynda Waldrop Lineberry, Tommy Litz, Ron Ludington, Irma Staro Magee, Bill Martin, Darrell Mathias, Helen Davidson Maxson, Debbie Might, Pam Milligan McDonald, Michael McGean, Tom McGinnis, Ramona Allen McIntyre, Joanne Funakoshi McLaren, Bonnie Patterson McLauthlin, Nancy Meiss, Anne Batdorf Militano, David Mitchell, Michelle Monnier, Irene Maguire Muehlbronner, Skip Mullins, Bob Munz, Miggs Dean Neenan, Dorothyann Nelson, Franklin Nelson, Christy Kjarsgard Ness, Ginny Baxter Newman, John Nicks, Helen Geekie Nightingale, John Nightingale, Lorin Caccamise O'Neil, Andree Anderson Jacoby Oseid, Ralph David Owen, Mike Paikin, Bobbie Parkinson, Bob Paul, Norvetta Tribby Pinch, Valerie Powell, Micaelia Randolph, Maxine Ceramin Rayner, Louella Rehfield, Kay Servatius Ringsred, Mary Miller Robicheaux, Evelyn Robson, Norma Sahlin, Rickie Rendich Samuels, Louise Samson, Donna Merrill Schoon, Evy Scotvold, Mary Batdorf Scotvold, Jan Serafine, Kristin Mittun Sharp, Coco Gram Shean, Eddie Shipstad, Jim Short, Sam Singer, Judy Schwomeyer Sladky, Carol Deuter Smith, Marjorie Parker Smith, Pat Creed Smith, Aja Zanova Steindler, Jimmy Stephens, Morry Stillwell, Sheila Muldowny Stone, Louis Stong, Jane Vaughn Sullivan, Dennis Sveum, Robert Swenning, Charlene Cruikshank Tagas,

Bette Todd, Bob Turk, Gene Turner, Yvonne Sherman Tutt, Ann Udell, Sally Schantz Urban, Stan Urban, Virginia Vale, Marlene Morris Van Dusen, Ben Wade, Barbara Wagner, Marcella May Willis Walker, Cindy Cheschier Walsh, Polly Blodgett Watson, Cynthia Hansen White, Bill Wilkins, Barbara Roles Williams, Joyce Underwood Winship, Carole Carlson Wolfswinkel, Tim Wood, Benjamin T. Wright, George Yonekura, Mary Ellen Young, Pat Farrell Zeiser, and Pam Zekman.

Non-skating friends also shared important insights, including Roberto Agnolini, Helena Bushman, Karl Bushman, Patty Williams Canary, Marshall Gage, Rose Hammond, Dave Harrower, Fred Heller, John Keith, Senator Edward M. Kennedy, Jason Lanning, Francis Lombardi, Julie Palmer Mayo, Dick Mills, Rodger Nordblom, Sean Overton, David Pinkham, Val Rodriguez, Kathryn Teague Schaub, and Judy Marienthal Wilson.

I would also like to thank individuals who were instrumental in providing contacts for me, including Ted Barton, Marjorie Birdsell, Judy Blumberg, Harland Burge, Tommy Collins, Dorothy Dotson, Jo Jo Starbuck Gertler, Joyce Hisey, Patty Tiffany Keller, Susan Keough, Marie Kingdon, Carolyn Kruse, Greg Mokler, Wynn Nordblom, Diane Parrish, Leslie Persali, Betsy Pickin, Donna Rosenstein, Ken Shelley, Barb Stott, Donn Walker, Audrey Wallace, and Don Watson.

Besides being interviewed, a number of individuals provided pictures or other archival information: Dudley Abbe, Richmond S. Abbe, Christie Allan-Piper, Joanne Heckert Bachtel, Patti Ballenti, Theda Beck Bartynski, Vicky Fisher Binner, Bradley Black, Bill Boeck, Robert Brewer, Joyce Butchart, Eleanor Banneck Curtis, Joanna Niska Delaney, Marilyn Meeker Durham, Carol Ann Peters Duncan, Lorna Dyer, Connie Espander, Jean Frazier Fahmie, Anne Frazier, Linda Adams Garl, Paul George, Wilhelmina Kipp Gozzard, Diana Lapp Green, Gretchen Gross, Lewis Hadley, Ruth Scholdan Harle, Lawrence Hart, Hank Hickox, Carole Harrison, Dan Hartshorne, Harry Hartshorne, Bradley Hislop, Dorinda LeMaire Howard, Jane Bucher Jones, Stephen Kelley, Bill King, Ruth Ann Kipp, Debbie Ganson Lane, Gerry Lane, Josephine Lawless, Terri Levine, Bruce and Johanne Lord, Mary Jo Turner Lloyd, Aloise Samson Lurtsema, Pam Thatcher Marsh, Cindy Kauffman Marshall, Bob McIntyre, Janet Roberts McLeod, Liz Herman McLouglin, Linda Michelson, Debbie Might, Anita Entrikin Miller, Nancy Moehring, Virginia Mount, Barlow Nelson, Yvonne Littlefield Nicks, Sharon McKenzie Nix, Kristy Panos, Joan Sherbloom Peterson, Ron Pfenning, David Pinkham, Glenda Rhodes Pugh, Sue Blodgett Rigney, Charlie Rizzo, Diane Yeomans Robins, Anita Andres Rogerson, Richard Rosborough, Ardelle Kloss Sanderson, Rich Sandvick, Ken

Shelley, Shirley Reflow Sherman, Marjorie Parker Smith, Diana LeMaire Squibb, Sylvia Clay Stoddard, Bill and Mary Swallender, Howard Taylor, Kim Troy, Sally Wells Van De Mark, Gary Visconti, Ben Wade, Dixie Lee Burns Wilson, the staff at the Professional Skaters Association, and the staff at the World Figure Skating Museum and Hall of Fame.

I am grateful for assistance from devoted librarians across the country, whether by mail, phone call, or in person, who were helpful in the retrieval of archival material, including those at the Allentown Public Library, Berkeley Public Library, Boston Public Library, Bridgeport Public Library, Harold B. Lee Library at Brigham Young University, Cleveland Public Library, Colorado College Library, Denver Public Library, Detroit Public Library, Downey Public Library, Eugene Public Library, Hartford Public Library, Indianapolis Public Library, Johnson County Community College Library, Johnson County Public Library, Lake Placid Library, Long Beach Public Library, Los Angeles Public Library, Michigan State University Library, Minneapolis Public Library, New York Public Library, Oakland Public Library, Ottawa Public Library, Pasadena Public Library, Pittsburgh Public Library, Powell Symphony Hall, Rye Public Library, Salem Public Library, Salt Lake City Public Library, San Francisco Public Library, Seattle Public Library, St. Louis Public Library, and the Miller Nichols Library at the University of Missouri-Kansas City.

I would like to thank the staffs of various schools and educational institutions who were helpful in providing information: the Air Force Academy, Allentown High School, Ashland High School, Banning High School, Berkeley High School, Boston Latin High School, Broad Ripple High School, Cathedral High School, Cheyenne Mountain High School, Fairfield Preparatory School, Hamilton High School, Ingraham High School, Narbonne High School, the National Museum of Roller Skating, Providence Day School, Redford High School, Roosevelt High School, Rye Country Day School, Swampscott High School, Trinity School, Troy High School, Winchester High School, and Xavier High School.

I found it important to visit, when possible, the resting sites of the victims of Flight 548, and I appreciated the kindness of the staff of the following institutions: Beechwood Cemetery, Calvary Cemetery, Cedar Hill Memorial Park, Evergreen Cemetery, Forest Lawn Cemetery, Green Hills Cemetery, Green-Wood Cemetery, Greenwood Union Cemetery, Holy Cross Cemetery, Mount Auburn Cemetery, Rest Haven Funeral, St. Joseph's Cemetery, Sunset Cemetery, Sunset View and Mortuary, Swampscott Cemetery, Swan Point Cemetery, Washington Park East Cemetery, and White Chapel Cemetery.

I would like to thank David Raith, Executive Director of U. S. Figure Skating, for his enthusiasm and support. The staff of the World Figure Skating Museum and Hall of Fame in Colorado Springs, particularly Karen Cover, was gracious in welcoming me on many occasions; its archival material on the 1961 World Team was essential in telling this story. I am grateful to Theresa Weld Blanchard, the founder and first editor of *Skating* magazine. The pages of *Skating* were an invaluable resource and provided many details I could not have found elsewhere. I am equally indebted to the variety of newspaper accounts from the fifties and early sixties, and express personal thanks to reporters who also wrote about the 1961 World Team in the last fifty years.

A sincere thank you to my production team, editor Lavina Fielding Anderson, cover designer Monika Fassi Stout, and Mark McCombs of the Covington Group, who elevated this work with their extraordinary talent.

I appreciate my extended family, whose emotional support was crucial. The writing expertise of my in-laws was a blessing. Claudia Bushman, who accepted the herculean role of first-round editing, will forever be my hero. Richard Bushman's enduring faith that I could accomplish the task at hand was inspiring. My mother, Theora Shelley, was a wonderful listening ear and supported me in a variety of ways, and I have felt the loving spirit of my father, Gene Shelley, throughout this experience. I thank my children, Peter and Shelley, for their patience.

This project would never have lifted off the ground without the help and encouragement of my brother Ken Shelley. From day one he provided names and telephone numbers when requested and was an enthusiastic supporter. My final thank you is to my husband, Serge Bushman. His editing skills and acumen have helped shaped this book in ways I could not have achieved on my own. It has been a wonderful gift to have the complete and absolute support from every member of my family.

Fifty years ago, when I stared at this list of names on the wall at the Iceland rink in Paramount, I had an overwhelming sense that these people were special. At the time I did not know why I felt that way. Now I do. I have come to admire each individual, and they have positively affected my own outlook. I am pleased to share with you, so you may discover for yourselves, the remarkable lives of the 1961 U.S. World Figure Skating Team.

Patricia Shelley Bushman
Overland Park, Kansas

GLOSSARY

While many of the following terms still exist in modern-day figure skating, these definitions are tailored to the time period covered in the book (1920–60s).

Axel jump	Named after its inventor, Norwegian skater Axel Paulsen, the axel takes off from the forward outside edge and is landed on the back outside edge of the opposite foot. A single axel is 1½ revolutions and a double is 2½ revolutions.
Camel spin	A spin on one leg with the free leg extended in a position parallel to the ice. The body remains in this "spiral" position while spinning.
Central Pacific	One of nine regional competitions. The top three competitors in each division advance to the Pacific Coast sectional competition.
Charlotte	Named for German skater Charlotte Oelschlagel who performed the move in the early 1900s. It is performed either forward or backward. The skater bends forward and glides on one leg with the other leg lifted into the air. The skater's head is as close to the grounded foot as possible; the skater's legs are almost in a straight vertical split position.
Combination spin	In this spin, the skater changes feet and positions while maintaining speed throughout the entire spin.
Compulsory dance	The compulsory dance is the first segment of the ice dance competition. The chosen dances have prescribed rhythms and specific steps that must be done in an exact manner with exact placement on the ice. All skaters perform the same compulsory dances in an event.

Competitive season   The competitive season (November–April) begins in the late fall with the regional competition, followed by the sectional competition, the U.S. Championships, and the World Championships. Prior to 1959, the World Championships were held before the U.S. Championships. The year of the regional competition, even though held in the fall, reflects the year in which the U.S. Championships are held (between January and April).

Crossovers   A method of gaining speed and turning corners in which skaters cross one foot over the other. Crossovers can be done either forward or backward.

Double jump   Any jump of two or more (but fewer than three) revolutions.

Easterns   One of three annual sectional competitions. The top three competitors in each division from three regionals—New England, North Atlantic and South Atlantic—advance to the Eastern competition. The top three competitors in each division at Easterns advance to the U.S. Championships.

Eastern Great Lakes   One of nine annual regional competitions. The top three competitors in each division advance to the Midwestern competition.

Edges   The two sides of the skate blade on either side of the grooved center. The inside edge is the edge on the inner side of the leg, while the outside edge is the edge on the outer side of the leg. Each edge is subdivided further to a forward and backward edge, equaling a total of eight different edges.

Figures   Also known as school figures or compulsory figures, there are nine levels of figure testing: preliminary and first through eighth. There are a number of required figure patterns, done on curves that must be perfected for each test. Types of figures include: eights, serpentines, threes, double threes, brackets, loops, counters, and rockers.

Flip jump	A toe-pick-assisted jump that is launched from the back inside edge of one foot. The skater lands on the back outside edge of the opposite foot.
Flying sit spin	In this spin, the skater leaps upwards, bends the entry leg while extending the free leg forward in a sitting position at the height of the jump, and lands in a sitting position.
Free dance	The free dance is relatively unrestricted, and skaters select the mood and tempo as long as they are danceable. Ice dancers are encouraged to display a full range of technical skills, interpretation and inventiveness. It is preceded by the compulsory dances.
Free skating	The free skate is the final part of singles and pairs competition. Skaters select their music and create their choreography to best display their technical and artistic skills. The free skate is limited to four minutes for ladies and five minutes for men and pairs.
Freestyle	Used to describe free skating sessions or the program performed in competition, the terms "freestyle" and "free skating" are used interchangeably by most skaters.
Gold dance	A skater has to pass at least part of the gold dance tests to compete at this level. Gold dance is the highest level of dance competition at the annual U.S. Championships. This event has had a variety of names over the years. For clarity, the term "gold dance" has been used throughout the book.
Gold figure medalist	When a skater passes the eighth figure test and freestyle test, he or she has become a U.S. gold medalist in figure skating.
Gold dance medalist	When an ice dancer passes all of the gold dance tests and the gold free dance test, he or she has become a U.S. gold dance medalist in figure skating.

Gold pairs medalist   When pair teams have passed their gold pairs test, they have become a U.S. gold pairs medalist in figure skating. Pairs tests came into vogue in the late fifties.

Guards   Skate guards are protective covers, usually made of rubber or plastic that protect ice skate blades off the ice.

Judges   The process to become a judge begins with trial judging tests and competitions. A judges' panel reviews the history of the trial judges' marks; the first appointment is low test. Judges work toward reaching successive levels. Judges are not paid, but their food, lodging, and transportation are covered by each test or competition committee.

Jump combination   The skater combines several jumps in a sequence; the landing edge of one jump serves as the take-off edge of the next jump.

Ice carnivals   Skating clubs put on shows to raise money for their club and to provide performance opportunities for their skaters. These shows were called ice carnivals.

Ina Bauer   Created by German champion Ina Bauer, this move is a variation of a spread eagle. The leading leg is bent and positioned in front of the plane of the torso, and the trailing leg is held straight and positioned behind the plane of the body. The torso may be erect but usually the back arches and the arms achieve a graceful pose.

Layback spin   In this spin, generally performed by women, the skater arches her back and shoulders facing up toward the ceiling while spinning; the arms are usually held in a circle above her body.

Loop jump   The skater launches this jump from a back outside edge and lands on the same back outside edge.

Lutz jump	A toe-pick-assisted jump takes off from a back outside edge and lands on the back outside edge of the opposite foot. The skater glides backward on a wide curve, taps his toe pick into the ice, and rotates in the opposite direction of the curve. The jump is named after its inventor, Alois Lutz of Austria.
Middle Atlantic	One of nine annual regional competitions. The top three competitors in each division advance to the Eastern sectional competition. Middle Atlantics was later renamed South Atlantics.
Midwesterns	One of three annual sectional competitions. The top three competitors from three regional competitions— Southwesterns, Eastern Great Lakes, and Upper Great Lakes—advance to the Midwestern competition. The top three competitors in each division at Midwesterns advance to the U.S. Nationals.
New England	This competition is one of nine annual regional meets. The top three competitors in each division advance to the Eastern sectional competition.
North Atlantic	This competition is one of nine annual regional competitions. The top three competitors in each division advance to the Eastern section competition.
Northwest Pacific	This competition is one of nine annual regional competitions. The top three competitors in each division advance to the Pacific Coast sectional competition.
Ordinal	A skater's total ordinals in competition are the sum of the judges' placements for each skater.
Pair lifts	Pair moves in which the man lifts his partner above his head with arm(s) fully extended. Lifts consist of precise ascending, rotational and descending movements.
Pacific Coast	One of three annual sectional competitions. The top three competitors in each division from three regionals—Southwest Pacific, Central Pacific, and

Northwest Pacific—advance to the Pacific Coast competition. The top three competitors in each division at Pacific Coast advance to the U.S. Nationals.

Patch

An individually reserved area of ice dedicated to practicing figure eights; patch sessions generally run forty-five minutes to an hour.

Regionals

The first of two qualifying competitions en route to the U.S. Championships. Skaters must place in the top three of their division to advance to the sectionals.

Referee

This official at a competition has full authority over all aspects of the event and is the chair of the panel of judges. The referee's responsibility includes ensuring that all rules are observed, that a high standard of judging is maintained, and that all technical aspects of the competition are satisfactory.

Salchow jump

Created by Swedish skater Ulrich Salchow, this jump is launched off the back inside edge of one foot and lands on the back outside edge of the opposite foot.

Scratch spin

An upright spin where the free leg is crossed over the skating knee and then pushed down towards the ice, as the arms are pulled in toward the chest.

Sectionals

Sectionals are the second and final qualifying competition en route to the U.S. Championships. Skaters must place in the top three of their division to advance to the U.S. Championships.

Silver dance

Dancers compete in the silver dance division if they have passed their pre-silver dance tests.

Single jump

A single is any jump of one or more (but fewer than two) revolutions.

Sit spin

This spin is performed in a sitting position, close to the ice and with the skating, or spinning leg, bent at the knee and the non-skating, or free leg, extended.

Southwest Pacific	One of nine annual regional competitions. The top three competitors in each division advance to the Pacific Coast sectional competition.
Southwesterns	One of nine annual regional competitions. The top three competitors in each division advance to the Midwestern sectional competition.
Spins	Skaters rotate on their vertical axes while maintaining contact with the ice with one or both skates.
Spiral	During a long glide across the ice, the skater extends the non-skating leg into the air behind him or her.
Spread eagle	A skater glides on both feet, toes turned out to the sides, heels facing each other; the legs completely straight and spread apart. It is performed on either the outside or inside edges.
Step sequence	This term refers to a sequence of steps that immediately follow one another, executed in time to the music and choreographically related to each other.
Stroking	Fluid movement used to gain speed in which a skater pushes off back and forth from the inside edge of one skate to the inside edge of the other skate.
Tank show	Tanks are small portable ice rinks, primarily used in hotel cabarets. Larger tanks were used in arenas that did not have their own ice surface, greatly expanding the number of venues where ice shows could operate.
Three turn	The skater turns on one foot from either forward to backward, or backward to forward. The ice skate blade makes the pattern of a "3" on the ice. Three turns are done from either an outside edge to an inside edge, or an inside edge to an outside edge.
Toe loop	This is a toe-pick-assisted jump that takes off and lands on the same back outside edge.

Toe pick	A toe pick is the set of teeth at the front of the blade used primarily for jumping and spinning.
Traveling threes	Also called "flying threes," a succession of forward and backward three-turns, down the ice, in a spiral position.
Triple jump	A triple is any jump of three or more (but fewer than four) revolutions.
Upper Great Lakes	One of nine annual regional competitions. The top three competitors in each division advance to the Midwestern sectional competition.
U.S. novice division	Skaters competed in novice men or ladies if they had passed their fourth figure test.
U.S. junior division	Skaters competed in the junior men or ladies if they had passed their sixth figure and freestyle test.
U.S. senior division	Skaters competed in the senior men or ladies if they had passed their eighth figure and freestyle test, and had placed in the top three in the national junior division in previous years.
Walley jump	In this jump, named after American skater Nate Walley, the skater jumps off the backward inside edge, makes one full rotation in the air, and lands on the backward outside edge of the same foot. The takeoff and landing are on the same foot, generally the right foot in a counterclockwise rotation.
Waltz jump	Skaters launch into the air from their forward outside edge and complete a half rotation, landing on a back outside edge on the opposite foot.

SOURCES

1. JoAnn Schneider Farris, www.figureskating.about.com/od/glossaryofskatingterms/Glossary_of_Skating_Terms.htm.

2. "Figure Skating Journal: Glossary," www.skatejournal.com/turnglide.htlml.

3. "Glossary of Terms," www.usfa.org/About.asp?id=60.

4. F. F. Hamilton Jr., *Ice Capades: Years of Entertainment* (Washington, D.C.: Penchant Publishing Company, Ltd., 1974).

THE DARKEST DAY

"It affected all of us for years. It still affects us. The worst thing that could happen, happened."[1]

February 15, 1961, was the darkest day in the history of figure skating. Americans remember where they were when President Kennedy was shot on November 22, 1963, or how they heard about the events of September 11, 2001. Similarly, members of the skating community remember where they were and how they heard about the events of February 15, 1961. Morry Stillwell, Pieter Kollen, and Barlow Nelson are just three of thousands of Americans who were numbed by the incomprehensible news about their beloved friends.

In 1995 Morry Stillwell became president of the United States Figure Skating Association (USFSA). Roller skating was his first love, but he and his wife, Elda, gravitated to figure skating in the early 1950s in Seattle, Washington. After moving to Southern California, they joined the Los Angeles Figure Skating Club and became officers and judges. The Stillwells found friendship and camaraderie with California skaters who were belatedly gaining national recognition. Morry was thrilled when four Southern California-based skaters medaled at the 1961 U.S. Figure Skating Championships and made the 1961 U.S. World Team. On the morning of February 15, 1961, Morry was headed to work, driving down Robertson Boulevard in Culver City, when he heard the radio news bulletin. The next thing Morry knew, he and his Porsche were across the street, against the curb, going the wrong way.[2]

Pieter Kollen did not plan to be a figure skater. As a young hockey player, he was conned into an ice show by the moms of the local figure skating club, who told him and his friends that they could wear official University of Michigan jerseys if they appeared in a hockey-themed number in the ice show. After realizing he loved to jump on ice, he traded his hockey skates for figure skates and began competing. After he and his partner, Dorothy-ann Nelson, placed second in junior pairs and third in silver dance at the 1961 U.S. Championships, they performed in several shows along the Eastern seaboard. Instead of flying home between shows, they cashed in their tickets and caught a train to Philadelphia to see friends compete at the North American Championships. Sleeping on hotel room floors, hanging out together, and cheering them on, they stayed for two days. On Monday, February 13, they said good-bye to their friends and headed to Lake Placid for another show. Two days later, Pieter awoke to urgent pounding on his hotel door at Lake Placid, accompanied by frantic screaming. Dorothyann was crying hysterically. Members of the British bobsled team had just told her some dreadful news. Pieter could not absorb the information. With heavy hearts, they performed in the show twelve hours later in honor of their fallen friends.[3]

Barlow Nelson discovered figure skating as a boy in Tulsa, trained as a competitor in Colorado Springs, and later trained in Boston while attending Dartmouth. After graduation, he joined the U.S. Navy and was assigned temporary duty at the Boston Naval Shipyard. Under normal circumstances, his competitive days would have ended, but his coach, Maribel Vinson Owen, personally knew Richard Jackson, the Assistant Secretary of the Navy. She arranged for Barlow to continue training for the 1960 U.S. Championships in Seattle. He then shipped out to sea and missed the 1961 U.S. Championships—his first absence in nine years. He kept track of the competition as an officer aboard the *U.S.S. Wrangell*. On February 15, in the middle of the Mediterranean, Barlow was a navigator on mid-watch when a radioman emerged from the radio shack and asked, "Mr. Nelson, weren't you involved in figure skating?" "Yes," Barlow replied. The radioman hesitated before handing him a transmitted teletype. "I thought you might like to see this." Barlow stared in disbelief at the message. The long list contained names of many close friends. Calling another officer to relieve him, Barlow went below to digest the devastating news. The plane carrying the U.S. World Figure Skating Team en route to the 1961 World Championships had just crashed.[4]

The newly formed team barely had time to catch their breath before departing for the 1961 World Figure Skating Championships in Prague, Czechoslovakia. On February 11 and 12, the team had competed for two solid days in Philadelphia at the North American Championships, a biennial event between Americans and Canadians. At the Sunday night party following the competition, various team members made last-minute pleas to colleagues to join them on their journey. The number of coaches, officials, and family members joining the delegation continued to balloon and shrink over the next forty-eight hours.[5]

On Tuesday afternoon, February 14, the eighteen-member team boarded a bus bound for New York City for the flight to Prague. The youthful group—eleven were teenagers—was giddy with excitement. The team was delighted to discover one of its own, Laurence Owen, on the cover of *Sports Illustrated* at the airport newsstand. An Associated Press photographer was on hand to take a picture of the team, arranged on the steps leading up into the plane. Normally the skaters traveled in small groups to the world competition; however, this was the first trip abroad for the majority of the team, and they wanted to travel together. There was another more compelling reason to stay together: At the height of the Cold War, the event was taking place behind the Iron Curtain.[6]

The team boarded Sabena Airlines Flight 548 for Prague, with one scheduled stop in Brussels, Belgium. The skating entourage consisted of eighteen skaters, six coaches, four judges and officials, and six family members. Including the crew, there were seventy-two individuals on board. The flight left on schedule at 8:30 P.M.[7]

Shortly before 10 A.M. Belgian time, the Sabena jet approached the runway at the Brussels airport. The traffic on the runway prevented the plane from landing. The pilot, a British Royal Air Force World War II veteran, retracted the wheels, and the plane lifted up again to make another attempt. The plane climbed to about 1,500 feet while banking to the left. The plane had difficulty coming out of the left turn, making three 360-degree circles around the runway.[8]

The control tower tried to contact the crew repeatedly. With no response from Flight 548, officials dispatched dozens of emergency vehicles. The American-made Boeing 707 was three miles north of the airport when something went horribly wrong. From a cloudless, blue sky, the plane plunged to the ground and burst into flames near the villages of Berg-Kampenhout. There were no survivors. The dead included sixty-one passengers, a crew of eleven, and a farmer working in the field where the plane fell. Of the forty-nine American passengers, thirty-four constituted the U. S. skating delegation.[9]

The news of the catastrophe spread quickly, hitting the front pages of almost every newspaper in the United States and abroad. Newly inaugurated U.S. President John F. Kennedy, in office for only three weeks, faced the first national tragedy of his administration. Telegrams from around the world flooded into the Boston office of the USFSA, as the world mourned the tragic deaths. The grief was particularly acute for the tight-knit figure skating community.[10]

In that era, competitive figure skaters resembled an extended family. They not only competed against one another but often trained side by side. There were a little more than a hundred rinks scattered around the country; and many of those rinks, especially on the East Coast and in the Midwest, shut down during the summer. Skaters gathered at summer skating centers, lived together in dorms, and became life-long friends. When the plane went down, most skaters across the country intimately knew some of the victims. Fifty years later, men and women still broke down as they remembered their terrible loss.

Added to the anguish of losing so many friends was the lack of information on the cause of the accident. Amid the despair and disbelief, questions flooded in after the fatal crash. Family members, skating enthusiasts, and even U.S. Congressmen wanted to know why the team flew together, and why they did not fly on an American airline. Sabena and Boeing executives were besieged with demands for explanations. The U.S. government ordered the FBI to investigate the possibility of foul play. Decades after this tragic episode, no concrete explanation has been given for the crash, causing additional sorrow and frustration.[11]

The USFSA, overwhelmed with the loss of so many talented skaters, wondered how the sport could ever recover. The rising generation of skaters was gone and, with them, many of the top-rated coaches. The USFSA needed to simultaneously continue its mission and find ways to remember this fallen generation.[12]

It had already taken the United States forty years to reach the top echelon of world figure skating, but then it was on a phenomenal roll, winning both the men's and ladies' Olympic titles in 1956 and 1960. Unlike many award-winning, modern-day skaters, the champions of previous generations retired after Olympic victories to allow the younger generation to take their place. That was true of the 1961 World Team. With the retirement of the skating elite, the next generation had trained relentlessly during the summer and fall of 1960, preparing for the 1961 U.S. Championships—the first formal step on the long, four-year road to the Olympics. There was every reason to believe that the United States would continue its domination at the 1964 Olympic Winter Games in Innsbruck, Austria.

The makeup of this new generation was a dramatic change from the years before and immediately after World War II. Competitive figure skating was no longer a sport primarily for the well-to-do. Skaters from all walks of life and socio-economic backgrounds were well represented on the 1961 World Team. It also meant that the parents of many team members made many financial sacrifices for their children to excel.

Although U.S. figure skating had brought home six Olympic gold medals by 1960, the sport was still relatively unknown to the American public. Financial resources were few and far between for elite skaters, and now that the nation's best had perished in a few unbelievable moments, it seemed impossible to recruit the new talent needed for Olympic competition just three short years ahead. Most people felt it couldn't be done. Eight to ten years was the conservative estimate before the sport could achieve international success again.

To comprehend the magnitude of the loss suffered in 1961 requires an understanding of why it took so long for the sport to evolve internationally; how American figure skaters successfully came to the forefront in the late forties; how the American skating community developed into a close-knit family; how skaters, coaches, and officials banded together in 1961 to rebuild skating in the aftermath of the crash, and why the devastating effect of the February 15 tragedy still reverberates today. The 1961 crash also facilitated the breaking down of long-held prejudices in the sport and, through the newly created Memorial Fund, allowed subsequent generations opportunities for financial support. Skaters over the last fifty years owe a huge debt of gratitude to the 1961 World Team.

To definitively tell the story of this pivotal moment in figure skating history is to discover and encounter the lives of the thirty-four members of the 1961 U.S. World Team delegation—whose talent, dedication, humanity, passion, and zest for life were readily apparent to family, friends, and the skating community. In many ways, the skaters led parallel lives, as did the coaches: hard-working kids who passed tests and usually rose up the podium quickly, and coaches who taught not only jumps, spins, and figure-eights, but life lessons to thousands of youngsters. Despite some similarities, each skater had to overcome personal challenges to represent his or her country at the 1961 World Championships in Prague. The skaters, coaches, officials, and family members, who hailed from cities across the nation, all had compelling reasons to fill a seat on Sabena Flight 548. The eldest was eighty-one; the youngest was eleven. Each has a story to tell.

CHAPTER 1

MARIBEL VINSON OWEN AND THE BIRTH OF U.S. FIGURE SKATING

At the 1953 California State Championships in Berkeley, California, coach Maribel Vinson Owen, displeased with the results of the competition, lost her temper, picked up several folding chairs at the Iceland arena, and hurled them across the coffee shop. Some patrons were aghast, while others didn't bat an eye—it was just Maribel being Maribel. Whether people admired her avant-garde skating style or were stunned by her blunt language and over-the-top personality, no one could deny Maribel Vinson Owen's love for skating. She was a great leader and worked tirelessly to advance the sport for several decades.[1]

Figure skating began in Europe—the first known skating club was established in Edinburgh in 1750—but the skating craze did not take off in America until Central Park opened in New York City in 1860; thousands packed its frozen ponds for daily skating. In Philadelphia, gentlemen who enjoyed skating on frozen lakes founded the first U.S. figure skating club, the Philadelphia Skating Club and Humane Society (PSC & HS), in 1861. The "Humane Society" attachment seems odd, but skating on ponds, rivers, and lakes entailed many risks. Club members carried a reel of stout twine which could be thrown to a hapless skater who had broken through ice. Other clubs opened in the East, including the Cambridge Skating Club in 1898, and the New Haven Skating Club and The Skating Club of Boston in 1912. New England became the center for American skating.[2]

As skaters banded together to form skating clubs, competitions developed in the USA and abroad. The first World Figure Skating Championships were held in St. Petersburg, Russia, in 1896. For the first thirty-five years, all World Championships (also called "Worlds") took place in Europe, and European skaters dominated. The initial event was men's singles; but Madge Syers of Great Britain entered the 1902 Worlds in London and placed second, forcing the International Skating Union (ISU) to rule that only men could compete in the world competition. The ladies' division was introduced four years later at the 1906 World Championships in Davos, Switzerland. Transportation limitations often prevented Americans from participating in these international meets. Instead, championships in the United States at the turn-of-the-century were informal and regionally based.[3]

The story of figure skating in America coincides with the story of the century-old Vinson figure skating clan, from the time of the Civil War through the early 1960s. Sumner Willard Vinson, himself an excellent skater, taught his four-year-old son, Tom Melville Vinson, to skate on the ponds of Roxbury, Massachusetts, in the 1870s. In 1893, Tom graduated from Boston University Law School and was the runner-up in the Championships of America, where American and Canadian skaters competed. Tom met his wife through skating. Gertrude Cliff, born in 1879, graduated from Radcliffe College magna cum laude in 1902. She first noticed him doing all sorts of tricks as she skated up the Charles River; later they were introduced at the Cambridge Skating Club.[4]

When Tom and Gertrude married, they settled in Winchester, a charming town twenty miles northwest of Boston. In 1911 Tom won his last skating competition, and Gertrude gave birth to their only child, Maribel Yerxa Vinson, on October 12, 1911. The Cambridge Skating Club made Maribel an honorary member at birth. She began to skate at age three on double-runner skates. Her parents taught her basic skating on Jamaica Pond in Winchester.[5]

Even before taking formal lessons, Maribel was goal oriented. "When she was just a little girl she told me she was going to be a champion," Mrs. Vinson said. "She worked and she drove herself." At age nine she began lessons with Willie Frick at the Boston Arena. Willie Frick, from Berlin, Germany, was a World War I prisoner of war and learned English from British soldiers; he came to the United States in 1920 and taught the majority of skaters at The Skating Club (SC) of Boston. Maribel, whom the skaters nicknamed Winch, trained as much as she could; but ice availability was a problem. "We would have trained more but we didn't always have the facilities" a Boston skater recalled.[6]

In 1921 seven clubs, primarily from the Northeast, took part in the formation of the United States Figure Skating Association (USFSA) on April 4, 1921. From the beginning, the SC of Boston was at the forefront of figure skating in America—many USFSA officials and national champions represented the club, and its official magazine, *Skating*, was published in Boston.[7]

Maribel, eleven, won the Cambridge Skating Club's ladies' competition in 1923. The next year she won the junior ladies' title in Philadelphia at the 1924 U.S. Figure Skating Championships (also called the "Nationals"). Advancing to senior ladies, she placed third in 1926 and was runner-up to Beatrix Loughran of The Skating Club of New York in 1927. Maribel was named a member of the 1928 Winter Olympic Team based on her second-place performance at the 1927 Nationals; the make-up of U.S. international teams was determined by the previous season's results until 1959.[8]

American figure skaters had medaled at the Olympic Games prior to 1928 but had yet to be major contenders. Twelve years after the first modern Olympic Games were held in Athens, figure skating made its debut at the 1908 Olympics in London. Seventeen skaters from five nations—Germany, Russia, Sweden, Great Britain, and the United States—took part in events for men, women, and pairs at the Prince's Skating Club rink. The sole American skater, Irving Brokaw of New York, placed sixth. Olympic figure skating was inactive for the next twelve years. The 1912 Games in Stockholm did not include figure skating, and the 1916 Games, scheduled for Berlin, were not held due to World War I.[9]

Twenty-seven figure skaters from nine countries competed in the 1920 Olympics in Antwerp, Belgium, Americans Theresa Weld and Nathaniel Niles among them. Weld won the bronze, the first Olympic figure skating medal for the United States, and she won the free skating portion of the event—although judges were aghast that her skirt flew up to her knees when she jumped.[10]

In 1924 the International Olympic Committee (IOC) staged a winter International Sports Week 1924 in Chamonix, France. Besides figure skating and hockey—which debuted at the 1920 Olympics—the Games included men's speed skating, men's Nordic skiing, and four-man bobsledding. Of the 258 athletes from sixteen nations participating, only thirteen were women, and they were all figure skaters. U. S. champion Beatrix Loughran took home the silver medal. The International Sports Week 1924 was an enormous success, and the IOC resolved to stage a separate Winter Games at four-year intervals, in the same year as the newly renamed Summer Olympics. The Chamonix event was then retroactively named the first Olympic Winter Games.[11]

Maribel Vinson looked forward to competing at the 1928 Olympic Winter Games at St. Moritz, Switzerland. Sonja Henie, who placed last in 1924, was the star, winning gold at the tender age of fifteen. Beatrix Loughran captured her second Olympic medal by winning the bronze. Maribel, sixteen, was second in figures but unfortunately dropped to

*Maribel Vinson Owen, at the
Cambridge Skating Club.
Source: World Figure Skating
Museum.*

fourth—still a respectable showing at her first Olympics, as *Skating* noted: "Maribel Vinson won the hearts of all by her good sportsmanship and youthful enthusiasm."[12]

After the Olympics, Maribel placed second to Sonja Henie at the 1928 Worlds in London. Everyone thought Maribel was on her way to international glory, but her innovative programs often seemed to penalize her, as she noted years later:

> When I at the age of fourteen entered my first national singles competition, the critic . . . [for] *Skating*, said, "Miss Vinson's free skating is also good—but the contents of the program has been accented too much on the border line of the spectacular." The spectacular at that point was a spread eagle with moderate lean, several standing and sitting spins, the jumps then popular, and a Charlotte ending in which my free leg was raised somewhat higher than the rest of the lady competitors! Yet it was only two years later that all these moves were a requisite part of every program, and by the Olympics of 1932 many more spins, more jumps, and more "daring" positions had been added to the championship repertoire.[13]

After Maribel won her first U.S. ladies' title in 1928, she graduated from Girls' Latin School in Boston with honors, enrolled at Radcliffe College, majoring in romance languages, and trained before and after classes at the SC of Boston. Besides training in singles, she and Thornton Coolidge won the U.S. pairs title in 1928 and 1929.[14]

North American skaters did not participate in the 1929 Worlds in Budapest, due to the time and cost of traveling abroad. Maribel won her second international medal when she took the bronze at the 1930 World Championships in New York City—the first Worlds held in North America. Receiving financial help from the USFSA, Maribel competed at the 1931 Worlds in Berlin, where she placed fourth in singles and fifth in pairs with her new partner, George E. B. ("Geddy") Hill.[15]

Figure skating took center stage for the first time in the United States when the III Olympic Winter Games were held in Lake Placid, New York, in 1932. Despite the worldwide depression, the Olympics proceeded as scheduled; however, few countries could afford to send a full team. More than 250 athletes from seventeen nations competed, although half of the competitors were from the United States or Canada. The Games in Lake Placid publicized figure skating to Americans as never before. The press attended every practice session and, for the first time, wrote about the U.S. figure skating team's chances for medals. Figure skating was the most popular of the five featured sports—a phenomenon which continued for decades. Crowds stormed the doors of the Olympic Arena and occupied every inch of seating space and standing room. American sports aficionados had finally discovered figure skating and wanted to see the world's best.[16]

Maribel, as the four-time U.S. champion, was more experienced going into her second Olympics. However Sonja Henie repeated her victory of 1928, and Maribel had to settle for the bronze. Beatrix Loughran and Sherwin Badger won the pairs silver medal. For the first time, the United States won the overall Olympic medal count with twelve medals. After the 1932 Olympics, the American press's skating coverage dwindled, and it was decades before American skaters became household names.[17]

Maribel continued to train for the 1936 Olympics but had limited success over the next four years. She could do no better than fourth place at the 1932 Worlds in Montreal, and the following year she skipped the Worlds in Stockholm. However in 1933 she won her sixth national title, passed her eighth figure test, and became a U.S. gold medalist (completing all figure and freestyle tests), and graduated from Radcliffe. Now that she was through with her studies, she put into action an unusual plan. She realized she had a great disadvantage at World competitions; the time and money required to travel to Europe for an international competition was significant—she was off the ice for weeks crossing the Atlantic, and she needed time to get accustomed to the different ice conditions. So instead, with the help of the USFSA, she spent the entire year training in Europe. She placed third at the European Championships ("Europeans") in Prague, but placed fifth at the 1934 Worlds in Oslo. In her absence, fellow Bostonian Suzanne Davis won the U.S. title, breaking Maribel's winning streak. After her European experience, Maribel felt strongly "that American and Canadian skating should continue its own development without paying too much attention to foreign ideas."[18]

Maribel wasn't ready to retire, but she was too ambitious to only skate. In 1934 she joined *The New York Times* as its first female sports reporter. There had been women affiliated with the sports pages before, but Maribel was the first female sports reporter with a byline. She added a new dimension to the sports pages in her "Women in Sports" column, moving from straight game reporting to a feature-oriented approach as she covered tennis matches, diving meets, and field hockey tournaments. Maribel's first day on the job illustrates the apprehension that Colonel Bernard Thomson, the sports editor, had in hiring her, as a *New York Times* reporter recounted:

> High anxiety permeated the sports room when Maribel checked in and sat at a desk, demure and ladylike. Something went wrong and the colonel exploded. "Dammit," Thomson began and instantly choked on the word, cognizant of a female in the room. He clutched at his throat and the flush surged to the roots of his hair. He stuttered, stammered, and made profuse apologies to the newest member of his department. Then he fled to another room, where he could talk more freely. As he departed he was overhead to mutter, "What have I done?"[19]

The men soon discovered that Maribel was a competent reporter and a sharp-witted woman who could spew as blue a streak as any of them. "She wore her black hair in a severe boyish bob and it gave severity to her sharp features, but her smile was warm and encompassing and her personality was bright, her intelligence high and she was a likable individual," summarized her journalist colleague Arthur Daley.[20]

Maribel didn't bother to attend the 1935 Worlds in Vienna; instead she saved her energy for the IV Olympic Winter Games, held in Garmish-Partenkirchen, Germany, in 1936. When Maribel arrived in Bavaria, she thought this was her best chance of winning the gold medal. Her biggest competition, she told reporters, would be Sonja Henie and British champion Cecilia Colledge. "Miss Vinson has improved so much in the past year that anything may happen," a New York reporter wrote. What happened was the expected: Sonja Henie won her third Olympic gold medal and Cecilia Colledge won the silver. Maribel finished fifth in both ladies and pairs with Geddy Hill. Maribel was not the only one shut out. None of her eight U.S. skating teammates stood on the podium either.[21]

With three Olympic gold medals in her pocket, Sonja Henie went to Hollywood, landed a lucrative contract with Twentieth Century-Fox, and made a fortune with her eleven skating movies and nationwide ice revues.

Sonja and Maribel were life-long competitors. Sonja respected Maribel's talent, acknowledging that she was both a great skater and extremely popular with the crowds. Polly Blodgett, who trained with Maribel, explained why Maribel could not surpass Sonja: "Maribel couldn't possibly compete with Sonja, who was petite and attractive and feminine. Maribel was just the opposite, and she was ill-advised on how to dress and how she put herself together."[22]

Maribel acknowledged that Sonja, a good friend, was a superb athlete, yet she had her own take on her closest competitor's success: "Sonja's routine is not as hard as mine, but she seldom makes a mistake." Maribel's programs were innovative, and she loved to toss in new movements. "Maribel did one of the first interpretive free skating programs," a skater recalled. "She wore black and really dripped, interpreting this sadness." The European judges did not respond favorably to the new things Maribel did. Her sports buddies at the *Times* agreed: "Maribel's routines were almost esoteric in their conception. The skating judges could score points easier with the familiar jumps, twists and turns. The new stuff baffled them."[23]

After winning two more U.S. titles in 1936 and 1937, Maribel retired, leaving an extraordinary record. Besides winning three national dance medals and the U.S. pairs title six times, her prime achievement was to reign as U.S. ladies' champion nine times—a record unmatched until sixty-eight years later by Michelle Kwan. Maribel's ten-year international competitive career, which included giving a command performance before King George and Queen Mary in London, resulted in one World silver medal, one World bronze medal, and one Olympic bronze medal.[24]

When Maribel announced her retirement in March 1937, she resigned from *The New York Times*, but she wrote articles about skating in newspapers, magazines, and books for the rest of her life. She turned professional and joined the Ice Carnival as its star and director. She soon formed her own touring ice show called Gay Blades. The show co-starred seven-time World champion Karl Schafer and Guy Owen, from the Minto Skating Club of Ottawa. Guy had won the Canadian junior championship in 1929, and was a student of Gustave ("Gus") Lussi. Maribel and Guy first met at the North American Championships, where he earned three gold medals in fours, an event with two men and two ladies skating in unison, from 1933 to 1937. Their friendship began at this competition; and over the years, romance blossomed.[25]

Guy was a banker in Montreal when Maribel encouraged him to join her show. As a pair team, Maribel and Guy were billed as the "foremost interpretive ice skaters." After spending the summer apart, twenty-five-year-old Guy Rochon Owen and twenty-six-year-old Maribel Yerxa Vinson were married at her parents' home in Winchester, Massachusetts, on September 3, 1938. After the wedding, they embraced a more stable life as coaches; however, they continued to perform in hotel nightclubs and arena engagements in North and South America while they coached. They first moved to Minnesota and taught at the St. Paul Figure Skating Club for two years. There Maribel helped mount the 1939 Nationals, produced the summer pops concerts (with skating exhibitions), and wrote two books: *A Primer of Figure Skating: A Primer of the Art-Sport*, and *Advanced Figure Skating*.[26]

In 1940 the Owens moved west to teach at the new East Bay Iceland rink in Berkeley, California, home of the St. Moritz Ice Skating Club (ISC). Four years earlier, they had performed at the St. Moritz carnival, an ice show, and the other skaters were astounded by their performances: "We had never experienced anything so spectacular. . . . The result was an improvement in most everyone's style," a club member recalled. Guy and Maribel settled in Berkeley and began their family. Maribel gave birth to a baby girl on April 25, 1940, who was named Maribel Yerxa Owen, after her mother.[27]

Maribel and Guy attracted many skaters from the surrounding Bay area and the St. Moritz club increased its membership to 1,000 members. The rink was so crowded that often times skaters doubled up on "patch"—the individual section of ice where each skater practiced figure eights. Every Sunday evening, the Owens gave skating seminars with blackboard talks and ice demonstrations and were at the rink night and day, teaching many students including their share of beginners. They introduced a more advanced competitive style of skating to the area, and Maribel took her students to state, regional, sectional, and national competitions.[28]

Maribel was a surprising revelation to skaters. She always wore a military-style coat and yelled at her students while pushing them through a figure eight. Her signature wardrobe and boisterous voice became as famous as her teaching techniques and champion students. Everyone knew when Maribel arrived at the rink, a club member recalled, because "if someone wasn't working on morning patch she'd yell from one end of the rink to the other . . . 'You'd better get to work!'"[29]

Throughout her career, Maribel had her fans and her detractors. Young skaters were shocked by her foul language, and some students took from her only briefly because of her frequent yelling. But many more students put up with her because they liked the results. As one club member recalled:

"Maribel was a dynamic influence, not only as a skating coach, but because her values of morality and character were imbued in us. We learned the importance of good sportsmanship and consideration of others."[30]

On Friday and Saturday nights throughout the summer, the Owens produced the pops concerts. In addition, Maribel produced and directed the annual St. Moritz show, and Guy did much of the choreography. Maribel was involved in every aspect of the show, from the music to costuming. Under her guidance, the skaters performed classical ballet numbers with the San Francisco Ballet Company, including pieces from *Swan Lake*, *Coppelia*, *Peter and the Wolf*, and *Carmen*. Wooden platforms were set on the ice for the ballerinas and members of the San Francisco Symphony Orchestra.[31]

Maribel and Guy regularly performed solos in the shows. Maribel was famous for her edge, speed, and technical competence. Her repertoire varied, but Guy had a signature piece. Adorned in a silk shirt and puffy pants, he perennially performed his famous gaucho routine. He opened the number with outside edges down the length of the rink, as skater Austin Holt recalled: "At the end of each edge he was literally off the ice. With his smile and verve he was so energetic. That's all he had to do and the house just fell over. He could take an audience and milk them like crazy. Guy was a real showman from the word go."[32]

These highly popular shows became grander every year. Maribel was the general-in-charge with many people to command. One year the children's number alone had 200 kids. The rehearsals were always late at night, and Maribel's loud voice came in handy during show time. "She had a voice that could shatter windows," Austin Holt declared. "About the second week of directing the show she became hoarse. When the show opened she was so hoarse she was whispering."[33]

Apart from mounting shows, Maribel's primary job was to coach competitive skaters. The USFSA chose the St. Moritz club to host the first U.S. Championships west of the Mississippi in February 1942. The bombing of Pearl Harbor on December 7, 1941, halted those plans, and the competition site was changed to Chicago. Star pupil Gretchen Merrill, the 1939 National junior champion from Boston, followed Maribel out west in 1943, and that year she won her first U.S. senior ladies' title.[34]

Maribel taught until a week before the birth of Laurence (pronounced Lo-RAWNCE) Rochon (Rah-SHONE) Owen, named after Guy's mother, on May 9, 1944. As Maribel took a few months off to be with Laurence, Guy taught and directed the summer pops concerts and ice ballet series. It was therapeutic for Guy to shine without his wife overshadowing him.[35]

After teaching five years in California, the Owens returned to Boston in 1945 to star in a twenty-by-twenty-foot tank show at the Copley Plaza Hotel and teach at the SC of Boston. A few Berkeley skaters followed the Owens back east. They competed at the Cambridge Skating Club's outdoor rink and every weekend gave exhibitions at the SC of Boston's four o'clock afternoon teas. Maribel's mother was always at the rink for exhibitions; she chatted with Maribel about how her students had progressed or where they needed improvement.[36]

Twenty-year-old Gretchen Merrill won her fourth U.S. title in 1946, but she had been unable to compete at the international level because the World Championships had been discontinued due to World War II. At the 1947 World Championships in Stockholm, seventeen-year-old Barbara Ann Scott of Canada took the crown and Gretchen placed third. Some people thought Gretchen, twenty-one, might have missed her prime moment for international stardom, but Maribel was undeterred as they returned to Berkeley; the St. Moritz club finally hosted the U.S. Championships in 1947. After winning her fifth title, Gretchen, accompanied by Maribel, headed to Boston to prepare for the 1948 Winter Games in St. Moritz, Switzerland.[37]

The 1940 Winter Olympics were originally scheduled for Sapporo, Japan, but the 1940 and 1944 Olympics were both cancelled due to World War II. When the Olympic Winter Games returned in 1948, a dozen years had lapsed. That gap in time, combined with war-torn conditions in Europe, gave American figure skaters the opportunity to catch up with the Europeans.[38]

During the last Games in 1936, a six-year-old boy had put on skates handed down from his brothers. Richard ("Dick") Button of New Jersey joined the Philadelphia Skating Club & Humane Society, trained with Gus Lussi, and spent summers in Lake Placid. At age fourteen, he won the 1944 U.S. novice men's title, the following year he won the junior men's title, and in 1946 became the senior men's champion. He introduced many new figure skating elements, including the double axel, consecutive double jumps, and the flying camel.[39]

Button won the U.S. title again in 1947, and attended the first World Championships in eight years in Davos. "It is difficult to apply an appropriate adjective to the impact of Dick Button's free skating on the Europeans who were seeing it for the first time," skating historian Benjamin Wright wrote. "It was a revolution compared with what they were used to before the War. Here was a young, very strong and athletic skater performing jumps and spins of great difficulty with comparative ease. The Europeans just did not know how handle it." Veteran Hans Gershweiler of Switzerland had a huge lead in figures but barely edged Button out of the 1947 World title. Button placed second, and it was the last time he ever won a silver medal.[40]

One thousand athletes from twenty-eight nations headed to the V Olympic Winter Games in St. Moritz, Switzerland, eager to compete after the long twelve-year hiatus. The Americans came away with three Olympic gold medals, including the four-man bobsled and skier Gretchen Fraser's win in the women's slalom—placing the United States third in the country medal count. Unfortunately for Gretchen Merrill and Maribel Vinson Owen, the 1948 Games were a disappointment. Canadian Barbara Ann Scott became the Olympic champion, and Gretchen finished in eighth place.[41]

This time around, the judges thought they were prepared for Dick Button's skating, but even they were amazed by his performance. All nine judges gave him the highest point total in Olympic history, and Button, aged eighteen, became the youngest man to win an Olympic title in figure skating. It was the first gold medal in figure skating for the United States in forty years of Olympic competition.[42]

The long road to Olympic glory had been paved with a variety of obstacles. The Americans felt that the European judges were prejudiced because there was a distinct difference between the European and North American style of skating. Europeans trained in close proximity and mirrored each other's style and maneuvers, just as Americans and Canadians skated alike.

Traveling to competitions had also been difficult for North American skaters. From 1896 to 1956, the World Championships had been held in North America only twice: in New York City in 1930 and in Montreal in 1932. Top-ranked American skaters had limited opportunities to compete abroad; the decision to compete usually depended on a skater's bank account. Sometimes the USFSA sent the best representatives; at other times, the USFSA gave spots to the well-to-do. Polly Blodgett made the 1936 Olympic and World Team in pairs; her family was well off but the costs were exorbitant. "Nobody had any money for the Olympic Team, so the USFSA only sent the top one," Polly explained. "I couldn't afford to go abroad, and no one was going to come up with the money. Jim and Grace Madden didn't even try out because he was laid up with a bad ankle at the time [of the Olympic tryouts], but they had plenty of money, so they went."[43]

Time was a further consideration. Dick Button took three months off from school when he sailed to Stockholm on the *Queen Mary* for the 1947 Worlds. Andra McLaughlin experienced difficulties on the *Queen Elizabeth* when she went to the 1949 Worlds in Paris: "It was fun on the ship, but we missed a full week of skating and then we had to compete," Andra recalled. "Coming across the North Atlantic was quite rough; there were storms and we got seasick. When we got on land we had rubber legs for a few days." It took time, money, and a lot of cooperation from family, educators, and skating officials to compete internationally. Button was fortunate to have everything working for him.[44]

Dick Button's numerous accomplishments in the 1948 season—Olympic, World, European, and U.S. champion—signaled a seismic shift in the perception of American skating, both in the USA and abroad. Prior to World War II, U.S. competitive skating had been relaxed. After Button's remarkable sweep, competitive skating in the United States finally became serious business. The 1948 season ushered in a new "Golden Age" of figure skating in America. Maribel Vinson Owen was a leading force in this new phase, too.[45]

The Owens left Boston and returned to Berkeley in the fall of 1948. They had lost many students in the interim, but one set of students remained constant—daughters Maribel Jr. and Laurence. They both began skating at age two and developed a love/hate relationship with the sport from the beginning. When the girls were supposed to take patch, they'd go off, like any small child, and go to the little girls' room. Maribel, in the middle of a lesson, would look around. If they weren't there, she'd head for the bathroom, yell at them, and drag them back on the ice. There was lots of screaming and crying.[46]

The girls' struggles with skating were not the only drama in the family. Returning to California couldn't reverse the difficulties in the Owenses' marriage. Friends conceded that Guy had a drinking problem that became too much for Maribel. They skated beautifully together, but off-ice their disparities were readily apparent. Maribel could accomplish anything and was not afraid to speak her mind—gender did not inhibit her. "People would always say to Maribel, 'You act just like a man!' and that really wounded her," student Ron Ludington declared. "She was very sensitive to that comment, but it was natural for her to take over and be in charge. In later years she worried that in some indirect way she had caused [her husband's] drinking."[47]

Instead of shining alongside his wife, Guy withered in her presence. However, his drinking was not evident to everyone, and he maintained his composure and demeanor while teaching. Guy taught for eight months in California, then left his family and took a position with the Sault Saint Marie Club in Michigan. The following summer he taught at Michigan State University in East Lansing and directed the MSU summer show.[48]

The divorce was disappointing, but Maribel remained steadfast. She accompanied Gretchen Merrill to Colorado Springs for her last Nationals in 1949. Gretchen was the defending six-time U.S. champion—only her coach had a longer winning streak with nine titles—but Yvonne Sherman of New York won. Maribel continued to teach in Berkeley and raise Maribel Jr., nine, and Laurence, five. She was active in the Professional Skaters Guild (later renamed Professional Skaters Association) and passed high-level ice dancing tests. At a Nationals party, she and pairs champion Robin Greiner performed a Charleston-Valentino combination "which had everyone clamoring for more." Maribel loved to try new things.[49]

Maribel had been the Iceland skating director for many years; but when U.S. pairs champion Robert Swenning arrived in town, he was appointed head professional. "There was never any animosity," Swenning explained. "She just said, 'Okay, that's the way it is. That's fine.' Her primary goal was to advance skating and she got along with everyone." Swenning did something nice for Maribel that everyone at the rink appreciated. One Christmas he bought her a new coat and told her, "I will only give it to you if you give me that other one." Swenning took her drab, olive, army coat, and she wore the new one.[50]

Under Maribel's guidance, many former students became judges and still judge today. She gave them encouragement and good advice—but not everyone agreed with her views, as judge Ramona Allen explained: "I had taken from both Nic [Howard Nicholson] and Gus [Lussi] and their styles were very different from Maribel's. A good judge has to accept a number of different styles, but when Maribel ran a judges' school for beginning judges, her way was the only way."[51]

As passionate as she was about her sport, Maribel's mantra was "skating isn't your whole life." After teaching in the morning, she played tennis in the afternoon. Many of her students congregated in her home—there was always a crowd of skaters and friends. The Owens lived in a marvelous house in the Berkeley foothills with a picturesque view of the Golden Gate and Bay bridges. Bob Swenning dined frequently at Maribel's, as did Robin

Greiner. "She had a wonderful maid who prepared dinner," Robin recalled. "After a candlelight dinner we would sprawl out on the floor with my [college] books and we'd discuss philosophy over a glass of sherry."[52]

As the primary breadwinner for her family, she also taught UC Berkeley P.E. classes, received small checks for writing assignments, and freely used her name and likeness to earn extra money. She endorsed Kumfortites, "the all-around sport accessory," Arnold Authentics skating and roller boots, and Wheaties cereal, as a "Breakfast of Champions" spokesperson.[53]

At the 1952 Winter Olympics, Maribel wore dual hats as a press correspondent and as a coach to Bostonian Tenley Albright. Tenley had won back-to-back victories as the 1949 U.S. novice champion and the 1950 junior champion, and in 1951 she was the senior ladies' silver medalist. A student of Willie Frick, Tenley also worked with Maribel during her periodic jaunts to Boston.[54]

Nearly seven hundred athletes from thirty countries participated in the VI Olympic Winter Games in Oslo. The vast Bislett Stadium—about the size of six regulation hockey rinks side by side—adequately staged the Opening Ceremonies. To make the space practical for the figure skating competition, a regulation-size rink was outlined in the center by a small, six-inch wall of snow. Jeanette Altwegg of Great Britain became the Olympic champion, and Tenley Albright surprised her countrymen by placing second. U.S. champion Sonya Klopfer placed fourth, and Ginny Baxter, who was "simply out of this world," won the free skate and pulled up from eighth to fifth place.[55]

Dick Button, now a twenty-one-year-old Harvard senior, dominated the headlines during the Games. Everyone expected the four-time World and 1948 Olympic champion to win again. After leading in the figures, Button performed a strong, innovative program, and his new moves quickly found their way into the skating lexicon. Button matter-of-factly explained his extraordinary repertoire to an admiring press: "I can't copy anybody because nobody has anything new." Besides performing three double axels in his routine, Button performed a triple loop jump— the first triple jump ever performed in competition. Button won his second Olympic gold medal, and Americans Jimmy Grogan and Hayes Alan Jenkins placed third and fourth, respectively. In pairs, Peter and Karol Kennedy won the silver. The United States had one of its best showings at these Winter Olympics. Norway won the country medal count with sixteen medals and the United States placed second place with eleven; four of those were in figure skating with one gold, two silver and one bronze—the most U.S. figure skating medals for any Olympics thus far.[56]

There was no way for Maribel to foretell the climactic events ahead of her when she returned from Oslo. Her ex-husband taught that winter in Spokane, Washington, and had planned to teach again in East Lansing that summer; but on April 21, 1952, Guy Owen died. The obituary in *Skating* failed to mention Maribel or their daughters. The months to follow brought further grief. On November 14, 1952, Maribel's father passed away. Thus, the two most important men in Maribel's life vanished the same year.[57]

Maribel continued to coach. After the 1952 Olympics, Tenley competed at Worlds, but she had to withdraw due to a serious bronchial condition. She came back the next year to win the 1953 World title in Davos. When Maribel returned from Switzerland, she prepared to move her family back east. Maribel would be a shoulder for her mother to lean on, and her girls would receive support from their grandmother. Coaching Tenley would also be easier.[58]

Before she left Berkeley, Maribel attended the 1954 Pacific Coast Championships. The proprietors of the Iceland coffee shop, who vividly remembered the chair-throwing episode from the year before, were prepared. A large banner draped across the coffee shop read: "Maribel . . . please leave our chairs alone." Bidding farewell to many dear friends, Maribel and her daughters headed to Boston in the spring of 1954.[59]

CHAPTER 2

MARIBEL IN BOSTON

Maribel's return to Boston in 1954 was officially announced in *Skating*: "Maribel Vinson Owen and daughters have returned to her mother's home in Winchester and Maribel is teaching at the Boston Arena and the Milton Academy rink." Her homecoming should have been a triumphant return of a favorite daughter, but Maribel was not allowed on staff at The Skating Club (SC) of Boston where she had victoriously won fifteen national titles.[1]

She was still a club member—having been inducted as an honorary member in 1935 as a tribute to her extraordinary competitive record and "her unselfish devotion to the Club's interest"—but she was denied teaching privileges. Some have suggested that her personality was to blame. "She was a very outspoken person and there was a lot of antagonism with the powers that be," a judge explained. "Maribel didn't put up with those people and she suffered no fools." A coach concurred: "She did her own thing and at that time the club was kind of hoity. They were pretty fussy about who could teach."[2]

It's true that the club was already well staffed when she arrived—Montgomery ("Bud") Wilson was head pro, plus Cecelia Colledge and Willie Frick, who had taught Maribel, along with others. Some felt that Bud Wilson of Canada was the primary obstacle in preventing Maribel from teaching there. A long-time rivalry existed between the Wilson and Vinson/Owen families. Bud's sister, Constance Wilson, had always placed above Maribel at North Americans, while Maribel usually beat Constance at Worlds; Bud and Constance usually beat Maribel in pairs, and Guy Owen was the perennial runner-up to Bud in the Canadian men's competition. By the time Maribel showed up to teach permanently in Boston, they had strong opinions of each other.[3]

Bud Wilson was only too keenly aware of Maribel's overbearing nature. "Maribel was not a diplomat," student Ron Ludington confirmed. "She was a controller, and she wouldn't conform. It was very 'dog-eat-dog' with coaches in those days, and Bud wouldn't let her join the staff." According to Paul George, who trained under both coaches: "It wasn't a bitter relationship, but it was a volatile one. However, when Maribel had difficulty coaching Laurence herself, she had Bud take over." While this step shows mutual trust, the two coaches were polar opposites. Bud was very gentlemanly and always arrived in a coat, tie, and tweed jacket, while Maribel was oblivious whenever she created a scene; and her lack of attention to conventional dress communicated her disregard for anyone else's opinion. "Maribel was like a messy bedroom running out of her house," student Ronna Goldblatt fondly recalled.[4]

Another theory revolves around Cecelia Colledge from Great Britain, who had joined the staff in 1952 and who could have been threatened by Maribel's presence. The two former competitors knew each other well— Maribel beat Cecelia soundly at the 1932 Olympics and Worlds; in 1936 Cecelia won the Olympic silver medal while Maribel placed fifth, and the following year Cecelia became the 1937 World champion. Even though they were friends, it would be understandable for Cecelia to want to keep her distance from Maribel and her audacious nature.[5]

The most likely plotters against Maribel were club officials, who were put off by her colorful language and demeanor. The Skating Club of Boston was very much a private country club with a socially exclusive atmosphere. The club officials of the few elite skating centers in the fifties wielded powerful authority; they controlled the business of the USFSA and some people felt they even influenced some competitions.[6]

Maribel openly defied people and institutions in an era when it was deemed inappropriate to behave in such a manner, particularly for a woman. She thumbed her nose at the USFSA officials within The Skating Club of Boston which, compounded with her unpredictable, rough language, would certainly have given them reason to exclude her. The club could not expel her because Tenley Albright, the 1953 World champion, took lessons from her, so she was allowed to teach Tenley at the club and, in time, her own daughters, but few others.[7]

Maribel would not have been happy working full-time at the club anyway, due to its exclusionary values. In her early days, Maribel befriended African American Mabel Fairbanks and gave her some free lessons; Mabel later coached hundreds of skaters in Los Angeles, including young Tai Babilonia and Randy Gardner. The club welcomed people with "money and manners," but also discriminated on religious grounds; they didn't want Maribel's students, including those who were Catholic or Jewish. "Their excuse was that she was too flamboyant and loud and crude in their eyes," student Frank Carroll said. "The truth is they didn't like her because she said

Maribel Vinson Owen, at the Cambridge Skating Club, 1960. Source: Photo by Franklin Nelson; courtesy of Barlow Nelson.

what she thought and she didn't hold back. She couldn't stand bigotry or people that were prejudiced."[8]

Maribel was vocal about her contempt for the club's attitudes. One time she verbally assailed a club official at a club dinner: "What about this skater? When is she going to be a member of the club? She's applied for membership!" "She won't," the official replied. "She won't ever be a member...she's Jewish!" Maribel rose up and screamed, "You bigot! Our soldiers went to war and gave their lives to put a stop to that sort of thing! How dare you! You should be ashamed!" Although the official always went out of his way to be nice to this student, she was never admitted.[9]

Occasionally Maribel implied that she had black ancestry, or told people she was Jewish, just to shame discriminatory individuals. Appalled by the restrictions at several East Coast clubs, Maribel once quipped, "To be a member of The Skating Club of Boston you needed to be a blue blood, but to be a member of The Skating Club of New York you had to have a letter from Jesus Christ." Of the club's exclusion, student Christie Allan said:[10]

Maribel had invisible opposition. Many of her students didn't realize how deep the malevolence was against Maribel. She was so outspoken that you understood how someone could be offended, but she would tell you something to your face and would never put a knife in your back. It was incredible that they wouldn't let the most illustrious member of their skating club who ever lived—and the most decorated woman in skating—teach there. [11]

The Skating Club of Boston, for all of its outdated practices, had an ideal training environment. The club owned the rink, so while hockey teams had practice ice and public sessions took place, the ice time was primarily dedicated to patch, freestyle sessions, dance sessions, club exhibitions, and social gatherings. The steady stream of national and world champions training there, including Tenley and Dick Button, led one skater to describe it as "skating with the gods." The focus was on winning, but club member Nancy Madden remarked that it was more than just skating: "The people at The Skating Club of Boston helped me change and grow up. The highs and lows were beyond belief but those were the happiest times of my life. When I left the club I was heads above my classmates in college. I had learned about classical music, time management, how to win and lose. . . . I learned many things. There were hard lessons to be learned at that club, but when I came out I was ready for life."[12]

Maribel taught primarily at other rinks. Her home base was the Commonwealth Club at the Boston Arena, next door to Symphony Hall. The kids liked the large seating area, but not everyone appreciated the old relic, as one skater noted: "The Boston Arena was the coldest rink in the world. It was a dreadful, awful dungeon, but Walter Brown gave Maribel the ice for free." Sometimes her students skated right after the Boston Bruins hockey team practiced, and they had to scrape all the snow off the ice. Walter Brown, owner of the Boston Gardens, "loved Maribel, so he made the ice at the Garden available for her too, but we never knew when that would be—we had to be ready to jump."[13]

Maribel and her students were vagabonds—they had a hard time finding ice and her students followed her all over the region, driving from Andover to Weymouth or Winthrop. She also had her students skate outdoors at the Cambridge Skating Club, the Milton Academy, and the Sidney Hill Country Club in Newton. "It was brutal," a skater vividly recalled. "On winter mornings we did figures outside for two hours and Maribel would not let us get off the ice—we were freezing to death." Once when a student asked why they were skating on a lake, she responded, "If you can do it on natural ice and then you put yourself on a commercial surface, it's a piece of cake."[14]

She often chauffeured her students. "Maribel would toot her horn if we overslept," Ronna Goldblatt recalled. When they did, she bought them a new alarm clock. Parents also dropped their kids off at Maribel's house in Winchester in the early morning; she would drive them to a hastily chosen rink, and bring them home in time for school. "She dragged us all over the place, but it was fabulous," Ronna said. "We didn't miss going to The Skating Club of Boston." The long trips to the Worcester rink, a converted bowling alley, were memorable. Everyone slept at Maribel's house the night before; and in the wee hours of the morning, everyone piled into her old woody station wagon—it had paneling with "mushrooms growing out of the wood," a skater recalled. "The doors were all tied shut with rope—I don't even remember how we got in." The kids often sat on each other's laps. Eventually a family bought her a new blue station wagon because her car wasn't safe for their children.[15]

Maribel used the captive riding time to give her students guidance. To Maribel, the only thing more important than skating was education and she continually stressed the importance of doing well in school. She told her students to bring their schoolbooks and do their homework in the car. She discussed history and English, quizzed them on vocabulary, gave them spelling bees, corrected their grammar or French pronunciation, threatened to fine them if they spoke improperly, and talked about SATs. She rarely talked about skating in the car.[16]

She expected her students to pursue higher education and was a pro-active mentor to college-age skaters. "She asked to see my first quarter grades from Dartmouth," Barlow Nelson recalled. "She said, 'My God! You can do better than that.' I felt chastised, but she was right." Maribel influenced Paul George's college choice. He had applied to Dartmouth, but Maribel said, "You're not going to Dartmouth. . . . I want you to meet Bob Watson," and she marched him right over to the Harvard dean of students' home. Paul went to Harvard because Maribel wanted him to. The long commute to Dartmouth had proved problematic for training, and Maribel told Paul, "I don't want to go through again what I went through with Barlow."[17]

Maribel's training included many off-ice activities. She encouraged students to take gymnastics and dance classes, attend plays, and sample other cultural events. One student went to see Marcel Marceau because Maribel had said: "I want you to be in the presence of somebody who communicates incredibly well with his audience without saying a word." She was concerned about her students' diets and often told them what to eat to keep their weight down. She suggested they eat steak for breakfast because protein was essential; if she saw someone eating an ice cream cone, she would take it and throw it away.[18]

In the summer Maribel's students congregated in Lynn, where the head coach, Lillian Tribby, had skated in Maribel's hotel tank shows. Lynn's was the only rink open in the summer, and a lot of people came to Boston just to take from Maribel. The skaters were delighted when Maribel, now in her early forties, occasionally skated alongside them in the more-relaxed summer environment.[19]

As an exception to this era of formality, her students were on a first-name basis with her. "It wasn't considered polite in those days, but everyone did," Christie Allan recalled. "Shortly after I started taking lessons, she stayed for dinner. I started to ask her something and I didn't know if I should say Mrs. Owen, Miss Vinson, or Miss Vinson-Owen. She must have read my mind because she laughed with her deep, throaty laugh: 'The name is Maribel, my darling!' So we all called her Maribel."[20]

Maribel's excellence in figures brought her many students interested in her technical expertise. She was a hands-on teacher; if a skater did not start a figure properly, she pulled her student back. Every time they skated an edge, she skated with them—inch by inch—putting their foot and hip in the right direction. In those days, figures accounted for 60 percent of the total competition score, so mastering figures was critical. There were nine levels of figure tests (preliminary and first through the eighth; passing the final eighth test resulted in a gold medal in figures); and at each level, there were four to eight new figures to master. Judges looked at the cleanness of the turns and the purity of the circles—their size, roundness, and alignment, the steadiness of lines, and the tracings. Once the first figure was laid down it needed to be traced two more times. By the time skaters had competed, they had made 8,000-10,000 tracings of each figure in practice. Senior-level skaters had to master twenty-four different figures for competition.[21]

Just as in Berkeley, Maribel's thunderous voice could be heard during the quietness of patch; and when music blared over the loudspeaker during freestyle sessions, she pumped up her voice several more levels. She began sessions hollering "Skate!" and made her students stroke with speed. If skaters slowed down, Maribel whacked them with a pair of faded, blue plastic skate guards as they went by, shouting, "You keep it up!"[22]

Maribel's freestyle instruction was unique. She had always skated intuitively. She expected her students to "find the feeling" and had little sympathy for those who couldn't. Maribel told her students: "Jump in the air, close your eyes, and pull your arms in. If you want to land it, you will."[23]

In freestyle she expected her students to have an in-depth understanding of what they should be doing. If something went wrong, she asked them to explain what happened, and they had to articulate it well. If they couldn't, she stared unblinkingly at them until they answered. A correct answer rarely received praise; her response was more along the lines of "you should have known that" or "why did you take so long to answer?" She also gave colorful advice, such as "squeeze the dime," which meant to clench the muscles of their derriere. On another occasion, she told a skater, "You're stiff; you need to bend your knees. You need to get down on the ice and mulch—like you're getting down in the soil and mulching the roses." Maribel then reached her hands down into the imaginary soil.[24]

Once at a party the discussion led to the ideal body shape for skating. Maribel said, "If you screwed my head around backwards you wouldn't be able to tell which way I was going—I find that advantageous for skating." A friend confirmed that Maribel was flat-chested and had no rump and, in addition to her natural ability, she indeed had a perfect shape for skating.[25]

Her students utilized every imaginable power adjective to describe her—from aggressive, assertive, and amazing, to forceful, fiery, and focused. "Maribel was one of the most energetic people I ever knew," a club member said. "She dashed onto the ice and never did anything half way." Maribel commanded that same kind of energy and respect from her own students.[26]

From the oldest to the youngest, she changed lives. "I loved Maribel because she made you feel important and good about yourself no matter where you were in the sport," a student reflected. She instinctively helped people out, even the students of other coaches from coast to coast. It was not unlike her to write letters to other skaters after the Nationals, critiquing their performance. "She was always kind in her critique, saying how impressed she was with me," one L.A. skater said.[27]

Even those who admired her were often overwhelmed by her. "I think everybody was afraid of her," a longtime student said. "She was larger than life and you didn't often meet people like that. She was the strongest personality I had ever met." Watching Maribel teach was never dull. "People would go nuts because Maribel would grab an arm and grab a leg and practically turn a kid into a pretzel to get them into the position she wanted," coach Red Bainbridge recalled. "You did it her way or she'd break your neck."[28]

Nancy Madden's first encounter with Maribel prepared her for what lay ahead. She had walked into the Lynn rink and listened to her scream at Little Maribel, who had failed her seventh test again. "I said to my mom, 'I don't want to take from her. I don't think this is going to work.' But I did take from her, I tried very hard, and I was always on my best behavior. She was very happy with me and only got mad once. I couldn't land a double salchow and she was frustrated. She told me if I didn't land it she would tear off my clothes, piece by piece—she would start with my gloves, and then my sleeves, etc."[29]

Maribel often threatened in jest, but some students actually felt her wrath. Frank Carroll once saw Maribel strike Tenley. "Tenley Albright was the goddess of all time and Maribel slapped her on the leg," Carroll remembered. "'My God,' I told myself, 'she touched the divine Tenley.'" Frank Carroll, in turn, was also a victim. Maribel, upset because Frank was not paying attention during a figure lesson prior to a competition, smacked him across the face with a skate guard. A long red mark was still visible on his face when he competed. Students often had bruises because Maribel had hands like steel. "No one could get away with what she did today," a student said. "She loved to swear—everything was bloody this and bloody that. She would constantly scream and yell at other people, and I would burst into tears and leave the ice. I finally had to stop taking from her." Surprisingly, despite Maribel's aggressive manner, most of her students remained steadfast. "They absolutely loved her," a coach declared, "because she certainly knew her stuff and they knew this was her way—the tough love." Ronna Goldblatt was one of many students who adored her: "In teaching, her word was everything to me. I never doubted one thing she said or did. I made sure everything I did was perfect—I had too much respect for her not too. She gave us so much confidence. Maribel was always loud, but in a loving way. It was never in a nasty or mean way, it was just her style to be loud. Maribel taught with passion and love—everything she said had such meaning."[30]

At competition time, Maribel was often combative with officials. At one Easterns competition a referee came close to throwing her out of the rink for sitting on the barrier and coaching during the warm-up for the event. Another time she approached the official playing the freestyle record during competition and put her hand on the volume control. When her student did a jump, she turned it up, to give the jump greater emphasis, and yelled out, "Great jump!" When coaches sat together at competitions, she made her presence known. If she did not like the judges' decisions, she led the crowd in boos. "It was done in Europe but not in the United States," coach Louella Rehfield recalled. "No one would do it in the U.S. except Maribel, and she got all the teachers to go along with her. All they needed was a little push."[31]

Maribel was a tireless worker, but finances were still difficult for the family. The Owen girls wore Hyde skates because Maribel had worked out a deal, as she told her daughters: "Mr. Hyde will make you a nice pair of boots and it will only cost you forty dollars. Why spend eighty-five dollars on Stanziones; Mr. Hyde's boots are good!" They were acceptable boots, but some girls thought they were unattractive. "If you look at the pictures of Laurence and Little Maribel's boots they have a chunkier heel and an ugly toe-box," Christie Allan recalled. "I felt sorry for them because their boots weren't beautiful like the rest of us who had Stanziones."[32]

Maribel accomplished so much by multi-tasking. Once she was teaching outdoors at the Milton Academy on Christmas Eve, and she finally got around to eating lunch at four o'clock. As she demonstrated a camel spin, she had a sandwich in her hand. She pliéd with her skating leg and reached down, whacking her foot, explaining to her student where her skate should be. When she came out of the spin, her sandwich had been consumed. Maribel taught practically every day—if she wasn't on the ice, she was in a car speeding toward another rink, sometimes driving with her skates on. She rarely had time for everyday tasks, and her pupils' parents often helped out, including doing her Christmas shopping and wrapping all the presents, too. Ron Ludington tells a well-known story involving the Owenses' Christmas tree: "It was almost Christmas and they had never bothered getting a tree. Dudley [Richards] and I decided that Maribel should have a Christmas tree so we bought one and brought it over. They had ornaments and everyone helped decorate it. After some time I said to Dudley, 'I think we'd better take it down.' By then it was April. For four months everyone just kept maneuvering around this completely withered tree. The ornaments barely clung to the branches. I thought we better remove it before the house burned down."[33]

Maribel's mother, Gertrude Vinson, was also devoted to skating and spent long hours at the rink. Everyone benefited from her presence. To most people she was "Grammy Vinson" and they treated her like a great-aunt. A tiny woman, she dressed like Queen Mary with a tweed coat, gray hat, gloves, and purse. She assumed the role of club matriarch and daily stood at rink side dispensing wisdom and advice. She had skated for more than fifty years and knew the sport well, as a club member recalled: "She taught me a king pivot and kept on my case until I learned it."[34]

Grammy drove her granddaughters and some of Maribel's other students in her old, beat-up, two-door Ford convertible—but she wasn't a very good driver. Once a visibly shaken Laurence arrived at the rink and told everyone that Grammy had driven the car on the wrong side of Memorial Drive. Ignoring Laurence's screaming, Grammy just exclaimed, "These people are all going the wrong way!" Another time she drove Laurence and a friend to the Lynn rink at 7:00 A.M., with the top down. As the freezing girls huddled in the back underneath a blanket, Grammy said, "Oh, isn't this delicious!"[35]

Several stories emerged because Grammy, near age eighty, had poor vision and hearing. "Grammy couldn't hear worth a darn," Paul George explained. "She would come into the rink and say, 'Have you seen what *so and so* is doing out there? It's terrible!' The whole rink could hear her." She sometimes wore an old-fashioned earphone; she would take it off and talk into it like a hand microphone, but when she was without it, she just yelled. Everyone became used to the riotous exchanges among the four Vinson/Owen women; but come competition time, they were always united. Even though Grammy refused to fly, she never missed a competition. "Seeing the three generations of that family at competitions—that was quite amazing," a skater recalled.[36]

Maribel's students intimately knew her family because skaters were constantly in the Vinson home on 195 High Street in Winchester. Built on a hill in 1803 by a Revolutionary War veteran, the large house was federal style, with a square colonial roof, four chimneys, and lots of stairs. The house had been in the family for three generations. Although Grammy had neglected home maintenance and the house usually looked unkempt, it was full of valuable treasures. The walls of the house breathed Maribel's illustrious career. All of her trophies were in one room, ashtrays and other mementos from exhibitions were scattered about, and years of pictures covered the walls going up the staircase.[37]

The Vinson homestead was typical of the Boston homes of old distinguished families who did not have a lot of money in the bank. Dinner guests sat at a beautiful Georgian dining room table elegantly set with individual silver salt and pepper shakers for everyone. "It was a stunning place with wonderful antiques," skater Peter Betts remarked. "I put my feet on this stool once and Grammy said, 'Oh, that's a handmade stool from 16-*whatever*. If you put your hand underneath you can feel the axe marks.'" At another party, Betts sat down in one of two antique chairs, which cracked in half. Maribel asked Laurence, "Did he sit hard in that chair?" Little Maribel and Laurence both said, "No, he went very, very carefully into it." She replied, "Oh well, I've always said furniture is meant to be used." Later on Betts learned there were only four of these chairs in the world—the other two were owned by the Shah of Iran.[38]

The Vinson/Owen home was open to people congregating on the weekends for barbecues and cookouts, and each year they held a big party for the club's annual Ice Chips show. The generous-sized house accommodated large groups, and skaters from all regions of the country stayed for a weekend, during the summer, or year-round. Most of them had positive experiences, but not all. "My parents left me at her home once when they went on a week's vacation," a student said. "I told them if they ever did it again I would run away. The yelling went on all the time, and I couldn't stand the turmoil." A friend recalled Laurence saying, "We had to have a large house so we could all yell at each other a long distance."[39]

Given Maribel's lack of public decorum, it seems ironic that she taught table manners in her home during formal dinners and was a stickler for proper etiquette. She lashed out at Ron Ludington when he used the wrong fork one night. Another time she unleashed her fury on a student who ran his finger over the top of a doorframe and showed Maribel the dirt on his finger. One skating father, who was a good friend of Maribel, loved to tease her. "One night after [a group] dinner my father deliberately left a spoon in his coffee cup and proceeded to drink—I thought Maribel would have a heart attack," student Julie Graham recalled. "She didn't say anything but just kept looking at him. Everybody else was bursting inside." Maribel did not hold her tongue when she thought Dick Button spoke too openly about a subject. "She looked at me sternly and told me there were certain things that gentlemen don't discuss too deeply," Button recalled. "Maribel was always straightforward." She achieved her finest transformation on bad-boy Ron Ludington, as he explained:[40]

> I adored her, but we also cursed at each other. I was basically a hoodlum and didn't know how to deal with people, and she was trying to rehabilitate me. She gave me an etiquette book to read, and in her home she had me set the dining table. She insisted I squire her to the theatre and it was so embarrassing—she looked and acted like Auntie Mame with a big, old, outdated fur coat, and I had to wear a coat and hat. She was a sight to see, but she didn't care what others thought of her. When the girls were young I often baby-sat them, and in the process that's how I became educated by Maribel. I took her good points and left the bad. She was the best thing that ever happened to me.[41]

Maribel attracted many new students when she settled in Boston in 1954, but her main focus was on Tenley Albright. After winning the 1953 World title, Tenley had a bad fall in Oslo in 1954, which cost her the title. Maribel wrote about the experience in *Sports Illustrated*: "Tenley went into a combination axel and double loop jump and promptly stunned the stadium and herself by inexplicably falling flat. Tenley went through the rest of her program in a deep trance. She never really recovered."[42]

Maribel and Tenley worked hard to recapture her title. They knew she'd be skating outdoors in Vienna in 1955, so more outdoor practice was in order. Maribel took several of her students to an outdoor rink at

Grossinger's resort hotel in the Catskills; their housing was near the rink but the main dining room was far away. "Maribel jogged down there every morning for breakfast so we'd have to jog down too, not to be humiliated," student Hugh Graham recalled. Maribel wisely engaged other coaches to help Tenley. Her good friend Gene Turner helped choreograph Tenley's program in Denver, and Maribel took Tenley to Lake Placid to work with Gus Lussi on her freestyle.[43]

Maribel was busy at the 1955 Worlds in Vienna, coaching and writing for *Sports Illustrated* and the Associated Press. She was up very early for training but spent every night in the bar with all of the reporters. One of her fellow writers said, "Maribel, how do you do it? You never sleep at all," and she replied, "Well, I sleep fast." At home Maribel slept for only a few hours each night. At four in the morning she'd wake up her daughters or any skaters in the house, saying: "It's time to get up. It's time for breakfast. We have to go!" Maribel read many books and worked on projects late at night—students spending the night could hear her furiously typing away. Surprisingly, her body just didn't need the rest.[44]

After Tenley successfully recaptured her World title in 1955, she was one step closer to the 1956 Olympic title. Maribel eagerly looked forward to a year of intense training. Tenley's triumph would indirectly fulfill Maribel's dream of achieving an Olympic gold medal.

CHAPTER 3

THE KING OF BROADMOOR

Maribel Vinson Owen was not the only coach training a potential Olympic champion. In Colorado Springs, the Broadmoor Skating Club began to rival The Skating Club of Boston in the number of champions it produced; and by 1955, it also had a prime candidate to win an Olympic gold medal. For years the Broadmoor management had recruited world-class coaches to lure the finest national figure skaters to their rink, but it took time to find the perfect head coach. To their great credit they eventually chose Edi Scholdan.

Edi (rhymes with "Teddy") Scholdan was only five foot five inches, but he loomed large in the world of figure skating. In his twenty years of teaching in the United States, he produced more World Team members than any other coach of his era. He was a great show producer and an innovative trainer, but his strongest teaching trait was enthusiasm. His students called him the "ultimate cheerleader" because of his positive mental attitude. They considered him "the most wonderful man they had ever met" and "everybody loved him deeply."[1]

Edi Scholdan's unprecedented success at the Broadmoor can be partially attributed to the obstacles he surmounted in his youth. Eduard James Scholdan was born on July 18, 1910, in Vienna, Austria. He was raised by an aunt after his parents died during World War I. He began figure skating at age twelve and became junior champion of Austria. In 1933 he placed sixth at the World Championships in Zurich, Switzerland.[2]

After participating at Worlds, Edi began teaching skating. He left Austria because of the rising Nazi regime and taught briefly in Switzerland and Sweden before moving to England. He was a staff member at the Sports Stadium in Brighton when its ice rink opened in 1935 and competed twice in the Open Professional Championship of Great Britain, placing fourth and seventh.[3]

Edi immigrated to the United States in 1938 and taught figure skating in the major U.S. skating cities before he settled permanently in Colorado. Two stories have circulated about how Edi came to the United States. Polly Blodgett and her mother, members of The Skating Club of Boston, were in

London during the summer of 1938, and Polly and Edi both performed in an exhibition in Brighton. Edi told the Bostonians he had been invited to teach in Cleveland, Ohio. "Cleveland!" they gasped. "Whoever heard of a club in Cleveland?" Mrs. Blodgett told Edi that the Boston Arena needed a coach and talked him into coming to Boston instead. The other story is that Boston sports promoter Walter Brown, on a visit to England, invited Edi to teach students at the Commonwealth Figure Skating Club. There is probably some truth to both stories.[4]

From the start of his American teaching career, Edi produced champions. In Boston, his student Wilhelm Junker won the novice and junior men's titles at the Easterns competition.[5]

Edi was still a developing coach when he came to the United States, but he was a seasoned performer. In those days, show skaters were primarily vaudevillians on ice who moved easily from show to show. Once in the States, Edi placed ads in *Skating*, describing himself as a "Famous European and American Skating Star, available for Carnivals with his novelty skating acts." The ad featured a picture of Edi juggling three hats while skating slalom between bottles lined up on the ice. In Europe, Edi had been briefly attached to a circus where he learned to juggle. His act, which he presented in small New York nightclubs and large metropolitan arenas across the country, varied through the years. He did intricate patterns as he slalomed through bowling ball tenpins, twirled a ring hoop on his free foot while juggling or balancing balls, and sliced through oranges or grapefruit as he slalomed on stilt-fashioned skates. In every performance, his infectious personality shone brightly and the crowds adored him.[6]

In 1941 Edi began to spend his summers at the Broadmoor Ice Palace. He was invited to teach but primarily to perform his juggling act in the Broadmoor Ice Revue. In subsequent summers, he helped mount the shows. Edi felt at home at the Broadmoor, which was reminiscent of his beloved Austria. Beginning in the early forties, many skaters across the country made the trek to Colorado for summertime training. Skaters appreciated the facilities, the excellent coaching staff, and the magnificent natural setting. In fact, the area's pristine beauty was the foundation for the most internationally renowned skating center in America.[7]

The Broadmoor Skating Club owes its existence to the creation of one of the most charming, Old World resorts in the country. The region's natural beauty bewitched Prussian Count James Pourtales, who immigrated to Colorado in the mid-1880s. He purchased land at the foot of Cheyenne Mountain, named the area "Broadmoor City," created a lake, established a private country club, and built a European-style casino. When the hotel burned to

Edi Scholdan, Head Professional of the Broadmoor Skating Club at the Broadmoor Ice Palace. Source: Courtesy of Ruth Scholdan Harle.

the ground, a new one was built; but the count left the area and the hotel fell on hard times. Spencer Penrose, a wealthy businessman who created the Pikes Peak Highway, became interested in the property. He envisioned a resort to cater to guests' every whim and bring worldwide acclaim. Penrose and his business partner Charles L. Tutt Jr. built a new hotel and kept the name Broadmoor, spelling it with a small raised "a": BROADMOOR.[8]

The Broadmoor resort re-opened in 1918 with several lavish parties attended by high society from all over the United States. The press dubbed it the "Jewel of the Rockies" and the "Newport of the West." Presidents, royalty, actors, musicians, athletes, and other dignitaries visited. The resort included beautiful golf courses and a grand equestrian stable. When a new stable opened in 1938, Penrose converted the old riding academy into an ice rink. The Broadmoor Ice Palace, with a 185' x 85' ice surface, became the home of the Pikes Peak Figure Skating Club (FSC).[9]

When Spencer Penrose died in 1939, Charles Tutt Jr. and sons Thayer and Russell took over management of the Broadmoor Hotel. In time the forward-thinking Thayer Tutt made the Broadmoor Ice Palace a sports destination by aggressively scouring the nation for top figure skating talent and actively recruiting amateur, collegiate, and professional hockey tournaments. The Pikes Peak FSC presented ice shows for conventions held at the Broadmoor and staged the first of its annual summer ice revues.[10]

As World War II came to a close, the Broadmoor hired Edi to begin a summer skating school. Edi had briefly served in the U.S. Army during the war, but what he did during active military duty is unclear. He later told some students he was attached to a ski troop out of Colorado Springs, but other skaters in the 10th Mountain Division ski troop do not recall him. At the end of the summer of 1943, he showed up in Lake Placid for an exhibition. There he approached the parents of Andra McLaughlin of New York City, telling them that he had just been discharged from the service, was building a stable of skaters, and wanted to know if they were interested. Andra was one of the first of many champion skaters that Edi brought to the Broadmoor.[11]

The Broadmoor provided a home for him near the resort when the summer skating school officially began in 1945. His day began with a stop at the Broadmoor for breakfast and then a short walk around Cheyenne (Broadmoor) Lake to the rink. Coaches didn't make much money in those days, so volume was important. Edi had lots of students and worked long days, teaching in a suit and tie.[12]

He began each day with figure lessons. While teaching, Edi wreaked havoc on patches. He sometimes smoked a cigar—his ashes falling on the figures. He followed his student constantly and skated all over the patch; his extra tracings looked as if four other people had skated there. To improve concentration Edi did unorthodox things—giving a skater a shove to throw him off his circle and then asking, "Why are you off the circle?" or making noises during the quietness of the patch session. "If you jumped, he would be upset with you because you weren't concentrating enough," a student explained.[13]

Free skating was Edi's forte. Despite a strong Austrian accent, his message came across clearly as he yelled "Stroke! Stroke!" at the beginning of sessions. During lessons, he shouted to his students, "Land that! Land that!" He once told a student who kept falling on his jumps, "Jump higher!" Edi was a great psychologist and knew his students inside out. When one student didn't enjoy jumping, he made her yell, "I will not panic! I will not panic!" as she went into her jumps.[14]

Edi's strength was his ability to get the best out of each student, as Andra McLaughlin observed: "He'd say 'Antie, you can do it higher' or 'Antie, you can do it faster.' He wouldn't tell you something was wrong, but what was right. Many coaches have used his way of teaching, including me." He was equally popular with the parents, and families often invited him over for dinner. One evening a skating mother asked what he would like for dinner, and he said, "I vill eat anything." "That will certainly be nice for whoever you marry," she responded. "Yes," he said, "my wife vill be lucky."[15]

As summers ended, Edi regularly headed eastward to teach in Boston, Providence, and New York City. During his time on the East Coast, Edi met Roberta Jenks. She had grown up in Providence and had skated competitively for The Skating Club of Boston, placing second in both novice and junior ladies in 1939 and 1941. Her father, Robert Jenks, served on the USFSA Board of Directors for a number of years, and the Jenkses were wealthy enough to send Roberta to London to train. Roberta was extraordinarily graceful on ice; she interpreted music well and was a great show skater.[16]

Roberta's family wanted her to continue competing, but at age eighteen she eloped with Richard D. Burns, a lieutenant in the Air Force. Her parents disapproved and cut her off financially. She moved in with her in-laws in Cincinnati, Ohio, while her husband served abroad in World War II, and their daughter, Dixie Lee Burns, was born on May 28, 1943. Even though she had a small child to raise, Roberta continued to skate. She moved back to Boston to train the next year and spent summers at the Broadmoor. She placed fourth in national senior ladies in 1946.[17]

The couple divorced after the war, and Roberta's path again crossed Edi's at the Broadmoor and on the East Coast. Edi had coached Roberta briefly, and she was impressed with his teaching skill. The Jenks family approved of Edi, and he helped Roberta get back in her parents' good graces. Edi also hit it off with three-year-old Dixie right away. Edi, thirty-six, and Roberta, twenty-one, were married in Providence, Rhode Island, on October 14, 1946.[18]

Edi and his new family moved to Chicago in 1947. Roberta continued to train, competing at Europeans in Davos in 1947 and in Prague in 1948. Between competitions, she gave birth to Edward James Scholdan, but the baby did not live long. After placing sixth at the 1948 Olympic tryouts in Chicago, Roberta passed her gold figure test. The following spring, James Edward Scholdan was born on April 18, 1949; and at age twenty-four, Roberta hung up her competition skates.[19]

In Chicago, Edi entered a professional partnership with Edith Palmer, executive secretary of the Chicago FSC and director of the figure skating program. They worked well together and made a formidable team. When Thayer Tutt approached Edi to come to the Broadmoor full-time in 1948, Edith Palmer was part of the package. She became executive secretary of the newly renamed Broadmoor Skating Club (BSC). In the late forties, the Broadmoor name did not yet have cachet in the skating world, but that transformation occurred when Edi and Edith moved to Colorado.[20]

After a string of head coaches, the Broadmoor management put their faith in Edi Scholdan, and Edi, in turn, put his faith in his students. Edi was especially appealing to the tots. One five-year-old passed her preliminary test after three weeks on the ice. "He always had this brilliant smile and his eyes were round, warm, and inviting—all that stuff that made you glue yourself to him," a student recalled. One parent, who came to Edi with her nursery school dropout, appreciated his playfulness. He had the youngsters do a shoot-the-duck (a squatting position with one leg outstretched) across the ice and the first one to cross the finish line received a piece of candy. If beginning students didn't hold their hands correctly, Edi put a quarter on the top of each little hand—if the coin didn't fall it was theirs to keep.[21]

Edi embraced beginners, but the Broadmoor management was looking for stars. Once Scholdan was on board they recruited the top American talent to train at their facility and represent their club. Edi's first World champions were Peter and Karol Kennedy. This brother-sister pair team moved from Seattle to Colorado in 1949. They had been training with Edi every summer for years, prior to winning their first national pairs title in 1948. By the time they represented the BSC, they were two-time U.S. pairs champions and two-time World silver medalists. At the Broadmoor, they won two more World silver medals and the 1950 World pairs title.[22]

Peter Kennedy acknowledged that Edi was a good pairs coach. "His strength was his patience," he said. "I know because I drove him crazy!" Peter and Karol were the first skaters to receive full scholarships to Colorado College. Karol lived at the Mayhurst dormitory and Peter lived in a thirty-two-room mansion with "Aunt Becky"—wealthy socialite Rebecca Sanders Miller, who was the Broadmoor club president and de facto godmother to the Broadmoor skaters.[23]

This formula—find the talent, provide housing, give them scholarships, and let Edi guide them toward championship titles—was repeated frequently in the coming years. The Broadmoor management invited skaters only if they were proven champions, but Edi continued to teach group lessons and developed homegrown talent, too. If he saw potential talent, he was proactive. "Edi took me out of a public session, told my dad I should be taking lessons, and gave me my first pair of decent skates," one student said.[24]

His coaching methods for both beginners and World champions were to pump up their energy and confidence, and increase their speed. At that time, speed was not considered a premium, but Edi demanded that his skaters "get the lead out." He would pick up a skate guard or walking cane, wave it around, and threaten to hit a skater, saying, "Move! Get going, get going!"[25]

Edi's focus on repetition—doing it right over and over again—drove his skaters crazy. His favorite phrases were "Do it again!" and "One more time!" He made his students work on the hardest things at the end of their program run-through. Edi would put the music on and say, "Okay, pick it up halfway through." At the end of the program, skaters could stop briefly to catch their breath, and then he said, "Okay, we will do it from the beginning and we will leave nothing out." The mental drill prepared his students for competition. When they got tired halfway through their program, they still knew they could finish because in practice they had done it twice. Edi pushed his students physically as far as he could, then mentally he took them one step further. He took pride in wearing his students out during their lessons.[26]

His students appreciated his technical expertise. He had a knack of looking at a jump, pulling it apart, telling students what went wrong, and explaining what needed to be done. "I don't think he could execute them himself but he knew how to teach and motivate you to do it right," one student observed. Like many coaches, Edi had a few idiosyncrasies. "He never allowed you to stand on two feet," a student remembered. "When you were listening to him in a lesson you had to shift from one foot to the other. The idea was that you would not rest in between anything while skating."[27]

Edi's high-pitched voice and his mangling of the English language amused his students. They kidded him when he said "point your finger-toe" instead of "point your toe." His mutilation of language included transposing words. After telling David Jenkins to "Turn your left head," David would respond, "Edi, it's turn your head left!" Edi also asked him to "go your program through." Edi loved to recite his favorite lines from movies, shouting them out for the amusement of others. After he saw *The Caine Mutiny* with Humphrey Bogart, Edi told students he had seen the most wonderful movie, called "Mutiny on the Can." The skaters imitated him and teased him about his language. As Edi choreographed a show number he wanted the girls in a V-formation, and they convulsed in laughter when he asked them to make a "we."[28]

Edi made up nicknames for students: Patricia Firth was Fitzy-First, Lorin Caccamise was Cacklemouse, and Christy Haigler was anointed Schfitznase—he told her it meant bird nose. Edi's version of English included comical phrases. "We had this long-standing joke," a skater remembered. "He always said 'bend your knees,' but because of his accent—and because coaches didn't make much money teaching then—he said, 'Benzeeknees, five dollars please.'"[29]

Aside from his playful approach to coaching, Edi encouraged his students to immerse themselves in the arts: "It is advisable for those who follow an artistic sport to study subjects of art . . . sculptures, paintings, the theatre, etc. Observance of good art helps to make one think, feel and evolve original movements in skating . . . [This will enable skaters] to get inspiration to create personality on ice . . . a very important factor in free skating programs." His students took ballroom dancing and ballet at studios around town, learned etiquette at Broadmoor tea dances, and went to cultural activities. "We'd go to these exotic ballets and I could never figure out why I was there except he wanted me to learn to appreciate what life was all about," a student observed. "He was very concerned about our development as a whole being."[30]

Edi involved his students in selecting music for their program. He took students to a music store where they could sit in a sound-proofed booth to preview music, and he suggested composers he thought they might like; they sat there together and listened until something clicked. He also encouraged his students to take an active role in choreographing their programs, saying, "Go out and feel the music. Show me what you want to do with it." He then tweaked whatever his students came up with.[31]

On ice he encouraged other forms of training. Andra McLaughlin's father thought things got dull at the Broadmoor in the spring when the competitive season was over. His sons had won speed skating medals in New York City, so Mr. McLaughlin suggested they have speed skating championships. Andra donned speed skates in Colorado and became the North American speed skating champion. Both Andra and Edi felt it improved her figure skating. Edi encouraged many of his students to speed skate for strength—increasing their stroke, speed, and stamina. Another fringe benefit was getting skaters off their toe picks; speed skaters have to push entirely with their blades because there are no toe picks.[32]

Edi had other novel ideas. In the summers, he took his students on field trips up into the mountains. He had them go into icy streams to build up their strength. His weekly gym classes, conducted on the green lawn outside the arena, included breathing exercises, stretching and limbering exercises, jumping over objects, and balancing on ladders. He encouraged his students to play tennis on the Broadmoor courts to develop agility and hone their natural reflexes.[33]

Students could not recall a specific diet, but he was concerned about weight gain. The Broadmoor Hotel drugstore was the local hangout; and whenever skaters had sundaes, they were always on the lookout for Edi. Andra McLaughlin recalled: "He always told us, 'You better lose weight! You better lose weight!' He never told us what to eat, but he would not be happy to find us splurging."[34]

As important as Edi's coaching methods were for grooming champions, his true strength was producing ice shows. He was a master at mounting the annual Broadmoor Ice Revue. Stars from the Broadmoor stable were featured alongside U.S. and international champions. An invitation to perform in the Ice Revue was often a skater's introduction to the mystique and allure of the Broadmoor resort and skating facilities. Skaters usually liked what they saw, and many could be persuaded to move to Colorado to represent the Broadmoor Skating Club.[35]

The Broadmoor Ice Revue was the highlight of the huge summer skating school, and the show incorporated hundreds of kids from coast to coast. As producer, Edi controlled everything. He chose the themes, selected the music, and choreographed the numbers. Edith Palmer was the co-producer, in charge of the logistics. The shows were a huge undertaking, and Edi was relentless. "If Edi wasn't getting the results he wanted, he kept us all night," a skater recalled.[36]

As an innovative show producer, Edi incorporated non-skaters into the show, including the Cheyenne Mountain Dancers (a folk dancing troupe), dancers from the Colorado Kiowa tribe (performing on wooden platforms), and the Broadmoor Hotel orchestra. Even an Olympic skier performed in the Ice Revue. Edi met Buddy Werner one day while skiing, and Buddy told him he was having trouble on the icy slopes. At the Broadmoor rink, Edi taught him how to ski on the ice, and Buddy performed in the show that year.[37]

Edi borrowed famous friends to perform in the Ice Revue, including comedians Frick and Frack, Freddie Trenkler, the Scarecrows, and the Three Bruises. Edi continued to do his act in the show. He had juggled for decades so he was always ready to perform. "He was so good, it was just unbelievable," a student said. He expanded his repertoire beyond juggling—he jumped over objects, performed a Charlie Chaplinesque routine, and squired a beautiful blonde in a dance duet.[38]

Eddie and Roy Shipstad and Oscar Johnson of the professional touring show Ice Follies loaned Edi costumes for the Ice Revue, and club member Ginny Might annually flew to the Follies warehouse in Los Angeles to retrieve them. It was a thrill for the skaters to wear Follies costumes, and they looked forward to the glamorous shows. In exchange, Edi steered potential show skaters to Follies. "After I performed in the Hollywood Ice Revue for three years I ended up in Ice Follies," Andra McLaughlin said. "I don't know how it happened, but Edi ended up with my contract and he signed me up."[39]

After seven performances of the Ice Revue, there was always an end-of-show party, usually a chuck wagon dinner in the Garden of the Gods. The

Broadmoor Skating Club was famous for entertaining the skaters throughout the summer: social teas, dinners at the Broadmoor Hotel, picnics at
Green Mountain Falls, Old West steak fries in Fisher Canyon, bonfires in
the mountains, attending the Pikes Peak or Bust Rodeo, making trips to the
Cheyenne Mountain Zoo, swimming at the Cheyenne Lake beach, or singing and dancing under the stars with a three-piece orchestra. Beyond the
impressive hospitality enjoyed throughout the summer, the culmination of
the season was test sessions. Edi took tremendous pride in the success of the
Broadmoor skating school as skaters passed dozens of figure tests.[40]

There were other shows throughout the year. Whenever there was a big
convention at the hotel, the skaters put on a show. Edi always had new numbers prepared for emergencies. In the fall of 1956, Patricia Nixon, the wife of
the U.S. Vice President, made a surprise visit; and the skaters scurried into a
quick performance. Several years later, the Broadmoor hosted a private skating party for the King and Queen of Thailand, and Edi gave Queen Sirkit a
free lesson. Broadmoor skaters performed at the drop of a hat.[41]

Producing shows and champions left little free time for playing golf,
Edi's huge passion. Whenever Edi went missing on the ice, his students
found him on the golf course, which was right next to the rink. He always
wore a golf cap, and skaters said that they probably wouldn't recognize him
without the hat. Edi involved his students in his love of the green. He asked
the girls to go into a pond to gather up his golf balls for him. He played
with many of his students' fathers, mixing business with pleasure. For example, Edi approached a Texan skating mother and said, "When your husband comes down, have him bring his golf clubs; I have to talk to him." As
they played a round, the two men agreed that Edi would teach the daughter year-round at the Broadmoor.[42]

When summer ended, Edi turned to his wintertime passion. The
Broadmoor ski resort was close and accessible. Edi's students weren't allowed to ski for fear of injury, but he was more relaxed after the competitive
season. He took national champion David Jenkins skiing when his mother
and brother were away. "Someone in my family skinned him alive," recalled
David, "because I had never been skiing before and he took me up on the
lift—and that's the last I saw of him that day. My family thought I might
break my leg because I was prone to do those things." Edi treated his own
children the same way. He took his daughter Ruth (born in 1953) to the top
of Aspen when she was tiny, saying "Okay, this is how you do it. I'll see you
down at the bottom." She couldn't keep up with him so she sat down and
waited for the ski patrol.[43]

Many skaters saw their lives flash before them when driving with Edi. "He was a terrible driver," student Sherry Dorsey remembered. "He drove fast and never paid attention. I just hoped I would make it out alive." After the competitive season was over, Edi invited some of his students to go skiing, but some parents would not let their children go—not for fear of a skiing accident, but a car accident. Edi bragged to his students about his many speeding tickets, garnered while driving down Cheyenne Mountain. When the cops stopped him he relied on his thick accent: "Don't speak-a the English."[44]

At home Edi kept busy with projects. In the basement, he perpetually worked on the landscape for an elaborate train set. The basement also doubled as a movie theater, where Edi showed his students memorable performances from the Olympics, as well as films he took of his own skaters for critiquing purposes. He also continuously worked on improving the skate blade. Edi never stopped for a moment. He had the ability to successfully juggle many aspects of his life, but his paramount goal was bringing an Olympic title home to the Broadmoor.[45]

The El Pomar Foundation, the umbrella organization that ran the Broadmoor, treated Edi like royalty, but it still expected him to produce champions. Edi had some outstanding skaters right from the start, including Andra McLaughlin, Helen Geekie of St. Louis, and Richard Dwyer of Los Angeles. Eleven-year-old Dwyer came to the Broadmoor during the summer of 1947 to perform in the Ice Revue. The Broadmoor invited Dwyer to train year-round after he won the 1948 U.S. novice men's title and the 1949 U.S. junior men's title, but his parents felt he was too young. After Dwyer placed third in U.S. senior men, producer and star Eddie Shipstad nabbed fourteen-year-old Dwyer to be his own replacement as Mr. Debonair in Ice Follies. "In all sincerity it was a temptation to work with Edi and compete for the Broadmoor," Dwyer acknowledged. "Edi was 'go, go, go,' and very charismatic." As it turned out, Dwyer decided to turn professional. He enjoyed a thirty-year career with Ice Follies.[46]

Edi lost Dwyer, but he was already working with an Olympic competitor. Jimmy Grogan grew up near Tacoma, Washington, and trained in San Francisco with Hans Johnson. When Grogan moved to the Broadmoor in the summer of 1949 at age sixteen, he had already won a U.S. senior men's bronze and two silver medals, and placed sixth at the 1948 Winter Olympics in St. Moritz. Under Edi's coaching, Grogan was runner-up to Dick Button at both the Nationals and Worlds in 1951 and won the bronze medal at the 1952 Olympics in Oslo.[47]

When Dick Button retired in 1952, Grogan was next in line; but Edi's plans for Grogan were thwarted when the nineteen-year-old skater was drafted and sent to Missouri. Grogan still planned to compete, but he was also competing head to head with Edi's newest star. The Broadmoor had invited Hayes Alan Jenkins, nineteen, and his brother David, fifteen, to train with Edi. Hayes was already accomplished. He had placed fourth in the 1952 Olympics right behind Grogan. The move to Colorado in 1952 was triggered because of financial need.[48]

The Jenkins dynasty included the brothers and older sister Nancy from Akron, Ohio. Early in their career, they joined the Cleveland SC and trained with Walter Arian. The Jenkins brothers spent the next six summers in Lake Placid, training with Gus Lussi, who coached Dick Button to two Olympic wins. Lussi, a phenomenal jump coach, gave the Jenkins brothers excellent training. Hayes became 1948 U.S. junior champion, and a member of four World Teams and the 1952 Olympic Team.[49]

Hayes was a freshman at Northwestern University when his father lost his job. The Jenkins brothers were offered a deal they couldn't refuse—free ice time, free lessons with Edi, a room they could share rent free in the employees' quarters in the Colonial House, and a scholarship to Colorado College. "With the finances running out, it was only because of the Broadmoor and the El Pomar Foundation that we could keep skating. They were wonderful to us," David said.[50]

Hayes appreciated the proximity of Colorado College to the Broadmoor. He had enjoyed studying at Northwestern, but it was not a good training set-up. The commute between Evanston and the arena in downtown Chicago was arduous, and Hayes hoped to stay in for four more years. "You didn't want to win the Worlds just once," he explained. "You had been at the game long enough that you wanted to prove that you were the champion. Dick had retired, and I wanted my shot at winning the World Championship—that was the large part of the reason I went to the Broadmoor to work with Edi."[51]

Observers have debated the importance of Edi's role in the Jenkins brothers' success. Broadmoor coach Eileen Seigh offered this assessment: "My father raised horses and he said, 'A good horse always makes a trainer look good,' and it's the same in skating. Hayes and David made Edi look like a star. In my estimation, Edi learned from them." Although the brothers were already formed when they went to the Broadmoor, Edi did all the right things. He instilled self-confidence and inspired them to do their best work.

Edi and Hayes worked together to create the outstanding freestyle programs that combined Hayes's athletic prowess, musicality, and polished style.[52]

When Hayes moved to the Broadmoor, he acknowledged that he arrived as a complete skater. "Gus gave me a marvelous foundation in jumping, but he was in Lake Placid which wasn't that convenient. Edi and I always got along extremely well, and he was a stabilizing influence. Edi wasn't teaching me but coaching me. There's a difference. He was very strong in the fundamentals and he helped me mature." Edi treated his students fairly and juggled two World competitors surprisingly well. Grogan and Jenkins had been competitors for four years, and Grogan had always beaten Jenkins. "Edi was willing to take me, and he continued to coach Jimmy, and it was never awkward for me," Hayes explained. "Jimmy and I roomed together when we did exhibitions, and we were very good friends."[53]

Jimmy Grogan was allowed to temporarily leave military service to compete at the 1953 Worlds in Davos, Switzerland, but he had only one month to train. Grogan won the figures, but Hayes Jenkins won the free skate and his first World title; Grogan settled for the silver. In 1954 Jenkins won his second World title in Oslo. Grogan again placed second, and David Jenkins placed fourth. After receiving his fourth career World silver medal, Grogan retired. In retrospect, Hayes believes that Edi would have liked to see Grogan win, since he had been with Grogan much longer.[54]

The Kennedy siblings, Jimmy Grogan, and the Jenkins brothers helped put the Broadmoor Skating Club on the map. Skaters nationwide flocked to the club to work with Edi. Being around the best was beneficial to everyone; the youngsters drew inspiration from training next to national and international competitors; similarly, the concentration of champion skaters kept the level of training consistently high. "Even though Edi had some incredible skaters, I never saw favoritism," a World Team member said.[55]

The Broadmoor was a wonderful place to live. The skaters' dormitory, the Mayhurst, was within walking distance of the rink. If the Mayhurst was full, upper-echelon skaters lived at the Colonial House or at the hotel. "In the summers my brother Monty and I had a small room at one end of the hotel, just above the Tavern [restaurant]," student Greg Hoyt remarked. "There was a faux balcony that opened into the atrium. We fell asleep to the strains of the orchestra, which played into the wee hours."[56]

The transition to the Broadmoor was not always easy. Frances Dorsey, the 1951 U.S. junior ladies champion, moved from Seattle to train with Edi. She was surprised when he told her she had to learn to skate all over again. For three weeks, she was not allowed to spin or jump; she spent every session stroking. Even though she was humiliated, Frances stayed. "I really loved him dearly," she said. "At first I thought he didn't like my skating, but then I realized he felt you had to stroke well and have a style, and he would not bend. He had a goal for all his skaters, and he knew how to put it all together. At times I was a little scared of him; but reflecting back, I recall the twinkle in his eye and his soft quality. If he asked me to jump over the Grand Canyon I probably would." His purpose was to guide skaters to the Worlds and the Olympics, and he did whatever he could to make that a reality.[57]

Edi's students won medals at the Midwestern, national and international levels; and by the end of the decade he had coached nearly twenty skaters who made the World Team. The Broadmoor organization valued its preeminent coach. "Scholdan was the greatest guy in the world," Thayer Tutt exclaimed.[58]

Everything went well for Edi except his marriage. Roberta had grown restless. She was twenty-eight when her second daughter, Ruth Thea Scholdan, was born on January 15, 1953. Roberta appeared in the annual shows, did a little judging, taught a little, did choreography, and filled in for Edi when he was away at competitions—but it was not enough.[59]

Edi and Roberta had been married eight years when she signed to skate with Ice Vogues, a professional ice show, in 1955. Dixie Lee was twelve, Jimmy was six, and Ruth was two when Roberta left the children with Edi and left the marriage. The separation was not a complete surprise: "It was a rocky road. . . . They fought like cats and dogs. . . . It was not a happy marriage," the skaters recalled. Edi was devastated but remained upbeat and steady in his coaching. Raised a Catholic, he had a great friend in Father Harrington of the nearby Pauline Catholic Chapel; they spent hours talking and walking around the lake.[60]

Edi eventually lost one student through the divorce. He had coached his stepdaughter Dixie since she was five. "I loved to skate; you couldn't get me off the ice!" she said; but Edi had been careful not to show favoritism. Dixie got the leftover ice, the end patch, and only if somebody cancelled did she get a lesson. "I was always the reject," she said, "but that's what he had to do, in his mind, in order to be fair to all of his students. He was a fabulous coach, and I always loved working with him." Dixie had been the 1954 Midwestern novice ladies champion and placed second in Midwestern junior ladies in 1955. She focused on her skating while Roberta was in Europe earning money so she could come back and collect the children. "We were waiting for her to return," Dixie said, "but she never showed up."[61]

Dixie longed to be one of Edi's national champions, but training proved difficult. She had to find her own way to the rink every day after school, among other challenges. "I kind of drifted away. It wasn't a conscious choice," she explained. "It was a response to my life being upside down at that moment. Edi would say, 'You know, this is your critical year. If you quit now, you can't come back.'" Instead, Dixie retired at thirteen, lived with relatives in Rhode Island, and became interested in other things. She regretted that she never finished her tests even though she detested figures. "I had this fantasy that someday I would go back and finish them—just to say I had done it."[62]

Although his stepdaughter had left, Edi had another World competitor in his stable of champions—Ronnie Robertson, a phenomenal free skater from Los Angeles. He was the 1950 U.S. novice men's champion and the 1952 U.S. junior men's champion, had placed fourth at the 1953 Worlds, and fifth at the 1954 Worlds. "Edi juggled Ronnie and me well, too; it was never an issue," Hayes remembered. Edi gave equal attention to everyone. He also worked with skaters whose coaches couldn't attend Worlds or the Olympics. "Edi always kept an eye on us," pairs skater Janet Gerhauser recalled. "He was very generous that way."[63]

The year 1955 turned out to be one of Edi's most rewarding. Hayes won his third World title, Robertson placed second, and David Jenkins was third—giving Edi and the United States a clean sweep of the men's awards. This extraordinary triumph occurred in his hometown of Vienna. Edi was justifiably jubilant in front of his countrymen.[64]

As the 1956 competitive season neared, Scholdan was confident—rightfully so—that his students would excel yet again, and not just internationally. He worked with dozens of students on a daily basis—and no one felt left out. He not only gave each one his time but supported everyone with his attentive, caring nature, as one skater recalled: "It's not what Edi taught me, but the moments with him where his humanity was so apparent." His stepdaughter Dixie pinpointed the reason why so many of his students did well. "He had the most incredible way to inspire you; he could make you feel like you were a million dollars. I saw him do it with Hayes, I saw him do it with David Jenkins, I saw him do it with everybody, and it certainly worked with me. He believed in your talent and there wasn't anything he didn't believe you could do."[65]

1956 WINTER OLYMPICS

A record number of athletes—924 from thirty-two nations—gathered in Cortina d'Ampezzo, Italy, to compete at the VII Olympic Winter Games.

The biggest excitement was the Russian team, which arrived for its first Winter Games. Cortina d'Ampezzo, a small town of 5,000, was a famed ski resort in the Dolomites. The figure skating events took place at two large outdoor rinks at the Olympic Stadium. The American skating team arrived early, expecting a dual win in the men's and ladies competition. However, a practice session changed all of that in an instant.[66]

Two days after the U.S. team arrived, two-time World champion Tenley Albright was skating backwards at high speed on a practice session. She quickly turned to avoid some skaters who were being photographed and caught her blade in a rut. As she fell, her left skate hit her right ankle with such force that the blade penetrated through her boot. "The blunt blade cut through a large vein and coursed obliquely downward, scraping the bone severely," her father, Dr. Hollis Albright, explained. Maribel Vinson Owen promoted a positive, hopeful outcome to the press, who hovered at the hospital to ascertain Tenley's condition. Under Dr. Albright's care, Tenley began skating three days after the accident. Her event did not start for ten days; but on the sixth day before competition, early signs of phlebitis (the inflammation of a vein) arose. She continued to skate up to the limit of pain every day.[67]

Meanwhile the Olympics officially began with the Opening Ceremonies. In figure skating, the men competed first; and Hayes Jenkins, Ronnie Robertson, and David Jenkins ended up "one, two, three" in the figures. For the free skate, the weather was cold and the ice was hard as steel. David did not skate his best; he later said that the sun on the ice was so bad that the glare made it hard to tell where the ice was when landing a jump. The battle for first place was between Hayes and Ronnie, now a Gus Lussi student. The American spectators rooted for both to do well. "I never felt such a strain; everyone was exhausted from it," Theresa Weld Blanchard, editor of *Skating*, confessed. Both men skated superbly. Robertson did "everything perfectly" and Hayes's program "was a masterpiece." Edi had barely watched Hayes's Olympic performance due to nerves. Afterward someone told Hayes that he stood next to Edi as he skated; every time Hayes jumped, Edi turned his back and asked, "Did he land it?"[68]

Robertson won the free skating, but it was not enough to overtake Hayes's lead in figures. Hayes Alan Jenkins won the first gold medal for the United States at the 1956 Winter Olympics. The entire men's team triumphed as well, with Robertson taking home the silver medal and David Jenkins the bronze medal.[69]

The Americans, elated with their historic sweep, were equally thrilled to learn that Tenley Albright could compete. The ladies, however, had difficulty with weather, too. Their first figure was skated in a heavy snowstorm, but the storm subsided and Tenley placed first, with Carol Heiss of New York right behind her.[70]

In the ladies free skate, Tenley skated beautifully; her only mistake was a slight falter on her double loop. Carol Heiss faulted on one double jump but otherwise skated a fast and intricate program. Tenley and Carol both received thunderous applause, but Tenley proved victorious. Carol Heiss won the silver and Ingrid Wendl of Austria won the bronze. American Catherine Machado placed third in the free skating and finished in eighth place overall.[71]

Tenley Albright's win went into record books: It was the first time the United States won the Olympic gold medal in ladies figure skating, and it was the first time U.S. figure skating won two gold medals at the same Olympics. Tenley's performance was made more remarkable after the Games when it was revealed that she had not been able to run through her program for twenty straight days.[72]

In pairs, the Austrians won the gold, and U.S. champions Carole Ormaca and Robin Greiner placed fifth. The drama during the pairs division involved the German team of Marika Kilius, twelve, and Franz Nigel, nineteen, who placed fourth. The crowd, objecting to the judges' low marks, booed, screamed, and threw oranges at the judges and referee; the ice had to be cleared three times.[73]

At their first Olympic Winter Games, the Soviet Union won the country medal count with a whopping sixteen medals. The United States won seven medals, five of which were in figure skating: two gold, two silver, and one bronze.[74]

After the Olympics, most of the athletes headed home; but the figure skaters proceeded to nearby Garmisch-Partenkirchen, Germany, for the 1956 World Championships. Most of the results mirrored the Olympic placements. The men pulled off another medal sweep—Hayes won his fourth World title, followed by Robertson and David Jenkins in second and third, respectively. In pairs, Austrians Sissy Schwarz and Kurt Oppelt won again, with Ormaca and Greiner placing fourth, and the British continuing their dominance in dance.[75]

The one big difference was the ladies championship. The top two American skaters were both incredibly accomplished, and either could have won both the Olympics and Worlds that year. Carol Heiss held a slim lead over Tenley Albright in the figures. Tenley performed well in the free skate, but Carol dazzled—"her near-flawless execution brought the chilled crowd to its feet. Even one of the judges broke into spontaneous applause," *Time* wrote. This time the scales tipped in Carol's favor.[76]

Although she was only sixteen when she became the 1956 World champion, it had been a long road for Heiss. Tenley had beaten her on eight previous occasions, but the victory was sweet for Carol for a more important reason. Her mother was dying of cancer, and she wanted her mother to see her win an international championship. Maribel Vinson Owen was disappointed that Tenley did not defend her World title, but the Olympic gold medal was a sweet victory for both coach and student.[77]

Besides guiding Tenley, Maribel had worn her press hat in Cortina, her third Olympics as the figure skating expert for the Associated Press. Sports reporters new to figure skating were grateful for Maribel's presence. Their ultimate resource was always, "ask Maribel—she'll know." Maribel was famous for quickly calculating the final score. For example, she figured that Austrians Schwartz and Oppelt won the pairs event, and the AP sent out the result, hours before the official results were announced. Later a competing service had a Canadian team as the winner. Maribel stuck to her guns and paced the AP office in Cortina for hours, anxiously awaiting the official announcement. "I know I'm right," she said. Maribel's confidence was vindicated.[78]

When Tenley Albright and Hayes Jenkins returned home, they received numerous parades, receptions, and commendations. On Sunday, March 11, 1956, Tenley and Hayes appeared on the hugely popular Ed Sullivan television show. In a matter of days, skaters across the nation flocked to Philadelphia to participate in the 1956 U.S. Championships. Tenley's injury had healed completely, and she skated with "unbelievable perfection." The final score for the U.S. ladies title was close, but Tenley won her fifth straight U.S. title, followed by Carol Heiss and Catherine Machado. Hayes Jenkins won his fourth U.S. title, followed by Ronnie Robertson and David Jenkins. Carole Ormaca and Robin Greiner won their fourth U.S. pairs championship, and Joan Zamboni and Roland Junso of Los Angeles won the dance title. After three back-to-back competitions for the Olympic and World Team, it was time to finally head home.[79]

As the 1956 competitive season ended, Edi Scholdan and Maribel Vinson Owen counted their blessings. Both had successfully coached their first Olympic gold medalists. Hayes Jenkins's win brought distinction to the Broadmoor; and now his brother was anxious for his shot at the World title. In 1954, the first time David Jenkins appeared on the international scene, he astonished the judges. The French judge approached Hayes and curiously asked, "Monsieur Jenkins, do you have any more brothers?" "David was doing big triple jumps very early on," Hayes explained. "He was always a powerful free skater. No one expected him to be so good off the bat—it was a bit of a shock to everyone." Edi Scholdan was sitting pretty with another dynamite prospect to be the next Olympic champion.[80]

The Skating Club of Boston had a long history of U.S., World and Olympic achievements. Dick Button represented the club when he won the 1952 Olympics, and now Tenley Albright had won the first U.S. Olympic gold in ladies figure skating. Maribel was at a crossroads. With the prospect of Tenley's retirement, Maribel looked for another skater whom she could groom into the next U.S. ladies champion. This time she looked within her own family.

CHAPTER 4

THE RISING GENERATION

After Hayes Jenkins's Olympic win, Edi Scholdan focused his attention on David Jenkins's ascension to the World title. The Broadmoor hosted the 1957 World Championships, the first time the United States had held the competition since 1930. Many European skaters came to North America for the first time.[1]

Besides seeing the United States, the Europeans were delighted by the physical setting of the championships: competing indoors at the Broadmoor Ice Palace. Outdoor conditions, such as those in Europe, made competitions unpredictable. The afternoon sun made the surface soft, wet, or like corduroy; in early mornings or late at night, the ice was hard and brittle. Skaters battled the frigid temperatures and the variable elements: wind, rain, snow, sleet, or glaring sun—all of which affected the outcome of competitions.

Europeans were used to these difficult conditions, but for U.S. World Team members, known as "hothouse skaters," their first outdoor competition was brutal. Ice dancer Sidney Foster wore a red taffeta dress at the 1956 Worlds in Garmisch; no one had told her to dress differently. She survived only because her Canadian roommate loaned her a wool undershirt and a warm-up jacket. To combat the cold, female skaters wore hoods, bonnets, and leggings. While competitors waited their turn to skate their figures, they huddled together in warming huts.[2]

The Jenkins brothers, members of fourteen World Teams, had faced a myriad of weather conditions over their careers. The 1955 Worlds in Vienna was particularly memorable as it snowed practically every day. Officials cleared the snow off the ice every fifteen minutes for figure competition; still, the snow caked under the skaters' blades, stopping them dead in their tracks. Free skating had even more challenges, as Hayes noted: "You had to really push and pump if you were going upwind; if you had it downwind it pushed you to the opposite end of the rink too fast. You tried to jump at an angle so you didn't jump directly into the wind. You made these adjustments instantly and instinctively." David Jenkins added: "The wind used to whistle through the stadium so that skating against it was like trying to skate up a mountain. . . . The ice sometimes got so cold that it . . . cracked, leaving cracks an inch or so wide."[3]

The fickle weather and the luck of the draw had a profound impact on one's competitive performance, as Bob Swenning (and partner Yvonne Sherman) discovered at the 1948 Winter Olympics at St. Moritz:

> On the day of the Olympics it was really snowing so I promptly went back to bed because I was sure it was cancelled. Then I got a phone call: "Come on, it's clearing up." Three-fourths of the pair teams competed in bright sunlight, and then it started to snow again. We were the last pair to skate; we were frozen and the judges were frozen. We wound up fourth because we couldn't hear our music and they couldn't see us. We went to Davos for the Worlds and the same thing happened. The other top skaters competed in the sunshine, and we wound up skating in a snowstorm and came in fifth.[4]

Transportation was another challenge. Jet travel for skaters didn't begin until 1958. Trips from New York to Europe for U.S. World Teams took anywhere from twelve to eighteen hours; a flight to the 1952 Olympics in Oslo was advertised as taking *only* sixteen hours. Generally the U.S. team traveled in shifts to Worlds: first singles skaters, then pairs, and finally the dancers. All flights were time consuming and costly.[5]

The Broadmoor organization rolled out the red carpet for the 1957 World competitors. They arranged a flight on a chartered DC-6 plane so that all the European skaters and officials arrived together in Colorado Springs. The championships had a western theme, and the large welcoming committee—including the mayor, skating officials, and U.S., Canadian, and Japanese skaters—were decked out in western clothing. They presented ten-gallon hats to the seventy-eight-member travel party, and the ladies received red roses. They traveled in limousines with police escorts to the Broadmoor Hotel.[6]

The Broadmoor had hosted several U.S. Championships; but even by its own high standards, it outdid itself. The Europeans and Japanese were dazzled by the Wild West ambience. "Whooping Westerners hustled the bewildered foreign skaters through mock branding ceremonies . . . and dragged them on lariats to the Broadmoor Hotel's front desk," *Time* wrote. Western TV star Montie Montana lassoed each competitor, Ute Indians in native costume danced, and a cowboy on horseback roamed the banquet hall as they dined. The city welcomed the competitors with a grand parade: fifteen convertibles, decorated with the national flags of all the competitors, carried the skaters through the streets of town, accompanied by a number of bands. On the eve of the competition, an international ball was held. Thayer

Tutt's special guests included movie stars Nelson Eddy, Mary Pickford, Buddy Rogers, and Agnes Moorhead. After days of celebration, interrupted by skating practice, the competition began.[7]

Hometown crowds were pleased by two American victories: Carol Heiss won her second World title, and David Jenkins, on his home turf, won his first World title. American dancers Sharon McKenzie and Bert Wright won the bronze. For the second time in his career, Edi Scholdan's students swept the men's division: David Jenkins, Tim Brown, and Charles Snelling of Canada. Maribel Vinson Owen had two new students at Worlds. Nancy Rouillard and Ron Ludington, who placed fourth in pairs, had been a team for less than two years. Ron had recently switched from rollers to ice skating; and after working with several different partners, he teamed up with Nancy, a New England junior champion.[8]

Two weeks after the World Championships, the American skaters gathered in Berkeley for the 1957 U.S. Championships. Carol Heiss and David Jenkins won their first U.S. senior titles. Edi Scholdan had five students on the podium, including junior ladies bronze medalist Stephanie Westerfeld. Maribel had three medalists: U.S. pairs champions Nancy Rouillard and Ron Ludington, and novice men's silver medalist Frank Carroll.[9]

For the fourth time, a West Coast club won the coveted Harned Trophy. The trophy, a gift from Bedell H. Harned of New York City, was instituted in 1939 and went to the club whose skaters earned the most points by their placement at Nationals. In the history of the Harned Trophy, the perennial winners had been East Coast: The Skating Club of Boston, The Skating Club of New York, and the Washington Figure Skating Club. Sharon McKenzie and Bert Wright, the 1957 U.S. dance champions, helped the Los Angeles Figure Skating Club win the trophy. The West Coast skaters, who had had only a sprinkling of national titles over the years, were finally gaining recognition.[10]

Even though East Coast skaters had dominated the U.S. Championships titles, there had been a fairly even number of competitors from across the country since the thirties. The USFSA had divided the country into three sections: the Pacific Coast (established 1936), Midwestern (est. 1933), and Eastern (est. 1938) competitions. The USFSA then divided the Pacific Coast and Eastern sectionals into three regions; the Midwestern sectional was not divided into regions until 1962. The first step on the road to the Nationals was to enter a regional competition. For example, if a skater placed in the top three in senior ladies at Southwest Pacific, she advanced to the Pacific Coast competition. If she placed in the top three in senior ladies at Pacific Coast, she then advanced to the Nationals.[11]

What came next was a bit confusing. Arriving at Nationals, the top three skaters from the Eastern, Midwestern, and Pacific Coast competitions all stepped down one division. The seniors competed in the junior division, the juniors in novice. Placing in the top three at the national junior level was the only route to compete at the national senior level the following year. Every skater's goal was to graduate to the national senior level so he or she could compete for a spot on the World or Olympic Team. The most vigorous competition at Nationals was thus the junior divisions: men, ladies, pairs, and the junior dance equivalent—silver dance. Winning the junior title meant you had arrived.

The year 1957 introduced a rising generation of skaters who would compete in either the 1960 or 1964 Olympics. The junior men's champion from the East Coast finally won after three years in the junior division, whereas the junior pairs champions from the West Coast were astonished to win on their second attempt. All three athletes were hardworking kids who had persevered and earned their success.

Bradley Lord

1957 National Junior Men's Champion

Bradley Lord was five years old when he saw his first professional ice show at the Boston Garden. "In 1945 I was taken to see a performance of Shipstads & Johnson Ice Follies," he said. "Ever since that day I have been completely thrilled by figure skating." Four years later his parents gave him a pair of figure skates; and from age nine on, skating became his life. Everyone rooted for Bradley because he put his heart and soul into skating. It didn't take long for Bradley to form two ambitions: to make the Olympic Team and to star in Ice Follies.[12]

Bradley Richard Lord grew up in Swampscott, Massachusetts, just north of Boston. Born on August 22, 1939, he was the second son of Roy ("Lefty") Lord and Mary Alfreda Lord. Roy was a former all-around athlete at Lynn English High School, in Lynn, Massachusetts. He had been a track star and was well known in the community. Alfreda had a background in ballet, and their two sons inherited their parents' talents. Bruce, two years older than Bradley, was a big, strapping kid who excelled in basketball, football, and baseball. Bradley was the opposite in height and build: five feet ten and a half inches tall and slender. His parents and his brother were strong supporters of his skating.[13]

Bradley's foray into skating began with a walk across the street. Every winter the park opposite the Lord home became a large makeshift ice rink, covering both the football and baseball fields. Brad first learned to get around on hockey skates. After he received a pair of figure skates, he was a constant fixture on the outdoor ice, as he noted: "Some days I would go skating from about 8 A.M. to 8 P.M.—time out for meals of course. My older brother would always wonder why I never became tired; but when one loves something, you never tire of it." When the North Shore Sports Center opened in Lynn, he trained there. Bradley progressed rapidly, first with coach Lillian Tribby, and then with Bud Wilson at The Skating Club of Boston; he continued to train at both rinks.[14]

Bradley was a member of the Commonwealth Figure Skating Club, along with those of less wealth and social standing than those in the private SC of Boston. The costs of skating were difficult for the Lord family to handle. Roy Lord designed shoes; he was a talented master craftsman but not wealthy. Bradley's aunt and uncle helped with his skating expenses, but the costs were still a challenge. The SC of Boston had few Catholic members in the early fifties, but club members recognized Bradley's potential, and invited him to join the club. This meant he had more time to work with coach Bud Wilson.[15]

From 1928 to 1939, Bud Wilson was the most accomplished male skater in North America, winning fourteen Canadian and nine North American titles in singles and pairs. A member of three Canadian Olympic Teams, he collected a bronze at the 1932 Games. He retired from competition in 1939, entered the U.S. Army, became a U.S. citizen, and after serving in Europe during World War II, moved to Boston in 1946. He became the SC of Boston's senior professional and director of its Ice Chips show.[16]

"Mr. Wilson," as his students called him, was a favorite among skaters, an excellent teacher, and a gentleman. From the beginning, Bud had faith in Bradley. His premier student, Dudley Richards, who was 1951 U.S. junior champion, was a good role model for Bradley, as were the many elite skaters who trained at the club.[17]

Bradley had a long and difficult commute to the SC of Boston, but he had company; he convinced his same-age cousin Frank Muckian to join him on the ice. They arranged carpools when possible or took mass transit to make the forty-five-minute trip to the club: a bus from Lynn to Haymarket Square, a trolley to Central Square in Cambridge, and then another bus to the rink.[18]

Bradley placed second in juvenile boys at the 1951 Easterns when he was eleven. He performed solos in ice carnivals along with Dick Button and

Bradley Lord, The Skating Club of Boston, 1957 Junior Men's Champion. Source: Courtesy of Bruce Lord.

Tenley Albright, including appearing in the Ice Chips of 1951 at the Boston Garden. The Lords went to Lake Placid for summer vacations, and Bradley passed figure and dance tests there.[19]

At the 1952 Easterns, Bradley placed third in figures in novice men, but dropped to fourth after the freestyle. "This was one of my first disappointments in skating," he said, "but to be a champion you have to learn to take defeat just as well as winning. So I told myself I'll just have to work harder and maybe next year I'll do better." Bradley spent the summer in St. Paul with Bud Wilson. He passed his fourth figure test and skated in the pop concerts at the St. Paul Auditorium.[20]

After placing second in junior men at the 1953 Easterns, Bradley was thrilled to make his first trip to the U.S. Championships held in Hershey, Pennsylvania. He placed sixth in novice men. The SC of Boston presented him with the Tozzer Award at its banquet. The Tozzer Award, named after three-time national champion Joan Tozzer, had been bestowed annually since 1941 on a young skater who showed the most improvement, demonstrated good sportsmanship, and maintained high scholastic standards.[21]

Bradley attended St. John the Evangelist parochial school in Swampscott. His competitive travels posed problems, and he had to diplomatically maneuver his way around school authorities. He had an ongoing problem with Monsignor Donovan, who frowned on his taking time off for competitions. In the Monsignor's mind, Bradley was neglecting his studies, even though Bradley remained a good student.[22]

Bradley, described as a mother's dream, was a shy, gentle individual who was completely devoted to his sport. Alfreda traveled with him to every competition, and the Lord family frequently attended the SC of Boston's Friday night dinners, enjoying a five-dollar meal cooked in the kitchen downstairs and delivered to the upstairs dining area by a dumbwaiter. The evening began with cocktails, and then people dined as they watched a practice session prior to exhibitions. Any club member could sign up to perform, and the exhibitions provided great performance experience.[23]

Bradley won the 1954 Eastern junior men's title and "a happier boy couldn't be found." *Skating* noted that he displayed "supple mastery of double jumps, spins and dance steps to capture the title." Bradley went to Los Angeles to compete for the second time in U.S. novice men. He got "tense on figures" and placed sixth, and was unable to move up in the freestyle. For the second year, he was sixth. "This was another disappointment hard to take but this time I was my own enemy by becoming nervous," he acknowledged.[24]

At age fourteen, Bradley wrote two pieces for *Skating*. One explained the best way to do an axel: "First, many people make the mistake of bending the free leg in the takeoff. If they would stretch their free leg (like kicking a football) they would get a much higher jump." His next article admonished figure skaters to cherish their sport: "Do not skate to see how many medals and triumphs you receive, skate because you love to."[25]

The next year Bradley turned in a superb performance at Easterns and placed second in senior men. Surprisingly he did not go to the 1955 Nationals. Bud Wilson felt his figures were not ready and advised him not to go. Brad also stayed home that summer—the first time in five years—because his mother was recuperating from an illness.[26]

In 1956 Bradley, sixteen, placed third at Easterns, but this time his coach was confident in Bradley's prospects for the 1956 Nationals. In Philadelphia Bradley landed one of his first double axels in competition and was thrilled to place third in junior men and receive his first national medal. His diligent training over seven years had paid off.[27]

At the SC of Boston Bradley had become a respected and popular member. He helped new members adjust to the protocol challenges. One skater recalled: "There was one little old lady who was like the Gestapo. She would rap her cane against the side and say to me, 'You can't get off the ice and you can't do this.' Bradley came up to me and said, 'Now, don't be afraid. I've had a rough time of it here too. . . . This is what you need to do.'" The youngsters were in awe of his work ethic and appreciated his friendship, as club member Gerry Lane explained: "A lot of the skaters treated the younger kids like they didn't know anything, but Bradley never treated me like I was a little kid. He treated me like one of the guys. He set a great example and was a mentor. He was kind and helpful, and lectured me if I wasn't working hard enough."[28]

Bradley's contemporaries at the club admired him, too. Peter Betts had competed against Bradley from novice on up; he knew Bradley would succeed because he was so focused. Not everyone got along, however, as self-described "rogue" Ron Ludington remembered: "Bradley worked hard and was so prepared—but there was no love lost between Bradley and myself. One time I fell on a jump and he came over and sprayed me [with ice]. Well, no one sprays me and gets away with it. I came over and slapped him!"[29]

If Bradley had any faults, it was his occasional temper. His outbursts during practices were surprising because he was normally calm, but his passion for skating overcame his pleasant demeanor. "If the first jump of the morning didn't go well, he would get mad," a club member recalled, "and the second jump would be worse, and on and on. Soon he would have these little holes all over the ice [from kicking]."[30]

Bradley spent the summer of 1956 in East Lansing, where the Michigan State coaching staff included Pierre Brunet, who brought his champion skaters: the Heiss siblings, Carol, Nancy, and Bruce, and over time, Canadian champion Don Jackson and French champions Alain Giletti and Alain Calmat. The elite summer skaters were impressed with Bradley's skating. Carol Heiss thought he was like Hayes Jenkins, the elegant, classical stylist. Bradley was very smooth and polished, with good spins, solid jumps, wonderful footwork, and good edges.[31]

On practice sessions, everyone understood that Bradley was all business on his mission to succeed competitively. One of his roommates, Bruce Heiss, saw how conscientious he was. "When he practiced, you didn't get in the way of Bradley Lord. He took over the ice and needed a lot of room for his double lutz. He landed very hard and flat . . . He even broke his blade one day." He skated barefoot and used thick sponges inside his skates for extra padding; even so, his feet often blistered and bled. His fellow skaters said he had the worst feet they had ever seen.[32]

Bradley had many female admirers who were attracted to his dark hair, wide eyes, long eyelashes, and dimpled smile. But his mother had a tight rein on him, and Brad knew he was in East Lansing to train. Although he rarely went to dinner with the other kids and didn't sneak out at night, he did some socializing. He drove into town with other skaters for banana splits or science fiction movies, or caravanned to Holland near Lake Michigan for weekend swimming. On Sundays, Brad and other Catholics went to mass.[33]

Bradley did have one serious summer relationship, with Nancy Heiss. Teenagers Brad and Nancy "dated" for a year—primarily through letters between Boston and New York City. "I wrote a letter every day and he wrote me back every day for a whole year," Nancy said. "We told each other we loved each other, but it meant 'I really like being with you.' It was ideal puppy love." She never had to buy shoes because Brad was always sending her new shoes from his father's company. Nancy has an enduring memory of Bradley: Once they were chicken fighting on the grass with friends, and another couple rammed them into a tree—she still has the scar on her thigh.[34]

Bradley's mother was well known to the MSU skaters. She had a strong Boston accent like her son and an infectious laugh. Both parents were in East Lansing when Brad passed his eighth test. Roy Lord had seen his son skate only in local competitions, but he explained in *Skating* why he was present for this significant achievement:

> To Mrs. Lord and myself, the importance of this event was not in whether he passed the test; it was in the realization that our son had learned some of the greatest lessons in life in his road up to this point. I realized that skating is just as rugged and hard as . . . football, baseball, hockey, etc. Perfecting jumps, learning programs and training for competitions is harder or just as hard a routine as any athlete has to follow. . . . It is a proud feeling to be the father of a gold medalist, but most of all it is a most gratifying feeling to know one's son has learned so much of the ups and downs of life at so early an age.[35]

To prepare for the 1957 Nationals, Bradley added an early bird morning patch and performed in winter carnivals at New England colleges. A month before the competition, he and his cousin Frank took the bus home from the club to Lynn. When they got home, they realized that Brad had left his skates on the bus. "He was devastated," Frank Muckian said. "We tried to keep it quiet for a few days. His parents knew, but we didn't want the word getting out right before competition. Days later we tracked down the bus driver and discovered he had found them and was keeping them safe."[36]

Bradley skated well when he won 1957 Eastern senior men's title, but he realized he had to do better to win the U.S. junior men's crown in Berkeley. In an essay he wrote for school, he described the competition:

All the way out [to California] I prayed and hoped that this would be my year and that I would be lucky enough to win. My prayers were answered when I won the figures by four [out of five] judges and also the free by four. A happier boy or Mother or Dad couldn't be found when I was announced as the new Junior Champion of the [United States]. I shall never as long as I live forget 1957 and all the wonderful things God gave to me. And now here's to the future and I hope my ambition of becoming a member of the World & Olympic Team can come true.[37]

The town of Swampscott presented Bradley with the key to the city and he received the local newspaper's "Bouquet of the Week." When he graduated from Swampscott High School that spring, his senior page listed his interests: "spends much time practicing figure skating [and] enjoys drawing and painting." His two post-school goals were to be a member of the 1960 Olympic Team and enter the Massachusetts School of Art. Bradley had received honors in art since fourth grade and intended to pursue commercial art. He liked to fuse his two interests; for club ice shows, he helped with the props and set design, and made miniature sets for visualization purposes. When he went away to competitions, the design of the various hotels interested him. Brad knew that one day, after the arc of his skating career had ended, he would make commercial art his living.[38]

After Bradley entered the School of Fine and Applied Arts at Boston University, he received excellent news. He had been named an alternate to the 1958 World Team. After nearly a decade of training, skating was still pure pleasure for him. He would need the ardent support from his coach and his own enthusiasm over the next three years to make the 1960 Olympic Team.[39]

Ila Ray and Ray Hadley Jr.
1957 National Junior Pairs Champions
Linda Hart Hadley, Professional

She was shy and quiet. He was the local heartthrob. Together, Ila Ray and Ray Ellis Hadley Jr. were the nicest kids in Seattle's skating community. They had been skating since they were toddlers. Their parents, who were their coaches, motivated and instilled a great work ethic in their kids. Ila Ray and Ray Jr. were not rebels and did exactly what they were told to do.[40]

The Hadley family moved from Portland, Oregon, to Seattle in 1951, the same year the Seattle Skating Club hosted its first Nationals. Ray Ellis Hadley Sr., born February 22, 1921, in Eugene, Oregon, was a roller skater and primarily taught roller skating in Portland. In Seattle he taught both roller and ice skating. Ray's earliest students on ice were roller skating gold medalists who made the transition to figure skating.[41]

Ray and Bette, whom he had met through roller skating, married young and had their children in quick succession: Ila Ray was born on September 18, 1942, and Ray Jr. was born on October 6, 1943. "Ray" was the maiden name of Ray Sr.'s mother. The siblings began skating when they were three and four years old, respectively.[42]

Ray and Bette divorced after the family moved to Seattle in 1951. Surprisingly, the children remained with Ray, though Bette continued to live in Seattle. Ray was awarded the children because "the mother wasn't suitable. She was wild," a relative said. A parent of one of Ray's students babysat the children. She drove them to visit their mother; but as time went on, Bette became less involved in her children's lives. Skating friends never saw Bette at competitions, nor did the siblings ever talk about her.[43]

Ray Sr. had worked at Boeing to supplement his teaching income; but in 1954, he had enough new students to teach skating full-time. He also had a new wife. Ray and Linda Hart were married in Seattle on March 8, 1954. Linda, born Alvah Lynn Hart on February 27, 1929, in Winfield, Kansas, was the youngest of seven children. When her family moved to Oregon in 1948, Linda learned to ice skate after mastering roller skating. Her family always called her Alvah Lynn, but she changed her name professionally to Linda when she appeared in the chorus of traveling skating shows on the West Coast. Ray and Linda met in Oregon when they both taught at a Portland roller rink.[44]

When Ray proposed, Linda was serving in the U.S. Army, and her army girlfriends made her a beautiful lace wedding dress. Linda became an instructor using her maiden name, Linda Hart. Ray was thirty-four and Linda was twenty-five. At that point, Ila Ray was eleven, and Ray was ten. She soon ran the Hadley household, a godsend for Ray Sr., who needed direction. Ray then blossomed as a figure skating coach. "Linda kept him in line and was the best thing that happened to him," a student declared.[45]

The Hadleys taught at the Seattle Civic Arena, located on the grounds of the future 1962 World's Fair site. The Hadleys ran "Learn to Skate" group classes, with 150 kids at a time, for fifty cents a lesson, yelling instructions into their megaphones. A large organ pumped away while students skated shoulder to shoulder in these overcrowded sessions. The Hadleys also conducted smaller group classes and private lessons, and attracted a fair share of beginning students and maturing competitors. Hungry for students, they took all comers.[46]

Linda Hart Hadley and Ray Hadley, Coaches, Seattle Skating Club, wedding photo, 1954. Source: Courtesy of Sharon Dowling and Lawrence Hart.

Linda was the brains of the pair, but the jury was divided on her popularity as a teacher. To some she was a great coach; to others she was demanding and domineering. Linda did not allow a lot of fraternization. At competitions she discouraged interaction with any skaters besides Hadley students, saying, "They're from the other camp. Stick with your own." Her students were not allowed to get off the ice to go to the bathroom, and she discouraged them from wearing mittens, which inhibited hand extension. On the plus side, Linda taught her freestyle students to do spins and jumps in both left and right directions. She was a good choreographer, due to former dance training, and she searched for the perfect music for each student. Her students practiced tracing figure eights, edges, and dance patterns on a chalkboard in a hockey room, called the theory room. [47]

Linda's military service contributed to her regimented attitude. "She ran everything like a boot camp and didn't take crap from anybody," student Linda Adams said. Her drill sergeant persona produced results but sometimes left a negative impression. She had no qualms about screaming at a student for leaving a patch to grab a Kleenex on the railing. She was known to leave the rink and secretly return, hiding in the bleachers to see if her students were misbehaving.[48]

Linda's intensity made her students nervous; skating parents, however, understood the need for discipline. Arvilla Kauffman praised Linda, who put her children, Ron and Cindy, together as a pair. "Linda was domineering, but she loved like nobody could. They treated my kids like they were their own and I just adored her." Her son Ron had only kind words for his coach. "She was always positive and there was never a hard word or any problems," he said. "Linda understood that our parents had made sacrifices for our lessons, and she was always prepared."[49]

Ray Sr.'s specialty was ice dancing. His dancers were known for their deep leans, strong edges, stretched legs, pointed toes, and close, precise footwork. His students had to respond "Yes, sir" or "No, sir" to his commands, and he used a skate guard if necessary. "He hit our little bottoms if we weren't standing up straight," Cindy Kauffman recalled. "We had to look up at our partners, which I hated because it was my brother. Ray said, 'Look him in the eye—you have to look him in the eye!'"[50]

As a team, Linda and Ray taught singles, pairs, and dance, and the Hadley kids participated in all three. The ice dominated their time; they skated in the mornings and after school. Before Linda arrived, they had mixed success. After competing in juvenile boys for three years, Ray Jr. placed fifth in the 1956 Pacific Coast competition. After three attempts, the siblings won preliminary dance at Northwesterns. After three years in junior pairs, they won the silver medal at the 1956 Pacific Coast.[51]

The Hadleys struggled financially. Linda's family didn't see her much after her marriage because she had no money to travel. Ray Jr. sometimes skated in borrowed tuxes. Ila Ray and Ray knew their parents were driving them toward success for financial gain and worked hard to fulfill their parents' ambitions. Any pro wants his team to do well to bring in more business. The more titles the kids won, the better off the family was. [52]

Other American skaters, like the Owen girls, also had a parent as coach, but the Hadleys had two pairs of eyes constantly watching them. Linda and Ray Sr. were civil to most of their students, but their friends noted that Linda was particularly tough on Ila Ray and Ray Jr. "She had a frightening look when she screamed at them, and it scared me," a student recalled. "Maybe she had to do that to get those kids motivated." Linda drove them to be perfect. If they fell or made a mistake she really came down hard on them. "She was unduly heavy-handed," a friend said. "She even knew who her kids spoke with and told them who they were not allowed to speak with."[53]

Ila Ray and Ray enjoyed being at the rink, where the younger skaters idolized them. However, their friends felt that they never really liked skating that much because they were pushed so hard. As children, they thought everybody lived as they did—going to an ice rink daily. The parental pressure, however, drove them together for mutual protection. They rarely called each other by name. It was always "Brother" and "Sister," a pet sarcasm. Because there were two Ray Hadleys, the skaters called the son by his first and middle name: Ray Ellis.[54]

Hockey limited the ice time at the Civic Center, so the Hadleys trained at the rink in the Ballard neighborhood of Seattle or at the Tacoma rink. In the winter, they taught at a rink in Yakima, 145 miles southeast of Seattle, for additional income. On weekends, they made the five-hour round-trip drive with other students in tow. The rink had a little apartment upstairs where the family stayed; skaters brought their sleeping bags and found places on the floor.[55]

Skating conditions were less than ideal. The outdoor rink in Yakima was across the river from a smelly slaughterhouse, and it was freezing, with temperatures ranging from the twenties to sub zero. A record player was in the tiny warming hut, where Linda put the music on for her students' routines. If they fell, she stopped the music, opened the door, and yelled, "Start over!" Students prayed, "Don't fall, don't fall!" Despite the freezing cold, Linda had them perform or do the hokey pokey with the crowd to drum up business.[56]

Linda and Ray Sr. trained other sibling pair teams, including Bob and Carol Deuter and Ron and Cindy Kauffman. Ila Ray and Ray formed close friendships with these other skaters, and they blew off steam together: zigzagging between the neophyte skaters during public sessions, exploring the full-size arena together, and playing hide-and-seek in the tunnels. The boys tried to get out of practice by hiding in the bleachers, where they enjoyed scaring the younger kids. Another prank was throwing their sisters into the Zamboni-created snow banks. "We put them up in a lift and threw them over the barrier into the snow bank—and then ran like hell," Bob Deuter recalled. "We got into a lot of trouble for that one."[57]

The Hadley kids bonded with the other siblings because they understood the hazards in pairs skating. At the end of one crowded session, the Hadleys tried to quickly squeeze in a few more lifts. Ray lifted his sister into the air. She came down wrong and spiked her calf with her skate, slicing all the way to the bone. "You could see the whole calf separate, but Linda quickly put a tourniquet on it," a skater recalled. On two other occasions, Ila Ray was more seriously injured. She collided with another skater on a dance session right before a competition in Montana and was cut badly. Ray Jr. applied pressure to the wound while waiting for medical treatment. The gash required twenty-four stitches, but she competed four days later; and the pair finished second. In Seattle, again before a major competition, Ray's blade tore a hole in her thigh.[58]

These mishaps were accidents, but all teams had their tense moments and the Hadley siblings were no exception. On one occasion, Ila Ray purposely kicked her brother with her toe pick; Ray also kicked her and intentionally dropped her once. "It was a brother-sister thing," Cindy Kauffman said. "Ronnie and I would get mad at each other, but we never drew blood on purpose." Bob Deuter agreed that both siblings were at fault: "Ray and Ila Ray did fight with each other. She'd grind her fingers into his shoulder blades in a lift and squeeze the heck out of him—and still have a smile."[59]

Away from ice skating, Ila Ray and Ray were regulars at the Ridge roller rink. In their younger years, they had appeared in roller shows there. The roller skating community knew that the family was strapped for cash and let Ila Ray and Ray skate for free. They did jumps and spins but primarily stroked to build up their leg muscles.[60]

In the summertime, Ila Ray and Ray spent more time at home. The Hadleys lived in the Ballard neighborhood of Seattle in a modest home on a corner lot with a willow tree and a white picket fence. There were two bedrooms on the main floor, plus an attic and a full-size basement. Ila Ray had a bedroom with two single beds, but Ray's room, in the basement, was sparse. "He had to sleep on a cot. He had nothing," a friend said. The kids also worked hard at home, doing the majority of the chores.[61]

At home Linda morphed into a different person. She grew beautiful orchids in little pots on her kitchen windowsill. She liked antiques and had her mother's beautifully ornate furniture. She listened to music for her students' programs and designed some of their costumes. "She was extremely talented and did a million things—I don't know how she had the time," Linda Adams said.[62]

Her main love outside of skating was raising poodles. She and Ray used the dogs as a bargaining chip for their students. Kids were promised a French poodle if they did well competitively. Once Ila Ray and Ray were promised a new dog if they won an upcoming competition; but when they came in second, Ray Sr. claimed the poodle deal was off. "Ray, give them the poodle," Linda argued. "No," Ray replied, "I made a promise. They came in second." Eventually Ray relented. "Honeybee," a white toy French poodle, became their mascot and went with them to competitions.[63]

Ray Sr. seemed almost passive at the rink, but at home he harshly disciplined his son. In an era when corporal punishment was common, Ray Sr. would order his son to take off his belt and then whack him with it. Linda

Ila Ray and Ray Hadley Jr., Seattle Skating Club, 1957 Junior Pairs Champions. Source: Courtesy of Linda Adams Garl.

Adams saw this episode occur more than once: "My dad was upset about it but my mother said, 'Don't make waves.'" Ray Jr. would get mad, but he never complained.[64]

Linda and Ray Sr. focused solely on skating, so the Kauffmans adopted the kids for other activities. Clarence Kauffman took Ray Jr. and Ronnie camping; the boys secured a gun safety certificate so Ray Jr. could go hunting. The Kauffmans also helped Linda and Ray Sr., by performing such maintenance jobs as reroofing their house. "We did a lot of things for them and they did a lot of things for us," Ron said. The two pair teams became as close as biological brothers and sisters. Ila Ray and Ray Jr. treated the youngsters as equals and were a good influence on the young Kauffmans.[65]

By the end of the summer of 1956, fourteen-year-old Ila Ray was five feet tall, had soft brown curls, and "was a sweetheart." Reserved around many people because of the sternness of the parents, she was friendly and outgoing with people she knew. The teenagers were not allowed to date much; but when she had the chance, Ila Ray enjoyed a night of ballroom dancing. "I took her to my senior prom but her mother was very much in control of the situation," Bill Wilkins said. "I enjoyed being with both Ila

Ray and Ray when their parents were not around because their personalities began to bloom."[66]

Ray Jr. finally grew several inches taller than his sister. He had dark, crew-cut hair, dark eyebrows, beautiful blue eyes, and light skin with rosy cheeks. All the girls—at the rink and his school—were attracted to him. He was so "drop dead gorgeous" that one skater got the shakes around him. "Ray was one of the most handsome guys I ever saw in my whole life. He was to die for," a skater gushed. At the annual ice show dinner party, Ray gave every girl a little bit of his time, and they were gleefully grateful. He was aware of their crushes, but he didn't let it go to his head. Linda tried to keep all the girls away, but they still found their way to him.[67]

After summer training, the siblings found school a pleasant diversion. Ila Ray was in ninth and Ray was in eighth grade at Jane Addams Junior High. Ila Ray was a member of the debate and drama clubs, a girls' club representative, and was named the outstanding student of the year. Ray was a member of the student council and was interested in all sports, but there was no time for after-school practices or games. Instead he took ballet with his sister, lifted weights to strengthen his arms, and ran four miles a day for endurance.[68]

Every fall the Hadley siblings appeared in the annual Ice Parade show at the Civic Arena along with 150 to 200 other skaters. The *Seattle Post-Intelligencer* sponsored the shows to benefit needy children in local area schools. Ila Ray and Ray always played a key role in the show, and the local Seattle audience saw the kids mature from year to year.[69]

Linda, after watching and copying freely from others, had matured into a good pairs coach. Now she created original moves for her kids. Ila Ray and Ray did a challenging and dangerous maneuver, going straight from individual axels into a flying camel pair spin. Another pair team tried it, hit each other in midair, and never tried it again. Another move was a pair of flying threes in unison; after four flying threes in tandem they pulled into a camel spin together.[70]

At the 1957 Pacific Coast competition, they won the junior pairs title. At the 1957 Nationals in Berkeley, Ila Ray, fourteen and Ray Jr., thirteen, were the youngest of the six pairs in contention for the junior pairs crown. The competition was extremely close, but they won first place by one point.[71]

The 1957 U.S. junior pairs title was a payoff for the Hadleys' persistence, and Linda was energized to go on a summer road trip to show off her new champions to East Coast judges and officials. The Hadleys and the Kauffmans drove a car across the country towing the Kauffmans' trailer.

The two families were squeezed into one car, with four kids in the back seat and three adults in the front. "We played cards on the top of our suitcases, which sat on our laps," Cindy Kauffman recalled. "We hung wet towels over the windows because there was no air conditioning." They rarely knew in advance when and where they'd be performing; their numerous stops included Sun Valley, Colorado Springs, Lincoln, St. Paul, and Lake Placid.[72]

Back at school in the fall, Ila Ray wrote a composition about her life:

> It is a proven fact that all skaters are "crazy." You must be eager to go to the rink on winter mornings (5:30) when the air that has been still all night is as cold as the inside of an icebox. It stiffens your muscles and freezes you clear through to your bones. You have to like the quiet concentration of long practice sessions on a gloomy, shadowy old rink when no one talks and the only sound is that of a skate on the ice surface, or your music being played over and over. You must like staying there all day and leaving all worn out, but with the feeling that you're lucky to come back the next morning and do it all over again, and still be able to face the school authorities when you miss school. You see, anyone who would spend hours at a time going around in circles, suffer falls, bruises, and pain must be a little crazy. But it is worth all the trouble, because if you can stand to be a figure skater, you can usually become anything else you set your mind to be. (Anyway, that's what they tell me.) [73]

That fall the Hadley kids learned they were named as 1958 World Team alternates. They quickly secured their passports. Instead of traveling in a cramped car with an old trailer, the Hadleys prepared to make their first international trip . . . to Paris.[74]

CHAPTER 5

DUDLEY AND
LITTLE MARIBEL

T he "Championnats du Monde, de Patinage Artistique et Danse," the
1958 World Figure Skating Championships, were held in Paris at the
Palais des Sports from February 13-15. A European venue meant twice the
competitors compared with the U. S. venue of the previous year. The most
novel aspect of this competition was the presence of seven skaters from the
Soviet Union, three men and two pair teams. No Russian had competed at a
Worlds since 1914—before the Bolshevik Revolution in 1917. The Russian
skaters were older than the other competitors and had little competitive experience, as *Skating* noted: "They have received no formal instruction but
have learned mostly from movies and books."[1]

The American skaters continued to dominate international competition. Besides two golds won by Carol Heiss and David Jenkins, American
dancers Andree Anderson and Don Jacoby won the bronze, and Tim
Brown, also coached by Edi Scholdan, won the men's silver. Edi's reputation
as a World coach had been enhanced in Paris. Besides coaching five U.S.
World Team members, he coached Ina Bauer of Germany. After placing
next to last in figures at the 1957 Worlds, Ina had trained with Edi at the
Broadmoor and placed fourth. Thus, Edi almost had three medalists at the
1958 Worlds.[2]

There were no huge surprises at the 1958 Nationals the following
month in Minneapolis—the 1957 senior champions easily retained their titles. Bradley Lord, in his first senior men's event, was third in figures. At the
senior men's free skate "you could fairly feel the tension and expectancy in
the entire arena," *Skating* wrote. Bradley skated well and the crowd was appreciative, but all the men skated superbly and unfortunately Bradley
dropped to fifth place. Ila Ray and Ray Hadley, who had just returned from
Paris where they performed exhibitions during the 1958 Worlds, barely
missed a medal by placing fourth in senior pairs.[3]

Southern Californian skaters swept the junior and novice singles divisions. Barbara Roles, who had withdrawn the previous year due to an injury,

became the junior champion, and the novice title went to Rhode Lee Michelson, a powerhouse from Long Beach. Jim Short of the Los Angeles Figure Skating Club upset the junior men's competition and edged out Greg Kelley of Boston to win the title.[4]

Edi Scholdan was again the most successful coach of the championships. His students won one gold, three silver, and three bronze medals. Maribel Vinson Owen's students brought home two gold, one silver, and two bronze medals. Maribel was especially proud of the two bronze medal winners. Her younger daughter, Laurence, placed third in junior ladies, and her older daughter, Maribel, placed third in senior pairs. Maribel Jr. was extremely lucky in her choice of partner—Dudley Richards had an enviable skating pedigree and was a favorite among competitors.

DUDLEY RICHARDS
1958 U.S. PAIRS BRONZE MEDALIST

Dudley Richards accumulated the longest competitive record of any skater in the fifties. From 1942, competitive skating was his life. He won every title on the East Coast, earned over a dozen regional, sectional, and national gold medals, was a member of six World Teams in two disciplines, and became a judge and USFSA official.[5]

As skillful a skater as he was, Dudley's popularity was due to his sterling character and warm disposition. He was extremely bright, well-spoken, and kind. "He was never pushy," his sister said. "He led quietly by example." He was a man born into privilege yet was a conscientious steward of his time and talents. He met adversity with courage and resolve and remained humble through a lifetime of achievements. "He was genuine and very balanced," a friend recalled. "He was always smiling and was such a happy guy. Everybody loved Dudley."[6]

Born on February 4, 1932, in Providence, Rhode Island, Dudley Shaw Richards was named after ancestor Thomas Dudley, an early governor of the Massachusetts Bay Colony. His parents, Byron Richards and Ruth White Richards, grew up in Pawtucket where Byron worked in an iron foundry business. The Richards were a tight-knit family; brother Ross was four years older than Dudley and sister Susan was four years younger.[7]

Dudley was a pond skater and played hockey. As he improved, he skated at the Rhode Island Auditorium, where the Providence Figure Skating Club was organized around 1938. Figure skaters saw Dudley's potential and invited him to join the club when he was nine. "Dudley was a super kid," a club member recalled. "Some kids are pains in the neck and others you remember as being special; he was a special one."[8]

Dudley was an honor student at the Providence Country Day School where he played all sports. In the summer, his family went to their cottage in Hyannis Port, and Dudley often sailed with family friend Ted Kennedy; the boys went on picnics to Egg Island and sailed down to Falmouth and Nantucket, taking their boats out overnight with friends. As a sailor, Dudley was "very, very competitive but always a good sport," Senator Kennedy recalled. "On the wall of the little Yacht Club at the foot of the Hyannis Port Dock are several placards with the names of race champions—some were won by Dudley and some were won by me. We were just teenagers then."[9]

During the wintertime, Dudley incorporated a daily skating regimen into his already full life. After winning juvenile boys at the 1943 Easterns, Dudley was invited to join The Skating Club (SC) of Boston and he commuted by train to work with Bud Wilson. Dudley, who "was especially outstanding in this class," won the novice men's title at the 1944 Easterns. He was chosen his club's outstanding skater and received the coveted Tozzer Award.[10]

Two years later, Dudley won the 1946 U.S. novice men's title in Chicago. The junior men's championship proved a more difficult accomplishment. At the 1947 Nationals in Berkeley, Dudley missed winning by one ordinal. His family wondered if age accounted for his placement. The champion, Robert Swenning, was in his early twenties and Dudley was only fifteen. They figured the judges thought he was too young and should wait his turn.[11]

Dudley was ready to take the title the following year, but his life took a dramatic turn. First he suffered a mild attack of polio, from which he recovered completely. Later in the summer, he was sailing at Hyannis and had finished a race when he decided to swim out and join his brother on another boat. Dudley dove off the ocean pier into shallow water and hit his head on the ocean floor. He was immediately taken to the hospital where the family's worst fears were realized. He had broken his neck. To repair his fractured vertebra, he was placed in a plaster cast for six months, which turned into a year. The accident took Dudley out of skating for a year and a half.[12]

When he returned to skating around Christmas of 1948, the junior men's division had changed significantly. The younger skaters coming up behind him, Hayes Jenkins and Richard Dwyer, surpassed him and won the junior men's titles in 1948 and 1949, respectively. Dudley never complained about his accident, but some family and friends felt that his injury negatively affected the quality of his skating from then on. One skater noted that he had an unusual way of holding his head because of his neck injury. "Dudley

Dudley Richards, The Skating Club of Boston, 1958 U.S. Pairs Bronze Medalist. Source: World Figure Skating Museum.

always had the goal of competing against Dick Button," Senator Kennedy said, "but that terrible accident really set him back because it occurred during a significant developmental time."[13]

Dudley worked hard to get back into shape. Within months, he gamely placed third in junior men at the 1949 Nationals. He achieved a significant milestone when he passed his gold figure test on July 28, 1949, in St. Paul. Dudley felt strong enough to win the elusive junior title in the upcoming season. At the 1950 Easterns, he placed first and Don Laws was second. At the 1950 Nationals in Washington D.C., Dudley placed first in figures; but in the freestyle, Laws thrilled his hometown audience when he won the title. Dudley didn't even earn a medal.[14]

During these setbacks Dudley remained grounded. Some skaters had private tutors, but the Richards felt that their son needed as normal a life as possible and school was definitely important. Byron Richards repeatedly told Dudley, "Today you win, tomorrow you're forgotten. Don't let it go to your head." Dudley was still an athlete in school, although his neck injury disqualified him from some sports. He initially wore a neck and shoulder brace as football manager. He later played baseball and tennis, enjoyed swimming, and was an avid golfer.[15]

Even though he lost time due to his accident, Dudley graduated early from the Providence Country Day School. He spent his senior year at the

Belmont Hill School near Boston. He was the school's skipper at the National Interscholastic Sailing Regatta in Annapolis, where the school's crew placed second. That summer he formed a pair team with Tenley Albright under the tutelage of Gene Turner at Denver University. In the fall of 1950, Dudley entered Harvard University, majored in history and science, and juggled skating and studies the next four years. One of his freshman roommates was his Cape Cod sailing buddy Ted Kennedy.[16]

Dudley attacked his studies and training equally. In his Harvard dorm, he did push-ups to strengthen his upper body so he could lift Tenley. Senator Kennedy recalled how conscientious he was: "Dudley got up every morning at 4:30. It was an ungodly hour for anyone, but he went to the Boston rink and skated for two hours. He came back, changed, and we went to breakfast together. He also skated late afternoons and on the weekends. He was strongly committed to his skating and his friends."[17]

Dudley also spent time with girls. Handsome and charming, he had many admirers. Joanne Scotvold first met Dudley at competitions in 1946. "We were just young kids but we liked being together. Later when I was in Ice Follies we dated. When I married, Dudley told my husband that he was supposed to marry me—he always liked to tease." At Harvard he took girls to school functions, jazz clubs on Massachusetts Avenue, or to Harvard football games on double dates with Ted Kennedy. "Dudley was personable and well mannered," Sheila Muldowny said. "He also had a strong New England accent and was a good sport whenever I teased him about it."[18]

In the fall of 1950, Dudley received an unexpected call from the USFSA—an invitation to be on the 1951 World Team. After World War II, the International Skating Union (ISU) allowed four U.S. single skaters to compete at Worlds because of America's international prominence. It was also easier for American skaters to compete abroad because travel time had been reduced significantly. Boat journeys in the forties took weeks; now the American teams crossed the Atlantic by air.[19]

That fall, Dudley and Tenley competed in the 1951 Easterns. They both won their senior titles plus the senior pairs; however after a fall and a minor injury to Tenley in practice, they decided not to compete at Nationals. She was on the brink of international success, and her father decided she should focus solely on her single skating.[20]

After placing fifth at the 1951 Worlds in Milan, Dudley focused his energies on the U.S. junior men's title. On his fourth try over five years, Dudley was victorious at the 1951 U.S. Championships in Seattle. Dick Button, who had just won his fifth U.S. senior men's title, exclaimed that seeing his fellow Harvard classmate win the junior men's crown was the biggest thrill of the competition. At the competitors' party, Dudley celebrated both his nineteenth birthday and this long-awaited achievement.[21]

Dudley had some setbacks the next year. He placed third at the Olympic tryouts in Indianapolis, but only two men were named to the 1952 Olympic Team because Dick Button was automatically on the team. At the 1952 Worlds in Paris, he placed fifth again. Dudley had wonderful figures and was a solid free skater, but he was overshadowed by one of men's skating's most phenomenal trio: Dick Button, Jimmy Grogan, and Hayes Jenkins. His fellow competitors, however, respected Dudley and acknowledged his talent. Beyond his strong, well-balanced fundamentals, they admired his footwork and musicality. Some thought Dudley had an unusual way of jumping, due to his neck injury. He wasn't necessarily precise in the air, but he usually managed to pull everything off. [22]

Dudley honestly assessed his competition and recognized greatness when he saw it. Few coaches accompanied their students to Worlds; Dudley's coach Bud Wilson usually had to wait several weeks before he knew the results. When Dudley came back raving about a young kid named Ronnie Robertson, Bud couldn't quite believe him, but Dudley graciously sang Robertson's praises, who then beat him out of a medal at the 1952 Nationals. Dudley, a veteran of two World Teams, placed fourth.[23]

International competitions and exhibitions swallowed Dudley's precious college time. Airline weight restrictions prompted creativity. He ripped up books and took the parts he needed to study. Once he took a test at Worlds at the exact same moment as his Harvard classmates to prevent any cheating. He was often overheard saying, "Pressure, pressure, pressure," which underscored the stressful academic environment he and other elite skaters encountered.[24]

Despite his setbacks in landing on the podium, Dudley was a great motivator for other skaters, especially at summer training camps. He had trained in St. Paul, Denver, and Lake Placid, and he always pushed everyone to better themselves. "With that little smirk of his he would say, 'Go faster, go faster,'" Sonya Klopfer recalled, "or we'd be skating along and he'd say, 'Do a double flip right now!' and you'd have to step out and do one. He was always supporting everyone else and never put himself up there." He also supported beginner skaters. He served as a low-test judge, and the young skaters thought he was "fabulous."[25]

After summer training was over, it was important for Dudley to relax and spend time with friends and family. At Cape Cod, he played softball and touch football with Jack and Bobby Kennedy, as well as his and Ted Kennedy's friends. The teams were the Barefoot Boys versus the Pansies. Skating friends visited at Dudley's invitation to play tennis at the Kennedys. The Richards family saw little of Dudley during the year; but when he was home, they'd throw a baseball in the backyard or play tennis. "My mother complained of tennis balls bouncing everywhere, but whenever Dudley was home, it was great," sister Susan said.[26]

The 1953 season did not begin well; Dudley dropped to sixth place at the 1953 Worlds. At the 1953 North Americans in Cleveland, he was third in figures, but Ronnie Robertson pulled ahead in the free skate and Dudley dropped to fourth. The Richards family had never seen Dudley compete nationally until the 1953 U.S. Championships in Hershey. It was a trip worth making. Dudley skated extremely well and placed third behind Hayes Jenkins and Ronnie Robertson.[27]

After winning the senior men's bronze medal, Dudley was committed to singles, but he also decided to give pairs another try. He and Sheila Muldowny had dated during Lake Placid summers, were both strong skaters, and had talked about forming a pair. Sheila applied to Radcliffe so she and Dudley could train in Boston; when she didn't get in to Radcliffe, she opted to train in Europe. So Dudley teamed up with Boston skater Anita Andres.[28]

Anita was astonished when Dudley approached her. She had not been successful in singles due to figures, but she was a good freestylist. Greatly admiring Dudley, she eagerly agreed. They enjoyed training together and became romantically involved. Dudley taught Anita pair lifts and choreographed their program. They won senior pairs at the 1954 Easterns and looked forward to Nationals. Dudley had been selected to be a member of the 1954 World Team in singles for the fourth consecutive year when he received a surprise letter from Uncle Sam.[29]

Years before when his cast was removed, the doctor had told him, "Dudley, you'll never have to worry about being drafted, because they'll never take you." The Korean War was in progress and Dudley applied for Officer Candidate School because he didn't want to go in as a draftee. But the Harvard ROTC programs—first the Navy and then the Air Force—rejected him because of his neck injury. As graduation approached, the U.S. Army drafted him, apparently ignoring the medical condition that made physical contact potentially dangerous. He passed up the 1954 Worlds and Nationals altogether, and his second pair partnership ended.[30]

Dudley graduated with honors in 1954. He had regularly appeared on the dean's list, and his Ivy League c.v. included the house touch football team, the Hasty Pudding Club, Varsity Club, Delta Club, and his brief stints in ROTC. The Harvard Athletic Association gave him a special honor: a varsity sweater. Only two other Harvard men had received a varsity sweater for non-college sports: golfer Bobby Jones and Dick Button. Dudley proudly wore his maroon sweater with the large white block "H."[31]

Dudley was inducted at Fort Dix, New Jersey, and to avoid activities that might aggravate his old neck injury, was assigned to the Special Services. He was sent to the U.S. Army entertainment division in Garmisch-Partenkirchen, where he was assigned to skate in the Casa Carioca nightclub.[32]

During the fifties, Garmisch was a year-round recreation center for American military personnel stationed in Europe. Soldiers came to this beautiful Bavarian town to snow ski, play golf, swim, water ski, and go boating. Garmisch had three ice surfaces. The larger rink, the Ice Stadium, was the site of the 1936 Winter Olympics; the second rink had been built for the cancelled 1940 Olympics. Right next to the Ice Stadium stood the Casa Carioca. The American military built and subsidized the nightclub, where a soldier could see a first-class show for a few dollars. After the show, a dance floor came out over the ice, and couples danced to the music of a seventeen-piece orchestra. The cast consisted primarily of European skaters, but American skaters serving in the military, like Jimmy Grogan and Dudley Richards, were incorporated into the show. A steady stream of Dudley's fellow soldiers from Harvard came to see him perform while on leave.[33]

Dudley was not a seasoned show performer, and Terry Rudolph, the producer and director of the show, complained that he was not artistic enough. Once she berated him in front of the other guys in the dressing room, concluding with: "You were just disgusting!" Dudley impressed the other skaters by calmly remarking, "Well, thanks a bunch for that!" Despite these reprimands, Dudley felt lucky to be there.[34]

Dudley was granted leave to attend the 1955 Worlds in Vienna. The Allied forces were still a visible presence in Austria in the mid-fifties. Although Soviet soldiers flooded Vienna, Dudley helped friends smuggle out a Czech female skater seeking asylum in the West. It was a brave act, considering he was an American soldier.[35]

The army gave Dudley permission to skate a few exhibitions on the 1955 World tour, and he performed one of his Casa numbers, "Deep in the Heart of Texas." Dressed in a cowboy outfit with chaps, his cap guns were supposed to go off to the beat of the music—"the stars at night, are big and bright, boom, boom, boom, boom"—but many times the caps failed to pop. "Every time they didn't go off we killed ourselves laughing on the floor," Catherine Machado recalled.[36]

The 1956 Worlds were held at Garmisch, and Dudley was delighted when friends came to see him perform at the Casa. Dudley had matured into a show skater. World Team members laughed hysterically at Dudley's portrayal of a clown in a ballet number. He performed at the Casa Carioca for the final year and a half of his service. Theoretically he was paid for performing, which should have jeopardized his amateur figure skating status, but his weekly army pay of fifty dollars was hardly scandalous.[37]

When Dudley returned from Europe in 1956, he found himself at a crossroads. He wanted to continue competing, but the younger men coming up, like David Jenkins and Tim Brown, had secured their positions at the top. He liked the idea of trying pairs again but didn't have a partner. Dudley performed exhibitions in ice carnivals around New England to keep in shape.[38]

During this sabbatical, Dudley began his professional life. He worked briefly for the Minneapolis-Honeywell Regulator Company, and then Rodger Nordblom, a fellow Harvard alum and Cape sailor, invited him to join the Nordblom Company of Boston as a commercial real estate broker in 1958. Dudley, working on a commission basis, handled commercial land sales and leases for office space in Boston and suburbs as well as industrial space along Route 128. He found his work stimulating and challenging, and looked forward to a lifelong career with the firm.[39]

However, the skating itch did not subside. In the fall of 1957 when Maribel Vinson Owen asked if he would like to skate pairs with her elder daughter, Dudley jumped at the chance.

MARIBEL Y. OWEN

1958 PAIRS BRONZE MEDALIST

If Maribel Jr. could have been granted any wish by a fairy godmother, it would have been to have any name but Maribel. Maribel Vinson Owen was a larger-than-life figure, and bearing her name would have been a burden for anyone. For much of Maribel Jr.'s childhood, her mother tried in vain to groom her to step into her champion skates, which created a complex relationship with her mother and with skating. Skating did not come easily for Maribel Jr., and her mother finally transferred her Olympic dreams to Laurence. Maribel Jr. persevered, nonetheless. She made good friends in the skating community, and with grit and determination, succeeded competitively. In time, Little Maribel grew to love the family's sport.[40]

Maribel Yerxa Owen was born on April 25, 1940, in Boston. She was rarely called plain "Maribel." It was "Little Maribel," "Young Maribel," "Mara," or "Maribel Jr." From her infancy, her parents were on staff at the

Iceland rink in Berkeley and were constantly on the ice, so it was natural for her to start skating at the age of two. Although she grew up on ice skates, it took her awhile to pass her preliminary test—three years instead of a year.[41]

Little Maribel was nine years old when her father moved away. The Owen women remained in Berkeley, where Little Maribel was a good student at Thousand Oaks Elementary School. She and her sister were making some progress at the Iceland rink, which she described to *Skating*:

> I love skating. Some mornings I go down to the rink at 6 or 6:30 and of course sometimes I don't go at all. In free style I'm working on a double salchow and trying to get more speed in everything I do. I have a six year old sister Laurence who is working on a lutz and an axel. My mother teaches very hard at the rink and when she gets time teaches us. The first half of the show last year was Cinderella. I was a maid of court and my sister was a lizard and did a short solo, which was very good for a five year old.[42]

The next several years were a bit of a roller coaster for Little Maribel. Her debut at the 1950 Pacific Coast was far from auspicious; she placed fifteenth in juvenile girls. In 1953 she placed ninth in junior ladies at the California State competition. Things were no smoother off the ice. In 1952, both her grandfather and her father passed away.[43]

As Maribel traversed the country with her children to coach Tenley Albright, Maribel Jr. began to show some promise. She placed third in junior ladies at the 1954 Northern California meet. After Pacific Coast she advanced to the 1954 U.S. Championships in Los Angeles but placed ninth in novice ladies. Maribel Sr., used to the competitive victories of Gretchen Merrill and Tenley Albright, was not expecting her daughter to come in dead last, and was obviously disappointed.[44]

When the Owen family moved east in the summer of 1954, Maribel finally conceded that her namesake would not be a singles champion. Little Maribel was tall with her father's lankiness and she wasn't a great jumper. Her free skating was conservative, and figures stymied her too. On the other hand, Maribel thought her daughter had the potential to be a successful pairs champion like herself.[45]

At the SC of Boston, Maribel noticed a handsome young man who was about the same height as her fourteen-year-old daughter. Maribel approached Chuck Foster, a twenty-year-old Harvard student from North Dakota, to ascertain his interest in forming a pair partnership. Chuck came from a skating family. His father became enamored of figure skating while attending medical school in Chicago; after learning how to skate, he helped raise the money to build an indoor ice rink in Fargo so his three children could skate. After spending summers training in St. Paul, Rochester, New York, and Schumacher, Ontario, Chuck headed to Boston in 1952 to attend Harvard.[46]

Chuck had previously skated pairs with his sister Sidney but inadvertently dropped her during a competition. Although Sidney was not injured, their mother was so angry that the partnership ended. The accident had spooked him but not badly enough to prevent his interest in Maribel's proposal. Like Little Maribel, Chuck admitted he wasn't succeeding in singles because of stiff competition from David Jenkins, Ronnie Robertson, and Hugh Graham, but he still wanted to compete. He was willing to give pairs a second try, so he and Little Maribel started training with Maribel. Chuck, who trained daily at the club, soon learned that Maribel's students had to train elsewhere; Maribel coached them at the Boston Arena, the Harvard rink, and in Lynn. Chuck discovered that Maribel was a great pairs coach because she had had extensive experience—two competitive partners and a twelve-year show career with her husband.[47]

The new duo won senior pairs at the 1955 New Englands, placed second in Easterns, and won the junior pairs title at the 1955 Nationals at the Broadmoor. Regarding their victory, *Skating* wrote: "The win in Junior Pairs by Maribel Owen and Charles Foster was a thrill to many 'old timers' but an especially big thrill for 'Mama' Maribel Vinson Owen." Chuck and Maribel turned out to be a good pair, but it was still a surprise to win a national title in their first attempt, as Chuck recalled: "Little Maribel was only fourteen at the time. She was cute and bubbly and full of enthusiasm, and I think that kind of sparked the old judges."[48]

National junior champions had often been named to a World or Olympic Team, but Chuck and Maribel were not included on the 1956 Olympic Team when the names were announced in the fall of 1955. Months later, Maribel and Chuck placed second at Easterns again; and at the 1956 Nationals in Philadelphia, they placed third in senior pairs. *Skating* cautiously supported the maturing duo: "Maribel Owen and Chuck Foster have a lot more skating to do together before they can catch the other pairs. However, they are pleasing to watch and had some nice separate moves." After less than two years in pairs, Maribel Jr. had won two national medals.[49]

Four-time U. S. pairs champions Robin Greiner and Carole Ormaca retired after the 1956 Olympics, and Maribel and Chuck were positioned to move up the senior ladder. In the fall of 1956, they were chosen as the first pick for the 1957 World Team. However, their partnership dissolved soon after the 1956 competitive season. Chuck had graduated from Harvard in

Maribel Y. Owen and Dudley Richards, The Skating Club of Boston, 1958 U.S. Pairs Bronze Medalists. Source: World Figure Skating Museum.

the spring of 1956 and wanted time to prepare for medical school. "Skating was not going to be my life; it was only a hobby," he explained.[50]

Chuck had found Little Maribel a hard worker, but sometimes their temperaments clashed. Their screaming matches had sent Little Maribel off the ice more than once in tears. "One time I thought Chuck was going to drop her on her head," a skater said. But Chuck and Little Maribel had achieved some nice success rather quickly; and Big Maribel didn't want to give it up. She was on the phone constantly, imploring him to return from Fargo. "They were desperate at that point because it left Little Maribel without anything, but I had to go," Chuck said. He entered the army in 1958 and was stationed in Korea.[51]

Little Maribel, back on her own, continued to compete in senior ladies at Easterns; in 1957 she placed fourth, while Laurence was sixth. It was the last time Little Maribel beat her sister. It was clear to Little Maribel that she would never be the skater that her mother was. One of her chores at home was to polish her mother's silver trophies. It must have been painful for her to face that beautiful sterling and realize she was not measuring up.[52]

Maribel Jr. was expected to do well academically, too. She attended Boston Latin, a prestigious school that counted Benjamin Franklin, John Hancock, Ralph Waldo Emerson, Arthur Fiedler, Leonard Bernstein, and

Maribel Vinson Owen among its graduates. Maribel Jr. was a bright young lady, but she didn't have her mother's academic talents either. She struggled in school, but a benefit of attending Boston Latin was the school's flexibility with her skating hours and competitive travels. Skating friends were aware of the pressures she faced. The commute from the school to the rink required several streetcar changes. Sometimes when she arrived at the rink, she headed straight for the women's locker room to change clothes and reappeared with twenty pieces of toilet paper in hand. "She just plunged past us crying," a sympathetic friend recalled.[53]

Maribel Jr. was worn out. She was supposed to be a straight-A student and go to Radcliffe like her mother. She was supposed to be a national champion and execute a beautiful spread eagle the way her mother did. "Everybody can do a spread eagle," Maribel Sr. had always said. But Maribel Sr. had a natural hip turnout and could fall into a spread eagle with no effort at all. She couldn't comprehend why any of her students couldn't master it, especially her own daughter. "Whenever Maribel Jr. did a spread eagle . . . her second leg was chattering," a club member said. "The blade was not on the ice smoothly—it went rat-a-tat-tat."[54]

In the frenetic Owen household, Little Maribel was the family peacekeeper whenever Laurence and her mother battled. "Laurence was just like her mother and had the same ferocity," a skater observed. "Little Maribel picked up the pieces after Laurence and Maribel and Mrs. Vinson went plowing through, stepping on people's feet in their oblivious way. Little Maribel apologetically made amends."[55]

Despite the stress, most of the time Little Maribel was cheerful, upbeat, and a favorite among the skating crowd, as Olympian Catherine Machado noted:

> Little Maribel was so much fun. In 1955 we went to Colorado Springs for the Nationals. At the start of the competition I walked into an auditorium filled with judges and officials and competitors—everybody was there. When Little Maribel sees me she stands up and yells at the top of her lungs, so everyone can hear, "I haven't heard a good dirty joke since the last time I saw you, 'Chado!" I thought I was going to die then and there. That's the kind of personality Little Maribel had.[56]

Little Maribel smoothly navigated around the opposite sex. Maribel encouraged her participation in subscription dances, which were a Boston debutante custom. Parents hosted dinner parties for students from a variety of private schools. After dinner the families chartered buses to take the boys and girls to a marvelous Beacon Hill townhouse (belonging to a student's family), graced with chandeliers, a sweeping staircase, and a magnificent ballroom where the kids danced all evening. "The guys were so smitten and enthralled by her, but she couldn't care less about them," a friend explained. "She was so totally poised and in her element. The rest of us girls were envious that she could talk to boys with such ease. But when she had to be on the ice and win things, that was hard for her."[57]

Maribel Jr. was well known in skating circles because of her name; but she also achieved a degree of fame on her own. "Maribel, Jr. was my peer and we always saw each other at Easterns," a skater remarked. "She was friendly and gave a lot of time to everyone. It made such an impression on me that she paid so much attention to others. She sincerely wanted to be with you and cared about you. Maribel Jr. was always that way."[58]

A year after she quit pairs, Maribel Jr. floundered in singles. She failed her seventh figure test many times. On the umpteenth attempt in Lynn, all the skaters patiently waited with her to receive the familiar dismal news. During the wait, a young skater went to the ladies' room, which was right next to the judges' room, put her ear up to the wall, and heard multiple voices: "What did you put? Did you pass her? Did you pass her? Okay, let's go tell her." Before the judges could officially inform her, the little girl ran to tell Little Maribel the good news. After achieving this long-sought goal, Maribel never attempted the final eighth test.[59]

Little Maribel would have been happy to retire, but that was not in her mother's plan. One day Maribel screamed loudly at her daughter across the rink, and Little Maribel screamed back: "When did you ever ask me if I wanted to skate?!" Another time around the dinner table, she sarcastically announced, "I'm taking up pairs now. This is another part of our wonderful sport!" On the positive side, skating friends became her extended family, and she realized she was lucky to have won a national title. "There had to be some willingness," a club member said. "It was difficult I'm sure, but when people said, 'Maribel's making them do this,' you can't push a rope."[60]

Naturally, when Little Maribel tasted success, it was a terrific feeling. She looked forward to being on a World Team and traveling abroad with her mother. Since most of her success had come as a pairs skater, she and her mother were both on the lookout for another partner. Talented, handsome, mature, and available—Dudley Richards seemed perfect.

Dudley and Maribel Jr. started training in the summer of 1957 with Maribel as their coach. They were a good match and clicked early on, even though there was an age spread; Dudley was twenty-five and Maribel Jr. was seventeen. Maribel Sr. had tremendous respect for Dudley and liked him a great deal. He was even tempered and kind. When things went wrong, as they invariably did in any partnership, Little Maribel would react with histrionics, screeching "Aaaaagghhh!" Dudley would patiently call her back to the task: "Now Maribel, let's try that again." He was the calming influence she needed, and her self-esteem began to blossom. Mama Maribel encouraged their friendship.[61]

Little Maribel opted not to attend Radcliffe like her mother but went to Boston University in the fall. She studied sociology and anthropology, and experienced the joy of learning as she followed her own path. She thought about becoming a teacher and, with the eyeglasses she wore to school, looked the part. But at the rink, she was the first club member to wear contact lenses for skating.[62]

Maribel Jr. competed in both singles and pairs at the 1958 Easterns. In preceding years, she had slowly advanced up the ladder in senior ladies, placing sixth, fifth, and fourth. But in 1958, she dropped to eighth place and wisely ended her singles career. Her sister had won the event. Maribel was happy for Laurence. They had always been each other's best friend and rooted for each other.[63]

Maribel Jr. fared much better in pairs. She and Dudley won senior pairs at the 1958 Easterns, and advanced to the 1958 Nationals in Minneapolis. The senior pairs division consisted of two World pair teams and four new entrants, including 1957 junior champions Ila Ray and Ray Hadley. Ron and Nancy Ludington had a solid first-place win, but the judging marks were all over the map for the second through fifth place teams. Maribel and Dudley barely beat out the Hadleys for the bronze medal. The year 1958 was the last year that the Worlds preceded the Nationals. Dudley and Maribel had shown they were competitive but had to wait another year to make the World Team.[64]

During the summer, Dudley and Maribel won gold pairs at the Lake Placid championships and spent the fall taking pair tests. The rules for pairs' competition were less stringent at the time, and formalized tests for pairs were coming into vogue. Dudley and Maribel rapidly passed every pairs test; and in only a few months, Maribel Jr. became a pairs gold medalist. Her persistence had produced grand results. Life had changed for Little Maribel. She looked forward to going to the rink daily to train with her good-looking and good-natured partner. Heading into the 1959 competitive season, Little Maribel had finally made a name for herself in the Vinson/Owen family.[65]

CHAPTER 6

THE TWO DYNASTIES

Dudley and Maribel were featured on the February cover of *Skating*, as competitors from across the country gathered in Rochester, New York, for the 1959 U.S. Championships. A total of 13,873 spectators, double the number at previous Nationals, attended the three-day event at the Community War Memorial arena. The competition chairman was Ritter Shumway, first vice president of the USFSA and a leading Rochester citizen. Competitors trained at the Ritter-Clark Memorial Ice Rink at the Rochester Institute of Technology (RIT), named after his grandfather, Frank Ritter, and George H. Clark, a forty-three-year trustee of RIT.[1]

David Jenkins won his third men's title, and Bradley Lord missed third place by just one ordinal. Carol Heiss won her third ladies title, sister Nancy placed second, and Barbara Roles of Los Angeles placed third. The Ludingtons won their third pairs championship. The 1958 junior pair champions Karl and Gayle Freed were second, and Dudley and Maribel placed third for the second year in a row. The Hadleys settled for fourth place, again.[2]

The junior men's champion was Gregory Kelley of Boston, and Laurence Owen was the junior ladies champion, followed by Stephanie Westerfeld, and 1958 novice champion Rhode Lee Michelson. Jerry and Judianne Fotheringill, a brother-sister team from Washington, won the junior pairs title, and Larry Pierce and Marilyn Meeker of Indianapolis won the silver dance title. Diane Sherbloom and Roger Campbell of Los Angeles were second and Robert and Patricia Dineen of New York took third.[3]

Rochester's Genesee Figure Skating Club ran a successful competition, shadowed by unexpected sadness. Novice skater Wanda Guntert placed third in figures; but prior to her free skate her father, David Guntert, a Southern California skating official, suddenly died of a heart attack. Wanda gamely finished the competition and won the bronze. "I'll never forget the kindness of Ritter Shumway and Maribel," Wanda recalled. "I knew who Maribel was but I had never spoken with her before. Both of them sought me out and gave me the courage to go on."[4]

For the first time, the U.S. Championships preceded the Worlds, and the USFSA announced the 1959 World Team at the end of the competition, which comprised the top three in each senior event. Because David Jenkins was a busy medical student, Bradley Lord went in his place to the North American competition in Toronto, where he placed fifth. In addition, Brad was allowed to represent the United States at the 1959 Worlds, which was held at the Broadmoor.[5]

The figure skaters were thrilled to return to the Broadmoor. The 1959 Worlds coincided with the "Rush to the Rockies" celebration, the 100th anniversary of the Colorado Gold Rush, and the competitors were given cowboy boots, skirts or shirts, a Stetson hat, and a silver-buckled belt. There were fewer competitors than in 1957; the Soviet skaters had had visa difficulties and were unable to come. The American team made a great showing, with World champions Carol Heiss and David Jenkins retaining their titles. Dancers Andree Anderson and Don Jacoby won the silver, and the Ludingtons and Tim Brown both won bronze. In their first World pairs meet, Maribel and Dudley placed sixth, and Bradley Lord placed eighth.[6]

While the 1959 U.S. World Team competed in Colorado, the U.S. junior champions had returned home from Rochester, eager to compete the following year for spots on the 1960 Olympic Team. The 1959 junior champions were the product of the two skating dynasties: Gregory Kelley and Laurence Owen, the junior men's and ladies champions, represented The Skating Club of Boston, while junior ladies silver medalist Stephanie Westerfeld, a long-time Edi Scholdan student, represented the Broadmoor Skating Club.

GREGORY KELLEY

1959 JUNIOR MEN'S CHAMPION

NATHALIE KELLEY

Gregory Kelley had such great natural talent that it was just a matter of time before he made a big splash internationally. He was "a polite, quiet young man, who always competed in the manner of the true sportsman, yet [was] modest about his achievements and generous to his competitors," skating historian Ben Wright wrote.[7]

An important factor in Greg's success was his eldest sister Nathalie. From the time Greg began training at The Skating Club of Boston, Nathalie was his chaperone, his driver, and his practice monitor. "Nathalie exemplified the value of helping others. . . . No more loyal sister ever existed," Wright said.[8]

Gregory Kelley, The Skating Club of Boston, 1959 Junior Men's Champion. Source: Courtesy of Stephen Kelley.

Gregory Eric Kelley was born on May 19, 1944, to an affluent family. His parents, Dr. Vincent and Nathalie Kelley, were Boston natives and met while working at the same hospital. Greg was the youngest of six children with three older brothers, Vincent, Kevin, and Stephen, and two older sisters, Nathalie and Judith. His siblings were eight to thirteen years older.[9]

Vincent Kelley was a prominent ear, nose, and throat doctor. The children grew up in a generous eighteen-room Victorian house in Newton. The family took regular trips to Canada and spent time at their New Hampshire retreat, called Greg's Place. Vincent Kelley, a fisherman, built a stream-fed pool and taught all his sons to fish. "Greg loved going to 'his place,' but at nighttime he had to go to bed before everyone else, and he was upset because outside his window he could see everyone else having a good time," brother Stephen remembered.[10]

Greg was anxious to emulate his brothers, who played hockey. Greg, tagging along, was wearing skates by age three. At age eight, he began figure skating for two reasons. His Catholic parochial school went to the SC of Boston for a weekly "Learn to Skate" program. The other inspiration was the stellar accomplishments of his neighbor, Tenley Albright. The Albright home, at the corner of Ward and Center, was three houses down from the Kelleys, who lived at the corner of Auburn and Center.[11]

The eldest Kelley, Nathalie Frances, was born on January 19, 1932, and named after her mother. She graduated from the Academy of Notre Dame High School in 1949, and began ferrying Greg to the rink while attending Emmanuel College, from which she graduated in 1955. She had majored in science and thought of becoming a doctor but became a teacher because she wanted to share her love of science with others. She taught biology and driver's education at Ashland High School. Nathalie, who still lived at home, continued to shuttle Greg to the rink; and as he rose in the ranks, she traveled with him to competitions. Nathalie smoothly juggled her school job and her role as Greg's skating chaperone. They became inseparable.[12]

Greg advanced quickly with help from his coach Bud Wilson. He passed three figure tests within a year and won juvenile boys at the 1955 Easterns. At age ten he was the youngest soloist ever to perform in Ice Chips at the Boston Garden. The next year, he won the U.S. novice men's title at the 1956 Easterns. That summer Nathalie accompanied twelve-year-old Greg to East Lansing to train with Bud Wilson, and he passed a multitude of tests: his fourth and fifth figure, and preliminary and bronze dance tests. After skating for only three years, he performed a solo in the summer show alongside World champion Carol Heiss.[13]

Back in Boston Greg had become a popular fixture at the club; he was outgoing and engaging with everyone. "Greg was a terrific kid," a club member said. "I was a little girl when I first met him and he could not have been nicer." The Kelley family came to the club when they could, but Nathalie was always present. She typified the skating mother; she continually looked out for Greg's welfare and was his shadow at the rink. "His sister was always doting on him," Ron Ludington said. "If she thought I was bothering him or interrupting his training she would say, 'You leave him alone!'"[14]

Sue Blodgett, who also lived in Newton, trained alongside Greg; and they won the New England juvenile, novice, and junior titles simultaneously. They skated in the morning from 6:00 to 8:30 before school, from 3:00 to 6:00 after school, and also put in several sessions on Saturday. Sunday training was more casual, with a tea in the late afternoon. Greg was an all-around skater; he was known for his high jumps and wonderful spins. He had a terrific work ethic and stayed focus on his training. "Gregory was very talented, but he was a ham too," club member Peter Betts said. "He loved performing and always pulled it together and did well—you could just count on it."[15]

In 1957 Greg continued his streak, winning the junior men's title at Easterns in Hershey. He took his first trip to the U.S. Championships in

*Nathalie Kelley, The Skating Club of Boston.
Source: Courtesy of Ashland High School.*

Berkeley. After creating a sizeable lead in figures, his strong free skating performance secured him the U. S. novice men's title. In Boston, Greg received the Rotch Award—named after the club's third president—for his achievements at the SC of Boston's annual dinner at the Harvard Club.[16]

Going into the 1958 competitive season, Greg's record had been extraordinary. He had competed for four years and had never lost a championship. He solidly won senior men's at Easterns in Troy, New York. "Greg is a short fellow with sparkling eyes and dynamite in his feet," *Skating* wrote. "He skated with abandon as if he were giving an exhibition rather than competing with the others in his class." But at the 1958 Nationals in Minneapolis, Greg came in second in figures to Jim Short of Los Angeles. Greg had skated well in the free skate but could not overtake Short. For the first time in his life, Greg placed second.[17]

Greg handled his defeat graciously. As important as skating was, it was not his whole world. He was a bright student at Sacred Heart, a first-through-twelfth-grade Catholic school in Newton. He kept up his schoolwork when he traveled, supervised by his resident tutor Nathalie. "She was devoted to him and helped him as he went up this ladder, both on and off the ice," brother Stephen remarked. Greg was academically motivated because he wanted to become a doctor like his father. Vincent Kelley avidly collected stamps and coins; his plan was to sell his collections one day to pay for Greg's medical schooling. His brothers were often asked why they had not entered the medical profession. They typically answered, "The only one who has the brains is Greg." The entire family realized he was a smart kid with tremendous potential. Greg was also an all-around athlete and enjoyed many sports. He continued to fish with his family whenever he could, and he spent weekends at the Longwood Cricket Club where he enjoyed swimming, diving, and playing tennis.[18]

In 1958 Greg and Nathalie made their annual summer trek to East Lansing. Greg trained alongside Bradley Lord and several international competitors. Greg and Brad, both Bud Wilson students, inspired each other to work their hardest. Nathalie sat in the stands at every practice and made sure Greg received Bud Wilson's time and attention.[19]

Although Greg understood Nathalie's role in his success on the ice, her constant presence inhibited his social opportunities. He rarely had the opportunity to hang out with the other skaters. An exception was Anne and Mary Batdorf, identical twins from Pennsylvania, who lived across the hall from the Kelleys at the Kellogg apartments. Mrs. Batdorf was a great cook and friendly, so they ate together often. Greg soon developed a crush on Mary Batdorf. "Greg was very nice but Nathalie was a tough cookie," Mary observed. "She was on him like a skating mother would be—you wouldn't want to mess with her. Mrs. Kelley [who visited briefly during the summer] was more relaxed and had a lot of fun with my mother, but it was Nathalie who made sure he got to patch at six in the morning and had the lessons."[20]

Passing his eighth gold figure test was the highlight of Greg's summer. In mid-August the skaters gathered at Shaw Hall for an end-of-summer party with a buffet supper and dancing with live music. Greg, fourteen, pinned a beautiful corsage on twelve-year-old Mary's tea-length dress and escorted her to the dance.[21]

Back at the SC of Boston the Kelley family regularly attended the Friday night dinners. The top club skaters, including Greg, Bradley Lord, Dudley Richards, Little Maribel, Laurence Owen, and others, performed at the weekly Friday exhibitions, and were invited to perform in ice carnivals all over New England. They caravanned to such colleges as Dartmouth and Bowdoin, and gave exhibitions at rink season openings.[22]

At the 1959 Nationals in Rochester, Greg solidly won the junior men's title and stood in the winner's circle with novice ladies champion Mary Batdorf. He was noted for his "well-planned and well-executed free program." Still, he had to share accolades with fourth-place finisher Doug Ramsay of Detroit, a dynamic free skater who "won the heartiest applause."[23]

Coach Bud Wilson was delighted with Greg's win. Since Greg's first steps on ice at the SC of Boston, Bud had been confident in his abilities and enthusiastic about his potential. Greg was the third Wilson student to claim the national junior title: Dudley Richards in 1951, Bradley Lord in 1957, and now Gregory Kelley in 1959.[24]

Returning to the SC of Boston as U.S. junior champion, Greg had everything going for him. He was a well-known freshman at his close-knit parochial school, he received excellent grades in his college-prep courses, and at fifteen he was a handsome young man with brown hair, blue eyes, and a cute, freckled face. "Gregory was my first crush," Ronna Goldblatt admitted. "He was a fabulous kid—funny, fun and terrific." Greg had a girlfriend or two at the club, and he took his dates to the movies or went on picnics, sometimes without his sister. Life couldn't be any better.[25]

Greg had reason to think he had a good shot at making the 1960 Olympic Team. There was only one problem. Bud Wilson also coached Bradley Lord. They had rooted for each other for years from the safety of different divisions. But now Bradley and Greg were head-on rivals, vying for a spot on the 1960 Olympic Team. Brad had competed in the senior ranks in 1958 and 1959, taking fourth place both times. However, he had competed at the 1959 Worlds and had a competitive edge going into the 1960 season. Bud had given equal passion to both students during their careers, but the Kelleys were concerned that his loyalties would now be divided. Though the family respected Bud Wilson, he had worked longer with Bradley and had a vested interest in his success. A rivalry became apparent as the two began training after Nationals.[26]

In the best interests of their son, the Kelleys sent Greg to Colorado to work with Edi Scholdan. Most skaters who received a special invitation to the Broadmoor made the move for financial reasons, but the Kelleys did not need that kind of help. The Broadmoor's sterling reputation and training environment had advantages for Greg. Edi Scholdan had already produced one Olympic champion and would likely have his second in the coming year. In the end, it was Greg's decision to break out of the familiar and try something new.[27]

Greg's move to Colorado made a deep impact in Boston. Bud Wilson was disappointed because he had been Greg's only coach and had treated him like a son. But the decision was certainly understandable from the Kelley family's point of view. A complex dynamic had developed between the two athletes, and the rivalry would have grown stronger in time. Bud may have juggled both students adequately, but the Kelleys wanted to avoid any potential problems and they understood the advantages of Greg working with Edi Scholdan.[28]

Greg's decision to move to the Broadmoor meant that Nathalie also had to make a decision. She had become head of the Science Department at Ashland High School, had joined the Ace of Clubs, an upscale women's club, and enjoyed equestrian activities. She was liked by the few skaters she knew well and had begun "a promising career as a skating judge" at the SC of Boston. The Kelley family agreed that twenty-seven-year-old Nathalie, a mother figure to Greg, should go to Colorado with him. She willingly put her life on hold, took a leave of absence from Ashland, and headed to Colorado with Greg in the late spring of 1959. "Nathalie was self-sacrificing and put her interest in the family at the forefront of her life," brother Stephen said.[29]

Although Greg's siblings were already established in their adult lives and had spent relatively little time with him, they were well aware of his character. "Greg achieved as much as he did because he was disciplined and was able to stand the heat of competition," Stephen remarked. "He was jovial and had an outstanding personality—he was a great kid."[30]

Laurence Owen
1959 Junior Ladies Champion

How do you describe a girl like Laurence Owen? Funny, dramatic, whimsical, a little rebellious, introspective, a character. She was extremely accomplished—she was an athlete, scholar, pianist, dancer, writer, linguist, and everyone's friend. She had an engaging personality and a megawatt smile that lit up a room or an arena. She smiled even in practice, as a coach noted: "She would toss her head around and her hair would fly behind her. With her big smile and big arms everything was grand and overly energetic—and yet unique."[31]

Laurence was foremost a figure skater, as Maribel had focused her to be, but she was much more. She was "the personification of youth's promise," her high school principal pronounced. "She was full of life—buoyant and happy. The challenges which her skating and her school work offered seemed only to make her more conscientious and determined. Few ever saw her discouraged or disillusioned. Although national fame turned the heads of many, Laurence was always sincerely humble and friendly. She was a wonderfully enthusiastic, vibrant, and mature person." Laurence developed into a beautiful human being who inspired many, but her life had not begun that way.[32]

Laurence Owen, The Skating Club of Boston, 1959 Junior Ladies Champion. Source: World Figure Skating Museum.

Laurence Rochon Owen was born May 9, 1944, in Berkeley, California, to Maribel Vinson Owen and Guy Rochon Owen and was named for her paternal grandmother, Laurence Rochon, of Ontario, Canada. Laurence's first exposure to skating was sitting in a playpen at the Berkeley and Boston rinks while her mother taught six-time national champion Gretchen Merrill. Older skaters babysat her while her mother taught.[33]

Laurence first put skates on at age two, but skating wasn't much fun. In her early years, she sat on the rink barrier and cried because things weren't going right. She was a tiny thing, but she knew what was expected of her, and skating wasn't always easy. She had difficulty maneuvering between skaters because she jumped in the opposite direction, from right to left, and skated against the flow of traffic. Maribel was not sympathetic with her difficulties.[34]

But skating every day produced results. In 1952 she placed third out of twenty-one girls in the novice division at the Northern California meet, and placed eighth in juvenile girls at Pacific Coast. No matter how she did competitively, Laurence remained optimistic. In a letter to *Skating* she wrote, "I hope to go in junures (*sic*) next year and come first." However, the next year she didn't even make the podium at the Northern California meet.[35]

Maribel would teach her daughters in the mornings until coach Bob Swenning showed up for patch. "I would find Big Maribel sitting on the boards crying," Bob said, "and I'd say, 'Okay, I'll take over now.' I taught them until I had enough. 'Okay, it's time for you to take them back. Laurence is going to drive me crazy.' Laurence was about nine and she was a little devil. My daughter was the same age, and they were two absolute terrors. Even at that age Laurence exhibited a lot of natural talent, but she and my daughter would hide someplace, and I would have to go find them."[36]

Laurence had bad rink manners. After falling on an axel, she would scream and bang on the boards; if she didn't want to do her program, she kicked her heels in the ice. When she got mad and sat down on the ice, her mother ignored her—Maribel was too busy making a living. Years later Laurence talked about her childhood in *Sports Illustrated*: "The years when I was 6 and 7 I really worked hard all the time. Then when I was about 8 I didn't work at all. I just thought I knew everything. I didn't compete at all that year except in pairs. I wasn't a very good pairs skater, to say the very least. The only thing that got me back to work was that Mummy said I couldn't go to camp, so I really got going."[37]

Maribel paired Laurence with Bill Hickox, whom she also taught in singles. Bill had been skating for three years when he and Laurence formed a pair. They placed third in junior pairs at California State in 1953. When Maribel moved her family to Boston the following year, the pair partnership ended.[38]

Though the girls had spent hours at the rink with their mother in Berkeley, neither sister had been motivated to train. Maribel hoped Boston would be a fresh start for Maribel Jr., fourteen, and Laurence, ten. Laurence herself was fed up with losing in competitions. On the West Coast, she had placed last in both juvenile and novice at Pacific Coast. After she finished last in juniors at the 1955 Easterns, Laurence was neither angry nor discouraged—just determined. She confided in skater Peter Betts. "Here I was last in all of those competitions in Pacific Coast and now last in Easterns." Then with a twinkle in her dark brown eyes, she announced, "Next year I'm going to win this!" When she won junior ladies the next year, she ran up to Peter Betts with the trophy and exclaimed, "I said I was going to win it, and I won it!" Laurence's success did not surprise Bob Swenning: "When she finally decided she wanted to do it, she really worked and then she blossomed."[39]

Laurence had also undergone a physical transformation since moving to Massachusetts. Between junior high and high school, she tweezed her eyebrows, gave her hair a pixie cut, and began to grow tall. The change was dramatic; and even though "Laurence wasn't one who would have thought about her looks," a classmate recalled, she stood out. Her fly-away bob, an unusual cut for the time, suited her and became a signature look.[40]

In Boston, Laurence also grew into her name. Her school friends only knew her as Laurie. "I had the impression she didn't like her name when she was in junior high school," a classmate said, "because some people thought her name was a man. As she got older she realized for whom she was named and she grew proud of it." When the press interviewed her, she always made sure they pronounced her name correctly: "Don't call it LAW-rence . . . it is Lo-RAWNCE."[41]

The year 1956 seemed like the golden year for Laurence. After winning Easterns, she made her first trip to Nationals to compete in novice ladies in Philadelphia. She placed fifth in figures but broke her wrist in a fall during practice and withdrew before the free skating event where, thirty-two years earlier, her mother had won the junior title at the same arena. Barbara Roles won the 1956 novice title while Laurence wound up ninth.[42]

Laurence had yet to mirror her mother's skating career, but she did inherit her academic strengths. Reading was Laurence's true passion, and she read the classics constantly. "Laurence used to come in with a pile of books and drop them all or invariably trip over something," a classmate recalled. "She was very awkward at the junior high school level but she was very bright and had many friends."[43]

Laurence moved up to senior ladies, and was now competing against her sister. At the 1957 Easterns, Maribel Jr. placed fourth and Laurence placed sixth. It was a huge disappointment to Mama Maribel—and also the girls—that they missed the opportunity to return to their former home and compete at the 1957 Nationals in Berkeley. The following year Laurence rebounded and won Easterns. "When she would land her spectacular jumps a delightful smile would spread across her face," *Skating* wrote. "When she ended her number, she just flung out her arms as if to say, 'Whee, I made it!' As she started to skate off she did a bunny hop, missed, and fell on her knees, but she just slid along, laughing, so great was her pleasure."[44]

At the 1958 U.S. Championships in Minneapolis, Laurence placed third in junior ladies behind Barbara Roles and Stephanie Westerfeld, respectively. After Laurence dropped out of Nationals in 1956 and failed to advance to Nationals in 1957, Maribel was thrilled that her fourteen-year-old won her first medal at Nationals; she also won many new fans. "Everybody knew Laurence because she was so visible in her grandeur," judge Newbold Black reflected. "She didn't have all of the super jumping ability that some other skaters had, but she had great presentation."[45]

Laurence sometimes wore a bandage around her "trick left knee" for support. Friends didn't know the reason, but one coach suggested she might have aggravated her leg due to the repetitious practicing of spread eagles. "Laurence didn't have a natural spread eagle but her mother insisted she practice it all the time," coach Tommy McGinnis said. "That may have caused some problems."[46]

The following year Laurence did not move up to the national senior level. Maribel wanted her to win the national junior title, just as she herself had in 1924. Laurence inherited her parents' skating genes, but she needed to work hard to be successful. She was agile and lithe, due in part to dance training. On Saturday mornings she went to the Alicia Langford School of Ballet, and she was just as graceful on the dance floor—the ballet school wanted Laurence to forego the ice and become a ballerina. Laurence was masterful at musical interpretation, and she infused her skating with soulful passion.[47]

Laurence's artistic expression captivated audiences, but her jumps needed work. She tended to cheat the landing (not completing a full rotation) on her jumps, as did a number of other female skaters. Her mother lacked strong jump expertise, as coach Ron Ludington noted: "In that era girls had their legs very open in the air in their jumps. Maribel never understood how to teach them how to get into the correct positioning for the landing. She let her students throw their legs out like an open flying camel in their jumps and hope for the best."[48]

Some of Maribel's students were recruited to help Laurence by demonstrating jumps in group lessons—an awkward situation for the girls who competed against her. "Maribel tried to give equal time to her other skaters besides her daughters," remarked Joanna Niska, who was a national novice medalist under Maribel. "However, I did leave Maribel because I competed against Laurence and it became too difficult." Rickie Rendich, from New York, had a different experience: "Laurence was coming up [in the ranks] at the time that Maribel was training me, but she believed in me and gave me everything. She was there for her daughter, but she was [there] for me too. There was no holding back. It was remarkable."[49]

Bud Wilson and Willie Frick also worked with Laurence because she did not always get along with her mother. Maribel felt she was never wrong, and Laurence, who had no qualms about challenging her, would respond with a loud, "But, Mother!" Maribel Jr. was meek like her father, but Laurence was like her mother, and they argued constantly.[50]

It would be difficult for anyone to have their own mother for a coach. Some accused Maribel of forcing her daughters to skate. "Maribel was pretty hard on Laurence," a friend conceded. "I can't say that [Laurence and Little Maribel] were necessarily passionate about skating, but it was so ingrained in them." Friends acknowledged that the girls had to be willing or they wouldn't have stepped on the ice every day. "They had the soul and spirit of skaters," a club member said. "A lot of people skate, but [the Owen girls] lived it." A club member succinctly summarized the Owen sisters' situation: "They did enjoy [skating], but there were days when they were mad at their mother, like all mothers and daughters that age are. So it may not have been the skating they were upset with but with their mother."[51]

Laurence was fully aware of how tethered she was to her mother, but often played it for laughs. Sometimes she would get on the ice late on purpose. Maribel would start yelling at her, Laurence would put her fingers in her ears, and Maribel would start chasing her around the rink. "Laurence was an actress and was hysterical," Ronna Goldblatt said. "She was a free spirit—absolutely free, like a bird. Laurence did have a passion for skating—on the ice you could plainly see her love for it."[52]

When the Boston rinks closed over the summer, Maribel coached in Lynn. Laurence and Maribel Jr. made the most of the summer, and sometimes pulled shenanigans, as adult skater Joyce Burden explained: "The kids would go to the beach and unbeknownst to us they would use us as the official chaperones [for an alibi] . . . like 'Joyce and Ernie are going to be there.' We usually didn't skate in the afternoon but one day we did and Maribel grilled us: 'I thought you were at the beach!' When Laurence, Little Maribel, and their friends came into the rink, Big Maribel lined them up against the lockers and screamed at them."[53]

Laurence explored other interests in the summertime. She enjoyed swimming, sailing, tennis, traveling, acting, and literary pursuits. Maribel said, "You can be talking to Laurence and see she isn't listening—she may go off to look for some paper and write a poem." Visitors to the Owen home didn't always see Laurence, because she'd be quietly in her room writing poetry. She entertained herself well and had a vast imagination. A friend said she was the kind of girl who would be out chasing butterflies in the morning and studying advanced mathematics in the afternoon. "She put 150 per cent into everything, and did everything," Ronna Goldblatt said.[54]

Music infused every aspect of her life. Laurence would enter the rink singing in a high operatic voice. She had studied the piano since she was young and had a vast knowledge of music, as her piano teacher of six years, Clinton Jonas, noted:

She was an extraordinary personality, not only talented and ambitious but her interest in music and the related arts was intense and genuine. She played Beethoven, Chopin, and Debussy beautifully and was able to assimilate advanced instruction in a manner unusual for a girl of her age. I believe that few outside of her family circle ever heard her play. Her skating activities prevented her from maintaining constantly a high standard of performance in her playing and this was important to her. Along with her poetry and stories she also wrote melodies which were harmonized and the work was entirely her own.[55]

When fall rolled around, Laurence rose at four o'clock to train before school. Instead of attending the Boston Latin School like her mother and sister, she matriculated with friends at Winchester High School. Her literary skills astounded her teachers. "She used to amaze me with her depth of understanding," her English teacher said. "There is no question that she had an unusual ability to write poetry. It seemed the perfectly natural way for her to express herself." She excelled in every subject; one classmate claimed that Laurence was the first person to achieve a perfect math score on the SATs. Laurence balanced her academic discipline with joie de vivre. "She was zany and pretty nuts, but everybody loved her for it. You just expected the unexpected from her," a classmate said.[56]

Maribel was stern with Laurence during practices as she prepared for the 1959 National junior ladies' title. She first won senior ladies at both the 1959 New Englands and Easterns. Her primary competition at the 1959 U.S. Championships in Rochester was Stephanie Westerfeld, who already had a bronze and silver in that division. Stephanie was strong in figures, but Laurence surprisingly placed first, then skated a strong freestyle program to win the event. The SC of Boston presented Laurence with the Rotch Award, which included a monetary prize of $500. "It was a great source of encouragement for the family and Maribel just absolutely burst into tears, which was very sweet," Dick Button recalled. Maribel had had a tenuous relationship with the club for years. It always bothered her that she was not accepted, and for her daughter to be honored was a huge validation. She enthusiastically worked with both her daughters at the SC of Boston and a myriad of other locales to secure two spots on the 1960 U.S. Olympic Team.[57]

STEPHANIE WESTERFELD

1959 JUNIOR SILVER MEDALIST

SHARON WESTERFELD

Stephanie ("Steffi") Westerfeld was one of the Broadmoor Skating Club's rare homegrown stars. She began skating as a tot and grew into the ice princess of Colorado Springs. She set a high standard at the Broadmoor Ice Palace. She was a lady at all times, she never lost her temper, and she was a role model for consistent, focused training. "Cute as a button and very special," remembered one friend. Everyone wanted to be just like Steffi.[58]

Stephanie Westerfeld became a skater because of her sister. Sharon ("Sherri") Westerfeld was the second child of Otto and Myra Westerfeld; their first child, a son, was stillborn. Sherri was born in Kansas City, Missouri, on March 1, 1935; and at age four, she put on ice skates during a family vacation at the Broadmoor. She liked skating well enough to continue in Kansas City. She skated on a frozen city pool and eventually trained with Canadian coach Mary Jane Halstead at the Pla-Mor ice rink before and after school every day.[59]

When Sherri was eight, Stephanie Westerfeld was born on October 8, 1943. Steffi followed her sister to the rink when she was four years old. She was nicknamed Popcorn because she spent more time at the rink's popcorn stand than on the ice. She also took from Mary Jane Halstead and was the youngest member of the Junior FSC of Kansas City.[60]

The Westerfelds returned to the Broadmoor every summer because the Pla-Mor rink was not open year-round. Sherri took lessons from Edi Scholdan in singles and from Walter Muehlbronner in dance. Steffi tagged along. Coached by Patty Sonnekson, Steffi passed her preliminary test and became the youngest skater ever to perform in the prestigious Broadmoor Ice Revue. At age five she wrote a letter published in *Skating*: "I am working on my first test and learning a solo 'The Waltzing Doll' for our Christmas party. I enjoy my many ice skating friends and am having lots of fun."[61]

The Westerfelds made a life-changing move in 1949. Sherri was in junior high and Steffi was six when Myra decided to move to Colorado permanently. Myra wanted the girls to skate year-round and take advantage of the coaching and facilities there. Otto agreed to remain in Kansas City to run his insurance business, with promises to visit the family when he could. Sherri competed at the 1950 Midwesterns in Chicago and placed eighth out of twelve girls in senior ladies. At the end of the year, she passed her eighth figure test—the third member of the Broadmoor Skating Club to become a gold medalist.[62]

Sherri never excelled competitively. She was adept at figures and graceful in her free skating, but she lacked strong jumps. At the 1951 Midwesterns she bettered her placement from the year before and placed sixth. Sherri made her first appearance at the U.S. Championships in 1952, held at the Broadmoor, where she placed fifth out of six participants in senior ladies. Her highest honor was being named as a second alternate to the 1953

World Team. At the 1953 Nationals, Sherri placed seventh in figures but withdrew before free skating.[63]

Sherri graduated a few months later from Cheyenne Mountain High School and then attended Colorado College. She retired from competitive skating but still performed in the Broadmoor Ice Revue and participated in summer dance competitions. Gregarious and attractive, Sherri was extremely popular at the rink and was crowned the "Beauty Queen of Colorado Springs" at the Broadmoor Hotel's annual beauty pageant. "Sherri was one of the most beautiful gals I had ever seen," Hugh Graham said. "If you ever saw her in person it was plainly obvious. She was stunning."[64]

Sherri was also very social. She enjoyed ballroom dancing and was a sought-after partner. At the Ice Palace, she flirted with the hockey players, had several boyfriends through the years, and developed serious relationships with two of the most talented men in figure skating. When she was seventeen, she dated Olympic bronze medalist Jimmy Grogan off and on. Some thought an engagement was imminent, but in 1952 the U.S. Army whisked Grogan away, ending any further romance. She next dated Hayes Jenkins. He eventually fell in love with Carol Heiss, but Hayes and Sherri always remained good friends.[65]

As Sherri's competitive skating moved into the background in 1953, her sister showed tremendous promise. Sherri became her sister's chauffeur, advisor, and personal confidante. Steffi always credited her sister for her success, saying she wanted to follow in her footsteps. When Steffi's skating surpassed her sister, Sherri was not jealous. "Sharon was just as proud as if she were doing it herself," a cousin recalled.[66]

Stephanie placed dead last in juvenile girls at her first Midwesterns in 1950—but she was only six. Two years later she won the event. One of her judges said she had the strongest wills to win he had ever seen, and one competitor remarked: "She was good and cute—like a tiny Sonja Henie." Steffi became the unofficial mascot of the Broadmoor Ice Palace.[67]

Right before the 1952 competitive season began, Steffi's beloved coach, Patty Sonnekson, died from complications of childbirth followed by pneumonia. Patty had taught for six years and was the first gold medalist from the Broadmoor. Her sudden death shocked the entire club. With a heavy heart, Steffi continued her training with Eileen Seigh Honnen, a 1948 Olympian.[68]

With her petite physique and curly hair, Steffi reminded everyone of Shirley Temple. She had more in common with this depression-era movie star than just looks. Just as Shirley Temple had danced with Bill ("Bojangles") Robinson on screen, Steffi danced with Jon Williams at the Broad-

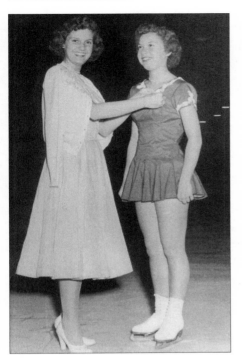

Sharon Westerfeld, pinning a gold medal on sister Stephanie, Broadmoor Ice Palace. Source: World Figure Skating Museum.

moor. After working with Fred Astaire to set up his Fred Astaire Dance Studios across the country, Jon and his wife, Vivian, settled in Colorado to teach ballroom dancing at the Broadmoor. They performed on Broadmoor's Terrace on summer evenings, and Jon always performed a number with nine-year-old Steffi.[69]

In 1953 Steffi won novice ladies at Midwesterns. She beat the skirts off the older girls. "Tiny Stephanie Westerfeld 'stole' the show with her skill and performance in an outstanding program to skate from fifth in figures to first place," *Skating* wrote. Unlike Sherri, Steffi found that jumping came easily to her even though she jumped from right to left. She changed coaches again, switching to Edi Scholdan when Eileen Seigh Honnen gave birth to her first child and moved to Denver. At age ten, Steffi sounded like a seasoned pro when she shared her thoughts with *Skating*: "As far as footwork and style are concerned, I feel your toes should be pointed at all times and your hands should never be carried above your waist, unless it is for a special move. I like to feel my music and have my program go with every beat, so every move has a meaning with the music."[70]

After her success in novice ladies, Steffi advanced to junior ladies; on her third try, she won the junior ladies title at the 1956 Midwesterns in Cleveland "with a superb and expressive interpretation of her music." At her first Nationals, she placed fourth in novice ladies in 1955. The following year, she unfortunately placed last in figures but pulled up to sixth place after the free skate.[71]

In 1957 Steffi won her first Midwestern senior ladies title in Sioux City, Iowa, and repeated her win the next three years. It wasn't much fun for her competitors, as one of them noted: "Steffi had an amazing ability to always deliver at competition time. Her figures were unbelievable, and she usually deserved to win." It didn't hurt that she had the Broadmoor machine behind her. "Of course she beat me," another competitor said. "She was a nice skater, but it helped that she was with a good club—Broadmoor skaters always won." This was a feeling shared by many skaters—the Broadmoor club's prestige and clout were assets at competition time.[72]

At the 1957 U.S. Championships in Berkeley, New Yorker Carol Wanek won junior ladies and thirteen-year-old Steffi placed third, winning her first national medal. She passed her eighth figure test that summer; a photographer captured Sherri pinning the gold medal to her sister's sweater, and the picture was splashed across the Colorado Springs newspapers. The Westerfeld girls were local media darlings. Ever since they moved from Kansas City, their faces regularly appeared in the Colorado papers, from skating at the Broadmoor to holding lion cubs at the Cheyenne Zoo. By the late fifties, the local press could put "Steffi" in their headlines and everyone knew who she was.[73]

After winning the 1958 Midwestern senior title in Troy, Ohio, Steffi appeared on a Dayton TV station; she had wonderful presence on camera and spoke eloquently about her sport. At the 1958 Nationals in Minneapolis, Steffi was one of the favorites in junior ladies. She placed second in figures and maintained that placement through the free skate. Barbara Roles won the event and Laurence Owen was third.[74]

Steffi was now a U.S. junior ladies bronze and silver medalist. The next year she planned to win and had what it took to be a national champion. She was good in both figures and freestyle. She was a gifted athlete and had a great figure skating body: petite and lean. However, because she had all the makings of a champion, she experienced a lot of pressure to achieve. When she didn't win or perform well in a show, she would privately burst into tears and upbraid herself.[75]

Much of that pressure came from her mother's expectations, and Steffi tried hard never to disappoint her. Mrs. West, as the other skaters called her,

Stephanie Westerfeld, Broadmoor Skating Club, 1959 Junior Ladies Silver Medalist. Source: Courtesy of Diane Yeomans Robins.

sat in the stands during every practice session with the other moms. "Steffi's mother was really hard on her. She had to behave . . . and be perfect," one skater recalled. Myra tended to be pushy, but Steffi never rebelled because she loved skating. Myra was so obsessed by her daughter's skating future that her marriage suffered. "It happens a lot in the skating world," Eileen Seigh Honnen explained. "The marriage breaks up because the mothers become so fixated on their girls they forget their husbands." Mr. Westerfeld visited from Kansas City once in a while, but "we all knew they were estranged," a skater said.[76]

Fortunately Steffi had an escape from the pressures of the rink. When she was seven, she began practicing the piano daily in their Cheyenne Arms apartment. She was extremely gifted and had won many competitions; she hoped to be a concert pianist. Piano teacher Esther Vance put pressure on her to quit skating and devote her life to music, but Steffi loved both equally and maximized every minute in her day so she could master both interests. Her piano expertise also enhanced her skating because she had a great affinity for music. Steffi was also an accomplished dancer—she took ballet, jazz, modern, and tap. She took cotillion classes and private ballroom lessons with other Broadmoor skaters. Steffi was a proficient ice dancer and competed in local dance competitions.[77]

Steffi was an honor student at Cheyenne Mountain High School. On campus she had an outstanding reputation. Like Sherri, she was very bright. Sherri studied psychology at Colorado College, pledged Delta Gamma sorority, and graduated magna cum laude. She became a more visible presence at the rink after she graduated and was instrumental in Steffi's success. Sherri was always positive and encouraging. "I never heard 'that wasn't good' or 'you messed up,'" a skater recalled. "It was always constructive and uplifting." Sherri was refreshingly wholesome, fun, and sophisticated, and Steffi emulated her. The Westerfeld girls were ideal role models for the other skaters at the rink; they supported all skaters and were happy when someone did well. "Steffi and I were rivals and were always neck and neck," Edi's daughter Dixie said. "Regardless we were really close friends."[78]

After performing as a headliner for the 1958 Broadmoor Ice Revue at summer's end, Steffi felt ready for the 1959 season. She won senior ladies for the third time at the 1959 Midwesterns in Denver. In Rochester, New York, Steffi hoped she could add gold to her national bronze and silver. However, Laurence Owen edged her out for first place. Steffi surprised observers by placing second in figures again and was unable to pull up to first. The following week *Sports Illustrated* featured Steffi, along with Laurence Owen, Rhode Michelson, and five other skaters, in an article spotlighting the next generation of skating champions.[79]

Most skaters would be thrilled to win a silver medal at Nationals, and Steffi was her usual gracious self about not winning. Still, it was a huge disappointment. She could move up to senior ladies and vie for a spot on the 1960 Olympic Team, but she and Edi Scholdan decided to give it one more year. On her fourth attempt, she was bound to win the U.S. junior ladies title. She returned to Colorado Springs with a bright smile and renewed commitment. Her presence at the Broadmoor Ice Palace continued to thrill and inspire the myriad of younger skaters who held her in high esteem. In their eyes she was already a national champion.

CHAPTER 7

THE LAKE PLACID
CONNECTION

Lake Placid inaugurated its first summer skating season after the conclusion of the 1932 Olympic Winter Games and, along with the Broadmoor, rapidly became a premier U.S. destination for summer skating. Many national and international champions trained there. Gus Lussi, who was at that first summer season, was the most prominent coach. Other coaches who taught during the summer season included Walter Arian, Willy Boeckl, Willie Frick, Howard Nicholson, Bill Swallender, Cliff Thaell, Walter ("Red") Bainbridge, Cecelia Colledge, Otto Gold, Jean Westwood, Bill Kipp, and Danny Ryan.[1]

Lake Placid was the most prominent summer ice dancing center in the United States. Every August, ice dancers from the Midwest, the East, and Canada headed there for Dance Week. Dancers passed tests, and USFSA dance officials conducted judges' clinics. The culmination of this two-week period was the largest dance competition in America. Dancers competed in bronze, silver, or gold divisions—the equivalent of novice, junior, and senior divisions. Couples performed a standardized set of steps and dance patterns to identical music at a specified tempo. Dancers had to pass dance tests— preliminary, pre-bronze, bronze, pre-silver, silver, pre-gold, or gold—to qualify for each of these levels and perfect a variety of dances for each test. Ice dances had some common names, like the swing, the blues, and the foxtrot, but also unusual names like the Fourteenstep and the Kilian. Numerous dance teams practiced simultaneously during crowded sessions to the strains of the "Westminster Waltz," or "Paso Doble." New partnerships were formed, new stars emerged, and dancers from across the nation gained inspiration from the variety of talent that gathered in Lake Placid every summer.

Three of the 1959 junior champions and their coaches had a Lake Placid connection. Both Danny Ryan and Bill Kipp trained there as competitive dancers, and returned in the late fifties as coaches. They picked up new students for the summer season and brought their own students as well, including Larry Pierce and Marilyn Meeker, 1959 silver dance champions, and Rhode Lee Michelson, 1959 junior ladies bronze medalist.

WILLIAM KIPP
PROFESSIONAL

Bill Kipp decided at a young age that figure skating would be his career. He worked toward competitive success, but his extraordinary talent pointed toward even greater performance opportunities beyond competition. Instead, as an adult he moved from a small town in Pennsylvania to the California coast, where he influenced many skaters as a coach. He was creative and had a terrific personality. "I was excited when I came to a lesson because I learned," a student exclaimed. "He had an electricity that made me feel very special, so I worked harder. I would have jumped over the great Niagara Falls for him."[2]

William Robert Kipp was born on July 15, 1932, the son of Martin and Wilhelmina Kipp. Bill grew up with three older brothers and two older sisters in Allentown, Pennsylvania. He was the baby of the family—eleven years younger than his nearest sibling. His childhood included building model airplanes and riding the roller coaster at Dorney Park.[3]

Asthma prevented him from participating in field sports, so his parents looked for a sport without dust and dirt. When he was young, he began roller skating, and "people used to stop and watch him," his brother Martin said. Bill learned to ice skate with his sister Wilhelmina ("Timmy") on the frozen ponds and creeks near their home. "The minute he got on the ice he stayed right up," she said. He pretended to skate in his bedroom slippers in the house and practiced jumps in their tiny backyard. He skated on many of Allentown's frozen ponds, including Rose Garden Park and Union Terrace Park, until a cousin invited him to accompany her to the Albeth Ice Rink.[4]

The Albeth rink did not have a coaching staff, so Bill taught himself. He joined the Penguin Figure Skating Club in 1946 and was fifteen when he passed his first figure test. Occasionally he went to Baltimore or Philadelphia to take lessons from Bill Swallender; by 1948 he made annual pilgrimages to Lake Placid, where his coach was in summer residence. Back home he began a dance partnership with Theda Beck, who was several years older. "He chose our music, choreographed routines, and taught me the dance patterns," Theda recalled. "He ran the show and was always positive." Bill was the resident coach at the Albeth rink and helped everyone out—he just never got paid.[5]

The Albeth manager said Bill "looked impressive on ice from the start and he developed into the best skater [I'd] ever seen." He won the Philadel-

William Kipp, Senior Professsional, Arctic Blades Figure Skating Club, Iceland, Paramount. Source: Courtesy of Anita Entrikin Miller.

phia Area junior championships in 1949 and was awarded the Philadelphia Bulletin Trophy for artistic performance. Bill and Theda were also Philadelphia's junior pairs and mixed dance champions—they did everything. Bill went to Lake Placid that summer and won two silver dance medals with another partner.[6]

In the 1950 competitive season, Bill and Theda placed fourth in silver dance at Easterns, where they were noted for "real expression and unity in their tango." They were allowed to compete in silver dance at the U.S. Championships in Washington, D.C., where they placed seventh out of fourteen couples. "We thought that was pretty good," Theda said. "We went without a coach but were so excited."[7]

Bill graduated from Allentown High School in 1950. His yearbook senior page focused on his passion: "Eats, sleeps, and drinks skating . . . sensational figure skater . . . won numerous medals . . . favorite pastimes are movies, records and dancing . . . sold on sharp clothes . . . hopes to make ice skating his career." Bill was a great show skater and several eastern clubs regularly invited him to perform exhibitions in their ice carnivals. Ice skating was his career choice, but the next two years tested his competitive endurance.[8]

Theda retired; and with no permanent partner, he sat out the 1951 season. The next summer, he suffered a major setback when he twisted his leg in practice. The injury was so severe that it kept him out of competition for the second year in a row. The following summer, he completed his gold dance test. Now that he was a dance gold medalist, all he needed was a partner.[9]

Bill joined forces with Janet Williams of the New Haven Skating Club that fall; both had musical interests and got along well. At the 1953 U.S. Championships in Hershey, Bill and Janet placed fifth out of five couples. Bill, undeterred, continued developing his skills by completing the ISU bronze and silver dance tests. He and Janet were chosen as first alternates to the 1954 World Team. At the 1954 Nationals, they just missed the podium, placing fourth.[10]

Bill passed his eighth figure test at Lake Placid that summer. At the time, he was one of seven individuals nationally who had ever passed the gold test in figures, freestyle, and dance. Bill never excelled competitively in singles despite the fact that his free skating was extraordinary. Slender at five foot seven and 130 pounds, Bill was a powerful skater. "He would scare me to death because he skated so fast," a skater remarked. "He could do a soundless double loop with no warm-up and land as light as an angel," another admirer recalled. Bill was featured prominently at the weekly Saturday night shows. He received enthusiastic applause because of his choice of music, sequined show costumes, and well-choreographed routines. "He felt music so intuitively and expressed it better than most," a coach remarked. He had more show biz than most competitive skaters, bringing down the house with his crowd-pleasing programs.[11]

The summer skaters did everything together: eating meals at the Mirror Lake Inn dining room, seeing movies, and hanging out. After the weekly Saturday night shows, they danced in roadhouses. Bill had a wonderful quality about him, as one skater noted: "He had this magical happiness about him that made you believe, 'Oh he really wants to spend time with me. I must be special to him.' We all felt we were his best friend." Bill kept his friends in stitches; he put words together which at first sounded improbable but were terribly funny. "He couldn't say two words without you laughing," Peter Betts said.[12]

Bill loved the Lake Placid atmosphere. "Every day at Lake Placid I practiced from seven to nine hours and then on Saturday night we had a show," he told a reporter. "I'm not kidding when I say that continual practice is not an easy grind." Bill now focused all his energies on ice dancing. He was double jointed, limber, and had deep edges. He was precise and had wonderful pointed toes. One time he rescued a friend who kept failing her blues test, saying, "I'm sick of you getting gypped." He partnered her for her test—it was the only one that passed that week. They celebrated with champagne.[13]

After Bill and Janet dissolved their partnership in 1954, he joined forces with Virginia ("Ginnie") Hoyns, who was twice national gold dance runner-up with Don Jacoby. Their coach was Jean Westwood, four-time World dance champion. In short order, they became a formidable team. They won senior dance at the 1955 Middle Atlantics and placed second at Easterns, where they "illustrated an exciting style. . . . [T]heir free dance was full of novel and surprising segments," *Skating* wrote. They became last-minute replacements at the 1955 North American Championships in Regina, Saskatchewan, Canada. Traveling into the region's harsh weather became an adventure, as *Skating* noted: "As [the team] approached the prairies [they] found a blizzard raging in full fury and air travelers were dumped unceremoniously at various points on the plains with no choice but to continue their journeys by train." Still, Bill and Ginny "pleased spectators with their smooth style" and took home the bronze medal—Bill's most prestigious win. Two weeks later they competed at the 1955 Nationals, where they finished a disappointing fifth.[14]

Bill had competed on the national level since 1950 and had little to show for his efforts. His North American bronze medal was evidence of his talent, but he rarely succeeded competitively. Friends suggested it was due to limited financial resources. They assumed his parents didn't have the kind of money needed for top coaching. Bill had trained with Bill Swallender and Gus Lussi, but only seasonally. He won medals in Lake Placid; but at the U.S. Championships, his competitive career seemed a matter of bad timing. He was not in the right place at the right time with the right partner.[15]

Actually, money wasn't the problem. Martin Kipp was a successful butcher of fine meats and had a lucrative business. Bill's siblings had grown up and moved into their adult careers, so there was more money available for skating expenses. His supportive parents traveled with him to many competitions, and his lack of success exasperated his family. At dance sessions, a select number of judges regularly chose him as their partner. "He knew all the steps perfectly and they all wanted to dance with him, so what does that prove to you?" Timmy said. "We'd see his performance and see the others, and we'd wonder what happened to him."[16]

Changing partners didn't help either. "The judges sometimes said he was too good for his partners," said sister-in-law Ruth Ann. Bill was most likely penalized because his home club, the Penguin Figure Skating Club, had little cachet in competitive circles. He would have been perceived more favorably had he represented the prestigious Philadelphia SC & HS. Bill's lack of medals was maddening for the family, but "he was too wonderful of a boy to complain."[17]

Bill turned professional in 1955 and was invited to join Ice Follies. He would have been a great asset to the show, but he turned down the offer to coach instead, following Jean Westwood to Los Angeles. Bill was twenty-three when he joined the staff of a special ice rink—Iceland, owned by Frank Zamboni.[18]

Frank Zamboni and his brother Lawrence owned an ice manufacturing plant in the 1930s. To replace the loss in their business due to the advent of refrigerators, they built Iceland in Paramount, California, in 1939. Frank invented a revolutionary ice floor, and Iceland became known for the high quality of its smooth ice surface, its generous 100' x 200' size, a pipe organ played weekly by manager Truman Welch, and its ice cleaning machine, called a Zamboni, which Frank invented in 1949. The Zamboni & Company offices were just a few blocks from the rink. If the Zamboni ever needed repair, Frank was just a quick phone call away.[19]

Bill soon had plenty of pupils. He gave his first lesson to dancer Sharon McKenzie, and her mother threw a big party in Bill's honor and presented him with his first five-dollar bill for a half-hour lesson. He and Jean coached Roland Junso and Joan Zamboni, Frank's daughter. They became the 1956 U.S. gold dance champions and students Aileen Kahre and Chuck Phillips were the 1956 U.S. silver dance champions. In his first year of teaching, Bill was the most successful American ice dancing coach in the nation.[20]

He and Jean were a winning professional combination. Jean brought her experience as British and World champion, and Bill was good at technique and a great choreographer. "Bill wanted us to fill out the rink, push the walls out, and make it as big and sweeping as we could," Aileen Kahre recalled. Bill, Jean, and Aileen lived in apartments near each other, which made a convenient car pool to the rink; Frank rented them midnight private ice for ten dollars an hour.[21]

Bill also worked with Sharon McKenzie and Bert Wright on midnight ice. Whenever Bert was late, Bill invited Sharon to skate his legendary "Night Train" routine with him. Sharon's father, a strait-laced minister, thought their dance movements were scandalous; but Sharon called skating with Bill "pure heaven, because he could lay on an edge and there was so much emotion in his skating." Sharon and Bert won the 1957 U.S. gold dance title; at the 1957 Worlds they placed third. Some of the judges thought their dance was shocking. They got in trouble because they dared to raise their legs waist high.[22]

Bill now had three teams who had achieved something he never came close to—a national dance title. His phenomenal success in coaching can be attributed to his teaching skills and his tremendous rapport with his students, many of whom were older than he. He taught with zeal and was forthright. "He explained things without making you feel like a dummy," Maggie Hosford said. [23]

Bill enjoyed the camaraderie of the adult dancers and joined them for movies, barbecues, and parties. A charismatic, free spirit, he livened up any event. "Billy was always full of hell and into practical jokes," a judge said. At one memorable soiree, Bill stunned hostess Gladys Mercer, who told guests to wear pants they wouldn't normally wear. When Gladys realized that the Ice Follies were in town, she cancelled the theme because cast members were invited. On Bill's invitation she wrote: "Forget about the pants." Bill arrived at the front door wearing a white shirt, a sport coat, a tie, socks and tennis shoes—but no pants. "I'll never forget the look on Gladys's face," a friend said. "I was surprised she didn't faint."[24]

Bill raved to his East Coast friends how wonderful it was to live in California. He loved the climate and was amazed that both the ocean and the mountains could be visible from one spot. "You can ski one day, swim in the ocean the next!" he exclaimed. He was a great skier; and whenever he could, he went to Mammoth Mountain. On other days, he left the frozen environs of the rink to spend a sunny day on the hot California beaches.[25]

Bill was equally happy at Lake Placid. After two years of teaching at Paramount, Bill returned to Lake Placid in the summer of 1957 with Jean Westwood, who was then teaching in Toronto. Their friendship and dance partnership continued over the next few summers. It didn't matter which national or World champion was on the Saturday night program. Bill and Jean were the stars. Their signature number, "St. Louis Blues," brought down the house every time. "The place went wild, simply wild," a fan enthused. Bill was an exceptional showman; his smile always drew the audience in. "When they performed, everybody's eyeballs nearly popped out," one skater exclaimed. They closed every show to standing ovations.[26]

Jean had a huge crush on Bill. From the first time she skated with Bill, she wanted him for a partner. He was phenomenally talented, and she was a fantastic dancer. Together, they made the perfect team. Jean paid him the highest compliment imaginable: "The oneness we had every time we stepped on the ice together gave me a joy of skating that I never experienced with the partner that I won the World titles with." Bill partnered Jean through all her American dance tests; when they performed the Kilian dance, they did ten sequences (normally three) before the judges stopped them. "I was just exhausted," Jean recalled. "I said to the judges afterwards, 'Why did you make us do it so long? What was wrong?' They responded, 'Oh, we were just enjoying it so much.'" Jean credited Bill for their magic on ice, but she also inspired him. "Any guy dancing with Jean could just hang on and soar," one dancer declared. "She made me do things I didn't believe I could do."[27]

From coast to coast, Bill acquired a legion of fans. "I adored Billy Kipp," raved Mary Batdorf. "[With his help] my sister and I improved leaps and bounds." Bill's motto was, "If anything is worth doing, it is worth doing right." Bill was a dynamic motivator. He tailored his message to each student, instilled self-confidence in them, successfully conveyed his performance style to them, and taught with humor. He understood that people remember what they laugh about. One California skater was fond of him because he called her "Ducky." "I was just a young girl, but I thought he was 'it.'"[28]

Bill was equally popular with skaters he didn't coach because he played fair. Once he told a competitor, "You got the royal screw on that last figure." She was impressed because his student was competing against her. Another time a skater fell on a double axel at Nationals, but otherwise performed well. Bill's pupil, who slid across the ice and hit the railing, placed ahead of him. Bill came up to the other competitor afterwards and said, "You should have beaten him." He had great affection for all skaters.[29]

Back in Southern California, Bill became the senior professional at Iceland and the hottest coach in town. He went through life with a huge smile, doing what he loved most. He took all skaters—singles, men or women, dancers, pairs—and gave them his best. He never gave up on anybody, and his students loved him for it, as one skater noted: "There was just something about that guy that brought out the absolute best in everybody." Bill was fortunate to have so many students who admired and appreciated him. He needed all his wits about him to tackle his most challenging and unique student ever—Rhode Lee Michelson.[30]

RHODE LEE MICHELSON
1959 JUNIOR LADIES BRONZE MEDALIST

In the fifties, the judges wanted their female skaters to be ladylike, quiet, and not make a ruckus. Rhode Michelson broke that code. Every facet of her personality was "vroom!" a friend noted. "Rhode was the wild, rebellious teenager that all of us wished we could be." If Maribel was the most colorful coach of her era, Rhode Lee Michelson was the most colorful skater. Some people avoided her because of her antics on and off the ice, but everyone admired her skating. She was a diamond in the rough, and Bill Kipp was the master jeweler who proudly worked on this gem.[31]

Rhode (pronounced RO-dee) was born on March 9, 1943, the eldest child of Arthur and Martha ("Marty") Michelson. They had a younger son, Wayne ("Mike"). Arthur was the foreman for a manufactured-homes company, and they lived in a modest tract house in Long Beach, California. Rhode had been born with a clubfoot, but her doctor suggested she take up a sport to strengthen it. Her father had skated on ponds while growing up in Minnesota; and on his way home from work one day, he passed the sign for the Iceland rink on the highway. He noted the information and brought the family for an outing. Iceland became their home away from home.[32]

Marty rarely skated, but the rest of the family more than made up for it. Rhode and Mike speed skated, and Arthur became president of the DeMorra Speed Skating Club. Rhode, who first started on speed skates, began figure skating when she was eight and joined the Arctic Blades Figure Skating Club. She also became a champion baton twirler. Skating soon crowded out twirling. By age eleven, she had passed four figure tests and lived for skating.[33]

Rhode took lessons from Jean Westwood when she arrived in 1955. Jean admired her talent and encouraged her inclination to skate fast. Rhode placed second in junior ladies at the Southern California Inter-Club competition in 1956; and at the 1957 Pacific Coast, she placed sixth in junior ladies. Rhode then began lessons with the new coach in town, Bill Kipp.[34]

Rhode spent her first summer away from home in Lake Placid when she was fourteen. At the end of the summer, she placed third in the junior division at the Lake Placid competition. More importantly, she was judged by East Coast officials for the first time.[35]

Rhode gained recognition on the West Coast, too. Her relative weakness in figures was counterbalanced with outstanding free skating. In that era, technical expertise between genders was vast. The men were usually a few steps ahead of the ladies, but Rhode's abilities easily matched those of the men of her day. Her double jumps, double axels, and even triples were better than those of some male counterparts. "The speed and the feeling of flying is what attracted me to skating, and Rhode could do that better than anyone," a competitor remarked. Her speed was phenomenal. "She skated a hundred miles an hour," said Barbara Roles.[36]

Her jumps were impressive but were nothing compared to Rhode's famous traveling camel. She often started her program with traveling threes, her body in a horizontal position, her arms spread out, flying down the ice at breakneck speed, with her free leg whipping. She traveled with such velocity that she seemed like a helicopter as she rotated down the ice. Finally hitting the camel spin was an incredible climax. "She was almost a blur," one skater declared. "It was death defying and a wonderful sight."[37]

Rhode was known for her explosive temper if someone got in her way while she was running through her program. She yelled at them to move or just mowed them down. When her music began, kids raced to the railings. "I knew better than to get in her way," one skater recalled. "But my coach said, 'Do you want to skate like her or do you want to hold the wall up?' So I learned her routine by heart and kept practicing."[38]

The beginning of the 1958 competitive season looked promising for Rhode. She made a huge impression at the Pacific Coast competition in Seattle, where she was runner-up in junior ladies. One of her competitors noted: "The rest of us had been competing against each other for years and all of a sudden there comes Rhode out of the woodwork. We had never seen her before. We did nice doubles and good spins but she had a double axel and skated like a man. Boy, could she jump!" Bill accompanied Rhode to Minnesota for her first U.S. Championships in 1958. She shocked her coach by winning the figures. After her dynamic free skate, she had three firsts and two thirds. Joanna Niska, a Maribel student, had the identical ordinal of nine, but Rhode had a majority of first place marks and won the 1958 U.S. novice ladies title.[39]

When Rhode returned to Lake Placid in the summer of 1958, she was a national champion. The eastern skaters considered her unpolished, and she became the epitome of a wild California girl. Her language raised eyebrows because she did not filter her thoughts. After a skater told her she was Jewish, Rhode said, "I've never seen a Jew before." Another skater's mother was a proctologist; and when she came to visit, Rhode said, "Oh, you're the ass doctor."[40]

Rhode did not have the traditional physique of a figure skater. She was short like most skaters, but had broad shoulders, a thick waist, and often led with her head while walking. She did not look like a skating champion; but when she took command of the ice, spectators were mesmerized.[41]

Rhode was accident prone. She broke her ankle one day while practicing doubles lutzes. Her foot was put in a cast, but she "fell out of the top of her bunk bed" and broke the cast open. Another time she smashed through a sliding glass door while looking backwards. But whenever she injured herself, she got back on the ice as soon as possible. Her fearlessness explained her superior jumping.[42]

Her flirtation with boys required constant supervision. "Rhode pressed the envelope pretty hard and was always game for a little adventure," a female skater said. The California skaters were fully aware of Rhode's wild ways. "Did Rhode fancy boys? Oh yes, yes, yes, yes!" one male skater emphatically stated. There were plenty of stories about Rhode and boys. She would corner a male skater in an elevator, just to shock him. At one Nation-

Rhode Lee Michelson, Arctic Blades Figure Skating Club, 1959 Junior Ladies Bronze Medalist. Source: Photo by Bill Udell, Courtesy of Linda Michelson.

als when an L.A. skater went to bed in his hotel room, his mother left the room, accidentally leaving the door open. Rhode walked down the hall, saw the door ajar, peeked in, and recognized her friend. She saw his mother coming down the hall so she quickly ran in and jumped into bed with him. "The look on my mother's face!" the skater laughingly recalled. "I was seventeen and she was fourteen. I thought it was incredible, given her age."[43]

Rhode liked getting a rise out of people. At Iceland, she repeatedly told a skating mother that the woman's husband was going to run off with her, just to unnerve the mother. The older East Coast guys thought she was cute but were wary of romance. One father warned his son, "You better watch yourself; you could get involved and not even know what was going on." She also chased the locals around town. "She would flirt like crazy whether you were sixteen, sixty, or a hundred," one dancer remarked.[44]

Rhode did whatever she wanted and stayed out late, creating a major headache for Bill Kipp. He was always getting her out of trouble and once remarked, "I'm surprised I'm not bald." Looking after her was a full-time job—and not just because of the boys. On a blistering ninety-five-degree day, she would skip taking a car back to the dorm and walk instead. Bill was incensed when she took risks that could affect her health.[45]

For all of her rambunctiousness, Rhode trained like crazy and was always on the ice for her 5:00 A.M. patch. In 1958 she placed first in junior ladies at the Lake Placid competition. Rhode prospered because ultimately she listened to her exhausted coach.[46]

Rhode was focused on the 1959 competitive season; however, returning home to Iceland the fall of 1958, she returned to speed skating and competed in the local Silver Skates race. She was a strong strider and "pretty good at it," her brother Mike admitted. The arrogant speed skaters called the figure skaters "fairy hoppers," but Rhode surprised them by her proficiency in racing and her ability to do an axel in speed skates.[47]

Rhode and her brother loved to knock each other down on the ice. She took derisive pleasure in intimidating others by skating in front of them or imitating their moves. Sometimes her teasing got out of hand. At one Pacific Coast competition, Rhode was in a devilish mood. Her friend was on the ice competing in figures, and the rink was as hushed as a library when Rhode, in the stands, heckled loudly: "Hee, hee, hee." Her friend laughed and started his figure on the wrong foot; fortunately he caught himself and the referee let him start again.[48]

Rhode's circle of friends was small because she was so competitive that friendship was a frequent casualty. But it was not a simple love-hate relationship between Rhode and other skaters; it was an admiration-frustration merry-go-round. As soon as she would start getting along with a skater, some new crisis would explode. One skater who had a series of run-ins with Rhode commented reflectively, "She was not a terrible person, just a little feisty. I believe she was a little insecure. Why else would she behave that way?" Club officials rationalized that she would be getting into more trouble if she weren't skating and grudgingly accepted her as a lovable rascal.[49]

The young skaters were her biggest fans, even though she teased them as well. One day she took young Billy Chapel to the Paramount Mortuary where a current boyfriend was working, and took Billy into the cadaver room. It creeped him out, and she laughed uproariously; but Billy still admired her. "Despite all her craziness she was a kind and wonderful person. She took me under her wing for some reason," Billy reminisced.[50]

"Rhode was my idol," Jennie Walsh agreed. "She couldn't get rid of me. I practically followed her around." Rhode was protective of her young friends, as parent Mary Miller noted: "If anyone said anything, did anything, or got in my daughter's way, Rhode was always there to play big sister."[51]

She was as much a trial to the coaches as to the other skaters. "At times I was so angry with her I just ignored her," a coach said. Bill didn't have that luxury, and they locked horns. He did not tolerate her kicking the ice, and he left her lesson whenever she was having one of her fits. If he asked her to do something and she wasn't in the mood, she told him to shut up. Even though she adored him—and vice versa—she still did what she wanted to do. Most pros would have dropped her as a student, but Bill believed in her potential.[52]

Rhode was equally loyal to Bill. Her friends knew she was crazy about him. She tried recruiting other students for him and was protective of his reputation. She had an "I can pick on him but you can't" attitude. With some notable exceptions, they got along famously. Rhode was fun and unpredictable. She was Bill's pride and joy, and he couldn't wait to show her off at Nationals again.[53]

In 1959 she won senior ladies at Southwest Pacific and again at Pacific Coast. At the 1959 U.S. Championships in Rochester, she placed third in junior ladies, behind Laurence Owen and Stephanie Westerfeld. Laurence and Steffi had competed in this division for a couple of years, but Rhode had won a medal her first year in juniors. She had the option of moving up to the senior ranks to vie for a spot on the 1960 Olympic Team, but Bill decided Rhode should stay in juniors one more year. Rhode left Rochester, flashing her impish grin but with the goal of being the 1960 U.S. junior ladies champion. With her determination, anything was possible.[54]

DANNY RYAN

PROFESSIONAL

Danny Ryan took up figure skating by accident during his college days and became one of America's most decorated ice dancers. His coaching career took him from Canada to the Midwest where he transformed the Winter Club of Indianapolis into one of the nation's rising dance centers. He accomplished all of this by determination and his three-letter motto: "Fun." "Danny was fun; the whole era was fun," an Indy skater recalled. Danny made the Winter Club of Indianapolis a destination and club members felt lucky to have him there.[55]

Daniel ("Danny") Charles Ryan was born on April 19, 1929, in Devon, Connecticut. Danny's childhood was filled with tragedy. Danny had a younger sister, Patricia, who died before her first birthday, and both of his parents died in their twenties. Danny was raised by his grandmother, Caroline Naylor, in Bridgeport. Danny excelled academically at Fairfield Preparatory School, a Jesuit school. Scientifically inclined, he liked physics and was known as the "wizard of the slide rule." Danny was friendly, comical, and famous for his watermelon-slice grin. At age fourteen, he discovered roller-skating at nearby Skate-Land and spent many hours at the rink.[56]

In 1947 Danny graduated from Fairfield Prep and moved to Washington, D.C., to attend Catholic University where he majored in psychology. Danny continued to roller skate, winning national medals in both novice and junior divisions. In the fall of 1948, Danny and two roller skating friends accidentally discovered the Chevy Chase Ice Palace. Danny had never been on ice skates before and gave it a try. He found the ice easy, and his love affair with figure skating began. On the ice that momentous day was Carol Ann Peters, who had begun skating at age eight in Buffalo. In 1942 her father took a job with the War Production Board, and the family moved to Washington, D.C. Carol competed in singles and danced with club member Ed Picken.[57]

Danny became a fixture at the Washington Figure Skating Club (FSC) dance sessions. Carol's coach, Osborne Colson, suggested that she and Danny dance together. Danny was nineteen and Carol just fifteen, but they got along well right from the start, due to Danny's outgoing nature. He made Carol feel at ease and she made ice dancing easy for him. Their skating styles meshed, and they soon won a small competition in Pennsylvania. Ed had to find another partner.[58]

Dance coach Lewis Elkin worked with Danny and Carol. In 1949 they won the Middle Atlantic silver dance, and placed third in silver dance at both Easterns and at the 1949 Nationals in Colorado Springs. At the Lake Placid Summer Dance Championships, they again won the silver dance.[59]

Despite his successful figure skating career, Danny continued roller skating. Washington club member Don Laws first recognized Danny from roller skating. The roller association used ice skating judges, and Don had judged one of Danny's tests. In 1949 Danny was runner-up in the senior men's division of the United States Amateur Roller Skating Association (USARSA) Nationals. When asked whether he liked ice or rollers best, Danny grinned and said he liked "both" best.[60]

Danny and Carol supplemented their training in London, Ontario, Canada, with Red Bainbridge, a national dance champion who recognized their potential. Coach and student were practically the same age, yet Danny listened to Red and absorbed everything quickly. "Danny was a natural, and it didn't take him long to get rid of the roller skater's stride," Red remarked. Red also thought Carol and Danny were a perfect match because Carol was quiet and shy, while Danny was fun and outgoing. Together they had great unison, and a fast-moving, bold style emerged. Danny and Carol trained at night and on weekends. They augmented practices by dancing at clubs; their expertise on the ballroom floor enhanced their skills on ice.[61]

Their second competitive season got off to a rocky start. At the 1950 Easterns, they placed fifth in silver dance; Ginnie Hoyns and Don Jacoby won. In a startling reversal a month later, Hoyns and Jacoby came in fourth while Carol and Danny won silver dance at the 1950 Nationals in front of their hometown crowd in Washington, D.C. Their triumph contributed to the Washington FSC's winning the coveted Harned Trophy for the first time. "It was a pleasure and a surprise to win silver dance," Carol said. She felt that their primary strength was their "style and expression." Danny also competed in the Fours (two pair teams). When someone backed out of a group and they needed a man at the last minute, Danny volunteered and ended up winning the silver medal. In just two years, Danny had become a versatile figure skater.[62]

Danny and Carol returned to Lake Placid for its nineteenth summer season. They enjoyed the rink facilities, the numerous training sessions, and world-class coaches. "Lake Placid was a great place because so many skaters trained there. Everyone got along so well and we had fun," Carol recalled. Ice dancers practiced "grass-hopping"—executing steps in time to music from a portable phonograph, with or without a partner, on the arena's side lawn. Away from the rink, they went on hayrides, partied at someone's home, or roller skated down the center of Main Street—a popular activity until police caught them one night.[63]

At Lake Placid it was evident that Danny loved to party. He competed with other dorm roommates to see who would get home the latest at night. "We were not necessarily doing anything bad, but we sure liked staying out late," Canadian Bruce Hyland said. Danny and Charles ("Lefty") Brinkman were party pals. Sometimes they went to Montreal for the weekend. Once, having failed to designate a driver, they were in a terrible car accident; fortunately no one was seriously injured.[64]

Danny was a ladies' man who enjoyed dating the top female skaters. Although not overly tall (five foot ten), he was handsome with brown hair and blue eyes. Even more appealing to girls was his terrific sense of humor. "Danny was jokester and a real character," Jean Westwood said. "He loved the ladies, that's for sure. We were pretty wild, our group." But even though Danny knew how to party, he was a disciplined skater and was always a serious competitor. At Dance Week, he and Carol placed second in the Fourteenstep event and third in gold dance.[65]

They continued to excel in 1951, placing third in gold dance at the Nationals in Seattle, second at North Americans in Calgary, and fourth in the second international dance competition in Milan. After these competitions their club, the Washington FSC, presented the Bachrach Trophy to them for winning the greatest number of points in competitive skating that year.[66]

Danny and Carol's training for the next season was interrupted when the U.S. Army drafted Danny. On April 1, 1951, Private Ryan left for Fort Knox, Kentucky. After basic training, Danny's military service was rearranged so he could continue training with Carol. She was attending St. Lawrence University in Canton, New York, and Danny was stationed at Camp Drum in Watertown, New York. Four times a week, Danny drove the two-hour roundtrip to St. Lawrence's Appleton Arena to practice. They also made periodic visits to Lake Placid; Danny, who had a pilot's license, sometimes flew them there in a small four-passenger plane on skis. When Danny and Carol participated in skating exhibitions, carnivals, or competitions, he wore his U.S. Army uniform.[67]

Their fourth competitive season brought major changes as ice dancing continued its evolution. Previously the dance competition had consisted of only set dance patterns, but in 1952 gold dance competitors also performed a free dance—choosing their own music and choreographing a three-minute routine. Carol and Danny considered themselves pioneers because the free dance was introduced during their generation. "It was fun to create something brand new, and it seemed revolutionary," Carol said. They participated in the 1952 U.S. Olympic tryouts in Indianapolis and placed second. The dance event was not included in the 1952 Olympics, but their silver medal placement secured them a spot on the 1952 World Team—the first time dancers were included. Danny and Carol first performed an exhibition at the 1952 Games in Oslo. Weeks later, they won the first World dance medal for the United States when they placed third at the 1952 Worlds in Paris. They moved up a notch at the 1952 Nationals and won the silver medal.[68]

U.S. dance champion Michael McGean thought highly of Danny's skills. "He was strong, well built, and quite muscular, which can work against a dancer, but he was smooth and always in control." Michael enjoyed competing against Danny because he was always positive. At one memorable moment at the 1952 Easterns, Danny tripped and fell. He shrugged off the fall and left the ice smiling. Michael sympathetically encouraged him: "There must have been a hairpin on the ice." Michael and partner Lois Waring skated next, and Michael fell in the exact same spot. Neither skater had bothered to go back and check the ice for an object; both men assumed their falls figured against them evenly by the judges.[69]

Carol and Danny were named to the 1953 World Team. Even though Danny was then stationed in Alaska, he was able to compete in Davos,

Danny Ryan with Carol Ann Peters at Lake Placid, Senior Professional, Winter Club of Indianapolis. Source: Courtesy of Carol Ann Peters Duncan.

where they placed third at Worlds for the second year in a row. International ice dancing was still evolving, as *Skating* noted: "In spite of the limitations on lifts, jumps and spins, many were used, and at least half of the programs would have done just as well in pair competition." In honor of their second World bronze medal, the editor of *Skating* composed the following limerick:

> A couple named Carol and Danny
> Dance in style that is surely uncanny
> In World competition
> They frighten opposition
> And bring credit to their Uncle Sammy.[70]

The year continued to be dazzling. They won the 1953 North American Championships in Cleveland. At the 1953 Nationals in Hershey they faced stiff competition. Their marks—three firsts, a second, and a fourth— tied in ordinals with Ginnie Hoyns and Don Jacoby. Danny and Carol had a majority of firsts, so they won the U.S. gold dance title. During the summer, Danny and Carol finally passed all their gold dance tests and their Canadian silver dance. After this achievement, they turned professional.[71]

In five short years, the Peters-Ryan duo had won bronze, silver, or gold in every event open to dancers. Danny, twenty-four, had just been honorably discharged from the army with the rank of corporal, skaters had no financial help, and he needed to earn a living. Danny moved to Ottawa, Canada, in the fall of 1953 to work as a dance coach at the Minto Skating Club (SC).[72]

While teaching at both the Minto SC and the summer school in Cobourg, Ontario, Danny met Rose Anne Paquette, who was also on the staff. Rose Anne, originally from Ottawa, had skated all over eastern Canada. "She was a wonderful girl and a good, respected teacher," a coach remarked. Even though Danny was an extrovert and Rose Anne was on the serious side, they began dating. "Rose Anne was just right for Danny because he was off the wall sometimes and she was the perfect lady," Red said. Danny, twenty-six, and Rose Anne, nineteen, married in Ottawa on May 5, 1955.[73]

Danny was offered a wonderful opportunity: teaching at the Indiana State Fairgrounds Coliseum, home of the Winter Club of Indianapolis (WCI). Established in 1940, the WCI skaters were elated when Danny and Rose Anne arrived in 1955. The Coliseum had a history of short-term coaches, including a hockey coach from the 1932 Olympic Team and Austrian champion Hedy Stenuf. Past pros had taught figures and dance, but very few had serious competitive experience before Danny.[74]

Danny and Rose Anne were both hired, Danny as head pro. He taught dance and pairs, they both taught figures, and Rose Anne taught free skating and kept the books. Danny was at the rink all day, teaching beginners, Girl Scouts—practically anybody. The Ryans started a Saturday morning basic skills class called the Earlybirds. The class was always full because "they made skating something you wanted to get up and go to," Sandy Schwomeyer said. Her ten-year-old sister Judy "couldn't get anywhere close enough to him." She would skate past Danny when he was teaching, just to look at him and hear what he was saying, hanging on his every word. Whenever students entered Danny and Rose Anne's office, he gave them a spearmint lifesaver.[75]

Danny's goal was to impart his dance expertise to a new generation, and the WCI was a heavy-duty dance club with people of all ages participating. Danny felt it paramount that dancers communicate romantic interest in their partner, which was sometimes a challenge. He was an advocate for technical perfection and a stickler on body positions; his dancers were known for their proper alignment. He used a novel approach for one skater who had a bad habit of ducking her head forward; he made her skate with a hairbrush tied to the back of her neck, dangling down her back.[76]

The Ryans made the Winter Club of Indianapolis an enjoyable place to be. Danny's penchant for creating fun sometimes backfired, when his older male students modeled his pranks. Danny had a red sports car that he dearly loved and parked close to the Coliseum every day. Student Pieter Kollen warned him that a hockey puck might fly out of the arena's open windows and hit his car. One day Pieter and Whitey, the skating manager, glued a puck onto the windshield and drew crash lines around it. Danny had a mild heart attack until he realized it was fake.[77]

Rose Anne had a full teaching schedule too. Known for her dry sense of humor, she was a fifties-era wonder woman. She juggled teaching and taking care of a husband, home, and four children. Danny and Rose Anne had started their family quickly, and in rapid succession Kevin was born in 1956, Patrick in 1957, Terri Ann in 1958, and Sheryl in 1959. Rose Anne kept teaching until it was time to go to the hospital. The Ryans had domestic help, including a Jamaican nanny, Lulu, and skating pupils who doubled as babysitters.[78]

Besides teaching, the Ryans directed the annual Ice Capers show and occasionally performed exhibitions. Every spring the family drove to St. Petersburg, Florida, for a month to visit Danny's grandmother. In the summer, they coached at a variety of summer skating schools, including Cobourg, Ontario, and Mount Royal, Quebec. The Ryans built a summer cottage outside Montreal, Canada; and when Danny started coaching in Lake Placid, they built a home there, too. Danny was happy to be back in the Adirondacks; and his wife and children came to love it equally.[79]

In the past, Lake Placid coaches had rarely shared teaching techniques with each other. That attitude changed with Danny, Bill Kipp, Red Bainbridge, and Cliff Thaell; they had all been skaters themselves and were less threatened by each other. Danny picked up many new students over the summer because he didn't scream, as some coaches did, and had wonderful free dance expertise. He had his own training techniques, but he was also open to students' ideas. Danny had a fatherly manner but was firm when he needed to be. One student noted: "I tended to oversleep and he would get so mad. I lived in a boarding house down the street from the rink, and one morning when I didn't show up he just walked into my bedroom, in his skate guards, and woke me up."[80]

Sunday, a day of rest in Lake Placid, included mass in the morning, lunch, and an afternoon of swimming and water skiing. There were lots of parties; and dancers, singles skaters, and pros all mingled. "It was a good environment," Red remarked. "Everyone worked hard on the ice, and off the ice we had good, clean fun."[81]

As a working woman, mother of four active youngsters, and wife to a busy, frequently absent husband, Rose Anne seldom had much time for herself. In Lake Placid she indulged in her seasonal passion—sweater shopping. When she found an ideal sweater at the Swiss Shop or Peck and Peck, she would put it on lay-away, paying a bit here and there. Over time she acquired a gorgeous sweater wardrobe. Whenever a student passed her gold test, she got to choose any one of Rose Anne's much-admired sweaters as a present for achieving her gold medal. "It's such a great achievement, and I was so proud of them," Rose Anne said.[82]

Back in Indianapolis, Danny practically lived at the rink and didn't have time for much else although he was an active member of St. Matthew's Catholic Church. The Ryans occasionally went to dinner or played cards with skating friends. He liked race-car driving, and the Ryans went to car races with WCI members. His primary focus, however, was his thriving career.[83]

Danny was contented in the Midwest. Not only did he have a large teaching pool at the Coliseum, but skaters from other locales flocked to Indianapolis to work with him. A group of skaters from Louisville, Kentucky, drove 120 miles every weekend to work with the Ryans. Pair team Karl and Gayle Freed drove two hundred miles roundtrip from Troy, Ohio, every Sunday. "He was good at teaching pairs, but he had trouble teaching Gayle this one lift," Karl said. "As he tried to put her in position, she whacked him in the nose." Danny led his pair team to the 1958 National junior pairs title, but his future success lay with his ice dancers. Indianapolis became a major center for ice dancing because of Danny. His growing reputation was cemented with the victories of a young couple he put together in 1955: Larry Pierce and Marilyn Meeker.[84]

LARRY PIERCE

1959 U.S. SILVER DANCE CHAMPION

Like Danny Ryan, Larry Pierce began skating competitively when he was older—at eighteen—and became one of its premier dancers. He enjoyed being one of the few top male dancers in a sea of beautiful female skaters. "Larry was a pistol," a friend recalled, "and he really loved the girls."[85]

Dallas Larry Pierce was born in Indianapolis on August 5, 1936, the second child of Dallas and Nellie Pierce. He had an older sister, Jan, and a younger brother, Russell. His father owned and operated the Dallas H. Pierce Plumbing, Heating, and Appliance Company. The family was unprepared for the financial cost of figure skating, but Dallas and Nellie were ardent supporters of their son and embraced his sport passionately.[86]

Larry learned to skate as a child when his family would join other members of the community on a frozen-over swimming pool in a public park. When he was nine, Larry joined friends from Frances Willard Elementary School on Friday night and Saturday afternoon public sessions at the Indianapolis Coliseum. When he was a teenager, girls vied for him as a partner for the popular Moonlight Skate. "The girls went ga-ga over him," a classmate said. Larry skated frequently but recreationally. He was a popular student at Broad Ripple High School where he was active in track and baseball. Outside of school, he enjoyed hunting expeditions with his father to Michigan and Canada.[87]

Larry became a more serious skater during his senior year at Broad Ripple. When he was eighteen, he passed his pre-dance test and his first two figure tests. That same year, he also appeared in the "Ice-O-Rama," a charity fundraiser for the *Indianapolis Times* Welfare Fund. This elaborately produced annual show had a fifteen-piece orchestra; five thousand spectators paid $1.50 to see a "whole galaxy of new talent." Larry Pierce was singled out in the "Big Man on Campus" number as "a good steady boy who will go places."[88]

Larry joined the Winter Club of Indianapolis the same time that Danny and Rose Anne Ryan joined the WCI staff. Larry's mother, Nellie, came to watch him train. The WCI did not tolerate the notorious "skating mother" syndrome common at other rinks. The WCI moms were "taught to sit back and shut up—period. And they would do it," a club member said. "They were great parents and they cheered us on."[89]

Dancers were generally adult skaters, but Danny groomed the young teenagers at the rink for his competitive teams. He was astute at pairing skaters, and one of his first teams was Larry Pierce and Marilyn Meeker. Marilyn had begun skating in 1949 when she was seven; by 1956 she had passed her bronze dance and third figure tests, but she had not excelled in singles. She had been to Midwesterns once where she placed sixteenth.[90]

Marilyn had first met Larry at the Riviera Club, a private family swimming and diving club, where Larry was a regular. Quite proficient in the high dive, he did competitive dives as well as silly stunts that no one else would try. He carried this adventurous spirit into the world of ice dancing with Marilyn, who was also a born ham. Despite the age spread in the trio—Danny was twenty-seven, Larry was twenty, and Marilyn was fourteen—they got along famously. Besides their skating skills, their personalities meshed, and the collaboration bore competitive fruit quickly. The duo had a good training system. Larry picked Marilyn up at 6 A.M., they skated for a couple of hours, and he drove her to school. After school they skated at Wednesday, Friday, and Sunday evening dance sessions, or skated on private ice from 10 P.M. to midnight.[91]

Danny sent three dance teams to the 1957 Midwesterns in Sioux City, Iowa. Larry and Marilyn won first place out of a field of twelve in bronze

dance. Indiana Governor Harold Handley sent them a congratulatory telegram. Larry quickly passed his pre-silver dance test as they advanced to the
silver level.[92]

Larry and Marilyn won silver dance at the 1958 Midwesterns in Troy,
Ohio. This was their passport to their first U.S. Championships in Minneapolis. There were ten teams in silver dance. Larry and Marilyn placed
fourth in compulsories and third overall. They returned home with their
first national medal and new friends from across the country.[93]

Skaters from other regions soon learned that Larry was a natural clown
and would do anything for a laugh. He did crazy things on the ice, like a
cantilever (leaning backwards in a bended-knee, spread-eagle position). It
was common to see Larry speeding around the entire rink in a supreme
limbo position. He did every zany thing he saw the professional ice show
comedians do. He loved to imitate Sonja Henie and run around on his tip
toes. "Goofing around and having a good time was what Larry was about,"
his brother Russell conceded. "However, he was serious about his skating."
At competition time, Larry delivered, and he and Marilyn had matured into
a stylish team. They created a signature move: holding her left arm, Larry
laid Marilyn out on the ice on her left side with the outside of her boot
scooting against the ice and her right leg high in the air. Then he would gallantly lead Marilyn across the ice to great applause.[94]

A number of Danny's students, including Larry and Marilyn, followed
him to Cobourg, Ontario, and then to Lake Placid for summer training.
Dancers practiced in the late morning and had the afternoons off. They water skied, went hiking, slid down the ski jump on cardboard cartons, or
swam across Mirror Lake, but their coaches chastised them if they were too
tired or sunburned to skate. Afternoons of outdoor fun ended with evenings
full of dance sessions. Sometimes they broke the monotony of training with
unusual challenges, such as doing the Argentine Tango backwards.[95]

Larry joined in the fun as much as possible, but he also had a part-time
job to offset the costs of skating. Many skaters had to pay their own way and
worked as lifeguards or hotel bellhops. Larry worked at restaurants and at
the Mirror Lake Inn whenever a big event was scheduled; sometimes movie
stars came to town and skaters made $100 in tips.[96]

When not skating or working, "Good-time Larry" had lots of fun, but
sometimes his clowning got out of hand. Larry and his friends sometimes
placed road signs that diverted traffic from Saranac Lake away from Lake
Placid. Eventually downtown merchants and police would catch on that
something was amiss. Once when a bridge was out, many cars were backed
up with nowhere to go. Another time he and Pieter Kollen brought a big

Larry Pierce with Marilyn Meeker, Winter Club of Indianapolis, 1959 Silver Dance Champions. Source: Courtesy of Rich Rosborough.

bucket of ice cream to share with everyone at the Ryan home but decided to have an ice cream fight instead and threw ice cream everywhere in the house. Upset with the mess, Danny made them leave. Instead of feeling chastised, Larry and Pieter climbed up on the roof. A fire was burning in the fireplace, and the boys covered up the chimney, sending black smoke throughout the house.[97]

Larry and his friends came up with their own signature greeting—their version of today's high-five. They held one hand up, fingers spread wide, as if holding the world in their palm. "It was something he would do often, when things were going well," Marilyn said.[98]

Larry was suave and a sharp dresser. At five foot ten, with a fashionable crew cut, blue eyes, and the horn-rimmed glasses that were de rigueur for the period, Larry enjoyed a great deal of female adulation. The younger girls were often tongue-tied in his presence. He was out-going and friendly, and had dated many girls. Larry enjoyed summers in Lake Placid because of the large pool of attractive women.[99]

The culmination of the summer was a two-week period called Dance Week. The men, dressed in formal shirts and bowties, switched off with a variety of partners in this high-volume competition. After the competition came dance tests. Girls facing a shortage of male partners came to Lake

Placid in hopes of finding someone to take them through their dance tests. Marilyn had to share Larry with lots of ladies during this time. The men received thank-you gifts like cashmere sweaters or gift certificates to local shops in exchange for test preparation.[100]

Back in Indianapolis, Danny prepared Larry and Marilyn for another shot at the U.S. silver dance title. To minimize training costs for skaters, Danny shrewdly negotiated a dollar-a-day rate with the Coliseum for each skater who had competed at Nationals, paid on the honor system.[101]

The Pierces were delighted to have their son home again. Every Sunday after attending the Broadway Methodist Church, the family went to watch Larry practice. The Pierce home also served as an unofficial boarding house for skaters, who stayed for months at a time, and they regularly provided weekly dinners for local skaters. Dallas set up card tables in the living room, and Nellie provided steaks, baked potatoes with sour cream, and plenty of desserts. The Pierces loved the skaters, and Nellie treated them like her own children. This generosity was a sacrifice because money was tight. They rarely traveled to competitions because they couldn't afford it but instead welcomed everyone into their home.[102]

Larry was equally generous with his time and talents. Skaters came to the WCI so Larry could partner them in tests. "He was very encouraging right from the start," a skater declared. "He got me into dance and took me through all my dances. Then Larry and Marilyn's parents helped me find a permanent dance partner." Larry visited many Midwestern cities to skate in a variety of club shows and partner girls for their dance tests. "I *loved* dancing with Larry Pierce," a Detroit skater said. "He was the best dancer I ever skated with."[103]

While training, Larry worked in his father's retail and plumbing repair business. He didn't enjoy the work but he wanted to help his father. Pieter Kollen, who often lived with the Pierces, joined Larry in the service truck and learned how to repair faucets on the job. "I wasn't paid, but I guess it was in-kind payment for my lodgings," he said.[104]

When he wasn't skating or plumbing, Larry was at the Speedway. Being an Indianapolis native, Larry loved going to the Indy 500 with the Ryans and other WCI friends. He regularly attended the Hoosier Hundred, a car race at the state fairgrounds track.[105]

Larry took business classes at Indiana University for two years, but his real goal was to become a skating coach like his mentor Danny. The U.S. government provided Larry with some temporary direction. He entered the Marine Corps in the fall of 1958 and did his basic training at Parris Island, South Carolina, reluctantly granting custody of his brand new 1958, powder-blue Chevrolet to his younger brother Rusty. In every letter Larry sent to Rusty, he wrote, "I know you're out charming the girls with my car. Don't speed. I know the police are looking for guys like you."[106]

The 1959 competitive season was nearing, and the Marine Corps generously gave Larry some flexibility. He returned to Indianapolis periodically to train with Marilyn. "It wasn't difficult for me because when he wasn't there we didn't have to train," Marilyn honestly reflected. His longest stint away from home was six months of boot camp; he was pleased that the military let him keep his signature flattop.[107]

Danny wasn't disturbed by Larry's military commitment because he had gone through the same thing during his competitive career. Danny wisely used it to his team's advantage. When Larry was away, Danny kept Larry's name alive with pictures and articles in *Skating* and the local paper. Danny knew that informing the skating world of the sacrifices his premier team was making could only reinforce its good image at competition time.[108]

Danny, Larry, and Marilyn traveled to the 1959 Nationals in Rochester, New York, with great hopes of winning the silver dance crown. After the compulsory dance, they placed second out of ten couples. "The competition in this class was tantalizingly close," *Skating* wrote. After the final dance, Marilyn and Larry received two firsts, a second, a third, and a fourth place from the judges, which was enough to pull them into first place. Roger Campbell and Diane Sherbloom of Los Angeles moved up from fourth place to second, and Bob and Pat Dineen fell from first to third.[109]

After four years of skating together, Larry, twenty-two, and Marilyn, seventeen, won a national title. "Timing was everything and we were very lucky," Marilyn said. She attributed their success to Danny, who had trained them well. "Things always worked out for us. We could be so awful in practice, and when the time came to compete, the good Lord willing, we were able to pull it out of us when we had to." The trio looked forward to their next goal: making the 1960 World Team.[110]

CHAPTER 8

THE 1960 OLYMPIC TRIALS

The United States Olympic Organizing Committee was in high gear the summer of 1959, as workers completed building projects for the 1960 Olympic Winter Games in Squaw Valley, California. It would be only the second time the USA had hosted the event. The 1932 Olympics in Lake Placid had utilized existing facilities, but the 1960 Games had to be built from scratch. Alexander Cushing, the force behind the United States' winning bid, deserved a gold medal for pulling off his brazen proposal.

When sports insiders first heard of Cushing's quest, they thought he was crazy. Squaw Valley was an old Indian retreat in the High Sierras, 200 miles northeast of San Francisco and forty-five miles southwest of Reno, Nevada. The name had been established centuries earlier when men from the Washoe tribe left their wives behind in a valley camp while they hunted. When the site was chosen in 1955, there was no winter resort—only a sleepy, scenic, mountain community with a few luxury homes, one ski lift, two rope tows, and one small lodge. The nearest amenities and services were seven miles away. Wayne Poulson, a Pan Am Airlines pilot, and Cushing, a socially prominent New York attorney and Harvard graduate who had come to Squaw Valley in 1947 to enter the ski resort business, were the chief local landowners.[1]

Since the first Winter Olympics in 1924, the Europeans had won most of the medals. At the 1956 Winter Olympics in Cortina, Italy, the United States had fallen short in every event except figure skating. Cushing realized that it was not in his power to improve the competitiveness of American athletes, but at least he could try to arrange for them to lose on their own soil. Since the Games had not been held in North America since 1932, he felt he had a fair chance.[2]

Cushing's maneuverings to win the Olympic bid were not illegal, but they were certainly creative. The other cities bidding for the 1960 Games were St. Moritz and Garmisch-Partenkirchen, which had already been host cities, and newcomer Innsbruck, Austria. Cushing anticipated that Austria's neighbors and the Iron Curtain countries would support the Innsbruck bid. With the help of *Chicago Daily News* foreign correspondent George Weller,

Cushing divided up the world; and the two embarked on a three-month international propaganda tour to secure votes. By the time Cushing headed to the IOC meeting, he had a dossier on each of the sixty-two delegates.[3]

The IOC members were surprised to learn that the Squaw Valley proposal had many things to recommend it. Building the Olympic site from scratch would allow a single community to host all the events. By contrast, the ski jump event at Cortina was three miles from town and the skating events were in a village eighteen miles from town. At Squaw Valley, every event could be staged in its entirety or finished in one area.[4]

Squaw Valley introduced another first: the Athletes' Village. The Olympic Village offered equality. At previous Olympics, athletes stayed at commercial hotels; the richer countries were at the finest hotels while the poorer ones had to scrounge around for something affordable. The Olympic Village could quarter 1,200 athletes, trainers, and coaches from every nation. Athletes could eat, sleep, and relax in private splendor, with the luxury of a five-minute stroll to most of the events. The final argument: Europe had dominated hosting the Olympics, and Innsbruck was only twenty-five miles from Cortina. A new locale "among the Pacific family of nations" was needed, Cushing argued. "This is not a question of countries but continents."[5]

The vote in 1955 was the closest finish in IOC history. Squaw Valley won, thirty-two votes to thirty. Squaw Valley's frontier bid turned out to be its greatest asset. Cushing's sales pitch, which painted humble Squaw Valley as offering the athletes of the world a chance to compete in a wholesome, unadorned, compact setting, had worked. "The mountains," remarked IOC president Avery Brundage, held "an opportunity to build an Olympic city from the ground up."[6]

Cushing belatedly informed American taxpayers that the Olympics would cost them one million dollars—and that estimate soon skyrocketed to eight million. Cushing and his promoters enthusiastically promised to make it "the finest and most novel winter games of all time." For example, in the heated ice arena, spectators could watch other events on a giant screen by closed-circuit television.[7]

Four years later, the valley had four-lane highways, hundreds of Alpine chalets, dormitory complexes, restaurants, lodges, two churches, and stunning contemporary architecture, particularly in the sports buildings. The mountains were laced with three tows and five ski lifts; and in the valley, speed skating ovals and an 8,500-seat indoor arena had been built for hockey and figure skating events. The Olympic Arena, an eight-story building that won first prize in the 1958 *Progressive Architecture* contest, was free of interior obstructions, thus providing better viewing. Squaw Valley, no longer remote, would be the center of the sports universe for two weeks in February 1960.[8]

While construction workers toiled in Squaw Valley, figure skaters concentrated on their training. The most pressure focused on Carol Heiss and David Jenkins. The nation expected them to win Olympic gold. Heiss and Jenkins were capable, but a variety of human factors could upset that prediction. Year after year, it was physically challenging and emotionally stressful to sustain their high quality. Fresher, younger talent was nipping at their heels, and they had to juggle their training with studies: Jenkins was in his second year at Cleveland's Western Reserve medical school, and Heiss was studying American literature at NYU.[9]

Carol Heiss spent the summer in East Lansing with coach Pierre Brunet. Taking classes at Michigan State distracted her from worrying about the Olympics; but by August, she regularly woke up in the middle of the night, unable to sleep. "This stress was self induced, knowing I had been silver medalist four years before, waiting for another four years, and now it was around the corner," she said. Talking to boyfriend Hayes Jenkins on the phone calmed her down; he understood exactly what she was going through, as Carol noted: "If you didn't win you didn't want to look back and say, oh if only I had worked harder or trained harder or had done this or that."[10]

David Jenkins spent his eighth summer at the Broadmoor with Edi Scholdan. As three-time World champion, David was highly independent by this point, but Edi kept his focus on his prize student. "I was very fond of Edi and the Broadmoor was such a wonderful place to train," he said. "They never asked anything of us; I guess it was a two-way street with the championships we brought to the club, but it mainly felt one way." David shared ice time with World teammate Tim Brown and newcomer Greg Kelley. Greg was grateful to train alongside Jenkins and derived a great deal of inspiration from him. David, in turn, thought Greg was an outstanding skater.[11]

One day in practice, David landed a jump near Greg, who was skating backwards. The back of Greg's skate sliced into David's leg. It was a bloody mess. Edi rushed Mrs. Jenkins out of the rink before she even knew what happened. Greg's blade had severed David's muscle in his lower leg, and the injury required thirty stitches. Greg came to the hospital to see David, who understood his anguish: "Greg felt bad and I felt so bad for him," he said. "You can imagine how he felt. He was fifteen and pretty crushed." Several days after the accident, Jenkins read a newspaper article saying it was doubtful that he could compete at the Olympics. "I thought, 'really?'"[12]

Jenkins was in a cast for a month and off the ice for another two months. For him the injury was not a catastrophe, but actually a kind of relief. "For me the mental twist was I really liked not having the conflict between skating and school," he confessed. David returned to Cleveland and concentrated on recuperating and studying; the accident gave him time to clear his head before the 1960 Games. David did not work with Edi again until three weeks before the 1960 Nationals. Edi would have preferred an earlier return to the ice, as David Jenkins noted:[13]

> Edi wrote letters to the dean of the medical school, appealing to their patriotism, to kick me out until after the Olympics. The dean called me in and showed me the letter and asked me what I wanted him to do. I told him he better write a nasty letter back, otherwise he would be getting a nasty letter every week from Edi! The dean was not offended by Edi's letter—he thought it was funny.[14]

Olympic medal hopefuls Ron and Nancy Ludington trained over the summer in Lynn, Massachusetts, with Maribel, who also coached their nearest rivals. Ron, Nancy, Dudley, and Maribel Jr. were the best of friends; there was a healthy rivalry and mutual respect among the foursome, but Maribel's desire to have her daughter succeed proved problematic. Ron and Nancy ended up doing a lot of training at night away from Maribel's eye. Otherwise any new maneuvers they created would end up in Little Maribel and Dudley's routine. "Maribel played to win and did whatever was necessary," Nancy said. "It depends on your perspective whether that was a good thing or not." Even though conflicts arose, the two teams always supported and cheered each other on, and the friendship remained intact. Maribel asked Tommy McGinnis, The Skating Club of Boston's newest coach, to choreograph Laurence's program for the new season. Laurence was excited to compete against Carol Heiss for the first time at the upcoming Nationals.[15]

At Lake Placid, Larry Pierce and Marilyn Meeker trained with Danny Ryan, while Bill Kipp worked with Rhode Michelson. At the summer's end, Kipp returned to Los Angeles but soon flew back home to Pennsylvania when his father, Martin Luther Kipp, passed away. "That was hard on Billy," sister Timmy said. "They had been inseparable growing up. When Billy skated at the Albeth rink, my father got up every morning at 5:00 A.M. and took him."[16]

The 1960 U.S. Championships were slated for Seattle in January, and Ila Ray and Ray Hadley Jr. were under intense pressure—90 percent of it at home—to win a place on the Olympic Team. During the summer, the siblings passed the newly required pairs tests, bronze through gold.[17]

Prior to the 1960 Nationals, regional and sectional competitions took place across the country. Bradley Lord, Laurence Owen, Maribel Owen, and Dudley Richards did not need to qualify for Nationals and sat out Easterns. At the 1960 Midwesterns in Minneapolis, Larry Pierce and Marilyn Meeker easily won gold dance. Doug Ramsay of Detroit won senior men and Stephanie Westerfeld won senior ladies for a record fourth time. Both Steffi and Doug planned to compete for the U.S. junior title.[18]

Prior to Pacific Coast, an exhibition took place at the Polar Palace in Los Angeles. Rhode Michelson, injured once again, was determined to perform, but Bill Kipp was trying to talk her out of it. She had stitches in her right foot after accidentally spiking herself while landing a jump. Her doctor told her not to skate—just putting on skates would hurt—but Rhode wouldn't listen. She laced up her boots, performed everything in her program, and cried with pain throughout the routine. When she finished, she plopped down on a bench and sobbed, "Get these off of me!" The stitches had broken, blood oozed from her skates, and her foot swelled. After her foot healed, she headed to Squaw Valley.[19]

1960 PACIFIC COAST

The 1960 Pacific Coast Championships were staged in Squaw Valley as a test run for the upcoming Olympic Games. Sponsored jointly by the St. Moritz Ice Skating Club and the organizing committee of the VIII Olympic Winter Games, the championships tested the recently completed Blyth Arena and utilized the Olympic accountants and timers, with IBM personnel on hand to test-run their electronic scoring, timing, and placement equipment—a first for the Olympics.[20]

The competitors, arriving in late December, discovered that the facilities were not entirely ready. Some competitors, coaches, and chaperones were quartered in the unfinished Athletes' Village. Skaters had to trudge in the snow from the lodge to the rink to find a bathroom. Competitors slept in bunk beds and ate food cooked by the U.S. Army. Some competitors had to stay in motels in nearby towns.[21]

Conditions for the competition, including the constant roar of nearby construction and the frigid weather, were difficult. The skaters competed in the partially open-air Blyth Arena. They enjoyed the beautiful view on one end that looked up to the ski jump but bemoaned the freezing temperatures. Many practices were held at night, when the temperature dipped to ten degrees below zero. Conditions were so brutal, due to the high altitude and cold weather, that a few skaters passed out. Competitors also trained at two other outdoor venues: a big patch of ice with no barrier (which could be dangerous if you slipped or jumped too far) or at the speed skating oval, which was slick and hard. Huge blowers cleared the snow off the ice, but both the blowers and the wind itself blew the skaters off their figures, as one Seattle skater noted:[22]

> I was so tiny that half way around my circle the freezing wind pulled me back. I was so mad because my coach, Linda Hadley, was sitting with my parents in the car with the heater on, while I was going around these stupid circles! Linda opened the window, screamed at me, got out of the car, stood there for a while, and then got back into the car.[23]

The arctic environment was especially hard on the Los Angeles skaters who were unprepared for cold weather: "It was so traumatic for us hothouse Californians," Don Bartleson recalled. "It actually snowed during the figure competition. We were shell-shocked." They borrowed sweaters from competitors and wore several pairs of tights or long underwear underneath their costumes. The spectators also suffered. The arena's cement benches had holes to blow out hot air, but the electrical seat warmers had not yet been installed.[24]

Eighteen girls competed in senior ladies. Judges used little brooms to brush away the snow to examine their figure tracings. Girls were so numb they ran hot water over their wrists. Only the top eight in figures skated their freestyle programs—the rest were grateful not to have to skate in their chiffon dresses. Rhode was fourth in figures; and despite her recent injury, she had a powerful free skate and took home the silver medal while Karen Howland took the gold medal.[25]

The arctic weather was just as brutal for the judges. They sat near the ice and most of them became ill. Very few of the officials were on hand to present awards at the competitors' party. The Hadleys won the senior pairs, Jerry and Judianne Fotheringill placed second, and Bill and Laurie Hickox of San Francisco placed third. Ila Ray also placed fifth in novice ladies, Ray placed second in novice men, and together they won silver dance. Those lucky enough to qualify for Nationals had three weeks at home for training before joining their fellow athletes from across the country in Seattle.[26]

1960 NATIONALS

At the 1951 Nationals in Seattle, an energetic eleven-year-old girl had won the novice ladies title and a fourteen-year-old boy had pulled up from fourth place in figures to win the junior men's title. Now Carol Heiss and

David Jenkins were the World champions. The 1960 Nationals seemed a mere formality before their quest for Olympic titles in Squaw Valley.[27]

Because of the "Kennedy Kids"—1950 World pair champions Peter and Karol Kennedy—Seattle was a skating-conscious city. The metro area was proud to have two more brother-sister pair teams vying for a spot on the 1960 Olympic Team: Ila Ray and Ray Hadley and Judianne and Jerry Fotheringill of nearby Tacoma. The local papers publicized the Hadleys as "the favorites in Senior Pairs." That was hardly the case, but on their third time in senior pairs they were expected to win a spot on the Olympic Team.[28]

Ninety-nine skaters participated in the 1960 U.S. Championships, held January 27-30. General admission tickets were $1; reserved seats were $2.50 and $3.50. On Tuesday, January 26, skaters gathered at the Tropics Motel for the drawing to determine the order in which they skated. It was bad luck for those who drew first, second, or third. Judges were hesitant to give too many good marks at the top of an event in case of better performances toward the end.[29]

Every event at the 1960 Nationals was important, but there was no denying the weight given to the senior men, ladies, and pairs divisions. The top three in each event would be named to the 1960 U.S. Winter Olympic Team. Of the current competitors, only Heiss and Jenkins had competed in the 1956 Olympics, where Carol had come home with the silver and David the bronze. Now twenty-one skaters were competing for the twelve Olympic Team slots.

Weeks before Nationals, one senior lady suddenly dropped out as another senior lady suddenly appeared. Three-time World Team member Nancy Heiss had a fluke accident during practice. She fell on a double axel, her leg caught beneath her. She heard the snapping sound in her ankle as she hit the ice. The doctor told her to stay off her foot for six days; but after a week, it was black and blue and swollen. Her coach took her to the New York Rangers hockey team doctor. He discovered she had a hairline fracture and put her in an air cast for two months. "It was a disappointment because I knew it was going to be Carol's last year and it would have been nice to be in Squaw Valley and room together," Nancy said. "We always gave each other sisterly support."[30]

When Stephanie Westerfeld arrived in Seattle, she was scheduled to compete for the fourth time in junior ladies. After her first day, she had a change of heart. She admitted she had been "skating scared" by remaining in junior ladies and wanted to compete in senior ladies instead. The skating officials approved her petition to switch divisions by the time senior ladies began on Thursday morning. There were no surprises as Carol Heiss took a commanding lead in figures. In second place by a narrow margin was Laurence Owen followed by Barbara Roles and Stephanie Westerfeld.[31]

That evening the festivities at the Civic Ice Arena mirrored the upcoming Olympics. To the accompaniment of an organ fanfare, a color guard of Boy Scouts holding the flags of the fifty states, formed a human tunnel through which the competitors, introduced individually, were presented. The first winners of the 1960 Nationals were novice champions Carol Noir of New York and Bob Madden of Tacoma. The junior pairs contest came down to a close battle between two young sibling pair teams: Bill and Laurie Hickox from San Francisco and Ronald and Vivian Joseph of Chicago. It was the second time both pair teams had competed at Nationals and the older teenagers prevailed. Bill, seventeen, and Laurie, fourteen, won over Ron, fifteen, and Vivian, eleven, by one ordinal.[32]

The senior men and junior ladies competed in figures on Friday morning. David Jenkins's stiffest competition was perennial runner-up Tim Brown. As usual, Tim took a slim lead over Jenkins in figures, followed by Robert Brewer, Bradley Lord, Gregory Kelley, Barlow Nelson, and Jim Short. Seattle's Karen Howland took an early lead in junior ladies. Rhode Michelson placed fourth. Once again, she would need a strong free skate to pull up into medal contention.[33]

That evening a near-capacity crowd of 5,100 gathered in the Civic Ice Arena. The junior men's competition was usually the most dynamic event, and this year there was a three-way battle for first place among Detroit's Doug Ramsay, Carol Heiss's younger brother Bruce, and Maribel's student Frank Carroll. Ramsay, in second place after figures, dazzled the crowd with his spectacular program. Heiss, currently in fourth, was noted for his sensational and artistic style, and Frank Carroll, the oldest competitor, gave the performance of his life. After the free skate, the marks were evenly divided among the three; their marks all added up to sixteen ordinals.[34]

In figure skating, the competitor who earned a majority of first-place marks was deemed the winner. If no competitor had earned at least three first-place marks, then the winner would be the competitor who garnered the majority of second-place marks, and so on. The individual marks were: Ramsay—1, 2, 2, 5, 6; Heiss—1, 1, 3, 5, 6; and Carroll—1, 2, 3, 4, 6. Since there was not a majority of "firsts," all of the first-place marks now counted as "seconds," and Ramsay was thus declared the winner with a majority of seconds. "The difficult judging and the high caliber of ability made this event an outstanding one," *Skating* wrote. Ramsay's victory was slim, but there was no denying the crowd's enthusiasm for him. The junior men's event was also noteworthy because New York's Scotty Allen, age ten, was the youngest skater ever to compete in U.S. junior men.[35]

Little Maribel Owen experienced two minor dramas before the senior pairs event. She broke her nose in an auto accident on the way to the Boston airport; and at the final practice session in Seattle, she had a terrible fall. People who had watched her smash into the boards were scared to death that she was badly injured, but Maribel went over to her daughter and said with a smile, "You look like you're all right." Despite these setbacks, Maribel and Dudley placed second in senior pairs, barely edging out hometown favorites Ila Ray and Ray Hadley, who placed third. The crowd gave their heartiest applause to Ron and Nancy Ludington, who won their fourth national title.[36]

The Hadleys benefited from performing in the rink they had trained in and skated "a difficult and imaginative number . . . in virtually flawless unison." The Fotheringills were not so lucky; they skated poorly and placed last. "It was our home territory and it was disappointing because we had a lot of friends in the audiences," Judianne said. Karl and Gayle Freed, the husband-and-wife 1959 silver medalists, had to settle for fourth place. "I didn't realize it at the time, but it mattered what club you were from," Karl said. "We were from Cincinnati, which was considered nowhere." The Hadleys were thrilled to be on the Olympic Team but were realistic about their prospects, saying "This one is for experience."[37]

Carol Heiss was nearly perfect in figures but she did not take her role as heir apparent for granted. She looked and skated like a champion in her free skate. Performing in a sequined black silk dress and a rhinestone-studded tiara, Carol had a slight falter on a double salchow but otherwise skated superbly and retained her title with a perfect final ordinal of five. A skating official enthused, "She's the best I've ever seen."[38]

Barbara Roles, in third after figures, brought down the house with her ambitious program of high-energy jumps and spins, all performed with an artistic flourish, but barely pulled above Laurence Owen to earn the silver. Laurence, who won the bronze, was equally appealing. Stephanie Westerfeld, who had entered at the last minute, skated creditably but had to settle for fourth place.[39]

Silver dance competitors Pieter Kollen and Dorothyann Nelson took a spill in practice the night before their event, and Dorothyann was carried unconscious from the ice. Rushed to the hospital, she was released just hours before competition. In the initial round, Patricia and Robert Dineen, a husband and wife team from New York City, placed first, followed by Ila Ray and Ray Hadley Jr. in second, and Dorothyann Nelson and Pieter

Kollen in third. After the final round, Pat and Bob Dineen, with "their smooth and stylish performance," became the silver dance champions. The Hadleys came in second by a half-point margin over Nelson and Kollen.[40]

On Saturday Bill Kipp's students Margie Ackles and Charles Phillips of Los Angeles won the gold dance. In second place was Marilyn Meeker and Larry Pierce, whose "chic free dance was provocative and imaginative." Audience favorites Yvonne Littlefield and Roger Campbell of Southern California won the bronze medal. Karen Howland won junior ladies, and the battle focused on who would come in second and third. Rhode, with her amazing repertoire of jumps and spins, placed second, Vicky Fisher of Minneapolis placed third, and Lorraine Hanlon of Boston slipped from second to fourth. Rhode was disappointed not to win, but was glad to take home the silver medal after winning bronze the previous year.[41]

During Nationals, Edi Scholdan boasted that David Jenkins would display "the most spectacular skating in the sport's history" in Squaw Valley. "Athletic agility isn't enough," he said. "It also demands artistic ability . . . brains, co-ordination and determination. David is the best skater in our time. Other skaters execute the triple salchow but David will have more in his program than any other." His claim suggested that Jenkins had fully recovered from his leg injury suffered four months previously. On Saturday night, the Civic Ice Arena crowd was anxious to see if Scholdan was correct.[42]

After four years in the spotlight, David Jenkins was truly the king of free skating and David proved his superiority without question. World silver medalist Tim Brown skated with mastery and placed second.[43]

The one-two placement of Jenkins and Brown was expected. The drama of the night was the battle between Robert Brewer and Bradley Lord for the coveted third spot on the Olympic Team. The two athletes had faced a similar battle in 1959, and Brewer had proved victorious. The judges were impressed and were evenly divided; the skaters tied with nineteen ordinals each. The figure totals gave the third place to Brewer, Lord placed fourth, Gregory Kelley placed fifth, Barlow Nelson placed sixth, and Jim Short placed seventh.[44]

Brewer, who had trained with Maribel over the past year, had daily trained on the same ice as Bradley. The outcome did not affect the friendship between the two long-time competitors, as Brewer noted:

> When I was young, there was animosity between me and my competitors in California. When I look back on it now, as a psychiatrist, I realize the animosity was not between us. . . . It was between our parents. The parents were negative and bad-mouthed other kids as we drove to and from the rinks. Once I got to be in the top echelon and on the World Team I became better

friends with my competitors. Bradley was a good, solid skater and a fine young man. Even though we were prime competitors, we talked all the time and were good friends.[45]

Missing the 1960 Olympic Team was a huge disappointment for Bradley, and he felt betrayed by one of the judges. An in-depth analysis shows that both skaters received identical marks: two thirds, two fourths, and a fifth. The figures' marks broke the tie, and Brewer had the higher cumulative mark. Bradley's sorrow was magnified when he looked at the judges' marks closely. Brad's chance to be on the Olympic Team was circumvented by a mark given to Gregory Kelley.[46]

Kelley's marks were three fifths, one fourth, and *one third*—given by the judge from The Skating Club of Boston. If the judge had given his third-place mark to Lord instead of to Kelley, Lord would have made the Olympic Team. In the judge's defense, there would be no way for him to know how the other judges' individual marks added up to declare each skater's placement. However, it was clear which skaters were in medal contention by their figure placement, their free skate, and the history of the skater—and this was Brad's third year in seniors. Of this disappointment, Bradley sadly wrote: "My greatest ambition of making the Olympic Team was a nerve-shattering experience that will always remain with me. I missed making the Team by .94 of a point! My own judge . . . failed to give me the other third place I needed and kept me off the team."[47]

Local television coverage fueled the traffic into the Civic Ice Arena for the Saturday night exhibitions. The finale of the competition was a dinner dance at the Washington Athletic Club. The Broadmoor SC was elated to win the Harned Trophy for team competition for the fourth time.[48]

Following the conclusion of each senior event, the formation of the 1960 U.S. Olympic Figure Skating Team unfolded. The twelve-member team included Nancy and Ron Ludington, Maribel Owen and Dudley Richards, Ila Ray and Ray Hadley Jr., Carol Heiss, Barbara Roles, Laurence Owen, David Jenkins, Tim Brown, and Robert Brewer. The Hadleys and Laurence Owen were the only newcomers to international competition. There was no greater joy than within the Owen clan. They became known as skating's first family because three members of the family were now Olympians.

The 1960 U.S. Olympic Team had only one day of rest. On February 1 the majority of the team left for Squaw Valley for two weeks of training. David Jenkins and Tim Brown both headed home to catch up on their demanding university course loads. Carol Heiss's plan for her first three days in California was to "simply rest, rest, rest." It would be difficult for any team member to thoroughly rest. The anticipation for what lay ahead was simply too great. Years of sacrifice and hard work, their coaches' passion and expertise, and their parents' pocketbooks and emotional support, were about to pay off.[49]

CHAPTER 9

1960 Junior Champions

As the 1960 U.S. Olympic Figure Skating Team headed to Squaw Valley, the junior champions headed home. Their wins positioned them as part of the new generation. Bob and Pat Dineen won silver dance on their fourth attempt, junior pairs champions Bill and Laurie Hickox won on their second attempt, and junior men's champion Doug Ramsay, coached by Bill Swallender, won on his third attempt. Swallender had previously coached skaters to national and international glory. However, the national title for Ramsay, whom he had coached from childhood, was one of his most personally satisfying wins.

Bill Swallender

Professional

"A sweetheart," "a teddy bear," and "a gentle giant," Bill Swallender was beloved by all. He was a tall man of Scandinavian descent with broad shoulders and a big chin, but he was not intimidating because he spoke gently and rarely yelled. When his students did well in competition, he gave warm fatherly hugs. He was also the quintessential gentleman as one student noted: "He was the most proper man I had ever met. I had the utmost admiration for him." Everyone who knew him agreed that he set the standard for "nice human being."[1]

Carl William ("Bill") Swallender was born in Minneapolis, Minnesota, on March 22, 1908, one of seven children. His father was an inventor and a machinist who, among other projects, designed streetlights in St. Paul and built a hydraulics machine for Caterpillar. Bill played tennis in high school and skated at the Minneapolis Arena.[2]

Skating coach Carl Gandry and former champions A. C. Bennett and Margaret Bennett prepared Bill for his first trip to Nationals. Representing the Twin City Figure Skating Club, Bill, twenty-five, won the junior men's title at the 1933 Nationals in New Haven. East Coast officials were shocked that someone unknown to them could win a national title. Bill expressed his

William Swallender, Coach, Detroit Skating Club. Source: Courtesy of Bill Swallender.

gratitude in *Skating* for the "courteous attentions received . . . for the opportunity of having competed . . . [and] for the friendly contacts I made."[3]

Moving up to the senior ranks was not as easy. Bill placed fifth in both the 1934 and 1935 Nationals. Finances and injuries prevented him from trying out for the 1936 Olympic Team. It was the middle of the Depression, his father had passed away, and Bill had developed knee injuries. His decision to retire was cemented when the Kansas City Ice Club, seeking him as their pro, told him he could name his own terms. "I set the price high, thinking they'd never meet it," he said. "But they snapped at the proposal, and that ended my Olympic dreams."[4]

Swallender moved to Kansas City in the fall of 1935, teaching at the Pla-Mor rink. He was the first coach for the newly formed Kansas City Ice Club with twenty-five members. They hoped that Swallender would stimulate more local interest. Bill took his students through their figure tests and to the Midwestern competition. He spread goodwill by giving free lessons every Saturday morning to club members' children, helped mount the club's show in 1936, and performed loop jumps and axels in his routine, dressed in a jacket and tights.[5]

Bill returned to Minneapolis the summer of 1936 to reconnect with Genevieve Nelson, a skater featured in Ice Follies. Bill and Gen first met at a Minneapolis rink when he was sixteen and she was ten. Gen and her three sisters, Vera, Virginia, and Marie, were famous in skating circles as the Four

Nelson Sisters. Their father, Julius Nelson, a former member of the Stockholm Ice Club, had taught his daughters how to skate. The Nelson Sisters had been America's foremost sister act in ice carnivals for over a dozen years and a favorite fixture in Ice Follies since its formation.[6]

Bill, twenty-nine, broke up the sister act by marrying Gen, twenty-three, on February 15, 1937. The newlyweds left Kansas City, which still had few skaters, moved to the much larger Ice Club of Baltimore, with five hundred members, and performed in the Ice Follies for a few engagements. In the late thirties and early forties, Bill spent summers at the Broadmoor, and served as its skating director in 1940. The following year, the Swallenders headed west to Chicago in 1941.[7]

Long-time skating official Harry Radix had purchased the Chicago Riding Club in 1936 and turned it into the Chicago Arena, home of the Chicago Figure Skating Club. The arena was a one-of-a kind rink with an enormous 280 x 100 foot ice surface, private locker rooms, and a cocktail lounge overlooking the rink. When the building was sold in the fifties, it became the home of the CBS Television Studio.[8]

Bill was a popular and respected teacher in Chicago. He had a commanding knowledge and explained everything in great detail. Known for his pleasant smile and quiet humor, he instilled confidence in his students. He told one competitor: "Oh my goodness, you are so fabulous and you're doing so well. You are so beautiful!" Years later, the grateful student still remembered that compliment, asking rhetorically, "What more could you ask for?"[9]

Swallender was very bright, and his mind was always racing. He thought faster than he could speak and sometimes stuttered, especially when he was excited or nervous. He told his students: "Sometimes you might have to get me to say it twice, and get it the second time around." His stuttering didn't slow him down nor was he embarrassed by it; one student used to mimic him, but it only made him laugh. At competitions his face became redder as his enthusiasm mounted. Sometimes he raised his voice, more in exhilaration than anger, to light a fire under his skaters. Students realized Bill's adrenaline rush stemmed from his eagerness to get on the ice. He took notes in a teaching notebook. When a student achieved a new move, he quickly wrote it down in his chart.[10]

Besides teaching in Berkeley the summer of 1942, Bill taught at Lake Placid throughout the forties and early fifties, teaching singles and dance, and helping to direct the summer shows. The pros were assigned a figures "teaching pen"—a twenty-foot-long block of ice reserved for each coach. Red Bainbridge, who taught next to Bill for years, said, "With some pros you always knew when they were in the rink because they were so loud, but Bill worked quietly at the far end of the rink. Some people would not even know he was there." At Lake Placid he found his first serious protégée, Virginia ("Ginny") Baxter of Detroit. Ginny had begun skating at age six and was a national competitor. She temporarily moved to Chicago to train with Bill.[11]

In the summer of 1943, Genevieve gave birth to their first son, William Nelson Swallender, at her parents' home in Minneapolis. After becoming a mother, she was rarely seen at the rink and became an enigma in the skating world; most people didn't know she had been an Ice Follies star. Unlike some coaches, Bill preferred a normal family life and kept his skating life separate.[12]

Bill moved his family to Philadelphia in 1947, taking over for Gus Lussi at the Philadelphia Skating Club & Humane Society. To Ginny Baxter, who lived with the Swallenders, Gen was a surrogate mother. "She was an honest, direct, and strong individual who handled her husband so well," she said. Besides coaching Ginny, Bill taught her how to drive and let her drive them home from the rink every day. That season Ginny won the 1948 junior ladies title in Colorado Springs.[13]

In Philadelphia, Bill taught other up-and-comers, like Bill Kipp and Newbold Black. "Bill was low key and didn't have the exuberant personality of some of the other coaches," Black said, "but he was a guy who built you up and never tore you down." When Bill worked with U.S. gold dance runner-ups Walter and Irene Muehlbronner, he taught them the laws of physics as part of their training.[14]

The Swallenders bought a home in Lake Placid in 1947, an attractive, melon-colored cottage with a large picture window on Cobble Hill near the base of a mountain. Bill cut down a hundred trees to provide a better view of the Adirondacks. The house was rather primitive. There was no electricity, so they used kerosene lamps, and every day Bill picked up ice for the refrigerator. They hosted picnics in their front yard and picked blueberries on the hillsides. When young Bill was eight, he wanted a tree house so his father built him one. It was a feature of the cottage for many years.[15]

Bill was extremely proud of his son and he encouraged him to skate, but young Bill was a recreational skater at best. When he was young, his father promised him a toy if he learned to skate backwards the full length of the rink. He had never skated backwards but his father said, "You can do this. Don't give up." He got the toy. At Lake Placid, Bill directed the weekly show featuring the Jenkins brothers, and one day he called his son over at the end of a session: "There's a show tomorrow night, you're in it, and we need to work up a routine. It won't be a big deal; you're only skating for two to three minutes." Young Bill quickly learned the few small jumps he would need for his program.[16]

Bill and Gen opened their home to boarding students, and other skaters frequently stopped by. "He was always happy to see you on a Sunday afternoon," a student recalled. Bill went out of his way to motivate his skaters. A student was preparing to take her eighth test; and her boyfriend, who was out of a job, liked to visit her at the rink. Bill gave him a job at his house, working on his roof, clearing brush, and anything else he could think of, just to get rid of the pest at the rink so she could pass her test.[17]

Ginny Baxter became Bill's first gold medalist when she passed her eighth figure test in the summer of 1948. She credits him for much of her success: "I learned a great deal from Nic [Howard Nicholson], but Bill polished me. He thoroughly addressed the what, why, where, and how you did things, and his explanations made complete sense. He worked me, saying, 'Don't miss anything in the program or you're going to start it over again until you do the whole thing right.' He was always steady and never cross; he was a very calming individual."[18]

After Ginny placed seventh at both the 1949 Worlds in Paris and the 1950 Worlds in London, the Swallenders moved to Ginny's hometown in the summer of 1950. Bill became head pro at the Detroit Skating Club (DSC) and ran its skate shop. He enjoyed sharpening skates and the extra income it provided.[19]

The DSC had just relocated to a new facility when Swallender arrived. Located on Seven Mile Road, the old Detroit Riding and Hunt Club was converted into a 175 x 75 foot ice surface. During the installation, all club members pitched in to clean, paint, install music equipment, and make other minor repairs. The DSC was the fifth club in the United States to have a private rink. The DSC president believed in the separation of the members and staff, but Bill made a point of stopping by the lounge to visit everyone; he felt it was important to interact with those outside his own circle of students.[20]

There was no heat in the Detroit rink, and with little insulation it still felt like a barn. At five o'clock in the morning, skaters' hands were so cold that they ran lukewarm water over them to bring them back to life. They spent much time near the radiators, and the ladies often wore two pairs of tights. Bill always wore business attire, teaching in either a suit or a sport coat with a tie and an overcoat.[21]

Bill won over new students and parents because he was patient and congenial. Parents appreciated the fact that he never flew off the handle with their children. However, he was a disciplinarian when it came to posture. If a skater's arms were too high during figures, he smacked the top of their hand with a leather glove; sometimes the free leg got the glove slap. His students were well known for their outstanding posture and posed for pictures demonstrating correct positions for 1948 Olympic champion Barbara Ann Scott's book on skating.[22]

Bill helped mount the DSC shows. For both shows and competitions, he chose appropriate musical selections for each skater. He choreographed some memorable routines, including Billy Kipp's "St. Louis Blues" show number—the "most outstanding routine I had ever seen," a skater claimed.[23]

After three years as senior ladies bronze medalist, Ginny Baxter was named to the 1952 Olympic and World Teams. Jeanette Altwegg of Great Britain won the Olympic title in Oslo, and Jacqueline du Bief of France won the World title in Paris, but Ginny won the free skate at both events. One admirer said: "Ginny could beat the pants off of anybody. She was the greatest free skater ever." After Ginny placed fifth at the Olympics and third at Worlds, she joined Ice Capades. Fortunately for Bill, the year Ginny retired, an eight-year-old boy with talent and star potential, Doug Ramsay, began lessons.[24]

Doug was a prodigy like Ginny. Bill recognized Doug's potential and treated him as his prize student. Whenever a possible conflict of interest arose with Doug, Bill dealt with the situation head on, as Pieter Kollen noted: "In those days if a coach had a hot skater he put all his marbles with that skater. Bill was very devoted to Doug. I took from Bill for a year and a half but when it came time when Doug and I were in the same division Bill called Gus Lussi, who took me on because of Bill's recommendation. I competed against Doug for several years and one time at Nationals I beat Doug. Bill was the first person to congratulate me. He was a big, sweet, wonderful guy and we always remained friends."[25]

Bill's family and career prospered in Detroit. Erik Edwin Swallender was born on March 5, 1953; and two years later, Bill achieved the life-long dream of building his own ice studio. Initially the banks, who had never heard of ice studios, were leery about lending him money, but studios were not a new phenomenon. By 1955 there were about two dozen ice studios in the United States. Some were as small as twenty by twenty feet and others as large as seventy-one by one hundred feet. Bill found space in a building connected to Ginny Baxter's father's insurance office.[26]

In 1955 Bill opened his $50,000 ice studio at 18630 McNichols Road West. The ice surface was thirty-seven by forty-three feet, about a sixth of a full-size rink. Bill proudly stated, "My freezing system allows me to have ice available in 106-degree weather and I think I have one of the finest indoor rinks in the country." A multitude of kids and adults passed through its doors for private lessons and group classes. Windows covered one side, for easier parent-viewing, and Bill installed mirrors on the other three walls; he wanted his students to see themselves as they practiced. The studio was large enough for small recitals, but too small for a program run-through; one benefit of the small space was learning how to jump with limited momentum.[27]

Bill put his family to work at the studio. Gen came out of retirement to run the front office: skates were rented, a showcase featured the family's collection of antique skates, and a small shop sold skating accessories. Gen occasionally taught children's classes but preferred not to be involved with the parents. Bill taught young Bill how to mount and sharpen blades, and resurface the ice, which was done manually. He cleaned the ice step by step with ripple shoes, which looked like a bunch of squeegees with forty to fifty blades on the soles.[28]

Bill closed the studio every summer for two months to teach at nearby East Lansing. His eldest son regularly went with him, hung out with kids in the dorms, and played sports with them. Young Bill recalled one summer when all the skaters jumped on a trampoline for hours and afterwards "couldn't skate worth a hoot. It threw them all off and they couldn't jump for several days. The coaches quickly banned the trampoline." Young Bill's passion was baseball, but he had been around rinks long enough that he was proficient in the dance sessions. He and Canadian Otto Jelinek tried to see who could skate the Kilian the fastest—with no partner—while weaving through the other dancers.[29]

Although young Bill never took up competitive skating, he regularly showed up for social events in Detroit and was popular with many of the female skaters. He looked just like his father and was "so gorgeous." Some coaches might have discouraged family fraternization with their students; but his son explained, "I don't think Dad minded if I ever dated any skater; besides, whom else was I going to meet?"[30]

When the family wasn't working at the studio, Bill and Gen enjoyed ballroom dancing and socialized with neighborhood friends. Bill took his boys to ballgames, especially if Ted Williams and the Red Sox or Mickey Mantle and the Yankees were in town. Bill worked long hours so the boys valued time spent with their dad, no matter the activity. Every Thanksgiving after the feast, the men raked leaves, cleaned the yard, washed windows, and completed other needed chores. Bill also took his family weekly to the Lutheran church.[31]

As in Lake Placid, the Swallenders opened up their Detroit home to skaters. Diana Lapp, a national competitor from Denver, lived with the family for several years when Swallender coached her. "Genevieve was a graceful, beautiful, strong woman who took good care of her husband, and they took care of me too, even throwing me a surprise sixteenth birthday party," Diana said. "Bill was able to leave his skating at the rink and was very jovial at home. He was a great big guy and had a great big chest. He would go outside and say, 'Hmm, smell that fresh air, Diana. It's a great day.' He loved life and it was wonderful to be around him."[32]

His protégé Doug Ramsay was a fifth member of the Swallender family. He and young Bill were close friends. Doug rode his bike over to the Swallenders on Saturdays to watch TV, play golf in their living room, or go to ballgames with the family. Bill took pride in Doug's success and treated him like a son.[33]

By 1960 Bill had enjoyed a twenty-five-year teaching career in nine cities. He had helped hundreds of skaters pass their tests and stand on the podium at competitions. After eight years of devoted, passionate training, Bill had great faith that Doug Ramsay would win the junior championship. In fact, everyone had faith that one day Doug would be World champion.

Doug Ramsay
1960 Junior Men's Champion

Doug Ramsay was admired widely. He was one of the most athletic skaters ever. His jumps seemed effortless. Diminutive and dark-haired, he was called Dick Button Jr. Doug's idol, however, was hockey's Gordie Howe of the Detroit Red Wings. Beyond his skating expertise, Doug was friendly and modest. "He was a good-spirited, happy, sweet guy," a friend said.[34]

Douglas Alexander Ramsay was born May 5, 1944, in Detroit. His family consisted of his parents, Alex and Jean, and three siblings: Judy, Christine, and David. The children were raised in the Detroit suburb of Redford, where his father owned a roofing company. Alex Ramsay had been an amateur hockey player in Canada; he wanted his son to play hockey, but at age six Doug saw an ice show on television and wanted to try figure skating. His sisters skated when they were young, but did not share his passion.[35]

Doug first skated on a makeshift pond on a vacant lot. In 1952 he began training with Bill Swallender at the DSC. At eight he was a tiny kid weighing less than fifty pounds, but he was a good skater right from the start. "Doug would rather skate than do anything else in sports," his mother said.

He jumped easily and spun like a top. He had the right combination to mature into a great free skater: small in stature and a natural-born athlete. Decades later, another skater of similar size and talent could have been Doug Ramsay's clone: 1984 Olympic champion Scott Hamilton. Though Doug had every right to be cocky, he remained modest about his athletic gifts.[36]

Doug was ten years old when he traveled with Bill Swallender and his students to the 1955 Midwesterns in Minneapolis. One rarely flew to competitions in those days, and it was an all-day train ride. "We had a wonderful time and there was great camaraderie," a DSC member said. After he won the Midwestern juvenile boys title, predictions emerged: "Many experts rate him as a boy who is on his way to a World crown," the press declared.[37]

Doug became a regular at the DSC and had to deal with the frigid conditions, as friend Gary Visconti noted: "Doug and I did twenty minutes of patch, ran off, took off our skates, put them on the steam heaters (radiators), and then put our skates back on. We burned our skates half the time. The only thing good [about the DSC] is that you didn't have the wind—otherwise it was just like being outside."[38]

Although the skaters were always cold, the DSC was a fun place. Remnants of the old equestrian stable lingered on. Even though no one was allowed in the attic because it was so decrepit, Doug and his friends made forts, played hide-and-go seek, and spooked the girls. There were empty lots around the club where Doug and the other boys played baseball.[39]

On the ice, Doug didn't goof around much, as a DSC official noted: "He never asked for any favors . . . . He was always pleased and grateful when he was allotted extra ice time to practice. Doug was the best skater at the club yet he always had time to give pointers and encourage the less talented ones." Doug impressed future Olympian Tim Wood, because Doug would skate his heart out even if there were only a few people in the bleachers. "Doug was my idol and I wanted to be just like him," Wood said.[40]

The DSC was family oriented. Family members came every Wednesday night for dinner. Everyone skated—even parents. Doug and two girls clowned around on the ice, pretending they were the three Heiss kids. As Doug got older, he became a member of the teen club. Parents supplied hot dogs and hamburgers, and the teens danced in their own room upstairs.[41]

Doug was a good-looking kid but not everyone noticed; they were blinded by his amazing talent. Doug had an astounding ability to jump and spin, as Aloise Samson noted:

> Dougie could stand in one place—not on skates—and revolve. I never saw anyone else who could do that on the ground. He was a bouncing spring, and sprang around all the time. It was amazing how easy it was for him to spin

Doug Ramsay, Detroit Skating Club, 1960 Junior Men's Champion. Source: Courtesy of Ron Pfenning.

in the air, even at a young age. He could do a double axel as easily as someone else doing a waltz jump. He was able to spin beautifully, too.[42]

People regularly compared Doug to 1956 Olympic silver medalist Ronnie Robertson because of their similar light, cat-like quality on jump landings. "You could drop both of them off a building upside down and they came out on their feet. It was instinctive," a friend said. Doug put unusual twists on his jumps: he did a double salchow out of a sit spin; he did a high double axel with his hands behind his back or with his arms crossed in front of him; and he could do axels on both feet. In fact he could do just about any jump in both directions.[43]

Over time, his overall free skating presentation matched his jumping and spinning prowess. His footwork had interesting, connective steps, and he exhibited great stamina. When he was young his coach sometimes had to keep him in line, but as he got older "he just couldn't wait to get the guards off and get on the ice."[44]

At the 1956 Midwesterns, Doug's free skating made a huge impact. Coach Danny Ryan had three of his students from Indianapolis compete in novice men. Prior to arriving in Cleveland, he told his boys they would end up first, second, and third. On their first practice session, one of them asked Danny, "Who is he?" It was Doug Ramsay whipping around the ice. "What division is he in?" another worriedly asked. When they realized he was their competitor, they said to their coach, "So what happened to one, two, three?" Doug won novice men with an outstanding performance.[45]

In 1957 Doug captured the Midwestern junior men's title in Sioux City, Iowa. He traveled to Berkeley, California, for his first Nationals. Greg Kelley won the novice men's title and Doug placed eighth in figures and seventh overall. Figures were his weakness throughout his career.[46]

Doug went to Troy, Ohio, for the 1958 Midwesterns but came down with scarlet fever. He was quite ill; friends who stopped by his hotel room could only wave to him as his door was quickly opened and closed. He recovered by the time the 1958 Nationals were held in Minneapolis, and the USFSA allowed him to compete. Jim Short won junior men, Greg Kelley was second, and Doug placed fifth. "While the crowd showed its appreciation for all [competitors] it seemed clear that young Douglas Ramsay stole their hearts with his inspired free skating," *Skating* wrote. Doug had yet to win a national medal, but he had garnered the most praise and applause.[47]

Doug would have already won a medal if it weren't for figures. "His figures were the worst; they were terrible," a friend frankly remarked. So even though he found figure eights boring, he persevered. He divided his time between the Swallender Ice Studio, which was a perfect place to practice figures, and the DSC, where he could run his freestyle program. When Doug was nine and ten, Bill took him to Lake Placid for summer training, and subsequently to Welland, Ontario, and East Lansing.[48]

Bill Swallender had worked with Doug for seven years, and they had a close relationship. He never yelled at Doug; he would bring him over to the rail, courteously give him directions, and quietly interact with him. Doug respected him, always called him "Mr. Swallender," and was never in trouble, as a friend noted: "He would say, 'I can't do that because Mr. Swallender wouldn't be happy with that.'"[49]

Bill was a father figure to Doug, and some skaters worried that young Bill got lost in the shuffle. "Mr. Swallender really doted on Doug, and Doug got a lot of attention," a friend observed. But Bill's namesake son was not threatened because he experienced his own success in other sports and understood his father's excitement and professional fulfillment in coaching a champion.[50]

At the 1959 Midwesterns in Denver, Doug placed second in senior men. Competing in junior men at the 1959 Nationals in Rochester, Doug placed seventh in figures and, after the free skate, pulled all the way up to fourth place. Greg Kelley, who had placed second the year before, won the event. "The winners skated well-planned, well-executed free programs, but it was Douglas Ramsay who, with a sizzling performance, won the heartiest applause," *Skating* reported.[51]

Doug was a regular at Michigan State for several summers. One room-mate described him as a happy, personable, and focused individual who "showed up and did his stuff." Doug practiced seven hours a day. His alarm went off at 4:30 A.M. in his first floor dorm room at Gilchrist Hall. After an eight-minute walk, he was on the ice for his five o'clock patch. After two patches, he ate breakfast at the rink's grill, then had a short rest in the dorms. A late morning free skate was followed by lunch at the Student Union. After lunch came freestyle and a dance session. After dinner were more high-test freestyle sessions. Everyone kept moving on these intense sessions; other-wise they would be run over.[52]

What set Doug apart was his jumping consistency. "He was very tal-ented," Bruce Heiss said. "I finally land a double axel and he puts his hands in his pockets and does one." The skaters tried to one-up each other in im-promptu jump games, but Doug consistently raised the bar. He landed dou-ble jumps seemingly without effort and could execute long series of jumps. His claim to fame was doing an encore of axel, axel, axel, double axel, axel, axel, etc. He tried difficult things and wasn't afraid to fall. People watching him thought he would never miss a jump, and he rarely did.[53]

Many skaters were active ice dancers during the summer, including Doug, who also regularly danced at the DSC. He didn't partner with many girls because of his size. When a young skater followed Doug's footsteps on the Argentine Tango, he stopped and kindly pointed out to her that he was doing the man's steps and not the girl's steps. "He was really wonderful about it," she recalled.[54]

The summer skaters practiced all day long; but during downtime, there were plenty of R & R activities on the MSU campus. They hung out in the Student Union, played cards, rode bikes, or sat outside in swimsuits on blankets. In the late afternoons, they went to the newly built Olympic-size outdoor pool across from the rink. Doug took advantage of other campus sports, too: tennis, canoeing, kickball, volleyball, and softball. The skaters had their own softball teams, the Heiss Flying Camels and the Jackson Spread Eagles. Neither team had an advantage because most of the skat-ers—except for Doug—were pretty pathetic ball players and could barely hit the ball.[55]

Dorm living could be rowdy. The big kids planned the pranks and turned the task over to the younger kids. They put shaving cream on the floors of the shower stalls, short sheeted beds, put scotch tape on the bot-tom of skate blades, and toilet-papered dorm rooms. Doug played practical jokes with everyone else but was never mean. The skaters sneaked out of their windows after the 10 o'clock curfew to get ice cream on campus. It was also a big deal to break into the rink's snack counter and filch a packet of saltines.[56]

At the end of the summer, all the skaters prepared for the Talent on Ice shows. Everyone, even the World medalists, helped design and paint the sets. Holiday on Ice, a professional touring show, stored costumes on campus and let the skaters borrow them. World competitors received top billing, but Doug always had a solo. He was a perennial show-stopper who enjoyed playing to the crowd.[57]

Despite his quiet demeanor and unrelenting focus on the ice, the arrival of the Batdorf twins one summer sparked his interest in girls. He could tell the identical twins apart because Anne had a little freckle on her face. Doug was fourteen and Anne was only twelve when he asked her to go to the end-of-summer dance. They became best friends and pen pals. "After the summer we wrote to each other and danced at the Nationals party every year," Anne said. "There was a part of him that was just like a kid; he was interested in so many things. He did well academically and competed in gymnastics at school. He was a well rounded individual and a boy in every sense of the word."[58]

After the Batdorf twins stopped coming to East Lansing, Doug became good friends with local skater Joanne Heckert. Doug went to her house for dinner or they went on group activities. "Back then things were so simple," Joanne said. "We went to the Lukon movie theater in town or the drugstore down the street for lime rickeys. It was idyllic and just like 'Happy Days.' We didn't realize at the time how perfect it was." Carol Heiss agreed: "All the skaters were respectful and kind to each other. There was no bad behavior."[59]

Doug's family was happy when he returned home, especially Jean Ramsay, her son's biggest fan. She periodically came to the DSC but quietly sat in the bleachers and didn't brag about her son. Her husband rarely came to the rink, but they were both supportive of their son; still, financing Doug's skating was a challenge. Bill Swallender helped by not charging him for every lesson, and the DSC helped with his expenses when he went to major competitions.[60]

In the fall of 1959, Doug began his sophomore year at Redford High School. He was an avid reader and brought his homework to the rink. When he wasn't skating he kept up with the local sports teams, the Lions and the Red Wings. He enjoyed watching NHL hockey and focused on the players' skating skills, such as pivoting, gliding, or back-pedaling. "I'm sure that if [Gordie] Howe had tried his hand first at figure skating instead of hockey he'd have wound up the best in the business. I just think he makes nice moves. And his reflexes are terrific," Doug said.[61]

At age fifteen, Doug had grown and gained weight, but he was still a mite at five foot three inches and 116 pounds. After passing his eighth figure test in the fall—the first male in Detroit to do so—he prepared for his fourth Nationals. Bill Swallender boasted of Doug's prospects to a local reporter: "Doug does all the double jumps, and he does them cleanly, with quality. He's also executed the triple Salchow, which few skaters his age do. The youngster has an excellent chance to become Detroit's first national senior men's champion . . . we have been bringing Doug along carefully. While he has far superior quality in his skating than any boy his age that I've seen, a talented lad like Doug can be ruined if you try to bring him along too fast. He's done everything we've asked him to do."[62]

Doug started the 1960 season on top, winning senior men at Midwesterns in Minneapolis. At the 1960 Nationals in Seattle, Doug eked out a victory in one of the closest junior men matches in history. He had his best showing in figures, placing second. His freestyle program included double axels, a delayed axel, a delayed double flip, and a walley combination. The field was strong with his MSU roommate Bruce Heiss and Frank Carroll of Boston also giving impressive performances. After the free skate, all three men tied for first place with sixteen ordinals. Doug broke the tie to win with a majority of seconds.[63]

Doug had achieved his first national medal and a national title; no one was happier than Bill Swallender, who said: "Doug is one of the finest looking Olympic prospects I've seen. The way he's progressing, he might wind up with a gold medal." Doug spent the spring performing in exhibitions, then headed back to East Lansing to focus on his next goal—a spot on the 1961 World Team.[64]

ROBERT AND PATRICIA DINEEN

1960 NATIONAL SILVER DANCE CHAMPIONS

Bob and Pat Dineen were destined to be together. Born just days apart in different boroughs of New York City, they attended different Catholic schools in Manhattan, learned to skate at different rinks, and competed with different partners. Four years after they formed a partnership, they won the U.S. silver dance title. Their win was unusual in the annals of the U.S. Figure Skating Championships. At the time of their greatest triumph, Pat was three months pregnant.

Robert Francis Dineen came from a distinguished family. His father, Benedict Dineen, was a New York State Supreme Court Justice. Bob was the youngest of Benedict and Mary's three sons, born July 8, 1935, in New Canaan, Connecticut. Bob was raised in New York City with older brothers Joseph and Benedict Jr.[65]

Bob began skating as a teenager and loved it immediately. He graduated from Xavier High School, a Manhattan Jesuit Catholic school, in 1953. During college days at St. John's University, Bob began serious ice dancing. Since brother Joseph became a doctor and brother Ben a college professor, Bob's pursuit of figure skating was an anomaly in this well-educated, professional family.[66]

Patricia Barbara Major was born to Edward and Ann Major on July 10, 1935, and she and brother Edward grew up in New York City. Pat attended Manhattan Catholic schools: St. Francis of Assisi, Holy Trinity Branch, and Cathedral High School. She excelled academically in her small class of thirty-two. Her classmates remembered her as a likeable, mature teenager who "exemplified being a Christian in her actions."[67]

Pat skated regularly before and after school. Near graduation she received a marriage proposal from a man she had met through skating. Sister Eugene, Pat's homeroom nun, discouraged the union because the man was older and of a different faith. She counseled Pat to turn down her suitor, quit skating, and go to college. Pat graduated from Cathedral High School in 1953, without telling the sister her decision.[68]

As matters turned out, Pat rejected all of Sister Eugene's advice. After she married Dave Schwartzer, skating became her primary focus. When the Brooklyn Ice Palace closed in 1955, Pat trained at the Iceland rink at Madison Square Garden, located between 49th and 50th Streets. Ice time was scarce if you were not a member of The Skating Club of New York (SCNY), a private club and selective in its membership. Still, club president Harold Hartshorne sponsored a weekly Thursday night dance session and invited non-club dancers. Pat took advantage of these "open" nights, also skating at New Jersey's Asbury Park and at Central Park's Wollman Rink.[69]

Bob Dineen and Pat Major met and competed against each other in the mid-fifties. They represented different clubs, the Manhattan FSC and the Metropolitan FSC. Pat and her partners tended to medal, while Bob and his partners usually missed the podium. At the 1956 Middle Atlantics, Bob and Ann Kamsley did not medal, while Pat and Peter Moesel placed second in silver dance. They made a big splash at Easterns, where they placed second: "The Major-Moesel team jumped into the competitive limelight almost out of nowhere," *Skating* wrote. "Mrs. Major is one of the exciting new finds in

Bob and Pat Dineen, Skating Club of Lake Placid, 1960 Silver Dance Champions. Source: World Figure Skating Museum.

dancing in recent years." At the 1956 Nationals, Pat and Peter placed sixth in silver dance. When the competitive season ended, Bob and Pat expressed a desire to compete together.[70]

Although Pat and Peter Moesel had just made their first trip to Nationals, Bob and Pat felt drawn together. Standing five feet five inches, Pat was a striking brunette with beautifully shaped legs and blue-green eyes. The female skaters admired her for her good looks and great figure. Bob had a blonde crew cut and blue eyes. At five feet seven and a half, he was just a little taller than Pat. On the ice, their relative size and skating styles complemented each other.[71]

Pat and Bob began training together. He was "head over heels" in love with her, but off the ice their relationship could not progress. When Pat married Dave Schwartzer after high school, he became a supportive spouse. Together Dave, thirty-one, and Pat, nineteen, had passed their pre-dance tests in 1954, but he never competed. Once Pat's skating surpassed her husband's, he committed himself to her success. He took her to Lake Placid, Lynn, and Schumacher summer sessions to work with dance coaches. Dave and Pat had been married a few years when Bob and Pat fell in love.[72]

Not many skaters knew Pat was married because she used her maiden name. She won the *Miss Lake Placid* contest one summer, leading to the

Miss New York pageant. However, she had to return her crown when pageant officials learned she was married. Her marriage had always been kept quiet, but her developing relationship with Bob Dineen led to plans for a marriage annulment.[73]

During this difficult period, Jean Westwood, who worked with them in Lake Placid, invited Bob and Pat to train in Paramount for the upcoming competitive season. Bob and Pat took the train to Los Angeles in the summer of 1956 where they took lessons from both Jean and Bill Kipp.[74]

Bob and Pat were immediately welcomed into the L.A. skating family. "They were incredible skaters, and as a team they were fabulous," dancer Eleanor Curtis said. They socialized with the dance crowd at weekend dinner parties in skaters' homes. Bob got a part-time job at a Los Angeles law firm; his long-term professional goal was to practice law like his father.[75]

Bob and Pat hoped to jumpstart their partnership in a new competitive region and changed their home club to the Arctic Blades Figure Skating Club. They were third in silver dance at Pacific Coast and fifth at the 1957 Nationals in Berkeley. With Bob, Pat had bettered her previous year's placement by one spot.[76]

Bob and Pat headed back to the East Coast in the spring of 1957; Bob returned to St. John's University to finish his degree, and both worked: Bob with the Pension and Welfare Fund and Pat as a statistical clerk for the Sterling Drug company. They trained most nights and ended their evenings socializing with other ice dancers. They went to late-night dinners at Al Mueller's, a German restaurant across from Iceland, or Pat's favorite, the Howard Johnson's on the corner of Broadway and 46th Street in Times Square. Everyone enjoyed hamburgers, French fries, and coleslaw but Pat, who starved all day so she could indulge in her favorite ice cream: the tasty tester dish featuring six different flavors. It was a lopsided diet, but it let Pat retain her beautiful figure. "No matter what you wanted to treat her to she wouldn't eat; she was just waiting for that ice cream," friend Marilyn Grace recalled. The evenings ended with arcades or movies on 42nd Street.[77]

On Saturday nights, Bob and Pat went regularly to St. Patrick's for late night mass, bringing non-Catholic dancers. Bob and Pat attracted a circle of faithful friends. "She was such a good skater I thought she would not bother with me because I was not at her level, but she was very friendly," a dancer said. Pat was bubbly and gracious. She never spoke ill of anyone. Bob was very happy-go-lucky and outgoing but also felt driven to succeed.[78]

The 1958 season showed early promise. The team placed second in silver dance at Middle Atlantics, while Pat's ex-partner, Peter Moesel, won with Gloria Grossman. Peter and Gloria also won Easterns, while Bob and

Pat placed third. Bob and Pat did not fare well at the 1958 Nationals in Minneapolis. They withdrew after placing eighth in the compulsories.[79]

After this disappointing competitive season, Bob's father, Judge Benedict Dineen, suffered a massive heart attack and died on April 3, 1958, at age sixty-eight. Two months later, Bob and Pat married. The timing was curious—either Bob's father did not approve of Pat, or the annulment had required a substantial length of time. Regardless, after two years of dating, Bob and Pat finally married on June 14, 1958. Monsignor Aloysius C. Dineen, Bob's uncle, had been instrumental in arranging Pat's annulment and officiated at their wedding at St. Agnes Church at 43rd Street and Lexington. The Monsignor, like Bob's immediate family, did not approve of Bob's skating career, but he supported his nephew's marriage to Pat.[80]

Pat was uncharacteristically late for her wedding, which was ironic because Bob was the notoriously late one. She was detained by a photographer and then got stuck in traffic. Bob kept asking, "Is she here yet?" Pat finally arrived and Bob happily shouted, "She's here!" Friends were concerned that Pat's ex-husband might appear and disrupt the ceremony, but the wedding proceeded smoothly.[81]

After they married, the Dineens trained with Sonya Klopfer at the West New York rink across the Hudson. She worked with them on their technique and increasing their speed. In 1959 the Dineens won silver dance at both the 1959 North Atlantic States and Eastern competitions. Heading to Rochester, New York, Bob and Pat were hoping to finally win a medal at the 1959 Nationals. Surprisingly they finished first in the compulsory phase but were unable to hold the lead into the finals, placing third in silver dance by just a fraction of a point. Marilyn Meeker and Larry Pierce were first, and Diane Sherbloom and Roger Campbell second.[82]

Bob and Pat planned to compete in silver dance one more year, and spent their summer training in Lake Placid. The Dineens lived and trained on their own dime, working at the Mirror Lake Inn during the day as waiters. Pat wore a uniform with a little white apron, and Bob wore a white jacket as they waited on all the younger skaters. "The Dineens were quiet and reserved and went about their business," Bob Munz recalled. "They weren't part of the rowdy group because they were trying to stay alive." They didn't have much time for socializing either. The Dineens went to the rink at the end of the day, skated until late evening, then woke up early to wait on tables. They usually looked worn out. Sometimes they skated in the middle of the night with friends Marilyn Grace and Charlie Rizzo. Marilyn's mother rented midnight ice so her daughter and friends could practice dance patterns without bumping into the swarm of Lake Placid dancers.[83]

The Dineens had represented several clubs throughout the years and were about to change home clubs again. The same day they passed their Argentine Tango test at Iceland at Madison Square Garden, Marilyn Grace slipped on a shredded rubber mat, broke her ankle, was taken away on a stretcher, and had a cast up to her knee for six weeks. When she decided to sue the Garden, the Metropolitan FSC president warned her that she would be banned from amateur skating. She dropped the lawsuit but also dropped out of the Metropolitan FSC, instead representing the Skating Club of Lake Placid. Bob and Pat joined her to demonstrate their support.[84]

In late 1959, Pat prepared to take Charlie Rizzo through his Kilian test. Charlie wanted to postpone the test due to a stiff neck caused by a fall but Pat protested that they had practiced too hard not to go through with it. "We were in the dance position," Charlie recalled, "and my hand accidentally slipped and landed on her stomach. I instantly realized something was different. After I passed the test she confided in me that she was pregnant." Pat kept her pregnancy private until after the competitive season was over.[85]

The Dineens did not need to qualify for the 1960 Nationals and went directly to the championships. On the way to Seattle, the plane had some trouble and returned to New York. The episode upset Pat, and she became uneasy about flying. But when they finally made it to Seattle, her nerves had settled. On their fourth attempt as a dance team, Bob and Pat won the silver dance crown, with a "smooth and stylish performance." Upon returning home, the Dineens were invigorated by winning the national title. They returned to training and looked forward to entering gold dance for the first time, even as they awaited their child's birth.[86]

BILL AND LAURIE HICKOX

1960 NATIONAL JUNIOR PAIRS CHAMPIONS

Fate had a hand in bringing Bill and Laurie Hickox, a popular brother-sister team, together, since Bill's parents had adopted Laurie as a newborn. They were devoted to each other. In looks and personality, they were very different, yet they became each other's best friend and brought out the best in each other. "They were regular kids, but to us they were bigger than life," a cousin said. "They were friendly, warm, and humble about their accomplishments."[87]

Bill and Laurie Hickox were the only children of Lute and Elinor Hickox. Lute Hickox was raised with five siblings near Portland, Oregon;

Bill Hickox, The Skating Club of San Francisco, 1960 Junior Pairs Champion. Source: Courtesy of Lorna Dyer.

his father was sheriff of Hood River County and a prison guard for the Oregon State Penal System. In the early 1920s, Lute traveled to China as a ship radio operator. When he returned, he attended college in San Francisco, where he met Elinor Hand. A native of the Bay area, Elinor graduated from University of California, Berkeley, in library science.[88]

The newlyweds began their married life in Sacramento where Lute was an auditor for the California State division of highways. They returned to the Bay area in 1940 where he worked as an accountant for the California Department of Agriculture. The Hickoxes waited nearly twenty years for a child and were thrilled when Elinor became pregnant. Lute was forty-one and Elinor was forty when William Holmes Hickox was born on March 28, 1942. Bill was a treasure to his parents, especially Elinor. He favored his mother in looks and was tall like his father.[89]

The Hickoxes wanted more children so they looked into adoption. Across town, a young pregnant woman decided to give her baby up for adoption. She was young and very much alone as her husband was far from home in the Merchant Marines. The grandmother wanted to raise the baby, but the expectant mother felt that her newborn would fare better with an older, established couple. Lute and Elinor were perfect. Laurie Jean Hickox was born at St. Luke's Hospital on December 6, 1945. Three-year-old Bill came to the hospital with his parents to meet his new sister. He brought his favorite toy, the one he never let anyone else touch, to give to his baby sister. From his first glance at her, Bill became a fond and protective big brother, and Laurie fully reciprocated his affection.[90]

From childhood, the Hickox children were goal oriented. Their accomplishments resulted from their mother's desire to have successful children and attain a social status that she herself desired. Her dutiful husband supported her wishes. The Hickoxes lived in a small Tudor-style home in Berkeley Hills, an exclusive enclave near the University of California at Berkeley. Everything in the Hickox home revolved around the children's potential. Skating was just one of their endeavors.[91]

Bill excelled at everything. He was an accomplished pianist and drummer, and both children were involved with their father's Masonic activities. Bill was a member of the Scottish rite, played bagpipes for a variety of functions, performed Scottish folk dancing, and achieved a Master's Degree in the Order of DeMolay, a Masonic youth leadership organization. He was an excellent student. In the midst of his full schedule, he spent much of his time skating.[92]

He began skating at Berkeley Iceland when he was seven. At age nine he took lessons from Maribel Vinson Owen and joined the St. Moritz club. After one year with Maribel, he passed three figure tests and two dance tests. At age ten Bill became a triple threat: he placed third in bronze dance with Sally Ann Kaufman at the 1953 Northern Inter-Club meet, won juvenile boys at the 1953 Pacific Coast, and won a bronze medal in junior pairs with eight-year-old Laurence Owen at the 1953 California State. Their partnership ended when the Owens moved to Boston in 1954.[93]

Bill focused on singles with coach Bob Swenning. In 1955 he won novice men at the Pacific Coast competition. In 1956 he placed second in junior men at Pacific Coast and advanced to his first U.S. Championships in Philadelphia, where he placed eighth in novice men. The following year the Nationals were held in Berkeley. Greg Kelley won novice men, and Bill dropped from fourth to sixth after the free skate.[94]

Laurie Hickox began skating when she was five. She passed figure tests, skated in shows, and began competing at age six. At the 1956 Pacific Coast, she placed eighth in juvenile girls. When the siblings formed a pair team, they achieved success quickly. They won junior pairs at the 1958 California State and placed second at Pacific Coast. At the 1958 Nationals in Minneapolis, they did not compete in pairs, but Bill placed fourth in novice men, missing the podium for the third time. After this disappointment, he focused entirely on pairs and ice dancing with his sister.[95]

Laurie Hickox, The Skating Club of San Francisco, 1960 Junior Pairs Champion. Source: Courtesy of Pam Thatcher Marsh.

In 1958 Bill and Laurie switched clubs and trained at Sutro's, home of The Skating Club of San Francisco. Sutro's was an amazing, one-of-a-kind ice establishment. Sutro's Baths was a series of buildings built in 1865 into a cliff overlooking the Pacific Ocean. Rising in successive levels from the ocean floor to the top of the rocky cliffs, the huge bathhouse had beautiful stained-glass windows and five swimming pools of variable temperatures. Eventually the baths closed and a full-size ice rink was built over the largest pool.[96]

Getting to the ice at Sutro's was an adventure. Skaters had to bypass the other pools, which had morphed into museums filled with Egyptian mummies, exotic birds, San Francisco memorabilia, and peculiar oddities and photographs from the late nineteenth century. Next came the daunting stairs. The rink was at the bottom of 140 steps, right next to the ocean. The large scenic windows were painted black so that the skaters would not be distracted by the majestic waves, seals basking in the sun, or the incredible view. The Zamboni ice machine shed its snow right on the beach.[97]

The ice at Sutro's was uneven because the proximity to the ocean caused constantly varying humidity; the ice tended to crack and the whole ice surface sloped, slanting down in one corner towards the ocean. The rink was noisy. Skaters were bombarded by shrill whistles from the nearby aviary and the roar of the ocean. "On one stormy day," a club member said, "the waves beating against the rocks rose to such height that they dashed against the windows and showered broken glass over one corner of the rink. However, the glass was quickly swept up and the skaters went on about their business." The skaters loved the space. After Saturday morning sessions, Bill and Laurie hung out with other skaters by an empty swimming pool.[98]

Bill and Laurie flourished at Sutro's and the family was active in The Skating Club of San Francisco; Lute began judging, and both kids were junior club officers. They won many medals in the 1959 season: at Central Pacific Laurie placed second in novice ladies, they placed second in bronze dance and won junior pairs. They repeated those placements in bronze dance and junior pairs at the Pacific Coast competition, then made their first appearance as a pair team at the 1959 Nationals in Rochester. The Fotheringills won the junior pairs, and the Hickox siblings placed third.[99]

Their first national success was a result of excellent coaching over the years. The consensus among their coaches—Maribel Vinson Owen, Robert Swenning, Gene Turner, and Bill and Julie Barrett—was that Bill made the most of his talent, while Laurie, who was young when they began pairs, was less motivated. "Laurie had to be pushed to do anything and tried to get out of skating at the slightest chance," Swenning recalled.[100]

In 1956 Gene Turner taught Bill and Laurie in pairs and singles. Gene didn't think he was intimidating; but after their first lesson, he overheard Laurie say, "He wasn't so scary." Gene liked working with Bill, but he found Laurie's focus hit or miss. "Her training was a bit erratic and her mood swings were in high gear as she became a teenager." Gene felt that the sibling bond between Bill and Laurie helped their development as a pair team.[101]

Bill and Julie Barrett had coached four-time national pairs champions Robin Greiner and Carole Ormaca; and starting in 1958, they helped the Hickox siblings prepare for national competition. "Bill was easy to get along with," Julie Barrett said. "He went through puberty like a dream and was so even tempered. He was an absolutely darling boy." Julie's enthusiasm over the other sibling was more restrained. "Laurie was a little temperamental because of her age, but she was still adorable. Both kids wanted to skate, worked hard, and were happy."[102]

The Hickox kids were popular. At Pacific Coast competition parties, they danced with everyone and hopped from table to table. Bill was good-looking, six feet tall, slender, freckle-faced, and redheaded with blue eyes. "Bill was like Ron Howard in 'Happy Days'—that's the kind of personality he had, so how can you fault that? Everyone liked him," an L.A. skater said. Bill wrote to skaters he met at competitions, and one of his first girlfriends was a fellow skater. The extent of their romance was secret hand holding.[103]

The siblings got along well despite the nearly four-year age difference. Bill was mature and protective of his sister, who needed looking after. Even at thirteen, Laurie had the "it" factor—an attractive figure with olive skin, dark brown hair, a beautiful round face, a gorgeous smile, dimples, and expressive brown eyes. Standing five foot seven, she was quite tall for a skater. Boys were attracted to her sensual and flirty personality. "She was stunning and a real bombshell," a friend said. "A parent's nightmare."[104]

Like her brother, Laurie was active in the youth organization of the Masons, becoming a Rainbow Girl while Bill was a prize-winning Caledonian Scottish dancer. Bill, whose room was filled with trophies, received most of the family honors; but Laurie was unfazed, perfectly happy to applaud her brother's achievements. He, in turn, was equally supportive of Laurie's other activities: ballet, modern dancing, Scottish dancing, modeling, and baton twirling.[105]

Elinor, a homemaker, was at the rink regularly to support her children. She joined the mothers' sewing circle and watched her kids practice. "Aunt Elinor was the driving force behind their skating, and all of these visions of greatness were built around Bill's potential. He was really the one they put all their hopes into," a cousin said. A friend added: "Bill had to succeed at everything, or she would have just gone nuts." Fortunately for family peace, Bill seemed to take these expectations in his stride.[106]

The Hickox kids trained in Sun Valley, Idaho, while their coaches spent the summer of 1959 in England. Elinor was hesitant about sending Bill, age sixteen, and thirteen-year-old Laurie away, but it turned out to be a productive summer. The siblings practiced all day long; on the weekends, they performed in the Saturday night show. In their few off hours, they socialized with the dorm kids from Seattle and Los Angeles.[107]

The strenuous training was offset by summer romances. Bill took a liking to dancer Lorna Dyer who was several years younger. They picnicked at the lake. "It was a two-hour drive and my dorm mother was nervous, but he was an honorable guy and totally trustworthy," Lorna said. "We rowed, walked around the lake, and drove home. My mother was concerned that I was dating somebody older than me, but when she met him all her fears were gone." Lorna's mother thought so highly of Bill that she began a life-long correspondence with Elinor Hickox. Laurie caught the eye of Seattle ice dancer Marshall Campbell, who was fascinated by her joie de vivre. "She was very lively and liked being the center of attention," he said. "I think she enjoyed skating because it meant that people were always watching her."[108]

After a fun summer in Idaho, Bill began his senior year at Berkeley High School, where he was a member of three clubs (English, math, and weightlifting—which helped with his pairs training), three bands (marching, concert, and pep), and two orchestras (concert and theater). Bill was the band student director and played percussion. The Berkeley High School band received an invitation to participate in the upcoming Winter Olympics along with dozens of other regional high school bands.[109]

Bill, a top student at Berkeley High School, aimed toward a career in science. His mother steered him toward the Air Force Academy in Colorado Springs; it was difficult to get into the academy, but Elinor felt it matched his talents and her plans. The academy had a sterling reputation, there was no tuition, and it was near the Broadmoor Ice Palace. Bill had the grades to get into the academy, and he also had a "connection." The head of the Air Force Academy, Commandant Henry R. Sullivan, was married to Jane Vaughn Sullivan, former two-time national senior ladies champion and a national figure skating judge. Bill applied to the academy and waited.[110]

Laurie, in her final year at Garfield Junior High, did well in school and enjoyed her many friends, who appreciated her kindness and sincerity. Though easy-going as a child, she was more temperamental and rebellious as a teenager. She wasn't easy to teach, but Bill helped to calm her and keep their partnership moving forward.[111]

Bill's romantic life took a more serious turn after meeting Anne Frazier. She was a skater from Walnut Creek who had first spotted Bill in a "Little Boy Blue" number at a St. Moritz show in the early fifties. Years later, at a Berkeley hockey game, she saw Bill and Laurie perform an exhibition between periods. She was surprised by how much his technique had improved and how handsome the "red-headed twerp" had become. Weeks later, she saw him at an SAT test and introduced herself. Both smart skaters, they had a lot in common and began dating, primarily holding hands on the ice and attending monthly Masonic youth activities together.[112]

Bill and Laurie worked with Gene Turner at Iceland and with the Barretts at Sutro's for the upcoming competitive season. They hoped to better their third place in national junior pairs. At the 1960 Pacific Coast in Squaw Valley, they won bronze dance and placed third in senior pairs behind the Hadleys and Fotheringills. Bill returned to Squaw Valley six weeks later to perform in the opening ceremonies of the 1960 Winter Olympics with the Berkeley High School Band.[113]

Bill received excellent news just before the 1960 U.S. Championships. He was one of eleven area candidates under consideration for an Air Force Academy appointment. The day before he left for Seattle, a telegram reported that he had been accepted. His appointment made the papers and featured a photo of Bill with U.S. Congressman Jeffrey Cohelan.[114]

Bill's euphoria over his academy acceptance only enhanced his competitive spirit. Bill and Laurie performed confidently "with a polished and interesting program." The Hickox siblings won the event, with two first and three second place marks, barely beating Ron and Vivian Joseph of Chicago.[115]

Bill had rarely disappointed his mother; but after he returned from Seattle, he informed his parents that he was retiring from skating. Elinor Hickox was devastated. As reigning national junior champions, her children had an excellent chance of making the 1961 World Team. The mechanics of how Laurie could train, live, and go to school in Colorado had not been worked out, but Elinor would have made it happen. Bill firmly discouraged his mother from making plans. He had skated for nearly a decade and was ready for a new chapter in his life. After he graduated from high school, Bill moved to Colorado Springs to attend the Air Force Academy. Elinor packed his skates—just in case.[116]

CHAPTER 10

1960 WINTER OLYMPICS

Weeks before the 1960 Winter Olympics in Squaw Valley, the international community was bad-mouthing the Americans. A French sports executive criticized the accommodations and the entertainment: "Can you imagine four women living together in one cramped room for a month? Ridiculous! How are we going to put our young men and women to bed at an early hour if there's a chorus line and Frankie Sinatra singing across the road?" The Europeans were aghast that Walt Disney was staging the Opening Ceremonies. The chancellor of the International Olympic Committee (IOC) griped, "All this hoopla has little to do with the Olympic spirit and I've wired the U.S. accordingly." Added Zurich's *Sport*: "Assigning the Games to Squaw Valley was a big mistake."[1]

Going beyond rudeness, a French skiing official forecast disaster: "The history of America's march westward is full of tragic adventures of pioneers perishing in the snow." The 1960 Olympic committee took the mud-slinging in stride, reassuring nations that, although the Olympic Village rooms adequately housed four people, the majority of female competitors would be housed in pairs. Although each country paid for its team's transportation and housing, for the first time Squaw Valley offered a subsidy of $500 per competitor.[2]

Olympic organizers had suffered five years of criticisms—dubious writers had called the complaints "Squawk Valley"—but they faded as the Games approached. The tab to turn Squaw Valley into an international sports center had risen to $20 million, and there was general agreement that the money had been well spent. The 665 athletes—522 men and 143 women from thirty nations—appreciated the newly minted Olympic site created just for them: new ice rinks, skating ovals, and ski runs on three mountains. The Olympic torch had been airlifted from Greece to Los Angeles, and schoolboys relayed it up the coast to the Sierra Nevadas. From February 18 to 28, 1960, the eyes of the world focused on Squaw Valley.[3]

The athletes were ready, but only 135,000 tickets from a total capacity of 385,000 had been sold just ten days before the Games were to begin. The weather had turned frigid, and 100 inches of snow fell just days before the

Opening Ceremonies. Fortunately, sales began to pick up. A large party of figure skaters arrived from San Francisco, including Maribel's former students and friends. Americans enjoyed the Games in the comfort of their own homes in the first U.S.-televised broadcast of the Winter Olympics on CBS-TV. In another first, two electronic computers tabulated results in minutes, instead of the normal three-hour delay.[4]

The state-of-the-art competitive venues delighted all, but the highlight was the Olympic Village. For the first time, all the athletes lived under one roof. One women's and three men's dormitories stood within a five-minute walk of most venues. The athletes ate and played together in a recreation center and huge dining hall that fed 900 at a time. "This is the first time that Olympic athletes have had their own self-contained world," the president of the organizing committee said proudly.[5]

Competitors could meet athletes from other sports and countries. American skaters interacted with the Russian hockey team, and ski jumpers and figure skaters supported one another, attending each other's practice sessions: "We thought we could never do that [ski-jump]," Carol Heiss said, "and they watched us practice and thought we were crazy!" Laurence Owen, who broke down barriers with the Russians by trading Olympic pins, interacted with as many athletes as possible: "I fell in love with the Japanese team.... [F]ifteen years ago we were bitterly fighting each other and today we are best of friends. I am really glad that this is so, for they are wonderful people."[6]

The recreation center contained game rooms, ping-pong tables, juke boxes, a dance floor, and two movie theaters open all day. Athletes enjoyed the nightly themed programs, including Western Night with staged gun battles and barroom fights. Movie and TV stars, including Danny Kaye and Art Linkletter, provided live entertainment every evening at the recreation center, and some were spotted at practice sessions, including Bing Crosby, Jayne Mansfield, and Liberace.[7]

Athletes arrived early to acclimate themselves. The practice sessions were held in the Ice Arena and three outdoor practice rinks. The outdoor rinks had their challenges, as Barbara Roles noted: "One evening we had a practice at midnight. Normally we went in groups of four countries, but nobody went that night except Carol [Heiss] and me. It was twelve degrees and there was a big crack down the rink. We had to jump over it so our blades wouldn't get stuck in it; the ice was pretty hard most of the time."[8]

During the training period, the weather was brutal. Linda Hadley sent a postcard to friends, saying: "Thanks a million for the boots. I'd be lost without them. It rains or snows every day—weather a mess. P.S. The snow is really as high as picture shows (three feet deep)." But then things turned around. The day before the Opening Ceremonies, another storm was predicted; but miraculously a bright sun lit the mountain-rimmed valley for the start of the competition, and the next ten days were sunny.[9]

The Opening Ceremonies on February 18 pulled out all stops. After a fireworks display, the Olympic band played "The Parade of the Olympians" as the athletes entered Blyth Arena. Vice-President Richard Nixon declared the Games officially opened. More than 1,285 musicians and a chorus of 2,645 from fifty-two California and Nevada high schools performed "The Olympic Hymn." The Olympic flag slowly ascended to the top of its pole, 2,000 "symbolic doves of peace" (white homing pigeons) were released, and a gun crew fired eight rounds, one for each of the Winter Games. Two-time Olympic gold medalist Andrea Mead Lawrence skied down Little Papoose Peak bearing the traditional Olympic torch and handed it to Olympic speed skating champion Kenneth Henry. The bands played "Conquest" as the Olympic flame was lit. After film star Karl Malden offered an Olympic prayer, the bands and chorus performed "God of Our Fathers."[10]

Carol Heiss took the Olympic Oath on behalf of all the participating athletes, the first time a female athlete was accorded this honor. After "The Star-Spangled Banner" played, fireworks, mountain chimes, colored flares, and the release of 20,000 colored balloons accompanied the athletes as they left the arena. Snow sculptures fourteen feet high, depicting the winter sports featured at the Games, stood outside Blyth Arena. These statues followed a tradition that began in 776 B.C., when sculptors created the likenesses of competitors for the Olympics in Athens.[11]

Observers agreed that, among the U.S. Team, figure skaters had the greatest potential for taking medals. The first event was the pairs division, held on Saturday, February 19. Unfortunately, the event, held in the early morning hours, drew only 2,000, leaving most of the 8,500 seats empty. An anxious moment came during the warm-up when the Hadleys collided with one of the Soviet teams. Fortunately, no one was injured.[12]

Three-time World pairs champions, Canadians Barbara Wagner and Bob Paul, were the clear favorites. "Their smoothness, complete unison, speed and difficult moves," resulted in unanimous first-place votes. They were the first non-European team to win the gold in pairs. Even with Squaw Valley's state-of-the-art computers, it took two hours to calculate the razor-thin margin between an American and German team for second place. Hans-Jurgen Baumler and Marika Kilius took home the silver with 76.8 points while Ron and Nancy Ludington received the bronze with 76.2 points. The Ludingtons won the first medal for the USA, even though

Nancy had the flu and needed oxygen after their performance. The Canadian team of Maria and Otto Jelinek ended up fourth. "Today people think fourth place means nothing, but we skated well and that's all we cared about," Maria said.[13]

The two other American teams did not perform well; Maribel and Dudley finished tenth while the Hadleys were eleventh. "Maribel displayed some nervousness and their performance did not have the life or spirit which they have shown in previous competitions," *Skating* lamented. The Hadleys also had breathing problems because of the high altitude; at one point, Ray Jr. almost threw his sister into the audience, and Ila Ray fell on an axel, executing "a second-base slide." The two Soviet teams finished sixth and ninth. Of the latter, Ludmila Belousova and Oleg Protopopov "gave a fair performance but showed [a] lack of skating ability and experience." Oleg bought his first movie camera and filmed everyone in an effort to improve their skating. The Russians' performance at the next Olympics would be a different story.[14]

Anything less than a gold medal in the ladies' division would be a disappointment for the U.S. Olympic Team. The free skating event, held on Tuesday, February 23, was a sunny yet cold day; only a heater allowed the announcer's microphone to function. Fortunately most of the ladies were prepared for the outdoor weather and wore wool jersey dresses. Whether it was the frigid weather, nerves, or the thin air, many of the women fell, and two girls collapsed after they finished.[15]

Carol Heiss had waited four years to fulfill her mother's wish of winning an Olympic gold medal. She had a commanding lead in figures with nine first-place votes; but as a veteran competitor, she knew it all depended on her four-minute program. Heiss was the seventeenth of twenty-six ladies to perform. There was a full house in Blyth Arena to watch Queen Carol claim her throne. They gave her an enthusiastic greeting, and she skated a near-flawless program. The highlights were her double axel and axels in both directions. The crowd cried "bravo" and "six, six, six" at the conclusion of her program.[16]

Believing the outcome decided, many spectators walked out after Carol's performance; they missed the fine performances of Canadian champion Wendy Griner, Sjoukje Dijkstra of the Netherlands, and the other Americans. Laurence Owen had one small fall on a double toe loop. When she fell, Maribel's face "registered sheer agony," but Laurence arose with a smile, completed her program, and left the ice laughing; the crowd thundered its approval. Her admirers thought her program was more exuberant than most, and her style "was a breath of fresh air." After twenty-five competitors, the final skater was Barbara Roles. She missed a flying sit spin but was enthusiastically received by the spectators; she placed second to Carol in the free skating and third overall.[17]

Carol Heiss decisively won and brought the United States its first gold medal of the Games. The U.S. Marine Band played "The Star Spangled Banner" when Carol, Sjoukje Dijkstra, and Barbara Roles received their medals at the Tower of Champions. For Carol, it was a relief to win. Her first Olympics had been fun, but this one was all business. As a previous medalist, she knew she was there to do a job, as she recalled:

> "*Sports Illustrated, The Saturday Evening Post*, [and] *Life* magazine were all predicting that the one sure [U.S.] gold medal would be in ladies' figure skating. So I really had to keep control of my nerves. . . . I just told myself, 'Look, you're well-trained, you've worked hard, just do your thing.' Once the marks went up, I knew I had won. I felt kind of numb. It wasn't until I actually held the gold medal that I realized I was an Olympic champion. There's absolutely no feeling like it, to know that you're the best at something. It isn't the thing that makes you happiest for the rest of your life, but there is a great feeling of pride."[18]

Laurence Owen, sixteen, came in a respectable sixth place in her first international competition. She became a mini-celebrity, as a reporter noted: "On and off the ice Laurence presented a pixie-like charm that made her a favorite with galleries. Her smile was her trademark . . . and she displayed surprising poise for one so young. She was highly popular with her teammates at Squaw Valley and actually seemed to take delight in being interviewed, as if she couldn't understand the reason for the fuss being made over her."[19]

The U.S. Olympic Figure Skating Team had one gold and two bronze medals, with the men's competition still ahead. David Jenkins's performance in Seattle indicated that he had fully recovered from his summer accident. After sixteen years of rigorous training, David was prepared, but he didn't hide the psychological toll. "I'm just tired of skating . . . and I've got my studies to think about. Of course I want to win an Olympic medal and match the one owned by my brother. But after that I've had it." For Jenkins, the Olympics was like "putting a period at the end of a long sentence."[20]

In figures Karol Divin of Czechoslovakia placed first, and David was second. The free skating was held on Saturday, February 27. Jenkins performed a flawless routine to a near-capacity crowd. After his five-minute, jam-packed routine—filled with two successive double axels, triple salchow, triple loop, and a flying open axel sit spin—he received a wild standing ovation. "Whoever originated the phrase 'poetry in motion' must have had David Jenkins in mind," a fan said. He received scores of 5.8 and 5.9, with one

6.0 by the Czech judge. When David came off the ice, his coach was not there to greet him. Edi had told David, "Your brother, he gave me an ulcer. I'm going to go enjoy myself this time." But Edi had been too nervous to watch and hid under the stands. Halfway through David's program Carol Heiss tried to grab him, exclaiming, "Edi, you've got to come out here and watch this. . . . It's a skate of a lifetime!"—but Edi wouldn't budge. He sat down with David afterwards and watched his inspired performance on television.[21]

David Jenkins brought the United States its third gold medal of the Games. Karol Divin placed second, and Canadian Donald Jackson pulled up from fourth to receive the bronze. Tim Brown, who uncharacteristically placed fifth in figures, was hampered by a strained muscle and remained in fifth, and Robert Brewer remained in seventh. After his win, David was a model of humility: "Any boy of the first eight or ten might have been on top. I was lucky." Everyone knew it was more than luck. Maribel, who sprang to her feet at the end of his number, screaming and stamping, said it was the greatest show in figure skating history.[22]

David's win contributed to new records: (1) He was the fourth consecutive U.S. gold medalist in Olympic men's figure skating, equaling a record set by Sweden; (2) It was the first time that brother succeeded brother for an Olympic figure skating title; (3) The United States was the first nation to achieve dual figure skating victories in two straight Olympics (Hayes Jenkins/Tenley Albright and David Jenkins/Carol Heiss); and (4) It was the first sweep of all three Olympic figure skating titles by North Americans.[23]

One of the busiest people at the Games was Maribel Vinson Owen. She coached six members of the twelve-member U.S. Olympic Figure Skating Team, one of her pair teams won the Olympic bronze, and she filed daily reports for both the Associated Press and the *Boston Globe*.[24]

On February 28 the competitors entered Blyth Arena for the last time. Several Americans chose to walk with the Russians, including Laurence Owen. "I feel that our problems arise mainly from our different political, social, and economic environments, and our ignorance of the other's way of life. If we could overcome, or at least understand these differences, all of us would realize in how many ways we are alike. This realization is our only hope of a lasting world peace." The closing remarks were pronounced, the Olympic flag lowered, and the Olympic flame extinguished.[25]

After ten days of competition, the VIII Olympic Winter Games closed. A strong showing in figure skating propelled America to third place among the competing nations, behind the Soviet Union and Germany. Besides the four figure skating medals, the United States won six additional medals: the gold in hockey, three silver in women's alpine skiing, one silver in men's speed skating, and one bronze in women's speed skating, an event that debuted at Squaw Valley. The 500-plus athletes who did not win medals took home wonderful memories and the reassuring words of the official Olympic Creed: "The important thing in the Olympic Games is not winning, but taking part. The essential thing in life is not conquering but fighting well."[26]

For most athletes their season was over, but the figure skaters had one more stop. They headed north for the 1960 World Figure Skating Championships in Vancouver, British Columbia.

1960 WORLDS

Although David Jenkins had announced his retirement in Squaw Valley, USFSA officials still expected him to compete at the 1960 Worlds, telling him he had a responsibility to the Canadian Figure Skating Association (CFSA), and threatened to suspend him. He wasn't planning to compete again, so he said: "Suspend me." Jenkins had brought the World title back home three times and had just won the Olympics. Now he needed to focus on making up three weeks of missed work at medical school.[27]

More bad news followed for the USFSA: none of the three male Olympians was going to Vancouver. Tim Brown, disappointed with his fifth place in Squaw Valley, decided it was time to concentrate on college, a decision reinforced by some health problems. After USFSA officials realized that Jenkins and Brown were serious about dropping out, they approached Robert Brewer: "You're going to Vancouver, aren't you?" As it turned out, Brewer had pulled a groin muscle during his training in Squaw Valley and had competed in the Olympics only because a team doctor injected his injured muscle with Novocain right before he went on the ice. The numbness "lasted about five to six minutes, which was the time I needed to finish my program," he said. Brewer was willing to go to Worlds and use Novocain again if his injury hadn't healed, but he was reluctant to ask his parents for more money; they had already paid for travel to three World competitions. Brewer told the USFSA he would go if the association paid his airfare and hotel. USFSA officials refused, explaining: "The U.S. champion gets his way paid, not the number one man on the team, so we can't do that." Brewer declined to go.[28]

The USFSA's decision seemed harsh. It had sufficient money to send Jenkins, and this plane ticket was an inexpensive ride up the Pacific Coast. However, the decision of the three male Olympians was a tremendous boon to the two World Team alternates. Bradley Lord, twenty, and Gregory Kelley, fifteen, were eager to go to Vancouver, and it made sense to have the next generation get some international experience.

Most of the competitors came to Vancouver directly from Squaw Valley, wearing their Olympic uniforms and looking tanned and healthy. The nine dance couples, from Great Britain, France, West Germany, Canada, and the United States, flew in from their home bases, anxious to compete after being shut out of the Olympics.[29]

Carol Heiss securely won her fifth World title with all nine judges awarding her first. Heiss, Dijkstra, and Roles received gold, silver, and bronze, the same medals they received in Squaw Valley. Barbara Roles showed she was next in line to be U.S. and World champion with her exciting performance. Laurence was seventh in figures but had trouble with her trick knee in the free skate and dropped to ninth place. Despite these difficulties, Laurence won new fans who were impressed by her artistry.[30]

The men's division was the most anticipated event of the week: The name "Jenkins" had been associated with the World title for seven years and Americans had owned the World title for twelve. International skaters were thrilled to have a clear shot at the men's championship. European champion Alain Giletti of France and Canadian Don Jackson were the primary candidates. Giletti placed first in figures, followed by Jackson; the American men made a fine showing, with Lord in sixth place and Kelley in ninth.[31]

In the free skating, Giletti executed two double axels and performed with control; he hoped it was enough to retain his thirty-three point lead. The partisan Vancouver audience tried to applaud Jackson into first place. Jackson won the free skate but it was not enough. Giletti became the first Frenchman to win the World men's title. Donald Jackson placed second, Alain Calmat placed third, and Bradley Lord and Gregory Kelley retained their sixth and ninth places.[32]

The new Olympic pairs champions Barbara Wagner and Bob Paul were victorious, capping their careers by winning their fourth World title. Canadians Otto and Maria Jelinek, having just missed a bronze in Squaw Valley, redeemed themselves by winning the silver. Third place went to Marika Kilius and Hans Jurgen-Baumler, the German team who won the Olympic silver medal.[33]

The pairs division was a disappointment for the Americans. The Ludingtons placed sixth, Dudley and Maribel placed tenth, and the Hadleys placed last—in twelfth place. The Ludingtons' poor showing was affected by their personal lives; after Worlds, they planned to divorce. "We went out for dinner after we won the [Olympic] bronze, but we didn't do anything special," Nancy recalled. "They were very difficult times." She felt that Maribel was in favor of their divorce, which made training sessions painfully awkward, both in Squaw Valley and Vancouver.[34]

The dancers, excluded from the Olympics (it would not become an Olympic event until 1976), finally had their moment. Britons Doreen Denny and Courtney Jones retained their World title; Americans Margie Ackles and Chuck Phillips placed fourth, Marilyn Meeker and Larry Pierce placed fifth, and Yvonne Littlefield and Roger Campbell placed eighth. According to Marilyn, she and Larry did not have a great beginning in the free dance: "Everyone tells me I walked onto the ice with my guards on and fell, but I don't remember it. When they announced our names to perform we looked at each other and it was like everything went totally out of our minds. Danny saw the look in our eyes; he just knew that we were scared to death. We were now a member of the elite, competing against these awesome champions. But Danny had prepared us well, the training took over, and we did our job."[35]

The championships were a resounding success. The competition was broadcast on Canadian television for the first time, and the crowd was standing room only on the final night. At the awards banquet, International Skating Union (ISU) official Walter Powell passed out the Radix pins to the three medalists in each event. After World War II, Harry Radix, a long-time USFSA and USOC official, had produced blade-shaped pins to give to U.S. and World champions as mementos of their accomplishments. For the first time, the Canadians had trumped the Americans. The host country won one gold and three silvers, while the Americans won only two ladies' medals, the fewest medals in seven years.[36]

At the conclusion of the meet, many American skaters retired. Two members of the U.S. skating delegation, however, were definitely not retiring. Walter Powell, eighty, the first and longest-serving American official in the ISU, had been a regular at Worlds for nearly fifteen years. On the other end, Roger Campbell, seventeen, had just experienced his first World Championships, and was poised for a long competitive career.

ROGER CAMPBELL

1960 WORLD TEAM MEMBER

MRS. ANN CAMPBELL

"Skating mothers can be a real psycho breed," one skater declared, and Ann Campbell was one such domineering skating mother who vociferously

*Roger Campbell with Yvonne
Littlefield, Arctic Blades
Figure Skating Club, 1960
U.S. Dance Bronze Medalists.
Source: Photo by Bill Udell,
Courtesy of Yvonne Littlefield
Nicks.*

defended her son's interests. Contradictorily, she was both loud and invisible. Although accessible to a lot of people, she rarely let anyone get close to her. Few knew her well and many did not remember her presence at all.[37]

Ann Bromloc Campbell was born on June 9, 1905. She and her husband, Alexander, were married in 1933 when she was twenty-eight and he was twenty-six. They waited nine years for their only child. On August 15, 1942, Roger Hunter Campbell was born in Portland, Oregon. Some skaters suspected he was adopted because he didn't look like his parents. Ann was vague about the circumstances surrounding his birth, fueling speculation that he was not her biological child.[38]

Roger discovered skating when the Campbells moved to California in the early fifties. They lived at 6724 Tujunga Avenue in North Hollywood, where Al managed the North Hollywood Manor apartments. Roger began skating in 1956 at age thirteen and joined the Los Angeles Figure Skating Club (LAFSC) at the nearby Polar Palace, part of the Paramount Studio lot on the corner of Van Ness and Melrose. Under coach Mabel Fairbanks, he trained in singles; but he didn't enjoy figures and free skating didn't come easy to him. In 1957 he gravitated toward dance and began passing tests. His first big competitive win was in 1958 when he placed second in bronze dance at California State with Anna Marie Hansen. A month later, they placed fifth at Pacific Coast.[39]

Diane ("Dee Dee") Sherbloom and Ray Chenson won both of these competitions. When Ray retired to attend college, Dee Dee began dancing with Roger, and they trained with Bert Wright, who had just won the 1958 U.S. gold dance title. Roger and Dee Dee quickly became a creditable dance team. That winter they placed second in silver dance at the 1959 Southwest Pacific competition. Weeks later they became the Pacific Coast champions. Within six months of dancing together, they were on their way to Rochester, New York, for the 1959 U.S. Championships.[40]

In Rochester they placed fourth in the compulsory dances. In an event where the final placement between the compulsories and the free dance rarely changed, Roger and Dee Dee moved up to second place. They received two firsts, two thirds, and a sixth, squeaking past Bob and Pat Dineen for the silver medal. The Dineens dropped from first to third, and Larry Pierce and Marilyn Meeker pulled up from second place to win.[41]

Roger and Dee Dee made a good partnership. Both sixteen, they had made an auspicious debut at their first national competitive appearance. However, at Dee Dee's request, they parted ways after the competitive season. Roger passed his pre-gold dance test that summer and looked for a new partner.[42]

Roger was going through a transition off the ice as well. He had attended the Hollywood Professional School, but his parents decided he needed more time for skating. He left the school without graduating, took correspondence courses, and studied interior decorating at night school. He was also interested in costume design; and at the rink, he often designed and sketched costumes.[43]

Roger got along well with the adult dancers. He was a popular partner because he was tall and talented. He and other top dancers were kind and helpful to the younger kids. "They were gods to me and I looked up to them," recalled young Billy Chapel. "They were so nice to me and I was just this up-and-coming kid." Another skater added: "Although Roger was four years older than me, we were friends. We would cruise around and talk about life, but his main passion was skating."[44]

Roger, though a good-looking guy, had a hard time socially. He mingled with single skaters his age and occasionally went with them to restaurants, but he often kept to himself. He was aware of figure skaters' disdain and lack of respect for dancers. They thought ice dancing was for old folks and didn't appreciate the restrictions in dance sessions. Single skaters retaliated. When dancers skated in public sessions, skaters earned a point if they "acci-

Ann Campbell. Source: Sketch by Carol Shelley Xanthos.

dentally" tripped a dancer or knocked him over. If Roger wasn't always friendly, the other skaters probably deserved it.[45]

Roger was teased a fair amount by both boys and girls. His manner was sometimes effeminate. "I personally used to tease him unmercifully; it was terrible," one female skater confessed. "In retrospect he was such a cool dresser and an all-around nice guy who got along with everybody. I finally realized he heard all of these comments people said about him, so I laid off his case." Roger was not part of the group of guys that hung out together.[46]

Skating officials told Roger to tone down his ostentatious presentation on the ice. Friends tried to help Roger fit in. "I knew Roger from the first day he got on the ice," an LAFSC member said. "I knew what the USFSA expected of skaters and I tried to shape him up. He was definitely talented. He had clever feet and that translated into being a champion."[47]

Roger's happiness was Ann Campbell's priority. Her husband was supportive of Roger's skating but was rarely at the rink; Ann's hovering presence caused the skaters to call Roger a "mama's boy." It was a vicious cycle; the more he was teased, the more aggressive she became. Ann "wanted her son to succeed at all costs," one skater said. She was a strong woman who openly expressed her opinion to skaters, other skating mothers, and officials. Her tirades were legendary.[48]

Roger considered turning professional. He tried out for one of the touring ice shows, but in those days joining a show for even one day would have terminated any competitive opportunities. Roger had already learned this lesson the hard way. Several years earlier, the USFSA had disqualified him from competing. His exact infraction is not clear, but it could have been performing in a show or an event not sanctioned by the USFSA, or receiving monetary compensation for skating. The USFSA later reversed his status at a U.S. governing council meeting, announcing the "reinstatement of Roger Campbell, LAFSC to full amateur status." Family and coaches persuaded Roger, sixteen, that his future was still in the competitive ranks.[49]

Besides passing dance tests, Roger had passed his second figure and silver pair test. Bill Kipp coached him and his new pair partner, Anita Entrikin. They competed in a few local events. Anita enjoyed working with Roger because he was fun and always focused. Whether practicing pairs or dance, Roger "was so intense," a club member said. "I've never seen anyone concentrate like that—every second on the ice was gold to him."[50]

Roger tried out different dance partners in 1959. In early spring he and Yvonne Littlefield won several medals in local competitions, both in dance and pairs. In the early summer he competed with Dona Lee Carrier, a recent transplant from the East Coast, also in dance and pairs. At the Southern California Inter-Club competition, they placed third, while Yvonne and partner Roland Junso won the gold dance. By the end of the summer, Roger decided to dance with fourteen-year-old Yvonne Littlefield. Yvonne had begun skating in Pasadena when she was young; and with her mother's encouragement, she skated singles, pairs, and dance. When she teamed up with Roger, the ice dancing became time consuming and her single skating waned.[51]

Roger and Yvonne trained with Bert Wright at Polar Palace. They were long-time LAFSC members but switched home clubs to Arctic Blades FSC because, as Yvonne pointed out, it was "a good club to be with if you wanted the support of the judges." The judges definitely liked the new partnership. Yvonne and Roger placed second in gold dance at both the 1960 Southwest Pacific and Pacific Coast. Roger's previous partner, Diane Sherbloom, placed seventh with Howie Harrold.[52]

At the U.S. Championships in Seattle, Roger and Yvonne were fourth in compulsories and after the free dance pulled up to third place. They won a spot on the 1960 World Team and drove up to Vancouver for the 1960 World Championships, where they landed in eighth place. They stayed in Vancouver long enough to pass the CFSA silver dance tests, and then returned to Los Angeles. Yvonne felt lucky to have teamed up with Roger. It was a coup to make the World Team at age fourteen.[53]

Off the ice, both skaters had to deal with each other's mothers, both strong and unbending personalities. At least one positive aspect of their partnership on the ice was that, while they were skating, Roger and Yvonne were free from both mothers. They enjoyed a great partnership: Yvonne was still maturing as a dancer; and Roger, talented and serious, was an excellent role model.[54]

Roger spent his days at the rink, attended night classes at North Hollywood High, and looked forward to the 1961 competitive season with Yvonne. Former U.S. Dance champion Sharon McKenzie was optimistic about his future: "Roger was a skater; that was his world. He was a fun-loving soul and was an up-and-comer, no doubt about it."[55]

WALTER S. POWELL
ISU REFEREE

Diminutive and dapper, Walter Powell was an affable gentleman who used his time, energy, and wealth to benefit American skaters. Described as a great-grandfatherly figure, white-haired Powell looked a lot like Kris Kringle. He was unassuming and generous with his resources. Although never a competitive skater himself, he became the highest-ranking American skating official in the world. Without children of his own, Powell was a father figure to all the U.S. World Teams and their chief promoter.[56]

Walter was born in Philadelphia in 1879. He was a vaudeville performer as a youngster but as an adult became a successful executive in the shoe industry. He went to work for the Moench Tanning Company in Gowanda, New York, before Brown Shoe bought it in 1926. He moved to St. Louis in the mid-1920s as Brown's manager of tanneries and a member of its board of directors. He left the shoe industry in 1951 at age seventy-two.[57]

Powell's move to the Midwest coincided with the formation of the St. Louis Skating Club (SC). Although he was fifty-six, Powell represented Holland in the Parade of Nations number for its first show in 1935. His foursome included Helen Lamb, who became a close friend. He eventually became the club's president.[58]

The Winter Garden, located on DeBaliviere Place between Delmar Boulevard and Forest Park, became Walter's home away from home. Built as a jai-alai arena, then utilized at the 1904 St. Louis World's Fair, the building was converted to an ice rink in 1916. A large mural featuring skaters on ice-covered lakes among snowy hills adorned three sides of the rink. For as long as any skater could remember, Walter was "old," but his elderly status did not prevent him from taking lessons and dancing with skaters half his age. As the dance sessions ended, either the man pivoted as his partner did a spiral, or all the dancers formed a chain and executed a "shoot the duck" down the length of the rink.[59]

Everyone liked Walter Powell. "He was the sweetest man in the world," a young coach exclaimed. He was known as a kind and caring judge throughout the Midwest. He helped start the Midwestern sectional competition, first held in St. Louis in 1933. Helen Lamb said Walter never uttered an unkind word about any skater or official. He quietly funded the training of several St. Louis skaters, including Ollie Haupt Jr. and Red Knoll, and mentored many local skaters. "Mr. Powell took me under his wing and advised my parents where to send me for summer training and which direction I should take in the sport," skater Helen Geekie said. "He was very generous with his time."[60]

The USFSA executives soon noticed Walter Powell's leadership skills and passion for skating, and invited him to join the USFSA board. He was second vice president in 1937, first vice president in 1940, and president from 1943 to 1946. He introduced uniform judging standards and programs to educate judges and skaters. He promoted summer skating schools, judging schools, dance conferences, and carnivals. He advocated strong public relations to encourage and promote the public's interest in figure skating, both as recreation and as an amateur competitive sport.[61]

Throughout World War II, national competitions continued except for the senior men's division in 1944 and 1945. During that time, Walter kept track of male skaters serving in the armed forces, as Austin Holt noted: "I had corresponded with Walter Powell, and when I returned he was instrumental in appointing me to go to Worlds." The 1946 junior men's champion, Dick Button, was ecstatic when Powell called him in 1947: "He told me I was invited to skate in the World Championships in Stockholm. It was the most exciting telephone call I ever had. Mr. Powell was always very personable and a great gentleman." During his presidential tenure, Powell visited many skating centers, especially if St. Louis-based skaters were training away from home.[62]

In 1947 Powell was appointed the first U.S. representative for the internationally based skating association, located in Davos, Switzerland. This organization's name had evolved from Internationale Eislauf-Verein to the International Skating Union (ISU). The ISU, which formulated the rules that governed all international figure skating and its competitions, was dormant during the war years. When Walter joined the organization, preparations for World competitions and the 1948 Olympics were already under way.[63]

Walter Powell, St. Louis Skating Club, ISU Referee. Source: World Figure Skating Museum.

Within the ISU, Walter became the spokesperson for both the USFSA and CFSA. His responsibilities took him to meetings and competitions in all the major European cities, and he often paid his own way. Walter formed a bond with his fellow international representatives at the 22nd ISU Congress in Oslo in 1947, as he noted: "Active contact with the fine men who lead our sport in these widespread countries, alert men of keen and upstanding personalities, provides real and lasting inspiration."[64]

Walter was elected to the membership council and soon proposed that his personal passion—ice dancing—be included in international competitions. His dream was realized five years later when ice dancing made its debut at the 1952 Worlds. The seeds he planted for Olympic inclusion took decades to germinate. At Walter's first congress, the delegates evaluated judging methods. No changes were made, but judging would be debated for many decades. During the fifties, Walter crisscrossed the United States, participating in judges' schools and judging at Nationals.[65]

On December 25, 1951, Powell married his long-time friend Helen K. Lamb in St. Louis. Walter and Helen had known each other for decades through their mutual love of skating. Helen did not spend as much time at the rink as Walter as she was the head surgical nurse at the Barnes Hospital. Walter's first wife had been committed to an institution many years before for causes unknown to his skating friends. After she passed away, Walter and Helen were married.[66]

judging, Walter was elected as an international referee. After ;, Walter was soon back on the road as a referee for the 1952 mpics in Oslo. His stature in figure skating rose higher when he was elected to the Board of Directors of the United States Olympic Association in 1954. He spearheaded U.S. figure skating involvement in both the 1956 and 1960 Winter Olympics.[67]

As the 1956 Olympics approached, Walter thought the U.S. skaters should have their own team practice uniform. He enlisted the help of former skater Shelia Muldowny who had her own sportswear label and was pleased with her design for the ladies: a navy blue wool leotard with a red and blue reversible skirt and a red and blue reversible hood. Helen usually stayed home when Walter traveled; but when he flew to Italy with the 1956 Olympic Team, Helen arrived later with a small company of USFSA officials and their wives.[68]

Sensing the Soviet Union's rising prominence in figure skating, Walter told the Soviet ISU delegate he would like to visit Moscow; a visit was arranged for him and Harry Radix. "We witnessed . . . a renaissance of figure skating in Russia," he said. "Bearing in mind the past great achievements of Russian Nationals in the field of athletics, music, ballet, etc., and witnessing their now seemingly renewed interest in our branch of the artistic sport, it seems to require no farseeing peep into the crystal ball to opine that before the present decade has passed we may be welcoming into our figure skating family a very creditable group of Soviet competitors." He took movies of Russian skaters and smuggled the films back to the United States. In St. Louis, he played the films for skating friends and said, "The United States better watch out for the Russians because they are coming up." Walter's remarks proved prophetic.[69]

Walter was well known, not only for his ISU executive skills, but also as an unofficial member of every U.S. World Team. Every year, no matter which American skaters constituted the World Team, Walter Powell was there. "He was quiet, soft-spoken, and just a delightful person," a team member said. Another added: "All of the skaters looked up to him and had a great deal of respect for him." The skaters learned from this veteran traveler. He always wore black shades over his eyes so he could sleep on the plane, and he traveled light, sometimes carrying his belongings in a large mesh bag. He always wore a dark chesterfield coat and a white silk men's scarf. His white hair was never out of place. He was elegant and classy.[70]

Powell was a great ambassador for the sport. He thoroughly enjoyed traveling and meeting people. Many people loved the glamour of figure skating, and Powell was one of them. He was young at heart, and he and the skaters thrived on each other's energy. The 1958 World Team performed behind the Iron Curtain for two weeks in the major capitals of Eastern Europe; they were the first American group into Hungary after the Hungarian uprising. "I believe Mr. Powell, with his international connections, had something to do with getting us in there and he probably spent some of his own money to make it happen," Claralynn Lewis said. He also helped skaters out in small ways. When Margaret Ann Graham ran out of cash after buying gifts for friends and family in Davos, Walter lent her money. "He was a very dear friend," Margaret said. "He would always say, 'Oh, look at the shoes you're wearing!' because he was in the shoe business."[71]

Walter and long-time friend Harry Radix helped finance each Olympic Team. "No one was more dedicated to a sport, and no one will ever know the amount of time and his own financial resources that he devoted to it," wrote skating historian Ben Wright. The degree to which he helped others is unknown; he chose to remain anonymous.[72]

The international skaters were aware of his sterling character. "Mr. Powell was very solid and one of the more upright officials within the USFSA," one Olympian said. In refereeing the 1960 Winter Olympics, he was fair with every skater. Canadian Bob Paul remembered Powell with great fondness because of a gaffe at the Olympics. He and Barbara Wagner had skated only one minute of their program when their record skipped two bars of music. The music system was primitive: a record player set up in the hockey penalty box. Taken aback, Bob and Barbara stopped skating. To their enormous relief, Powell interceded with the judges on their behalf. "Everything's fine. Don't you worry," he told them. "I just have to officially walk across the ice and talk to them and get the okay." The Canadians had a moment to catch their breath during Powell's leisurely walk. They started over from the beginning and actually skated much better the second time.[73]

As American skaters celebrated their 1960 Olympic victories, Walter was already planning for the future. He was on the 1964 U.S. Olympic Committee for the Winter Games in Innsbruck. He would be eighty-four when the international athletes gathered in the Tyrolean Alps, but he was in excellent health and had no plans to slow down. The Powells, celebrating their ninth wedding anniversary, had moved to a luxury top-floor apartment overlooking beautiful Forest Park in downtown St. Louis; they often entertained and were well known in St. Louis social circles. They were also patrons of the St. Louis Symphony—Helen's real passion—and were friends with other prominent society couples who also served on the St. Louis SC board.[74]

The Powells attended weekly club sessions at the Winter Garden. Walter enjoyed stroking around the rink, talking with everyone. Helen, more reserved, did not interact with others as much, but she was a source of encouragement for a few competitive skaters. Like her husband, Helen knew the dances and skated with younger partners, but she and Walter squabbled playfully whenever they danced together. One club member recalled how entertaining it was to "hear one of them say, 'You're not doing this right!'" Walter's close skating friends knew that he planned to leave his extraordinary wealth to U.S. figure skating. He had made a great deal of money during his working years but he was also frugal; over several decades, he had accumulated a significant fortune.[75]

Walter had been a staple of the St. Louis skating scene for more than thirty years, but Helen had family in Massachusetts and persuaded him to move to Boston. Living in Boston had its advantages; the city was the headquarters of the USFSA and Walter had many friends in The Skating Club of Boston. But before Walter and Helen could seriously plan a move, Walter had another major trip. At the ISU Congress in Baden-Baden, West Germany, in June 1960, the ISU would choose the location of the next World Championships. No matter where it was held or who would be named to the 1961 U.S. Team, it was a given that Walter Powell would be there.[76]

CHAPTER 11

SUMMER 1960

The day after the 1960 Worlds was over, the American skating community speculated who was in and who was out for the 1961 competitive season. Before any skaters announced their retirement, they basked in the glow of welcome-home celebrations. Carol Heiss enjoyed a ticker-tape parade in New York City. New York University, the borough of Queens, and the mayor of New York City hosted receptions in her honor. David Jenkins received a huge welcome at the Cleveland Airport, and the city of Cleveland and the Cleveland Figure Club honored him.[1]

The top three U.S. men all retired. David Jenkins joined Ice Follies, performed in the show for one year to pay for his school expenses, and then finished medical school. Tim Brown returned to the University of California, Berkeley, having earned four U.S. silver medals, one World bronze, and two World silver medals. After the Los Angeles Figure Skating Club threw a party for Robert Brewer, he hung up his skates, returned to college, and took a part-time job. Then he received a call from Maribel. "Everybody has dropped out and your figures are wonderful," she told him. "If you come back here and really train, you could be the next World champion." Brewer told her that finances were an issue. "I won't even charge you. You can stay at my house for free." Brewer appreciated Maribel's kind offer but wanted to get on with the rest of his life. He declined.[2]

In the ladies division, Carol Heiss was the only one who retired, and her personal life soon became public. Sixteen days after the 1960 Worlds, "the most interesting romance in the skating world" became official when Hayes Alan Jenkins and Carol Heiss announced their engagement. Carol had confided to friends that Hayes had teased her about competing in Vancouver, suggesting that she wanted to win one more gold medal than he did—Hayes won four World titles, Carol five. After an April wedding at the St. Thomas Episcopal Church in New York City, Carol signed a contract with 20th Century-Fox to make a motion picture in the fall. In the interim she moved to Akron, Ohio, where Hayes was a lawyer with B.F. Goodrich.[3]

The Arctic Blades Figure Skating Club hosted a reception for Barbara Roles upon her return home. In the spring of 1960, she turned nineteen, skated in a number of carnivals, and looked forward to competing the next year for the U.S. ladies title. As the Olympic bronze medalist, she was favored to inherit Carol's crown. Winchester High School gave Laurence Owen a special award in honor of her Olympic experience.[4]

Both the 1960 U.S. pairs and dance champions retired. Ron and Nancy Ludington skated in several ice carnivals before going their separate ways. Margie Ackles married that summer, and Chuck Phillips became an ice dancing coach.[5]

The senior skaters who remained competitive were anxious to learn the location of the 1961 World Championships, which the ISU would determine in June. There was a strong likelihood that the event would be awarded to a European city. The last three international competitions had been held in North America: the 1959 Worlds at the Broadmoor, the 1960 Olympics in Squaw Valley, and the 1960 Worlds in Vancouver. If the Worlds were held in Europe, it also meant that an exhibition tour would be scheduled in European cities following the competition. For many skaters, this alluring prospect alone was worth twelve months of grueling training.

H. Kendall ("Ken") Kelley was particularly aware of the comings-and-goings of the senior skaters. As the USFSA International Chairman, he was the American liaison for the 1961 World Championships. Kelley, a World War I veteran and graduate of Cornell and Harvard Business School, had started skating in 1936 when the Cleveland SC was organized. He became a World figure and dance judge and served as the USFSA president from 1952 to 1955. He was noted for being "ever patient and calm in the consideration of vexing problems," but those virtues would be tested as the plans for the 1961 Worlds became the most challenging ever.[6]

In the run-up to the 1961 Worlds, at least eighteen senior-level skaters left the field. They retired, dissolved their partnerships, or remained at the junior level. In the days when amateurs were not allowed to earn from their skating, finances were the primary reason athletes retired short of achieving their goals. The USFSA provided no financial assistance to skaters. Home clubs produced elaborate skating carnivals, sponsored midnight skating parties, and held other fundraising activities for competitors, but there was never enough money to go around.[7]

When the USFSA was organized in the early twenties, elite competitive figure skaters were from well-to-do East Coast families. By the fifties, Carol Heiss and the Jenkins brothers were the first champion skaters with middle-class backgrounds. Among the rising generation, financially secure upper-echelon skaters included only Dudley Richards and Gregory Kelley. Times had changed since the day when the majority of international skaters, like Dick Button and Tenley Albright, did not worry about skating expenses. The Jenkins brothers and Carol Heiss had been subsidized by the deep pockets of the clubs they represented. Other skaters depended on their families' sacrifices. Parents worked two jobs or mortgaged their homes. A few lucky skaters had a wealthy sponsor.

A competitor's expenses included four to six hours of ice time six days a week; four to eight private lessons a week; two pairs of skates for freestyle and figures; ballet classes; a dozen sets of practice clothing; two to four competitive outfits; show costumes; transportation, food, and dorm costs for summer training; recording costs for competitive programs; transportation, food, hotel costs, and entry fees for various competitions; and hotel costs and transportation to competitions for their coach. These annual costs ranged from three to five thousand dollars a year, which, for some families, was 20 to 30 percent of their annual income. Most of the potential 1961 World Team members, who were teenagers or college students, left the fiscal management in their parents' care as they faced their own trials and unexpected joys throughout the summer of 1960.

High atop the Iceland rink at Madison Square Garden, one skater's weight had rapidly advanced. Pat Dineen was tall and carried her baby well; for a long time most skaters did not know she was pregnant. As Pat's delivery date approached, the dancers looked out for her. They yelled, "Watch out, watch out! Here she comes!" No one wanted to trip her. Pat planned to skate until her due date, which concerned her coach. Sonya Klopfer pled with Bob Dineen to make Pat stop, but he said, "No, she's fine. Pat should keep skating if she wants to."[8]

When Pat started getting big, Bob borrowed his brother's car for dance practices and gave their friends a ride home. They invariably stopped at Howard Johnson's; and one night, Pat suddenly announced, "I think my water broke!" She was only eight months along. The group piled into the car and sped toward New York Hospital, where Robert Dineen Jr. was born on June 17, 1960. The baby was christened at St. Michael's Church, followed by a party at the New Yorker Hotel. Marilyn Grace was the godmother and Bob's brother, Ben, was the godfather.[9]

Pat was back on the ice a week after her delivery. The extra pounds flew off and she quickly returned to her beautiful shape. Pat's pre-birth exercise had helped to produce a healthy, adorable baby boy. Bobby slept in the daytime because his parents were up late at night. Pat sometimes brought the baby to the rink, and friends watched him as Pat and Bob danced.[10]

The Dineens had little money but they were passionate about skating, cherished their friends, and deeply loved their little boy. They occasionally worked odd jobs, but neither had a career. Bob had put his law ambitions on hold. They lived with his mother, Mary Dineen, who did a lot of babysitting and helped them with their expenses.[11]

Bob and Pat enhanced their training with additional coaching from new pro Ron Ludington, who had competed against them when he won the 1958 U.S. silver dance title with Judy Lamar. Ron taught in Norfolk, Connecticut, and a group of New York City dancers regularly drove up there. Ron helped the team with their presentation, improved their free dance routine, and introduced them to a healthier diet—goodbye, Howard Johnson's.[12]

Training with a baby was not easy, but the Dineens were committed to their goal of joining the World Team. Their strength as dancers had always been their deep mutual love, now intensified by the birth of their son. Their free dance routine, set to the Jule Styne/Sammy Cahn tune "It's Been a Long, Long Time," reflected their long quest for a national title and their unusual romance.[13]

Larry Pierce and Marilyn Meeker had been on the move since Worlds. After a brief trip to Los Angeles, Larry completed his annual hitch with the U.S. Marine Corps at Camp Lejeune in North Carolina. Back in Indianapolis, they quickly passed their gold dance and gold free dance tests before the Coliseum closed for the summer. Then Larry, Marilyn, and the Ryan family packed up their belongings for another Lake Placid summer.[14]

In the summer of 1960, Larry Pierce fell hard for Sally Schantz, a seventeen-year-old dancer from Buffalo who was ice dancing with Bob Munz. "Larry talked to me about Sally," Bob said. "He wanted to know who she was." Larry and Sally had fun together, as she noted: "On Sundays we went water skiing or to the movie theater on Main Street. There were plenty of parties but we were there to skate and train and that was mainly what we did." The skaters noticed a dramatic change in Larry, who instead of pulling pranks, left little notes for Sally on the barrier of the rink as she skated her patch. He also buckled down in his training with Marilyn as they worked with Danny to improve their set dances and expand their free dance repertoire, which included several unique upside-down moves. "We were in the era of long, low deep edges, and the Blues and the Argentine Tango became our best dances," Marilyn said.[15]

Danny and Rose Anne Ryan were happy to be back at their Lake Placid home. Several of their Indianapolis students lived with them and doubled as babysitters for their growing family. Rose Anne continued to teach although she was pregnant again; a fifth child was due in January. That summer Danny bought a boat for water skiing. Having fun was just as important as guiding his students to winning championships—and win they did. Marilyn and Larry cleaned up at the Lake Placid Summer Dance Championships, winning three events.[16]

In Boston, Bradley Lord still smarted from the outcome of Nationals. "Brad's main struggle with the sport was when he was nosed out of a placement because of judges, which he considered unfair," brother Bruce said. Bradley felt that politics was at play, but he realized that he should be diplomatic about the situation. His ultimate goal, beyond competing at the 1964 Olympics, was to star in Ice Follies. Bradley had a verbal agreement with Eddie Shipstad to join the show when his competitive days were over. He secretly wanted to replace Richard Dwyer as Mr. Debonair; dressed in white tie and tails, Dwyer brought a bouquet of roses to a lucky "grandmotherly type" sitting in the front row at the beginning of his number. Ice Follies treated the Lords to front-row seats whenever they were in Boston, and Dwyer always brought the flowers to Alfreda Lord.[17]

Richard Dwyer, the Dick Clark of the skating world, was still young and had no plans to retire. "I kept thinking I should quit and become a lawyer, but I just kept skating, and it seemed like it was meant to be," he said. The longevity of a skater was usually limited, but Dwyer skated in professional shows for over forty years. "I knew Bradley liked my style and how I handled my career; that was a great compliment. I'm sure the show would have grabbed him, and who knows what would have happened?"[18]

Brad returned to East Lansing for the summer and practiced seven hours a day. If he made the 1961 World Team, his Canadian friend, Don Jackson, who also trained at East Lansing, would be his chief competition. Don, the Olympic bronze medalist, was a skilled jumper and executed several triples—a jump Bradley had yet to master. Only one young American skater in East Lansing had a triple jump; Doug Ramsay had mastered a triple salchow and a triple toe loop.[19]

After winning the 1960 junior title, Doug's visibility increased. "I had a huge crush on him," said Jan Serafine, then ten. "The world rotated around Doug Ramsay in my eyes." Doug dated Joanne Heckert that summer and gave her a bracelet for her birthday. "Doug was a really fun kid," Joanne said. "He was so unpretentious that I didn't realize how good he was."[20]

Back in Detroit, Doug began his junior year at Redford High School, with plans to attend Michigan State University. He was dedicated to school and his training at Detroit Skating Club and the Swallender Ice Center. Doug's coach, Bill Swallender, had gone through his own metamorphosis by dieting away nearly fifty pounds.[21]

Edi Scholdan flew to San Francisco, helped polish the new Ice Follies show, and saw David Jenkins briefly; it was the first time in eight years that Edi would not be coaching him. Edi's long winning streak with his male students had included Jimmy Grogan, Hayes Jenkins, David Jenkins, Ronnie Robertson, and Tim Brown; next in line was Gregory Kelley, with whom Edi worked well. Greg, who had a commanding presence on the ice, was an inspiration to the other club members. "He had great speed and just owned the ice," Christy Haigler said.[22]

Edi put many of his promising pupils into a half-hour group class with Greg and Steffi Westerfeld, who analyzed their jumps. Greg was earnest and resolute when training; he could be light-hearted and joke around with the other kids, but the constant presence of his older sister, Nathalie, limited his socialization. Greg, who had taken college prep classes at his Catholic high school, was now homeschooled and thrived academically thanks to his sister's skills. Nathalie also tutored other skaters.[23]

During the summer of 1960, Cupid's arrow struck its two premier skaters. Through training together, Greg and Steffi became close friends. Steffi had been chosen Homecoming Queen by the nearby all-boys school, Fountain Valley, and had many admirers at the rink; but club members soon realized she was very fond of Greg.[24]

The two had an inside advantage over other senior competitors. The 1961 U.S. Championships were slated for the Broadmoor—the rink Steffi had trained in for over a dozen years. She told the *Denver Post*, "If nothing unforeseen happens, I'll skate toward the 1964 Olympics. I'd love to win the Olympic medal." She was a conscientious worker, but the younger competitive skaters inadvertently hampered her training by seeking her counsel. When they had difficulties, Steffi would invariably say, "Let me take a look at it." She mentored many students, as Christy Haigler noted: "We'd say, 'Steffi can you watch my axel and tell me what I'm doing wrong?' She would give, give, give, and finally she wasn't working anymore. So then we'd have the big lecture from Edi, and he told us we could not ask Steffi to watch us anymore. There was a positive working environment at the Broadmoor and a very good spirit between Steffi, Greg, and Edi."[25]

Steffi took her ice time seriously because she understood its value. Her mother was always well dressed, and their apartment complex was one of the best in the area, but money was tight. Otto and Myra Westerfeld were divorced, and Otto had married Joan, a woman who was not much older than Sherri, who had just given birth that summer to Otto Jr. The family received some financial support from Otto, but it wasn't enough. Sherri had worked at Bryan & Scott Jewelers since 1956 to help with Steffi's skating expenses. That summer, Ice Follies offered Sherri a choreographer's position, but she put that opportunity on hold to help Steffi make the World Team. Broadmoor club members became the Westerfelds' surrogate family. "Steffi and Sherri regarded my dad as their father and the Westerfelds came to our home for dinners and parties all the time," skater Skip Mullins said.[26]

Greg and Steffi were the stars of the Broadmoor Ice Revue along with guest star Barbara Roles. After the show, the cast enjoyed a steak dinner in Fishers Canyon, entertainment by a local orchestra, and an old-fashioned sing-along. Throughout the summer, Greg and Steffi kept each other focused and confided in one another. In the middle of the summer, the site for the 1961 Worlds had been announced: Prague. Greg and Steffi couldn't believe the chosen location and dreamed of flying there together—hopefully as the 1961 U.S. men's and ladies champion.[27]

The location for the 1961 World Championships was hot news. The ISU Congress meeting in Baden-Baden narrowed the pool of potential host cities to Vienna, Prague, Bratislava, and Budapest. The four cities were near each other, and three were under Soviet control. After weighing many factors, the ISU awarded the location to Prague in Czechoslovakia. Great Britain had applied for and was provisionally awarded the 1962 World Championships.[28]

The Worlds had been held once before in Prague—in 1939 on the eve of World War II. But 1961 was the height of the Cold War. Going to a Communist country was a surprise. The young American skaters realized that going behind the Iron Curtain might be the chance of a lifetime. But for one Canadian pair team, this location was the worst news imaginable. Otto and Maria Jelinek, the 1960 World silver medalists, had begun skating at six and four in Prague, their hometown. Born into a family of wealth and privilege, they lived in an ancient stone mansion with huge windows that overlooked the Old Town. Their palatial home included sweeping staircases, crystal chandeliers, vaulted ceilings, parquet floors, stone fireplaces, multiple vast bedrooms, a magnificent library, an enormous kitchen, pantries, wine cellar, a playroom, and a gymnasium.[29]

Their father was part of the Czech resistance during World War II, and the family had endured many harrowing episodes with the Gestapo. After the war, the Communist regime was equally terrifying. In 1948 the family left their ancestral home and tremendous wealth, escaped to Switzerland, and settled in Oakville, north of Toronto. Otto and Maria resumed their skating and became Canada's second-place pair team. Having won one bronze and two silver World medals over the previous four years, they were the top pick for the 1961 World pairs title.[30]

When Prague was announced as the site for the 1961 Worlds, their father was firm: "It is unthinkable. You are not going!" Otto and Maria were devastated. Henry Jelinek consulted the Minister of Foreign Affairs in Ottawa who warned him not to send his children to Czechoslovakia. Although they considered themselves Canadians, the Czechoslovak regime considered them to be still Czechoslovak citizens. The Canadian government would be powerless should the Czech government decide to arrest them. Canadian officials said the only way out would be if the Communist government released Maria and Otto from their Czechoslovakian citizenship.[31]

Such an event in the middle of the Cold War was highly unlikely. The Communists' propaganda machine declared that no one would willingly leave their country, and they did not welcome visitors like the expatriate Jelineks, who were well known by the Czech people. The ISU, CFSA, and USFSA threatened to choose a different site if the citizenship issue was not resolved favorably. The Jelineks, who had trained in Lake Placid and East Lansing, also had many American friends. Otto and Maria continued to train the summer of 1960 and prayed for a miracle.[32]

Pacific Coast clubs anticipated a strong presence on the 1961 World Team after securing half the spots on the 1960 World Team. In Seattle, the Hadley parents coached at three different rinks, but their children were their primary focus. "Linda was so busy with Ila Ray and Ray and a few other kids that she didn't care so much about the rest of us," a student lamented. Linda was unrelenting in pushing her kids to their limit. However, they were starting to push back. Ila Ray was almost eighteen, and Ray was almost seventeen. They were old enough to spread their wings and had begun to resist Linda's tight control.[33]

School had become a refuge for the youngsters. Ila Ray excelled at Roosevelt High School but didn't graduate with her class because she had taken the fall semester off to train for the Olympics. She attended summer school and officially graduated in August. Ray was not a gifted student like his sister and sometimes struggled, but what he lacked in brains he made up in charisma, as Linda Landin noted: "He had girlfriends all over the place at school. He used to give them some of his medals, because it was all he had." Ray seemed debonair because he had traveled all over the country, had been to Paris, and had girls writing to him regularly. "He was to die for. The girls were drooling all over him," a female skater said.[34]

Ila Ray wasn't a flirt like her brother; but during the 1960 Nationals and Worlds, she had developed a crush. Friends said it was on the "ice dancer who wore glasses." It's easy to see why Ila Ray was attracted to Larry Pierce—a funny, charming man, who was probably unaware of her admiration. Back in Seattle, ice dancer Bill Wilkins had just started dating Ila Ray. His dance partner, Diane Anderson, dated Ray Ellis and they double dated frequently, going bowling, to the movies, or roller skating.[35]

After a highly controlled childhood, Ila Ray began to explore other interests. She interviewed skaters for her club's newspaper, *The Skating Blade*, and blossomed as a reporter. Ray and Ila Ray spent the summer trying to exert their independence. "They stuck together because they had to wrangle things to help each other out," a friend said.[36]

Other Washingtonians trained outside of the state. Judianne and Jerry Fotheringill and Karen Howland spent the summer in Sun Valley. They were the featured skaters, along with Chicagoans Ron and Vivian Joseph, in nine weekly carnivals. In California, Tim Brown had supposedly retired but he was still skating in Berkeley, passing his ISU bronze and silver dance tests that summer.[37]

Laurie Hickox was planning to compete in singles, but she sorely missed Bill, who left before the end of the school year. "They brought the plebes in early and put them through this awful hazing, but he did not seem depressed about it," girlfriend Anne Frazier said. "Attending the Air Force Academy was something he really wanted to do and he was committed; he had no intention of returning to skating."[38]

Without Bill to focus on, Mrs. Hickox turned to Laurie. When Elinor discovered that another skater was using Laurie's music for her program, George Gershwin's "Rhapsody in Blue," she raised a ruckus. She was also upset when Laurie didn't prepare for her fourth figure test. Laurie did just enough to get by and luckily passed.[39]

Laurie had her own issues over the summer of 1960. She made friends with men who were much too old for her and became obsessed over a John Huston film called *The Unforgiven,* starring Audrey Hepburn and Burt Lancaster. Audrey played a Native American who had been adopted by a white family; in the course of the movie she learns her ethnic background. "We saw that movie four or five times," Anne Frazier said, "and it didn't occur to me at the time why she loved it." Laurie's curiosity about her own origins preoccupied her.[40]

In Paramount, California, Bill Kipp coached at Iceland for the first time in three summers. He initiated the first Iceland Summer Skating School and prepared his pupils—Rhode in particular—for the upcoming competitive season. Bill asked his close friend, coach Dory Ann Sweet, to work with Rhode on her musicality. Dory chose Bernie Wayne's "The Man and His Music" for her new competitive program. The music was powerful, up tempo, and fast; it was pure Rhode.[41]

Rhode was maturing a bit, and she and Bill were closer than ever; but her quirky personality stayed the same. "A couple of times we stopped at this same restaurant," a friend recalled, "and she always ordered the same thing: bacon, eggs, hash browns, and pancakes. She mixed them all together before she ate. I couldn't even look at her. It was so disgusting. I said, 'Rhode, what are you doing?' She replied, 'You know, it just saves wear and tear on my stomach. I have more important things to do.'" All Rhode could think of was making the 1961 World Team.[42]

Bill Kipp missed Lake Placid, but he had recently moved into a swanky new apartment with a blue-white swimming pool in Downey, just a ten-minute drive to Iceland. Bill helped mount the Iceland Revue, the climax of the summer season. Club president Deane McMinn coordinated the production, which starred Barbara Roles, Rhode Michelson, Roger Campbell, and Yvonne Littlefield.[43]

As an Olympic medalist, Barbara Roles had spent a busy spring traveling coast to coast with carnival engagements. She trained intensively in Pasadena with her coach Nancy Rush and at Iceland in Paramount. Barbara and Rhode, "The California Girls" as they were known, developed a friendly relationship and were direct competitors for the first time.[44]

<hr>

Maribel put more pressure on Laurence than ever before, and once again engaged other coaches to limit mother-daughter tensions. Laurence took lessons with Gus Lussi at Lake Placid and a few with Bud Wilson in Boston. He stood at the gate during her practice sessions; and even though Maribel was always nearby, she willingly turned the reins over to others. She'd do anything to help Laurence win.[45]

During the summer, Maribel, Laurence, and choreographer Tom McGinnis chose selections from Berlioz's "Symphony Fantastique" for Laurence's new program. Tom recalled: "The music was cutting edge for its time and her program was theatrical and a bit avant-garde. She was game to try anything." Tom helped Laurence design a unique dress which looked like a pleated, Venetian shade on the front, with the skirt coming up on the hips and a low skirt in the back, creating a tail in the back to make her "look like a little fish, traveling fast over the ice."[46]

Laurence had a new hurdle in her life. As a young girl, she was lean with long legs and never had to worry about her weight. However, she had evolved into a big-boned girl with broad shoulders and, at five foot six, was now taller than her mother. She watched her calories and avoided sweets. Whenever a *Sports Illustrated* writer contacted Laurence, she dieted until the appointment; after the interview she ate up again. Whenever the writer returned, she trimmed herself down.[47]

Laurence found a release from the pressures of skating in academics. During the summer, she took second prize in her town's Lincoln and Lee history essay contest, and Harvard awarded her a scholarship for an experimental language immersion program. For six weeks, she attended a daily four-hour French class, finishing this difficult intensive course with high honors.[48]

Her sister concentrated on studies, too. After missing school because of the Olympics, Worlds, and spring carnivals, Maribel Jr. caught up on her Boston University courses and emerged from her finals with honors. During the summer, she took two courses to reduce her schedule for the upcoming winter term.[49]

Little Maribel trained with Dudley every morning and in the evenings after his work at the Nordblom Company. Professionally he was a natural. He served a one-year apprenticeship and impressed upper management.

"Dudley's work ethic and dedication to the job at hand was outstanding," Roger Nordblom said. "He was disciplined and was good at everything to which he devoted himself. He was on track to become a huge success in the real estate business."[50]

After skating at the club, he did weight training at the local gym. Dudley was not a large man, and he was self-conscious about his ability to do the lifts. Despite his advanced age of twenty-eight, he had tremendous stamina and resolve. After his career in singles, Dudley had settled comfortably into his role as a pairs skater. "Pairs is more sociable," he told a reporter. "I've reached the point where I'm a sociable skater."[51]

On weekends, Dudley spent time with friends on Cape Cod; in town he spent more time off the ice with Little Maribel. Maribel had encouraged Dudley's friendship with her daughter, now a mature twenty. "Dudley treated her so nicely," a friend recalled. "He was so attentive and sweet, and Little Maribel felt safe with him." It was not a surprise that Dudley fell for his pair partner. "Everyone had a crush on Little Maribel," skater Ronna Goldblatt recalled. Most skaters knew that she and Dudley were close; but only a few were aware of a budding romance. When Ron and Nancy Ludington had visited Dudley in his Commonwealth Avenue apartment, which he shared with two former Harvard classmates, Little Maribel was there. However, Nancy was not surprised: "I knew she had a crush on him and they worked very hard at keeping it a private matter."[52]

Maribel Jr. had dated other skaters. One summer she dated a New Yorker who trained in Lynn. He was an Elvis Presley ringer with black hair. Not surprisingly, her mother was not too thrilled about him. Some people at the club thought she had a serious relationship with someone at Boston University. A few close friends were aware that she and Dudley were dating, but Little Maribel rarely volunteered information about her love life to others. Mama Maribel had yet to suffer over boy troubles from Laurence, who was sixteen and still only a flirt. Ever practical about her social life, she quipped: "When you have to get up at 5 A.M. who dates?"[53]

In an ice show in Rochester at the end of the summer, Laurence showed how much she had become like her mother. An orchestra performed from sheet music provided by the skaters. During rehearsal, the conductor led Laurence's music, but fifteen seconds into her number she stopped, saying "I'd like that tempo to be increased." The orchestra started again, and fifteen seconds later she stopped again. "No, that's not right." She did this four times. Finally the conductor said, "Laurence, come here. Here is the baton. Why don't you lead the orchestra?" That's exactly what she wanted. She led the entire piece at a frenzied pace, then handed the baton back to the conductor, and said, "Okay, do it just like that." When she finished conducting, the orchestra gave her a standing ovation.[54]

Maribel Sr. was busy with her own projects. She spent the year writing her third book, *The Fun of Figure Skating*. The book included all of her family members: Dudley and Maribel Jr. appeared on the cover; Maribel Sr. and Laurence, along with students Joanna Niska, Robert Brewer, and Barlow Nelson, demonstrated techniques in photographs. The dedication included her late ex-husband. On the book jacket, she trumpeted that she had taught more than 4,000 pupils in her career.[55]

After training in Lynn and at Tabor Camp in Needham, the Owen family returned to The Skating Club of Boston. Mama Maribel hoped for at least one new national title. She was realistic about Laurence's chances of winning because she was up against Barbara Roles. With the Ludingtons retired, Dudley and Little Maribel were next in line for the U.S. pairs title. If they won, they would take possession of the trophy that listed Maribel Vinson's name six times. Maribel was optimistic that Little Maribel's name would be inscribed near hers.[56]

By the end of the summer, Karen Howland, Rhode Michelson, Bruce Heiss, and Scotty Allen had passed their eighth test in figures and freestyle; however eleven-year-old Scotty remained in junior men. Jerry and Judianne Fotheringill, Janet Harley, and Jim Browning achieved their gold medal in pairs, along with Ron and Vivian Joseph, who elected to stay in junior pairs another year. There were eight new gold dance medalists: Larry Pierce, Marilyn Meeker, Elva Traxler, Marshall Campbell, Jan Jacobson, Karen Howland, Yvonne Littlefield, and Dona Lee Carrier. Most, but not all, of these dancers had partners. Only a few months of fall training were left before the 1961 season began. The roster of senior competitors was seemingly set.[57]

When Tim Brown stepped back into the picture, he surprised the skating world. Tim had skated for over a dozen years. His father was in the military, so the family had moved often. Consequently, Tim had passed figure tests in Spokane, Washington, in the late forties, trained in Baltimore when he became the U.S. novice champion in 1952, and then moved to Los Angeles. Under the coaching of Eugene Mikeler, he became the 1954 U.S. junior champion. When Tim entered senior men's, Hayes Jenkins, Ronnie Robertson, and David Jenkins were the top three skaters in the world, and he had to wait until the champions retired.[58]

Tim was multi-talented. He played the piano well, spoke multiple languages, and was academically gifted, but he was best known as an eccentric. He would ride a motorcycle in the rain, with an umbrella, while reading a book. "He used to drive me to the rink in the morning in his convertible because my mother didn't want to take me," Barbara Roles recalled. "Driving with the top down he would say, 'Isn't this refreshing? It just wakes you up and gets you ready to skate.'"[59]

In the mid-fifties, Brown moved to Berkeley, entered the University of California, and trained with Gene Turner. In 1957 he moved to the Broadmoor to work with Edi Scholdan and attended Colorado College. He had to get straight A's because of his scholarship; he rarely went to class, but he was so smart he pulled it off. "Tim was always reading and was one of those super-genius, over-the-edge type people," a skater said. "Tim just did whatever." That attitude carried over to the ice; he choreographed his own programs and he made up footwork at the drop of a hat, sometimes in the middle of a competitive performance.[60]

Tim was superb in figures—they were precise and accurate. When he was fourteen, he told *Skating* that "the remedy for any fault in figures is practice . . . faithful practice." Beginning in 1957 Tim habitually won the senior men's figures at Nationals, but then David Jenkins overtook him in the freestyle. Tim was second fiddle to David Jenkins at the Broadmoor and was lax about arriving on time for practice. Christy Haigler recalled: "He would run into the rink because he was late for patch. He leapt onto the ice with his guards still on, followed by a big crash."[61]

Tim thought there would be some revelation in working with Edi, but it turns out Tim was the revelation. Edi thought his figures were wonderful and would bring David Jenkins over to see them. David noted that Tim looked at skating as an intellectual exercise: "He was a very smart guy and he would think about it. He didn't really train very hard but since he was my major competition I didn't mind. He was fine in figures and I really enjoyed his free skating. Tim did interesting footwork and choreography. His programs could go off the deep end or they could be quite interesting; I loved what he did with [Dvorak's] 'The New World Symphony.'"[62]

Tim was runner-up to David from 1957 to 1960 at the U.S. Championships, and runner-up to David at Worlds in 1957 and 1958. He went on the European tour after the 1958 Worlds in Paris, and was constantly on the verge of igniting an international riot. "We were the first people to go into Budapest after the Hungarian Revolution, and the country was still occupied by Soviet troops," Bobby Brewer said. "After we performed, Tim got into a fight with one of the Russian soldiers. We were told to return to the dressing rooms but Tim got mad because he was still signing autographs. I kept saying, 'You don't understand. He's got a gun!'"[63]

After deciding to compete in 1961, Tim trained a little with Gene Turner but primarily worked on his own at Berkeley's Iceland. Tim's reentry was terrible news for his competitors. Bradley Lord, who had been considered the front-runner, was no longer the favorite. In the fall of 1960, more changes and surprises lay in store.[64]

CHAPTER 12

FALL 1960

After daily six-hour workouts at summer sessions across the country, skaters returned home to the grind of fitting skating between the demands of school, homework, and work. The USFSA was also busy, preparing for the 1961 World Championships in Prague, Czechoslovakia. They arranged for the participation of U.S. officials, alerted potential World Team members of international travel requirements, and worked with the Czech organizing committee, which proved to be the most daunting task of all.

The USFSA filled a quota of international judges for every World competition, for which American skaters were always grateful. All international competitors felt that it was advantageous to have their own countrymen judge them. Nevertheless, American skaters often felt U.S. officials bent over backwards to be fair to all competitors, while judges from some countries seemed biased towards their own competitors.[1]

Arranging for American judges had been easy the previous few years, when the World Championships had primarily been held in North America. Prague was another matter. The city itself was not the problem; many judges would enjoy the chance to go behind the Iron Curtain. USFSA officials sent inquiries in March 1960 to potential judges for the 1961 Worlds. Margaret Ridgely of Baltimore and Mary Louise Wright of Boston were initially designated and were confirmed until the fall, when they both had a change of heart. Margaret felt that her career in real estate and insurance was too demanding to allow a trip abroad, and Mary Louise declined because her mother was ill, and she wanted to be with her for a scheduled surgery in February. The alternate, USFSA Secretary Colonel Harold B. Storke of Boston, wanted to go but had become seriously ill with a long-term condition.[2]

Other possible judges were unavailable. Deane McMinn had already accepted the assignment as 1961 World Team Manager and was not allowed to judge simultaneously. Harold Hartshorne was willing to judge, but he was a member of the ISU Dance Technical Committee, and as such he was not allowed to judge at international competitions. The ISU, aware of the USFSA's judging situation, authorized both Margareta Drake of Chicago and Edith Shoemaker of San Francisco to act as judges for the 1961 Worlds. However, Margareta already had a ninety-day round-the-world trip planned with her husband, so she declined; why Edith Shoemaker excused herself is unknown.[3]

In the meantime, the USFSA entertained a proposal from a British official who disapproved of holding the championships behind the Iron Curtain and proposed moving the meet to another location, possibly Davos. The USFSA briefly considered not sending a team if judges could not be found. The United States had enjoyed an incredible thirteen-year streak, winning seven ladies and twelve men's World titles, but International Chairman Ken Kelley feared that American dominance might be waning. In a letter to a U.S. official, he confessed, "I wish there were some way that you could fire the team with enthusiasm! I can just feel the hot breath of the European wolves thirsting for the blood of the Americans."[4]

By November, the USFSA had only one official to represent the United States abroad—the ever-devoted Walter Powell, serving as a referee. Harold Hartshorne had asked the ISU for a special exemption to judge in Prague but was refused. Hartshorne finally requested a release from his committee post so he could serve as a dance judge in Prague. Lacking other options, Ken Kelley, a World figure and dance judge, agreed to judge singles.[5]

The USFSA now had three officials and a team manager for the Prague competition. One more official, Eddie LeMaire, planned to travel with the team. LeMaire, a national judge from Rye, New York, was ostensibly a spectator; but in fact, the USFSA planned to promote Eddie to a World judge prior to the 1962 Worlds and had an understanding with him that he would observe the judging as orientation for what he would face the following year. There had been rumors of vote trading by international judges, and the USFSA wanted someone who would counter these corrupt practices.[6]

In November, nearly three dozen senior skaters received the long-awaited letters on USFSA letterhead announcing the upcoming competitive schedule: the 1961 Nationals at the Broadmoor the end of January, the North American Championships in Philadelphia the second weekend in February, and the departure date for Prague: February 14, 1961. The schedule provided for a week of training in Prague before the competition and a two-and-a-half-week post-World European exhibition tour. Unlike the expense of traveling to and from Europe on their own dime for most of the 1961 World Team members, the exhibition tour was a free ride, as host clubs and associations covered the expenses."[7]

The USFSA had solved its staffing problems, but the ISU was still having trouble ensuring safe passage for Otto and Maria Jelinek. The siblings had been naturalized Canadian citizens for twelve years, so the ISU made a formal request to cancel their Czechoslovakian citizenship. This move was necessary to prevent the possibility of arrest by Czechoslovakian authorities, but the Communist government had not budged. The Americans found the Czechoslovakians difficult to work with as well. There was constant communication between Ken Kelley in Cleveland, the USFSA offices in Boston, and the ISU headquarters in Davos. If these problems could not be resolved, Canadian and U.S. officials would put pressure on the ISU to move the location of the 1961 World Championships.[8]

When the European-chartered plane arrived in Colorado Springs for the 1957 Worlds, the large welcoming committee, including greeters dressed as cowboys, met the delegation. As ISU officials and the judges stepped off the plane first, the cowboys drew their guns and fired a few blanks in salute. From inside the plane, a skater exclaimed: "My God, they've shot the judges!" It was a small but significant token of the tensions. A love-hate relationship existed between judges and skaters, but the American officials going to Prague—Deane McMinn, Eddie LeMaire, and Harold Hartshorne—were popular and well respected and would admirably represent their country behind the Iron Curtain.[9]

DEANE MCMINN
1961 WORLD TEAM MANAGER

Deane McMinn was a prominent Pacific Coast USFSA official and an ambassador for skating. Although quiet and retiring, Deane was intelligent and well-liked. He devoted his life to figure skating.[10]

Deane Everett McMinn was born on November 28, 1916, the eldest of three children. His family moved from Nevada City, California, a town north of Sacramento, to Southern California in 1932 during his high school years. He graduated from Nathaniel Narbonne High School in Harbor City in 1934; activities included the basketball team, Spanish club, junior class treasurer, yearbook business manager, and dramatics. Deane graduated from the University of Kansas in marine engineering. During World War II, he enlisted in the Navy and served on PT boats in the South Pacific.[11]

Deane had begun skating in 1939 at age twenty-three and was a charter member of the Arctic Blades Figure Skating Club. He picked skating up

Deane McMinn, Arctic Blades Figure Skating Club, 1961 U.S. World Team Manager. Source: Courtesy of Janet McLeod.

again after World War II and became a regular at Iceland's Sunday night dance sessions with partner Elvira ("Betty") Sonnhalter. They also danced to live music from Truman Welch at the Wurlitzer organ every Monday night.[12]

At the advanced age of thirty-three, Deane passed his preliminary figure and bronze dance tests and focused on dance competition. In 1950, Deane and Betty competed in bronze dance and placed third at California State and second at the Pacific Coast competition. They won the bronze dance championships at both events the following year and moved up to silver dance, placing second at the 1952 Southern California Inter-Club competition. In 1953, they won the gold medal at the Inter-Club meet.[13]

Although Deane and Betty were on a winning streak, they retired after winning the gold, and Deane began judging. Within a few years, he had become an intermediate and silver dance judge. By 1957 he was selected to judge at Nationals. Betty Sonnhalter also became a judge and an Arctic Blades FSC officer. Deane was often her escort to parties and events.[14]

Deane was single, and most people thought he was a bachelor or widowed. He never discussed his marital status, so only a few close friends knew he was divorced from his wife Midge. When not judging, he enjoyed playing golf and tennis, swimming, and spending time with his niece and two nephews. The Treasury Department employed him as an accountant with the U.S. Coast Guard at Terminal Island. Outside his full-time work, he traveled frequently to all the western states to judge tests and conduct judging schools.[15]

Deane was a tough judge, mainly because he wanted to prepare West Coast skaters for national competition. He was soft-spoken but did not compromise his high standards. "Deane was a judge who liked to fail me," an L.A. skater ruefully recalled. "On my sixth test he failed me by 3/10ths of a point. In those days the judging had to be unanimous so I had to wait and take it again. I asked for the same three judges. This time Deane passed me and another judge failed me by 3/10ths of a point."[16]

Deane had the perfect temperament for judging. He wanted both to improve the sport and to support the skaters. Whether it was critiquing skaters or assuaging fears, he helped skaters in a non-threatening way. One young skater recalled that, when he refereed her event, "We were all scared and he held our hands as the judges held up the marks."[17]

Deane's ideas and methods were cutting edge within the USFSA, and the Arctic Blades FSC had the reputation of being progressive because of McMinn. For example, after competitions he critiqued skaters' performances and offered feedback. In a friendly way, he told them what he didn't like in their programs and offered suggestions for future competitions. The skaters accepted his advice and flocked to him because of his positive and open manner. For many years, judges and skaters had not communicated, but McMinn broke down these long-standing barriers.[18]

He was a skater's ally. After Jim Short won the 1958 U.S. junior title, he had to pass his seventh and eighth tests to compete in seniors the next year. When a test session was on the verge of being cancelled, Deane used his influence to ensure that judges showed up so Jim could qualify for the upcoming competitive season.[19]

Deane always had the best interests of Arctic Blades club members at heart, but he was fair and treated all skaters with respect. He rapidly became an elder statesman in the Los Angeles area, visible at every competition and many test sessions at every rink in the valley.[20]

Deane was active in the Southern California Inter-Club Association (SCICA), comprised of four local clubs. In *Skating* he championed interclub associations because they "tend greatly to bring the members closer together and create a feeling of goodwill." When the SCICA mounted the 1954 Nationals in Los Angeles, Deane was chairman of the event. After the competition, the USFSA nominated Deane to its executive committee. Over the years, he chaired the Rink Cooperation, Dance Judging, and Test Standards committees. In *Skating* he encouraged skaters to produce better figures:[21]

> The thought of spending many hours . . . in the monotony of figure practice is not appealing to anyone. The rinks are cold and unfriendly places [at]

these times. The confidence imparted to a skater through the knowledge that the figures in a test are mastered . . . will be evident in the results, and will prove to be of infinite value in combating the butterflies in the stomach, and the sponge-rubber knees that are prone to show up when appearing before the judges.[22]

At the 1959 USFSA Executive Committee meeting in Chicago, McMinn did an enormous favor for skaters nationwide. Until that time, the three judges had to be unanimous to pass a figure test with the result that many skaters ended up taking tests multiple times because of that rule. The executive committee approved Deane's proposal to change the figures test standards to a majority of a three-member panel.[23]

Money was tight for many top competitive skaters, and Deane encouraged clubs to help their members in higher-level competitions. "In order to arrive at the level of proficiency needed to compete under today's standards, a considerable sum of money must be expended for ice time, lessons, costumes, boots, blades, tests, etc. These expenses must be borne by the skater or parents of the skater. . . . This is the reason for the Club Competition Fund." Deane suggested a variety of ways to raise these funds, including club dues, shows, raffles, and other creative fund-raising events.[24]

McMinn played a pivotal role in the success of the Arctic Blades FSC at Frank Zamboni's Iceland in Paramount. As a board member, he had resurrected the Arctic Blades ice show in 1954, which had been suspended in 1949. In 1960 he served as president for the 200-member club.[25]

Deane also recruited new judges. If you asked any L.A.-based judge in the fifties how they started, the judge would say: "Deane McMinn was responsible for my going into judging." McMinn found candidates from all over Southern California and guided them into this society. "I give him one hundred percent credit for getting me started," judge Maggie Hosford said. He created a judges' school for adult skaters. Once a group of prospective judges judged a test that they had thought was a training exercise. Afterwards McMinn told the three judges that they had just judged a real test and reviewed their marks. The lucky skater passed.[26]

In the fifties, you could be a lower-test judge and also compete. Deane encouraged many young adults to join the judging ranks, as LAFSC judge Eleanor Curtis noted:

> The judging wasn't always good when I was skating so I thought I should do something about it. Young people were not involved in judging then but Deane was instrumental in putting us forward. When he was refereeing he would put me on panels. He just pushed and pushed and said we were exactly what skating needed. I was just eighteen at the time. He would constantly re-

assure us and say, "We need your type of judges and you should be doing this." He was a big reason why I became a judge. I just adored him.[27]

McMinn continued to rise in the judging ranks himself. The USFSA promoted him to a gold dance judge in 1957. Deanne regularly judged at Nationals and had recently judged all the senior events at the 1960 Nationals in Seattle. One of the thrills of his life occurred a month later when he judged at the 1960 Olympic Winter Games in Squaw Valley.[28]

Deane spent most of his free time at the rink, and he often socialized with club members. They had dinner together or went to a club member's home for dessert after dance sessions. Everyone enjoyed his company. "Deane's birthday was very close to mine," Maggie Hosford said. "I was much younger than Deane. When we first met we struck this deal; every year we celebrated I'd get a year older and he'd get a year younger. By 1960 we were both the same age."[29]

In October 1960, Arctic Blades club members surprised President McMinn with a reception. He had just returned from the USFSA Executive Committee meeting where he was nominated a World judge and named 1961 World Team Manager. The celebration included two large cakes decorated with a world motif. McMinn, forty-four, felt honored and excited to be named team manager. "He was so happy to have been chosen to go on this trip," said his mother, Pearle Sutherland. Only one thing could make his selection as team manager sweeter—if L.A.-based skaters were named to the 1961 World Team.[30]

EDDIE LEMAIRE
NATIONAL JUDGE

Eddie LeMaire's early skating pedigree was similar to that of Maribel Vinson Owen. His parents strapped skates on his feet as soon as he could walk. He had been a child vaudevillian skating star, regional speed skating champion, national roller skating champion, twice national figure skating champion, and a national figure skating judge. The USFSA counted on his fearlessness to ensure fairness in international judging.[31]

Edward LeMaire was born on October 26, 1924, to a well-known vaudeville skating pair, Francois Edward LeMaire from Salt Lake City and Maud Amelie Reynolds LeMaire from Chicago. She was a member of the famous Reynolds circus family. The LeMaires skated in ice shows across the country, including the Chicago World's Fair, the Texas Centennial Exposition, and countless nightclubs. Besides performing unique dances, Fran's

Eddie LeMaire, The Skating Club of New York, National Judge. Source: Courtesy of Diana LeMaire Squibb.

specialty was performing serpentines around candles. He also taught skating in New Haven, Providence, St. Louis, and New York.[32]

During his childhood, Eddie and his younger sister Patty criss-crossed the nation with their parents. By age four, Eddie was the darling of the family's vaudeville act. Wearing shorts, long socks, and a beret, he jumped over barrels on the ice. Eddie attended schools in Nova Scotia, Connecticut, Pennsylvania, Illinois, Indiana, Missouri, and Texas. When he was eight, he performed an exhibition between hockey games at the 1932 Winter Olympics in Lake Placid. An avid speed skater, he won his first race medal at age four and in time became Silver Skates Champion in New York City, Illinois Western Champion, Ozark Champion, and New England Champion in that sport.[33]

Eddie's parents settled in New York City in the thirties and Eddie began to take figure skating seriously. He regularly skated at the newly opened Rockefeller Center ice rink and was popular with the crowd. When he was fifteen, The Skating Club of New York (SCNY) invited him to join. Most of the club members were well-to-do, and one club member sponsored him, paying for his skating lessons, facilitating his acceptance into the Trinity School, and paying his educational expenses.[34]

Eddie trained with Willy Boeckl and also went to Philadelphia to train with Gus Lussi. At the 1940 Nationals, Eddie placed second in novice men.

In addition to his speed, he was known for his intricate footwork. He was a good spinner and had great flexibility. His style was smooth and effortless.[35]

He tried pairs, eventually clicking with partner Dorothy ("Dottie") Goos. Both were excellent singles skaters of about the same height. When a friend asked him how he could lift her, he confided that Dottie jumped so high all he had to do was grab her in the air and break her fall. They were the 1942 U.S. junior pairs champions. In 1943 they were U.S. senior pairs bronze medalists, and Eddie won the U.S. junior men's title.[36]

In 1942, Eddie launched a brief career as a roller skater as the result of a dare. Skating friend Bob Swenning bet Eddie he couldn't learn to roller skate, and Eddie boasted that he could. He bought a pair of roller skates, practiced for three weeks, competed in a roller skating championship, and won the senior men's gold medal.[37]

At Trinity School, Eddie was a well-rounded athlete, participating in baseball, basketball, volleyball, and tennis. He also captained his intramural water polo team. When he graduated in 1942, the school paper published his "last will and testament," which announced that, since he was leaving for Yale, "mothers of New York City could now let their daughters out of the house."[38]

Eddie soon had his eye on a new SCNY member: silk heiress Muriel Gerli. She was half-British, half-Italian, and "incredibly beautiful." A recent divorcee, she moved to New York and took up skating for exercise and diversion. While she was practicing her figures one day, "some idiot" kept jumping and spinning right in front of her. Muriel was incensed at the impertinence of this whirling dervish. A friend identified the smart aleck as Eddie LeMaire and commented that she thought they would make a good couple. Muriel's response was crisp: "Not a chance in hell."[39]

Then she attended a dinner party at which she found herself stuck between an elderly deaf man and Eddie LeMaire. By the end of the meal, the impish young man had charmed her and she had forgiven his obnoxious behavior at the rink. Still, her appraisal was, "No way." He was eighteen—six years her junior.[40]

Despite Eddie's plans to enter Yale, he enlisted in the Navy in 1943, ironically ending up at Yale as an aviation cadet in the V-5 program. He later was stationed at Cornell, New York; Chapel Hill, North Carolina; and Glenview, Illinois; for advanced training. His ultimate assignment was in Corpus Christi, Texas, as a Navy pilot. Ensign LeMaire "recorded the highest scores in Instrument Flying and in Navigation on record," said his granddaughter Wendy Howard, and was thus made an Instructor of Advanced Flying.[41]

Eddie and Muriel were married on June 23, 1945. After the war, they moved to Reno where Eddie pursued a degree at the Mackay School of Mines, at the University of Nevada. The LeMaires bought houses in Reno and Lake Tahoe, California, and invited New York friends to spend the summer with them. They went sailing and hunted out old mines. Eddie flew his guests to San Francisco and other destinations in the SNHJ-5 Navy plane that he had bought after the war.[42]

Son Richard was born in 1947, and daughters Dorinda and Diana followed in 1949 and 1950. The family moved back to New York in 1952 where Eddie first worked for the Crucible Steel Company, then joined the brokerage firm of Talmage and Company and became a member of the New York Stock Exchange. He switched companies twice more: first joining Osborne and Thurlow, then Adams and Peck in 1957.[43]

When his work on Wall Street stabilized and his children were old enough to skate, he took his daughters to the Playland ice rink in Rye every Saturday morning. "Daddy always put us on his shoulders," Diana recalled. "He'd go flying around the ice and he was so incredibly fast. I had a little pixie haircut and what little hair on I had on my head stood straight up in the air." He returned to the SCNY, skated in its ice carnivals, and kept up his other sports: skiing, golf, tennis, shooting, swimming, and sailing. A Naval Reserve pilot, he flew each year with his group.[44]

When his sister Patty performed in ice revues, Eddie became a judge and loved it immediately. He was made a national judge in just three years. Eddie was confident of his judging abilities because of his skating experience; in the early days, few judges on the national level had been competitive skaters. Eddie put a lot of time, energy, and effort into judging.[45]

His sense of humor influenced his judging career. He was extremely irreverent and wanted to shake up the staid judging world. Newbold Black, one of the youngest judges in that era, said, "He always had a laugh and always had something funny to say. He called it as he saw it as far as judging goes."[46]

Once when judging a men's event, Eddie gave the skater a 6.0 (the highest score). He then got called on the carpet by officials, who told him "Nobody's perfect." Eddie retorted: "Find me the mistake and I'll reverse it." The mark remained. Another time Eddie and Newbold were on the faculty of a judges' school. An audience member asked the panel what they liked and didn't like in the sport. Eddie, eschewing the solemn technical answers of the others, said, "Let me tell you one thing I really, really don't like—girls who wear yellow dresses when they free skate. I can't stand yellow dresses." After the meeting was over, someone asked him, "Why did you say that,

Eddie?" His playful reply was that he "just wanted to see what would happen. I bet nobody sees a yellow dress for five years." Eddie's prediction proved true.[47]

Judging took him away from home constantly, affecting his kids more than his wife. "He wasn't always there for Father's Day and he wasn't always at school for Parent's Day," Diana said. Years later, in evaluating his sacrifices, she realized how much he cared about judging. Without pay, he had given up professional time, family time, and personal time. His children accepted his passion for skating and cherished his moments at home. He was a wonderful father, partly because of his youthful verve.[48]

Eddie's admirers included the top skaters of the day. He was a fixture at the SCNY. World champions Tenley Albright and Carol Heiss were among his fans. "At dance sessions, we'd always do a couple of turns of his favorite dance, the rocker foxtrot," Carol said, "and he would talk about my program with Mr. Brunet, giving complimentary comments or suggesting constructive changes." Eddie made sure he was in Squaw Valley to support Carol for her greatest skating triumph.[49]

Eddie was confident, cocky, and free-spirited. He was always the life of the party, and his enthusiasm was contagious. His energetic outlook infused his brokerage business, his family life, and the world of skating. The USFSA thought his independence and toughness would help him withstand the influence of judges on the international circuit. Eddie looked forward to the new challenge.[50]

HAROLD HARTSHORNE
ISU DANCE JUDGE
LOUISE HARTSHORNE

Harold Hartshorne, born into wealth and privilege in turn-of-the-century New York, was a talented designer and yearned to be an architect, yet he followed in his father's footsteps and became a successful Wall Street broker. He excelled in sports and was drawn to dramatics. An avid photographer, he traveled the world constantly, documenting his own life with extensive diaries and photographs. When faced with an early tragedy, Harold turned to the thing that gave him the most pleasure—ice dancing.[51]

Harold Hartshorne (pronounced HEARTS-horn) was born in New York City on September 8, 1891, to James Mott Hartshorne III and Mary Shufelt Hartshorne. Harold's grandfather, James Mott Hartshorne II, created one of the first successful brokerage firms on Wall Street in 1865. His timely entrance into the market and his business acumen resulted in spectacular financial returns. Harold's father built on that success and retired at age thirty.[52]

Harold was raised in luxury, growing up in two side-by-side four-story buildings. Franklin D. Roosevelt's mother, Sara, liked the Hartshorne house so much that she asked her architect to design a house like theirs and built it across the street from them on East 65th Street, as a wedding present for Franklin and Eleanor. "There was an air of formality about Harold," grandson Tom said. "However there was more to Harold than his wealth. He represented honesty, concern, gravity, and devotion to family."[53]

The summer before Harold entered Princeton, he met the love of his life. His parents owned a home in Oconomowoc, just outside Milwaukee, and the family went there every summer. Back in New York, Harold's younger sister Eleanor rode her ponies in Central Park with school friend Marietta Chapin. Eleanor asked Marietta how she moved her ponies out to Lake Geneva, Wisconsin, every summer, and Marietta facilitated arrangements for Eleanor's horse to ride in the Chapin boxcar. Harold met Marietta when he picked up Eleanor's horse in Lake Geneva. The Hartshornes invited Marietta to Oconomowoc for the weekend, and a friendship began. Harold was eighteen and Marietta was fifteen.[54]

Harold entered Princeton in 1909 where he majored in English. He had an artistic bent and, interested in photography, liked being both behind and in front of the camera. For two years, he was the main photographer for the *Princeton Review*. Harold embraced all sports. He was a tennis champion, excelled in track, and played scrub hockey games on Carnegie Lake. With his speed he could have excelled in hockey; however, he spent more and more time on the ice as a skater. Grandson Tom attributes the eye that gave Harold his pleasure in photography as an influence on his skating: "He was aware of how he looked and was fascinated by the form that he cut on the ice. Hockey probably seemed less dramatic and less individualistic to him. In skating he was the ultimate focus."[55]

In the middle of his Princeton studies, Harold took a year off and made a round-the-world trip, stopping in most of the European capitals but also visiting Egypt, the Suez Canal, Ceylon, Burma, India, Siam, China, and Japan, photographing every step of his journey and filling four diaries. The Chapin family was also traveling in Europe, and Harold more than once would track their movements and "spontaneously" show up. Harold had fallen in love with Marietta Chapin.[56]

When Harold returned to Princeton, he indulged his other passion: theatre. He was president of the English Dramatic Association and was involved in every production his senior year. He might have pursued theatre professionally had it been more socially acceptable at the time. After graduation in 1914, Harold went to Europe for a brief vacation and was there when World War I erupted. Instead of going home he became an intelligence officer—his rank that of a second lieutenant in the Department of Criminal Investigation. Harold, who had learned German at his mother's knee, interrogated prisoners and took photos of the front lines.[57]

When Harold returned home, he made a life-changing decision. Although he had planned to be an architect, that course of study would take six years. He was deeply in love with Marietta and wanted to marry her and maintain her family's comfortable lifestyle. Marietta's well-to-do father, Simeon Chapin, had moved his stock and bond business from Chicago to New York in 1906. Harold decided to go into brokerage like his father, grandfather, and future father-in-law. "He was there every day, whatever the hours were, and was a good stockbroker," Tom said. "He enjoyed it but it never quite became his passion. His love was for other things: skating, traveling, and everything else."[58]

Harold and Marietta married in 1916, honeymooned in Jamaica, and set up housekeeping in a tenth-floor apartment on East 79th Street. Marietta shared his love of sports and literature; in the evenings, they frequently read aloud to each other. Harold adorned his young bride with jewels, including a necklace with gold leaves and green jade grape bunches designed by Lewis Comfort Tiffany. They were prominent members of the New York social scene and enjoyed a charmed, full life.[59]

Marietta's first pregnancy was difficult, and the birth was tragic. Although she had excellent medical attention, she had wanted to give birth at home. The baby died, and Marietta almost did, too. But she was committed to having a family. Their next child, Harold ("Harry") Hartshorne Jr., was delivered safely in a hospital.[60]

Marietta became pregnant again when Harry was eighteen months, and she refused to return to the hospital. Despite a physician's attendance, complications developed. "Father ran all over New York trying to get a specialist and the saline solutions she needed, but she was gone by the time he got back," Harry said. "Had she listened and gone to the hospital she would have been fine. It was really needless and it was terribly hard on Father." They had been married only four years, a loss made all the more poignant because Harold and Marietta seemed an ideal couple. The inscription on Marietta's headstone, "Love endureth forever," aptly described his adoration. It would be difficult for any other woman to measure up to Marietta.[61]

Harold Hartshorne with Sandy Macdonald, The Skating Club of New York, Madison Square Garden Ice Carnival. Source: Courtesy of Harry Hartshorne.

Harold picked up figure skating again to help overcome his grief. In 1923, three years after Marietta's death, Harold married Mary Bryan, daughter of a socially prominent family from the South. Together they had three children: James, Anne, and Margaret ("Peggy"). Harold was one of the founders of The Skating Club of New York (SCNY) and spent much time at the Iceland rink, adjacent to Madison Square Garden. Harold found great happiness on the ice, but "Mary was a little irritated because he was having fun at the rink and was never home on time for dinner," Harry recalled. Mary took up skating, too, to share Harold's interest; but her skills did not match Harold's and she had three children to raise, plus Harry, whom she treated as her own.[62]

Harold finally got to be an architect when Mary wanted a different home for the growing children. Harold bought an apartment on East 78th Street for city dwelling and bought eighteen acres in Little Silver, New Jersey, on the Shrewsbury River for an eleven-room Tudor-style mansion. Working alongside his architect cousin, Harold spent every free moment designing "Halcyon Bight," completed in 1929.[63]

When not overseeing his dream house, Harold performed in ice carnivals sponsored by the SCNY at Madison Square Garden in which skating champions from all over the world made their appearance. Leon Leonidoff, famed producer of the Radio City Music Hall shows, brought along his design team and staged the carnivals. New York high society, including the Rockefellers, Rothschilds, Roosevelts, Kennedys, Guggenheims, Whitneys, and the Vanderbilts, financially supported the shows.[64]

New York society also joined the SCNY. Many members were bank presidents or CEOs. Most of the adult skaters were ice dancers, and the men, often elderly, were on the prowl for young dance partners. Marjorie Parker was seventeen when she and five other Brooklyn girls were invited to join. "My dance partner, Joseph Savage, was president of the club and to me he seemed 108," she said. "Skating was mostly a hobby for businessmen. They were wonderful dancers and I learned a lot from those I danced with, like Harold."[65]

The club held many theme parties, which provided dress-up opportunities. Harold loved outlandish costumes—the funnier the better. Once he dressed as a pirate with a live parrot on his shoulder; another time he played a farmer and took piglets out on the ice.[66]

Harold loved to perform, but he also enjoyed competition. He had great posture and an erect carriage, which was ideal for ice dancing. Harold was the key driver in consolidating previously fragmented titles, like waltz, original, and Fourteenstep, into a national dance title. Marjorie Parker and Joe Savage were the first U.S. dance champions in 1936 and Harold and Nettie Prantel placed second. "Harold was upset, of course!" Marjorie said, "because he had done all the work to make it happen." Harold and Nettie were victorious the next two years.[67]

After winning in 1937 and 1938, Harold ended the partnership "because he thought she was too old," commented Marjorie, even though Harold, at forty-seven, was much older. Harold next competed with Sandy Macdonald, then in her early twenties. He coached her constantly, and their hard work resulted in three U.S. dance titles (1939-41).[68]

Sandy retired after she and Harold placed second in 1942. Harold coaxed Nettie to become his partner again, and they placed third the following year. Harold competed on the national level one more year with Kathe Mehl, placing second in 1944. Harold had competed nationally for almost a decade and ice dancing tastes had begun to shift away from his careful, precise style toward a more free-spirited ballroom interpretation. The time was right for Harold, a five-time national dance champion, to retire. Kathe Mehl went on to win the 1945 U.S. dance title with twenty-year-old Robert Swenning.[69]

Harold had competed in his last Nationals at age fifty-two. During World War II, he had tried unsuccessfully to get a commission and reluctantly sat out the war. "My father was such an active guy and so physically erect you would never know he was [over fifty]," his son explained. "He exercised his whole life and always had good health."[70]

He might have wanted to go to war to leave behind his troubled home life. Harold had wanted a divorce in the early 1940s; and when Mary refused to cooperate, he went to Reno where residency requirements and acceptable grounds were notoriously easy. According to Harry, while Harold was putting in residency time in 1942, he was invited to play tennis in a foursome. Barbara Hatch, twenty years his junior, was in the foursome and also ending a marriage. She came from a wealthy, socially prominent New York family whose Madison Avenue property, opposite the Carlyle Hotel, spanned the entire block.[71]

Harold was enchanted by this charming socialite. After they were married in 1942 in New York City, Harold bought a triplex on East 79th Street that occupied the tenth, eleventh, and twelfth floors. The large triplex was soon filled with Harold and Barbara's three children: Daniel, Gail, and Daryl. Harold was fifty-seven when his seventh child was born.[72]

Harold continued to skate frequently. "He left the minute he could from Wall Street and raced over to the skating rink," recalled son Dan. Barbara also "took up skating and got half-way decent." But this marriage also unraveled; and in 1950 Harold and Barbara divorced. "It was a messy split and there was friction with our father because we [three children] were loyal to our mother," Dan said. Harold was attached to all seven of his children and visited them at boarding school, college, in the service, at the family farm, or in Mexico, where two of his children had settled. His three youngest moved from place to place, until they finally settled in Colorado.[73]

During these troubled decades, skating remained a constant source of joy for Harold. By the late forties, Harold had become a USFSA official, chairing its Dance Committee and guiding the development of ice dancing in the United States. At home, he sketched designs for the dances and constantly listened to ice dancing records. "He played the music repeatedly to determine the exact speed for the dance," Gail said. He also designed and financed a number of trophies for club, sectional, regional, and national competitions.[74]

Harold became a skating judge and traveled frequently for tests and competitions. He knew many dancers by name and took an interest in their progress. Every summer he ran dance conferences at Lake Placid and even competed in its annual dance championships. Every winter Harold also competed in veterans' dance at Easterns; his friendly nemesis was USFSA first vice president Ritter Shumway. Harold won in 1950, 1952, and 1953. In 1954 Harold designed and paid for two new Eastern veterans' dance championship trophies, which Ritter won from 1954 through 1960, except for 1959. Harold and Florence Schaefer won that year when Ritter did not compete.[75]

Harold had become an international dance judge in 1951 and a dance referee in 1953. He sponsored weekly dance sessions at Iceland, welcoming skaters from all metropolitan clubs. He was a popular partner at the SCNY because he was a great dancer, but he also enjoyed presenting thoughtfully chosen gifts to other skaters. "Harold was handsome, tall, and a grand fellow," a club member stated. "He would come into the club with a whole bunch of boxes all done up as little gifts for all the ladies in the dance session. When you first met him, you thought he was rather austere, but he was actually pleasant and friendly; he had all the ladies twitterpated."[76]

If any of them aspired to become the fourth Mrs. Hartshorne, their hopes were dashed when Harold married forty-four-year-old Louise Heyer at the Riverside Church on September 26, 1953. Club members were surprised, even though divorce and remarriage constituted something of a revolving door at the club. "No one saw it coming," a club member said. "She was different in background than the rest of us, and not the type we thought he would have married. She was quiet and unassuming; you would not notice her in a crowd." Louise was not in the same social class as Harold and his three previous wives, and their paths would never have crossed had it not been their mutual interest in skating.[77]

Louise, known by some as "Bunny," was one of the regular SCNY dancers. She and Harold had known each other for years. Since 1946 she had competed against Harold in veterans' dance. Louisa Heyer, as she was christened, was of German ancestry and had never married. She lived alone and worked in a psychologist's office. The bright spot in her life was practicing figures and skating in dance sessions. Although she started skating late in life, she was gifted with persistence and worked hard to progress.[78]

Louise quit her job and became the ideal fifties wife, devoted to making her husband happy. She was undemanding and accommodating. Harold, now in his sixties, had a long-established lifestyle and Louise joined his world, which included skating, music, languages, favorite restaurants, and movies. "She entered his life at just the right time and made him very happy," Harry

Louise and Harold Hartshorne,
The Skating Club of New York,
at Sun Valley. Source: Courtesy
of Harry Hartshorne.

said. "She was conscientious about his diet and kept him young. There were no emotional upheavals. She was so wonderful to Father."[79]

Louise kept their home spotless, cooked their meals, exercised regularly, volunteered teaching children, and did handicrafts. Harold and Louise went skating, traveled frequently, and fully lived the life of empty-nesters. In 1957 it all changed when Barbara suddenly died and Harold assumed full custody of his three youngest children, ages fourteen, twelve, and ten. Louise was unprepared to become a mother to teenagers; she had little experience and the kids were challenging. "We were three bratty youngsters when we first arrived," Gail conceded. "We flew kites out our thirteenth story window and the kites sailed over the buses coming down Fifth Avenue. We were always on the verge of destroying ourselves or someone else." When Harold and Louise went skating at night, the kids "caused all hell" until they heard the elevator doors open.[80]

In retrospect, Dan felt that Louise did as well as she could. "It came as a shock to her," he said. "She was an orderly person who suddenly had three kids in her life and she hadn't planned on it."[81]

It also took time for the kids to warm up to their father again, and Harold connected with his children in ways he knew best. He advocated education and supported any athletic endeavor his kids pursued. He was a disciplinarian but rather than punishing them he would say, "Let's get busy on something good." He wanted them to be adventurous and try new things.[82]

Louise's background of working for a psychologist proved helpful. "She was always telling us we were going through a stage," Daryl recalled. She fixed the girls hair and instructed them on nutrition. "She was a very sweet person, but she was used to running everything and she was rigid"—completely different from Barbara, whom Gail called "definitely wild and crazy." Harold and Louise spoke German to each other whenever they didn't want the teenagers to understand what they were saying.[83]

"Louise tried with all her heart, and how loving is that?" commented Gail. "I have the utmost admiration for someone who tried so hard to be the right focus for my dad and the right focus for us, and she never blew her own horn. To me it was a small miracle how she handled everything." Dan agreed: "Louise was very stable and provided needed structure. She was grounding for our father and we knew we could rely on her too."[84]

In time all three children went to boarding school. Harold and Louise traveled to Europe for skating competitions. Louise wholeheartedly supported Harold's skating activities, organized the judges as test chairman, and appeared in the ice carnivals at Madison Square Garden with Harold.[85]

Louise and Harold competed together once, taking the silver at the 1954 Easterns, but they then reverted to different partners. Louise eventually retired from competition, but Harold continued, competing against fortysomethings even when he was in his late sixties. "At one competition I thought he was going to pass out on the ice," Dan said. "He was so exhausted when he came to the rail but after he got his shot of orange juice he was all right again." Harold and Louise regularly took the three kids with them on summer skating trips to Sun Valley.[86]

As president of the SCNY, Harold had been instrumental in the club's financial support of skaters, persuading the club to back Carol Heiss and her siblings. He even anonymously donated some of his own money to cover her expenses. He derived great pleasure from helping skaters financially.[87]

When Harold received his assignment to judge at the 1961 World Championships in Prague, there was no question that Louise would accompany him, as she had most of his trips. Although he had traveled extensively, Harold was eager to go to a Communist country. After seven years together their marriage was strong. Louise, fifty-one, had survived a crash course on motherhood and Harold, sixty-nine, had found serene contentment. They looked forward to a new adventure behind the Iron Curtain.[88]

In September a tumultuous cacophony arose from the Polar Palace ice arena in Hollywood. Dance partner musical chairs had become common in Los Angeles; but when a World Team partnership split because of their mothers, skaters around the valley took notice. Three mothers—Ann Campbell, Edith Littlefield, and Eleanor Carrier—were the only ones who knew exactly what was said, when, and where; but all of the Polar Palace skaters recalled the screaming. One day 1960 World Team members Yvonne Littlefield and Roger Campbell were training and the next day they were not— Yvonne was out as a partner and Dona Lee Carrier was in. The scuttlebutt, finger pointing, and accusations continued until Dona Lee and Roger left town for national competition.

Dona Lee Carrier had never been a serious competitor. As one East Coast skater remarked, "Of all the skaters I ever met, Dona Lee seemed the least likely to end up in a major competition. It is definitely a result of her perseverance." Perseverance aptly describes Dona Lee's skating career. It is also what brought Dona Lee into this world.[89]

DONA LEE CARRIER

"We have the only daughter in the world" is how the Carriers felt about their child. They had waited seventeen years before being blessed with a child, and they poured all of their energies into their beautiful daughter. Although they believed their daughter to be special above all others, Dona Lee never presented herself that way nor was she a spoiled girl.[90]

Floyd and Eleanor Carrier were married in 1923, but it wasn't until October 23, 1940, that Dona Lee was born in National City, California. The Reverend Floyd Carrier was thirty-eight and Eleanor was thirty-six. Three years later, Rev. Carrier became Director of Church Relations for the Council on Alcohol Problems, which required frequent family moves. While the family was living in Seattle in 1951, eleven-year-old Dona Lee began skating.[91]

By 1955, the Carriers had settled in Troy, New York. Dona Lee became a member of the RPI Club, its name taken from its home rink, which was located in the Rensselaer Polytechnic Institute Field House. The Carriers lived modestly and some members of the extended family helped pay Dona Lee's skating expenses. She was aware of the sacrifices her parents and others made so she could skate.[92]

Her coach Mary Lou Butler recalled that she was "a nice skater, but not one I expected to become a champion." Her figures were average and her freestyle lacked strong jumps. More than anything else her body shape—

tall with a long torso, wide hips, and heavy thighs—was not ideal for a skater. She stressed about her weight for years.[93]

Dona Lee had had little competitive success in singles. She participated in Easterns only once, placing last in junior ladies. After passing her fifth test, she could have easily called it quits, but at her coach's urging she continued ice dancing. "She was one of those skaters who had these flexible, rubbery knees where she could dance like the wind," Mary Lou said.[94]

Dona Lee's biggest problem was finding a dance partner. During the summer of 1957, she competed in a "Girls Only" dance competition in Rochester, worked with Bill Kipp at Lake Placid with a variety of partners, and socialized with dancers Pat Major, Bob Dineen, and Marilyn Grace. But she never found a partner.[95]

At eighteen, Dona Lee graduated from high school. She had not made her mark in skating, even locally. In the RPI annual carnival, she was only in the chorus of a precision number. She might easily have faded into anonymity, but her father received another transfer to Los Angeles. In the late fifties, Southern California was the center for ice dancing and featured a supportive environment, with gold-level dancers often helping the bronze-and silver-level skaters. Outside the rink, the large Los Angeles Figure Skating Club (LAFSC) community dined, went on picnics, and went on weekend skating parties to Lake Arrowhead. Dona Lee became fast friends with many skaters, including young Jennie Walsh. "Dona Lee was beautiful from the inside out," Jennie said.[96]

Dona Lee passed her sixth figure test and then focused solely on ice dancing with coach Bert Wright. She skated at the club's Monday and Wednesday night sessions and soon passed her pre-gold test. Her next challenge was finding a partner. Los Angeles had more male dancers than some locales, but it also had an abundance of female dancers.[97]

Dona Lee couldn't find a partner in time for the 1959 Southwest Pacific competition but was allowed to compete at Pacific Coast when she found partner Howie Harrold. They placed fourth out of six teams in gold dance.[98]

After the season, the musical chairs began. Howie left Dona Lee to join forces with Diane Sherbloom, who had just left her partnership with Roger Campbell, who in turn joined up with Yvonne Littlefield. Despite this association, Roger teamed up temporarily with Dona Lee over the summer. They competed in several local dance and pair competitions, then Roger rejoined Yvonne before the end of the summer. Dona Lee was out in the cold again.[99]

As the 1960 season rolled around, Dona Lee stepped down from the gold level to partner Dr. Robert Wilkins in silver dance. They placed second at Southwest. At the Pacific Coast competition in Squaw Valley, they did not fare as well, placing ninth. Over the summer of 1960, Dona Lee teamed up again with Howie Harrold and placed second in gold dance at the Inter-Club competition; Roger Campbell and Yvonne Littlefield took first. Dona Lee had yet to win, but she finally had some medals to show for her hard work. One medal was particularly rewarding; that summer she passed her gold dance test.[100]

Despite her lack of a permanent partner, Dona Lee's two years in California had seen a metamorphosis. She had transformed herself from a brunette to a blonde with cascading curls. She broke out of her sheltered upbringing and discovered California boys, and also lost weight in her thighs. She had always been careful with her diet and had a small waist, but genetically she was stuck with heavy legs. She needed focused weight loss in the right places. How she managed this success was never clear. Some thought a series of shots of some unidentified substances had knocked off the inches. Everyone, admiring her new legs, agreed that she "had something done." The treatment and whatever it required fulfilled Dona Lee's longing to be "a beautiful dancer."[101]

Her reward was a new dance partner—Roger Campbell, L.A.'s most talented male dancer at the time. Again, no one quite knew how it happened. As Roger Campbell and Yvonne Littlefield started training in September for the competitive season, Roger suddenly switched partners, informing Yvonne he would now be skating with Dona Lee Carrier; no reasons were given. Roger and Yvonne had been training all year and were credible candidates for the national title. It was a serious jolt. "My mom was a really honest person," Yvonne said, "and when we found out the Worlds were in Prague, she told Mrs. Campbell that we could not afford the trip unless we won." Yvonne's father, a milkman, worked a second job and her mother had a daycare center in their home to provide for their four children and Yvonne's skating.[102]

When the breakup occurred, Mrs. Littlefield told Yvonne that the Carriers had promised the Campbells they would pay for Dona Lee to go to Worlds if the pair made the team. However, the Carriers didn't have much money either. The true reason for the breakup may have been the slowly deteriorating relationship between the two mothers. At least some observers felt that, as animosity grew between Mrs. Campbell and Mrs. Littlefield, a growing friendship emerged between Mrs. Campbell and Mrs. Carrier. Together, they arranged for their children to become partners.[103]

At the rink, the mothers had more than one screaming match, and the environment became toxic. "It obviously wasn't pretty," said a club mother. During the tumult of emotions, skaters and parents took sides and some stopped speaking one to another. "It was horrible," recalled judge Eleanor Curtis. "The mothers would yell at the judges too, and say all kinds of unbelievable things." It became so bad that, within a matter of weeks, the LAFSC told the mothers that they could not attend club sessions.[104]

As for Dona Lee and Roger, they wisely took their partnership out of the Polar Palace rink where Bert Wright was coaching and made a fresh start with Bill Kipp at Iceland. Bill, who had groomed several national silver and gold dance champions, was ecstatic to have a new team. He quickly chose their music and choreographed their free dance.[105]

Dona Lee, two years Roger's senior, assumed a big sister role. She stood up for him and made skating fun for both of them. Her positive attitude smoothed over the turbulence of their pairing. Conversely, Roger's expertise helped Dona Lee with her dancing. "They both presented well, but she was like fire on the ice," a friend said. "She was elegant and the sparkle [of the team]." Prior to their first competition, Roger took Dona Lee through her gold free dance test.[106]

Roger and Dona Lee not only skated together but also now lived near each other. The Carriers and Sherry, Dona Lee's little dog and constant companion, moved into one of the five hundred apartments managed by Roger's father in North Hollywood. The Campbells also lived at the apartment complex, within walking distance of the Polar Palace. The move was a slight financial relief for the Carriers, who now focused on gathering funds for Dona Lee's potential trip to Prague.[107]

Dona Lee practiced six hours daily, and her parents were at the rink constantly, supporting her efforts. She hoped that competitive success would help her eventually turn professional; she wanted to give back to her sport through teaching. "Dona Lee was so caring, and I was grateful for the kindness she bestowed on me," said Jennie Walsh. "Her charm and grace made a lasting impression." Dona Lee, who had once been an introvert, had many fans.[108]

Yvonne Littlefield continued to train and competed in all disciplines. She won senior ladies at an LAFSC competition and partnered with Howie Harrold to compete in gold dance at Southwest. Being on the same ice with Roger was awkward for Yvonne, but he called her occasionally and told her he missed skating with her. Those calls meant a lot to Yvonne during this difficult time. "It was uncomfortable," she confessed. "I'm sure we were all civil to each other but there was a lot of resentment." The three kids only

Dona Lee Carrier with Roger Campbell, Los Angeles Figure Skating Club. Source: Photo by Bill Udell, Courtesy of Sylvia Clay Stoddard.

wanted to skate and compete but were the pawns in the games their mothers played.[109]

In November 1960, the Hadleys realized a long-sought dream. They opened their own ice rink, the Hadley and Hart Studio, located at Aurora and 98th in Seattle. Many skating families helped the Hadleys convert the existing building into a small ice studio by pushing in wheelbarrows full of sand for the ice surface and painting the interior. One parent made an ice cutter from a riding lawn mower. The Hadleys encouraged some families to invest in the studio; Linda Adams, for one, recalled: "The Hadleys wanted our family to re-mortgage our house to get money for the studio, but we really couldn't afford that."[110]

The rink was billed as the largest studio in the Northwest. The ice surface was sixty by eighty feet. There was enough room to practice jumps, spins, and lifts, but not to skate a routine. On the far wall were full-length mirrors, another wall was a mural of a Swiss mountain scene with trees and ice ponds, a third wall was windows separating the parents' observation room from the rink, and the fourth wall was a series of windows that could be opened to the outside world. "It was fabulous," a student exclaimed. "In the summertime we opened up the doors and it was heaven."[111]

The studio did a brisk business right from the start. Linda and Ray wanted a controlled environment, which was why they designed a parents' waiting area and simultaneously banned parents from the ice barriers. The studio had a lounge, which doubled as a ballet/exercise room, a bathroom/changing room, and an office, which doubled as the music room. Ray Ellis had a job sharpening rental skates every Saturday afternoon. Arvilla Kauffman ran the studio; and for her work, Ron and Cindy Kauffman got one lesson a week.[112]

Across the country, other prospective World Team members trained in earnest, secured their passports and shots, and negotiated with their schools, as Janet Harley noted: "I was enrolled at Butler University in Indianapolis, and they were not happy that I would have to miss school just to go to Nationals." In addition the senior skaters had to explain why they would miss an entire month of school should they be named to the 1961 World Team.[113]

At the end of fall, the USFSA sent a second letter to potential World Team members. They had made arrangements to get the Czech visas for all the team members. At the completion of the 1961 Nationals, a closed-door meeting of the International Committee would choose the 1961 North American and World Teams. A chartered bus would leave Philadelphia two days after North Americans and go directly to the Sabena terminal at Idlewild Airport in New York City. "It is planned to invite all our Team and the persons accompanying them, and also any of the Canadian team members and their party who may wish to make the Prague flight with us," the letter stated. The USFSA requested that all team members travel together, except the judges. "Others who wish to go at a different time may do so, but must make their own arrangements as to planes, entry into Czechoslovakia, hotel, etc." The USFSA had reserved thirty seats on the Belgian national airline Sabena (Societe Autonyme Belge d'Exploitation de la Navigation Aerienne).[114]

One person guaranteed a seat on that plane, based on her past performances, was Barbara Roles. She had won her first championship at age twelve. When she won the 1958 U.S. junior ladies crown five years later, it was her thirteenth gold medal in a row. Barbara was a superb free stylist; her strengths were solid jumps, speed, and showmanship. Barbara's competitive philosophy helped her to excel: "I was brought up to do the best I could do and never to evaluate myself against other people; I skated against my own standards." The Olympic judges at Squaw Valley were captivated by her and gave her the bronze medal.[115]

She appeared on the cover of the December 1960 issue of *Skating*; the accompanying caption read, "Barbara Ann Roles . . . will be one of the leading contenders for the open title of U.S. Lady Champion." The magazine editors were completely unaware that Barbara had already announced her retirement on the West Coast, and had married Ron Pursley in November. Her coach, Nancy Rush, and her mother, Bunny Roles, an accountant, club official, and judge, had hoped that Barbara would be the 1961 World Champion, but Barbara was soon pregnant. Barbara's retirement was an opportunity for her competitors who now had an open shot for the 1961 U.S. ladies title.[116]

CHAPTER 13

DECEMBER 1960

A s 1960 came to a close, there was trouble in the LeMaire household in Rye, New York. The USFSA had asked Eddie LeMaire to go to the 1961 Worlds in February, but his son Richard ("Dickie") had just been expelled from the prestigious Rye Country Day School. Dickie was an extremely bright child who was getting into trouble because he was bored. Dickie was a precocious boy who had already been through a great deal of adversity by the time he was thirteen.[1]

RICHARD LEMAIRE

Richard Osborn LeMaire, born on August 2, 1947, in Greenwich, Connecticut, was the eldest of three children and his mother's favorite—"the crown prince" as one friend described him. Except for his blond hair, he was a younger version of his father with his round face and impish grin. As a young teenager, he terrorized his two younger sisters, Dorinda, eleven, and Diana, ten, playing tricks on them. But his sisters loved him anyway because he was so much fun. The children were raised with two big collies in a large three-story home which sat on five acres in Rye, New York. All three children attended the Rye Country Day School.[2]

Dickie, who would have preferred to be an only child, used to say to his mother: "Just where are you getting all these babies from?" But he eventually accepted his two younger sisters and ruled the roost. He hooked up a walkie-talkie between his bedroom and Dorinda's bedroom closet, and they would talk together all night long. When his parents went out in the evening, Dickie regularly subverted the babysitter's plans. As the sole inhabitant and "lord of the castle" on the third floor, he was allowed to stay up because of his age. He would liberate his sisters from their bedrooms and include them in his shenanigans. One winter evening, after the girls were put to bed at 8:00, Dickie came down the stairs, got the girls out of bed, and took them out through the basement while the sitter watched TV and talked on the phone. Outside, Dickie had set up a sledding course down the hill from their home next to a golf course. He had put lighted candles on the

Dickie LeMaire, soccer goalie at Rye Country Day School. Source: Courtesy of Dorinda LeMaire Howard.

outdoor terrace stairs. The LeMaire siblings slid down the hill for hours. After they were exhausted, they sneaked back upstairs and watched television in his room until midnight.[3]

His sisters were recreational skaters, but Dickie didn't spend much time on the ice, except to play hockey on a frozen pond near their home. He played many team sports at school and dreamed of playing football for Yale, his father's alma mater. In 1959 he accompanied his father to Boston for the Harvard-Yale game; and from the Harvard stands, he yelled mightily for his Bulldogs, even in defeat.[4]

Dickie had a distinct, high-pitched voice—a result of how interesting he found everything and how excited he was about life. "He was a bright star that shone brightly around others," a friend said. Dickie had great energy and spirit in part because he had already conquered a serious affliction. On Thanksgiving Day 1956, when he was nine, Dickie had a fall and developed a staph infection, osteomyelitis, in his leg. In the fifties, it was a serious malady. After he spent seven weeks at United Hospital in Rye and three weeks at home, a high fever alerted doctors to the continuation of bone disintegration. At Roosevelt Hospital in New York City, the doctors told the family he might never walk again, but more importantly, Dickie's worried mother could see that the doctors were fighting to save his life. Dickie stayed at Roosevelt Hospital for four months as he endured multiple surgeries and daily injections of penicillin. Dickie was finally sent home, and three months later he gave up his crutches. He missed the entire fourth grade, but he still passed his exams at the end of the year.[5]

When the hospital released Dickie, he was barely walking. Doctors encouraged him to resume sports as part of his physical therapy. He began with swimming and eventually played a little soccer as goalie.[6]

The year after his illness, he went to a summer camp in Colorado run by a family friend. The LeMaires thought the hiking and the outdoors would help strengthen his leg. In Colorado he fell in love with the magnificent rocks, immersed himself completely in geology, and began collecting, avidly ordering specialized stones from catalogs and magazines, and amassing an impressive library on geology and mineralogy. He visited the geology departments of several East Coast universities and boasted to his family that his rock collection was better. At Princeton he took a tour with a professor, who was astounded by his knowledge of each rock in their collection. The professor told him: "I'm saving a place for you at Princeton, whenever you want to come."[7]

He forced his passion upon his sisters. If they misbehaved, he pulled them into his room and said, "Okay, you're going to have a test." Under a soft fluorescent light, Dorinda and Diana stared at what seemed like "jillions" of rocks and had to identify them and their properties. The sisters became proficient because he threatened to put real spiders in their beds if they didn't pass. Even though he made them study rocks, he also did their homework when asked. He often took Diana's math sheet to his room and left it in front of her door, completed, the next morning.[8]

By the fall of 1960, Dickie was in the eighth grade at the Rye Country Day School. He was due to graduate in June 1961 and was scheduled to enter Taft Prep School in Connecticut the following fall. Academically he should have been in tenth grade or higher. His father had skipped two grades, but Dickie was not emotionally mature enough to take that step. Consequently, his boredom fostered innocent yet disruptive anarchy. He shot rubber bands at his teachers and classmates, flew paper planes, and "God knows what else," Diana said. The final straw came when Dickie told his strict match teacher that he didn't need to do his homework because he "already knew the answers." As the fall semester came to a close the exhausted and exasperated school officials suspended him.[9]

Eddie and Muriel also didn't know what to do with their son. With Eddie leaving for Prague in the coming weeks, they discussed the possibility of Dickie accompanying him. Both parents felt it would be better for Dickie to do something fun and educational compared to the alternative of sitting at home, bored to tears, and teasing everyone in the family. Eddie and

Dickie made plans for a six-week trip abroad, traveling through Iron Curtain countries and touring western Europe in addition to their ten days in Prague. As father and son excitedly made their plans, they learned of another father and son planning a similar journey. The two fathers were happy to know their sons would have someone their own age on this adventure. The traveling companions were Edi Scholdan and Jimmy, nearly twelve.[10]

JIMMY SCHOLDAN

On April 18, 1949, Edi and Roberta Scholdan produced an heir. If Edi's dream had been realized, James Edward Scholdan would have followed in the footsteps of Edi's protégés, Olympians Hayes and David Jenkins. In some ways, father and son were alike; both were short, enthusiastic, and full of life. Jimmy, however, looked like his mother. She had performed in the Broadmoor Ice Revue when she was pregnant with Jimmy, but he didn't gravitate toward figure skating. He eventually discovered a passion for skating, but it was for hockey and speed skating.[11]

Jimmy grew up in a small carriage house located in front of the Broadmoor Hotel on Lake Street. Jimmy had two sisters: Dixie Lee was five years older, and Ruth was four years younger. Jimmy attended the Pauline Chapel School next to the Broadmoor resort. The school nuns and skating parents thought he was charming; his friends considered him the craziest and most fun person they had ever known.[12]

Jimmy's sisters both skated. Dixie had won championships and Ruthie, who had had special skates made for her at age two, skated every day and was the youngest performer in the ice shows. Despite Edi's encouragement, Jimmy didn't progress much beyond preliminary figures and a few jumps and spins. Instead, he often played hooky from the rink, walked around Cheyenne Lake with friends, or stole a boat for a joy ride.[13]

Edi had Jimmy regularly perform in the large children's number in the Broadmoor Ice Revue. Christy Haigler, a young rising star, appeared in these numbers with Jimmy and was the target of his teasing. Christy remembered Jimmy as a "character who enjoyed being obnoxious." One of Jimmy's friends said that Jimmy targeted Christy, primarily because she was "cute and was the girl they all wanted to marry."[14]

The children's number was near the beginning of the show. Once it was over, Jimmy was unleashed for fun. He and a friend, Fred Chescheir, stole canisters of carbonated drinks and set up their own soda fountain underneath the seats of the Ice Palace while the show continued. One rainy night he and Fred left the arena, netted 150 salamanders from Cheyenne Lake, and spilled them in front of the exit after the show just when the crowd was coming out.[15]

When Jimmy wasn't terrorizing people at the rink, he was speed skating or playing hockey. He was a standout player in the ragtag hockey teams and fearlessly banged into people. He and his teammates were known as the "woolly bullies." However, his small size worked against him, and one time he even suffered a broken leg.[16]

Jimmy preferred speed skating. Sponsored by the Broadmoor Hotel, the Broadmoor Speed Skating Club (BSSC) was organized in 1947. Soon the arena was hosting national and North American meets. As a young boy he joined the BSSC, competed in local events, and saw the best speed skaters in the country. Edi flew with him to St. Louis for the Silver Skates meet in 1959 when Jimmy was nine. He didn't win any races, but he did well in his age group and continually improved. However, Jimmy never looked like the other speed skaters. "Jimmy was a free spirit," said speed skater Phil Cagnoni. "He always seemed a little out of control. If he were an adult, I'd say he had an extra quart of champagne in him." Edi, who encouraged many of his students to take up speed skating, was proud of his son's success.[17]

The three Scholdan siblings grew up at the ice rink, but Jimmy preferred the outdoors. He climbed trees, jumped in creeks, and went fishing in Cheyenne Creek, where a reservoir runoff created a little pool full of brook trout. Fishing rods were discarded for a more strenuous form of hand-to-hand combat: jumping into the pool, chasing the fish, and picking them up when they wore out. Another favorite activity was sneaking into the annual Pikes Peak or Bust Rodeo. The rodeo stadium was about fifty yards from the Broadmoor Ice Palace, and the challenge was to slip in for free.[18]

Jimmy spent time at the rink, school, or running around outside because life inside their home wasn't ideal. The parents' union had become strained, and Edi and Roberta often quarreled. When Jimmy was six, Roberta went abroad to perform in the Ice Vogues, a version of Holiday on Ice, and settled in Vienna. Dixie moved back east to live with her grandparents and attended Smith College.[19]

As traumatic as divorce can be for children, the separation brought peace at home. The Scholdans had a black housekeeper/nanny named Miriam who had been managing the household for years. She essentially raised Jimmy and Ruthie, cooked the meals, and made Edi pay his bills on time. Miriam was a wonderful stabilizing force in this chaotic household. Miriam often let Jimmy's friends spend the night, and he often showed up at friends' homes for dinner.[20]

Jimmy Scholdan, age nine, Pauline Chapel School, Colorado Springs.
Source: Dixie Lee Burns Wilson.

Jimmy enjoyed the security of a close relationship with his father; however, he still drove Edi crazy. Once he took one of Edi's watches, one bequeathed from his jeweler father, and took it apart to see how it worked. Then he couldn't figure out how to put it back together. "It was a special watch, so it was kind of a big deal that he had taken it apart," Ruth recalled. Another time Jimmy and Ruthie got in Edi's new 1959 Chevy, pretending to drive it. Suddenly the car started down the inclined driveway. Jimmy panicked and jumped out, leaving seven-year-old Ruthie in the car as it went down the driveway, crossed the street, and landed in a ditch. "He didn't get in trouble for taking the car—he got in trouble for leaving me in the car!" she said.[21]

Edi couldn't turn Jimmy into a figure skater, but he taught him how to ski. Jimmy was fearless and a pretty good skier. "You just pointed him down hill and he wouldn't stop," Ruth said. "He would ski into these big bales of hay, and that's how he would stop. We called him Bonzo Jimmy."[22]

By the fall of 1960, eleven-year-old Jimmy had made great strides in speed skating and planned to compete in the national speed skating championships in Illinois in mid-February. He was working toward this event when his father offered another option. Edi, who most likely would have two students on the 1961 World Team, invited Jimmy to go with him to Prague so his son could see his mother in nearby Vienna. Edi actually wanted to take both Jimmy and Ruthie. He discussed the matter with Father Harrington of St. Pauline Church, who favored the idea, but the nuns who taught Jimmy and Ruthie didn't think the children should go on a long trip, especially not Ruthie, who would see little of her father during the competition. They persuaded Father Harrington that Ruthie should stay home. Father Harrington agreed but felt that Jimmy's situation was different. The travel would be a great education for him. Jimmy wanted to see his mother, and he would have Dickie LeMaire to hang out with.[23]

Jimmy could either go to Europe or travel to the speed skating championships. Jimmy was eager to travel with his father; he had always wanted to accompany him to international competitions, but in the past he had been too young. Edi, who had been to fourteen consecutive World championships and four Olympics, loved the idea of taking his kids with him.[24]

Both Edi and Jimmy were excited about their upcoming journey. Edi looked forward to a reunion with his ex-wife. He had never lost hope that Roberta would come back, and his children thought his plans for the trip included reconciliation. "He always said that he loved her," a friend recalled. Edi was also anxious to return to his roots. He told a local reporter, "I'm going to take Jimmy with me to Worlds. I want him to see my old home in Austria."[25]

Bill Hickox had been in Colorado Springs since June, attending the Air Force Academy. With his grueling schedule, he had not had time to skate at the Broadmoor rink, but he had received his appointment to be a low-test judge and he went with friends to see the Ice Follies in Denver. When he heard that the 1961 Nationals would be at the Broadmoor, he thought about competing in junior men, but his chances for getting practice time fell through. He then pursued the idea of speed skating and had ordered a pair of speed skates in October. However, his mother had other ideas.[26]

When Elinor Hickox found out that the 1961 Nationals were slated for the Broadmoor, she urged Bill to compete in pairs one more time. When a USFSA letter arrived in Berkeley encouraging potential World Team members to get their passports, it only fueled her resolve. She contacted the academy to see if Bill could train. "This was her idea, not his," girlfriend Anne Frazier said, "and I don't think he could stop the juggernaut.[27]

When Bill put his skates on at the end of November, it was the first time he had been on the ice in 162 days. "[At first] I felt as if I'd never been on skates in my life," he said. "After an hour, though, I was landing axels and clean double toe-loops." After Laurie Hickox placed second in junior ladies at Central Pacifics in early December, she took a leave of absence from Berkeley High where she was a freshman. She and her mother found lodgings in Colorado Springs near the arena, and Elinor arranged for a private tutor.[28]

Edi Scholdan was delighted to have a new pair team, but they had only six weeks to prepare for Nationals. By the end of December, the close siblings had found their rhythm again on the ice. "Sis and I are skating like mad now," Bill wrote in a letter. "We went down to Broadmoor yesterday and we had the 'red carpet' rolled out for us. They are arranging all kinds of ice time. The skating is coming along real well, . . . [and] I'll bet that I have the only spit shined skates in the Nationals."[29]

As a member of "The Blue Zoo," Bill arrived at the Broadmoor arena in his bright royal blue cadet outfit to train with his sister. To Bill's astonishment, the Air Force Academy agreed to let him train five days a week (three weekdays plus Saturday and Sunday). In his first semester at the academy, fourth-class cadet Bill Hickox had compiled a brilliant scholastic record and had recently made the dean's list. The academy classified him as a varsity athlete and put him on the inter-collegiate squad list. "I might even get a letter!" he enthused. Even though Bill knew he couldn't have entered the academy and continued his skating career at the same time—and had made the choice to focus on school—he considered the Nationals a one-time-only competition. Even if he and Laurie made the World Team, he was doubtful that the academy would give him the time off to go to Worlds.[30]

The landscape for prospective 1961 World Team members had changed dramatically during the year. The exit of Barbara Roles left the way open for the ladies title. In the men's division, prospects for the championship title were upset when Tim Brown reentered the race. Jerry and Judianne Fotheringill, the 1959 junior pairs champions, had been favored for the third spot in senior pairs; now there was additional competition from the Hickoxes, the 1960 junior pairs champions.

Of all the disciplines, the dance division proved to be most volatile. Bob and Pat Dineen were still planning to compete even though they had become parents. Roger Campbell had dropped his World Team partner Yvonne Littlefield to train with the relatively unknown Dona Lee Carrier. The only stable partnership was Larry Pierce and Marilyn Meeker of Indianapolis.

Larry and Marilyn felt that the U.S. dance crown was within their reach. Coach Danny Ryan had choreographed a terrific routine, Marilyn's competitive dress had been designed and made, Larry had his skating tux ready, and they had secured their passports for Prague. After seven more weeks of training, they could see themselves skating their way to victory.[31]

In early December, Larry and Marilyn ran through their free dance routine, just as they had every day. They executed a move in the program where Larry pushed Marilyn so she would glide on her side. This time she inadvertently caught her heel and fell. The skaters at the Indianapolis Coliseum were alarmed when Marilyn was carried off the ice. When she took off her boot, she immediately knew something bad had happened. A doctor gave her the grim news: She had chipped a bone in her ankle and there was no quick-fix remedy. The doctor put her left foot and leg in a cast and told her she would be off the ice for months. "This season's over, kiddo," the doctor matter-of-factly told her. Marilyn thought she was going to die.[32]

Danny Ryan was heartsick for his team. The threesome had been together since Danny had arrived in Indianapolis. They loved working together and Larry and Marilyn had steadily climbed the competitive ladder. Now the dance crown had disappeared in seconds. Danny and Larry did not want to give up. Larry was already twenty-five years old and his chances for success would lessen with time. He had to become the new reigning champion in 1961; after that, if he and Marilyn consistently delivered good performances they could count on the national dance title for a number of years. Danny and Larry formulated a game plan and brought Marilyn in to make the final decision.[33]

Marilyn's injury was not permanent. The doctor thought she would be back on the ice by spring. The idea was to find Larry a temporary partner for the 1961 competitive season, three to four months at the most, and then Larry would resume skating with Marilyn. The three agreed that this was best for the team. Marilyn knew it was the right thing to do but it was a bitter decision. She wanted the dance championship as badly as Danny and Larry. She cried over her misfortune and "wondered why God hated me so much."[34]

The next big question—who could replace Marilyn? Sally Schantz was not an option; she was only at silver level. Danny and Larry immediately thought of Diane Sherbloom. When Larry and Marilyn won the 1959 U.S. silver dance title, Diane and Roger Campbell were the runners-up. Larry had also skated with Diane once before—when Larry went to Los Angeles after the 1960 Worlds. Larry knew that their skating styles were compatible because he had partnered Diane on some gold dance tests. Although they had heard she had retired during the summer, she might be available. In the second week of December, Larry called Diane.[35]

Diane Sherbloom had graduated from high school, was working and applying for college, and had a boyfriend. She had enjoyed her national skating success in 1959, but 1960 had not been as fruitful and she felt her career was over. What Larry and Danny didn't know was that another dancer had already coaxed her back into competition.[36]

DIANE SHERBLOOM
1959 SILVER DANCE SILVER MEDALIST

Diane Carol Sherbloom, born September 21, 1942, was the elder of Thomas and Ruth Sherbloom's two daughters. The Sherblooms lived in a modest house on Lanier Street in Los Angeles. Joan, three years younger, followed Diane onto the ice.[37]

Tom Sherbloom had a unique and glamorous occupation—that of an ice sculptor in Hollywood. His childhood, however, was clouded with trauma and misfortune. He had been crippled as a child when he fell down the stairs and broke his hip. His father died from a broken neck when Tom was nine. His sister drowned, and his mother died in a fire when he was fourteen. He eventually went to art school, learned ice sculpting while working at a hotel, and became the only full-time ice sculptor in the United States. His clients included the Beverly Hills Hotel, the motion picture industry, restaurants, and posh private parties. His work was featured in *Life* magazine. He sculpted many famous faces, including Bob Hope and Mickey Mouse, but his favorite subject was his daughter Diane, whom he sculpted in a bathing suit in the summer of 1958. His work was lucrative but it could also be seasonal. The exorbitant cost of his daughters' skating proved difficult for the Sherblooms.[38]

As a toddler, Joan had trouble pronouncing her sister's name and called her "Dee Dee." Diane's good friends used the same nickname throughout her life. In 1953, when Diane was ten and Joan seven, they started skating at Jerry Page's Ice Studio in Los Angeles and at Blue Jay, where they met members of the Los Angeles Figure Skating Club (LAFSC). They were soon skating at the Polar Palace, the club's rink. Bill Udell, a photographer and LAFSC pro, said, "I saw Dee Dee take her first stumbling steps on ice. I saw her grow into one of the most beautiful little girls you ever saw."[39]

Diane took dance lessons from Helen Gage Moore and Joan Zamboni, and passed her pre-dance and bronze dance tests at fourteen. Ray Sato, a long-time fixture at the LAFSC, also taught her many of the dances. Under Bill Kipp's guidance, Diane and partner Ray Chenson won their first championship, the bronze dance title, at the 1957 Southern California Inter-Club competition.[40]

Diane and Ray continued to improve and skated at dance sessions all over the valley, in Culver City, Paramount, Pasadena, and Hollywood. Their hard work paid off in the 1958 competitive season with a bronze dance double win—at California State and two weeks later at Pacific Coast in Seattle—over eleven other couples, including Roger Campbell and Anna Marie Hansen who placed fifth.[41]

Ray attributed part of their success to the tremendous support they received from the crowds. Ray realized that Diane's natural beauty helped their skating. "I was told that the man's duty was to show off your partner," he explained. "Therefore my job was to sit back and make her look good. Dee Dee had a great smile so she made my job easy." Ray and Diane had a harmonious relationship. Diane's mother was often present at the rink, but she didn't join the gossip as many other skating mothers did, or try to micro-manage her daughter's career.[42]

Ray and Diane easily passed their pre-silver and silver dance tests prior to the next year's competition, but their plans changed when Ray received his appointment to West Point. Diane understood his desire to take advantage of this opportunity, and the two parted amicably. She easily found a new partner. Roger Campbell and Diane were both sixteen, and she was initially happy with their partnership. They joined forces with coach Bert Wright to prepare for the upcoming competitive season.[43]

At the same time, coach Austin Holt approached Lorin Caccamise and suggested he and Diane do pairs. Lorin had to talk Diane into it, but he also had to face the "death threat" of the judges who told him, "If you drop her we are going to kill you." They thought Diane was headed toward dance stardom, and they were wary of this new partnership, but it didn't last long. They didn't do any big lifts, and Diane was afraid of doing an axel—or any jumps for that matter. It was hard for Lorin to be aggressive with her. "Dee Dee was so cute I couldn't ever yell at her," he said. They competed in one summer competition and performed a trio with young Peggy Fleming in an Arctic Blades club show, then called it quits.[44]

Diane then focused solely on dance prior to the 1959 Southwest Pacific competition. Surprisingly her ex-partner also entered the competition. Before Ray Chenson went off to West Point, he and partner Sandra Richardson won the silver dance, while Diane and Roger placed second. A month later, they reversed positions, and Diane and Roger won silver dance at Pacific Coast, ahead of Ray and Sandra. Prior to leaving for the 1959 Nationals in Rochester, Diane and Roger performed in a club exhibition held as a fundraiser to help meet their traveling costs.[45]

Diane Sherbloom, Los Angeles Figure Skating Club, 1959 U.S. Silver Dance Silver Medalist. Source: Courtesy of Sylvia Clay Stoddard.

At the 1959 Nationals, Diane and Roger placed fourth in compulsories. After the final round, they pulled up to second place. The winners were Larry Pierce and Marilyn Meeker; in third place were Bob and Pat Dineen.[46]

Diane had had an incredibly successful year; she was just one placement away from a national title. Roger and Diane had skated together for only one year and were an impressive team. But when she and Roger returned to Los Angeles, she told him she didn't want to skate with him any longer. Diane got along with Roger, but his mother was overbearing and Diane didn't feel comfortable in her presence. Roger, a talented dancer, quickly found a new partner, Yvonne Littlefield.[47]

Diane was extremely popular and didn't worry about finding a new partner. Some thought her shy, but no one disputed her good looks. She was a beautiful blonde with blue-gray eyes, slender and petite. "She was someone you wanted to be like," Yvonne Littlefield said. Diane went with judges Jack and Eleanor Curtis to church many Sundays. "She was very sweet and had a great personality," Eleanor recalled. "She was delightful and everyone loved her."[48]

Diane teamed up with Howie Harrold for the 1960 competitive season. They placed seventh in gold dance at Pacific Coast at Squaw Valley. Her former partner Roger Campbell and Yvonne Littlefield placed second. Diane returned home to finish her senior year at Hamilton High School in Los Angeles. A cheerleader with many friends, she was also a good student, enjoyed languages, science, and math, and was an artist like her father. She enjoyed drawing in her free time.[49]

As Diane neared graduation, she contemplated taking a break from skating. She was anxious to explore other opportunities and found no resistance at home. Her mother had said, "If you want to skate, skate. If you don't want to skate, we won't go." So Diane's decision to quit did not upset her family. Her competitive career had lasted just a few years, and her family anticipated that she would now have time to excel in other areas. When 1960 U.S. dance champion Margie Ackles invited Diane and Dona Lee Carrier to be bridesmaids at her May wedding, Diane enjoyed the festivities, then took a sabbatical from the ice.[50]

In December 1960, Diane was working as an information operator for the Pacific Telephone Company and liked making money. She had recently returned to the ice to partner dancer Ray Sato in the Southwest Pacific competition. When Larry Pierce called, she saw it as a golden opportunity to make the 1961 World Team. Larry's parents promised to house and chaperone Diane like a daughter, a promise that reassured Diane's parents, who gave the project their blessing. Diane skipped competing at Southwest, said good-bye to Ray, obtained her passport, and left Los Angeles for Indianapolis on December 18 for an exciting new adventure. If she made the 1961 World Team and went on the European tour, her family would not see her for three months.[51]

Larry welcomed Diane with relief; he had been without a partner for two weeks and the competition was in less than five. Danny immediately taught Diane the free dance routine, and she worked many hours a day to make their team competitive. She would wear Marilyn's competition dress and new matching sweater on the practice ice in Colorado. Marilyn was still suffering emotionally when she came to visit one of their sessions. After the practice, Diane and Larry autographed her cast. A newspaper photograph accompanying the story shows Marilyn sitting by the rink barrier wearing a wool coat, her right foot in a saddle oxford shoe and her left foot in a cast, smiling gamely for the photographer.[52]

Diane first lived with Danny and Rose Anne Ryan. They had moved into a new ranch home, and out-of-state students periodically lived with them. Even though Rose Anne was used to houseguests, she was in her seventh month of pregnancy, so Diane moved in with club members Newton and Bette Todd. The Midwest was new to Diane, and she was entranced by the novelties of the area, including the flatlands and the cornfields. "A live cow especially intrigued her," Bette recalled. "She had never seen one before."[53]

Three-time Olympic champion Sonja Henie and Maribel Vinson competed against each other nine times. They were good friends and respected each other's talent. *(Collection of the World Figure Skating Museum)*

Maribel, performing a spin at Rockefeller Center in the thirties, exhibited her natural hip turn-out, which enabled her to easily execute spread eagles. *(Collection of Patricia Bushman)*

The Vinson/Owen clan in a light-hearted moment during a party. Left: Mary Louise Wright, Maribel Jr., Laurence, Maribel, Gertrude ("Grammy") Vinson. *(Collection of the World Figure Skating Museum)*

Edi Scholdan learned to juggle in Europe and brought his juggling act on the ice to the United States. *(Collection of the World Figure Skating Museum)*

Edi Scholdan at the 1956 Olympic Games in Cortina d'Ampezzo, Italy, with bronze medalist David Jenkins and Olympic champion Hayes Jenkins. *(Courtesy of Ruth Scholdan Harle)*

Stars of the 1952 Broadmoor Ice Revue. Left back: Edi Scholdan, Kay Servatius, Patricia Firth, Hayes Jenkins, Tenley Albright, Eileen Seigh, Ronnie Robertson, Claralynn Lewis, Jane Holmes, Carl Chamberlin. Left front: David Jenkins and Eleanor Soneman. *(Courtesy of Debbie Might)*

Bradley Lord was a smooth skater like his muse, Richard Dwyer of Ice Follies. *(Collection of the World Figure Skating Museum)*

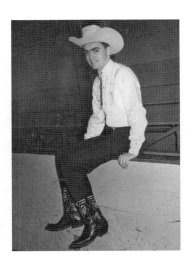

Bradley Lord received western clothing as a competitor at the 1959 Worlds at the Broadmoor. *(Courtesy of Bruce Lord)*

Ray Hadley and Linda Hart began coaching together at the Seattle Civic Ice Arena after they married. *(Courtesy of Sharon Dowling and Lawrence Hart)*

Ila Ray and Ray Hadley Jr. won the 1957 U.S. junior pair title when she was fourteen and he was thirteen. *(Courtesy of Joan Sherbloom Peterson)*

Both siblings and best friends, Ila Ray and Ray Hadley Jr. were the most popular kids in the Seattle Skating Club. *(Courtesy of Sharon Dowling and Lawrence Hart)*

At the Providence Skating Club in the late thirties, Dudley Richards skated with a young female club member. *(Courtesy of Dudley Abbe)*

Dudley Richards competed in his third Worlds in singles at Davos, Switzerland, in 1953. *(Courtesy of Dudley Abbe)*

Maribel Jr. and Charles ("Chuck") Foster won two national medals in their two-year partnership. *(Collection of the World Figure Skating Museum)*

Greg Kelley flew from Boston to Berkeley, California, where he won the 1957 U.S. novice men's title. *(Collection of the World Figure Skating Museum)*

Greg Kelley, after he won the 1959 U.S. junior title, moved to Colorado Springs to work with Edi Scholdan. *(Courtesy of Gerard Lane)*

Laurence Owen, in her early days in Berkeley, California, skated on St. Moritz club sessions at Iceland. *(Courtesy of St. Moritz ISC)*

Laurence, Maribel, and Little Maribel Owen in Boston used this image for a Christmas card. *(Collection of the World Figure Skating Museum)*

Laurence Owen, who charmed audiences in Squaw Valley, placed sixth at the 1960 Olympics. *(Collection of the World Figure Skating Museum)*

Sherri Westerfeld, in junior high, moved to Colorado with her sister Steffi and their mother to train year-round at the Broadmoor. *(Courtesy of Diane Yeomans Robins)*

Steffi Westerfeld, coined a "little Shirley Temple on ice," looked like the childhood star from her youngest days. *(Courtesy of Diane Yeomans Robins)*

For years, Steffi Westerfeld was the unofficial mascot of the Broadmoor Skating Club. *(Courtesy of Diane Yeomans Robins)*

Steffi Westerfeld won the Midwestern senior ladies title four years in a row. *(Courtesy of Diane Yeomans Robins)*

Bill Kipp and Jean Westwood were the stars of the Lake Placid summer shows. *(Courtesy of Wilhelmina Kipp Gozzard)*

When Barbara Roles dropped out of competition in 1960, Rhode Michelson became the new ice princess in Los Angeles. *(Courtesy of Anita Entrikin Miller)*

Rhode Michelson, who made a big splash at the 1958 Pacific Coast competition, placed second. Left: Rhode Michelson, Sharon Constable, and Linda Galbraith. *(Courtesy of Linda Michelson)*

Danny and Rose Anne Ryan, on ice at the Winter Club
of Indianapolis, teach their oldest son, Kevin. *(Courtesy
of Rich Rosborough)*

Marilyn Meeker and Larry Pierce
won the 1958 Midwestern silver
dance trophy. *(Courtesy of Marilyn
Meeker Durham)*

Larry Pierce and Marilyn Meeker
made the 1960 World Team when
they placed second at the 1960 Nationals. *(Courtesy of Rich Rosborough)*

Genevieve and Bill Swallender were the Broadmoor skating directors in 1940. *(Courtesy of Virginia Mount)*

Thirteen-year-old Doug Ramsay, the 1957 Midwestern junior champion, appeared at the Cleveland club show. *(Courtesy of the Detroit Skating Club)*

Doug Ramsay, on his third try, won the U.S. junior men's title in Seattle in 1960. *(Courtesy of Ron Pfenning)*

Bill Hickox along with his sister, Laurie, spent the summer of 1959 in Sun Valley. *(Courtesy of Anne Frazier)*

Laurie and Bill Hickox won the U.S. junior pairs title on their second try, in 1960. *(Courtesy of Patti Ballenti)*

The 1960 U.S. Olympic Figure Skating Team. Left back: Carol Heiss, Maribel Y. Owen, Laurence Owen, Team Leader Amy Fisher, Nancy Ludington, and Barbara Roles. Left front: David Jenkins, Ron Ludington, Tim Brown, Robert Brewer, and Dudley Richards (Ila Ray and Ray Hadley Jr. absent). *(Courtesy of Dudley Abbe)*

Pat and Bob Dineen (right) competed against their good friends Charlie Rizzo and Liz Herman. *(Courtesy of Liz Herman McLoughlin)*

Yvonne Littlefield and Roger Campbell competed locally in pair and dance before they became a dance team in 1959. *(Courtesy of Yvonne Nicks)*

Walter Powell, a friend to all U. S. World Team members, visited with Tenley Albright and Jimmy Grogan in Davos, Switzerland. *(Courtesy of Debbie Might)*

1943 National champions at Madison Square Garden. Left: Buddy Vaughn, Ann Robinson, Dottie Goos, Gretchen Merrill, Jane Zeiser, and Eddie LeMaire. *(Courtesy of Dorinda LeMaire Howard)*

Eddie LeMaire with his Naval Air Corps, Yale 1945 Unit; Eddie is third from the right. *(Courtesy of Dorinda LeMaire Howard)*

Dickie LeMaire, after four months at Roosevelt Hospital, was happy to be home. *(Courtesy of Dorinda LeMaire Howard)*

Harold and Louise Hartshorne spent several weeks every
summer in Sun Valley with Harold's children and New York
coach Fritz Dietl. *(Courtesy of Harold Hartshorne Jr.)*

Dona Lee Carrier, prior to her blonde
transformation, partnered with Dr.
Robert Wilkins in silver dance. *(Courtesy of the Los Angeles Figure Skating
Club)*

Before the 1961 North Americans, Dona
Lee Carrier and Roger Campbell trained
with coach Bill Kipp in Allentown, Pennsylvania. *(Courtesy of Anita Entrikin Miller)*

In 1959, Diane Sherbloom and Roger Campbell won the Pacific Coast title and the U.S. silver medal in silver dance. *(Courtesy of Joan Sherbloom Peterson)*

Diane Sherbloom and Larry Pierce posed for photographers during their training at the Ardmore rink in Philadelphia. *(Courtesy of Joan Sherbloom Peterson)*

Bill Kipp worked with Rhode Michelson at the Albeth rink in Allentown, Pennsylvania, prior to the start of the 1961 North Americans. *(Courtesy of Anita Miller Entrikin)*

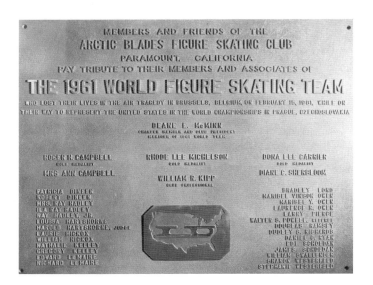

The Arctic Blades FSC memorial plaque, which lists all thirty-four names, still hangs in the Iceland rink in Paramount, California. *(Courtesy of Anita Entrikin Miller)*

The Broadmoor memorial skate blade bench, in honor of Steffi and Sherri Westerfeld, Edi and Jimmy Scholdan, Greg and Nathalie Kelley, and Laurie and Bill Hickox. *(Courtesy of Dudley Abbe)*

Prior to the 1961 Midwesterns in Troy, Ohio, Edi Scholdan spoke to the Broadmoor competitors on behalf of all the coaches: "You are all going as a team. No one person is better than the other person. I expect everybody to support their teammates and cheer for them." In Troy it was obvious which skaters were from the Broadmoor because they wore team uniforms both on and off the ice. On ice the women wore gray pleated skirts and navy blue blazers with the Broadmoor logo.[54]

Newlyweds Janet and Jim Browning won senior pairs and Vicky Fisher of Minneapolis won the senior ladies title after a four-year sweep by Steffi Westerfeld. Edi had recently invited Vicky to train with him at the Broadmoor, but she declined.[55]

The majority of potential World Team members, who had already participated nationally at the senior level or had placed in the top three at the junior level, did not need to compete in sectionals and could go directly to the 1961 Nationals. Larry Pierce and Roger Campbell had to compete in sectionals since they had new partners, but Larry and Diane were given special permission to bypass Midwesterns due to the recent formation of their partnership.[56]

At the 1961 Easterns, Harold Hartshorne was runner-up to Ritter Shumway yet again in the veterans' dance. Bob and Pat Dineen elected to compete and won the gold dance. As new parents, they reviewed their priorities and asked former coach Jean Westwood what she thought of their chances to make the 1961 World Team. "Quite honestly, you could make the team because the champions have retired," she responded. "However, you should really think of following in your father's steps as a judge now that you have a baby. You may want to think of that [responsibility] rather than the chance of making the World Team."[57]

The Dineens pressed onward. However, Pat had a premonition that something was going to happen to her. Dottie Otto recalled that one day, while they were lacing up their skates for a dance session, Pat said she had a feeling that she was going to die. "Pat didn't act concerned or puzzled; she shared this premonition matter-of-factly." Pat also confided to Charlie Rizzo that she kept having the same bizarre dream: "I dream of a black curtain, floating in the wind, and I get tangled up in it."[58]

Dona Lee Carrier and Roger Campbell won gold dance at Southwest Pacific, beating out ex-partners Yvonne Littlefield and Howie Harrold. Dona Lee had never won first place before, and she had never looked better in her life. Her renewed confidence was reflected in her performance at Pacific Coast, held at the Polar Palace. Dona Lee and Roger won gold dance again; Yvonne and Howie elected not to compete.[59]

After ten years of skating, Dona Lee was going to the Nationals for the first time. Several exhibitions were held at Iceland and Polar Palace to help finance their trip. Roger and Dona Lee felt confident they would make the World Team and didn't expect to return to Hollywood for months.[60]

A week before Nationals, Rhode seemed up to her old tricks. She coaxed skater Marlene Morris into skipping practice and driving in Rhode's old station wagon to the Paramount Mortuary so she could leave a note on her boyfriend's car. On the return ride, however, she asked Marlene what she wanted to do with her skating:

> I was older and I told her I just wanted to do the best I could. I was having problems with my current coach and she said, "I can probably get Bill to take you on as a student, but you'd have to promise that you will really work because he's not going to take someone who's not willing to work." Rhode really wanted to be on the World Team and she told me, "You really have to want it to get it. You can't be afraid to go out after it."[61]

Even though Rhode had her heart set on making the team, school was a different matter. Unlike most top skaters, Rhode had never done well in school. She told the press she wanted to be a doctor, perhaps an attempt to mold herself into Tenley Albright, who was now a surgeon. Rhode had attended Progress High School, a Lutheran private school in Long Beach, but then transferred to Banning High School where she was a senior. She took a leave of absence to prepare for the Nationals but planned to graduate after competition.[62]

Bill Kipp was leaving behind many students during the five-week competition schedule, including twelve-year-old Peggy Fleming. Rhode rubbed shoulders with all the young figure skaters. She gave Jennie Walsh one of her old dresses before she left for Nationals, saying "Jennie, you'll grow into this dress one of these days."[63]

Rhode slowly began winning over some of the skating moms. "I always felt secure knowing that Rhode was at the rink because she mothered my daughter," Mary Miller said. Mary threw Rhode an impromptu party before she left for Nationals, and all the kids from the rink came. With Barbara Roles's retirement, Rhode was the new ice princess in Los Angeles.[64]

Teachers at Redford High School in Detroit willingly rearranged Doug Ramsay's schedule so he could practice six hours daily. "He was a good student ... and a credit to himself," said the assistant principal. Although Doug had planned to attend Michigan State, he recently learned he had a chance to enter Harvard because of his high scholastic standing. "It made him work even harder at his studies," sister Judy said.[65]

There were just a couple of weeks left before skaters from across the nation arrived at the Broadmoor for the 1961 U.S. Championships. One day during a practice session, everyone stood at the boards, and one by one started imitating each other. Ardith Paul recalled: "Greg Kelley did an attitude spin (free leg bent behind, raised and stretched outward) and everyone said, 'Oh, that's Ardith, that's Ardith!' and we just laughed and laughed. It was a real tension-reliever just before competition." Greg, sixteen, knew the Broadmoor expected him to continue its winning streak in senior men. He loved competing, but his ultimate goal was to become a doctor like his father. After the 1964 Olympics, at age nineteen, Greg planned to hang up his skates for good. He told a reporter: "The pressure of competitive skating would become so great that it would cut into a normal college life."[66]

There was no question that Steffi planned to compete at the 1961 Nationals in her hometown rink, but she still had to make a choice. If she made the team, she would have to turn down her invitation to compete in a national piano contest in February. She had won the piano division of the Colorado State High School Music Contest and was scheduled to compete at the national championships in Philadelphia around the time the team was scheduled to fly to Prague. Her piano teacher was upset with her final decision, but Edi was pleased. He had just written Roberta in Vienna, telling her that he and Jimmy were coming but that Ruthie was too young to travel to Europe.[67]

Bill Hickox's girlfriend, Anne Frazier, made a stop in Colorado Springs on her way home from Smith College on her Christmas break. She went with Bill to a dance at the Air Force Academy, but otherwise saw very little of him. Mrs. Hickox would not allow Anne to go to the rink to see him practice. Anne and Bill's sister, Laurie, had spent a lot of time together that summer, and Laurie had done things that upset her mother, who in turn blamed Anne, who clearly understood the dynamic: "She was trying to find something to be mad at me about, because I was the girlfriend." Still, the trip ended on a high note at the Colorado Springs airport where Bill and Anne decided to marry after they graduated from college—even though it was three and a half years away.[68]

Greg and Nathalie Kelley had just returned to Colorado after spending Christmas in Boston. The Boston skaters had not seen Greg much over the past year and a half, and he had grown up considerably, as Christie Allan noted: "He wasn't little Gregory anymore, he was a young man. He said, 'Hello, Christine,' very seriously. I remember thinking, 'Oh, Gregory, don't you realize I love you still! Even though you left Mr. Wilson, it doesn't mean I am mad at you.' He came back thinking that we would all be partisan to Bradley, that we would not be his friend, but we were all happy to see him." Bradley Lord took a leave of absence from his senior year at Boston University to concentrate on the upcoming Nationals. School was important, but attaining the 1961 senior men's title was paramount at the moment.[69]

Laurence and Maribel were back at each other's throats, primarily because of the pressure. With Barbara Roles out of the picture, Laurence was a favorite to win, but mother and daughter quarreled non-stop. At one dramatic point, Laurence ran off the ice and into the ladies' room. Maribel followed her, hauled her back on the ice, and locked the gate leading out to the rink.[70]

The Owen girls' stress translated into a short fuse on the ice. They would send younger skaters scampering when they shouted, "Get out of my way!" during their programs. When the press made periodic visits, however, they presented well-schooled positive fronts. "Both girls [are] the products of their mother's relentless drive to make them champions, but neither ever showed resentment," one reported optimistically. "Certainly it's tough," Laurence said, "but I love every moment of it." Laurence's pressure-cooker intensified when she fell, injuring her right knee. She took some time off but soon returned to the ice despite the pain.[71]

At school Laurence was thriving. Her senior class at Winchester High School had voted her "Best Figure" and "Most Likely to Succeed." Despite her heavy skating schedule, she participated in extra-curricular activities, was a member of the National Honor Society, and had won early admission to Radcliffe, her mother's alma mater. She took her midyear exams early so she could compete at Nationals and North Americans.[72]

At Boston University, Maribel Jr. joined the Sigma Kappa sorority, the Student Christian Association, and had just been chosen a homecoming queen candidate. One of her professors scheduled a final exam at the exact time she was scheduled to compete at Nationals. When she went to the professor to explain the predicament, he responded, "Well, Miss Owen, I am sure when you think it over you will realize which is more important." "Yeah, so I won't be there," she said with a grin. She was cocky about it, but the stress took its toll.[73]

At the rink, Little Maribel worked hard and tried to avoid trouble with her mother, but the goodwill didn't last. Maribel discovered that her daughter's infatuation with Dudley had grown into a serious relationship. Dudley had taken Little Maribel down to his family's home in Providence several times. "I liked [Little] Maribel," his sister said, "but I never had a real opportunity to get to know her because they hardly had any free time." Mama Maribel thought the world of Dudley—he was any mother's dream catch—but she wanted all of their energies focused on their training and not on each other. Again, Maribel turned her daughter's coaching over to someone else. "Maribel was fighting with them all the time," Ron Ludington recalled. "She called me and said, 'I can't deal with this!' All hell broke loose so I came to work with them."[74]

Maribel's role was not easy. Besides being a mother to her children, she was their coach, friend, greatest booster, and severest skating critic. Although she was a strong individual, Maribel admitted to close friends that the past year had been personally overwhelming. "The last year had been so difficult for Maribel," Ronna Goldblatt said. Even though Maribel seemed to manage perfectly fine on her own, "she was lonely and tired. She was just trying to get through the season."[75]

Part of her concern may have been over her elder daughter. Little Maribel had developed ulcers, and the pharmacist at the Winchester apothecary worried that her university studies and the pressures of skating were too much. She was losing weight drastically, and Dudley confided in Ron Ludington that he feared she was seriously ill. "She spit up a lot and had trouble skating through her programs," Ronna Goldblatt said. "She did not have much stamina."[76]

———————

On the other side of the country, Ila Ray Hadley had the opposite problem. She was as tall as Ray and lifting her was a struggle. She strove to lose weight and he strengthened himself by running five miles every morning or evening.[77]

Ila Ray attended Edison Technical School in the evening, taking geometry and literature classes, and planned to enter the University of Washington in the spring; she longed for something in addition to skating. Now that she was eighteen, she realized that she was legally an adult and could make her own decisions. As soon as they finished the competitive season, the siblings planned "to get out of here," either by leaving the sport or by training at the Broadmoor or some other facility.[78]

The Hadley parents were unaware of the potential mutiny. They thought they were making necessary sacrifices on behalf of their children to raise champions. Their training methods, which were completely acceptable for the time, produced positive competitive results but stunted their children's emotional growth, a result that became apparent only in retrospect. Linda's unrelenting drive may have been fueled by the fact that she did not have any personal competitive experience and may therefore have worked hard to make a success of both herself and her children.[79]

The Hadley kids put on their game faces and kept practicing. Before they left for Nationals, their fellow club members cooperatively gave them an extra wide berth on the Civic Center ice. Local club members put on a special skating exhibition to raise money for the Hadleys, in case they made the trip to Prague. At the club Christmas party, Ila Ray advertised her burgeoning independence by appearing in a stunning red dress.[80]

Before leaving for Colorado, Ila Ray and Ray still fantasized about leaving Seattle, as Darrell Mathias noted: "They came down to the Civic Arena the night before they left for competition. Ray and Ila Ray made a pact with a couple of friends that, when they got back from their competitions, somehow we were all going to go and escape, just get away for a couple of days. Ray said, 'This is going to happen. It will happen.'"[81]

⸺⸺◆⸺⸺

During the 1960 Olympics, Maribel mused to a reporter about how figure skating had changed:

> It isn't like it used to be. . . . We skated in the winter time only. . . . But nowadays a figure skater has to skate 12 months of the year. . . . Once I hesitated whether to steer Laurence and Maribel into skating. But they enjoyed it so. And I became so proud of the way they developed. Skating was a joy and a passion with me. I think it is with Laurence. More so than Maribel. [Laurence] has such wonderful rhythm, such fine co-ordination. I think some day she may do what her mother failed to do—win a gold medal in the Olympics.[82]

Even though the year had been extremely taxing, Maribel was on a mission to get her daughters to Colorado and return home with two new U.S. champions. Grammy Vinson and the girls were hoping for the same goal. A reporter had recently asked Laurence why she went through "the long hours of tortuous training for a small piece of hardware and a title, which at best, was transient. 'Oh,' she said, 'I have to. It's like a mountain. It's there. No one knows why a person climbs a mountain. . . . No one knows why a person figure skates.'"[83]

CHAPTER 14

1961 NATIONALS

In the middle of January, Marilyn Meeker finally got her cast off. The same week, Larry Pierce and Diane Sherbloom gave a dazzling performance for the Indianapolis press. The audience didn't realize how impressive it actually was; Diane had the flu including a 100-plus temperature. Marilyn wished Larry well before he left with Diane for the 1961 Nationals in Colorado Springs.[1]

After an intensive month of practices, Larry, Diane, Pieter Kollen, and Dorothyann Nelson piled into Danny Ryan's station wagon. The intrepid travelers caravanned with another car full of Ryan's students toward Colorado. Danny, Larry, and Pieter took turns driving non-stop all night, while the girls slept in the back in sleeping bags. At Nationals, all of Danny's students dressed in matching outfits so everyone could recognize his dancers. He understood it was in his best interest to reinforce his role as a leading dance coach. Because ice time at the Coliseum was seasonal, his master plan was to raise money to build a private rink in Indianapolis.[2]

When the competitors arrived at the Broadmoor, the rink looked different. With renovations and a new name—the Broadmoor World Arena—the ice surface had increased from 185 by 85 feet, to 190 by 100 feet, the seating capacity had been increased from 3,200 to 5,000, a new south side entrance had been built, and the main entrance had been remodeled. The hotel itself was undergoing renovation. The Broadmoor Hotel was now the Broadmoor Main and an adjacent Broadmoor South building was under construction, as was the Broadmoor International Center.[3]

The Colorado press heralded the upcoming competition. Daily news accounts previewed the skaters in each event and publicized how unusual it was that no senior defending champions would compete. Since 1946, the men's and ladies titles had been won by the defending champion or the previous year's runner-up. This year spectators would witness the emergence of six new champions.[4]

The Broadmoor Skating Club (BSC) had won the Harned Trophy for team competition the past two years and was eager to retain the honor. The Skating Club (SC) of Boston, the strongest challenger, had eight competitors, four of whom were returning World Team members, while the Broadmoor had only six competitors.[5]

The Boston-based USFSA dealt a blow to the BSC by announcing that Greg Kelley could not compete for the Broadmoor. He had transferred his membership from the SC of Boston only recently. Under USFSA policy, a skater had to wait a year to change a home club membership, thus preventing clubs from grabbing potential prize-winning pupils prior to a competition. The BSC also lost Tim Brown, now representing Berkeley's St. Moritz club.[6]

On Friday, January 20, 1961, most skaters took time out to watch John Fitzgerald Kennedy sworn in as the thirty-fifth president of the United States. In his inaugural address, he invited the Communist world to join him in a "quest of peace." Ken Kelley no doubt hoped the Czech organizing committee would take this message to heart. Bill Hickox had been scheduled to play with the Air Force Academy Band at the inauguration but felt he needed to stay in Colorado and continue training with his sister. Dudley Richards was President Kennedy's personally invited guest, but he also chose to spend the time training in Colorado.[7]

On Sunday, January 22, as the 100 skaters gathered in Colorado Springs, they were stunned to learn of the passing of USFSA President Howard D. Herbert at age seventy-three. The forty-fourth U.S. Championships were dedicated to his memory. On the eve of the competition, the first vice president, F. Ritter Shumway, was suddenly thrust into the limelight as acting president.[8]

As they practiced, most skaters were affected by Colorado's high mountain altitude. The BSC president dryly remarked, "It was the general opinion that the altitude wouldn't affect the winners at all but would be the determining factor to the losers." Practice time at the Broadmoor World Arena proved livelier than usual, as a club member noted:

> Several near catastrophes almost occurred when the Zamboni threatened to scoop up several competitors who diligently tried to get in a last three change three or a split twist before the next practice group took the ice. On one occasion some found themselves in the midst of a full fledged hockey game as the Colorado College hockey team roared on the ice for a practice session. . . . Complaints were heard concerning the fact that the rink was closed at one o'clock in the morning and didn't open again until 5 A.M. and it seemed a shame to let those precious four hours of ice time go by.[9]

Ticket sales for the four-day meet had been robust. The entire series cost between $4.00-$7.50; daytime performances were a mere sixty cents a ticket. For the first time, the four senior events would also be televised nationally.[10]

Dick Button had had the foresight to suggest broadcasting the 1961 Nationals. He had no doubt that skating would be popular with the American public and that television coverage would dramatically increase skating's fan base. He did, however, have trouble convincing television executives. Even though "nobody wanted anything to do with it," he was able to arrange the broadcasting rights with CBS. Sportscaster Bud Palmer, who had worked with Button during the 1960 Winter Games, joined Dick again to describe the action for a Sunday session on CBS Sports Spectacular.[11]

The day before the competition began, the judges and officials arrived, including Deane McMinn and referee Walter Powell. They received fur hats as a thank-you gift. A minor crisis developed when judge Dorothy Burkholder, allergic to the fur, sneezed and sniffled throughout the competition. Newbold Black vividly recalled his first Nationals judging experience in 1961: "The male judges wore black tie for all the evening events, and every night chief referee Hank Beatty held a cocktail party in his suite before dinner." Despite this hospitality, the judges were restrained. "We did not want the appearance that we may be intoxicated."[12]

On the eve of competition, the Broadmoor treated competitors and officials to a chuck wagon dinner. Broadmoor titans Charles and Thayer Tutt were hosts in the new Winter House, a chateau located at Ski Broadmoor on Cheyenne Mountain. The evening glittered with a smorgasbord, a performance of rousing German and Austrian songs, a roaring fire, a picturesque snowfall, and torchlight skiers carving the slopes. As always, the Broadmoor orchestrated a memorable spectacle.[13]

―――――――

The 1961 U.S. Figure Skating Championships began on Wednesday, January 25, with novice division figures. Many novice and junior skaters were making their first trip to a national competition. "I was a kid in a candy store," Billy Chapel said. "I spent the whole time watching these amazing people. . . . It was so much bigger than anything I was used to." Gary Visconti agreed: "Broadmoor was like an Olympic Village. You saw everybody all the time—lobby, elevator, everywhere. It was nice because we felt free. We could go out and do what we wanted to do, but we knew our parents were still on the same property."[14]

As competitors finished their events, they enjoyed the resort's amenities. Some swam in the outdoor heated pool, while others went horseback riding in the mountains. But most skaters had brought their schoolbooks and studied in their rooms between events; some university students were required to take exams at Colorado College. The senior competitors needed a good night's rest as the next day their quest to qualify for the World Team began.[15]

Beginning in 1961 the senior events became gender specific: only men judged the men's event and only women judged the ladies event. Early Thursday morning five female judges walked onto the ice to judge the senior ladies figures. They were dressed in heavy coats and snow boots, and they carried clipboards, papers, and pens. Laurence Owen took an early lead, but Steffi ended on top with three first place votes; Laurence placed second, Karen Howland third, Vicky Fisher fourth, and Rhode Michelson fifth.[16]

Junior men's figures followed and Monty Hoyt of the Broadmoor captured the lead, with eleven-year-old Scotty Allen in second. That evening, tiny Tina Noyes of Boston performed a brilliant free skating program that pulled her all the way up from sixth place to win novice ladies. Peter Meyer of Buffalo retained his lead and won novice men.[17]

The junior pairs climax came Thursday evening. Ron and Vivian Joseph of Chicago dominated the competition with a dynamic, well-executed program. Dick Button had CBS film the youngsters. "In my opinion it won't be many years before they're World, and even possibly Olympic champions," he said.[18]

After Thursday night's performances, the local paper wrote: "This should be one of the most suspense-packed tournaments over U.S. skating laurels in a decade or more." Even though the skaters performed brilliantly, the altitude was taking its toll. Junior pairs competitor Paul George was one of many skaters who were affected: "I was interviewed by the *Denver Post* early in the week and I commented that the altitude didn't bother me a bit. Then we skated our program and we ended up fifth; the altitude clearly bothered me." The altitude meltdown was obvious to the audience. One girl in a pair team collapsed against her partner due to oxygen depletion.[19]

Most skaters had come to Colorado early to get acclimated. Pair team Jim and Janet Browning used an alternative strategy—to come in at the last moment and go for it full blast, as Janet noted: "The MSU hockey coach told us to take iron pills and we didn't have as much trouble with the altitude as other skaters. Many stumbled off the ice and looked like zombies."[20]

The altitude problem suddenly seemed trivial when a news story appeared on Thursday announcing that the Worlds in Prague "have been definitely cancelled." The details modified this stark pronouncement. The ISU warned; "Unless the Czechoslovakian Government furnished proof of its good intentions by next weekend, the union [would] award the meet to another European city." The ISU board had voted unanimously that the championships would not be held in Prague unless Otto and Maria Jelinek could be assured of safe passage to and from Czechoslovakia.[21]

The senior men took the ice early Friday morning. Tim Brown, the perennial winner in the figure competition, demonstrated uncharacteristic vulnerability. A seesaw battle between Bradley Lord and Greg Kelley ensued with Kelley holding a slim lead at the end of six figures. Bradley placed second, even after stopping in the middle of one of his figures. Tim Brown placed third, followed by Bruce Heiss and Doug Ramsay.[22]

On Friday evening, the junior men's finals concluded. Broadmoor's Monty Hoyt won the event and Scotty Allen placed second. Even though Tommy Litz of Hershey placed sixth, he made a big impression. Litz weighed in on that memorable competition: "I was having difficulty with the altitude but my teacher told me the third day would be the worst and then I would feel more acclimated, and he was right. By the time I did my program I had a terrifically clean performance." Litz was one of only two competitors to execute a perfect triple salchow.[23]

The final event on Friday night was senior pairs. Dudley Richards, who was competing in his fourteenth Nationals, had more on his mind than winning a title. Olympian Bobby Brewer, who drove from Los Angeles to Colorado at the last minute to see his friends compete, recalled:

> One day I was at the Broadmoor Hotel and Dudley said, "Bobby, why don't you come with me? I want to talk to you." I went to his room and we talked as he changed clothes. "I have something to tell you." "What is it?" "Well, I've asked Little Maribel to marry me and she said yes. When we get back from the Worlds I'm going to announce it." "Gee, that's wonderful. I'm so happy for you." "Please don't tell anybody. The reason I wanted to tell you is that I feel you are like part of the family. You're going to be out in L.A. so I wanted to tell you now, person to person, because it will be the last chance I have to do that."[24]

Brewer was amazed because he had never thought of Dudley and Maribel as a romantic couple when he lived in the Owen home, from the spring of 1959 through winter 1960. "Dudley used to come around a lot. Maybe I was naïve and didn't understand what that was all about," he said. Nearly a year had gone by since Brewer left the Owens and a great deal had transpired since his departure. Still, Dudley and Little Maribel's relationship was a well-kept secret.[25]

The senior pairs competition began that evening, with television cameras filming the performances. Skaters soon discovered the negative side of television production. "They used power lights that gave off so much heat," Gary Visconti said. "It was hot and stuffy, and the altitude was bad on top of that. It definitely made a difference." Another competitor concurred: "They had these bright lights all over the arena, and I got lost and didn't know which end was what."[26]

CBS-TV commentator Bud Palmer, dressed in a suit with a thin black tie, and a young Dick Button, casually dressed in a white turtleneck and a wide-striped cardigan, introduced the broadcast. Button recapped the unusual nature of this competition: "Bud, they're going to be wide open. After the Olympics most people drop out, turn professional or decide to stop skating. So this year we're going to have an exciting competition. . . . Everybody's fighting for the title."[27]

Ray Hadley quickly brushed the front of his suit and Ila Ray did some deep knee bends before stepping onto the ice. She wore a dark, lace-trimmed dress with a V-shaped neckline, and he wore a tailored suit with a USFSA patch on his sleeve, a tradition at the time. The Hadleys performed to "I Could Have Danced All Night" from the Lerner and Loewe musical *My Fair Lady*. Their program was full of jumps, lifts, and pair spins. Their unique moves included axels into a flying camel, an axel lift into a back pair sit-spin, and an unusual combination: side-by-side traveling camels into a pairs waltz jump into a flying camel. The Hadleys skated conservatively, but their program was executed without any mistakes, and they received a hearty ovation. The attending nurse, a matronly woman dressed in a starched white uniform and cap, helped Ila Ray on with her coat when she stepped off the ice.[28]

Button acknowledged that they had skated much better here than they had in Squaw Valley. The judges gave two marks: the first for "contents of program," which ranged from 5.0 to 5.6, and the second for "manner of performance," which ranged from 4.9 to 5.6. The highest mark attainable was 6.0.[29]

Bill and Laurie Hickox followed. The local press supported the town's adopted pair team, and Edi Scholdan, a master at spin, boasted that Bill and Laurie had a strong chance to win. "They are very well matched and work together unusually well," he said. Laurie wore a beautiful dress with a bejeweled bodice, and Bill wore a short-jacketed tux, which was his Air Force Academy mess dress uniform. They skated with great flow, had inventive footwork, beautiful spread eagles, and many lifts, including an overhead, axel, and split lutz. Despite an extra three turn on Laurie's second axel, they skated extremely well.[30]

When Maribel Owen and Dudley Richards stepped on the ice, she did a little curtsy and he nodded to the crowd while testing his blades; he had broken one the day before and had replaced it with one from a five-year-old pair of skates he had fortunately brought with him. Maribel wore an elegant, golden-yellow dress with a fur-trimmed scoop neckline and Dudley looked smart in his tailored suit with his USFSA patch over his heart. Little Maribel tossed a quick smile to Big Maribel.[31]

Dudley and Maribel burst through their first twenty seconds with incredible speed, executing three lifts, a pair-spin, side-by-side double loops, and multiple single jumps. Maribel and Dudley held onto each other as they did spread eagles. Their slow section included five lifts and a spiral sequence into back camels. They ended their program with double salchows, axels, and a nice cartwheel lift in the final seconds.[32]

Their program was almost flawless. Dudley nearly slipped after his walley and Maribel put her foot down on her double salchow, but Button commented that "double salchows are very difficult for pair skaters to do." The caliber of their lifts was similar to the Hadleys, but Maribel and Dudley had the edge with their speed and individual jumps. "They had a harmony together that at the time was unmatched by anybody," a competitor said. Their marks ranged from 5.6 to 5.8 and 5.5 to 5.6. The judges clearly placed them first, making it difficult for the other teams to beat them.[33]

Tacoma-based siblings Jerry and Judianne Fotheringill were favored for third, but their performance went terribly wrong. To Judianne, it was a performance she'd rather forget:

> We had been skating well and were trained to go out and do it that night, but we did not. We had contracted Howard Cracker [who filmed skaters] to record our performance, and even today it is painful to watch. It was dreadful. The mistakes we made were not your run of the mill mistakes. We didn't fall on jumps, but we muffed things and some of the lifts didn't go as planned. It just looked pretty ragged.[34]

Janet and Jim Browning, newlyweds from Indianapolis, felt they had a shot at third place. The Brownings felt the high altitude worked in their favor because it made their jumps higher and lifts easier. "You are not used to being so light, and you almost had to be careful that you didn't go out of your partner's arms," Janet said. "I thought we did a great job."[35]

After the results were tabulated, Maribel and Dudley received unanimous first-place votes to win their first U.S. senior pairs title. This was Dudley's third national title, after winning novice men in 1946 and junior men in 1951. Little Maribel now had a second national title, along with her 1955 junior pairs title. The Hadleys earned the most applause of the evening, but placed second.[36]

The marks between the Fotheringills and the Hickoxes were razor-thin for third place. The Fotheringills received two seconds and three fourths and the Hickoxes received four thirds and one fourth—each had a total ordinal of sixteen. The Hickox team had a majority of thirds and were thus awarded third place. Bill and Laurie Hickox had just made the 1961 World Team, thanks to the encouragement of their mother. "It was the best opportunity they ever had, and I'm sure Bill and Laurie felt the same way," former coach Julie Barrett said. "It was an experience they had lived for—for years."[37]

Bill and Laurie's good fortune contrasted with the Fotheringills' heartache. They were surprised to be in fourth place because the Hickox kids had never beaten them before. "They probably deserved what they got and we probably deserved our placement," Jerry said, "but we were upset with ourselves at the time." Judianne added, "It was very justified that we were not put on the team, but it was disappointing." Bill Hickox acknowledged that the only reason they made the 1961 World Team was because the Fotheringills didn't skate well.[38]

The Brownings placed fifth, although some people, including several coaches, thought they should have been placed higher. Maribel told them they had been robbed, adding, "You should have come earlier." Janet replied, "Maribel, we couldn't afford to come any sooner." Maribel retorted, "You couldn't afford not to! You should have been here so the judges could find out who you are." It was classic Maribel—encouraging her daughter's competitor because she wanted everyone to be at their best.[39]

The senior ladies took to the ice at 9:45 P.M. First up was Rhode Michelson. Currently in last place, she was ready for the fight of her life, as a skater noted: "When she took her guards off to get on the ice she said she was going to pull up if it killed her." Attired in a rhinestone-studded red dress with a multi-layered chiffon skirt, she stepped onto the ice and remained in position for the first fifteen seconds of Bernie Wayne's "The Man and His Music"—and then exploded like a ball shot out of a cannon.[40]

In rapid-fire succession Rhode performed a double loop, a double salchow, a double toe loop, and her signature traveling camels going into a camel spin. Her high-octane beginning prompted Button to exclaim, "She's pushing very hard. I hope she can sustain this for the four minutes." Her slow section included two double axels in a row, cleanly landed. The final portion of her routine included a double lutz, a double salchow, two walleys, and a closing spin with tremendous power.[41]

Rhode was very popular with the crowd and had a huge rooting section, composed primarily of Lake Placid skaters. Bill Kipp gave her a hug as she got off the ice; and Edi Scholdan, standing nearby, generously clapped for her. Her marks for content and manner of performance ranged from 5.0 to 5.4—embarrassingly low, since she was clearly the strongest skater in the group. Granted, her extension in her arms and legs was lacking. Regardless, the audience was bowled over by her performance. "Rhode Lee Michelson was exciting to watch because she was so athletic. She was a real fireball out there," a fan said.[42]

Karen Howland, currently in third, was a versatile skater. She had first begun on roller skates and started figure skating when she was seven. She never made a permanent switch; she could do double axels in both kinds of skates. She came into the competition as the 1960 U.S. junior ladies champion. Her coach in Seattle, Hans Johnsen, was not able to accompany her, and Edi Scholdan agreed to put her on the ice. She felt ready to win the bronze, but instead "did not skate a clean program. I absolutely bombed," she said. "It was very warm in the rink, but I wouldn't use that as an excuse. I just didn't skate well. Usually freestyle was my strong point, so I was pretty devastated. Edi Scholdan was standing by the rail waiting for me when I got off, and even he couldn't believe I did that poorly."[43]

The next competitor was Stephanie Westerfeld, with the goal of being the first skater west of the Mississippi to hold the U.S. ladies figure skating title. In her favor she had the familiarity of the Broadmoor ice and the mile-high altitude, the partisan hometown crowd to cheer her on, and the local press: "Steffi Bids for Ladies Title in National Figure Skating Meet." All of the young Broadmoor girls tried to clap Steffi into first place: "We stood around saying, 'We're going to cheer really loudly and maybe that will impress the judges.'"[44]

Currently in first by the smallest of margins, Steffi knew the Broadmoor had also set its hopes for a national title on her. She suspected that some judges and officials felt that Laurence Owen was the rightful heir to the senior ladies' crown because she was the daughter of Maribel Vinson Owen. However, not all USFSA officials were Owen family supporters.

Sherri Westerfeld, who had been ferrying records to the record booth as a music committee member, was close at hand to lend moral support. Steffi's grandmother, watching Steffi compete for the first time, was in the audience with Myra. Steffi skated onto the ice in a scarlet dress with a beautiful rhinestone neckline. She flashed a huge smile as she began and kept it throughout her performance.[45]

Skating to Puccini's *La Boheme*, she opened with a solid axel followed by a double axel that was plainly cheated. Her first falter came with her double flip. She singled out of it but recovered with a flying camel combination spin followed by a spin/double salchow combination. In the slow section of her program, she executed a double toe loop, but singled out of a double loop. As the music tempo changed, some nice footwork led into another double axel and a double axel into a spin. In her final minute she performed a beautifully executed Ina Bauer, two double salchows, an axel, a split jump, and finished with a fast toe spin.[46]

Steffi grabbed her guards and was greeted warmly by Edi. She had skated with grace, but it was not the performance she had intended. "Steffi was usually a solid and steady skater, but she was not perfect that night," a club member said. "There was a lot of pressure on her and it may well have been in her own mind because it was her own turf." Despite a couple of mistakes, Steffi drew a huge round of applause from her hometown crowd and received strong marks from the judges. Now she had to wait and see how Laurence would do.[47]

Laurence Owen took off her large coat, stepped onto the ice, and headed toward the center of the ice, wearing a soft green dress that flattered her tall figure. She quickly pulled the snow off each blade before the music started. She struck a regal pose, like a queen awaiting her crown. She looked as if she had already won.[48]

Skating to Berlioz's "Symphonie Fantastique," Laurence opened with great speed and performed a large waltz jump, an axel, and an axel into a back sit spin. She followed her opening with a double salchow and a double loop but fell out of her double flip. That mistake was followed by a cheated double axel, a series of walleys into a double toe loop, and an incomplete double lutz. In her slow section, she took her time interpreting the music and her ballet training was fully evident. She executed a beautiful layback spin, two split jumps, and a graceful spread eagle. She seemed to tire near the end but finished with nice spins: a flying camel and a flying sit/crossfoot combination spin. She threw her arms up triumphantly at the end to the excitement of the enthralled audience.[49]

When Laurence stepped off the ice, she fell into her sister's arms and the two clung together. Big Maribel pulled Little Maribel away, and Laurence returned to the ice on her own initiative for another bow to the audience. "Despite the fact that she skated very well she also made some errors and I'd say it's really a tossup as to who will win this championship," Button said. "She seems very popular though."[50]

She was, in fact, popular with the judges, receiving marks of 5.5 to 5.8 for content and 5.5 to 5.7 for manner of performance. Each judge marked Laurence higher than Steffi. Laurence had won the freestyle, but it was not clear whether her marks were high enough to place her in first overall. The three Owen women departed together, arm in arm.[51]

No matter the outcome, Laurence had accumulated a new set of admirers. Everyone liked her distinctive, pixie-cut hairstyle. "Everyone else wore a bubble with every hair in place. Laurence's hair wasn't and that was very interesting," a Broadmoor skater said. She especially captured the hearts of men in the audience. Besides being wholesome in a sexy way, they thought her skating transcended the athletic, as a fan noted: "Laurence was just so free and floating, as though she was released from being in handcuffs. It was her time and she knew it. It didn't matter what she did, she was going to win."[52]

Vicky Fisher of Minneapolis, in fourth place, was affected by the altitude and did not skate her best. She acknowledged, "I got fatigued like I never have in my entire life. It was hard physically to get through my program, and you could see it on everyone else. Nobody skated well, but Rhode skated the best. In my program I wrote 'No' by everyone, but by Rhode I wrote 'Yes!'"[53]

Laurence ended up in first place with four firsts and one second; Steffi was second with one first and four seconds. The girls had had similar content and had made similar mistakes, but Laurence had the edge in her presentation. "Laurence was such a dynamic figure and she had these big jumps, whereas Steffi's jumps were rather small and kind of cautious," a Broadmoor skater said.[54]

The margin was agonizingly close between third and fourth. Karen Howland received two thirds, two fourths, and one fifth; Rhode Michelson received the exact same marks. Both girls had a total ordinal of nineteen; the skater with the largest point total would win the bronze. Karen had 911.90 points and Rhode had 913.49. Rhode won third place by 1.59 points, primarily on the strength of her powerful free skate. Vicky Fisher had to settle for fifth place. "I was last, but I was okay [with it] because I didn't skate that well," she said.[55]

Near midnight, Little Maribel and Dudley were awarded the Henry Wainwright Howe Memorial Trophy for the U.S. pairs title. Bud Palmer joined Little Maribel and Dudley on the ice, and asked him what was up next: "Skating wise we go on to Philadelphia for the North American Championships and then to Prague for the World Championships. . . . [T]hen I'll have to get back to my real estate job in Boston."[56]

The Gertrude Cheever Porter trophy for the U.S. ladies title went to Laurence. "Maribel Vinson" was engraved at the top of one column, and "Laurence Owen" would now be engraved at the top of a new column. It was the first and only time a mother and daughter both won the U.S. senior ladies title. Bud and Dick joined Laurence on the ice. "Now here's a very happy young lady, Laurence Owen, our national ladies champion. Congratulations to you," Bud said. "Oh, why thank you, Mr. Palmer. Golly, I feel terrific right now," Laurence beamed. "Dick, you were certainly pulling for Laurence, weren't you?" Bud asked. "I certainly was, Bud," Dick replied, "and I'm just delighted that she won; she did a wonderful job."[57]

Stephanie Westerfeld was disappointed that she didn't win, but the silver medal was a great achievement. "Steffi didn't skate well at all the seven days before the competition, so it was a pleasant surprise when she made the World Team," a skater recalled. No one was prouder than her sister, Sherri, who had never competed internationally; it would be Sherri's first trip abroad, too.[58]

Karen Howland was devastated by her performance, and the day after the competition she could not be found. After her poor performance, she had found Edi Scholdan waiting for her at the railing, and he had announced: "You're going skiing. . . . You need to let off steam and go have fun." She had never skied before, but Edi took her up the mountain and quickly taught her, as the USFSA searched for her. Edi's prescription was good therapy, but the USFSA "scolded" both of them roundly, Karen recalled. She had been named to the North American Team, and the USFSA had nightmares that she might get hurt.[59]

Rhode Michelson, the third-place finisher, also laid low the next morning. Few people knew that she had skated despite an injury. "Rhode hurt her ankle before the competition and it flared up again in Colorado," Gary Visconti said. "My mom had brought a red plastic heating pad and we gave it to Rhode. She was a wild one—saying what she felt and not giving a darn about anybody." Rhode, however, was trying hard to be on her best behavior. She needed to be ladylike because now she would be her country's representative behind the Iron Curtain.[60]

The debate about where to hold the 1961 Worlds concluded on Saturday. Cables had zipped between Prague, Davos, and Colorado Springs during the previous days with Davos or the Broadmoor under consideration as possible replacements. Even though the Broadmoor was busy hosting the Nationals, it hoped to also host the 1961 Worlds, now less than one month away. After the ISU threatened to yank the competition, the Czech government sent it "an unheard-of-letter which attacked the ISU in the strongest terms and accused it of mixing sports with politics." The ISU did not back down. The next day a humbler cable from Prague confirmed that the Jelineks' Czech citizenship had already been withdrawn on December 27. On Saturday, January 28, ISU president Dr. James Koch announced that the 1961 Worlds would be held in Prague because the Jelineks' nationality problems had been settled.[61]

The same day, the silver dance title was decided. Ila Ray and Ray Hadley Jr., the 1960 silver dance runner-ups, were expected to win. The silver dance competition, however, was a surprise, as Pieter Kollen noted: "In 1960 the Dineens won and moved up [to gold dance]. The Hadleys were second, Dorothyann [Nelson] and I were third, and Stan Urban and Wilma Piper were fourth, so we thought one of us would be first." Instead, David Owen and Rosemary McEvoy of Brooklyn won. "We couldn't believe it. The Hadleys were second, we were third, and Stan and Wilma were fourth—two years in a row."[62]

In junior ladies, placements remained intact after the freestyle, and Lorraine Hanlon of Boston won the title. The altitude and overheated arena continued to be a problem. "I could do my program twice in a row at sea level but I was having a lot of trouble with the heat," said Michelle Monnier of San Francisco.[63]

The senior men's final didn't begin until 10:15 P.M. because the schedule ran late. Each competitor had an impressive resume. Greg Kelley was powerful and had big jumps; Bradley Lord was a lyrical skater with solid jumps and good speed; Tim Brown's talent lay in step sequences and innovative choreography; and Doug Ramsay had phenomenal jumps. "It was a magnificent time in skating," one competitor said.[64]

Tim Brown, a familiar presence at Nationals and a former Broadmoor skater, received a warm welcome from the crowd. Button noted that Tim "has one of the most interesting programs," and he wasn't exaggerating. Tim often inserted or deleted maneuvers during competition; on this occasion, he seemed to make up the program as he went along. After a long sequence of footwork circling the ice several times, Tim fell out of a double flip, followed by more footwork, a split jump, a spread eagle, and several camel spins. Dick was speechless, not knowing what would happen next. An attempted double lutz turned into a half-completed single lutz. When Tim did a double loop, the crowd cheered at the first fully completed double jump. As Tim did more footwork, the flummoxed Button exclaimed, "With Tim it's very difficult to know what he's going to do."[65]

Tim looked very tired in the last minute of his program, which consisted of a waltz jump, a series of walleys, a double salchow, and a scratch foot spin. At the conclusion of his program Button exclaimed, "Watch this coming up now. I believe . . . it's an ending," and then described the final seconds: "There's a split jump and watch what he's trying to do. Oh!" The exclamation was echoed all over the arena. On Tim's second split jump, he purposely landed off the ice. No one had ever ended a program by jumping off the ice and landing in the exit area. Tim kept going and headed into the locker room, with a nurse chasing after him.[66]

Skaters expected the unexpected with Tim, but this performance seemed bizarre. Several skaters recalled Tim struggling for breath. "I saw his eyes roll up into his head and I thought he was going to pass out," a Broadmoor skater said. After Tim reached the locker room, he fainted. The organizers had anticipated that some skaters would have this problem; and medical personnel, their ambulance parked just outside the arena, swiftly administered oxygen. Tim soon revived.[67]

Tim's marks ranged from 5.2 to 5.6 for content and 5.0 to 5.5 on manner of performance. The content marks were generous, as he completed only two double jumps and didn't execute an axel. Tim had logged many noteworthy performances before the 1961 Nationals, but his lack of practice had caught up with him.[68]

Bruce Heiss, then in fourth place, had an excellent opportunity to move up to third, but he was another altitude victim, as he noted:

> I arrived only a few days before the competition. I "walked" through my number during training sessions, saving it for competition. About three and a half minutes into my five-minute number I was having a little hypoxia; the altitude was getting to me. Next thing I knew I woke up and the regulator was going off on the oxygen. They said I made it to the sidelines at the end of my program, and then they gave me oxygen.[69]

Doug Ramsay, who now had a better chance to move up from fifth place, had prepared well all week. "At the end of one hour-long practice session everybody had left the ice except Doug," Pieter Kollen recalled. "He was kind of beat and just perspiring, but Bill Swallender kept urging him on, saying 'Come on Doug, do it again. I feel good.' The more Doug did, the more Bill got excited."[70]

Doug, dressed in a dark tailored suit, white shirt, and bow tie, opened his program with a walley sequence, jumping in both directions. His program was packed with difficult jumps and exciting spins, including multiple flying camels and a flying camel/sit spin/axel into a back sit spin combination, a beautiful delayed axel, axels in both directions, double toe walley, double loop, double lutz, two double axels, including one with his arms folded, and a triple salchow. Then, in a giant circle, he popped off a double toe loop, double loop, double salchow, and a double flip. He ended his number with a split jump and a flying sit spin. The arena exploded into enthusiastic applause and cheers.[71]

Doug Ramsay developed an instant fan club. Dick Button was elated with Doug's effortless jumps and cried "beautiful" after every one. "He was destined to be the next David Jenkins—he was that good," Pieter Kollen said. Doug quickly bowed four times and gave a modest nod before stepping off the ice. Bill Swallender stretched out his hand to Doug and wrapped his other arm around Doug as they went into the locker room together.[72]

While the battle had been fought for third place, the senior men's title was still at stake. Greg Kelley's parents were in the stands, as they had been for every Nationals, hoping to see their son crowned the 1961 U.S. men's champion. Since Steffi was unsuccessful in winning senior ladies, the Broadmoor hoped Kelley would retain the men's crown. Scholdan felt Greg could do it: "Hayes was a brilliant artistic skater and there has never been a better jumper than David, but now Gregory has advanced to a position where he is combining Hayes' artistic touch and David's jumping." Greg also had the support of the Colorado press: "Kelley is regarded to be the finest free skater in the United States and should have little trouble wrapping up the senior men's championship."[73]

Greg wore a light-colored two-piece suit with a cross tie and his World patch on his sleeve. As he began skating to selections from the opera *Pagliacci* he performed his signature move, a delayed axel, followed by a double flip. He executed big jumps throughout his program, including a double salchow and a double lutz. After some musically inspired footwork came the most ambitious moment in his program. He performed a clean, high double axel, did a three turn, and performed an equally magnificent double axel. He ended his program with two walleys, a split jump, and a flying camel. After his flawless program, Scholdan and Greg's sister, Nathalie, exuberantly embraced him. Greg had done his best, and his superb program raised the bar for Bradley Lord.[74]

In order to win, Bradley could not make any mistakes. His long career led up to this critical moment. Wearing his World patch on his sleeve, Brad skated to "Malaguena." He began with great speed and didn't let up. He executed a large opening axel, a double salchow, a giant sit spin, and a pair of walleys. After a double toe loop, he accelerated rapidly for his reverse spread eagles, followed by some fast footwork into a double flip, an axel sit spin, and a double loop. He received a big "ooh-aah" from the crowd when he did a reverse pivot swiftly across the ice. Button commented repeatedly on Bradley's speed at each step of his program. Bradley finished with a double lutz, an axel, a split jump, a flying sit spin, and a very fast scratch spin.[75]

Yet at the conclusion of the competition, there was no clear winner. Doug Ramsay had the most technically ambitious program with a triple salchow and two double axels, but he was far behind in figures. Greg Kelley had the biggest jumps and had executed two beautiful double axels, but wasn't as fast on the ice as Ramsay and Lord. Bradley was technically solid, but he didn't include a double axel in his program. To balance that, however, he had skated with terrific speed throughout the entire number, as friend Peter Betts noted: "He skated like the wind. He was so good he just had to win." Brad, receiving marks of 5.4 to 5.7 for content and 5.7 to 5.8 for manner of performance, beat Doug Ramsay in the free skating marks.[76]

As the senior men's results were tabulated, the dancers took to the ice. The press had chosen Bob and Pat Dineen, the 1960 silver dance champions, as the couple most likely to win. This assumption was based on the fact that the past two medalists, Larry Pierce and Roger Campbell, had new partners. Larry had a new partner out of necessity; but for the last three years, Roger had competed with a different partner. It was anyone's guess which team would win.[77]

Throughout the week, everyone had noticed Larry Pierce because of his high spirits. "He went up and down the hallways all night at the Broadmoor hotel," a competitor recalled. "He was such a free spirit, and he didn't care if people thought he was bad or good." Coach Bill Kipp, who had sprinkled compliments to competitors all week, told Larry's coach Danny Ryan, "Larry's cha-cha-ing better this year."[78]

The gold dance initial round was held late Saturday afternoon. Larry and Diane Sherbloom were first after the compulsories, Roger Campbell and Dona Lee Carrier were in second, and Bob and Pat Dineen placed third. The marks were close enough that anyone in the top three could win.

The dancers had an easier time in the finals than other senior competitors as their free dance program was only three minutes long.[79]

First up were Roger Campbell and Dona Lee Carrier. When Dona Lee stepped onto the ice, her friends from the East barely recognized her. "We couldn't believe it was the same girl. She made a total change. It was wonderful," Irma Staro said. "Dona Lee was so proud of the weight she had lost right before Nationals," dancer Maggie Hosford explained. "She came running up to me and said, 'Guess what? I bought a pair of red plaid pants!' She was so excited about getting into those pants."[80]

Dona Lee was dressed in a slimming black sequined dress and Roger skated in a black tuxedo suit, wearing his 1960 World patch on his arm. They skated to a medley of Gershwin tunes: "Bidin' My Time" and "Let's Call the Whole Thing Off." Dona Lee wore her blonde hair up on her head with a headband around her forehead, looking like a twenties flapper straight out of the Gershwin era. Throughout their program, they skated with great assurance and musicality. The judges' marks were consistent: 5.2 to 5.3 for content and 5.1 to 5.3 for manner of performance. [81]

Larry Pierce and Diane Sherbloom, wearing Marilyn's red dress with a plunging V back, were next. Their music included "Pennies from Heaven" and a blues and cha-cha section. At times, both Larry and Diane skated tentatively, but overall their performance was remarkably good. Their marks ranged from 5.1 to 5.5 for content and 5.0 to 5.4 for manner of performance. Their marks were slightly higher than Roger and Dona Lee's.[82]

Pat Dineen, skating in a beautiful turquoise dress, partnered by Bob Dineen, skated to "Tip-Toe through the Tulips" and "It's Been a Long, Long Time." Their coaching from both Sonya Klopfer and Ron Ludington in the past year had been worthwhile. They performed a polished program.[83]

Larry and Diane won the 1961 dance title with four firsts and one second. Roger and Dona Lee won the silver, and Bob and Pat Dineen received the bronze. Marshall Campbell and Jan Jacobson of Seattle pulled up from fifth to fourth, Roy Speeg and Thomasine Pierce of Cincinnati dropped to fifth, and Peter Betts and Katrine Neil of New York remained in sixth. "I went to [USFSA official] Harry Radix's party before my free dance," recalled Peter Betts, then twenty-four. "He kept pushing me to drink two gin and tonics. I figured I could have one drink because I knew we weren't going to medal anyway, but I almost threw up."[84]

Harry Radix presented the new Radix Trophy for the dance championship to Larry and Diane. Bud Palmer asked Larry how they could pull off a victory in such a short time. "We have a good pro, Dan Ryan," Larry explained. "We think he's one of the best pros in the country—*the* best pro in the country."[85]

Bill Kipp was elated that Roger and Dona Lee made the team. He now had three World Team members, as did Maribel. Edi Scholdan had four. In the absence of Ron Ludington and Sonya Klopfer, who were unable to travel, Danny Ryan agreed to keep an eye on the Dineens.[86]

When the dance competition finished, Bradley Lord was ebullient because the men's results had just been posted. He learned that he was victorious with three firsts and two seconds. Greg Kelley won the silver, Tim Brown received the bronze, and Doug Ramsay pulled up to fourth place. Bruce Heiss was devastated that he placed fifth. "I was so far ahead of Doug Ramsay in figures it was unbelievable, but Doug got the position as alternate."[87]

Bud and Dick joined Brad on the ice after the awards. Bud congratulated Bradley and then asked Button, "Would you consider this an upset or not?" "Not only would I consider this an upset but an excellently done championship. You really skated beautifully and congratulations," Button replied. When Bud asked if he thought Greg could achieve the coup of remaining in first, Bradley responded tactfully, "I sort of thought he would, too. It depended on how I skated. After I skated, I felt I had done the best that I could. I didn't know if it would be good enough to pull up, but as long as I had done my best I'd be happy." Alfreda Lord was there to see her son win. "It was thrilling for her," Brad's brother said. "It was a complete surprise because we thought the altitude would hurt him, but he skated a magnificent program."[88]

Bradley's joy increased when he realized that Ice Follies management had witnessed his gold medal performance. Ice Follies and Ice Capades scouts came to Nationals every year, where they found 80 percent of their talent. Ice Follies' Roy Shipstad and Oscar Johnson became big fans of Laurence. Shipstad said he had seldom seen a young skater with as much natural talent, and Johnson said, "She's not only a great skater but she has that quality that few other skaters posses. It's called showmanship."[89]

Roy and Eddie Shipstad, who regularly went to Worlds, had planned to attend the 1961 Worlds with Edi Scholdan, but family life took precedence. "Roy's wife was expecting a baby soon and something came up that prevented my grandfather from going as well," Eddie Shipstad III said. Both Shipstads cancelled their trip.[90]

Also sitting in the audience was Bradley's former competitor, Olympian Bobby Brewer. "I was standing next to Maribel near the ice when they presented Bradley the gold medal. Maribel said, 'If you had just stayed in you would be out there right now getting that gold medal.' I said, 'Maribel, I appreciate that, but you make a decision in life and you just have to go for it.'"[91]

Coach Pierre Brunet also closely watched the senior men's event. The confident Frenchman felt that his student Don Jackson would win the 1961 World crown. "Zum of deez young skaters may develop in the next few years, but zey aren't of championship form yet. Skaters like Carol Heiss and David Jenkins come along only vonce in many years."[92]

Although Brunet was unimpressed by the American athletes, Dick Button was delighted by what he had just witnessed. "There were a couple of upsets and the emergence of a couple of very good skaters that are coming up for the future," he said. "Usually after the Olympics the level of skating is very low, because skaters drop out for one reason or another. This championship proved that there are some awfully strong skaters in this country." After observing that the United States had dominated skating for the past ten years, he added: "Let's hope we keep it up."[93]

The commentators had done a wonderful job with the inaugural Nationals telecast. Button's trademark bluntness was apparent in that first telecast. He was caught off guard by Bud's ignorance of figure skating. After Bud had commented that the girls in ice dancing had the tougher steps to perform, Button corrected him: "It seems to me . . . that they are pretty much performing the same steps." When Bud seemed impressed that Rhode practiced six hours a day, Button quickly interjected, "That's usual, Bud." The most perplexing aspect of his job was when skaters altered their program. Tim Brown's spur-of-the moment routine gave Button apoplexy.[94]

At the end of the competition, the 1961 U.S. World Figure Skating Team was named—a formality as the top three in each senior division were usually chosen. The eighteen-member team included Bradley Lord, Gregory Kelley, Tim Brown, Laurence Owen, Stephanie Westerfeld, Rhode Michelson, Dudley Richards and Maribel Owen, Ila Ray and Ray Hadley Jr., Bill and Laurie Hickox, Larry Pierce and Diane Sherbloom, Roger Campbell and Dona Lee Carrier, and Bob and Pat Dineen.

Tim Brown had reentered competitive skating hoping to win the championship title but his erratic performance was underwhelming, and he didn't bother showing up at the awards ceremony. He may have felt that the USFSA had dumped him; but even if he had wanted to go to Prague, there was a reason to stay home. Tim had experienced severe chest pains related to rheumatic fever after his performance, and the doctors told him he shouldn't risk the stress of long-distance travel and intense competition. "His father died from heart problems at a pretty young age, so he knew he needed to take the advice seriously," Barbara Roles said. Tim left Colorado without letting USFSA officials know his intentions.[95]

The Harned Trophy was awarded to The Skating Club of Boston for winning the most points; its skaters won three of the four senior titles. The award-winning team included Bradley Lord, Laurence Owen, Maribel Owen and Dudley Richards, junior ladies champion Lorraine Hanlon, novice ladies champion Tina Noyes, and junior pairs siblings Paul and Elizabeth George. "This marks a renaissance for us," Dick Hapgood of the SC of Boston said. Not since 1924 had the club swept the big three national titles.[96]

The Skating Club of Boston had had a long list of senior men's champions throughout its history, including Nathaniel Niles in the teens, Sherwin Badger in the twenties, Roger Turner in the thirties, and Dick Button in the fifties. "The Broadmoor performance . . . was [Bradley Lord's] greatest ever, for despite the altitude and the competitive pressure he must have been under, he skated swiftly through the five minutes without a miss and carried off the title," a club official said. The Boston victory marked the first time in eight years that the Broadmoor had not won the men's crown.[97]

One of the most heart-warming wins was that of Dudley Richards. He had been an outstanding role model for figure skaters for nearly twenty years and had begun to fulfill a promising role within the USFSA. He was chairman of the College Figure Skating Committee and was a high test judge. Named to his sixth World Team, he was chosen as the first newly designated team captain. He was also the oldest team member, his twenty-ninth birthday less than a week away. He had participated at the 1943 Easterns before more than half of the team was born. He had achieved periodic success, but this win was long-deserved recognition of his talent and perseverance. "It was important for them to win that national championship," Paul George said. "Dudley knew how critical it was to have that American gold medal for international competition."[98]

No one could have been happier about the 1961 Nationals than Maribel Vinson Owen. Never before had two sisters won a senior championship in the same year. Grammy Vinson, who never missed a competition, was there to see it all, even carrying her granddaughters' skates in and out of the arena. The Vinson/Owen family was now skating's premier dynasty.[99]

The dance championship crown was significant because it brought attention to Midwestern and West Coast clubs. Larry Pierce brought the first U.S. senior title to the Winter Club of Indianapolis. It was Danny Ryan's first national senior title as a coach, and a nice complement to his own 1953 U.S. gold dance title. Diane Sherbloom represented the Los Angeles FSC, which had won the national dance title in 1957 and 1960.

The Skating Club of Boston won the Harned Trophy, 1961. Front left: Maribel Y. Owen, Tina Noyes, and Elizabeth George. Back left: Bradley Lord, Dudley Richards, Lorraine Hanlon, Laurence Owen, and Paul George. Source: World Figure Skating Museum.

All the skaters donned their best party attire for the competitors' party in the Broadmoor Hotel, which capped a week of competition, a year of training, and a year of dieting. Everyone heartily ate roast beef with all the trimmings and tirelessly bunny-hopped and jitter-bugged. "This affair continued until after 3 A.M. when little by little the crowd thinned and even the diehards slowed down to a walk," according to a club official.[100]

The competitors' party was a time for skaters to unwind, interact with coaches, and seek new friendships. Ron Pfenning, from Detroit, had never met Rhode until that week, but they gravitated to each other at the party. "She told me after her skating career was over she might want to be a funeral director, but then she might have been fabricating a wonderful story line" he said. Rhode was the hit of the party and had made the rounds with competitors the entire week.[101]

The competitors' party concluded a week of flirting; and in at least two cases, Cupid's darts hit home. The first was Peter Dunfield, coach of junior pairs champions Ron and Vivian Joseph, and Sonya Klopfer, coach of the Dineens. They met late one night while walking around Cheyenne Lake. "It was instant and everything went from there," Dunfield said. The other romance ignited between Bobby Brewer and the new first lady of skating. Bobby recalled:

> Laurence and I had always gotten along very well; but when I lived with the Owen family, she was this little girl. Now she was seventeen and had be-

come this beautiful young woman. She asked me to take her to the competitors' party, and it developed into a quasi-romantic thing. I took her back to her room and kissed her goodnight. She was going off to Prague and I was going back to L.A., but we were going to work something out so I could see her again. We didn't know where it was going, but I told her we would definitely get together again because sparks were flying.[102]

Saturday night also capped a week's worth of nightly parties organized by the new generation of coaches. "All the skaters that I skated with were now coaches," said Sonya Klopfer, "and they had all made it to Nationals that year with their pupils, like Danny Ryan, Billy Kipp, as well as Maribel and Bill Swallender. We spent so much time with each other that week and it was so great." Former World Team member Hugh Graham took part in the coaches' nightly shenanigans:

> One late night we had a steeplechase at the Broadmoor with furniture we had re-arranged. We'd tip the chair over and you had to jump over that, then you had to go down and perch on the top of the escalator. It was pretty silly but we had a marvelous time. Dick Button was there and Dan Ryan, Billy Kipp—the whole crew practically. Edi wasn't there because he was older and didn't participate in that silliness, but Young Maribel came with Dudley. The parties always ended on the mezzanine level, just hanging out together.[103]

On the last night, the coaches had a fabulous party, progressing from room to room partying, until someone had a brilliant idea. The Broadmoor Hotel has a fountain in the lobby. All of the coaches knew the fountain scene from the movie *An American in Paris*, someone had the Gershwin music, and someone else had a portable record player. "We went downstairs, put on the music, and we reenacted the whole scene from *An American in Paris*—dancing and lifting the girls, all around the fountain. We had the best time," Peter Dunfield said. "Most of us were fairly young, budding coaches; and the world was ours. We all loved that music and could fantasize quite easily. We went from the lobby, from one room to another, dancing in the hallways. We just went on and on."[104]

The week in Colorado Springs had been a great success for the 1961 Nationals' organizers, many of the competitors, and especially the 1961 U.S. World Team. The years of toil, sacrifice, and dedication had made their dreams come true. They were the nation's preeminent figure skaters about to embark on a grand adventure—the North American Championships in Philadelphia and then the World Championships in Prague. All participants, coaches, family, and friends came away with wonderful memories of their time at the Broadmoor World Arena the week of January 23—cherished memories that acquired deeper poignancy in the weeks to come.

CHAPTER 15

1961 NORTH AMERICANS

After the parties and a few hours of sleep, the 1961 U.S. World Team, along with coaches and family members, gathered for a meeting on Sunday, January 29, with team manager Deane McMinn. The team alternates and junior champions who had been invited on the European tour were also there with their coaches and family members. The one notable absence was Tim Brown.[1]

The 1961 U.S. World Team was more geographically diverse than ever before. Eight skaters came from the West Coast, four from the Midwest, and six from the East Coast. Deane gave each skater two USFSA team patches and 1961 chevrons for their skating clothing, and five USFSA pins to swap. Deane circulated a clipboard, and attendees listed their passport information and verification of vaccinations. A photographer took visa pictures as the group filled out Czech visa applications.[2]

After the meeting, some headed home and some stayed to watch the telecast of the 1961 U.S. Championships on the CBS Sports Spectacular. The program featured performances from all World Team members except for the third-place Dineens and the Hickoxes. In their place, CBS showed the program of 1961 junior pairs champions Ron and Vivian Joseph. The show's sponsors included Schlitz beer and L & M cigarettes.[3]

Danny Ryan, Larry Pierce, and Diane Sherbloom piled into Danny's station wagon for the long ride home to Indianapolis. Before she left Colorado, Diane called her little sister to share her excitement over winning the dance crown. Her mother was delighted that the USFSA would pay her way to Prague. Diane had already been gone for six weeks. The schedule called for another six weeks' absence.[4]

Steffi Westerfeld, Greg Kelley, and Bill and Laurie Hickox continued training at the Broadmoor World Arena. Steffi and Greg were disappointed over their second-place finishes. Even on their home ice, they had been unable to maintain their leads going into the free program. Edi Scholdan, with complete confidence in his budding champions, told reporters that his skaters would surprise everyone at the upcoming Worlds.[5]

The Hickox siblings were in shock. They had made no plans for a Prague trip because they had not expected to make the team. The Air Force Academy was hesitant about letting Bill miss too many classes and, equally, about allowing Bill to go to a Communist country. Lute Hickox was also unenthusiastic. He was equally concerned about Bill's schooling and felt that the kids were unlikely to do well. Elinor Hickox, however, was un-daunted and took it upon herself to overcome problems with the academy.[6]

Ila Ray and Ray Hadley returned home to Seattle to train while their parents figured out expenses for the entire family's trip. At over $600 for each plane ticket plus hotel costs, they needed more than $2,500. They or-ganized car washes, bake sales, and skating exhibitions; a large contribution jar labeled "Hadley Skating Fund" greeted skaters at the Hadley & Hart Studio. Skating friends donated five dollars at a time; some kids donated their allowances. "We knew there was a possibility that they might not go, so we all worked hard to help them," Ron Kauffman said. Their support base in Seattle was strong, and friends were generous.[7]

The USFSA, concerned that the Hadleys could not fund their trip, con-tacted coach Peter Dunfield and told him that Ron and Vivian Joseph might be competing. The Josephs had been invited to perform on the tour, but their parents didn't want them flying early with the team because they needed to stay in school; Ron was a high school junior and twelve-year-old Vivian was a seventh grader. But an opportunity to compete was a different matter. The USFSA sent them plane tickets, and the Chicagoans waited to see if the Hadleys could raise the money.[8]

Bob and Pat Dineen couldn't believe their good fortune in making the team. They returned to New York City to see their baby and faced two ago-nizing dilemmas: whom to leave their nine-month-old son with, and how to fund their trip. Money was as serious an issue for them as it was for the Hadleys. However, there were no dance alternates. If the Dineens did not go, the United States would send only two dance teams.[9]

Bill Kipp took his three World Team members to his hometown of Al-lentown, Pennsylvania, for training. Theda Beck Bartynski, Bill's first part-ner, happened to be at the Albeth rink when they arrived, and Bill danced the blues with her. When the local paper heard that Bill was in town, a re-porter rushed to the rink for a "hometown boy makes good" article. Bill skillfully deflected attention to his students, claiming that his sole purpose was to develop champion figure skaters. He may have been thinking of Rhode when he commented: "The general public is starting to realize the importance of skating in regard to curbing juvenile delinquency." However, Rhode most likely stunned her coach when she later told a reporter that, in

Roger Campbell, Dona Lee Carrier, Bill Kipp, and Rhode Michelson at the Albeth Rink, Pennsylvania, February 1961. Source: Photo by Jack Lapos, Courtesy of Wilhelmina Kipp Gozzard.

addition to making the 1964 Olympic Team, she planned to enter the University of Southern California as a pre-med student, become a doctor, and looked forward to marriage, a family, and a home.[10]

The Bostonians returned home to glory and honor. Maribel put her champions—Laurence, Little Maribel, and Dudley—through their paces as she pored over invitations for them to skate in ice carnivals after Worlds. The long European tour prompted many carnivals to reschedule their shows so World Team members could participate.[11]

Bradley Lord, Swampscott's favorite son, received a key to the city for the second time—the only resident to have been honored twice. He trained in Boston for a week, then headed to Marblehead for a break, visiting his brother Bruce and wife, Johanne, who was eight months pregnant. If the baby was a boy, Bruce and Johanne planned to name him Bradley.[12]

The big unknown was whether Tim Brown would take his place on the team. His erratic performance, his collapse after the competition, and the dire report from the doctors led the USFSA to assume he would not go to Worlds. Doug Ramsay and Bill Swallender had returned home to Detroit, unaware that the USFSA was preparing to ask Doug to take Tim's place in Philadelphia and Prague.[13]

Another fourth-place finisher, Karen Howland, was definitely heading to Philadelphia. The Canadian Figure Skating Association (CFSA) had earlier requested that the ladies' event be enlarged from three to four contestants from each country. Karen had the opportunity to compete at North

Americans, but would not continue on to Prague. At least that was the plan before she arrived in Philadelphia.[14]

———◆———

The 1961 Canadian Figure Skating Championships were held in La-chine, just north of Montreal, the same week as the 1961 Nationals. The CFSA had advised potential World Team members to pack for a six-week trip because they had been invited on a European tour with the Americans. While the USFSA funded travel for first-place finishers, the CFSA did not provide travel funds for any skaters. Unlike the suspense of the 1961 Na-tionals—each of the four senior championships were wide open—the Ca-nadians had three returning 1960 champions and all easily retained their ti-tles: 1960 Olympic bronze medalist Donald Jackson, Wendy Griner, and dancers Virginia Thompson and Bill McLachlan. With Olympic gold med-alists Barbara Wagner and Bob Paul retiring, Otto and Maria Jelinek finally won their first Canadian pairs championship.[15]

Canadian skaters were not concerned about their own welfare behind the Iron Curtain—only for the safety of the Jelineks. Maria was stoic about their predicament: "We stayed focused all year because we had to keep training for the Canadian Championships. We knew it would be dangerous to go back [to Prague] because we had escaped, and the Czech government needed to understand that we were now Canadians. If it was not resolved our parents would not have let us on the plane. If it didn't work out this year, we knew there would be next year."[16]

———◆———

Ken Kelley continued to negotiate with the Czechs as the Canadians and U.S. Championships were in progress. The Czechs repeatedly sent the USFSA the same letter, stating that once they received a complete list of names of all the skaters and others in the traveling party, they would advise their Washington Embassy to issue visas. Unfortunately, the USFSA held the Nationals the last week of January, and the team could not be selected until then. This schedule left only two weeks for the necessary paperwork before departure. Kelley, frustrated by the red tape, vented his mounting frustration to Deane McMinn: "If we don't get a hotel maybe we should all bring tents and bedding rolls? Who in hell ever decided to hold this thing in Prague, anyway?!"[17]

On January 24, Ken sent a letter to the Czech organizing committee with the U.S. team's travel plans. The delegation was divided into two groups. More than two dozen people would arrive in Prague on Wednesday, February 15, giving the team a week to recover from jet leg and become acclimated to skating conditions. The rest of the delegation, primarily officials and family members, would arrive on Monday, February 20. After the competition, the European tour would last from two to three weeks. Ken diplomatically requested information on practice times, rinks, and the hotel.[18]

The USFSA shared with the ISU concerns about possible Cold War harassment of the American skaters. The USFSA contacted the State Department, advised it of travel plans, and requested an official State Department escort for the team in Prague. In the meantime, the USFSA received final word from the ISU that the Worlds would be held at Prague. "The Czechs have given every assurance of safety in, during and out to all skaters and accompanying people, including Jelineks." The Czechs did not want the Americans and Canadians to boycott the Worlds. The two countries represented nearly a third of the competitors.[19]

The USFSA provided the airfare and an allotment toward room and board for the six champions. All other skaters had to pay their own transportation, room, and board. The USFSA paid everyone's competition fees. With time short, USFSA personnel tracked down individuals whose paperwork and checks were delinquent. Tim Brown got a special delivery letter because he had "skipped out without telling them anything." Deane knew that Bill Hickox's status as an Air Force cadet might prevent him and his sister from going to Prague. Deane doubted that Tim and the Hickoxes were going abroad.[20]

Meanwhile, Elinor Hickox sent word that Bill and Laurie would compete at North Americans, although clearance for Worlds had not yet been obtained. The Brownings, the fifth-place pair, had received word that they might go to Prague in place of the Hickoxes. They trained in Indianapolis while waiting to hear the outcome of the military's decision on Bill. Surprisingly, the fourth-place Fotheringills heard nothing.[21]

On February 5, Doug Ramsay received the news that he was going to Prague because Tim Brown was staying home due to his heart condition. "It's wonderful," Doug said. "It's the biggest thrill of my life." Jean Ramsay wanted to go with her son, but there was no money for such a trip; even coming up with the money for Doug was a challenge, but the Detroit Skating Club offered to pay part of Doug's expenses. Bill Swallender was ecstatic for his star pupil: "It is a fine break for Doug's career." Bill asked Ginny Baxter to take over his studio classes while he was away. Bill had never invited his family to a competition before, but Gen, Bill, and Erik joined him in Philadelphia because he told them "they needed to be there."[22]

The Hadleys received good news from two sources. A Seattle newspaper, hearing of the family's financial plight, wrote a story asking for donations. The Seattle Skating Club also offered a $2,000 loan to help the family get to Prague. Linda flew with the kids to Philadelphia; and Ray, who stayed behind to keep teaching till the last moment, would join them later in Prague. Just a few days before the start of North Americans, the USFSA informed Peter Dunfield that the Hadleys would be going, not the Josephs.[23]

Bob and Pat Dineen cleared away the obstacles. They entrusted their baby's care to Ben Dineen, Bob's brother and the baby's godfather. Their financial fairy godmother came in the form of Bob's mother, Mary, who loaned them the money. They said good-bye to Bobby Jr., handed him to Ben, and piled into friend Marilyn Grace's car for the three-hour drive to Philadelphia.[24]

Elinor Hickox was elated when Bill was cleared to travel abroad. Under Commander Sullivan's direction, the board of athletics met and granted Bill a temporary leave to participate at Worlds, because of his high grades. He could have flown to Prague inexpensively on a military transport plane, but fifteen-year-old Laurie would not have been allowed to travel with him. Elinor wanted her daughter to stay with Bill, so they elected to fly with the team.[25]

On Wednesday, February 8, some team members made their way to the City of Brotherly Love. They had packed in anticipation of a month of European travel. David Jenkins and Carol Heiss had written a helpful travel guideline, entitled "Skating Abroad on 44 Pounds." Carol advised the female skaters to bring a suit for plane and train travel, a cocktail dress for parties, black heels, comfortable flats for sightseeing, and an ample supply of Danskin tights, nylons, and Kleenex tissues. For the males, David suggested a dark suit for banquets and parties, a sport coat, drip-dry white shirts, and oxford shoes for walking. Both men and women should, they advised, have in their carry-on bag the most essential items: two pairs of skates, competition records, cameras, extra shoes, a pair of slippers for the plane, and school books. Some packed more than that; understanding the unavailability of items from the West, Bill Hickox had taken four dozen Hershey and Heath candy bars, eighty packs of gum, and two cartons of cigarettes, for "goodwill."[26]

Competitors looked forward to the skating tour, which allowed American skaters to be seen by European audiences and international judges who would judge them later. The tour usually included the top five World competitors in each event, but the entire 1961 U.S. Team was invited on an ambitious European tour after the competition, with stops in Czechoslovakia, Hungary, Poland, Switzerland, Italy, France, and Germany.[27]

Skaters customarily dressed well for trips abroad. Friends generously loaned or gave personal articles to team members so they would look their best. Lorin Caccamise gave Bill Hickox a suit for parties. Seattle club members bought Linda Hadley a new coat and new clothes for the kids. The Haigler family gave money to Sherri Westerfeld, who was traveling on a shoestring. Jack and Eleanor Curtis loaned Dona Lee Carrier and Roger Campbell their matching sweaters. Bill Kipp helped himself to his brother Elmer's new hat for the trip. Walter Powell took a friend's insulated winter boots. In short, the suitcases of the 1961 Team were filled with the physical good wishes of many friends.[28]

Doug Ramsay gave an exhibition the night before he left. The DSC had had two previous World Team members: Ginny Baxter and Miggs Dean in the late forties and early fifties. Doug was the first male World Team member from Detroit, and the hastily planned send-off included dinner, champagne, a sheet cake decorated with a pair of skates and "Bon Voyage, Doug," in frosting, and a gift of luggage. Oscar Klausner, the eighty-three-year-old patriarch of the DSC, taught Bill and Doug some Czech phrases and gave them sightseeing tips. It was a great party; but Doug was, rarely for him, feeling downcast. He told Gary Visconti, "Everybody is here and it's my party and I skated terrible." "Doug, it's just a club exhibition. . . . Who cares?" The club members, unfazed, had applauded enthusiastically and shouted "Good luck!"[29]

Bradley Lord, Laurence Owen, Little Maribel, and Dudley Richards had also performed at a club exhibition the night before leaving for Philadelphia. Like Doug, everyone was off. Laurence couldn't land anything. "It was terrible," a coach recalled. "It had always been hard to skate at the club exhibitions, and none of them skated well."[30]

Dudley and Maribel's poor performance may have been due to health problems. Little Maribel had dealt with ulcers before, but close friends suspected cancer. Ron Ludington went with Dudley to pick up boxes of Metrecal for Dudley to take to Prague. Maribel had been drinking cans of the dietary supplement to keep her weight up. If Maribel Sr. had concerns, she didn't voice them. As she told Ken Kelley, "We're holding the thumbs up for the North Americans, the next step."[31]

Doug Ramsay and the Swallender family flew to Philadelphia on Thursday. Doug was granted permission to leave school because he was doing so well academically and promised to make up his schoolwork the next summer. Doug's mother flew out the next day to watch him compete.[32]

Denver Post reporter Lee Meade came to Stapleton Airport to see off Edi and Jimmy Scholdan, Steffi and Sherri Westerfeld, and Greg and Nathalie Kelley. Meade had planned to accompany the skaters to Prague but his publisher, Palmer Hoyt, told him he had to wait for a year. So instead, he joined his friends for lunch while they were waiting for their flight. While dining, Scholdan informed his students that Brussels would be the first stop on their international flight. "You will love Belgium," Edi told them. "It is one of the friendliest countries in the world." He then pontificated on his students' prospects to Meade:

> I don't expect too much at the North American Championships. That will be a battle between the champions of the United States and Canada and both countries will be working to build up their titlists for the World meet. The judges will overlook the fact that Steffi and Greg came as close to winning as possible in our national championship. But it will be different in Europe. The European judges will be more neutral and I predict Steffi and Greg will head the American squad in the World meet. I have never worked with a pair of skaters who got along as well together as Laurie and Bill. They have a great deal on the ball and can go a long way.[33]

Before they boarded, Lee poked fun at Edi's well-known dislike for flying. Pointing to an imaginary plane, he said, "Edi, I know why your plane is late. I see it in smoke out there and it's burning." Scholdan didn't bother to look out the window. "Lee, whenever you can tell me my plane is burning that's just fine. When the day comes that my plane is burning and you can't tell me, that's when I'll be upset."[34]

Danny Ryan had had a busy two weeks in Indianapolis. Between continuing to work with his dance champions, he paid brief visits to his new baby son in the hospital. Michael Ryan was only eight days old when Danny headed to Philadelphia. Before he left his wife and five children at home, he told his oldest son, five-year-old Kevin, "You take care of your mom." Rose Anne had planned to go to Prague, but her doctor had refused; she wasn't strong enough yet. Michael had been born ten days after his due date, their only child not to come on time or early. If Michael had followed this pattern, Rose Anne would have gone with her husband.[35]

Soon after Larry Pierce and Diane Sherbloom arrived at the Philadelphia Skating Club and Humane Society (PSC & HS) for practice, news photographers flocked around the handsome couple. Pictures of Diane and

Larry graced the pages of several metropolitan papers. Bradley Lord and Laurence Owen were already on the ice practicing alongside their two chief Canadian rivals—Don Jackson and Wendy Griner.[36]

Rhode Michelson shared a cab to the arena with Karen Howland, and told her: "No one belongs on the top pedestal of the podium except me." It was her way of psyching herself up; and by the time Karen got out of the cab, she almost believed her. Rhode whipped around the ice as usual, but she had a terrible fall in the middle of practice and had to leave the arena with severe back pain and big bruises on her hip. That night she talked on the phone with Barbara Roles, who said, "There was such excitement in Rhode's voice. Such joy in living. I almost wished I had been going with them." The indomitable Rhode was back on the ice the next day.[37]

———※———

Skating fans converged on the practice rinks on Friday before the competition began. Besides the local crowd, many skating friends decided to come at the last minute, including Midwesterner Sally Wells who convinced her mother to drive her and two friends fifteen hours through a violent storm to support Doug Ramsay and Larry Pierce. After performing at St. Lawrence University, Pieter Kollen and Dorothyann Nelson cashed in their plane tickets and took the train to Philadelphia, sleeping on the floor of Larry Pierce's and Diane Sherbloom's rooms. Carol Peters Duncan, Danny Ryan's dance partner, came from Washington, D.C., with her husband to see him. Eddie LeMaire came to visit Canadian friends and introduce them to his son Dickie.[38]

Dick Button spent the day with the competitors. After successfully covering the 1961 U.S. Championships for CBS, he would follow up by doing solo commentary for the local CBS affiliate in Philadelphia. He watched practice sessions and asked skaters to outline their programs.[39]

The competitors were eager to know each other personally. Bradley Lord and Doug Ramsay invited Brad Black and his coach to lunch one day after practice. Shirra Kenworthy bonded quickly with Steffi and Laurence at practice. The three arrived so early at the arena one day that most of the doors were locked; they laughed at their predicament as they circled the building, looking for a way to get in.[40]

Sports Illustrated (SI) photographers arrived at the ladies' practice to do a photo shoot of Laurence and Wendy Griner. The magazine's reporters had already interviewed both sixteen-year-old girls for an upcoming article, seeing them and European Sjoukje Dijkstra as likely contenders for the World title. Within days, Laurence would appear on *SI*'s cover for the February 13 issue.[41]

During the ladies' session, Rhode again fell badly on a double axel, aggravating the injury from the day before. Reports unevenly listed her injury as a bruised hip, an injured ankle, a stress fracture in her right leg, and a sore back. She probably suffered from all four afflictions because for once she conceded defeat. The doctors told her to nurse her injuries or she would be off the ice for months. To Bill Kipp's amazement, Rhode withdrew. "I'm going with the team to Europe anyway and I'll resume training in Prague," she told the press. Karen Howland, on the same practice ice, believed she might get to go to Prague. The USFSA doubted Rhode would be ready in time, but they didn't know Rhode. Watching her competitors at rink side, she told the local TV affiliate, "I don't want to miss the Worlds. They mean an awful lot to me."[42]

Bill Kipp turned his attention to Dona Lee and Roger. Dona Lee was skating well and riding on a wave of family support. Her mother had arrived from Los Angeles and her father had sent a letter any athlete would love to receive:

> Darling Dona Lee: By the time you get this letter it will all be over. . . . I want you to know that regardless whether you come in 1st, 3rd, or last you will still be the same to your old Dad . . . [This is] the culmination of eight years of hard work and the fruition of the hope your mother and I have had as we watched you practice, work and play through the years. Remember too—there are other years and other competitions, no one can win them all—someone has to lose, and to be a good loser is as important as being a humble winner. So remember, Darling, win or lose, be a real sportsman in the knowledge that you have done your best. Love from, Your Dad[43]

Instead of flying in two groups as originally planned, the Americans were now flying together on Valentine's Day. Danny Ryan eagerly told the Canadian coaches about their upcoming flight: "It's so exciting. For the first time we've got all our reservations together—all the skaters, all the coaches, all the officials, all the family—we're all going on the same plane and it's going to be so nice." Some of the Canadian team, including Don Jackson, the Jelineks, and Shirra Kenworthy, had trained with the Americans, who encouraged them all to join the Sabena flight.[44]

Canadian dancers J. D. and Donna Lee Mitchell also wanted to fly with the Americans, but their coach Jean Westwood felt her pupils needed to unwind. She suggested they fly straight to her hometown of Manchester, England, before heading to Prague. John Mitchell, who wanted his children to fly with the American team, accused Jean of wanting to visit friends in Manchester. Jean was insulted at the accusation and gave him an ultimatum: "Fine. You go with the Americans. I'm going right back to Vancouver. As you're not going to listen to me now, you're not going to listen to me ever. That's it!" Under threat of losing their coach, the Mitchell family agreed to fly to Manchester.[45]

On the eve of competition, coach Sheldon Galbraith pulled Wendy Griner's mother aside and implored her to change their airline tickets. Weeks ago, unaware of the USFSA's plans, Mr. Galbraith, Mrs. Griner, and Wendy had booked tickets on the same Valentine's Day Sabena flight as the Americans. Mr. Galbraith didn't want his star pupil arriving with the Americans, dwarfed by the fanfare surrounding the huge U.S. delegation and especially not Wendy's chief competitor—Laurence Owen.[46]

Plans for travel to Prague were made and changed as the 1961 North American Figure Skating Championships began in the Philadelphia suburb of Ardmore on Saturday morning, February 11, at the PSC & HS rink. The United States had a slight advantage in officials: three American judges and two Canadian judges for each event. The American judges included Deane McMinn and, as referees, Ken Kelley and Harold Hartshorne.[47]

The men's competition began at 8 A.M. with six figures. Don Jackson was expected to win but coach Bud Wilson felt Bradley Lord could beat him. "Bradley has something going for him that he never had before. He's got the confidence that goes with being the national champion." Brad received good marks for his bracket and rocker figures, but it was not enough to overpower Don's cumulative score. Bradley sized up the situation prior to the free skating event: "I'll try my best, of course, but he's too good for me just now." Despite Jackson's first-place standing, the Americans had done well, with Lord, Kelley, and Ramsay placing second, third, and fourth, respectively.[48]

The dance compulsories, which included the Fourteenstep, the Westminster, the Paso Doble and the Blues, were held late morning. Canadians Virginia Thompson and Bill McLachlan, the 1960 World silver medalists, placed first. U.S. champions Larry Pierce and Diane Sherbloom had received a lot of press, but they were eclipsed by Dona Lee Carrier and Roger Campbell, who placed second. Paulette Doan and Ken Ormsby were third, Larry and Diane were fourth, J. D. and Donna Lee Mitchell were fifth, and Bob and Pat Dineen were sixth. Dona Lee quickly sent her father a Valentine's card: "We were second in compulsories. . . . [K]eep your fingers crossed for us."[49]

The ladies' figures began after lunch. Laurence, wearing a dress with a large lace collar, and Wendy Griner, wearing white gloves and a Canadian

Maple Leaf emblem on her dress, began their quest for the ladies title. Steffi Westerfeld faltered for the first time in figures, while Laurence took an early lead. She performed an excellent paragraph three and rocker, but lost her balance on the final figure, the paragraph loop, and Wendy closed the gap. Maribel didn't stay for the results, but pulled Laurence through the crowd to get to the practice rink, groaning, "We lost it on that last figure." Actually Laurence had the lead but only by the slimmest margin, just 5/10ths of a point ahead of Wendy.[50]

That afternoon, the Jelineks were executing a lift in practice when Otto's skate hit a hole in the ice. He collapsed, with Maria tumbling on top of him. His head was slit open and blood flowed freely onto the ice. Maria's right thigh was cut by her brother's blade, spilling more blood. Maria slowly rose but Otto remained motionless. Several Canadian coaches, reporters, and a doctor immediately hopped over the boards. They helped Otto to the first-aid room where Dr. Hugh Ormsby diagnosed a concussion and temporary lapse of memory. An ambulance took the Jelineks to the hospital; riding in the ambulance with them was their worried coach, whose wife was expecting their first child in Toronto at any moment.[51]

Otto was treated for a wrenched back and a mild concussion. He received three stitches on the back of his head. Doctors disinfected Maria's wound and gave her a tetanus shot; she had a bruised left hip, a pulled muscle, and a gash on the upper part of her right thigh. Back at the rink, the ice resurfacer cleaned up the grisly scene before the men began their practice. That evening at a competitors' dinner, the talk centered on the Jelineks' catastrophe. However, Otto had already checked himself out of the hospital. The doctors told him he needed to stay, but he insisted he was okay and did a handstand to prove it. "Otto decided [his accident] wasn't going to get in the way," Maria said. "When he decides something, that's it." Coach Bruce Hyland watched him carefully over the next twenty-four hours. Maribel and Dudley, who had just received a good luck telegram from Ted Kennedy, had a chance to win if the Jelineks withdrew.[52]

⸻ ❍ ⸻

On Sunday the competition moved to The Arena in downtown Philadelphia. The opening ceremonies began at 2 P.M. with more than 4,000 spectators in attendance, while hundreds of thousands watched at home on Philadelphia station WFIL-TV.[53]

The first event was the dance finals. Diane Sherbloom and Larry Pierce performed well, though they knew they were unlikely to move up. Pat and

Bob Dineen, with nothing to lose in sixth place, impressed the crowd with their strong edges and interesting footwork.[54]

Like Larry and Diane, Canadians Paulette Doan and Ken Orsmby had just paired up; they were particularly rhythmic, considering they had been skating together for only six weeks. Dona Lee Carrier and Roger Campbell performed their program with great flair and vitality. The judges responded favorably to their expert timing and precision.[55]

The last dancers to skate, reigning North American champion Bill McLachlan and partner Virginia Thompson, gave an outstanding performance and won the event. "We were strong and on a roll," Virginia said. "We had come in second in Worlds in 1960 and it was fresh in everyone's minds. We thought it was our year for the World title." After the competition, Danny Ryan approached Virginia and said, "You are going to be World Champion. You have so much talent and you are only fifteen—what are you going to be like when you're eighteen or twenty!" Virginia was bowled over by so much enthusiasm from an American coach.[56]

The dance results were identical to the compulsory placements. The Canadians placed first, third, and fifth, and the Americans placed second, fourth, and sixth. Dona Lee and Roger, hoping for a bronze, were thrilled to win the silver. Bill Kipp was elated that Dona Lee and Roger had surpassed his personal best in 1955.[57]

One of Danny Ryan's last wins had been the 1953 North American dance title, and he had hoped that his team would duplicate that achievement. Larry and Diane were disappointed with their fourth-place finish, but Larry told a Canadian reporter, "Your dance pairs were much better, but wait until Prague—then it will be a different story." His disappointment was softened by the fact that girlfriend Sally Schantz had been in the audience all weekend. Diane quickly shrugged off the disappointment, sending her sister a card: "Life is really very wonderful. Never forget it."[58]

Pat and Bob Dineen were not disappointed to finish sixth. They were thrilled just to be at their first international competition. Pat shared with friends her excitement over the upcoming European trip. Her only disappointment was not having her baby with her, and she told everyone how hard it was to be separated from her nine-month-old son.[59]

The ladies final proved to be the most controversial event. Steffi Westerfeld was the first to skate her four-minute program. She successfully landed all of her jumps except her double loop. Without the pressure of being first in compulsories, as she had been at Nationals, she skated a smoother, cleaner, and more expressive program.[60]

All eyes were on Wendy Griner as she stepped onto the ice in a red dress with a sparkling neckline. She successfully executed a double axel, double salchow, double loop, double lutz, and a double flip into a camel/sit spin combination. She tripped once after a split/double flip/sit spin sequence, but recovered quickly. She skated beautifully, with high jumps, and was "light as a feather." Wendy felt she had skated well and had done enough to come in first. She received marks of 5.2 to 5.5 for both content of program and manner of performance.[61]

Laurence skated after Wendy. As she moved to the strains of "Symphony Fantastique," Maribel loudly clapped the rhythm, calling, "Come on, Baby! Delightful," at every move. "I just tried to keep her in step with the music," she said. "She had to be at her best to beat Wendy." The crowd buzzed in amusement at Maribel's antics, but she was oblivious to everything but Laurence on the ice.[62]

Technically speaking, Laurence skated better than she had at Nationals. She landed all of her jumps, losing her balance only on one double axel. She covered any imperfections with consistently dramatic endings for her jumps: arms extended high, making a statement that shouted, "Yes, I did it!" Canadian team members rooted for Wendy but were inspired by Laurence's unique showmanship. "She was carefree and joyous on the ice," Debbi Wilkes said. "I was totally enchanted by her."[63]

Maribel cheered wildly when Laurence finished. Her content marks ranged from 5.1 to 5.6 and her performance marks ranged from 5.2 to 5.6. Both Laurence and Wendy had made one mistake. When all the marks were tallied, Laurence, by the narrowest of margins, ended up on top. She managed to win with 931.5 points and seven ordinals, compared to 929.6 points and eight ordinals for Wendy. Laurence had matched her mother's 1937 North American title. The press asked Maribel if she felt she were on the ice with Laurence: "You bet. I skated every stroke with her."[64]

The Owens painted a picture-perfect skating life to the press. "I like to watch my girls skate because they have fun," Maribel said. "People frequently come up to me and say that my daughters look as if they are really enjoying themselves. They are." Maribel said she would have no objection if the girls found the life too strenuous and gave it up; her only impatience was with half-hearted performances. Even while basking in her daughter's victory, Maribel stated that competitive skating required a decade of hard work and sacrifice, "and even then all you might get is heartbreak." Laurence had the final word: "Mother deserves all the credit for our victories."[65]

Wendy Griner had to settle for second, followed by Sonia Snelling, who pulled up from fourth to third place. Steffi, who was sixth in figures, turned in a sensational performance and finished fourth. She admitted that she had been nervous in her first international competition but overall she was satisfied with the results. Shirra Kenworthy, recovering from the flu, dropped from third to fifth, Frances Gold placed sixth and Karen Howland placed seventh. Even though Karen came in last, her well-skated program was a great compensation for her unfortunate performance at Nationals.[66]

As much as the crowd was captivated by Laurence, some thought that Wendy's sparkling performance should have won. "It was so very close between Laurence and Wendy. It could have gone either way," Don Jackson said. "I know Laurence had beautiful positions, but Wendy was good too." The Canadian press, feeling that Wendy had been robbed, noted that three of the five judges were Americans. Wendy and her coach, Sheldon Galbraith, realized that she would have to earn a first from at least one American judge—and, in fact, she did. What they hadn't counted on was a Canadian judge who placed her second.[67]

Wendy was stunned by the loss. Canadian judge Melville Rogers, a lifelong friend of Maribel, approached Wendy and her mother after the event and apologized: "I'm very sorry to say I placed you second. I meant to place you first, but I put the wrong marks down." Wendy was shocked by the revelation. This was not the first time a judge had inadvertently held up the wrong marks, but for Wendy the timing could not have been worse. The European judges would now perceive Laurence as the stronger of the two champions. Although Wendy's second place was a crushing blow, she vowed to work harder to produce a different result in Prague.[68]

The disastrous accident that put Otto and Maria Jelinek in the hospital had been widely reported in the local press. Competitors and coaches thought it impossible that they could skate. "Immediately after the accident I seriously wondered if we could compete," Maria said. "We were all banged up, cut up, bleeding, and we could hardly walk, but we were young and we recovered pretty quickly." To everyone's amazement, Otto and Maria stepped onto the ice for their warm-up; invisible from the stands were the bandages on Otto's head.[69]

In pairs, Canadians Gerty Desjardins and Maurice Lafrance included a split turn lift, twist lift, and a death spiral in their program. Dudley and

Maribel followed with a clean program, which included a twist lift, Baier lift, and several side-by-side jumps.[70]

Canadians Debbi Wilkes and Guy Revell had many remarkable lifts in their programs, including a double twist; and when the judges revealed their low marks, including a fifth and sixth placement from the American judges, four thousand spectators booed for two minutes. When the Hadleys followed the popular Canadian team, the crowd appreciated their mistake-free routine.[71]

The audience greeted Maria and Otto Jelinek with hearty applause. They performed most of their elements, only omitting their cartwheel lift. For their heroic performance, they received first placements from all the judges, including their first 6.0—the highest mark. "We were being very, very careful and didn't let loose; that's why we skated so well," Maria said. After Otto's win, coach Pierre Brunet told him, "You are the only skater in the history of the North American championship who won the title with a hole in your head."[72]

Although they knew they were not in medal contention, Bill and Laurie Hickox skated with great aplomb and placed sixth. The Canadians were first, third, and fifth, and the Americans were second, fourth, and sixth. Dudley and Maribel ended up with the silver medal while Debbi Wilkes and Guy Revell took home the bronze. Regarding the controversial judging, Dudley candidly told a Canadian reporter, "Debbi and Guy were judged too low. I have never seen them skate better. They deserved to come second."[73]

Don Jackson, defending his 1959 North American men's title, was favored to win, but he couldn't relax because three strong American free skaters were right behind him. Don skated confidently, his "power permeated the crowd." He fumbled one triple jump, but easily landed a triple flip, and multiple double jumps. He received enthusiastic applause and high marks from the judges. His victory was solidly secured.[74]

Spectators, believing they had already seen the best, were unprepared for the program that followed. Doug Ramsay, in fourth place, moved through his program landing double jump after double jump with a triple thrown in. The crowd went wild. Despite missing one double axel, he received thunderous applause and foot stamping when he landed a double axel with his arms folded. He was the clear favorite with the crowd. After his performance, Don Jackson remarked to a reporter, "Did you see that double axel he performed with his arms folded? I've seen him do it with his hands in his pockets. He has a great future ahead of him."[75]

Bradley Lord, who did not exhibit the same fire as he had in Colorado when he won the Nationals, still skated a superb program with speed, grace, and cleanly landed jumps. Greg Kelley, skating last, had the most memorable opener of all: a thrilling delayed axel. He distinguished himself by his wonderful spins and well-executed jumps, especially his triple salchow. Besides his sister Nathalie, Dr. and Mrs. Kelley were there along with most of the Kelley siblings to see Greg win the bronze medal.[76]

The Americans had their best showing in the men's division. Although Don Jackson won the event, Bradley, Greg, and Doug placed second, third, and fourth, respectively. Doug Ramsay did not win a medal, but he won many new fans.[77]

After the men's event, the champions performed an exhibition; Laurence performed a memorable program to "The Flight of the Bumble Bee." "She was a free spirit—like [U.S. champion] Janet Lynn," Gerty Desjardins said. "It was beautiful to watch her and so inspiring. We were just amazed by her."[78]

The officials presented the trophies and medals that night. The Canadians were disappointed that Wendy Griner did not win, but they had reason to rejoice, scoring their biggest win in the history of the North American meet with three gold, one silver, and three bronze medals. A Canadian reporter asserted: "With a little less obvious diplomatic judging, our skaters could have registered a clean sweep in the competition."[79]

The organizers hosted a glamorous competitors' party at the Treadway Inn. Forming an unlikely threesome were Bob and Pat Dineen and Virginia Thompson. The Dineens were in their mid-twenties, married with a small baby; they had placed last, while Virginia was the new dance champion at age fifteen. They had become friends, and Pat had promised to purchase several pair of tights for Virginia and bring them to Prague because Danskins were hard to find in Canada. All of the Canadian and American skaters had become fast friends and looked forward to being together behind the Iron Curtain.[80]

Maribel celebrated with Peter Betts, who had recently placed sixth in gold dance at the Broadmoor. She encouraged him to keep competing: "Make sure you get a really good-looking young partner, and you'll be fine. Go for it! Do it. Do it!" Betts decided right then he would find a new partner and compete the next year.[81]

The U.S. team tried to recruit more passengers. The Owen sisters blindsided Peter Betts: "Oh, you should come to Worlds! Eddie LeMaire has two extra tickets! You should come. . . . We'll have a good time!" He had seen the extra tickets posted on the New York club's bulletin board; Eddie had written "Tennis, anyone?" next to the offer. Betts, passing by the board daily, had thought, "I should really take those tickets," but something kept telling him not to do it.[82]

The Owen sisters approached Boston judge Mary Louise Wright, who had declined her invitation to judge Worlds. The girls gave Mary Louise a hard time, saying, "We're still mad you're not going with us." Wright reassured them, "I'll be the first one on the plane next year." The Dineens asked Ron Ludington once more if he could accompany them. Ludington, who had been to the last four Worlds as a competitor, could not afford to go. Ron wished them all well and said his good-byes.[83]

Dick Button shared his unfortunate news with the American team; he would not fly with them as scheduled. When he couldn't sell the 1961 Worlds to the American networks, the Canadian Broadcasting Corporation (CBC) hired him, but the contract had not yet arrived. The next morning, he left for New York to finalize production of the North American telecast. Days later, he would head to Lake Placid to perform in a carnival and then would fly to Prague after his CBC contract had been signed.[84]

Coaches and other adults cut loose at the open bar while the skaters danced into the night. Maribel Vinson Owen could not contain her excitement over Laurence's win. Later that night, hotel guests were shocked to see a woman doing cartwheels in the lobby.[85]

Early Monday, February 13, Jean Ramsay kissed her son good-bye as he slept at the Treadway Inn, left a note at his bedside, and returned to Detroit. The team had the day off and most of them slept in—a rare treat for a competitive figure skater.[86]

Across town, Maribel and her family were houseguests of the Goodrich family. Their sleep was interrupted by an early call from a Boston reporter. "I'm still so thrilled, so excited over Laurie's winning," Maribel said in her froggy voice. Laurence took the phone and recapped her recent triumph. "I won't have a chance to calm down before the excitement of the trip and the World championships at Prague. The competition will be tops. Some of the other girls are very, very good. There's the Dutch girl Sjoukje Dijkstra for one. And Wendy Griner, the Canadian champion I just managed to beat. . . . I'll slave to keep up in my work while I'm abroad . . . and I'll still have lots of makeup work when I get back to Winchester High."[87]

The Owens said good-bye to eighty-one-year-old Grammy Vinson, who would not make the difficult trip to Prague. Friends had asked Maribel if she thought it safe for all of her family to fly on the same plane. Grammy was concerned too, but Maribel replied, "Don't you worry, Grammy. Everything will be all right." Grammy said good-bye to her family, including Dudley, her "adopted grandson."[88]

Bill Swallender took his family to the airport. He had one last request. His eldest son had worn his father's brand-new green tie all weekend. "I need it back," Bill stated. Young Bill, laughing, handed it over. Then Bill took off his ring, a beautiful star sapphire, and handed it to Gen, saying "I want you to keep this." Bill kissed his wife and family good-bye and flew back to Detroit. The Swallenders' twenty-fourth wedding anniversary fell on February 15, so they planned to celebrate when Bill returned from Europe.[89]

Harold Hartshorne's daughters, Gail and Daryl, had spent the weekend with their father and Louise in Philadelphia. He had picked them up from their nearby boarding school to watch the competition and spend time together. The girls went back to school as Harold and Louise returned to New York City to prepare for their journey abroad.[90]

Bud Wilson wanted to fly with Brad Lord, but the powers-that-be at The Skating Club of Boston insisted that he return to prepare for the annual Ice Chips show. Bud flew back to Boston but had a ticket to fly to Prague later in the week. Bud, who had helped coach Laurence the last four weeks, planned to work with her in Prague, too.[91]

Acting USFSA President Ritter Shumway spoke to the team before he headed to Washington, D.C. He encouraged this energetic group, made up mostly of teenagers, to be statesmen behind the Iron Curtain. "A great opportunity [lies] before you. You are going to be ambassadors for the United States, ambassadors of good will."[92]

There were still openings on the Sabena plane for the 1961 U.S. junior champions, but three of the four skaters had already declined. Monty Hoyt and his mother, Helen, had planned to be on the flight but Helen had changed her mind. She later called it a premonition. Monty's parents also concluded that he would miss too much school because of the tour's length. The Joseph family also felt that school was important for Vivian and Ron, so they had tickets to fly over later for the exhibition tour.[93]

Lorraine Hanlon, 1961 junior ladies champion, wanted to go with the team, but she was attending a Boston private school, Winsor, and administrators had told her that, if she went to Prague, she should look for another school. Her parents left the difficult decision up to fifteen-year-old Lorraine; and after an agonizing weekend, Lorraine, who wanted to attend medi-

cal school, tearfully told her parents on Monday morning: "I'm not going."
She informed the USFSA that she would not fly on Tuesday.[94]

The Canadian skaters began to scatter. Coach Bruce Hyland flew back
to Canada to see his new son, who was being born while the Jelineks won
the pair title. One quick visit to his wife and baby and he was on another
flight to New York to catch his international flight on Tuesday. Jean Westwood said good-bye to Bill Kipp before she flew to England with her students. Jean was still in love with Bill, and they planned to rendezvous in Europe. "See you in Prague!" were their parting words.[95]

Ken Kelley flew to New York City with his wife, Joan, to make a connecting flight to Europe. They flew to Brussels on Sabena Flight 548,
twenty-four hours before the U.S. team's flight, then flew on to Vienna for a
little vacation before the competition began. As one of the 1961 Worlds
judges, he wanted to fly separately from the team because he would be judging them in a few days.[96]

That evening, coach Sheldon Galbraith, Wendy Griner, and her mother arrived at Idlewild (now JFK) Airport in New York City. The threesome,
who had changed their tickets from Sabena Flight 548 on Tuesday, now
boarded a SwissAir flight for Prague. They arrived Tuesday morning and
settled in at the competitors' hotel, the Jalta. Wendy began training for her
next showdown with Laurence and Sjoukje Dijkstra. The competitors had
been told that a new arena had been built for the 1961 Worlds, but Wendy
and Mr. Galbraith discovered that it wasn't ready. Wendy practiced in the
rickety old arena, situated on an island in the middle of the Moldau River,
and waited for her competitors to show up the next day.[97]

TUESDAY, FEBRUARY 14

There was little time for training or for valentines on this lovers' holiday, as the skaters shopped, packed, headed to New York, and called and
wrote to family and friends before they traveled behind the Iron Curtain—the first time for most of them.

Harold Hartshorne, the most seasoned traveler in the delegation, had
developed a fear of flying. In particular he didn't like landings. His daughter
Daryl recalled that, whenever she sat next to him on flights, he was visibly
tense. For years, Harold had preferred to fly on one airline, Scandinavian
Airlines (SAS), another sign of aviation anxiety. An SAS flight was unavailable, so Harold and Louise had tickets on Air France. They were scheduled
to fly to Paris and from there take a train-bus combination to Prague.[98]

Like Ken Kelley, Harold preferred not to fly with the team because, as a judge, he did not want to show favoritism to the American skaters. Over the previous forty-eight hours, however, Harold had been talked into changing their plane tickets and flying with the delegation. He called his son James to ask what he knew about Sabena Airlines and its safety record. Louise, who usually accompanied her husband to competitions, had developed a bad cold in Philadelphia but resolutely packed up anyway.[99]

On Tuesday afternoon, a chartered bus took the team from Philadelphia to Idlewild Airport in New York City. Karen Howland saw the team off on the bus. Rhode Michelson was hell-bent on going to Prague; but the USFSA, still uncertain about Rhode's ability to compete, gave Karen a plane ticket for Wednesday. She was scheduled to room with Laurence in Prague.[100]

After the Hadleys got on the bus, they realized they had forgotten their music. Karen ran back to the lobby, retrieved their record case, and passed it through the bus window to them. There were other mishaps. No one realized that Dona Lee Carrier had missed the bus entirely. She had been shopping at a local department store and was late getting back. Bob Pearce, manager of the Treadway Inn, asked an assistant manager to rescue her, telling him, "You said how cute she was, so you can chase down the bus." The assistant manager rose to the occasion, put Dona Lee in his car, and drove at top speed, finally catching the bus near the Pennsylvania border. On the shoulder of the New Jersey turnpike, an embarrassed Dona Lee got on the bus to the cheers of everyone on board.[101]

The rest of the Canadian team also headed to New York City. Don Jackson and his coach Pierre Brunet wanted to fly with the Americans, but the CFSA wanted them to fly with the Canadians. Actually, Don was too ill to even fly with the Canadian team that night. He had won the North American title with a 103-degree fever, a reaction to a flu shot he'd had before the competition. When he arrived in New York, his worried coach advised, "I think you should stay here because the hospitals are better." They decided to wait a day or two before flying to Prague.[102]

Late in the afternoon on Valentine's Day, Eddie and Dickie LeMaire packed their bags into the family car, prepared to leave Rye for their month-long journey. Ten-year-old Diana said good-bye to her father and gave him a big hug. Thirteen-year-old Dickie exhibited classic older-brother behavior: "See you, squirt," he said, giving her a noogie. Eleven-year-old Dorinda was jealous that Dickie got to go with their father and thought, "Maybe next time it will be my turn." Muriel, Eddie, and Dickie drove out of sight toward Idlewild.[103]

That evening, the Ice Follies opened in Boston. David Jenkins had invited Edi Scholdan to see his show-stopping performance, but Edi had called him the day before with apologies: "Sorry, David, but I can't make it. These kids have never been abroad, and I really should go with them."[104]

Bradley Lord would normally have been at the Ice Follies opening. He was anxious to compete in Prague but was not excited about getting there. Like Edi Scholdan, Brad was not fond of flying. When he had flown back from the 1961 Nationals with a member of his club, he had gripped her arm during the landing, muttering, "I really hate this." Bradley had several trips ahead of him. After the European tour, the six U.S. champions had been invited to go to Japan.[105]

Broadmoor's Thayer Tutt was flying to Europe too, but not until Wednesday. After attending the World Hockey Federation meeting in Geneva, Switzerland, he planned to meet up with Edi. Broadmoor was slated to host the 1962 World Hockey tournament, and the two were planning to work out additional details. Tutt asked Edi, who spoke half a dozen languages, to be his interpreter. Edi had an extra ticket for the Sabena flight and had invited Mimi Haecker, a long-time club member who helped Edi with the shows, but she declined.[106]

At Idlewild, the bus discharged the passengers into a private Sabena lounge. Sabena did not charge the skating delegation for excess baggage, such as skates, boots, etc. "This [was] an $18,000 order for Sabena and they [were] going all out for us," Ken Kelley said. In the Sabena lounge, a State Department representative spoke with the delegation. Later Maribel called press contacts, informing them she could be reached at the Jalta Hotel.[107]

At airport newsstands, Laurence's smiling face greeted the Americans. Snapped in a brilliant red dress on a frozen pond at the Cambridge Skating Club, her cover girl article in *Sports Illustrated* had hit newsstands the day before. The article, "Mother Set the Style," chronicled the "basically insane Owen plan of existence" as their lives swirled around their intensive skating regime. The article concluded by recording the sisters' long-term ambitions: Maribel Jr.'s desire to teach and Laurence's interest in travel, acting, and writing.[108]

A partial Canadian delegation had arrived at Idlewild for their overnight KLM flight. Wendy Griner and her coach were not the only ones who had changed tickets. Coach Bruce Hyland had earlier changed plane tickets from Sabena to KLM for all three pair teams. He wanted to get a jump on the Americans and arrive in Europe first so they could get settled and make training arrangements. Brad Black's coach, Ron Vincent, did not get his visa in time. He and Brad planned to fly on Wednesday evening with Don Jackson, Don McPherson, Sonia Snelling, and Shirra Kenworthy.[109]

The final count on the KLM flight delegation was still fluctuating. At first there wasn't any room on the KLM flight for Ken Ormsby and Paulette Doan, and the American skaters told them, "You can go with us." At the last minute, space became available on KLM. Paulette did not have time to let her parents know of the switch, so they assumed the couple had flown with the American team.[110]

Otto and Maria Jelinek were still up in the air. Dudley Richards and other American skaters had invited them to fly with the U.S. team. The Jelineks were very close to the Americans, especially Dudley and Little Maribel. When Mrs. Jelinek said good-bye to her children in New York, they told their mother they would fly with the American team. They were in the middle of changing their tickets when their coach directed: "You're a Canadian, and you should fly with the Canadians."[111]

Numerous stories later emerged why the Jelineks did not board the Sabena flight; the primary one was that their coach would not let Otto fly without him because he was a womanizer and party animal. The truth was that Bruce Hyland wanted Otto and Maria to fly with him because he was worried about the political problems they had had with the Czech government. As Canadian team coach, Hyland had diplomatic immunity for the whole team and wanted to make sure that the Jelineks arrived safely.[112]

The KLM flight left Idlewild at 7:00 P.M., an hour and a half before the Americans. The Canadian skating delegation was small—eight skaters, one coach: Bruce Hyland, Maria and Otto Jelinek, Gerty Desjardins, Maurice Lafrance, Debbi Wilkes, Guy Revell, Paulette Doan, and Ken Orsmby. A couple of parents accompanied the group, but Debbi Wilkes's mother almost didn't make the plane because of a delayed visa. If the visa didn't get to the airport in time, her backup plan was to fly with the U.S. team. The visa was delivered in time. The Canadians flew to Amsterdam, changed planes, and boarded a Czech airplane for Prague.[113]

The American delegation had fluctuated over the past few days. Besides the eighteen-member team, the delegation included six coaches: Linda Hadley, Bill Kipp, Maribel Owen, Danny Ryan, Edi Scholdan, and Bill Swallender; six family members: Ann Campbell, Louise Hartshorne, Nathalie Kelley, Dickie LeMaire, Jimmy Scholdan, and Sherri Westerfeld; and four officials: Deane McMinn, Harold Hartshorne, Eddie LeMaire, and now Walter Powell. He had planned to fly on KLM with the Canadians, but he called Ken Kelley several days before the flight and requested to fly with the team. Helen Powell said good-bye to her husband that night and flew back to St. Louis. Deane received a telegram at the airport from Ritter Shumway, asking Walter to call him, and sent his "best wishes to all for interesting and successful trip."[114]

Scott Allen and his coach, Fritz Dietl, had tickets for the Sabena flight. The eleven-year-old would have been the third young spectator, along with eleven-year-old Jimmy Scholdan, and thirteen-year-old Dickie LeMaire. Dietl had a skating studio in Westwood, New Jersey. Three days before the plane took off, his compressors broke. He had to wait for parts to come in and fix the problem before he could go. Dietl was Scott's chaperone so they both delayed their trip.[115]

There was almost another member of the young spectator group. USFSA official Carl Gram and his wife Anne had reserved three seats on the plane for them and their twelve-year-old daughter, Coco, as a birthday surprise. Changing their minds for unknown reasons, they gave up their seats. Carl, who was Dickie LeMaire's godfather, had planned to see the team off, but a snowstorm stranded him in Chicago. Anne came to the airport to say good-bye to the LeMaires.[116]

During the pre-board wait, some in the delegation bought airline insurance. Marilyn Grace, who brought corsages to the airport for Pat Dineen and Dona Lee Carrier, pulled Bob Dineen aside, and said, "Listen, whatever you do, you better take insurance because you have this baby and this responsibility. What would happen if something happened to you?" Bob sneaked off to the insurance counter, and Dona Lee followed. Many of those who took out insurance had always done so, like Larry Pierce. "My father taught Larry and me to take out the maximum insurance so the airplane couldn't afford to go down," Marilyn Meeker said.[117]

Ann Campbell had a panic attack and didn't want to get on the plane at all. She had flown with Roger to competitions before, but something felt different this time. Two days earlier, she had called her husband, told him she felt that something was going to happen, and announced that she was canceling her trip. After he had calmed her down, she resolved to go. Now, with the clock ticking away the final minutes, her jitters returned. She called Al again in Los Angeles. "I'm afraid to get on this plane," she wailed across the country. "Then don't get on it," he responded. "Jump on a plane and come home." Al Campbell spoke with Roger, whose nerves were equally frazzled, due to his mother's hysteria. After Ann talked at length with her husband, she again changed her mind. Her desire to be with her son outweighed her nagging fear; still, she took some medication to calm her nerves. Before she boarded, she stopped at the kiosk and took out a large insurance policy.[118]

Ann Campbell was the only parent of skaters on the flight besides Maribel and Linda Hadley, who doubled as coaches. For the first time, Alfreda Lord did not accompany her son to competition. She had seen Bradley compete right up through North Americans that weekend, but she had recently had surgery and was scheduled to see her doctor. Alfreda saw Bradley board the Sabena plane and flew back to Boston that night.[119]

Elinor Hickox had flown to Philadelphia for North Americans and went to New York City to see her children off. The exorbitant cost was keeping her home; but she was grateful that Maribel was on the plane. Bill had taken lessons from her in Berkeley, and it gave her peace of mind that both Edi and Maribel were there for her kids. After Elinor left them, she spent the night at an airport hotel.[120]

Eleanor Carrier also saw Dona Lee safely on board, and then flew to Chicago to visit family. Jean Ramsay desperately wanted to go with her son, but they couldn't afford it.[121]

Ruth Richards had accompanied her son to only one of his fourteen national competitions, but she had made arrangements to go to Prague. At the last minute, though, she changed her mind. She had back problems and decided she wasn't up to such a long trip. The Richards family sent a farewell telegram to Dudley, but he didn't receive it before the plane left.[122]

Rhode's mother, Marty Michelson, was scheduled to join her daughter on Flight 548, but had caught the flu prior to North Americans, and her doctor wouldn't give her the shots necessary for international travel. Rhode's friends back home, knowing of her injuries in Philadelphia, were surprised that she flew with the team to Prague. Before Rhode boarded the plane, she took a moment to mail a note to Mary Miller, thanking her for her going-away party. Mary loved the homemade card—a little witch sitting on a broom—though she wasn't sure if the witch referred to Rhode or herself.[123]

Danny Ryan called his wife, busy at home with five small children, including two-week-old Michael. Larry Pierce realized the sacrifice Danny was making to accompany them but felt that Danny's coaching in Prague would be the difference between winning and losing a medal. Besides hoping to bring home a medal, Larry planned to buy an engagement ring while he was in Europe.[124]

More last-minute calls provided happy news. Laurence Owen talked to Bobby Brewer in Los Angeles; he congratulated her on her win, and they made plans to meet after Laurence returned from Europe. Doug Ramsay received word that the DSC directors had voted to create a skating fund in his name to cover travel expenses for international competitors. The Hadleys learned that the Seattle skaters had held another fundraiser for the family. The Westerfeld girls called their mother. They "were having the time of their lives," Myra said. "Both were in high spirits and excited about going to Europe."[125]

Ritter Shumway, who had spent the day in Washington, D.C., to hear President John Kennedy's first speech to American business leaders, had returned to Rochester, New York. He had already spoken to Walter Powell but felt the urge to talk with the team and called Idlewild again. "Gee, I wish I could go," he had told them. "They were all hyped up and really looked forward to going," he recalled. "You could just feel the excitement . . . the sparkle over the telephone."[126]

Team family members and New York skating club members also saw the group off at Idlewild. While waiting for the flight to be called, shutterbugs in the Sabena VIP lounge took farewell pictures. Dickie LeMaire, wearing a sport coat with a Skating Club of Boston patch on his lapel, smiled broadly next to his father.[127]

Associated Press reporter Francis Stilley and photographer Matty Zimmerman were covering the team's departure. Zimmerman took group photos: Steffi, Laurence, and Rhode; dancers Dona Lee and Diane looking dreamily at a skate held up by Pat Dineen, and the unofficial Owen family on the tarmac—Maribel, Laurence, Maribel Jr., and Dudley.[128]

Boarding paused as Zimmerman caught a priceless moment in time—the eighteen skaters, plus their team manager, grouped by divisions on the steps of the Sabena plane. Laurence, Steffi, and Rhode stood next to Deane McMinn; behind them were Doug, Greg, and Brad. Going up the steps were the pairs: Maribel, Dudley, Bill, Ray, Laurie, and Ila Ray. The dance teams filled the flight up to the door: Larry, Diane, Roger, Dona Lee, Bob, and finally Pat, who was near the door. Laurence held a hand-made sign proclaiming: "U.S. Figure Skating Team." Many of the girls wore corsages from friends and family pinned to their warm coats. Everyone held bags of skates and record cases. Laurence, Steffi, and Rhode, for unknown reasons, each held a second coat.[129]

Zimmerman's soon-to-be-famous photo caught Larry Pierce in a moment that created much speculation. The picture showed him holding his right hand up with fingers spread wide. Many thought it was an obscene gesture; a well known vulgar symbol times five. The inference was that he was cocky, holding the world in his hands. His friend Pieter Kollen cleared up the mystery: "The gesture was an 'in thing' that a group of friends developed. Instead of today where you would do a thumbs up, it was our way of saying 'Hey guys, this is it!' There was nothing obscene about it."[130]

Laurence Owe
Vinson Owen,
Owen, and Dudley
Richards, before boarding
Sabena Flight 548,
Idlewild Airport, February
14,1961. Source: Photo by
Matty Zimmerman,
Courtesy of Dudley Abbe.

As the last flashbulb went off, the entourage turned and dashed into the waiting silver and blue Boeing 707 plane. "They were a healthy, eager group of youngsters . . . full of life and confident-looking," an airline employee stated. It was nearly 8:30 P.M. when Sabena Flight 548 left Idlewild to cheers and waves from family and friends.[131]

The U.S. team took up more than half the plane. The remaining twenty-seven passengers included European and American businessmen, young wives making their first flight, and several young soldiers. The team's joy and excitement was infectious. They were on a quest to be the best in the world and were exactly where they wanted to be. Their thoughts were focused on the upcoming competition and the weeks of fun ahead of them as they performed in the major European capitals. Their current state of joy could only be exceeded by the future, which held unlimited possibilities.

Members of the skating delegation could be categorized a number of ways. Sherri Westerfeld and Nathalie Kelley were on the plane because of their siblings' success. Family members Dickie LeMaire and Jimmy Scholdan were there for personal reasons. The individuals who confirmed their participation at the eleventh hour included Doug Ramsay, Bill Swallender, Bill and Laurie Hickox, Ila Ray, Ray, and Linda Hadley, and Bob and Pat Dineen. Those who flew even though they were not well included Rhode Michelson, Maribel Owen Jr., Louise Hartshorne, and Ann Campbell. Some who had changed their flights at the last minute were Walter Powell and Harold and Louise Hartshorne. Some were there, including Dona Lee Carrier, Roger Campbell, Larry Pierce, and Diane Sherbloom, because they had formed partnerships late in the season. More than half the delegation had overcome multiple obstacles to make that flight.

Those left behind were skaters whose hopes to make the team had been dashed, including Marilyn Meeker, Yvonne Littlefield, Judianne and Jerry Fotheringill, Jim and Janet Browning, Jan Jacobson and Marshall Campbell, Tim Brown, Bruce Heiss, Vicky Fisher, Barbara Roles, and their respective coaches and chaperones. Family members, judges, and professionals who hadn't been able to make the trip included Ruth Scholdan, Alfreda Lord, Elinor Hickox, Eleanor Carrier, Jean Ramsay, Ruth Richards, Marty Michelson, Rose Anne Ryan, Mary Louise Wright, Margaret Ridgely, Margareta Drake, Edith Shoemaker, Colonel Harold Storke, Ron Ludington, Sonya Klopfer, Carl, Anne, and Coco Gram, Mimi Haecker, Eddie Shipstad, and Roy Shipstad. Junior champions who had received the coveted invitation but declined, included Monty Hoyt, Ron and Vivian Joseph, Lorraine Hanlon, and their parents and coaches. Looking forward to joining the group but taking later flights were Karen Howland, Bud Wilson, Ray Hadley Sr., Fritz Dietl, Scott Allen, and Dick Button. Those who had contemplated flying with the team but had made other arrangements were Ken and Joan Kelley, and the Canadians: Wendy Griner, Mrs. Griner, Sheldon Galbraith, Donald Jackson, Pierre Brunet, Otto Jelinek, Maria Jelinek, Bruce Hyland, Gerty Desjardins, Mrs. Desjardins, Maurice Lafrance, Debbi Wilkes, Mrs. Wilkes, Guy Revell, Ken Ormsby, Paulette Doan, Ron Vincent, Brad Black, and John, Billie, J. D., and Donna Mitchell. More than seventy-five other people had considered flying with the American team.

In retrospect, moments of uneasiness at the separation—natural for a transoceanic flight to a Communist country at the height of the Cold War—became bitterly regretted premonitions. Pearle Sutherland, mother of team manager Deane McMinn, couldn't sleep at all, plagued by a certainty that something was not right. In the early hours of the morning, she was afraid to turn on the radio or television. Marilyn Meeker, whose partner was on the plane, had a disturbing dream, in which the plane took off and disappeared from sight.[132]

Bill Hickox's girlfriend, Anne Frazier, had had a bizarre experience six weeks before the Sabena flight. Her Smith College assignment book had fallen open to February 15. She felt the room turn icy cold and a disembodied voice, not her own, said, "This will be the worst day of your life." More puzzled than alarmed, she wondered, "What on earth could possibly happen?" Several weeks later, after a dorm Valentine's Party, she walked upstairs to her room, then remembered that the next day was February 15. She racked her mind but could only think that her "horrible English teacher"

1961 U.S. World Figure Skating Team, with Team Manager Deane McMinn, before boarding Sabena Flight 548, Idlewild Airport, February 14, 1961. Source: Photo by Matty Zimmerman, Courtesy of Dudley Abbe.

might make her read her paper out loud. She hadn't made the connection that Bill and his teammates were leaving on the plane. In a few hours, the whole world would learn the fate of the 1961 Team.[133]

CHAPTER 16

FEBRUARY 15, 1961

The 1961 World Team, with their high spirits and enthusiasm, continued the party atmosphere as they boarded the Sabena plane, even after the flight left at 8:30 P.M. When it was time to settle down, everyone had reading material, including copies of the recent *Sports Illustrated* with cover girl Laurence Owen.

The plane crossed the Atlantic uneventfully. It was 3:00 A.M., New York time, when the plane neared the coastline, 9:00 A.M. European time. Normally the sun would have streamed in, waking anyone with an open shade. However on this morning, Captain Louis Lambrechts, the fifty-three-year-old Belgian pilot who had been in the British Royal Air Force during World War II, alerted his passengers to an eclipse of the sun. The moon dramatically slipped in front of the surface of the sun, turning day to night. From 33,000 feet above the Atlantic Ocean, the total eclipse was a magnificent sight.[1]

The passengers came to life as the plane neared the Brussels airport for the scheduled stop en route to Prague. The weather was perfect with cloudless skies and bright sunshine. At 9:40 Captain Lambrechts told controllers that "everything was normal on board." He closed his flight log, noting nothing more serious than a few burned-out bulbs on the instrument panel. Co-pilot Jean Eugene Roy talked with Belgian airport traffic controllers eight times to set course corrections in the final ten minutes before the scheduled arrival time of 9:50. The plane made a right turn near the village of Kontich for its final, ninety-second approach to runway No. 20. Initially the traffic controllers treated Flight 548 as a typical flight. The villagers, however, knew something was amiss.[2]

Three small but densely populated communities abutted the runways of the Zaventem Brussels Airport, eleven miles northeast of the city. The novelty of the big jet airliners had worn off, and the residents of Berg, Kampenhout, and Steenokkerzeel scarcely looked up any more when they heard the roar of engines. Nonetheless, on Wednesday morning at 9:45 A.M., many villagers pricked up their ears—the engines roared intermittently instead of their normal hum. The air traffic controllers became alarmed when they could not contact the cockpit again to ask for final status and give clearance to land. The tower tried reaching Flight 548 on several frequencies, but received no response.[3]

The Sabena plane appeared to be fine when the pilot dropped down for a landing right on schedule. Captain Lambrechts, a veteran of the jet age, made a wheels-down approach, but at 300 feet off the ground, he overshot the runway, pulled up his landing gear, and climbed to about 1,500 feet while banking to the left. Some observers thought he pulled up because a Caravelle jet was moving along the runway, ready to take off. Captain Lambrechts appeared to come around for a second approach, but the engines sounded strange and the flight path looked erratic. Streams of smoke pouring from the jets brought curious villagers out to observe the scene.[4]

Pilot Jacques Genot, who was in the airport briefing room filing his flight plan, saw the Boeing "dip and ascend like a bucking bronco." He suspected the pilot was fighting for control. He watched Flight 548 abort its approach to Runway 20 and try to land on adjacent, non-operational Runway 25 Right. He surmised that Lambrechts was undertaking an alternative because a mechanical malfunction—involving the wing spoilers or the tail stabilizers—prevented a normal landing. Airport personnel, watching from the tower with field glasses, saw the plane make a series of strange turns, as it would during a test or training flight.[5]

On Lambrecht's second approach he came in too low—breasting the flat fields nearby at 500 feet—increased his speed, and wrapped the giant 707 into an almost vertical bank. The plane never came out of the left turn, making, in total, three 360-degree circles around the three-mile long runway.[6]

During the last fifteen minutes of the flight, Captain Lambrechts had not contacted the Brussels airport tower. Realizing that the plane was in crisis, the Brussels tower flashed the emergency signal. Many villagers had called for fire engines. Rescue workers, in fireproof rubber clothing from eleven fire companies, raced toward the field in fire trucks, and ambulances, sirens screaming, rolled down the landing strip. A motorcycle policeman patrolling a nearby road joined the speeding emergency vehicles.[7]

Villagers watched the airliner turning overhead at 600 feet in an abnormal manner. The jet struggled to gain altitude, wobbled in the air, cartwheeled with wings almost perpendicular to the horizon and dropped its nose toward the ground with landing gear extended. Then, narrowly missing three houses in the village of Berg-Kampenhout, three miles north of the airport, it crashed at a seventy-degree angle in a small farm field near a grove.[8]

On impact the fuel tanks burst, engulfing the fuselage in flames and spewing debris and smoke into the clear blue skies. Fire engines were already on the scene, but there was no way to immediately control the flames. Firemen watched helplessly. The plane burned with a temperature estimated at 1,000 degrees centigrade. A state policeman said, "The heat was so intense I saw pieces of aluminum melting like butter." Because the plane had plunged almost straight to the ground, no windows were broken in the houses just a few hundred feet away, but the thick, black smoke signaled the disaster for miles around.[9]

The crew and passengers apparently knew the plane was in trouble. Firemen found the passengers strapped into their seats in the crash position—crouched over, head down, knees together. "It all took place at a terrifying speed," an airport official said. The control tower tried to explain the unexplainable: "All seemed all right, then suddenly we realized something was going wrong. There were no more contacts. The plane appeared out of control. It fell like a bomb." Pilots interviewed at the airport suggested that the controls on the left side of the plane had suddenly failed to function. From the severity of the crash and the massive, erupting fireball, it was apparent the passengers and crew had died instantly. The only living creature found in the wreckage was a German shepherd, severely injured, in the cargo hold. A merciful police officer quickly euthanized the suffering animal.[10]

Besides the seventy-two people instantly killed on board, one man was killed on the ground. Ironically, the seventy-third victim was another sports figure. Theo De Laet, twenty-one, was a well-known cyclist who had been released from military service two months earlier. Both he and Marcel Lauwers, twenty-seven, were working in the chicory fields that morning in the bright sunshine. Neither farmer heard the warning cry of a neighbor, who was flung against a shed and knocked unconscious by the explosion.[11]

Bertha Goovaerts had been cutting a crop of endives nearby when she heard the explosion. As she turned to see what had happened she saw her nephew, Marcel, crushed under the flaming wreckage. Hit by white-hot metal debris, his leg was severed. Bertha raced to Marcel, a rolling log of flame, and stripped off his clothes to save his life. Another rescuer quickly applied a tourniquet to his shattered limb.[12]

The police interrogated airport officials and villagers from the surrounding hamlets, but the accounts, at times, were contradictory. Farmer Wilhelm Verbaume said he saw the plane approach the airport and everything appeared normal. "But then it began to zigzag and rapidly lost height," he said. "It grazed a row of houses and smashed through telephone wires before crashing in the field." Another local farmer, Mr. Verhoeven, said he thought pictures were being taken from inside the plane because it was such a beautiful day.[13]

Three times the big silver and blue plane had skimmed over the nearby villages and a number of people had rushed out of their homes to watch. Mrs. Croon said the plane was "making much more noise and was much lower than they usually are." Mrs. Mariette Peeters had hurried outside when she heard the repeated roar of the engines: "There was a sudden silence followed by the noise of a crash . . . I saw the plane go down, nose-first." Viscountess Pierre de Biolley was on her doorstep: "The plane was making an unusual noise [and] flying extremely low. I saw it balancing in the sky, then, as it flew over a small nearby wood it seemed to recover power and pointed upwards and then it suddenly fell. It looked as if the pilot had made a deliberate effort not to hit the houses." Mrs. Heloise Vereycken of Steenokkerzeel concurred: "I believe the pilot did not want to crash on the houses, but was desperately looking for a clear spot."[14]

Mrs. Joseph Verhoeven from the nearby village of Berg had a close-up view:

> It was so low. I could see people looking at me from inside the plane and gesturing. I held my hand up to them. Then the airplane stopped right in the air. It was as if it were hanging there on something. The whole thing was shaking terribly, as if it were struggling to get started moving again. But something was holding it back. Then an amazing thing happened. The plane began to point to the sky. The whole nose began to rise upward. In a few seconds, the plane was straight up, absolutely straight—pointed right to heaven. It fell then like a stone, straight down, until it hit the ground. I could see the people inside waving at me, and I kept waving back.[15]

Many passengers on a Liège-Brussels express train skirting the airport saw the disaster. One passenger said: "The plane appeared to be making a normal approach to land when, on nearing the ground, it suddenly reared up, pointing almost vertically nose up into the sky. Then it fell back like a giant stone and we heard an explosion."[16]

The plane's movements reminded a number of eyewitnesses of war. Marcel Verhoeven, a reporter for a suburban newspaper, saw the plane as he rode his bike. He said he hadn't seen a plane behaving like that "since he was a frightened boy watching World War II bombing maneuvers." Francois de Kleermaeker, a coal merchant, said, "The plane took a tight turn, then turned again and fell. It was like during wartime when planes fell after being hit."[17]

Father Joseph Cruyt, a Roman Catholic priest from the nearby St. Servatjus Church, hurried to the scene after seeing the plane nose-dive into a field near the woods and seeing the smoke mushroom into the sky. "I snatched the holy oil and jumped into my car. . . . The blaze was so hot I couldn't get near the plane. I stood at the edge of the road praying and I gave a general absolution."[18]

Dozens of eyewitnesses watched the tragedy and gave the police and press conflicting accounts. Some said the wheels never came down, while others said the wheels were lowered and retracted twice; airport personnel confirmed that the plane let down its landing gear, then withdrew it unexpectedly on its first attempt. One eyewitness saw objects falling from the aircraft before it crashed, but no other reports confirmed this. A state policeman, among the first to arrive, spoke of $100 bills scattered around, but no one else did. The most surprising fact is that half said the plane nose-dived, while the other half plainly saw the plane's nose go up in the air and then "fell like a stone," crashing on its tail.[19]

Accounts from airport officials, who watched the plane until seconds before the crash, suspected a fault in the electrical and hydraulic mechanisms that work the plane's control. "The Boeing came over Brussels airport too high and too fast, we think," an airport official said. "The pilot apparently tried to gain height after coming in to land but failed. It looked as if the plane's controls had been lost completely. Suddenly the plane fell in a series of spins. It literally disintegrated."[20]

Some relatives had been waiting at the Zaventem Airport. The pilot's wife, Mrs. Lambrechts, was among dozens of relatives and friends who had watched from the airport window. Hostesses tried to comfort them after Sabena officials broke the grim news—"No survivors." One set of parents, seeing the plane in distress, left the airport and hurried to the crash site; the elderly Brussels businessman later led his weeping wife away from the dreadful scene, saying, "We lost our son there."[21]

The state police quickly established a cordon around the horrific crash site. Flaming, twisted, tangled wreckage had been spewed over a 200-yard wide radius. The plane's wheels were perched on top of a five-foot high pile of smoking metal, an engine was half buried in the ground, and plane fragments and luggage contents were strewn about: skates, shreds of costumes, a crumpled nylon stocking, an unscratched valise, and passport scraps settled across the blackened farm field. The stench of kerosene and fire hung in the air as an airport tank truck sucked up a lake of jet fuel that had poured from a part of the plane thrown free of the initial blaze. Investigators and rescue searchers were ankle deep in mud as firemen sprayed water and fire-extinguishing foam to prevent new fires from breaking out.[22]

According to an account in the *Boston Globe*, the firemen had never encountered a disaster of this magnitude before. "It was like an atomic explosion," an airport fire brigade member declared. Oscar De Ryck had raced his fire truck alongside ten other units. De Ryck got as close as possible to the bonfire as he climbed to the roof of his truck from which he directed his hose to extinguish the blaze. After several fourteen-hour days among the ruins, De Ryck disinfected his hands twice on doctor's orders, showered before leaving work, and when he arrived home showered again and changed clothes. "I still had the smell of death on me," he said. Another firefighter, Victor Brouckmans, had fainted at the scene. Brouckmans was transferred to another airport unit, never to fight a fire again.[23]

The investigation began before all the bodies had been removed. Minister of Public Works Omer van Audenhove arrived to help, along with other officials and authorities. Desperate for answers, some speculated that the total eclipse of the sun had affected the plane's electronic equipment. Sabena officials dismissed this idea because the eclipse ended an hour before the crash. As the wreckage cooled, investigators examined pieces for clues. Despite the violent crash and intense heat, the flight recorder and several other instruments were recovered. The Belgian government impounded tapes of the tower conversations with the aircraft.[24]

Willem Deswarte, Sabena director general, said everything was normal "when there took place an incident, the nature of which has not yet been determined, but which certainly affected the control of the aircraft." Deswarte said the undercarriage was not faulty and that engine trouble had been ruled out. His opinion was that something had gone wrong with the controls; the only alternative was that the two experienced pilots had suddenly lost consciousness at the same time, which he considered impossible. Other Sabena Boeing planes flew throughout the day because officials determined the crash was no cause for grounding other planes; the Flight 548 plane had recently been through a complete overhaul.[25]

Belgian officials did not consider sabotage a possibility, despite worldwide demonstrations at Belgian embassies and at the United Nations, following the suspicious death of deposed Belgian Congo Premier Patrice Lumumba. That morning a Sabena Boeing had flown into the Zaventem Airport from the Congo.[26]

A Sabena spokesman said positive identification would be difficult. By noon thirty bodies had been pulled from the wreckage, placed in Red Cross wagons, and transferred to a temporary mortuary at Melsbroek, the former Brussels airport.[27]

United States embassy officials, Belgian Premier Gaston Eyskens, cabinet members, and a representative of Belgium's king appeared at the scene within an hour of the accident. King Baudouin and his bride of two months, Queen Fabiola, soon arrived. The grave-faced king talked with dozens of salvage workers as they recovered bodies from the wreckage. The queen, her dark eyes full of tears, murmured, "It is terrible. It is terrible." The royal couple visited Theo De Laet's widowed mother and the wife of Marcel Lauwers. The king and queen then went to the hospital to visit Lauwers, and subsequently drove to the morgue at nearby Melsbroek to pay their respects to the dead.[28]

For King Baudouin and the Belgian nation, it was a difficult period. Belgians had recently experienced a mine disaster, floods, a village engulfed by a sliding slag heap, the escalating Belgian Congo crisis with its strikes and riots—and now the worst plane crash in their country's history. The village eyewitnesses told the royal couple that the pilot deliberately swerved the plane and came down at a steep angle to avoid hitting the nearby rows of brick houses. The villagers felt the disaster could have been much worse.[29]

The fact that a Boeing was involved in the crash added to the Belgians' distress. These planes had earned the nation's high regard after airlifting Belgian refugees from the Congo the previous summer. From July 9 through July 28, 1960, five Boeings, including the one that crashed, made sixty-two round-trip flights between Belgium and Africa, ferrying thousands of Europeans on mercy flights. This particular Boeing had recently returned to passenger service.[30]

⎯⎯⎯⎯⎯⎯⎯◦⎯⎯⎯⎯⎯⎯⎯

As firemen and rescue workers toiled in Brussels, the Canadian skating delegation arrived in Prague. They had first landed at Amsterdam's Schiphol Airport for a scheduled layover on a KLM Dutch Royal Airliner DC-1; an hour later they continued to Prague on another KLM flight. Although the Americans had left after the Canadians in New York, the U.S. team had a shorter layover in Brussels and had been scheduled to arrive before the Canadians in Prague. When the Canadians arrived in Czechoslovakia, they immediately knew something was wrong.[31]

After the KLM plane landed, Otto and Maria Jelinek were escorted off the plane. The skaters assumed the Jelineks' lives were in jeopardy because of their problems with the Communist government; they didn't understand that Otto and Maria were singled out because they spoke Czech. "A group from the Czech skating association came to greet us at the plane," Maria said. "I didn't know who they were, but right away I said, 'Are the Americans here yet?' And they said, 'No, the plane crashed in Brussels and nobody's alive.' I started crying, and the rest of the team thought we were being arrested."[32]

When the skaters saw Maria sob uncontrollably, they panicked. As they got off the plane, military police immediately took their passports. Fourteen-year-old Debbi Wilkes approached their contact—a stereotypical Communist wearing a long, heavy gray coat and coke-bottle glasses—and asked, "Where are all the Americans?" In her staccato English, she replied: "They've all been killed." "That was all she said," Debbi recalled. "I thought they had been lined up in front of a firing squad."[33]

Marie Vichova, a sixteen-year-old Prague skater whose parents had allowed her to skip school to watch the competitors practice at Zimni Stadion, was at the arena when the other skaters received the news. "I saw them crying and hugging each other," she said. "In a few minutes everybody in the building knew what had happened."[34]

The Canadians, who had just been with the Americans that weekend, could not comprehend what had happened. "I was already terrified about this Otto and Maria thing and going behind the Iron Curtain," Debbi Wilkes admitted. "I had this very fourteen-year-old concept—I probably thought there was a real iron curtain." The plan had been to meet up with the Americans in Prague and all go into the city together on a bus; stunned and bewildered, the Canadians huddled in the bus as it left the airport, inching through the traffic. "We couldn't move through the streets because they were teeming with a million people," Debbi recalled. "Demonstrators, protesting the death of [Belgian Congo Prime Minister Patrice] Lumumba carried huge black and white placards. People were leaning up against the bus and we were afraid the bus was going to be pushed over."[35]

The rest of the Canadian team in North America was in limbo. Don Jackson, coach Pierre Brunet, Brad Black, coach Ron Vincent, and Shirra Kenworthy were scheduled to fly out from New York Thursday night on KLM. Don Jackson, who was staying with friends, got a frantic call from his mother who had just learned of the crash and was terrified that Don had been on the plane. On the way to skating practice, Shirra Kenworthy bought newspapers, thinking: "I have to show this to all the American kids when we get to Prague—then it hit me that they were gone." J.D. and Donna Lee Mitchell had trained with Jean Westwood that morning in Manchester, and learned about the accident after seeing it on television. Their mother, Billie Mitchell, a Canadian Figure Skating Association (CFSA) board member, phoned Ottawa to let them know that her family had not been on the plane. The CFSA asked her to fly to Brussels to help identify the bodies; the entire Mitchell family and Jean Westwood flew to Brussels.[36]

The anguish was not confined to the skating community of family and friends. Thirty-eight other people had perished, including seventeen Belgians. The all-Belgian eleven-member crew consisted of a four-man cockpit team: the pilot, Captain Louis Lambrechts, co-pilot Jean Eugene Roy, navigator Jean-Marie Kint, and Lucien Eduwaere, the flight engineer. Working in the cabin were five stewards: Marcel Demaeyer, Paul De Vos, Pierre Vanden Bussche, Henri Vernimmen, and Robert Voleppe; and stewardesses Jacqueline Rombaut and Jacqueline Trullemans. Captain Lambrechts was Sabena's most experienced pilot flying Boeing planes. Mme. Helin, a long-time Sabena employee, said Lambrechts was "one of the best in Belgium."[37]

The remaining Belgian passengers were Pierre Balteau, Marcellin Deprince, Vernier Dominique, Franz J. Offergelt, Jean L. R. Verbruggen, his wife Germaine Verbruggen, and Robert Raulier. Raulier was the son-in-law of Henri Cornelis, who had served as governor-general in the Belgian Congo from 1958 to 1960—the last governor-general before the Belgian Congo received its independence and inaugurated Patrice Lumumba as the nation's first native prime minister.[38]

The twelve other Americans on board were diverse. Five were Texans. Dayton Alexander and George Young were en route to jobs in Libyan oil fields. Three Trans-Texas Airlines flight attendants, Iris Jean Duke, Linda Foster, and Daurice Herring, were embarking on a European vacation.[39]

Five passengers had a military connection. Nineteen-year-old Juanita Dauzet Lemoine of New Orleans was taking her first plane trip to meet her serviceman husband, Private James Lemoine, in Frankfurt. Twenty-year-old Margaret Lovering Pozzuolo, pregnant, was also en route to Frankfurt to join her husband, a cook in the U.S. Army. Private first class Robert Stropp, eighteen, was returning to Paris after his first leave. Captain Richard Robinson, thirty-six, was returning to Germany with his twenty-eight-year-old Belgian bride, Jacqueline Samples Robinson, after visiting his parents during a six-day honeymoon trip in Indiana.[40]

The majority of other passengers were businessmen. Julian Baginski was a restaurateur en route to Warsaw to visit his dying mother. Max Silberstein from Westport, Connecticut, was a diamond importer and partner in the jewelry firm of Morris Silberstein of New York City. Harold G. Kellett of Bronxville, New York, was an executive of Scott & Williams, a manufacturer of knitting and hosiery machinery. Howard R. Lillie was a renowned scientist and executive with the Corning Glass Works in Corning, New York. H. Herbert Myers of East Orange, New Jersey, was president of the Charles Beseler Company, manufacturers of photographic equipment. Little is known of Jacob Herschkowitz, from Queens, New York; his neighbors said they only knew that he was "a quiet man, hard working."[41]

Several businessmen were European expatriots. Martin S. Soria, a native of Berlin, was a Michigan State University professor and an international authority on Spanish art. Chicagoan banker Francis C. Medina came from a prominent Latin-American banking family. The Reverend Otmar Boesch, a Swiss Roman Catholic priest serving in Seattle, was making his first visit home in five years to St. Gall. The only Canadian on board, Victor Maes, was a tobacco farmer from Vanessa, Ontario.[42]

Sadly, there were twists of fate for a number of the Sabena passengers. The Texan stewardesses missed a connecting flight and joined Flight 548 at the last minute. Juanita Lemoine changed her flight a day early to make international connections. Private Stropp missed an earlier flight and had endured a twenty-four hour layover. Victor Maes missed his plane in Montreal to attend his mother's funeral, so caught a flight out of Idlewild. The family of Herbert Myers thought he had already cheated death—just a week before the Sabena flight, he had survived an armed robbery during a Las Vegas business trip.

It was truly a loss felt on two continents. President John F. Kennedy, in office for only four weeks, led the nation in mourning the deaths of forty-nine Americans, including the thirty-four members of the U.S. figure skating delegation. Within hours of the catastrophe, the nation's chief executive extended sympathy to the families and friends of the victims from the White House:

> I was distressed and saddened to learn of the airline crash in Brussels this morning. This disaster has brought tragedy to many American families and is a painful loss to the international community of sports as well. Our country has sustained a great loss of talent and grace which had brought pleasure to people all over the world. Mrs. Kennedy and I extend our deepest sympathy to the families and friends of all the passengers and crew who died in this crash.[43]

Secretary of State Dean Rusk telegraphed Ritter Shumway: "I wish to express my personal condolences and those of the Department of State to you and ask that you convey them to the families of the United States Figure Skating Team. That they lost their lives while on their way to represent the United States in the World Championships in Prague only increases the tragedy, for I am certain that these fine Americans would have served their nation well by their presence."[44]

After Ritter Shumway, in Rochester, New York, learned of the crash, he issued a statement: "The human tragedy involved in the loss of the United Sates Figure Skating Team in the crash of the Sabena airliner in Belgium simply cannot be expressed. I can only extend my sympathy to the families and friends of all those involved."[45]

Increasing the pain, all of the 1961 Team's families heard about the fate of their loved ones before the USFSA or Sabena Airlines had a chance to notify them. Muriel LeMaire always kept a little transistor radio on whenever her husband flew. When she heard the news, she called several close friends who hurried over. "My sister and I woke up for school and came downstairs," Diana LeMaire said. "We couldn't figure out why these people were at our house at 6:00 in the morning."[46]

In Los Angeles, an Arctic Blades club member heard about the accident on the radio at 2 A.M.; the first report—a shocking misstatement—was that the plane had been "shot down." Fortunately, that rumor was not repeated. The club member immediately called Rhode Michelson's family, and tried to find the words to convey the news gently. In Boston, Bradley Lord's parents heard the report on the radio, as did Lute Hickox in Berkeley. Lute quickly made a plane reservation to join his wife, who was still in a hotel near Idlewild Airport. Anne Frazier, who heard the news at Smith College, called Lute to see if Bill was on the plane. Devastated by the news, she flew home to San Francisco—only then did she remember her premonition.[47]

Others saw the news on television. Ruth Kipp Kline, Bill's oldest sister, saw the first early morning newscast, and called her sister Timmy; together they went to break the news to their mother, who lived with her son Elmer in Allentown, Pennsylvania.[48]

Perhaps the cruelest way to hear the news was when reporters called to ask for comments. That's what happened to Genevieve Swallender, recently returned from Philadelphia, when she took a call from a *Detroit News* reporter. In Colorado Springs, a reporter woke up Broadmoor club president Bill Haigler, informing him of the crash. He and his wife Fran, a close friend of Myra Westerfeld, arranged for a doctor to go with them to tell Myra, but she had already received a telephone call from another reporter.[49]

Some reporters actually showed up in person. Mary Dineen, answering the door bell at 4:30 A.M., found a reporter asking if she knew that her son and his wife had died. Diane Sherbloom's mother had already left for work and her father was still in bed when reporters arrived at 8 A.M. Fifteen-year-old Joan threw some clothes on to answer the door but paused to answer the ringing phone. It was Larry Pierce's sister, Jan. Joan ran next door to her godmother, evading the reporters outside her door. "It wasn't until that evening we got a telegram from the airlines," she said.[50]

A number of families were apart when they heard the news. Reverend Floyd Carrier was in Los Angeles while his wife was in Chicago visiting relatives; she made plans to fly home immediately. "If I can only hold out until my wife gets home," Rev. Carrier said. "As a minister I have seen much tragedy. But it's different when it's personal." Rev. Carrier received Dona Lee's Valentine's card just days after the crash.[51]

Rose Anne Ryan's parents had been helping their daughter for the two weeks after baby Michael's birth and had just left Indianapolis. Mr. and Mrs. Henry Paquette, en route to their home in Ottawa, Canada, did not learn of the crash until they reached Buffalo. They turned around and drove back to Indianapolis late Wednesday night to be with their daughter and grandchildren.[52]

The three youngest Hartshorne children were all in boarding school. Dan's teacher approached him in hushed tones, telling him about a horrible accident in Belgium. Dan called his grandfather, who reassured him that his father had flown on Air France. "He called me back within two hours," Dan said, "telling me he was dreadfully sorry to inform me that Dad was indeed on the plane with Louise." Hartshorne's oldest son, Harry, was stunned to learn his father and Louise were on the plane. The last plans he had heard had them traveling to Europe by steamship.[53]

For some, the crash wiped out their entire immediate family. Helen Powell had just been with her husband in Philadelphia for North Americans but was home in St. Louis when she received the news. The phone rang at the Hadley home in Seattle in the middle of the night, giving Ray Hadley Sr. the grim news. "I just don't know what to do," Ray said in quiet desperation. "We should have gone together."[54]

Dr. Hollis Albright and Rev. John Ellison broke the news to Grammy Vinson shortly after 10 A.M. Dr. Albright gave her a sedative and discussed jet planes—how fast they traveled and their landing speed. "As the news came in she knew it would be bad," Dr. Albright said, "and then she said to me, 'They are all dead.' She repeated this several times and then added, 'I would rather have them dead then coming back all mangled.'" Dr. Albright added, "I simply cannot describe the courage this woman showed."[55]

No matter how this devastating news was communicated, it was a life-changing moment for the families. Stephen Kelley was asleep on the third floor of their home when he heard a piercing scream from the first floor. Jolted awake, he ran downstairs to his mother, who had just learned of the crash. After Dallas Pierce heard the news, he was so shaken his family sought medical attention for him.[56]

The press contacted Tim Brown at his parents' home in Carmichael, California. "They were all close friends," he said. "I've known some of them for ten years. . . . I got a letter yesterday from Dudley, telling me he hoped he would see me when the plane took off," he said. "It is terrible for those killed and even more tragic for the relatives and friends who survive."[57]

Some friends and family immediately flew to Brussels. Fred Heller, Dudley's best friend, was in Europe and contacted the Richards family, offering to fly to Brussels on their behalf. "I put his death down as the biggest loss in my life," Heller said of Dudley, who was the godparent of one of his sons. Roberta Scholdan, whose plan to meet Edi and Jimmy in Prague had been scrapped when the Czechs denied her a visa, flew to the crash site after being notified at the Vienna Ice Arena.[58]

Skaters, coaches, and officials across the nation struggled to find words for their shock and grief. USFSA official Harry Radix said, "Some of the most wonderful people in skating were in that group. . . . It was like a family." Francis Turner, a Skating Club of Boston official, said, "All my children have been taken away." The overwhelming loss was felt beyond the American skating community. In shops and bars across the Atlantic, Europeans approached Americans and expressed their sympathy.[59]

Every metropolitan paper published the Sabena passenger list. Despite this clarity, friends believed a few other skaters were on the plane, including Jim and Janet Browning, Dorothyann Nelson, and some Canadian team members. Canadian papers listed Wendy Griner's name on the roster and her school announced to her classmates that she had died in the plane crash. The families of Paulette Doan and Ken Ormsby thought they had been with the U.S. team, because that was the last word they had heard.[60]

Coach Tom McGinnis filled in for Maribel at the Boston Arena, teaching her Haus Frau Club, which met every Wednesday morning. The ladies knew Maribel would want them to skate, but they were too numb. By the time McGinnis returned to The Skating Club of Boston, the rink looked like a morgue with an abundance of floral arrangements. The club members could not bring themselves to skate either, and a prowling TV news crew didn't help. That afternoon during a hockey game, in a bizarre doubling of disasters, Ted Benshimol, a young hockey coach at New Prep in Cambridge, collapsed while playing in an annual alumni game and was pronounced dead on arrival at the hospital.[61]

The Boston press bombarded the Ice Follies stars at their hotel that morning. "Edi Scholdan . . . was like a father to me," David Jenkins said. "I knew practically everyone on the plane. They were wonderful dedicated youngsters." Jenkins shook his head and murmured, "I can't even think of the loss to skating—it is simply incalculable; and the loss to their loved ones is so great." Ice Follies impresario Eddie Shipstad, who had almost flown to Prague, said, "I'm heartbroken. . . . [T]here has been nothing like it in the skating world. I lost many close friends."[62]

True to the show business adage, the Ice Follies gallantly performed at the Boston Garden Wednesday night after spectators and performers had stood for a moment of silent tribute. After the show, the shaken skaters huddled together to support one another, when the Lords and Kelleys suddenly appeared backstage. A half dozen Boston skaters were in the show, and the families said it made them feel better to be with friends of their children. "The Lords were like family to the show and had already been invited because of Bradley," Richard Dwyer explained. "They were brave people and my heart went out to them."[63]

School friends struggled to deal with their sorrow. At Ingraham High School in Seattle, the usually noisy halls were hushed. "Everyone knew Ray [Hadley] because he had been on the Olympic Team," skater Bob Deuter said. "Everybody knew—a thousand students—and it was just dead quiet." At the Air Force Academy, the Cadet Wing—particularly the 7th Squadron—was overwhelmed with grief but had to carry on, even as they dealt with the untimely death of one of their own: Fourth Class Cadet Bill Hickox.[64]

The large U.S. flag at Winchester High School in Massachusetts was lowered to half staff. Students wept as Principal Howard Niblock addressed the school's 870 students over the public address system: "The skating world lost some outstanding skaters and we lost a very fine friend," he said. "If there is a happy note on this sad occasion, it is that Laurence died at the moment of her greatest triumph—National and North American women's figure skating champion. Words are hollow at a moment like this so let a moment of silence and our prayers express our sorrow."[65]

Despite the overwhelming sorrow, the ISU had to quickly decide whether to hold the 1961 World Figure Skating Championships. Just hours after the crash, the Czechoslovakian Figure Skating Section sent a sympathy telegram to the USFSA; simultaneously the ISU announced the cancellation of the championships "as a sign of mourning for our sports comrades." The USFSA made a sportsmanlike gesture in encouraging the Worlds to proceed as planned. Ritter Shumway cabled a "carry on" request to the ISU:[66]

> Skaters from all over the world have trained for years for these events and many already are in Prague. We feel that the members of the United States team, all of whom were such fine sportsmen and completely dedicated to the sport of figure skating, would have wanted the championships to go on. They were all good troupers, wonderful young people. We appreciated the tribute to our skaters, but in fairness to all the other competitors we [think] the competition should continue as the skaters, I know, would want it that way.[67]

The Czech organizing committee made it clear they were definitely in favor of holding the competition, "although we are all extremely depressed by the tragic incident." ISU Secretary General Georg Hasler and ISU President Dr. Jacob Koch fielded queries from ISU executive board members about whether a cancellation was appropriate. Hasler and Koch cabled the opposing views of the ISU and the Prague organizers to the executive committee members for a telegraphic ballot.[68]

On Thursday, February 16, Hasler revealed that a "substantial majority" of the ISU executive board members voted to call off the championships but declined to name those holding pro and con positions. However, delegates from Sweden, Norway, and Denmark made public statements. While acknowledging that cancellation would mean a huge financial loss for the Prague organizers, they felt that staging the championships would be too emotional given the magnitude of the crash. Koch agreed: "This is the only correct decision. The tragedy is too enormous to go on with the championships. It is impossible to hold them. There would be no joy in such a championship."[69]

The Prague organizers were stunned by the news. The Czechs asked the ISU to reconsider and argued from a precedent: fifteen members of the Czech hockey team had been killed in a plane crash en route to London in 1947, "but in spite of this the world championships was held." Preparations had cost more than $140,000 and arrangements had been completed for a sixteen-nation European television hookup of the competition. They also argued that most of the skaters had already arrived in Prague. It was true that skaters from seven countries had arrived, but those from nine countries had not. Only half of the Canadian team was there; the other scattered team members were told to, "Stay where you are. We're not sure what is happening."[70]

All the international skaters were in limbo. British dancer Doreen Denny was in England but her partner Courtney Jones was in Zurich on business, and she didn't know how to reach him, nor did her association know what to tell them. German skater Christa Von Kuczkowski was training in Milan with her coach, 1953 World bronze medalist Carlo Fassi, whom she had recently married. "It was upsetting for Carlo because he knew quite a few of the people," she said. "Dudley [Richards] had just called him three days before, saying he was looking forward to seeing him in Prague."[71]

Surprisingly, a few U.S. skaters were on high alert. Bruce Heiss's guardians told him to get ready to go to Prague, in case the USFSA decided to send another team over. Lorraine Hanlon continued to train because she heard a new team might depart for Prague. These instructions may have come from parents or coaches, because the USFSA never sought a replacement team.[72]

The Czech organizers wanted the skaters to stay in Prague, providing them with further ammunition against cancellation. The competitors bonded outside the rink as they waited for the verdict. "I have pictures of all of us sitting on a hotel bed, just chatting and waiting for a decision to be made," Wendy Griner said. When some skaters went to Zimni Stadion to train, they were startled to find fans who had waited outside the stadium for hours. "They were so excited to have us there," Debbi Wilkes said. "The stadium itself was terrible, but it was practically full with fans, who gave us little gifts as we left the arena."[73]

The organizers probably didn't ask the athletes if they wanted to compete. The Czech organizing committee, consisting of Czech skating officials and parents from the local clubs, had had to work with a difficult Communist regime to make the necessary preparations for a world-class event. They had already jumped over insurmountable hurdles and spent an enormous amount of money. Their anxiety was understandable. The Czechs once again requested the ISU to reconsider.[74]

On Friday 17, the ISU once again turned down the Prague request, officially cancelling the 1961 World Figure Skating Championships. The meet had never been cancelled before except during wartime, 1915-21 and 1940-46. No other World organizing committee had faced such an extraordinary crisis. The Czechoslovakians, as Marie Vichova explained, were very poor: "The tickets had all been sold and all the money had to be refunded, but as the host country we still had to pay all the expenses for the skaters, judges, etc. The government was unhappy with the cancellation, but the majority of the skaters and the skating federation wanted to do something to honor these people." It was some consolation that Prague was immediately awarded the 1962 World Championships.[75]

The skaters were relieved by the news. "It just didn't seem appropriate," Paulette Doan said. "If they had told us the competition was being held we would have skated, but no one was in a competitive mood." World dance champion Doreen Denny agreed: "We were skating better than ever and probably would have won our third title, but there's no possible way I would feel good about competing and winning." According to British pairs champion Peter Burrows, the athletes stopped the event because they didn't think it should be held. "There would have been a sour feeling to the whole event had it gone on." Native son Karol Divin was a favorite for the World title, but from the moment he heard about the disaster as he practiced at Zimni Stadion, he was too full of sorrow to compete. When Worlds was cancelled, "I felt a great relief," he said. "I agreed with that decision very much as I felt that was the only possible solution."[76]

The skaters packed their bags. "It was sad that the championships would not be held 'til next year," Marie Vichova said, "but it was more sad knowing that these wonderful skaters had disappeared forever. Even though we didn't know them personally, they were part of our lives." Many European skaters performed at a special exhibition in Garmisch on behalf of the 1961 U.S Team, and the Canadians went on an abbreviated exhibition tour to a few cities in Czechoslovakia and Switzerland. At the beginning of each show, the skaters went to the center of the ice while the announcer called out the names of every skater who had died in the crash.[77]

Ritter Shumway, who had encouraged the 1961 Worlds to proceed, was grateful for the ISU decision: "I know I speak for all members of the USFSA when I say we are deeply moved by this expression of sympathy. The sincere feeling of fellowship evidenced by such a sacrifice eases the burden that all of us in the United States feel and indicates the high personal regard in which our skaters were held throughout the world." Still shaken, Shumway admitted that the personal tragedy of the crash had overwhelmed him.[78]

The Czech organizers had persuasive arguments and USFSA support, but one of the factors toward cancellation may have been the death of Walter Powell. He was the first North American ISU executive committee member, representing both the United States and Canada, and had served in his post for fifteen years. The ten-member ISU executive committee was a tight group, and at age eighty-one, Powell was a highly respected peer due to his longevity and experience. Ritter Shumway, who had accompanied Powell to two ISU Congresses, said: "If ever an ambassador was 'persona grata' it was

Walter Powell among his colleagues of the ISU." The ISU hierarchy may have been most affected by losing one of their inner circle so tragically.[79]

Canadian official Nigel Stephens, who had voted to hold the championships, voiced his disappointment to the ISU, and wrote to the CFSA membership: "We were all very upset by the shocking disaster, but felt that the cancellation of the championships would only add to the unhappiness of the skaters, bearing in mind the extensive preparation of those concerned from all over the world during the last year." The Canadian team, positioned to win several World titles, had more at stake than any other country. Ritter apologized to the CFSA:

> I am only sorry that our tragedy, which we must in the end bear by ourselves, had to be the means of inflicting a substantial sacrifice on our good friends among the Canadian World Team by the cancellation of the World Championships by the Council of the I.S.U. From my public statements I am sure you know that we in the United States felt that this was quite unfair to the other competitors. . . . We, of course, deeply appreciate the tribute that has been paid to our skaters and we look forward particularly to a renewal of the very fine and friendly competition with Canada at the North Americans two years from now.[80]

Back in Brussels, the U.S. Consulate continued the verification of American bodies. The Belgian government, Sabena, and the U.S. State Department requested the co-operation of the FBI, and President Kennedy authorized a four-man FBI disaster squad, who had recently worked on a New York air collision in December 1960, to head to Brussels. Identification was sometimes confirmed by scraps of passports or engraved wristwatches; fingerprints sent by the FBI helped in some cases.[81]

Friends of the American team assisted the FBI, including coach Jean Westwood, Billie Mitchell of the CFSA, Roberta Scholdan, Dudley Richards's friend Fred Heller, who flew in from the Canary Islands, and Edward Marshall, president of The Skating Club of Boston, who flew in from Paris. Representing the USFSA was Ken Kelley, who had flown with his wife on Sabena Flight 548 on Monday night in advance of the team delegation and was in Vienna at the time of the crash.[82]

When Ken Kelley visited the crash site on Friday, February 17, nothing had been disturbed. The area was roped off and well guarded by police. The left wing and the main cabin were shredded; the right wing had snapped off and broken into several pieces, some of them otherwise nearly undamaged.

The cabin of the plane and the four engines had torn eight-foot pits in the ground, while the tail remained whole and untouched by fire. In the three foot pile of charred personal belongings, Kelley found Mrs. Campbell's Sabena ticket absolutely intact and pristine. "I took a number of pictures of the shocking and fearful scene," Kelley wrote to Shumway. "This was not with a ghoulish intent—in fact, I wish I could forget the scene but fear I never will."[83]

The most frightful aspects of newspaper reportage had finally stopped. A number of initial statements had been erroneous, including ". . . here and there were couples locked in frantic embrace . . . dismembered bodies were strewn everywhere and some were found speared in the earth." In fact, the FBI confirmed that all bodies had remained intact. The Belgian Association of Pilots and Navigators acknowledged that certain statements made to the press on the day of the accident had contained inaccuracies. It was a muted way to describe sensationalism that increased the agony of those who had lost loved ones.[84]

On Saturday, Kelley took Fred Heller, Roberta Scholdan, and Private Lemoine, whose wife had been on the plane, with him to the Sabena offices. Kelley described Lemoine as "a pitifully crushed lad lost in a maze of foreign language and red tape." By Monday, February 20, fourteen members of the skating delegation had been positively identified. The U.S. Army took responsibility for Bill Hickox, and Fred Heller accompanied Dudley Richards's coffin home on Wednesday, February 22. Jean Westwood, flying the same flight, was unnerved when the plane developed temporary engine trouble.[85]

At the time of the accident, the Brussels airport commander said it could take six months to establish the cause of the crash. The U.S./Belgian investigating team imposed a strict news blackout, saying it was too soon to disclose findings. An existing international convention required that international airline accidents must be investigated by experts beyond the country in which the crash occurred. Besides a Belgian government inquiry and judicial investigation, investigative experts from around the world descended on Brussels within days of the crash, including a team of Boeing technical experts. The remains of the plane were moved to Melsbroek, an old civil aerodrome near the airport, where investigators tried to reconstruct the plane. All objects found, including the plane's recorder, flight log, and thirty other instruments, were seized. Among the salvaged items was the plane's altimeter, which could provide clues to the plane's final movements.[86]

Because there were no adverse weather conditions, there was great speculation as to what caused the plane to crash. The Belgian newspaper *Le Soir* suggested that the plane stalled because of "reduced speed or because the controls jammed." But it added that the latter possibility seemed remote because the "Boeing 707 has so many alternate power supplies for each piece of control equipment." The French daily newspaper *L'Aurore* suggested possible terrorism, stating that "the accident might have been caused by a passenger running amok with a submachine gun." An airport official, counteracting this assertion, responded: "This is highly unlikely, and belongs more to the style of a novel than to present day conditions of international travel with severe luggage checks by customs."[87]

Sabena said that Boeing 707 OO–SJB had had trouble with its undercarriage just three days before the accident. On February 12, a Brussels to Leopoldville flight was delayed because of a "minor incident concerning its undercarriage" that was repaired immediately. A complete overhaul was not called for because "the plane had only recently undergone a complete revision." After its return from the Congo, the jet flew to New York and picked up passengers for the Valentine's Day nonstop return flight to Brussels. After this statement was released, Sabena reversed itself; William Deswarte, Sabena's general manager, stated that speculation that the Boeing's undercarriage was at fault was "erroneous."[88]

Investigations by Belgian national authorities, the U.S. Federal Aviation Agency (FAA), and the Montreal-based International Civil Aviation Agency yielded no definitive cause for the crash. Airline investigators suspected a fault in the electrical and hydraulic machinery affecting the plane's controls; the spoilers or stabilizers were the most plausible culprits. An official report revealed that the plane's stabilizers had seized on earlier flights, making it difficult to turn right. Sixteen official complaints had previously been filed, but none by Captain Lambrechts. Investigators concluded that it was "impossible for the pilot to bring back to neutral simultaneously all lateral control surfaces." In other words, once the wings were tilted, Lambrechts wouldn't have been able to return them to a level position. The FAA quickly proposed new regulations for airlines to file more detailed and explicit reports on failures and malfunctions. The FAA noted that the most plausible hypothesis for the crash was a malfunction of the stabilizer adjusting mechanism that had consequently allowed the stabilizer to accept a nose-up position of 10.5 degrees, when the normal angle is one or two degrees.[89]

The official, fifty-two page Belgian accident report presents an in-depth analysis of the data, and in so doing clears up some lingering questions. Although some witnesses observed an object detach itself from the plane, a systematic search did not support that observation; the debris on site proved conclusively that the "aircraft structure was intact before impact." Among a number of hypotheses, the report also focuses on the possibility of problems with the spoilers. It deduces that the pilot could have corrected the erratic functioning of the spoilers by "activating the pump pressure control switches of the hydraulic pumps." However, the commission acknowledged that: "If we admit the sequence of events as explained heretofore, it was impossible in the time available and under the circumstance in which the crew found itself to identify with certainty the failures in which it was confronted. What is more, it must be noted that is nearly impossible to observe the spoilers from the cockpit, which in itself would render the identification of the cause more difficult."[90]

The "King's Report" states that the "flying controls" were the most likely reason for the jetliner's crash but, in the end, does not commit to that hypothesis:

> Having done all possible reasonable investigations, the Commission concludes that the cause of the accident must be looked for in the physical failure of the flying controls. However, while it was possible to advance certain hypotheses relative to this possible cause, it must remark that they generated certain objections and can therefore not be considered as entirely satisfactory. Only the physical failure of two systems can lead to a complete explanation, but leaves the door open to an arbitrary choice because there is not sufficient evidence to corroborate it.[91]

The exact cause of the crash remains a mystery. Decades later, the FBI released 120 pages of once-classified documents, including cables from FBI offices of interviews with grieving relatives. The FBI documents suggested no sabotage. Ritter Shumway, in a letter to FBI director J. Edgar Hoover, thanked the FBI for sending a team of experts to Brussels to investigate and help identify the victims. Hoover replied, "Any technical aid and skill which we are able to contribute on such occasions can never equal our earnest desire to be of greater service."[92]

The Sabena Flight 548 crash was one for the record books. At the time, its death toll of seventy-two was the deadliest crash involving one passenger jet; the worst accident involving a single commercial jet aircraft; the first disaster involving a Boeing 707 on a passenger flight; the first major air disaster of 1961, and the greatest one-accident loss to American athletics. The deaths of multiple family members—brothers and sisters, fathers and sons, mothers and daughters, mothers and sons, and husbands and wives—was a catastrophic blow to ten skating families.[93]

The public demanded an accounting of Seattle's Boeing 707 jets. Before February 15, the huge jet had suffered three crashes during training flights, resulting in the deaths of fifteen crew members. The Boeing 707, which ushered in the jet age, had a capacity of 181 passengers and a cruising speed of 600 mph—two-thirds faster than its closest propellered rival.[94]

Sabena was one of the first carriers to order 707s—a total of five Intercontinentals. Sabena had been operating the Boeings since early 1960; these five Boeings had transported 139,000 passengers, 2,500 tons of freight and mail, and had covered more than six million miles. The crash was the worst suffered by Sabena and the first for the Belgian airline in fourteen years of service between New York and Brussels.[95]

The airline industry worried that the first fatal Boeing 707 commercial accident would result in declining airline patronage, as an editorial in *The Oregonian* noted:

> The traveling public likes the fast new jets, but does not yet have full faith in them or their operators. . . . [J]et air travel is as safe as any modern means of transport, if not safer. Yet since jetliners are so new and spectacular, and since they carry so many passengers likely to be prominent, their mishaps are certain to be widely publicized and have an impact much greater than that of, say a train or bus wreck. This is a situation the airlines industry simply must endure, since it hardly seems likely the time ever will come when airplanes will be perfect, traffic control systems infallible, and pilots immune from error.[96]

Although the deaths of eighteen members of the U.S. Figure Skating Team, six coaches, four officials, and six family members, immediately took its place as "the worst disaster in the history of sports travel," several earlier airline accidents had involved sports teams. One of the earliest occurred on May 4, 1949, when thirty-one people were killed in a plane crash in Turin, Italy, including the Italian national soccer team consisting of the fourteen-man squad, two directors, coaching staff and three journalists.[97]

On February 6, 1958, Britain's championship soccer team, Manchester United, was returning from a European Cup match in Belgrade, Yugoslavia, when its chartered plane crashed at Munich's Remi Airport. Among the twenty-two killed were eight team members, eight British sports journalists, and three club officials. The Manchester United Club was among the first groups to express sympathy to the USFSA. "We can appreciate only too well what a blow this must be, not only to relatives, but to the sport as a whole. As the Munich crash affected soccer, so this new tragedy will affect skating."[98]

There were two sports accidents in 1960. On July 16, eight of Denmark's leading soccer players were killed in a chartered plane crash near Copenhagen. On October 29, a chartered plane carrying the California Polytechnic (Cal Poly) San Luis Obispo football team crashed at the Toledo, Ohio, airport. Twenty-two of the forty-eight people aboard were killed, including sixteen Mustang football players, the team's student manager, and a Cal Poly football booster. For four months, it had been considered the worst sports air disaster in history. Now that dubious honor belonged to the United States Figure Skating Association.[99]

Since the Manchester United crash, American professional sports leagues had begun to think about disaster plans. By 1961, most of the professional sports teams in the United States routinely traveled by air because their games were scheduled coast to coast. The risk was considered part of doing business. As the owner of the San Francisco 49ers said, "I know people who have suffered food poisoning and died, but our players haven't given up eating. I'm sure they won't give up flying either."[100]

On the day of the crash, airline industry records and the general state of sports travel should not have been the primary focus, as a sports columnist noted: "American skating officials predict that it will be at least three years before this country can again compete on equal terms with skaters of other nations. At the moment this doesn't seem very important. The tragic loss of life transcends all else. What's a mere gold medal when weighed against a human life?"[101]

The grief over the loss of these thirty-four people was indescribable. Traumatized skating friends fled to the rinks, wrapped their arms around family members, and tried to make sense of this unbelievable tragedy. "We walked into [Iceland in] Paramount that morning and that place was packed—it was wall-to-wall humanity and everybody was in tears," Mary Miller recalled. Skaters embraced the families of victims in their homes. Pieter Kollen hitch-hiked from Lake Placid to Indianapolis to be with Rose Anne Ryan and waited with her until Danny's body was flown home. In Detroit, friends visited the Ramsay home, sitting and talking quietly on the couch with Jean. Ice Follies' performers consoled Boston team families, who continued to attend the show. "The Lords would just drop in and reminiscence," Richard Dwyer said. "It gave them some comfort to be surrounded by Bradley's friends."[102]

Sonya Klopfer spoke for the entire skating community when she said, "Skating [was] such a small sport and we were all so close, that it felt like my whole world was wiped out in that crash." For families, skaters, and friends across the nation, it was time to mourn.[103]

CHAPTER 17

A TIME OF MOURNING

Family members were understandably anxious to have their loved ones' bodies home quickly. Belgian officials had reassured some families that identifications would be complete by the day after the crash, but a Sabena spokesman said identification had proven difficult.[1]

After the first victims were identified, their bodies were laid in a small airport chapel. King Baudouin supplied beautiful caskets made of zinc-lined Belgian oak with the royal seal. An ISU representative met Ken Kelley at the chapel and delivered a small speech about the skaters but broke down before finishing. "It was pretty tough," Kelley said. "We are trying not to let go until we get this job done, and would just as soon avoid any more heart-tearing ceremonies until the end."[2]

A memorial service was held in Belgium commemorating the victims. On February 22, King Baudouin, Queen Fabiola, Belgian government officials, and U.S. Ambassador William Burden attended a service at Minimes Catholic Church; other attendees included Ken and Joan Kelley, Jean Westwood, Billie Mitchell, Roberta Scholdan, and Fred Heller. After the service, Ken and Joan flew to Paris to recover from their sad duty. "We never can thank you enough for all you did," *Skating* editor Theresa Weld Blanchard wrote, "nor be thankful enough that at least you two were spared." On March 1, they flew to New York to see Ritter Shumway, then returned home to Cleveland.[3]

The loss of American life was particularly acute for three cities: Los Angeles, Boston, and Colorado Springs, where Mayor William Henderson instituted a three-day period of official mourning and ordered flags flown at half staff. Massachusetts Governor John Volpe ordered all flags at the State House at half staff, and the legislature adopted a resolution extending sympathy to the families of the seven Boston-area victims. In Los Angeles there was no official tribute, due to the sport's relative local obscurity; but the local skating community planned to honor the dead with a special service.[4]

Two memorial services were held for Walter Powell even before his body was released. The first was held at Trinity Church in Boston on Friday, February 17, with USFSA officers and Ice Follies skaters in attendance.

"Walter's service to international skating [was] . . . one of the most distinguished careers ever established in the administration of our sport," Ritter Shumway said. "[He] kept active right up to the end . . . long past the age when others would have found these burdens too heavy. . . . [F]igure skating throughout the world lost a great spirit, a dedicated friend, a wise counselor. His place can never quite be filled." Another service for Powell was held in St. Louis on Sunday, February 19, at the Ladue Chapel.[5]

A memorial service was held for Dudley Richards on Saturday, February 18, at the Congregational Church in Barrington, Rhode Island. The minister acknowledged Dudley's many virtues: "We thank thee for his grace both of body and mind, his earnestness, his loyalty to family and friends, his willingness to bear the burdens of others, to aid and sustain and to lead. For his maturity, his affectionate nature, his regard for children, his competitive nature ennobled by concern, friendship and regard for his competitors, his sincerity and warmth, we thank thee." Dudley had been one of the first to be identified—by a St. Christopher medal that Fred Heller had given him years earlier. Dudley was buried in the Richards family plot at the Swan Point Cemetery in Providence.[6]

On the same day, at Colorado College's Shove Chapel, a memorial service paid tribute to the eight Colorado Springs residents. Filling the chapel were members of the Air Force Academy 7th Squadron and friends and relatives of the skaters. The Colorado Legislature passed a memorial expressing the state's regret and sorrow for the tragedy and sent a copy of the tribute to the four Broadmoor families.[7]

As the FBI worked to identify victims in Brussels, Ritter Shumway worked the phones from Rochester. As coordinator of information for the victims' families, he was frustrated with how slowly information was trickling in from Brussels, which only prolonged the ordeal for the agonized families. Ritter contacted his friend, New York Senator Kenneth Keating, to expedite the process.[8]

Many friends took individual action. Bruce Lord's employer sent catered meals to the Lords' home for two weeks and called the Brussels ambassador every day, pressing him for identification information. The Kelley family was indebted to friend John W. McCormack, the House Majority Leader. "We couldn't find out anything in the beginning," Stephen Kelley said. "I called [McCormack in] Washington and told him we were not getting any information—eventually we started to get a little."[9]

On Thursday, February 23, when the Brussels Consulate reopened after Washington's Birthday, Shumway received good news, which he passed along to Senator Keating: "I received information that something had happened to change the attitude of certain people in the consulate in Brussels and that all was proceeding expeditiously and with the best of cooperation, understanding and good will. Many, many thanks for your effective help."[10]

It had taken an endless nine days to cut through the red tape. Senator Keating and others made countless phone calls on behalf of the bereaved families. The person responsible for getting everyone home, however, was most likely Muriel LeMaire. Muriel turned to the president of the United States; they had been friends when she was married to her first husband. "They used to go down to Hyannis and she and Jack hit it off," Diana LeMaire said. "It had been about twenty years, but she said, 'I'm going to call Jack Kennedy,' and she called the White House. She gave her name and the President knew right away who she was, and said, 'I know exactly what this is about.' He got [my brother] home the next day."[11]

On Thursday, February 23, Brussels authorities finally made the long-awaited announcement: "Identification of the 73 victims of the Brussels-bound jet airplane is complete." Sabena began transporting the bodies back to the United States that day. The father of skater Gerry Lane was in charge of the Catholic Cemeteries in the Boston Archdiocese, and he went with the Kelleys and the Lords to Logan Airport to receive the bodies and make arrangements.[12]

Ritter Shumway wanted to attend all of the services but could not. Instead, he asked USFSA representatives in each area to represent him at the funerals across the country. He sent a condolence telegram, copies of President Kennedy's and Secretary of State Dean Rusk's telegrams, and a handwritten letter. When possible, he called families prior to the services. In addition, Ken Kelley sent a 1961 World Team shoulder patch, a copy of the Sabena-produced black-bordered invitation to the Brussels memorial service, and photos of the service.[13]

The children of Harold Hartshorne invited Ritter Shumway to speak at the service honoring their father and Louise. Ritter, who was a close friend and Harold's competitor for over a decade, said that he had never done anything so hard in his life. The memorial was held at the Unitarian Church of All Souls in New York City on Friday, February 24. The overflow crowd was a cross-section of Harold's multi-layered life, including the denizens of Wall Street, New York society, and The Skating Club of New York. "I was stunned by how many people were at the funeral," son Dan said. "People came up to me and said, 'You don't know this but your father was a great man.' Dad had touched a larger group of people than I had suspected." Harold and Louise were buried in the Hartshorne family plot, next to Harold's first wife, Marietta, at the Green-Wood Cemetery in Brooklyn.[14]

Services were also held on Friday 24, for Bill Kipp in his hometown of Allentown, Pennsylvania. The memorial service, attended by family and a few close friends, was held at St. Peter's Lutheran Church, followed by interment at Cedar Hill Memorial Park.[15]

On Saturday, February 25, the farewell for Maribel, Maribel Jr., and Laurence Owen took place in Winchester, Massachusetts. An hour before the services began at the Church of the Epiphany, the five hundred seats had filled up; three hundred mourners were seated in the nearby Hadley Hall, where a loud-speaker system had been installed. Attendees included a large delegation from The Skating Club of Boston, the principal at Winchester High School, a delegation of faculty and Laurence's classmates, the Boston University student body president, Governor John Volpe and his wife, town officials, and Boston team families. Attorney Walter Baldwin escorted matriarch Gertrude Vinson into the church. Two nieces, one nephew, three cousins, and skater Ronna Goldblatt sat with her on the front row. Mrs. Vinson was dry-eyed, saying, "You can't live to be as old as I am and not learn to deal with it."[16]

The standing-room-only service was silent. "If any of us had spoken we would have just broken down sobbing," Christie Allan recalled. Snow carpeted the ground outside the church, but it was a very warm day; the snow evaporated up into the skies, along with great clouds drifting through the air. "It was misty and thick—you could hardly see through it," Christie said, "but we were all grateful because the weather masked all of our tears." Although Mrs. Vinson was stoic in public, in private she admitted her "overwhelming sorrow" and her "distressed spirit." The cremated remains of Maribel Yerxa Vinson Owen, Maribel Yerxa Owen, and Laurence Rochon Owen were placed in the Story Chapel mausoleum at Mount Auburn Cemetery in Cambridge, Massachusetts.[17]

During the Owen family service in Boston, a similar service was being held for the Owens at St. Clement's Episcopal Church in Berkeley, California. Jack and Amy Fisher, Owen family friends from their time in Berkeley, organized the service. Many friends and former students were in attendance, including two pair partners: Geddy Hill, Maribel's partner from 1930 to 1937, who lived in the Bay Area, and Chuck Foster, Little Maribel's first partner, who happened to be in San Francisco on business.[18]

In death, the "First Family of Skating" perpetuated the *Sports Illustrated* (*SI*) curse, which predicted quick tragedy for those appearing on the magazine's cover. American skier Jill Kinmont was paralyzed in a spill several days after she graced the cover in 1955, and auto racer Pat O'Connor was the cover boy the week he died in a pile-up during the first lap of the Memorial Day Indianapolis 500 in 1958. Now, after her February 13 cover story, Laurence Owen, and indirectly her thirty-three companions, had become part of the *SI* curse.[19]

In Rye, New York, Richard Osborn LeMaire returned to his mother, Muriel, and two sisters. The family held a memorial service for both Dickie and his father, Eddie, at Christ's Church on Saturday, February, 25, although only Dickie's body had been returned. After his interment at the family plot at Greenwood Union Cemetery in Rye, Muriel received word from the State Department that Eddie's body was also on its way home. A service was held at the William H. Graham Funeral Home on Monday, followed by a briefer graveside gathering as Eddie was buried next to his son.[20]

Just south of Rye, a double memorial service was held at St. Agnes Church in New York City for Robert F. Dineen and Patricia Major Dineen on February 27. Presiding was Bob's uncle, Monsignor Aloysius Dineen, who had married Bob and Pat at the same church. Bob and Pat were buried next to Bob's father in the Calvary Cemetery in Woodside, Queens, New York.[21]

Three memorial services were held for Bill and Laurie Hickox—the first at the Masonic Temple in San Francisco, where the Hickoxes were members. A multitude of Scottish dancers, Rainbow Girls in their capes, military personnel, and the Bay Area figure skating community were in attendance. Family members carried Laurie's casket while the military carried Bill's casket. Another Berkeley service was held at the Northbrae Community Church. At the Air Force Academy, a third service honored Bill in Arnold Hall on Monday, February 27. Members of the Cadet Wing, military personnel, academy employees, and Broadmoor Skating Club members were present, along with Lute and Elinor Hickox. Bill and Laurie Hickox were buried at the Sunset View Cemetery in El Cerrito, California.[22]

On Tuesday, February 28, three services were held for team members. In Los Angeles, a memorial service for Deane McMinn was held at Gamby Chapel in Lomita. The pallbearers included Bob McLeod, one of the many judges Deane had nurtured. Deane Everett McMinn was laid to rest at Green Hills Memorial Park in Rancho Palos Verdes, California. His marker included his military credentials, "MOMM1 MTB Squadron 29, USNR" and an engraving of a USFSA skating pin.[23]

Just hours after the McMinn service, all of the Arctic Blades members gathered at the Dilday Chapel in Long Beach to pay tribute to Rhode Lee Michelson, who was also interred at Green Hills Memorial Park. Rhode's mother, who could not accept that her daughter was dead, couldn't stop sobbing. Skating coach and photographer Bill Udell reflected on Rhode's life: "She always thought she could do anything and do it better than the best. How could someone like that simply not be any more?" The back-to-back funerals numbed the local skating community.[24]

In Detroit, services were held on Tuesday, February 28, for Doug Ramsay. The Ramsays invited only a few close friends to the wake held Monday night at the Ramsay home. On Tuesday, more than 350 people, including Detroit skating club officials, judges, skaters, and students, attended the memorial rites at the McCabe Funeral Home in Farmington Hills. Among the mourners were Genevieve, Bill, and Erik Swallender. The pallbearers were primarily Doug's skating friends: Gary Clark, Bruce Heiss, Paul Pepp, Ronald Pfenning, Gary Visconti, and Donald Tripp. Douglas Alexander Ramsay was laid to rest at the White Chapel Memorial Cemetery in Troy.[25]

There were five services on Wednesday, March 1. A rosary service for Eduard Scholdan and James Edward Scholdan was held Tuesday evening at the Law Mortuary. On the following morning, a special high mass was held at St. Pauline's Catholic Church. Scholdan family friend, the Reverend Michael Harrington, officiated, and all of Jimmy's classmates from the St. Pauline School were in attendance. Roberta had initially requested that Edi and Jimmy be buried in Vienna near her, but instead father and son were interred at the Evergreen Cemetery in Colorado Springs.[26]

Private services were also held on Wednesday at the Swan Funeral Home in Colorado Springs for Sharon and Stephanie Westerfeld. Myra Westerfeld forewent a formal funeral and settled on a graveside service for only family and a few close friends. Initially she could not decide whether to bury the girls in Colorado or in their hometown of Kansas City. Then one day she remembered that Sherri had said, "I always want to live here because I love the mountains." The sisters were buried in plots facing the mountains in the Evergreen Cemetery in Colorado Springs.[27]

Also on Wednesday, March 1, another double funeral took place in Newton, Massachusetts, for the Kelleys. School buses full of nuns and other visitors arrived at the Kelley home on Tuesday evening for the wake. On the day of the funeral, two hearses rolled down Main Street, side by side. The service for Gregory and Nathalie Kelley was undoubtedly one of the largest. More than a thousand people gathered at the Sacred Heart Church, including a delegation of two hundred from The Skating Club of Boston and a delegation from Natalie's school, Ashland High School. The honor guard for Greg was composed of his classmates from Sacred Heart High School. The Reverend Eric MacKenzie called Greg "an unspoiled boy, quietly unwilling to talk about his triumphs lest he should seem to boast, [and] sincerely ready to praise his rivals." Of Nathalie, he said that her pupils "respected and were loyally devoted to her. Her chief purpose in life was to care for and assist her youngest brother." Nathalie Frances Kelley and Gregory Eric Kelley were interred at St. Joseph's Cemetery in West Roxbury, Massachusetts.[28]

At the same time, a memorial service was held at Boston University's March Chapel for students Bradley Lord and Maribel Owen. University students and officials gathered to pay tribute to both Bradley, a commercial art major, and Maribel, a sociology major in the College of Liberal Arts. In time, Boston University awarded Maribel her degree posthumously.[29]

On Thursday, March 2, there were six funerals. The wake for Bradley Lord was held on Wednesday night at the T. W. Rhodes Funeral Home in Lynn, Massachusetts. In Bradley's honor, all city flags were lowered to half-staff—a sign of respect normally reserved to mark the death of town officials. Mourners at the St. John Evangelist Church on the Seaside included skating and school friends, team family members, citizens of the community, and a dozen town officials, including the fire chief and the Swampscott High School principal. Boys from St. John's School formed an honor guard and pallbearers were cousins Peter Hunt and Frank Muckian and skaters Roger Collard, Peter Betts, Paul George, and Don Jackson. Bradley Richard Lord was buried at Swampscott Cemetery.[30]

Indianapolis remembered Daniel Charles Ryan on March 2. A rosary was recited on Wednesday night at Flanner & Buchanan Broad Ripple Mortuary with a Thursday morning service held at St. Matthew's Catholic Church. Burial followed at Calvary Cemetery. A USFSA representative said that the family was "doing very well under the circumstances."[31]

That afternoon at the same mortuary, services were held for Dallas Larry Pierce. He was entombed in a mausoleum at Washington Park East in Indianapolis. The services for Danny and Larry were well attended. "There were people from out of town and they were so many—they were just pouring out of everywhere for both of them," a skater said.[32]

Services were held for Carl William Swallender in Detroit and in his hometown of Minneapolis. On Wednesday, March 1, a memorial service was held at the family's church, Gloria Dei Lutheran, near the Detroit Skating Club. On Thursday, March 2, services were held at Sunset Memorial Park Chapel in Minneapolis, before the burial at Sunset Park Cemetery.[33]

Ray Hadley Sr. returned to his hometown of Eugene, Oregon, to bury Linda, Ila Ray, and Ray Jr. After a private service at the mausoleum at the Rest Haven Memorial Park on Thursday, March 2, the Seattle Skating Club held a memorial service in Seattle several days later.[34]

Dona Lee Carrier's funeral was March 2, at the Little Church of the Flowers at Forest Lawn in Glendale, California, with interment following in its Garden of Honor. Her father, Reverend Floyd Carrier, spoke to the standing-room-only crowd. The skaters noticed the absence of the now-familiar narrow European casket from Belgium; Eleanor Carrier had wanted a special coffin to differentiate her daughter's from the others. Dona Lee's epitaph reads:[35]

> Our Beloved Daughter, Dona Lee Carrier, October 23, 1940–February 15, 1961; Gold medalist and member of the U.S. Figure Skating Team representing the United States in world competition which was to be held in Prague; She perished at the peak of her career with all her teammates in the Sabena Airlines crash in Brussels, Belgium; "She was beautiful, talented and good;" "Like a cup of gold on the ice;" "Her grace and sweet spiritual fragrance touched lives;" "Her loveliness glowed from within;" "I will come again and receive you unto myself." John 14:3.[36]

The last individual funeral was for Diane Sherbloom on Saturday, March 4, at the St. Augustine Catholic Church in Culver City, California, with burial following at Holy Cross Cemetery. Apart from their sorrow, the service was difficult for other reasons. Mr. Sherbloom, on crutches, had been in a car accident the week before the plane crash. Joan Sherbloom had already attended three funerals by the time of her sister's service. "We went through the motions," Joan said. "I got through the whole thing and then my mother broke down and well, that was it. My mother was in shock. Who thinks of losing their daughter at age eighteen?"[37]

A memorial service was held for Linda, Ila Ray, and Ray Hadley Jr. at the University Baptist Church on Sunday, March 5, in Seattle. The large gathering included skaters, school friends, the public, Linda Hadley's elderly father, and Ila Ray and Ray's birth mother. "Everybody was whispering that it was Mrs. Bette Bell back there," a skater said. "She sat on the back row and someone overheard her say, 'I've been in the background all of their lives and that is where I will remain.'"[38]

The Arctic Blades club sponsored a memorial service at the Lafayette Hotel Ballroom in Long Beach on Sunday, March 5, to honor all seven of the Southern Californians who perished. "I don't think any of us will ever forget it," a club member said.[39]

It was the last of five farewell gatherings in the Los Angeles area. Each service had a multitude of flowers, including huge wreaths sent by the USFSA. The strongest memory was the rain—it had poured during every funeral and at every graveside service. "It was as if heaven was crying and the skies were weeping with all of us," Sylvia Clay said. "I had to throw out the coat I wore because it was just shapeless by the end of the week."[40]

No one recalled a separate funeral in Los Angeles for Ann and Roger Campbell. Al Campbell buried his wife and son at the Big Hill Cemetery in Providence, Kentucky. The Los Angeles funerals ended the thirty-one services, held in twelve states, through seventeen days of official mourning.[41]

The skaters returned to the ice rinks, still consumed by the crash. Instant folklore erupted about why certain people didn't go: Coach Bud Wilson had been on the plane but got off because Brad Lord had forgotten his boots; Fritz Dietl, Scott Allen's coach, had been in the cafeteria, but missed the plane because he didn't hear the flight call; Roberta Scholdan had witnessed the tragedy as she waited for Edi and Jimmy at the Brussels airport; Edi had joined Flight 548 at the last minute because he had stayed behind to have Steffi's skates sharpened; and Dudley Richards, as team leader, was to have purchased airline insurance for all the team members but had run out of time. All of these rumors proved false.[42]

Ritter Shumway was steadfast at his post, consistently and rapidly communicating any news that became available to the twenty-two families of the thirty-four victims and working to dampen the spread of rumors. He became the de facto minister and personal counselor for many family members, providing guidance and comfort.

Ritter counteracted the most hurtful rumors head on. "[Ken Kelley] has assured me in his phone calls and in his letters that, contrary to some statements which you may have seen in the public press, there was no dismemberment, and the end must mercifully have come instantaneously. While it is very difficult for me to write all of this I believe that you are entitled to direct and accurate information, especially when I also believe that it will be of some comfort to you." Ritter consistently praised Ken Kelley, who courageously worked with the FBI team in Brussels. "I am convinced beyond any shadow of a doubt that once the FBI team announced a [person's] identification, it was positive."[43]

Ritter maintained his correspondence with the families throughout 1961, and the families' gratitude breathes through the correspondence for the lifeline he represented. "Please accept our humble thanks for your prayers, letters, calls and all other thoughtful deeds," Mr. and Mrs. Pierce wrote. "You'll never know how much they have meant to us. Your call on the dark day helped so much then, and thinking back we realize it was one of the things that really helped us through those trying days. Larry really went to Europe and didn't return to us. However, we know he was most happy and played a part in that happiness which is a great satisfaction to us."[44]

Ritter also had to deal with distraught skating coaches, officials, and most notably, Congressman Walter Rogers of Texas, who had investigated the television quiz show scandals of the fifties. A month after the crash, he turned his attention to the Sabena disaster. "Since this accident I have had quite a number of people ask me why a team representing the United States in international competition should be traveling to the scene of the competition on an airline of a foreign country rather than an American airline." He demanded answers.[45]

Patiently, Ritter answered both Congressman Rogers and the skating community in a thoroughly detailed letter. Sabena was the only airline that offered a flight to Prague on American-manufactured equipment (a Boeing 707 to Brussels, and a Douglas aircraft to Prague). The connecting flights on both Pan Am and TWA were with Czechoslovak Airlines, which flew Russian-made planes. Sabena was also the only airline that gave one-carrier service from New York to Prague, and guaranteed that the connection from Brussels to Prague would be made on the same day. Weather delays were a frequent occurrence in winter, and Sabena promised to hold the flight to Prague should the New York flight be late. Furthermore, Sabena, who had contacts with the Czechoslovakian embassy in Washington, offered help in securing visas for the newly formed team, a critical factor given the limited two-week time period. Only Sabena offered this service.[46]

Ritter assured Rogers that the USFSA's decision to fly the team on Sabena Flight 548 was made only after extensive and exhausting planning. No one could have foreseen the disastrous outcome. The USFSA's reluctance to fly on Soviet-made Ilyushin aircraft was not unfounded. Cold War tensions aside, there were concerns about the aircraft's safety. A month after the Sabena crash, a Czechoslovak Airlines Ilyushin plane crashed thirty miles north of Nuremberg, Germany. Fifty-two perished, many of them children.[47]

Ritter invited the families to a memorial service on Saturday, May 6, 1961, at the Hotel Roosevelt Ballroom in New York, held in conjunction with the annual USFSA Governing Council Meeting, where Ritter Shumway was inducted as the association's fourteenth president. Besides the thirty-four members of the 1961 World Team delegation, the memorial service paid tribute to USFSA President Howard Herbert, who had died in January, and USFSA Secretary Colonel Harold B. Storke of Boston, a long-time World and Olympic judge and referee who had passed away in April. At the service, Shumway said: "On the table before us are thirty-six American Beauty roses—one for each of our dear friends whose memory we have gathered here today to honor." During this critical moment in U.S. figure skating, it was fortuitous that, at the helm, was Ritter Shumway, an ordained minister. In its darkest hour, spiritual leadership provided steadfastness and meaning for the distraught skating community. Ritter's inspirational address struck a chord with the mournful crowd, as he encouraged them to move forward:[48]

> We came here . . . not to grieve, but to honor, not to look back upon what cannot be changed, but to look forward to a future which lies within our power to shape, not to lament but to try to find in this experience the lessons for life that God wants us who remain to learn. . . . We must understand that what for us is a sorrowful human parting from friends and loved ones, is for them a release from the weights and errors that beset them here, and prevented them from realizing that perfection . . . that perfect understanding for which they were always striving, and which they can now experience. Just as they, and we too, rejoiced greatly as they took each step closer and closer to perfection, and passed each Test in their progress . . . so should we also rejoice for them . . . now that they have passed the Supreme Test and are at the very fountain-head of perfect judgment, discernment and understanding. They have attained the perfection that they wanted so much. . . . For their sake, in their memory, to their honor and glory, and to the honor and glory of God, let us go forward as they would have us go.[49]

Ritter's thoughtful gestures on behalf of the families included sending them the television footage of the last two competitive performances of the 1961 Team. The 1961 Nationals film reached the families in June, through the cooperation of CBS and the Eastman Kodak Company. Though acquiring the North Americans competition proved more difficult, Ritter assured families "that we will eventually obtain them." He persisted until this goal was achieved more than a year after the accident. Gertrude Vinson expressed the sentiment shared by all the families: "How can we ever express adequately our appreciation and deep gratitude[?] . . . [T]his interest and kindness is unique in my skating experience . . . . Whenever [team families] meet, we always speak gratefully of your thoughtfulness in our behalf . . . . We thank you from the bottom of our hearts."[50]

Months after the New York memorial service, Ritter sent a copy of his remarks to all the families. Gertrude Vinson said they were one of her most prized possessions. "In the printed word I have it with me always, where, at need, I can find peace of mind and inspiration of soul and body from . . . [the] words giving us help and strength."[51]

All of the families welcomed Ritter's address at the memorial service, but he was even then in the process of creating a more memorable keepsake. The USFSA offices had been deluged with messages of sympathy. Letters of condolences, cables, and telegrams arrived from international skating associations, sport federations, and Olympic committees from around the world. Besides written tributes, "moments of silence" in honor of the team were held at many skating exhibitions and other sporting events. The unofficial period of mourning lasted throughout the year.[52]

Ritter compiled a selection of the tender notes, cards, and letters for an "In Memoriam" booklet for the families. The printer, moved by the circumstances of the booklet, personally supplied the French-imported mould-made paper. Ritter sent the gift as "a record of the understanding and compassion of our friends throughout the world. It is our hope that it will provide some further solace to you through the knowledge that your grief has been shared by so many."[53]

The memorial booklet was received in the spirit it was intended. Muriel LeMaire read the entire book upon arrival. "I was so deeply touched, not only by the many lovely messages of sympathy printed on its pages, but also by its own mute expression of sympathy and affections which represents all the thoughts and care of so many kind people in conceiving and publishing such a magnificent testimonial." Lute and Elinor Hickox were overwhelmed by this permanent record of sympathy: "We shall always cherish it. . . . [I]t is comforting to know that other people are thinking of us and the other families affected by this tragedy."[54]

The USFSA office became the conduit for making connections with the 1961 Team families. Many of them asked for address information so they could be in touch with other grieving parents. Other families used Ritter as a clearinghouse of information about retaining attorneys and reaching settlements with Sabena Airlines.[55]

Ritter helped families throughout the year when they had specific requests. When Diane Sherbloom moved to Indianapolis, she took all of her skating medals with her, and then packed all of her belongings for the trip to Philadelphia and Prague. The Sherblooms asked the USFSA if they could obtain replacements of Diane's regional and national medals; within months the newly made medals were sent to the Sherblooms.[56]

Many families honored their children with memorial trophies. Ray Hadley and Lute and Elinor Hickox thought of donating a new senior pairs trophy for Pacific Coast competition. The USFSA reached a deal with the families; new trophies for both junior pairs and senior pairs at Pacific Coast bore the names of both Hadley and Hickox.[57]

Many letters concerned orphaned Bobby Dineen, inquiring who would raise him. Some wanted to start a fund to care for him. Shumway felt a great deal of concern for the child. "While all of us feel very deeply and keenly the loss of our good friends and skaters . . . my own greatest concern and sense of tragedy concerns Bobby Dineen Jr." Both families wanted to raise the little boy. According to the USFSA, both Bob and Pat took out life insurance and the $60,000 payment was ample money to care for the child. Although Pat's mother, Ann Major, wanted custody, the baby ended up with brother Joseph Dineen.[58]

Ritter Shumway served as president of the USFSA until 1964 and was instrumental in the rebuilding of competitive skating in this country. However, his name was forever linked to the 1961 U.S. World Figure Skating Team, and he continued to be a good friend to many 1961 Team families. Dallas Pierce acknowledged that there had been "long, hard months in spite of everything we tried to tell ourselves. Yet, with a faith in our Heavenly Father and friends like you and countless others we know we must go on." The families experienced the nationwide outpouring of love and felt affirmed by the great compassion. Mr. and Mrs. Richards said, "We have received from people of all religious creeds their types of memorials, which makes us all closer in our respect for each other and our Creator."[59]

By the end of 1961, the competitive wing of the USFSA was already moving forward. The 1962 Nationals would take place as usual in a few weeks. The skaters were still shaken by the events of the 1961 Brussels tragedy, but they strove to follow the counsel set forth by Ritter in his memorial tribute address: "Let us run the race that is set before us. Let us . . . carry on the high traditions of excellence, of sportsmanship, of devotion, that they so well exemplified and have now entrusted to us. For their sake, in their memory, to their honor and glory . . . let us go forward as they would have us go."[60]

CHAPTER 18

THE REBIRTH BEGINS

As a result of the crash, the future of American figure skating looked bleak. USFSA secretary Carl Gram Jr. summarized the situation: "These were the finest skaters in the country. . . . They represented years of hard work and practice. Now we will have to start from the beginning—with our juniors and kids. It's a long road back." Pierre Brunet, coach of Olympian Carol Heiss, concurred: "Skating has received an incalculable setback . . . It'll be two Olympics before we can hope to have a strong, representative team here again. If then!"[1]

Decades later, at the 1994 Goodwill Games, Dick Button was bothered by the overscheduling of the younger skaters, particularly Michelle Kwan. He told the press: "This is not a time for a 14-year-old to be in competition. She needs some time to train and work, and most importantly, kids have to have time to be kids." But in the spring and summer of 1961, the kids had to grow up quickly—and deal with grief beyond their years. That task was difficult because skaters felt as though their own family members had died. "I cried when there weren't even any tears left," dancer Marshall Campbell said.[2]

Skaters in Boston were stabbed at every turn by reminders. The Boston team members had all converged at the club before heading off to Philadelphia, and their cars still needed to be driven home. The club secretary had recently received a check in the mail from Laurence for practice sessions, with a letter apologizing for forgetting to turn it in before she left. Dozens of wreaths and floral arrangements crowded the lobby so that the skaters had to make their way to the ice through poignant reminders of loss. It was a step in the direction of healing when the skaters themselves requested that the wreaths be removed.[3]

Joan Sherbloom said she would never put skates on again; but in a matter of weeks, she was back on the ice, and so were scores of skaters. One skating family explained why: "We can never give back these loved ones to their families. We can, however, rededicate ourselves to youth of the future by lending a hand in molding their lives."[4]

One New Jersey family eloquently summed up the feelings of the skating community nationwide:

> The loss belongs to the whole country. It belongs to the world. Then how long shall we mourn? Should we weep long and loud until free of ache and shock or shall we estimate their staunch courage, draw strength from their determination, which is the pre-requisite of champions such as they all were and do as they would ask us to do—carry on for them as well as for ourselves. . . . Soon we must stop our lament. We must mend our hearts and dry our eyes. We must show our departed friends that we were worthy of their friendship. . . . We must support our skaters every way, every place.[5]

For many skaters across the country, putting their skates back on was a form of healing. Working hard and focusing on goals was the fabric of their lives. Channeling their grief provided a way to ease the pain.

At The Skating Club of Boston, the annual Ice Chips show was transformed into both a tribute to the 1961 World Team and a USFSA fundraiser. First-time producer Dick Button assisted director Bud Wilson and succeeded in selling the national broadcasting rights to CBS. "I had to pay everything; there was no such thing as commercial sponsorship then," Button said. "The network was so pleased with the impact of the show. . . . For me it was a very moving and cleansing thing to be involved in it."[6]

The show, held at the Boston Garden, was a veritable who's who of skaters: Olympic champions David Jenkins, Barbara Wagner, and Bob Paul; 1961 Canadian World Team members; 1961 U.S. junior champion Lorraine Hanlon, 1961 U.S. junior silver medalist Scott Ethan Allen, and 1961 U.S. novice champions Tina Noyes and Peter Meyer. One performance was of historical importance—two-time Olympic champion Dick Button skated his last full program. Before the show began, Ted Kennedy read a special tribute from President John F. Kennedy.[7]

The Canadian team members found it therapeutic to perform and were happy to support the cause. "It was breathtaking and the highlight of my career," Debbi Wilkes said. "I was bowled over by all of the most famous names in skating." Wendy Griner, Laurence's toughest competitor, took time after the performance to visit Gertrude Vinson in her home. Canadian team members went on their own tour throughout Canada and parts of the United States on behalf of the newly created Memorial Fund. "Mr. Shumway and our [CFSA] president, Mr. Kimball, got together and decided to have the tour," Don Jackson said. "I don't remember how many cities we did. We just did whatever they asked."[8]

The Ice Chips show was the first of many spring and summer fundraisers for the "1961 U.S. World Figure Skating Memorial Fund," which was created a week after the crash, to honor the 1961 U.S. World Team and to revitalize figure skating in America. Past champions, such as 1951 U.S. champion Sonya Klopfer, skated in a New York City memorial show, and Tim Brown helped organize a benefit in Squaw Valley. Money poured into the USFSA's Boston office as clubs across America donated proceeds from their spring carnivals.[9]

Skaters headed to summer skating centers and buckled down to train in honor of their fallen friends. "Everybody who trained referenced rebuilding," Patti Gustafson of Boston said. "This tragedy would have served no purpose for people to have stopped what they were doing."[10]

Coaches and USFSA officials speculated about who would fill in the gap, but no one really knew who would lead the next World Team. Over the next four years, some of the most obvious contenders dropped out, while some of the major players at the 1964 Winter Olympics were largely unknown in the spring of 1961. The USFSA would not know the competitive status of senior skaters until the end of the summer season, and they were clearly worried. Besides contacting current senior-level skaters, they sent letters to skaters who had retired, some as far back as five years ago, and implored them to come back and compete. They encouraged coaches to move every junior-level skater up to the senior level for the 1962 season. The strict policy of junior skaters needing to place in the top three at Nationals was temporarily thrown out the window. [11]

A number of long-time competitors did not come back. Tim Brown, who had already resumed his studies at UC Berkeley, said his decision to give up skating was strengthened by the crash. There would be no competitors from the Heiss family for the first time in fifteen years. Carol was in Hollywood filming a movie, Bruce planned to start college in the fall, and Nancy was a junior at Michigan State. She had been off the ice for more than a year; but after the crash, she returned to the MSU rink. After a few days, she realized she wanted to focus on college. Olympian Robert Brewer was also knee deep in college.[12]

Just after the accident, Broadmoor's Thayer Tutt had said: "In honor of these fine people, we at the Broadmoor intend to continue our skating program with even more concerted effort." He wasted no time in finding a successor for Edi Scholdan. Tutt had already planned to contact 1953 World bronze medalist Carlo Fassi because Edi had requested an assistant and had suggested him. Now Tutt headed to Italy to plead with Carlo to replace the legendary Scholdan. "He was settled in Italy and doing well, but I urged him to go," his wife Christa said. "I had never been to America before and I was excited."[13]

Carlo, like Edi, hated to fly, and jumpy because of the crash, insisted on taking a ship to the States. Tutt and Broadmoor club officials hosted a large, elegant ceremony upon his arrival in Colorado in May. Fassi, thirty-three, who had summer skated in Lake Placid, loved being in Colorado from day one, but Christa, nineteen, was homesick—which was ironic, given her initial excitement. "Two days after I arrived I found out I was pregnant," she recalled, "and I had a lot of morning sickness. Also, we had left a very nice apartment in Milano; and at the Broadmoor we lived in the employees' housing, which was pretty bad. We bought a house two years later because we had two children by then."[14]

Carlo was a seamless fit at the Broadmoor because he and Edi were both European, had strong accents, and had their idiosyncrasies in speaking. There were differences, however, between the two. The major plus was Carlo's figures' expertise, which had been Edi's main deficiency. "Carlo had a very mathematical, technical mind, so that's why he was good at teaching figures," Christa said. Whereas Edi had been a grand cheerleader rallying the troops, not everyone warmed up to Carlo. Greg Hoyt, comparing the two men, noted that Carlo, unlike Edi, was "temperamental and theatrical . . . Christa, who taught less experienced students, went on to teach international competitors, but I don't think she received her due as a coach. Carlo was center stage."[15]

Broadmoor scouting agents looked for top talent for Carlo to train. Jerry and Judianne Fotheringill contemplated retirement after their disastrous 1961 Nationals performance, but the USFSA urged them to remain competitive. They summer skated in Sun Valley while working at the resort. After *Denver Post* sports reporter Lee Meade saw them in a weekend show, the Broadmoor invited them to work with Carlo. They were thrilled because their training would be subsidized and the facilities were the best, as Judianne noted: "In Tacoma we trained on a substandard size rink; we had always done our routine in sections because we couldn't fit it in the rink all at one time. It was a huge handicap and made us ill prepared for competition." The Fotheringills clicked with Carlo right from the start, and the Broadmoor paid for their ice time, coaching, and travel expenses. It even provided scholarships to Colorado College.[16]

At the Broadmoor, everyone still talked about their friends on the 1961 Team. Steffi Westerfeld had left her guards behind, and they became a treasured memento for one young skater. The most permanent reminder of the team was the granite bench shaped like a skate, designed by Broadmoor Club President Bill Haigler, which listed the eight names of the Broadmoor club members. The bench, paid for by donations from friends of the victims, was placed in front of the rink on the edge of Cheyenne Lake.[17]

Edi Scholdan was uniquely remembered within the walls of the World Arena. "People always thought Edi's ghost was in the rink," Christy Haigler said. "They believed his spirit had come back. Many people had this experience, particularly the janitors. They saw his little white hat, which was a very distinctive part of him." Coach Doreen Denny-Routon, who came to the Broadmoor in the mid-sixties, reported a sighting during a midnight dance session:

> There were two people sitting next to each other, a man and a lady. He was sitting on the outside of an aisle seat and she was sitting next to him on the inside. He was wearing a cap and she had a purse on her lap. It was a smoky state and that's all I could see—there were no faces showing. I thought, who in the heck is sitting there . . . and when I turned around again they were gone. They were there one minute and then they weren't. There was no time to get up and walk out.[18]

A casualty from the crash was Edi's long-time right hand, Broadmoor club secretary Edith Palmer, who was laid off. Helen Davidson Maxson, who had trained under Edi before she starred in Ice Capades and Ice Follies, assisted Carlo Fassi as the new secretary. Edith was getting older and the club had wanted to put someone younger in place for years. Edith's son, Dick Palmer, later became head of Ice Capades.[19]

There was a big void in East Lansing without Bill Swallender, Doug Ramsay, and Bradley Lord. "A pall hung over everything and it was unbelievably depressing," skater Coco Gram said. Still, new senior skaters came out of the MSU farm club. Joanne Heckert and Gary Clark did a parody of a pair team in the summer show and discovered they liked pair skating. "There really was no one there to take their place, but we were terrible for the longest time," Joanne said. Jim and Janet Browning, who had placed fifth behind the Fotheringills, planned to retire since Jim was attending MSU and working. However, they were pressured to continue, as Jim noted: "People said, 'Get serious. . . .We're trying to identify a new team.' Well, that's easier said than done when you don't have any money." They trained during the summer of 1961—even though Janet was expecting their first child in November.[20]

At Iceland in Paramount, California, Frank Zamboni wanted Jean Westwood to come back and replace Bill Kipp, but she couldn't face all the memories. Zamboni next pursued British pairs champion John Nicks. After winning the World title in 1953 with his sister Jennifer, Nicks spent five years in an ice show in South Africa. He turned to teaching after breaking his foot backstage, which required a long time in a cast. His role models included his coach Gladys Hogg and Edi Scholdan. "Gladys built mutual respect between athlete and coach, and encouraged her students to try their best at all times," Nicks said. "Edi taught me the American way of teaching, which was based on avoiding heavy criticism." After a brief return to England, he visited his sister Jennifer in Canada, who told him there were many teaching prospects in North America.[21]

Nicks received four offers—in Cleveland, a club in Canada, at Sutros in San Francisco, and Iceland in Los Angeles. "I picked L.A. because I knew the Arctic Blades Figure Skating Club was a very strong club," he said. After waiting for his green card, Nicks officially arrived in Paramount in September.[22]

The beginning was slow for Nicks because many of Bill Kipp's students had already found other coaches. Although most people were welcoming, some coaches weren't happy about a newcomer. Dory Ann Sweet, Bill Kipp's close friend, had thought she was going to step into his position, so there were hurt feelings and unwarranted resentment. In time, Nicks picked up some of Bill's students, including Wanda Guntert and Ronnie Frank, and new students, such as pair team Alicia ("JoJo") Starbuck and Ken Shelley. Peggy Fleming was training with Dory Ann, but would soon switch to Nicks.[23]

It was a happy surprise when Barbara Roles showed up at Iceland. Initially she had been too traumatized to think about returning. After her daughter Shelley was born, the USFSA talked to Barbara's mother, Bunny Roles, about Barbara's return; but unbeknownst to them, she was already on the ice. "When I had my baby the doctor told me I was too fat and that I ought to skate to lose weight," Barbara said. "I wasn't thinking about competition, but I got the bug again." She appeared in the Iceland Ice Revue in August, just two months after giving birth. Training with a baby was hard, but she lost the weight quickly; and in a matter of weeks, she felt as if she had never left the ice.[24]

Peter Betts felt compelled to follow Maribel's advice—to compete one more time with "a really good looking young partner." There were only two viable gold-level dancers: Marilyn Meeker and Yvonne Littlefield. Bunny Roles thought Peter and Yvonne would be excellent partners and played matchmaker, sending Betts a letter. "I was bored with my job on Wall Street and had always wanted to go to L.A.," Betts said. "Marilyn Meeker was already training in Lake Placid, so I decided to go to California to see what kind of partner Yvonne would be." Betts arrived in August and clicked with Yvonne right away but wasn't prepared for fresh reminders of grief. He recalled, "One time Barbara and I walked into Iceland and somebody was skating to music that somebody used who had been killed in the crash. We both looked at each other and just started crying."[25]

Jim Short, the 1958 U.S. junior champion, also returned. He had retired in 1960 and was working for a high-end furniture store. "Barbara and I vowed we would never skate again. It was just too hurtful," Jim admitted. "At first I didn't even want to go into an ice rink. Four months later, I felt the USFSA needed me to come back, so I did." Jim was soon drafted for military service. He managed to get an assignment at a Pasadena missile site but had only two hours a day to train.[26]

There was a big void at Lake Placid without Bill Kipp, Rhode Michelson, Danny Ryan, Larry Pierce, and Bob and Pat Dineen. "People trained just as hard, but it was different because there were so many people missing," Bob Munz said. Ron Ludington, a new coach filling the void, lucked out with some great talent, including Pieter Kollen, Dorothyann Nelson, and Ron and Cindy Kauffman. Ludington was beholden to Danny Ryan for his good fortune. "Danny wanted us to work with him [in 1960] because he had said Ron was the up-and-coming coach," Kollen said, "so we went with Ron the summer of 1961." Ludington seized the opportunity because he thought it would be fleeting.[27]

Ron and Cindy Kauffman first trained with Ray Hadley, but his life had fallen apart. "It seemed to be common knowledge that he was drinking," Cindy said. The Kauffmans went to Lake Placid to take lessons from Ludington, despite the distance. For eight summers the family drove from Seattle to Lake Placid; Arvilla Kauffman rented a house and was dorm mother to eleven additional skaters. During the school year, Ron and Cindy skated in Seattle and took instructions over the phone from Ludington.[28]

A familiar face at Lake Placid was Rose Anne Ryan. "She kept going because she had to; she didn't really have a choice," Pieter Kollen said. Rose Anne rented a home next to Kollen and his gang, and Sally Schantz helped look after her kids while she taught. Kollen and Rusty Pierce, who had spent summers with his brother Larry in Lake Placid, trailered Danny's boat from Indianapolis to Lake Placid for Rose Anne. After a summer of skating and water skiing, they drove the boat up to the Ryan cottage in Canada for a little relaxation and remembrance of happier times.[29]

Coach Red Bainbridge had invited Marilyn Meeker to Lake Placid and paired her with Stan Urban. The Pierce family visited Marilyn at the end of the summer. "Those fine young people seemed to realize they had extra work to do, and were equal to it," Dallas Pierce told Ritter Shumway. During Dance Week, Marilyn and Stan placed second in two events. Stan en-

joyed skating with Marilyn, but his fondest memory was the honor of staying in the dorm room that Bill Kipp had used."[30]

At the end of the summer, Red Bainbridge transferred to the Broadmoor. Marilyn and Stan planned to follow, but Stan's parents did not want
him to move because he was only sixteen and still in prep school in Buffalo.
"He didn't go to Colorado, but I did," Marilyn said. "I finally got my life's
desire—going to Colorado Springs to skate for the Broadmoor—but I had
no partner!" The Broadmoor provided housing and a job for Marilyn in the
hotel's main office. When Stan backed out, Red brought in Marshall Campbell from Seattle. He had placed fourth at the 1961 Nationals but had already told his partner, Jan Jacobson, that he was quitting. The crash had
torn him apart. "The passion had just left," Marshall said, "but when I got
the call from both Red and Marilyn, I changed my mind and went to Colorado. Jan got all mad at me and I don't blame her."[31]

Julie Graham, a Maribel student, also trained with Red Bainbridge at
the Broadmoor. After an automobile accident sidetracked her single skating, L.A. dancer Howie Harrold contacted her. "I don't know how he heard
about me," Julie said, "but he came to Colorado. As it turned out, we did not
get along. I was feeling, 'I can't stand you, I hate you,' but we danced anyway."[32]

Aileen Kahre came out of a six-year retirement to support U.S. figure
skating. Bill Kipp had coached her in Los Angeles when she won the 1956
U.S. silver dance title, and she had since returned to her native San Francisco. The USFSA invited silver dance competitors Howard and Georgia
Taylor, who had two sets of twins, ages ten and thirteen, to compete in gold
dance. When Georgia declined, Howard approached Aileen. They had
time for only two dance sessions a week because they both worked. With no
coach, Howard cut the music and choreographed their program. "People
on the sessions were encouraging and watched out for us," Aileen said."[33]

———————◦—————

Aileen Kahre and Howard Taylor were two of 107 competitors at the
1962 Pacific Coast Championships, held at Great Falls, Montana, the first
week of January. Reminders of the 1961 World Team pervaded the competition: Ron and Cindy Kauffman, former Linda Hadley students, won senior pairs; Buddy Zack, an Edi Scholdan student, won senior men; and
Michelle Monnier, who won senior ladies, was the first recipient of the
Rhode Lee Michelson Memorial Trophy. Mrs. Carrier presented the Dona
Lee Carrier and Roger Campbell Memorial Trophy for Best Free Dance to

Yvonne Littlefield and Peter Betts. "That was rather an awkward moment," Yvonne admitted. Peter Betts, who was good friends with Dona Lee and her family, recalled the emotional day: "Mrs. Carrier had tears in her eyes and said, 'This trophy is for you. You richly deserved it.'" Despite the fresh emotions, Eleanor Carrier was thankful she went: "It was healing to hear the skaters speak of the inspiration they obtained from 'our youngsters' and of their determination to do their best to carry on. Seeing them work, I feel it won't be long before our ranks will be closed again, with the terrible gap well filled."[34]

Former Hadley students were also well represented at Pacific Coast. Word had spread about Ray Hadley's excessive drinking; he spent little time at the rink and his studio floundered. Compassionate Seattle skaters wanted to reverse his self-destructive course. Retired skaters called each other and said, "Let's go back and see what we can do." Dance teams were formed at the Hadley & Hart Studio and many teams qualified for Pacific Coast; Ray almost seemed like his old self again. In an amazing achievement, Ray's students won three medals in silver and bronze dance.[35]

Thirteen-year-old Peggy Fleming placed second in figures but became nauseated during the junior ladies freestyle. Everyone agreed that she had thrown up on the ice, but no one was sure about the reason. After she left the ice, her chance to advance to the U.S. Championships was over.[36]

Peggy's friends rallied around her. Jean Westwood scooted under the rope and said to the referee, "You've just got to give this girl a bye. She's already beaten all these other girls [at Southwest Pacific]." Peter Betts called officials in Boston, site of the 1962 U.S. Championships, to plead Peggy's cause. Even though she had placed eighth, she was allowed to compete at the 1962 U.S. Nationals.[37]

The Midwestern section had finally been divided into regions, and medal winners from the Southwestern, Upper Great Lakes, and Eastern Great Lakes competitions headed to Denver for Midwesterns, where once again Broadmoor skaters reigned supreme. Edi Scholdan's former students, now coached by Carlo Fassi, swept the awards in senior ladies, junior ladies, novice ladies, and novice men. The legacy of Doug Ramsay was manifest in the men's divisions: his friend Gary Visconti won senior men; and Tim Wood, who also trained alongside Doug in Detroit, won junior men. Vivian and Ron Joseph, 1961 Team alternates, won senior pairs for the first time, and Darlene Streich and Charles Fetter Jr., former Danny Ryan students, won silver dance.[38]

Marilyn Meeker competed at Midwesterns, but her life had already changed dramatically, as she noted:

The house mother at Holly Hall had this big Christmas party every year at the Broadmoor Hotel. She invited a family from Georgia who were new to the area. She was fond of one of the boys who had been a summer waiter and invited him, his dad and his brother to the party. She said, "Marilyn, please pay attention to these people because the family is recently divorced and I love this kid so much, so just be nice." I said I could do that. Well, it wasn't the little brother I fell for but his older brother.[39]

Marilyn and John Durham were inseparable. He accompanied her to Midwesterns, where she and Marshall won gold dance, but that didn't stop Rose Anne Ryan from noticing a change in Marilyn. "It doesn't look like your heart is in this," Rose Anne said. "No, it's not; I'm not having very much fun," Marilyn replied. The absence of her long-time partner became more acute at competition time. Her skating had always been intertwined with Larry Pierce; in time, they had wanted to turn pro and join a show. Now, winning the Midwestern gold dance title for the second time had lost its charm. "It was only by the grace of God that we did win because I was in terrible shape," Marilyn admitted. "I don't know if it was the altitude, too much partying, or not enough skating with Marshall, but I was not at my best."[40]

For Marilyn, it was more than having a new partner or falling in love. She had survivor's guilt. "I thought, 'God wanted all of these people to do a skating show up in heaven, but he didn't want me?' Really nutty stuff. Skating was never the same for me. Rose Anne had said, 'I hate a quitter,' but I said, 'I'm not a quitter. I'm just changing my course.' Personally, it was helpful for me to go in a different direction. I got swept off my feet and I forgot about the rest of the world. You don't [normally] know someone twenty-eight days and then marry them. It was my lot in life."[41]

Marilyn was embarrassed to inform the Broadmoor management that her skating days were over. "Thank God I was young and didn't know what a stupid thing it was to do," she admitted. It was even harder telling her new partner that she was not going to Nationals. When Marilyn left Colorado, Marshall had little choice but to return to Seattle. "I felt abandoned and thought, 'What am I going to do now?'" He called his former partner, Jan Jacobson, and begged her to compete with him. "That took some doing because she was still upset with me and she had every reason to be," Marshall said. "She had even stopped skating by then." Jan did not make it easy for him; but with less than three weeks to prepare a new program, she agreed to be his partner.[42]

Easterns was also held the second week of January at Lake Placid. Maribel Owen's former students did well, but there was a noticeable absence in the veterans' dance—Harold Hartshorne had been a competitor in that division for thirteen years. As the sectional champions headed to the 1962 U.S. Championships, they didn't know what to expect.[43]

1962 NATIONALS

The Skating Club of Boston, celebrating its golden anniversary in 1962, hosted the U.S. Championships on February 1-4. As with the 1961 Nationals, there were no defending champions. The senior division was an unusual assortment of competitors; and as one USFSA official commented, "Anybody could win anything."[44]

The practice sessions—at The Skating Club of Boston, Harvard University's Donald C. Watson Rink, the North Shore Sports Center, and Boston College's McHugh Forum—revealed new names and new partnerships. "There was a 'go for broke' attitude and everyone was going into every event because the World Team was wide open," dancer Lorna Dyer said. The officials treated the competition like any other, and their professionalism helped; but many competitors were melancholy. They couldn't shake the fact that they were competing for the first time on the national level in the shadow of the crash.[45]

Holding the 1962 Nationals in Boston was difficult because the "wounds were still open and hadn't healed yet," admitted coach Louella Rehfield. The Skating Club of Boston, the site for compulsories, held too many memories of those team members who had died. Gertrude Vinson and Lefty and Alfreda Lord came to the competition, and Christy Haigler visited the Kelley family after the competition. People spoke of the accident in muted tones. "Before we arrived everyone had wondered, 'What are we going to do? All of our top skaters are gone,'" coach Peter Dunfield said. "So everyone went [to Boston] hoping that talent would surface, and that we would be able to compete at the top level that year."[46]

The 1962 Championships opened with a celebration of the fiftieth anniversary of The Skating Club of Boston and a history of the USFSA. Boston had the best record of U.S. champions, and many of them returned for the festivities. The one champion notably missing was Maribel Vinson Owen. The competitors' program was filled with the history of the club and dozens of photos of the past—but no pictures of the 107 competitors.[47]

The finals were held at the McHugh Forum, which could seat 4,000. On Friday, Robert Munz and Susan Bright won the silver dance, Diane Sherbloom's ex-partner, Ray Chenson, placed second, and Larry Pierce's former girlfriend, Sally Schantz, placed fourth.[48]

On Friday night, Pam Schneider of New York won novice ladies, but *Skating* gave its highest kudos to Jennie Walsh, Rhode Michelson's eleven-year-old shadow. Peggy Fleming, who worked with Cecelia Colledge during the competition, pulled up from fifth to second place. In novice men, Detroit's Tim Wood won, followed by Paul McGrath of Boston and Billy Chapel of Los Angeles.[49]

Paul and Elizabeth George, who now trained with Bud Wilson, won junior pairs, a bittersweet victory that the siblings saw as a tribute to Maribel. "We skated the program that Maribel had choreographed and we felt her pulling for us on the other side," Elizabeth said. Linda Hadley's former students, Ron and Cindy Kauffman, placed second—clearly on their way to become one of America's top pairs. The new pair team of Joanne Heckert and Gary Clark placed third. "No one wanted to talk about it, but we all felt undeserving," Joanne said. "We all knew we wouldn't be there if it weren't for the accident."[50]

On Saturday evening, the junior ladies performed. Under Carlo Fassi's tutelage, Christy Haigler won junior ladies. Myrna Bodek of Detroit won the silver medal, and Tina Noyes of Boston won the bronze. The evening concluded with senior men. Monty Hoyt, who was known as "Mr. Figures," won both the figures and the free skating with five unanimous first-place votes, and became the new senior men's champion.[51]

The star of the senior men's competition was five-foot, ninety-seven-pound Scotty Allen. "Displaying maturity of style far beyond his years, twelve-year-old Scott Allen performed an amazingly polished and strong program to earn him a silver medal," *Skating* wrote. In 1960, his mother had told the press she hoped her son would compete in the 1964 Olympics—and he was on his way toward accomplishing that goal. David Edwards of Philadelphia placed third. Jim Short, who had trained while in the army, wasn't too disappointed he missed the podium. "I did as well as I could," he replied. "My skating was kind of a shadow of what it had been."[52]

At the awards dinner held late Saturday night at the Sheraton-Plaza—the first time the party was held before the competition ended—the usual gaiety was cut short by a tribute to the departed 1961 Team members. The remarks unleashed the buried feelings the competitors had tried to control. "We all fell apart," remembered Julie Graham. "Everything was so depressing and we spent more time crying—it was bad." Pam Zekman agreed: "There was a certain sadness—an emptiness—over the whole competition. . . . They had been a fixture for years and then they weren't there."[53]

Sunday was the final day of competition. Tommy Litz of Hershey, Pennsylvania, won the close race for the junior men's title. "The fast, complete rotation of two successive double axels, a high flying sit spin culminating in a fast cross-foot spin, the effective 'Litz' double Lutz, were outstanding in a program which had no weak spots," praised *Skating*. Gary Visconti, who had hoped to honor the memory of his friend Doug Ramsay by winning the junior title—as Doug had in 1960—skated well and was happy to place second.[54]

The Boston skating community hoped that Lorraine Hanlon, the 1961 junior ladies champion, would win the senior ladies title. *Skating* had put her photo on the January cover, proclaiming her as "Boston's best hope to mirror Laurence's win . . . on home ice." Superb in figures, Lorraine had spent the summer in Europe passing ISU figure tests. She had the hometown advantage, but the majority of the competitors looked to Barbara Roles as the heir apparent. "Seeing Barbara at Nationals was like seeing a ghost," more than one competitor said. She had competed for years with the 1961 Team members and was indelibly tied to that era. Everyone knew that, except for the birth of baby Shelley, she would have been on the ill-fated plane.[55]

The other top contender, Karen Howland, had almost flown with the 1961 Team because of Rhode Michelson's injuries. However, this year Karen had her own health issues. She had caught the flu while training in Minnesota; and when she arrived in Boston, she couldn't even walk. She deplaned in a wheelchair. "We went to Tenley's dad [Dr. Albright], and no one knew what it was. I wanted to try skating, and I said, 'I can do it, I can do it.'" Dr. Albright let her skate because she was determined—but she couldn't put any weight on one foot and withdrew. "I was heartbroken because I thought it could have been my year," she said. It was later determined that Karen had Guillain-Barre, a paralytic illness that begins in the feet and moves up the body. It took her six months to recover. She remained in Boston to watch, but "it hurt mentally and emotionally to be at the competition."[56]

Karen's withdrawal reduced the senior ladies field; Barbara Roles was almost another casualty when she narrowly missed the figures competition. She had already qualified for the 1962 Worlds on the basis of her third place at the 1960 Olympics and Worlds, but she still had to compete. Barbara almost defaulted due to her tardiness, and according to the *Boston Herald*, "many people thought she should have been" dropped. The *Boston Herald* published the "officially released" story:

> After worried conversation with referee and judges, the blonde . . . was allowed onto the ice. "Another minute or so and she'd have been out of luck,"

said [a] referee. . . . If her composure was ruffled this was not manifested by Barbara's eloquent blades that carried her to first place in the compulsory figures. Mrs. Pursley, whose seven-months-old daughter Shelley slept on the sidelines, said she thought the event was scheduled to begin at 12:30 P.M. but the schedule said noon. Then, on the way from the hotel, her car ran out of gas, and she finally arrived at 12:20.[57]

Peter Dunfield, who coached senior ladies competitor Vicky Fisher, told a different story. On Thursday evening, during the ladies' practice, officials posted the start time for the Friday figure competition but changed the time after the ladies left the rink. They notified all of the women except Barbara, who was staying at a different hotel. When she came to the rink Friday afternoon, pushing her baby in a stroller, her warm-up group was already on the ice. "Barbara, they've changed the time! Didn't they let you know?" Dunfield asked. "No, I didn't know," she replied. Dunfield ran to tell the officials while she quickly got on the ice and warmed up. "The story circulated so fast in the arena. Everybody immediately took sides."[58]

Decades later, Barbara explained the controversy:

> Most people treated me fine, but there were a couple of people that were not too kind because they wanted Lorraine Hanlon to win. For instance, the referee. The night before they changed the starting time—they put a newspaper clipping over it. I wasn't late for the regular time. I was late for the time change. They didn't call and tell me. I came in a taxi (the running-out-of-gas story was false). When I arrived they were starting to warm up. They let me skate because somebody else showed the referee that it was posted underneath and it was not out in plain view. There was only one official that yelled at me, but he died of a dreadful disease.[59]

Apparently, there was prejudice against Barbara. "At the time it was not socially acceptable for a competitor to be a mother," Dunfield explained. "Many people thought Barbara shouldn't even be competing. You're sending a woman [to Worlds] who's just had a baby?" Some dancers had had children, like the Dineens, but they were regarded differently because they were generally older. Still, the USFSA frowned on any World Team member having a baby.[60]

Barbara regained her composure after her near-miss and placed first in figures. The marks, however, were close among the top three: Barbara, Frances Gold, and Lorraine Hanlon. Lorraine was disappointed not be in the lead because figures were her specialty. Barbara performed exquisitely in the free skate—a remarkable feat considering that her conditioning had been so brief. "She was the only lady of the competition who had to regain her figure as well as her figures," the press predictably joked. "With maturity and control shining through her performance, Mrs. Pursley enthralled a turn-away crowd of 4,000 at McHugh Forum with a free skating triumph. She had that much more poise than the other girls and it showed. She'd been through tougher competition and was there to win." After Barbara won the senior ladies title, she acknowledged the difficulties of the past few months: "The figures—mine and the skating—were tough to get right . . . [but] the free skating came back easily." Lorraine pulled up from third to second, Vicky Fisher moved from fourth to third, and Frances Gold dropped from second to fourth.[61]

The next event was the dance championship, which had the most participants of all the senior events. Peter Betts, twenty-five, and Yvonne Littlefield, sixteen, won with four firsts and one second. "I don't know if I was surprised that we won because we were prepared," Betts said. "We had as good a chance as anybody because of the partner shifting. We thought, 'Let's just go out and do it, and see what happens.'"[62]

Dorothyann Nelson and Pieter Kollen, who placed second, felt lucky to medal because Pieter had been in bed with a bad cold before the competition started. "I got out of bed thinking, 'I don't have a lot of strength,'" he recalled. "It was so cold in some of those Boston rinks that I wore a surgical mask so I could breathe." Lorna Dyer and King Cole of Seattle placed third. It was Lorna's first Nationals, and they were startled to medal at all.[63]

There was great disappointment for the four other dance teams, all of whom soon retired. The 1961 silver dance champions, David Owen and Rosemary McEvoy, placed fourth and were shocked not to make the World Team. "I thought we should have won," David said. Marshall Campbell and Jan Jacobson, who had reunited in the past few weeks after Marilyn Meeker quit, placed fifth. "I fell right on my butt and pulled Jan down too," Marshall said. After the competition, Marshall stopped skating because of the pessimistic attitude of the USFSA: "We had been told that the new team was going to be at the bottom of the barrel internationally because they didn't have the experience of the old team. Our own officials were telling us we would not perform well for ten years."[64]

The Berkeley team of Aileen Kahre, twenty-five, and Howard Taylor, in his late thirties, placed sixth. The competitors had been welcoming, and officials hoped they would return next year, but they had felt like fish out of water around the "young whipper-snappers" and did not plan to return. Julie Graham, who placed last with Howie Harrold, was thrilled not to make the World Team: "We had footwork that went the entire length of the ice, whereupon I dropped down and did a split on the ice, while my partner had forgotten the whole thing. I didn't feel badly because I didn't get along with him. I got off the ice and never laid eyes on him again."[65]

The final event was senior pairs, in which several teams had realistic expectations of winning. Pieter Kollen and Dorothyann Nelson had competed in gold dance just an hour and a half before the pairs final. They won the senior pairs title with "a good deal of dash [and] pleasing lifts." The Fotheringills, who placed second, had hoped to win because they had placed fourth the year before, but they felt Pieter and Dorothyann deserved the crown. "They were a little bit older, more athletic, and more sophisticated than we were," Jerry said.[66]

Bronze medalists Ron and Vivian Joseph, the 1961 junior pairs champions, felt that the judges were against them. "My father had a discussion with one of the judges after the competition," Ron said. "He basically said they would never have a Jew on the American team. Knowing these obstacles existed just made us work harder." Coach Peter Dunfield was fully aware of the prejudices that existed in U.S. figure skating and commented: "You knew the ground rules and you had to work around them. The Joseph parents had already fled a very unaccepting world [in Germany] and were not very accepting [of the discrimination] as it happened."[67]

Jim and Janet Browning placed fourth. Janet had given birth to a daughter in November, and therefore had only two months to prepare for competition. She had trained every morning at 4 A.M. During their performance, Jim heard their daughter crying in the stands and thought, "We're really not in a position to do this." But the disaster moment came when they were literally tripped up by the judges' platform on the ice. Jim caught his heel and slid from one end of the arena to the other. "If we had skated really well I would have been disappointed [not to make the top three]," Janet said, "but we made mistakes."[68]

The Brownings were among a number of competitors who had made many sacrifices to help rebuild U.S. skating the year after the crash. Another was junior lady Pam Zekman, who hung in for one more year—but with disastrous results. She didn't have much time to train during her freshman year at UC Berkeley. "I trained a little at St. Moritz, and then crash-trained with Peter Dunfield just before the competition," she recalled. "I destroyed my ankles because I was on the ice for ten hours a day during vacation. I ended up competing but barely able to walk."[69]

At competition's end, the Arctic Blades Figure Skating Club, buoyed by the dual titles of Barbara Roles in senior ladies and Yvonne Littlefield and Peter Betts in gold dance, and Peggy Fleming's silver in novice, won the coveted Harned Trophy for the first time. Gretchen Merrill Gay, Maribel

Vinson Owen's first Olympian, summarized the 1962 season: "Skaters, the tension and year of mourning [are] over now. Were those who were with us in spirit in Boston able to say it to you, I think it would be, 'Good job.' Our country has a firm foothold on a progressive path forward. We have the Memorial Fund in their honor to work for, [and] a magnificent group of competitors."[70]

The International committee selected the 1962 World Team. In previous years, the USFSA sent three entrants in each division. The ISU had predetermined that the USFSA could send only two entrants in each division, except ladies, where it allowed three because Barbara Roles was a past World and Olympic medalist. However, the thirteen-member team actually consisted of eleven skaters because Kollen and Nelson represented the United States in two divisions. The press ballyhooed the youth of the new team, primarily because of twelve-year-old Scott Allen; but at the other extreme, Barbara Roles, Pieter Kollen, Dorothyann Nelson, and Peter Betts were in their twenties.[71]

The 1962 Nationals was historic on many fronts. Barbara Roles was the first senior ladies champion west of the Mississippi, and the first with a child. Scott Allen was the youngest U.S. World Team member to that point. Monty Hoyt was the first person since Dick Button to win junior and senior titles in successive years. Pieter Kollen and Dorothyann Nelson made the World Team in more than one event—the first time in eight years.[72]

Barbara Roles and Yvonne Littlefield had a unique bond: They were not only former World Team members, but they were also both from the same club and had both narrowly missed the tragic consequences of being 1961 World Team members. Although Barbara's daughter was with her in Boston, she had remained home in California when her mother and ten other members of the 1962 U.S. World Team flew to Prague.[73]

1962 WORLDS

For the first time in sixteen years, Americans had no expectations to medal at the 1962 World Figure Skating Championships. Still, the eyes of the country were on the event as it was televised in the United States for the first time. On the day of the crash, Al Campbell had complained to the press: "Too few people paid attention to the efforts of those kids. Maybe this tragedy will focus attention on future United States skaters." Dick Button had been unsuccessful in arranging for a television broadcast of the 1961 Worlds, irked that the project had sat for months on the desk of Roone Arledge of ABC Sports. The enormous publicity of the crash persuaded

Arledge to take a chance on the 1962 Worlds. "It turned out to be the most successful show that year for ABC," Button said.[74]

The new USFSA policy precluded the team's traveling by air as a unit; instead, they flew with chaperones and coaches in small groups. For the first time, the USFSA, through the Memorial Fund, paid for transportation costs for the entire team; it was also the first time the USFSA provided accident insurance. Some of the 1961 Team families were unnerved that the 1962 Team was flying to Prague. Ritter Shumway addressed their concerns: "[We will] send the team on two or three different flights to Germany, where they will assemble at one convenient place . . . and will then travel probably by train to Prague. You may be sure that we are sympathetic with your point of view and are doing everything possible to avoid a repetition of last year's tragedy." All of the Americans arrived safely, but Pieter Kollen and Dorothyann Nelson's suitcases didn't arrive with them. A Canadian pair team shared their practice outfits and toiletries.[75]

No one expected much from the U.S. team. Previous teams numbered between eighteen and twenty-two competitors, compared to the 1962 World Team of thirteen. Some people unfairly categorized this team as second string. However, the competitors greeted the new American team with great admiration for their courage in making a showing. "There was the sense that we needed to do our best because some of the best weren't there," Scott Allen said. "There was a tremendous camaraderie among all the skaters, and that really made a difference." The Canadians helped the new team members feel welcomed—showing them the ropes and being available to talk with them. "We felt a tremendous loss [for the 1961 Team], and we couldn't even begin to comprehend how that loss was felt at home," Debbi Wilkes said.[76]

The Czechs' reception of the Westerners was overwhelming. Practice sessions had stands teeming with spectators. "Every time we stepped onto the ice it became a performance," Judianne Fotheringill said. "They were always asking for autographs and taking pictures—it was like becoming a movie star overnight." Thirteen-year-old Marie Vichova was one of many kids who skipped school in order to watch the daily practices. "Skating was as popular a sport here as Little League baseball was in the U.S.," Marie said. "Every school had a courtyard that was flooded and frozen, and the kids skated every day; in each of the four Prague skating clubs there were over five hundred competitive members."[77]

Besides admiring fans, the competitors also had KGB escorts. Three men were assigned to the team—one stayed at the hotel, one took them shopping, and one took them sightseeing—but it made them jittery to have an armed soldier 300 paces behind them. The skaters were never allowed out on their own and found microphones in their hotel rooms. Still, they considered their stay in Prague a great adventure.[78]

Tickets for the championships had been sold out since the previous year. The new Julius Fucik Stadium had seats for 14,000 and room for 4,000 to stand. *Skating* correspondent Jane Vaughn Sullivan considered the crowds "the most receptive and interested I've ever seen. When the music has a strong beat, everyone claps hands in unison and whenever a skater falters or falls, the audience groans."[79]

In pairs, Pieter Kollen and Dorothyann Nelson performed well and received marks that ranged from fourth to tenth. They ended up in eighth place. The Fotheringills, who skated first, placed tenth. The American pairs knew there was a pecking order and were not shocked by their placements. "We were not in a position to even wildly imagine that we would medal," Judianne Fotheringill said, "so there was very little pressure on us."[80]

The entire crowd greeted Otto and Maria Jelinek with great excitement. Skating to the melodies of Czech composers Dvorak and Smetana, the Jelineks "held everyone breathless while they performed a beautiful program with very high floating lifts," *Skating* reported. The Jelineks won the World title and enjoyed the adulation of their native countrymen, who admired them because they had successfully fled Communism. "There were a lot of people who left, assimilated into some other country, and then you never heard from them again," Marie Vichova said. "The Jelineks had made a whole new life for themselves and had triumphed."[81]

The Jelineks' strongest competitors, 1960 Olympic silver medalists Marika Kilius and Hans Baumler of Germany, collided during their performance—Marika accidentally kicked her partner—and had to withdraw. Russians Ludmila Belousova and Oleg Protopopov, whose performance was like a "dance on ice," placed second.[82]

At the men's competition the following evening, Sullivan described the skating as the most thrilling she had ever witnessed. "Scotty Allen took [the audience] by storm. . . . He fell on his double axel but went right ahead without hesitating. The crowd admired his courage and 'aplomb,' and clapped harder than ever. After his performance they wouldn't let the next skater on until Scotty took a bow." Scott pulled up from tenth to eighth place. "He immediately became the darling of the teenage world," Marie Vichova said. "He was our age, very smiley, so fast, and everybody loved him." U.S. champion Monty Hoyt skated well except for one fall, in which he slid into the referee. He later said he was the only skater who had a conversation with the referee during his performance. Hoyt began and ended in sixth place.[83]

The spectators were certain that native son Karol Divin, with a huge forty-five point lead, would be crowned the first Czech World men's champion. He skated well, receiving marks from 5.2 to 5.8. The audience responded with a prolonged standing ovation.[84]

Few thought Canadian Donald Jackson had a chance to overtake Divin, but Jackson had a triple lutz—a jump no one had ever tried in competition. "He had been doing it in practice," Marie Vichova said, "so when you saw him coming up for the lutz [in the competition] everyone just held their breath." Sullivan described the play-by-play action as Jackson took to the ice:

> A hush fell on the stadium. The strains of Carmen broke the silence as Donald started his program, gathering speed slowly around the rink in a series of steps which culminated in a terrific triple lutz! The audience cheered wildly as Donald skated the most fantastic program I have ever seen. He jumped higher, spun faster, did the most intricate footwork, jumped double and triple jumps with the greatest ease and grace—all magnificently choreographed with the music. Everyone agrees it rates as the greatest free skating performance of all time as well as one of the greatest of all athletic feats. When he finished everyone knew that here was the new World Champion. The Czech people stormed and cheered, and again stopped the [event] from continuing. It was heartwarming to see how they appreciated and admired Donald's skating.[85]

The judges rewarded Jackson's extraordinary performance with seven 6.0s, which insured him the World title. The judges' marks fell along Cold War lines: Jackson received five firsts from the western countries, and four seconds from Communist countries. The next triple lutz in competition did not occur for two decades.[86]

The final men's results gave the gold, silver, and bronze medals to Canada, Czechoslovakia, and France. Marie Vichova remembered: "Karol wasn't really upset because he was best friends with Donald. He congratulated him because it was a totally historic moment in skating." Jackson, who had switched coaches from Pierre Brunet to Sheldon Galbraith, included a gesture of homage to Doug Ramsay in his program—his signature double axel performed with crossed arms. "I had seen Doug do it and I liked it because it showed control," Jackson said.[87]

British dance teams had won every World dance title since its inception in 1952. Doreen Denny and Courtney Jones, the 1960 World champions, retired when the 1961 Worlds were cancelled. Canada's Bill McLachlan, with a bronze and three silver World medals with two different partners, was expecting to win. Instead, Czech siblings Eva Romanova and Pavel Roman, with the audience on their side, won. "Their wild enthusiasm must have infected the skaters because they gave an inspired performance," Sullivan noted.[88]

The Canadians were surprised to place third. "We got screwed," Bill said. They had three strikes against them. The Europeans, who had been wearied by the American sweeps, were not interested in a new Canadian sweep; after the Jelineks and Don Jackson won, there was "no way we were going to win," Bill said. Second, Virginia Thompson was recuperating from the Asian flu. Finally, from their perspective, the judges had played dirty. A friend of the Canadian champions overheard the Czech and French judge make a trade at the opening night cocktail party. "Nobody did anything about it in those days; it was like a dirty family secret, but everybody still knew," Virginia said. "The Czechs won and the French came in second. Neither had beaten us before, and we placed third by a hundredth of a point." To make matters worse, a British judge approached Bill and Virginia after the competition to apologize, saying she had meant for them to be second, but she had put down the wrong mark.[89]

In contrast, the American dancers expected their poor placement: Dorothyann Nelson and Pieter Kollen placed seventh and Yvonne Littlefield and Peter Betts placed eighth. "I don't think they knew what to do with us," Betts said. It was the fourth time in the history of World dance that the Americans had not won a medal.[90]

In the ladies division, Barbara Roles placed fifth in figures, putting her in medal contention. In the finals, she skated "with assurance although not up to her past performances," *Skating* wrote. She received high marks but remained in fifth. Lorraine Hanlon, who had competed with a broken bone in her foot, barely made it into the top ten. Vicky Fisher, who had the bad luck of drawing first for the freestyle and had skated while people were still entering the stadium, ended up sixteenth.[91]

Sjoukje Dijkstra, the European champion, skated confidently with great power, and became the 1962 World champion. Wendy Griner, who performed a polished and difficult program, was disappointed to win silver: "When the competition was cancelled [in 1961] it was a disastrous decision for me. I was in good condition and I felt that I could have won. Sjoukje then established herself. After having a champion from across the ocean for so many years, Europeans felt it was time for a European champion."[92]

The Canadians dominated the competition with two golds, one silver, and one bronze; every team member placed sixth or higher. In contrast, Barbara Roles placed fifth and the rest of her U.S. teammates placed between sixth and sixteenth. Nevertheless, the United States was proud of the team. *Skating* had judged that they had done "a commendable job. Their conduct off the ice was of the highest caliber; they demonstrated good manners and fine sportsmanship."[93]

Even though the Americans came home empty-handed, the 1962 Worlds had been a great success. Fortunately for the skaters, preparations had improved from the previous year. They had better hotel accommodations and competed in a spectacular new arena. Any fears of going into a Communist country were dispelled. The Americans were won over by the beauty of Prague and the enthusiasm of the Czechoslovakian people, who were welcoming hosts. They had enjoyed the discovery that an athlete in a Communist country is considered a superstar. "We were always surrounded by hundreds of adoring kids," Pieter Kollen said. After the competition, the U.S. team went on an exhibition tour to Switzerland, West Germany, the Ukraine, and Russia.[94]

But inevitably, there were the moments of "might have been." The 1961 U.S. World Team would have been equally well received by the citizens of Prague. They would have clapped as heartily for their performances as for the 1962 World Team. "Even though the [1962] team was not the top people, they were still great skaters," Swedish skater Ann-Margreth Frei said. "With the Americans, no matter what happened, there was always somebody else that was great that would step right in." The USFSA hoped for the best as there were less than two years before the 1964 Winter Olympics in Innsbruck. But after the 1962 Worlds, the possibility for any Olympic medalists was remote . . . and more defections were to come.[95]

CHAPTER 19

1964 AND 1968 WINTER OLYMPICS

By January 1963, the preparations for the 1964 Winter Olympics in Innsbruck, Austria, were in full swing. But U.S. figure skating was still experiencing a merry-go-round of champions. All of the 1962 senior champions had either retired or were dethroned at the 1963 U.S. Championships.

During the week-long competition at the Long Beach Arena in Long Beach, California, the ladies crown was one of two titles vacated. Barbara Roles had retired for the second time. Boston's Lorraine Hanlon, who was first in figures, kept her lead after the freestyle, and finally became the 1963 senior ladies champion. Christy Haigler, the 1962 junior champion, pulled up from fourth to second place. Karen Howland, thrilled to be back at Nationals after her debilitating illness, dropped from second to third. "I skated really well," Karen said, "but a judge came up to me afterwards and said she basically screwed me; it was a political thing."[1]

The U.S. pairs title was vacant because Dorothyann Nelson had joined Ice Follies to skate with Richard Dwyer, leaving Pieter Kollen to find a new partner. Jerry and Judianne Fotheringill, in their third year in seniors, became the new U.S. pairs champions, Ron and Vivian Joseph placed second, and Pieter Kollen with new partner Patti Gustafson placed third.[2]

In the first outright reversal from the previous year, Tommy Litz executed effortless triple jumps and became the new U.S. men's champion. "I wanted to be a national champion so bad that it was indescribable," Litz said. "It was a magnificent honor to win." Scotty Allen, skating with ease and confidence, placed second. The 1962 U.S. champion Monty Hoyt, who had a commanding lead in figures, placed third. Monty, who had been working with coach Sheldon Galbraith in Canada, was disappointed to lose his title but, according to his brother, "bore no ill will."[3]

Dance champions Yvonne Littlefield and Peter Betts presented a free dance "rich in content and showmanship," but they could not overcome the lead Sally Schantz and Stan Urban had taken by placing first in compulsories. Sally and Stan, coached by Ron Ludington, did not expect to win because it was their first time competing at the gold level.[4]

The Harned Trophy changed hands again. The Skating Club (SC) of Boston had won in 1961. But when Boston hosted the 1962 Nationals, it relinquished the trophy to the Arctic Blades Figure Skating Club. In yet another reversal, when Arctic Blades hosted the 1963 Nationals, the SC of Boston regained the trophy for the eighth time.[5]

The 1963 U.S. World Team made a quick trip to Vancouver, British Columbia, for the 1963 North American Championships, where they made the worst showing ever for an American team. The Canadians swept every event for the first time since 1941. Tommy Litz won the men's silver, Scotty Allen the men's bronze, the Josephs the pairs bronze, and Sally Schantz and Stan Urban a bronze in dance. The U.S. ladies were shut out completely. The results did not bode well for the upcoming Worlds, but Ron and Vivian Joseph were only one-tenth of a point away from second place, and Litz, who had pulled up from fifth to second place, once again performed a spectacular freestyle program.[6]

The open-air ice stadium at Cortina d'Ampezzo, Italy—where the United States had won its first double Olympic win in figure skating in 1956—was the site for the 1963 Worlds, but the Americans didn't expect to medal. Tommy Litz went to Cortina but did not compete. After North Americans, he had had an accident at an outdoor rink in Pennsylvania: "I did a double flip, and when I toed in my ankle went over, collapsed, and twisted—the pain was excruciating, and that was the end of that," Litz said.[7]

Germans Marika Kilius and Hans-Jurgen Baumler, who had been runners-up four times, won the World pairs title, and Ludmila Belousova and Oleg Protopopov placed second. The judges clumped the Americans together—the Fotheringills placed seventh, the Josephs placed eighth, and Kollen and Gustafson placed ninth. Canadians Debbi Wilkes and Guy Revell had been favored to medal, but they withdrew. While posing for pictures on an outdoor rink before the competition, Guy lost his balance on the slushy ice while Debbi was in the air. She suffered a skull fracture and was off the ice for several months.[8]

The men's World title, vacated by the retirement of Donald Jackson, was captured by Canadian Donald McPherson. Scott Allen placed fifth, although many thought he should have been placed higher, according to British reporter Dennis Bird: "Allen . . . demonstrated such brilliant jumps, spins and footwork that many people felt sure he is a coming World Champion." Monty Hoyt placed seventh in figures but slipped to eleventh after the free skate. "If you didn't go in as the American champion, you were not perceived as well," said his brother Greg Hoyt. "Therefore, he slid in the rankings." Litz, watching the men's event with his father, wasn't as depressed as he thought he'd be. "These poor guys were out there in twenty below zero weather, and I thought, 'I'm glad I'm not out there.' It was horrifying."[9]

World dance champions Eva Romanova and Pavel Roman won for the second time. The Americans were again bunched in the middle—Sally Schantz and Stan Urban placed seventh and Lorna Dyer and John Carrell placed eighth. Yvonne Littlefield and Peter Betts, who eloped right before Worlds, were ninth in the compulsories. In the middle of their program, Peter's blade fell off, the whole heel separating from the boot. After securing the blade with screws, they went back out and tried it again. "We were having the best day we ever had; we got to the exact same place in the free dance and it happened again, so we had to withdraw," Betts said. The judges could only mark half of their content and they ended in seventeenth place. "Two judges told us they would have placed us third in the free dance if we had continued," Betts said.[10]

The ladies competition was the final event, and the Americans did not show well. After the free skate, Lorraine Hanlon dropped from seventh to tenth, Karen Howland pulled up from thirteenth to eleventh, but Christy Haigler dropped from fifteenth to nineteenth. Sjoukje Dijkstra, of the Netherlands, retained her World title, and Wendy Griner, the 1962 World's silver medalist, placed fourth. "Competing outdoors was an absolute nightmare," Wendy said. "It was not an equal playing ground. Sjoukje skated when the sun was out, while I was second to last on the program, and had to skate when it was dark and bloody cold. Being on the ice at midnight changed the whole texture of the ice—it became brittle and it shattered. It just wasn't fair."[11]

Scott Allen's fifth place was a strong showing for the United States, but most of the other placements in each division were comparable to 1962. The 1963 World Team included only half of the 1962 Team; and after the European tour, the defections began. Karen Howland decided she had had enough: "The attitude seemed to be, 'Well, the team is gone . . . there is no way you can be near the top for several years.' That's difficult to take when you train very hard."[12]

The 1964 Nationals in Cleveland, Ohio, provided surprises and upsets—a rare occurrence in an Olympic year. "Perhaps in the years to come, it can be said that the United States' re-entry to prominence in the international figure skating picture stemmed from this competition," *Skating* noted. That statement proved prophetic. ABC hired Carol Heiss Jenkins, now a resident of Akron, Ohio, as TV commentator to cover the U.S. Championships.[13]

In the fall of 1963, separate accidents knocked two teams out of competition. U.S dance champion Stan Urban damaged his leg in a college intramural football game and was in a cast for seven weeks. Five weeks before Nationals, Pieter Kollen caught his edge on the ice with Patti Gustafson in the air, and they both crashed down. Patti was in the hospital for a month.[14]

Along with the defections came a surprise reappearance. Ice Capades was interested in having Barbara Roles join the show but first wanted her to be a member of the 1964 Olympic Team. "The galleries buzzed with excitement over the appearance of Barbara Ann Roles," *Skating* noted.[15]

Twenty-three-year-old Barbara faced younger competitors, including fellow club member Peggy Fleming. In 1963 Peggy had worked with John Nicks and placed third in national junior ladies. Nicks discovered what other Fleming coaches had encountered: "She had real nervous problems, her endurance was limited, and she got tired quickly. However, Peggy was very talented and over time she conquered her nerves." Peggy again switched coaches and now worked with Olympian Bob Paul. Most of the senior ladies had been featured in advance publicity; but Peggy, who had trained in Cleveland early in her career, had been left out of the spotlight.[16]

After a year off the ice, Barbara Roles placed sixth in figures, reflecting her lack of patch time. Lorraine Hanlon, Christy Haigler, Tina Noyes, and Peggy Fleming each won individual figures, but Christy ended in first. In the senior ladies free skate, Barbara Roles received a warm ovation, although her sixth placement in figures made it difficult for her to make the Olympic Team. Five senior ladies from 1963 returned in 1964, but it was two new young ladies who broke through. Tina Noyes, the 1963 junior champion, skated a high-content program which propelled her from fourth to second place.[17]

Peggy Fleming was in third place when she stepped onto the ice for a defining moment. Eyewitnesses remembered every step and nuance in her program. She "left nothing undone as she electrified the crowd with a dynamic free skating program which included five different double jumps," *Skating* noted. Peggy said, "I just let myself go. When I skated off the ice, I really wasn't thinking anything about how I had done."[18]

No one had predicted that Fleming would win—even Peggy herself. "I was just hoping to make it into the top six," she said. "It was a complete surprise to me that I won." The U.S. Championships preceding the Olympics had always been business as usual because American champions fared better in international competition when they had year-to-year continuity. "She accomplished a feat which usually has been considered next to impossible," the *Plain Dealer* noted. The women had been the weakest division since the plane crash, and Fleming was the first skater to emerge with what looked like the potential of being the next great champion.[19]

Peggy Fleming, fifteen, became the youngest U.S. senior ladies champion. Tina Noyes, fifteen, won the silver, and Christy Haigler, sixteen, the 1963 runner-up, won the bronze. "I had a good chance at the 1964 title, but I actually didn't skate my best," Christy admitted. The teenagers prevailed; and the older girls, including 1963 ladies champion Lorraine Hanlon who dropped from second to fourth, were left behind. Barbara Roles was disappointed not to make the team, "but I could tolerate it," she said.[20]

Monty Hoyt and Scotty Allen battled for first place in figures, and Scotty triumphed. In 1963 Tommy Litz had pulled up from third in figures to win the title, and he hoped to do it again. His program included a triple salchow, a triple toe loop, and two consecutive double axels. He received the highest free skating marks, but it was not enough to put him up in first place. Scotty Allen, whose program included many double jumps, intricate footwork, and reverse spread eagles, maintained his lead and became the 1964 U.S. men's champion. Fourteen-year-old Allen became the youngest U.S. senior men's champion. Litz, the newly dethroned champion, was magnanimous about the outcome: "We respected each other and I was happy to be on the Olympic Team."[21]

Each of the three men on the 1964 U.S. Olympic Team had won the U.S. men's title. Bronze medalist Monty Hoyt boasted of the strength of the men's team going to Innsbruck: "I feel that the three skaters we send will do better than any other three from any other country." Gary Visconti, who came in fourth for two years in a row, was disappointed not to make the 1964 Team—partially because of Doug Ramsay. "Everyone at the club wanted to fill his shoes," Gary said. "We were carrying the torch for him."[22]

The dance crown had been vacated by the departure of Sally Schantz and Stan Urban, and Darlene Streich and Charles Fetter of Indianapolis became the 1964 U.S. dance champions by a slim margin. "It was our first year in gold dance and we had no expectations to win," Darlene said. In fact, they had barely made it to Nationals. They passed part of their gold dance test just three weeks before Nationals and had placed third at Midwesterns. Darlene had been thirteen when her coach Danny Ryan died in the crash. "I decided to move forward because I loved to skate," she said.[23]

There were only four entrants in senior pairs until the week of competition. Patti Gustafson, who had just been released from the hospital in Boston, stopped by the rink on her way home and discovered she was able to skate. She made a quick call to Pieter Kollen, and they asked USFSA officials to put them back in the competition. They had just two days to practice. But during the warm-up for the short program competition—the first year of new pairs compulsories—the referee informed them that they would not be allowed to skate. It put an end to their career, which had seemed glorious until their accident. They had been excited about their programs and thought "a medal at Olympics and Worlds was possible."[24]

The Fotheringills pulled up from second to win their second pairs title—the only repeating champions in the past three years. The Josephs won the silver for the second year in a row and Ron and Cindy Kauffman placed third. The Josephs were thrilled to be on the 1964 Olympic Team, but they and their coach were stunned that they dropped from first to second. "It was blatant that the judges were not supportive. The [USFSA] was run very deeply by the same people who ran restricted clubs for so many years," Dunfield explained. The Josephs were disappointed with the silver because they knew you had to be the American champion if you wanted to do well at the Olympics.[25]

In retrospect, it seems incomprehensible why, in light of the tragedy and the effort to rebuild U.S. figure skating, these old prejudices were not cast aside for the good of the sport. "The anti-Semitism in skating wasn't an organized situation, but it was there," Ron said. "My parents had said, 'Get a good education and be a great athlete, and you'll go on in the world.' They never thought it would be a problem in skating until we ran into it. Therefore, we tried to be better than everybody."[26]

Nearly half of the 1964 World Team had been coached by 1961 World Team coaches, and almost everyone on the 1964 Olympic Team personally knew the 1961 Team. The three senior ladies had a direct connection with their 1961 counterparts. Peggy Fleming had trained alongside Rhode Michelson, Tina Noyes had trained with Laurence Owen, and Christine Haigler had trained with Steffi Westerfeld. The 1961 Team was there in spirit as the new Olympians flew to Innsbruck, Austria.

1964 OLYMPICS

ABC covered both the 1964 Nationals and the 1964 Winter Olympics in Innsbruck, Austria. Prior to the 1964 Games, ABC ran a series of fifteen television programs on the history, personalities, and skills of the world's outstanding winter athletes, with Carol Heiss as the series' leading expert on figure skating.[27]

As the 1964 U.S. Olympic Figure Skating Team gathered to fly to Innsbruck, people wondered if they were ready. Three years had passed since the crash, and the perception remained that the Americans were not competitive internationally. "The night after the crash I got a call from a reporter," judge Newbold Black recalled. "He wondered if it would take five, ten, or twenty years before the United States would be back [competitively]. I said we would win at least one medal in the Olympics in 1964." Black was more optimistic than most in those dark days. There had been little stability; every year there had been new champions, with the exception of the Fotheringills.[28]

Every 1964 Olympic Team member knew that he or she had made the team because of the crash. "The team didn't travel together and it was always in the back of your mind; *knowing why*," Cindy Kauffman said. They felt honored to be on the team, "but would Peggy Fleming and Christine Haigler and I have been on it otherwise? I don't think so," Tina Noyes said. "There were too many other skaters who had seniority."[29]

The official poster for the IX Olympic Winter Games depicted a snow crystal, but Innsbruck experienced its mildest weather in fifty-eight years. The Games officially began on January 29 with 60,000 spectators at the Opening Ceremony at Bergisel Stadium. The procession of teams had significantly increased—the number of athletes skyrocketed from Squaw Valley's 655 to 1,091 in Innsbruck, with 891 male and 200 female athletes from thirty-six nations. This surge was due, in part, to new events in established sports, and the addition of new events, including luge, tobogganing, and bobsledding.[30]

The first figure skating event was the pairs. The 1963 World champions, Germans Marika Kilius and Hans-Jurgen Baumler, were in a heated competition with the now-married Russians Oleg and Ludmila Protopopov for the Olympic title. The Germans skated cautiously, and "in risking nothing, they lost all," *Skating* noted. The Russians, however, outshone everyone because of the "marvelous artistry of their performance." Kilius and Baumler had previously beaten the Protopopovs nine times, but the Russians won the Olympic title and the Germans had to settle for the silver—the same medal they had won in 1960.[31]

The three American pair siblings skated well. Judianne and Jerry Fotheringill, recognized for their "pleasantly smooth style," placed seventh. Cindy and Ron Kauffman's performance, was "one of the three or four most interesting programs of the evening," *Skating* noted. The Kauffmans, who placed eighth, made a strong first impression, but their Olympic experience was bittersweet. "Ron [Ludington] had plans for us, but Linda [Hadley] had had that plan for us too," Ron Kauffman said.[32]

The marks between third and fourth place were extremely close. Canadians Debbi Wilkes and Guy Revell's stellar performance indicated that Debbi had made a complete recovery from her serious injury the previous year. Vivian and Ron Joseph, who were fortunate to be the last pair to compete, were "startlingly good," *Skating* noted. Ron Joseph recalled, "It was one of those performances where we were in the zone." The total ordinals for both Wilkes and Revell and the Josephs were 35.5. The Canadians received the bronze medal by 3/10ths of a point. The Josephs did not win a medal but were grateful for the opportunity to compete for their country. "It was a great place with unbelievable athletes," Ron said, "and it was a spectacular experience competing in the Olympics."[33]

Sitting among the 11,000 spectators in the Eisstadion on Sunday, February 2, was the entire Dutch royal family—Queen Juliana, Prince Bernhard, Crown Princess Beatrix, and Princess Margaret of the Netherlands—there to support Sjoukje Dijkstra, who had already built up a commanding lead in figures. Thirty girls contended for Olympic hardware. Christy Haigler, in sixth place, was the first American on the ice and landed every jump. Tina Noyes, in ninth place, missed her triple salchow, but otherwise had an outstanding performance. Peggy Fleming, in eighth place, also had one fall, but *Skating* saw a bright future in her: "She is a thoughtful skater who has considerable capacity for development." The American ladies, typically bunched together, did as well as could be expected: Peggy pulled up to sixth, Christy placed seventh, and Tina rose to eighth place.[34]

The highlight of the event was the performance of Sjoukje Dijkstra. "Never before has there been a woman skater of such power and athletic skill; there are not many men who can exceed the speed and height of her double axel," *Skating* noted. Her Olympic gold medal, the first her country had ever won, pleased the royal gallery. Regine Heitzer of Austria won the silver, and Canadian Petra Burka won the bronze.[35]

Wendy Griner, the 1962 World silver medalist, placed tenth, which was not far from her twelfth placement at Squaw Valley. She knew the Olympics would be a disappointment before she even arrived in Innsbruck, because of the Canadian Championships. "[The judges] decided after the second figure that they were going to dump me," she said. After new champion Petra Burka was crowned, Wendy knew she was sunk internationally. "When I got to Europe, the first thing everyone said was: 'What happened to you?'

Of course I said, 'Nothing,' but I was finished." Wendy then quit the sport because she had had enough.[36]

The Canadian men had reigned supreme in World competition the past two years. The two Donalds—Jackson in 1962 and McPherson in 1963— retired after winning the World title. Alain Calmat of France was the favorite, but Manfred Schnelldorfer of Germany captured the lead in figures, with Karol Divin of Czechoslovakia in second, and Calmat in third. Scott Allen was not far behind in fourth place, Monty Hoyt was sixth, and Tommy Litz was thirteenth out of twenty-six competitors.[37]

Even though he was down in the pack, Tommy Litz gave an electrifying performance at the men's final. His speed, freshness, and jam-packed program—two double axels, a triple salchow, and a triple toe loop—brought storms of applause from the spectators. Most of the judges marked Litz in first place in freestyle, but surprisingly the American judge placed him ninth. "American judges are widely respected for not marking up their own skaters merely for patriotic reasons," *Skating* wrote, "but in this case a 5.4 and 5.3 for Litz surely carried impartiality rather far." The Russian judge and the American judge were the only ones who gave him anything less than 5.7. Even though "Monty Hoyt [had] improved . . . since Cortina," he dropped from sixth to ninth place.[38]

Some of the men in medal contention faltered, including Alain Calmat who fell on two jumps. When he left the ice, he was so unnerved he burst into tears. When the judges gave him high marks anyway, the German fans screamed *"Schiebung! Schiebung!"* [Fix! Fix!] These performances opened the door for Scott Allen, who skated a "dazzling program, reeling off double axels, a triple salchow, split jumps, double lutzes, all linked together with good spins and intricate footwork. . . . [He] is a skater of immense talent," *Skating* noted.[39]

Manfred Schnelldorfer was the last skater and had the advantage of knowing that Divin and Calmat hadn't skated their best. He gave the best performance of his life and became the first German Olympic men's figure skating champion. Joining him on the winner's stand was Alain Calmat, who pulled up to second place.[40]

In third place, to the happy surprise of the Americans, was Scott Allen. Fourteen when he competed (his birthday was two days after his performance), Allen set a new record by becoming the youngest-ever medal winner in any Winter Olympic event. "The American youngster Scotty Allen stole the show," the official Olympic journal reported. Scott felt that his performance was one of the greatest skates of his life. To him, it was a huge benefit that no one expected him to win a medal:

The top competitors seemed extremely nervous, but because I was fourteen, I didn't have a care in the world. I just wanted to land my triple salchow
and have a good run in the program. I was ecstatic with the way I skated. . . .
Nothing can describe the elation and joy of getting up on the podium. It
doesn't matter what color the medal—you're in your Olympic outfit and the
flag is going up. The medal ceremony was one of the most exciting things
that has ever happened to me.[41]

Litz won the freestyle, but his thirteenth position in figures raised him
to only sixth place; however, he was still pleased with his Olympic experience. "I never felt a bias against the Americans or a low expectation because
of what had happened [in 1961]," he said. "I always tried to extricate myself
from the whole political aspect of skating."[42]

Overall, the USA had won six Olympic medals: a gold in men's speed
skating, the bronze in men's figure skating, and four medals in alpine skiing.
For the second Olympics in a row, the USSR won the nation's championship
with twenty-five medals—almost twice as many as any other country. In fact,
it was the 1964 Winter Olympics that began a Russian domination in figure
skating. It began in pairs, spread to dance in the seventies, and finally to the
men's and the ladies' divisions in the eighties and nineties. Coach Peter Dunfield saw first-hand the kind of dedication the Russians brought to skating:
"[The Josephs'] dressing room cubicle was next to the Protopopovs—[their]
pre-competition warm-up routine lasted an hour. I thought, 'They're not going to have anything left!' Their off-ice warm-up was similar to ballet dancers—we had never seen that in skating before. They were way ahead of their
time, and I greatly admired and respected them."[43]

Besides introducing new artistry and training methods to figure skating, the Russians brought controversy. Western athletes realized that the
East Bloc athletes had no other responsibilities. Training was their job,
which blurred the line between being an amateur or a professional. This
monetary difference was first recognized during the Soviet Union's inaugural appearance at the 1956 Winter Games. "I have heard $35 million men-
tioned as the sum set aside by the Soviet government for its state-subsidized
athletic program," Andre Laguerre of *Sports Illustrated* reported. Russian
pair teams first emerged in Squaw Valley; and in four short years they came
away with a gold medal. The American domination in figure skating was
evaporating.[44]

The USOC recognized the strength of the Communist opposition but
believed they could put into effect "a program which will enable the USA to
hold its own with any nation in the world." But programs meant funding,
which was slow to come. In time, U.S. skiing was a magnet for U.S. dollars

from corporate sponsors and other sources, but U.S. figure skating and other winter sports lagged behind for years.[45]

The 1964 U. S. Olympic Team was stunned and delighted that Scott Allen had won a bronze medal. Nearly everyone said that U.S. figure skating couldn't come back after the 1961 plane crash—and yet it had. This accomplishment was a tribute to the talent and exuberance of young Allen, but it was also a pat on the back for the entire U.S. skating community who rallied to move beyond the crippling crash.

Tina Noyes had said there was no way anyone could "fill the skates" of the 1961 Team, and the skaters of the 1961 Team were sorely missed. Pundits speculated how the 1961 Team might have fared in the 1964 Olympics. "The 1961 Team definitely would have done very well at the 1964 Olympics," said Barbara Roles.[46]

Some skaters, judges, and officials over the years have suggested that the 1961 Team was actually weak—young, unseasoned, and lacking international credentials. It's true that a good majority of the team was teenagers, but the team also included seven skaters in their twenties. They had passed innumerable tests by being named to the 1961 U.S. World Team. Their opportunity to compete at Worlds was a first for half of the team; and at that point, most of the skaters still had many more competitions ahead of them. Although their chance to compete on the international stage was cruelly snatched away, they were, in fact, well positioned to medal at Worlds or at the 1964 Olympics.

The men's division had been the strongest. Ardelle Sanderson, who had judged them at North Americans, was convinced the men would have excelled in Innsbruck: "Doug Ramsay was an absolutely fantastic skater and the Boston boys, Greg Kelley and Bradley Lord, were awfully good, too." Lord, Kelley, and Ramsay made a team equal to other great U.S. men's teams: Dick Button and Jimmy Grogan; and Hayes Jenkins, Ronnie Robertson, and David Jenkins.[47]

Laurence Owen also had a good chance to become World or Olympic champion. She needed to perfect her jumps, but she had artistry and politics on her side, as coach Peter Dunfield acknowledged: "Laurence never quite did what you felt she could do, but you backed her because she had so much to offer. Her mother was a former Olympian and at that time, the politics was still intense. Everybody in the world who was a skater or judge knew her mother and had watched Laurence grow up. She would still have to produce, but she would be in the select group with the judges before she even stepped on the ice."[48]

The other ladies also had strong potential. Steffi Westerfeld had the Olympic experience of Edi Scholdan to guide her. Rhode Michelson's figures needed work, but her freestyle was equal to that of Olympic champion Sjoukje Dijkstra. Vicky Fisher, who had competed against the 1961 ladies, thought Rhode was the shining light among the three.[49]

The new Russian dominance in pairs was formidable, but the American teams still would have been competitive. Friends, however, wondered if all three teams would have stayed until 1964. Dudley would have been thirty-one if he had competed in Innsbruck. "Had Dudley and Little Maribel placed at the 1961 Worlds, they probably would have gotten married and that could have been it," Paul George surmised. Dudley, who was on track to become USFSA president, would have been an effective leader. "He had a wonderful mind and related to people terribly well," Peter Dunfield said. "He was an innovator and was always coming up with something different about training or a new direction for skating."[50]

The one thing for certain about the 1961 Team is that it had tremendous potential, but where it may have led will remain a mystery. "It makes you sad because you don't know what their promise was," Olympic champion David Jenkins said. "They were gone before they really had a chance to express their skating."[51]

•

The 1964 Worlds were held in Dortmund, Germany, one month after the Innsbruck Olympics. Marika Kilius and Hans-Jurgen Baumler won their second World title in their native country. The Protopopovs placed second, Debbi Wilkes and Guy Revell placed third, and the Josephs again placed fourth, with the Kauffmans and Fotheringills placing seventh and eighth, respectively.[52]

In men's competition, Olympic champion Manfred Schnelldorfer repeated his win. Tommy Litz gave the performance of his life and won the free skate, pulling him up from eighth to sixth place. Scott Allen placed fourth in figures and retained his placement after the free skate, while Monty Hoyt placed eleventh.[53]

Sjoukje Dijkstra won her third World title and finished her career with a wonderful tribute; more than six thousand people came from Holland to see her skate. The American ladies did well. Christy Haigler fared the best, placing fifth, with Peggy Fleming in seventh, and Tina Noyes in ninth place.[54]

Eva Romanova and Pavel Roman won their third World dance title. Americans Lorna Dyer and John Carrell were fifth, Carole MacSween and

Bob Munz were sixth, and Darlene Streich and Charles Fetter were eighth. Had the crash not occurred, Larry Pierce and Marilyn Meeker would surely have made it to the medal stand by 1964. So would Dona Lee Carrier and Roger Campbell. But the Dineens might have bowed out early, due to financial and family demands.[55]

For the third Worlds in a row, the Americans were shut out of medals; still the team's spirits had been revived with Allen's Olympic bronze. In time, the Americans won an additional Olympic medal. Not long after the medals were awarded in Innsbruck, a protest was officially filed against silver medalists Marika Kilius and Hans-Jurgen Baumler on the grounds that the pair had already turned professional. And, in fact, pictures and merchandise of the German pair team had been sold right outside the Olympic arena.[56]

The official protest said the Germans had prematurely signed a professional ice contract prior to the Olympics, which would have been a violation of amateur regulations. Baumler admitted that they had signed a contract with Holiday on Ice but that they had done so several months after the Games. Two years later, a ruling went against Kilius and Baumler, and they had to forfeit their Olympic silver medal. New silver medals were produced and given to bronze medalists Debbi Wilkes and Guy Revell. During his first year of medical school, Ron Joseph and his sister Vivian received their bronze medals from the Canadians.[57]

But the story wasn't over. The decision was reversed in the eighties, and Kilius and Baumler asked for their medals back. The German Olympic Committee had new medals pressed, identical to the originals. However, no one from the ISU or the IOC ever notified Wilkes and Revell and the Josephs that the decision had been reversed, and they still have their silver and bronze medals.[58]

The Skating Club of Boston lost more friends in 1964. Willie Frick, who was Maribel Vinson's coach, died after a long illness on July 29, 1964. Walter Brown, general manager of the Boston Garden and a good friend of Maribel's, died on September 9, 1964. Although Bud Wilson was considered lucky for missing Flight 548, he discovered he had cancer and died on November 15, 1964, age fifty-five.[59]

The top skating clubs still produced great skaters, but the next four years brought new talent from a wider variety of clubs in all divisions. "It was like a great farm club of a baseball team," former national champion

Gene Turner said. "The backups were so good that they really helped bring everything up very fast." [60]

There were many shake-ups prior to the 1965 season. Although Tommy Litz, Monty Hoyt, and the Fotheringills had retired, the three young ladies—Peggy Fleming, Tina Noyes, and Christy Haigler—had performed well at both Olympics and Worlds and were eager for the next season. Furthermore, Olympic medal winners Scott Allen and Ron and Vivian Joseph planned to continue competing.

The United States had a reason to be proud of its champion skaters, but there were still doubters. When skaters nationwide converged in Lake Placid for the 1965 U.S. Championships, the national perception reflected in the media was still focused on loss. An article about Tenley Albright in *Sports Illustrated* contained this stinging sentence: "With the loss of the entire U.S. team [in 1961], American figure skating virtually ceased to exist. The American youngsters who will supersede Tenley in people's minds have not appeared, possibly have not been born, even yet."[61]

Nothing could have been further from the truth. At the 1965 Nationals, Vivian and Ron Joseph won their first U.S. pairs title, Peggy Fleming retained her title, and Gary Visconti dethroned Scott Allen in a very strong, emerging men's field. The 1965 U.S. World Team made a brief stop in nearby Rochester for the North American Championships. After a dismal showing at the 1963 event, the United States successfully recovered three trophies: Gary Visconti won the men's title, the Josephs won the pairs event, and Lorna Dyer and John Carrell won the dance crown. Peggy Fleming came in second to Petra Burka in the ladies event.[62]

The 1965 Worlds were held for the third time at the Broadmoor. Alain Calmat of France, a ten-year-veteran of World competition, finally won the men's title and Canada's Petra Burka won the ladies title. Olympic pairs champions Ludmila and Oleg Protopopov and World dance champions Eva Romanova and Pavel Roman both won. The U.S. Team, competing on home turf, medaled in every division: Scott Allen pulled up from fourth to win the silver, Ron and Vivian Joseph won the silver in pairs, Lorna Dyer and John Carrell won the bronze in dance, and Peggy Fleming won the bronze—her first World medal.[63]

As a comeback, it was stunning. The Americans had won medals in every division at Worlds for the first time since 1959. This competition also saw the emergence of Peggy Gale Fleming as America's next skating star. Dick Button described her as "a skater who has a unique combination of athletic ability, technical control, great style and immense musicality. . . . [S]he does certain small things which I know from experience are difficult, hard to do and hard to learn, but some [judges] can't even realize she's doing them." Joey Heckert, who was on the World Team with Peggy, offered her assessment: "When Peggy skated, she was in the zone. She did not play to the crowd, but as you watched her, you felt as though she was letting you into her space—which was a great place to be."[64]

Following the 1965 Worlds, the Fleming family solved its financial difficulties by moving to Colorado. The Broadmoor absorbed Peggy's skating expenses and gave Al Fleming a job. Peggy conquered her endurance problems by training at the Broadmoor year-round, perfect preparation before going to 5,164 feet for the 1966 Worlds at Davos, Switzerland. Bob Paul had transformed Peggy's free skating, and now Carlo Fassi took her to the next level in figures. Carlo got along well with Peggy and, more important, with her mother, Doris Fleming.[65]

Christy Haigler, a Fassi student who placed fourth behind Peggy at the 1965 Worlds, fortunately had decided to retire. "Carlo was genuinely wonderful," Christy recalled. "He came to my family and said, 'I have this opportunity to work with Peggy, but I don't want to upset you.'" The Haiglers said, "Bring her in," and Peggy's figures improved dramatically under Carlo's guidance. Eventually, Tina Noyes worked with Carlo too, which meant that Fassi ended up coaching the entire 1964 U.S. ladies figure skating team.[66]

Carlo Fassi had yet to produce any World champions for the Broadmoor, but he had coached four World Team members since 1962. "Carlo had his own inner drive to succeed," Christa Fassi said. "He was competitive in everything. Even if he was playing Monopoly with his son he wanted to win. That was his nature." Carlo determined that Peggy would be the next World champion and took her to Colorado College's outdoor hockey rink to simulate her upcoming Davos experience. As Carlo worked on her figures, Bob Paul remained Peggy's choreographer. "She was made to work hard and she was very obedient and took all the advice," Paul said. "Peggy was very adaptable and had tons of natural talent. This girl floated through the air."[67]

Peggy was on her way to a World title, but Ron and Vivian Joseph retired. When they won the 1965 U.S. pairs title, they broke through the wall of anti-Semitism in U.S. figure skating. "I felt absolutely no bitterness whatsoever," Ron said. "I tell my kids it's a matter of training as hard as you can, working as hard as you can, and luck. Luck plays a huge part in all of this . . . and we had a good time doing it."[68]

When the 1965 Worlds were held in Colorado, the national press was a no-show. But the following year, all eyes were on Peggy Fleming. At the 1966 Nationals in Berkeley, Peggy won her third U.S. title, Scott Allen regained his U.S. title, the Kauffmans won their first U.S. pair title, and dancers Dennis Sveum and Kristin Fortune won their second title. Finally, there was some stability in the ranks as the 1966 U.S. World Team traveled to Davos, Switzerland. Davos had been a popular location for skating competitions for many years, but this year marked its final World meet because the outdoor conditions had been difficult and unfair for many of the competitors.[69]

Peggy continued to impress spectators at Davos. Her figures were nearly flawless as she piled up a strong forty-nine-point lead; Petra Burka, the 1965 World champion, came in second. "That's it!" a U.S. Team official pronounced. "Unless Peggy falls flat on the ice, she's got it in the bag." Peggy could have played it safe in the free skate, but she did not. She nailed all of her jumps with confidence and exhibited impressive stamina; the highlight of her number was her spread eagle-double axel-spread eagle combination. The capacity crowd rose to its feet as she finished her program. Peggy, conscious of pressure from the USFSA to win the World title, said, "Gosh, I'm glad the big scare is over."[70]

Suddenly everyone wanted to understand Peggy Fleming. Carlo Fassi, who worked the press with the same skill as Edi Scholdan, said, "[Peggy] has an excellent disposition, which makes her forget a bad practice in 10 minutes. But at the same time, she learns from all her mistakes. There is no doubt in my mind she is the best in the world." Featured on the cover of *Sports Illustrated*, she was, in the magazine's terms, "the most impressive U.S. skater in a decade."[71]

Petra Burka had lost her title, one of only four defending champions to lose their World title in the sixty-year history of the ladies division. Peggy certainly deserved her win, but Petra Burka had performed with a handicap, the circulatory problem known as Raynaud's phenomenon. Her legs went numb in cold weather, so she usually performed her warm-up with skates loosely laced, and then tightened them before she competed. "As the first skater in her group for freestyle, she didn't have time for the loose-laced warm-up, and during competition she couldn't feel her legs at all," *Sports Illustrated* explained. Petra had not skated her best, but Peggy's lead was so large she would have won anyway. Gabrielle Seyfert of East Germany placed second, and Petra had to settle for third.[72]

All the leading national magazines carried articles about Fleming's victory in Davos. The Americans did extremely well in all divisions, but the press continued to dwell on the crash. Typical was *Time*'s report: "The news from Davos, Switzerland last week still echoes that grim day of Feb. 15, 1961. Scotty Allen, the U.S.'s No. 1 male skater, finished fourth at the 1966 World Championships. The top American pair wound up third, the best U.S. dance team placed second behind a couple of Britons. Bad news indeed for a nation that had won 21 World figure-skating championships in 13 years before the 1961 crash."[73]

On the other hand, the USFSA was surprised that, only five years after the tragedy, a World champion had emerged. "In 1966 we probably had the best medal count at Worlds," dancer Dennis Sveum said. He and his partner Kristin Fortune won the silver, dancers Lorna Dyer and John Carrell won the bronze, Ron and Cindy Kauffman won the bronze in pairs, and Gary Visconti won the bronze—five World medals in total. For Peggy Fleming, the excitement of winning her first World title was diminished by news of her father's third—and fatal—heart attack. Albert Fleming, forty-one, who drove a Zamboni every morning at the Broadmoor, died weeks later while Peggy performed to appreciative audiences on a European tour.[74]

Pushing beyond her grief, Peggy easily won her fourth U.S. title at the 1967 Nationals, held at the Ak-Sar-Ben Arena in Omaha, Nebraska. Scott Allen and Gary Visconti had battled back and forth for the past two years, and Gary Visconti ended up with his second U.S. title. The Kauffmans won their second straight pairs title, and Lorna Dyer and John Carrell won their first U.S. dance title.[75]

The 1967 Worlds were held at the Vienna Ice Club, celebrating its centennial. Austrians had won thirty-two World championships, while the United States had only twenty-two. The outcome of this championship depended on five-foot-four-inch, 108-pound Peggy Fleming, who said, "I have everything to lose." By the end of three days of figure competition, she was ahead by sixty-nine points. Gabrielle Seyfert's mother/coach said with sad resignation, "Peggy is practically unbeatable."[76]

And, in fact, Peggy seemed unstoppable until the first minute in her free skating program, when she fell on her opening double axel. The audience gasped, but Peggy remained steady. "It crossed my mind that I had blown the event, but I refused to let that shake me." She skated the rest of her program perfectly, as if nothing had happened. Near the end of her number she successfully landed a double axel. The audience gave her a standing ovation, and all the judges gave her first-place votes. Still Fleming reproached herself: "I got a little behind my music and I was trying to catch up, and I got a little too close to the wall. That makes me mad, doing something I've done right in practice so many times." Peggy was hard on herself, but her competitors were in awe. "Peggy has no weaknesses," Gaby Seyfert said. "Everything Peggy does is pure ballerina."[77]

Peggy wasn't the only American making an impact. Gary Visconti vowed to pull up from fifth place; he blasted through his routine and won the bronze medal for the second year in a row. Ron and Cindy Kauffman won their second straight bronze in pairs, and Lorna Dyer and John Carrell won the silver in dance. Heading into the 1968 Olympics, the press predicted at least three medals for the USA.[78]

1968 OLYMPICS

At the 1968 U.S. Championships in Philadelphia, Peggy Fleming won her fifth straight title with one of the greatest performances of her life. The ladies team included Tina Noyes and newcomer Janet Lynn. Scott Allen and Gary Visconti, who had both won two U.S. titles, lost to Tim Wood of Detroit. Wood had placed tenth at the 1967 Worlds and had dropped out of college to spend more time on his figures. Visconti placed second; and an up-and-coming sensation, John Misha Petkevich, placed third. Surprisingly, Scott Allen, the wunderkind who had pulled off the impossible in 1964, placed fourth. The USFSA named the teams for the Olympics and Worlds—they sent Petkevich to the Olympics and eighteen-year-old Scott Allen to Worlds. Allen, who had been fourth at the 1967 Worlds, was a victim of the U.S. figure skating's incredibly strong men's division.[79]

Peggy Fleming was considered unbeatable for the Olympic gold medal in Grenoble, France; Gary Visconti, Tim Wood, and the Kauffmans were also considered potential medal winners. The American press anticipated Peggy's win. Her pre-Olympic fame had been enhanced by Charles Schultz in his nationally syndicated "Peanuts" cartoon when beagle Snoopy had a long-running dream of skating with Peggy. She got the biggest boost from ABC Sports, which broadcast same-day television coverage of Olympic events, for the first time in color, and generally in prime time.[80]

At the Opening Ceremonies, 1,150 athletes from thirty-seven nations paraded before French President Charles de Gaulle, while perfumed paper roses cascaded from the sky and school children waved sparklers. Alain Calmat, the 1965 World champion, lit the torch to open the Xth Olympic Winter Games in Grenoble. IOC President Avery Brundage pronounced, "May the sacred Olympic flame burn through the fog of misconceptions and misunderstandings." But politics soon erupted through this virtuous sentiment. As *Newsweek* noted, "The Russians held a news conference and denounced U.S. involvement in Vietnam."[81]

The ladies figures event took place soon after the Games began. Peggy was surprised by the whiteness of the ice, making it difficult to see figure tracings. However, after two days of figure competition, she had an extraordinary 77.2 point lead. On February 10, when the ladies free skating was scheduled, Peggy was too nervous to eat. "I felt an enormous burden of responsibility not to let myself or my country down," she said. Dressed in a chartreuse dress that her mother had sewn for her, "Peggy displayed her extraordinary grace while maintaining a degree of caution," *Newsweek* wrote. Her performance was marred by two missed jumps and Peggy later said, "I think I could have skated better." But her elegant style mesmerized the crowd who gave her a rousing ovation. As she came off the ice, she saw her mother, "which was wonderful. I only wish my father had been there." With a lead of more than eighty points ahead of her closest competitor, Peggy solidly won the Olympic gold medal.[82]

At the awards ceremony, Peggy stood tall on the winner's podium as "The Star-Spangled Banner" played. "This feeling," she said, "can never be shared—even by the richest people." Also on the podium were silver medalist Gaby Seyfert of East Germany and bronze medalist Hana Moskova of Czechoslovakia. Tina Noyes placed fourth, her best showing ever, and Janet Lynn placed ninth out of thirty-two competitors.[83]

Roone Arledge of ABC Sports, sensing there was something special about Fleming, devoted an entire evening of Olympic programming to her quest for the gold, making her an instant American celebrity. Her performance popularized figure skating. Every little girl wanted to be Peggy Fleming. More than anything else, Fleming's performance climaxed seven years of rebuilding U.S. figure skating. She entered the elite circle of American figure skating Olympic gold medalists: Dick Button, Tenley Albright, Hayes Jenkins, Carol Heiss, David Jenkins . . . and now Peggy Fleming.[84]

The United States was delighted with the gold medal, but there were more events. On Valentine's Day, the seventh anniversary of the 1961 Team's flight to Europe, the pair teams competed. The Kauffmans were third after compulsories; but after two falls in their five-minute program, they finished sixth, a huge disappointment. The Protopopovs won their second Olympic pairs title, with Tatania Zhuk and Aleksandr Gorelik of the USSR in second, and Margot Glockshuber and Wolfgang Danne of West Germany in third. The two other American teams, Sandi Schweitzer and Roy Wagelin, and JoJo Starbuck and Ken Shelley, placed seventh and thirteenth respectively.[85]

The men's final commenced two days later. The 1967 World champion Emmerich Danzer was expected to win, but fellow Austrian Wolfgang Schwarz held a slim lead over Tim Wood in figures. After the free skate, the margin was extremely close, but Wolfgang Schwarz became the 1968 Olympic champion. Wood received the silver medal; however, the possibility of two American gold medals had been within reach, as Tim Wood noted:

> When the [freestyle] marks went up, everyone told me I had won. I knew something was wrong when my coach said, "We have a problem." [It seems] one judge . . . made a mathematical mistake. He computed the marks the way you would at Worlds, and not at the Olympics. The USOC tried to fight it, but the rules wouldn't allow it. [The judge even] told the referee, but they couldn't do anything about it, because he had already written down the mark. Now it's different; if they make a mistake they can change it.[86]

To the delight of the French audience, native son Patrick Pera received the bronze medal. Emmerich Danzer had to settle for fourth, while Gary Visconti placed fifth, and John Petkevich placed sixth. Visconti did not win an Olympic medal, but he retired as two-time U.S. champion and two-time World's bronze medalist. "It made me feel good that I could be on the podium at Worlds several times, because [Doug Ramsay] would have been on the podium," Visconti said. "I was always thinking of Doug at those times."[87]

In light of Peggy's historic win, Tim Wood's silver medal performance did not receive the limelight it deserved. If Tim had won the men's gold, he would have received more press, but not as much as Peggy had. Olympic champion David Jenkins explained:

> It is just part of skating that the girls get more press. I never felt bad about it, but I will say that skating is better appreciated in Europe, where we would skate for crowds of 15,000. In the U.S. it was much different. We weren't going to make the front pages of anything but our local sports section. European men have more permission to express themselves aesthetically than men do here. It is an athletic sport with very strong artistic overtones. At its best, it is a wonderful combination; at its worst, it is the worst of all combinations. Since the time of Sonja Henie, figure skating was perceived as a woman's sport, and skating queens have existed ever since.[88]

The United States won seven Olympic medals in Grenoble—one more than in 1964. Besides Fleming's gold and Wood's silver in figure skating, the five other medals came in speed skating—more than U.S. speed skaters had accumulated in nine previous Olympics. Bob Paul, who coached Peggy along with Fassi, felt she deserved all the accolades she received. "Even though people would like to deny that [U.S. figure skating] would have come back anyway, it wasn't just that she snuck in there and won," he insisted. "She walked away with it. It was a tremendous boost for U.S. figure skating morale." The attention and adulation for the only American gold medalist of the 1968 Grenoble Olympics made Fleming a star. President Lyndon Johnson invited her to the White House, she performed in Ice Follies and Holiday on Ice, she starred in five NBC television specials, and she signed lucrative endorsements. Her fame has lasted for decades.[89]

Three decades after Fleming's Olympic win, six-time World champion Michelle Kwan said, "When you look back 100 years from now at figure skating, you'll still see Peggy Fleming." But in 1968, Peggy was unaware of the historical importance of her Olympic win. "I didn't have a clue," she said. "We were all naive on the impact we were having back then. I'm just happy the world was able to latch onto and appreciate such a beautiful sport."[90]

Recently *Sports Illustrated* named Fleming as one of the most influential athletes of the twentieth century. She is one of figure skating's most recognizable ambassadors, due to her work as an ABC sports commentator and as a spokesperson for breast cancer. Though Peggy got a boost because of the instability in the ranks due to the 1961 tragedy, fellow Olympian Carol Heiss said, "I think Peggy would have won the 1968 Olympics one way or another." For U.S. Figure Skating, Peggy Fleming will always personify the rebirth of skating in America.[91]

CHAPTER 20

THE MEMORIAL FUND

After Peggy Fleming's Olympic victory, U.S. figure skating was back on track. Between 1969 and 1972, Americans won eleven World medals, including two men's titles that Tim Wood brought home in 1969 and 1970. When Janet Lynn won the only U.S. figure skating medal at the 1972 Olympic Winter Games in Sapporo, Japan—a bronze just like Scott Allen's 1964 Olympic bronze—it seemed like déjà vu. But U.S. figure skating rebounded in subsequent Winter Olympics. Since 1968, there have been seven U.S. Olympic gold medalists: Dorothy Hamill in 1976 in Innsbruck, Scott Hamilton in 1984 in Sarajevo, Brian Boitano in 1988 in Calgary, Kristi Yamaguchi in 1992 in Albertville, Tara Lipinski in 1998 in Nagano, Sarah Hughes in 2002 in Salt Lake City, and Evan Lysacek in 2010 in Vancouver. In the eleven Olympics since Grenoble, American skaters have also brought home nine silver and eight bronze medals. In World competitions beyond 1968, American figure skaters have won twenty-eight gold, twenty-eight silver, and forty-five bronze medals.[1]

There are similarities between today's skaters and the 1961 Team: They train many hours daily on ice, they watch their weight, their expenses are exorbitant, and competitions remain a great social gathering.

In other ways, however, the 1961 Team would be surprised by today's competitive environment: the disappearance of figures from competition; intensive off-ice dance instruction; weight training and other fitness regimes; fewer club shows and more competitions; multiple coaches and frequent switching of coaches; the higher number of injuries due to the degree of difficulty in jumps, spins, and maneuvers; the ability to make money from skating; the abolishment of restrictions at private skating clubs, and the most jarring change—the new judging system.

The most significant change, however, is the financial support available today that simply didn't exist a half century ago. Prior to 1962, a middle-class family had to shoulder the costs of figure skating on their own. "You mortgaged your home to compete, many times over," one skater said. The family of Sarasue Gleis of Los Angeles was typical of many skating families in the late fifties:

My parents were able to pay for my lessons and go to local competitions, but the first time I made Pacific Coast, there was no money available for travel. My mother gave up smoking so I could afford to go. I had two sisters and a brother, and my dad worked two jobs. He worked at the racetrack all day, came home, had a quick dinner, and then worked at Hughes Aircraft at night until four or five o'clock in the morning, slept until nine, and then got up in the morning and did it all over again.[2]

Another example is that of Mary Batdorf Scotvold, coach for Olympic silver medalist Nancy Kerrigan. Mary and her twin sister, Anne, had both competed at Nationals—Mary won the novice title in 1959—but their father pulled both girls out of Easterns in 1961 because he thought the judging was crooked. "He wanted to make a statement and he did," Mary said. "We were only fourteen and I was devastated." Beyond the judging, however, the enormous cost of keeping two kids in skating had become too much. The girls lived at Lake Placid nine months of the year to work with Gus Lussi, who was the highest paid coach in the United States. Their grandfather funded their skating, but over time the money ran out. "In those days, you just had to quit—there were no other options," she said.[3]

Ten years later, after they were both coaching, Mary and Anne learned there had, in fact, been another option—one of the few that existed in the fifties. Their father told them that Edi Scholdan had approached him, inviting both girls to train under the Broadmoor umbrella. With free ice and lessons, both girls could have continued on their competitive track. "He told us if he had to do it over again he would have done it, but he knew that I was a total Lussi student and I could never have taken from anybody else," Mary said. "But if it meant I could continue to skate, I may have changed my mind."[4]

Other high-profile skaters also left competition prematurely due to finances. The USFSA picked Richard Dwyer to be a member of two World Teams, but he didn't go and instead turned pro. "There were times when I wished I could have gone to Worlds, so I could have had the experience," he said. Many skaters joined Ice Follies, Ice Capades, or Holiday on Ice because competitive skating had broken the family bank.[5]

At a time when every penny counted, World Team members did what they could to stretch their parents' dollars. Andree Anderson, who won two World dance medals in the late fifties, picked up a needle and thread. "I had a maroon dress and my partner, Don Jacoby, had a maroon monkey suit, as we called them, and I sewed both of them. The first year I competed, I made a dress with some red knit jersey for $1.98 a yard, and put some pearls on it; I only needed a yard so the dress cost $2.00."[6]

Sometimes a coach helped out a promising student who lacked funds. Slavka Kohout Button, coach of five-time U.S. champion Janet Lynn, is a case in point. She recalled:

> Walter Williamson, who ran the Wagon Wheel rink [in Rockton, Illinois], helped Janet with her expenses. This man gave me the opportunity to teach there, so I couldn't charge him for Janet's lessons. After the first two years of teaching Janet, I never charged another lesson. I needed to put something into it because Mr. Williamson paid for the European expenses and travel [for both Janet and me], so that's what I did.[7]

Occasionally, a wealthy skating patron individually sponsored an upper echelon skater. "There was a lot of sponsoring going on behind the scenes," Ron Joseph said, "but it was never offered to us, and it was definitely a struggle for my parents."[8]

From time to time, elite skaters received gifts for their exhibition performances. When U.S. World Team members went on exhibition tours, host countries gave them small gifts or small amounts of money to purchase souvenirs, but skaters had to be extremely careful to avoid jeopardizing their amateur status. Skaters from Communist countries, however, didn't seem to have the same restrictions, as Ron Joseph noted: "After we skated the World exhibition tour with the Protopopovs, they wound up with a stereo and a car from their government. [IOC President] Avery Brundage looked at us [funny] if we got a fifty-dollar watch. When we went to the Olympics, all we got was a coat, a patch, and a pair of great slacks."[9]

The need for American figure skating funding was acute even before the crash. Walter Powell, after seeing Russian skaters in Moscow in the late fifties, foresaw the new Russian revolution. Their contributions were undeniable—the Protopopovs introduced ballet, and Irina Rodnina and Alexei Ulmanov introduced power and phenomenal speed; their influence changed the sport forever. The controversy surrounding the Communist skaters, however, concerned their government-paid training. To the westerners, it screamed "professional" and it seemed unfair. The American skating community had long been aware of the need for serious funding, because the way it existed wasn't viable.

U.S. figure skating, along with other Olympic teams, was critically under-funded in the 1960s, but the broader athletic community seemed unsympathetic. When ABC did a series of programs highlighting sports prior to the Summer Games in Tokyo in 1964, *Sports Illustrated* thought it was terrible that the series raised the issue of money with the American viewing audience. "Various American athletes of Olympic ability come on to shill for funds to send the U.S. summer-games team to Tokyo . . . [T]heir slogan, 'Raise the colors more in 1964,' is about as un-Olympic an idea as you can find."[10]

The USFSA needed to raise money for its own athletes, and the need was dire after the 1961 tragedy. To address the problem, the "1961 U.S. World Figure Skating Team Memorial Fund" was established a week after the crash, on February 23, 1961. Once the USFSA announced the creation of the Memorial Fund, skaters were eager to contribute. "The Memorial Fund was a brilliant idea because there was no money—there was nothing," Peter Betts said. "It was a wonderful thing to do because everyone wanted to do something, and it made everybody feel better, to have helped out."[11]

The Memorial Fund was created before it was determined how the money would be used. The vision was broad: "for the general education of and the development of public interest in the art and sport of figure skating; and to help and assist figure skaters to reach their goals and objectives." Skaters made suggestions: trophies; scholarship funds; a college for skaters; an endowment to help worthy skaters attend competitions; a new USFSA building; or a skating museum. Some clubs wanted to donate money to help the families left behind.[12]

The Memorial Fund executive committee decided the fund should be used to help the living. By the end of the year, they established four objectives: (1) "To conduct figure skating clinics . . . to fill the gap left in the ranks of our top figure skaters;" (2) "the preparation of pamphlets and films . . . available for the use of those participating in clinics, clubs or judging schools;" (3) "Assisting in the travel expense of competitors to World Championships;" (4) "Providing a plaque in memory of the skaters, officials, relatives and friends lost in the Brussels disaster, to be hung in the Boston Office of the Association."[13]

The Memorial Fund accumulated $33,000 in its first year. The largest contribution was $13,000 from the Boston Ice Chips Benefit, held one month after the accident. "I worked my fanny off on that one, but it was a labor of love," producer Dick Button said. "Number one, I wanted to memorialize the crash. Number two, I thought it was a great opportunity for all of us to get together. Number three, I wanted it to be professionally good, and lastly, it was an emotional experience for us." The second largest contribution, more than $7,500, came from a benefit performance of Ice Capades in Pittsburgh. The USFSA solicited money directly through every U.S. skating club. Besides setting aside money toward the competitors' expenses for the 1962 Worlds, $4,000 was set aside for free clinics in twenty cities.[14]

Celebrating its fiftieth anniversary in 2011, the Memorial Fund has enjoyed its longevity because of one man—Ritter Shumway. His heartfelt devotion to figure skating, combined with his individual wealth, went a long way toward helping countless U.S. figure skaters.

Frank Ritter Shumway was born on March 27, 1906. After graduating from Princeton in 1928, and receiving a master's of divinity degree at University College, Oxford, in 1931, he became assistant pastor of the Larchmont Presbyterian Church in New York. Three years later he joined his family's business. His grandfather Frank Ritter, an industrialist, helped found the Mechanics Institute in 1885, the forerunner of the Rochester Institute of Technology. He also established the Ritter Company, which manufactured dental equipment and furniture. Ritter started with a salary of twenty dollars a week in 1934 and twenty years later was president of the company. He made a fortune. "In dentists' offices for years all you saw was 'Ritter'—that was their family," a coach said. "He owned all of that dental equipment—he did not sell it, he leased it." In 1968, he founded the conglomerate Sybron Corporation and was its chairman and CEO.[15]

Ritter was a modern-day Renaissance man. A sailor, he was commodore of the Rochester Yacht Club and was chief commander of the United States Power Squadrons, a non-profit maritime educational organization. He was active in business and civic activities, serving as president of the U.S. Chamber of Commerce in 1970. A noted philanthropist, he was once dubbed the "richest man in Rochester." He eventually gave away much of his fortune, estimated at fifty million dollars. His interest in young people and the community led him to leadership positions within the YMCA, Boys' Club, and Girls' Club. He gave generously to countless local and national organizations.[16]

Like fellow businessmen Walter Powell and Harold Hartshorne, Ritter had a tremendous zeal for figure skating. He was a pond skater as a boy and fell in love with figure skating after seeing the Ice Follies in 1939. After World War II, he began ice dancing lessons. In 1955, Shumway co-founded the Genesee Figure Skating Club on an outdoor rink. Needing a place to train, he donated money to the Rochester Institute of Technology to build an indoor ice rink on its campus. The Genesee club moved into the Ritter-Clark arena in 1955. Thirteen years later in 1968, a new rink, the Frank Ritter Memorial Ice Arena, opened, named for Ritter's grandfather.[17]

Ritter passed his pre-gold dance test at age fifty-five, and began competing in the veterans' dance at Easterns in 1953. With five different partners, he amassed a total of fifty-three gold, nine silver, and four bronze medals. "He had oodles of companies around the world, and no matter where he went, his skates were in his suitcase," coach Mary Lou Butler said. He joined the USFSA executive committee, became a national dance judge and ref-

F. Ritter Shumway, USFSA President, 1961-64; Chairman of the Memorial Fund, 1971-92. Source: World Figure Skating Museum.

eree, and rapidly acquired the expertise of an accomplished competition chairman.[18]

Ritter saw first-hand the need to provide better funding for international competitors. Gold dance runner-ups Andree Anderson and Don Jacoby became the de facto first place team in 1958 when the champions bowed out. "At first the USFSA wasn't going to give us any [money for the 1958 Worlds in Paris], but my mother called them," Andree recalled, "and said we were now the first place team so they gave us one airplane ticket . . . and that's where Ritter comes in. He had a tea dance to raise money, and they gave us luggage and the other plane ticket."[19]

Beginning in 1971, Shumway served as chairman of the Memorial Fund and raised money for the fund his entire life. In the early days of the fund, "Ice Folliettes," the show's chorus girls, fanned out through the audience to collect money during intermissions at performances. At club carnivals and competitions, volunteers solicited contributions from spectators during intermission. These activities soon waned, but Ritter never stopped. At many competitions, he personally collected donations in the stands and passed out patches and buttons to contributors. Ritter loved to skate in honor of the 1961 World Team; he and his partner Harlene Lee made themselves available for any benefit, performing their crowd-pleasing "New York, New York" number.[20]

In his own unique way, Ritter persuaded friends and colleagues to personally donate to the fund. In USFSA board meetings he would shift into his ministerial voice, "encouraging" each board member to dip into their own wallets to help out the skaters. As Ritter slowly wore them down, checkbooks would appear. Driving donations to the Memorial Fund became his personal mission.[21]

The skating world recognized Ritter's numerous contributions with his induction into both the U.S. Figure Skating Hall of Fame and World Figure Skating Hall of Fame in 1986. Two years later, the International Skating Union presented him with the Georg Hasler Medal in 1988 for outstanding service and personal dedication to figure skating, and the Professional Skaters Guild of America honored him in 1989 with a National Recognition of Achievement Award in his name, for "unending dedication and significant contribution to the sport of figure skating." Ritter didn't hang up his skates until failing health forced him to retire in 1991. The following year, Ritter Shumway died of neck cancer on March 9, 1992, just three weeks shy of his eighty-sixth birthday. Many old-timers sorely miss him to this day. Ritter personalized the story of the Memorial Fund by regularly getting on the ice and talking about all the wonderful people who died in the crash. "One of the greatest shining lights in skating has been Ritter Shumway," Peter Dunfield acknowledged.[22]

The Memorial Fund has gone through many transformations over the past five decades. Fundraising efforts have varied from appeals in competitive programs, to direct mail solicitations, to promos on television during Nationals, to special benefit exhibitions, to email solicitations. One funding source derives from the fact that judges are never paid for their services; beyond the compensation of transportation, hotel, and food stipends, competition organizers frequently give judges a small gift for their time and service; recently, these small gifts have sometimes morphed into a donation in their name to the Memorial Fund. *Skating* now regularly lists donations given either "In Memoriam" or "In Honor" of skating friends. This public acknowledgment has fueled regular contributions and kept the need for donations in the public's eye.

From its inception, the Memorial Fund has supported skaters when they reach certain benchmarks. Beginning with the 1962 World Team, the USFSA covered the international travel and lodging expenses for all team members. After awhile money went to high-level skaters for direct expenses such as coaching, skates, ice time, clothing, etc. However, a skater was never allowed to receive any cash whatsoever; skaters submitted receipts for reimbursement. Beginning in the eighties, donors were allowed to set up trust funds to help a designated skater.[23]

Currently there is a formula in place that allows equitable compensation for skaters receiving financial assistance from the Memorial Fund. Skaters must apply and meet eligibility requirements. One factor is that the skater must have placed in the top six in sectional, national, or junior national competitions. This means that support for young, maturing skaters can begin at the juvenile level, although most of the money makes its way to national novice, junior, senior, and international competitors. There are two levels of assistance: one for elite skaters and the other for collegiate skaters. For the former, the formula for financial distribution is based on how the skater has placed in competition, combined with an evaluation of financial need. For the latter, skaters must also submit a college transcript; more credit hours and higher GPAs may result in greater financial assistance. All applicants must submit a tax return.[24]

The chair of the Memorial Fund chooses the committee members, made up of skating officials, coaches, and at least one athlete from the Pacific Coast, Midwest, and Eastern sections, and together they review the applications. Although juvenile and intermediate competitors have an opportunity to receive funds, the majority of funds go to top-level competitive skaters. The amount of money distributed to each skater is not divulged, but it is only a fraction of a skater's yearly expenses. Over the last ten years, the Memorial Fund has provided athletic scholarships and academic grants to skaters totaling more than $3.8 million.[25]

The creation and existence of the Memorial Fund were critical in laying the foundation for future growth and accomplishment. However, the dynamics of need have changed now that competitive skaters can earn money. Some contributors worry that Memorial Fund money is funneled to those who receive lucrative endorsements and other sources of funding, but this is not the case. Memorial Fund money goes to competitors based only on financial need. Even though contributors do not know how the funds are distributed, the skating community agrees that continuing the fund is crucial, as coach John Nicks noted: "Sometimes it's been criticized, but I think it's been pretty well run. Some of my students were helped, but not a lot of money was involved. The big problem is . . . that those fourteen-year-olds coming up are good—but not that good yet—and still struggle a little." The Memorial Fund committee constantly reviews its policies, ensuring that funds support international competitors, while also boosting young novice level-skaters who are new to the U.S. Championships.[26]

Surprisingly, the USFSA has never obligated any skaters who reaped financial rewards to pay back into the fund, although many elite skaters have. A case in point is the Carruthers family. The Memorial Fund money was critical in helping Peter and Kitty Carruthers train for and ultimately win the Olympic silver medal in pairs at the 1984 Sarajevo Games. In their early years, their parents struggled to fund their children's skating; father Charlie Carruthers even sewed Kitty's costumes out of felt. Ritter often asked the family if they needed more help, saying, "You give those children everything they need, and it will be taken care of." Charlie replied, "It would certainly make things a little bit easier." After they retired, the Carruthers family reinvested in the fund.[27]

Memorial Fund contributors think the Carruthers' example should be emulated. "When my husband passed away we had some of the donations go to the Memorial Fund," long-time judge Bette Todd said. "A lot of the kids who made a lot of money could really give back to the Memorial Fund. It is the honorable thing."[28]

Many coaches, who were personal friends of the 1961 Team, are distressed that people don't know why the fund was established. That frustration would be lessened if Memorial Fund recipients had at least a working knowledge of the fund's genesis. "The younger generation knows absolutely nothing about the older generation," 1960 Olympic champion Barbara Wagner said. "A skater gets $1000, and she doesn't even have a clue what the Memorial Fund is about, the number of lives that were changed, how the direction of skating changed, or [any knowledge] of those that were lost, and how great they were." Some coaches have suggested that before skaters receive funds, they should learn about the history of the fund. This knowledge would greatly enhance their appreciation of the money and the value of this investment in their future would increase when they understand why the Memorial Fund was created.[29]

The birth of the 1961 World Figure Skating Memorial Fund did not prevent the creation of separate memorials across the nation. The Seattle SC set up the "Hadley Memorial Fund" and the SC of San Francisco established the "Bill and Laurie Hickox Memorial Fund." Both funds subsidized competitive travel. The Lake Placid SC renamed its existing annual scholarship the "Pat and Bob Dineen Memorial Scholarship," and the Providence FSC created the "Dudley Shaw Richards Memorial," an annual award given to the skater who made the most progress in skating, personality, and sportsmanship.[30]

Memorial trophies were also created. The Kelley family offered a trophy in honor of Gregory and Nathalie for the newly created Southwesterns competition. The Broadmoor club honored Sharon and Stephanie Westerfeld with a Midwestern juvenile ladies' trophy. In addition to the Roger Campbell and Dona Lee Carrier Memorial Trophy for the Gold Free Dance, the Southern California Inter-Club Association presented three other Pacific Coast trophies: the Diane Sherbloom Memorial Trophy for the bronze dance, the Rhode Michelson Memorial Trophy for senior ladies, and the Deane E. McMinn Memorial Trophy for the club winning the most points. Rose Anne Ryan donated the Daniel C. Ryan Memorial Trophy for dance competition at the Winter Club of Indianapolis. The Sun Valley FSC honored Harold and Louise Hartshorne with the Hartshorne Memorial Trophy for outstanding achievement in ice dance. Memorial trophies were named after many of the team members; but over the years, quite a few of these perpetual trophies have been retired, as decades' worth of names have filled up all of the trophies' available space.[31]

The Owen family was honored outside the skating world. A Vinson-Owen Memorial Scholarship Fund at Radcliffe College provided room and board and full tuition for one student each year; a new elementary school in Winchester was christened the Vinson-Owen School; and Laurence and Maribel Y. Owen were named to the Winchester Sports Foundation.[32]

The tragedy of the 1961 Team became the benchmark for every international skating victory or disappointment. If the U.S. Team bombed, it was measured against the fate of the 1961 Team; if any American skaters excelled, reports of their triumph also referenced the team. One of the worst-performing World Team showings in recent history was at the 1993 Worlds when American skaters were shut out of medals—ironically, in Prague. Coincidentally, the 1993 Canadian World Team won three medals, including the men's title and pairs' title, just as Don Jackson and Otto and Maria Jelinek had in 1962.[33]

The following year, at the 1994 Worlds in Chiba, Japan, the Americans did not win any medals for the second consecutive year, and U.S. standings declined in every event. The competition was the worst U.S. showing since 1936, and "even worse than the rebuilding years after the 1961 plane crash." Two years later, the Americans rebounded at the 1996 Worlds in Edmonton, Canada. Winning four medals, including the men's and ladies' title won by Todd Eldredge and Michelle Kwan respectively, was "reminiscent of the glory days of the 50s—the days before the 1961 plane crash."[34]

The legacy of the 1961 Team has been celebrated intermittently over the years. The USFSA celebrated its own sixty-fifth anniversary jointly with the twenty-fifth anniversary of the Memorial Fund in a skating benefit extravaganza called "Celebration . . . America On Ice!" in Indianapolis in 1986. Besides being the largest single gathering of U.S. champions in one place at one time to date, the highlight of the evening was a tribute to the 1961 Team, with video clips from its 1961 Nationals performances, accompanied by a song written by Jordan Bennett for the occasion: "A Time to Remember."[35]

One of the largest celebrations fittingly occurred in Boston, which hosted the 2001 U.S. Championships—the first time Boston had hosted Nationals since 1962. The New England Sports Museum at the Fleet Center staged a three-month exhibit dedicated to the 1961 Team. One day, 400 students from the Vinson-Owen Elementary School in Winchester visited the exhibit and watched the competition. Stories about the tragedy appeared in the program but featured only the Boston team members.[36]

Later in the year, a fortieth anniversary show, "A Skating Tribute," was scheduled for October 14, 2001, in New York City. The planning committee, made up largely of contemporaries of the 1961 Team, tracked down many of the 1961 family members and invited them to the event. But anticipation for this once-in-a-lifetime gathering was shattered by the events of September 11, 2001. The uncertainty about whether to hold the 1961 Worlds after the February 15 tragedy was similar to the debate about whether to proceed with the show. Many people wanted to cancel the event, but some felt that the story of skating's rebuilding after the 1961 tragedy was appropriate in light of the events of September 11.

The Madison Square Garden event went forward, although there were challenges. The peculiar circumstances altered the usual atmosphere of a skating show, as U.S. dance champion Charles Fetter noted:

> Outside the Garden [the air] smelled like wires burning, and you didn't really want to breathe. They were still working out security; there were long, long lines and police stationed everywhere. Later in the show, some big bang happened way up in the rafters. Everyone in my section ducked and looked. We were distracted because we knew this thing was happening on the ice, but other things were pretty important.[37]

The program featured a who's who of figure skating: five Olympic champions, nine World champions, and twenty-one U.S. champions. Performers included Linda Fratianne, Scott Hamilton, Rosalyn Sumners, Brian Boitano, Kristi Yamaguchi, Todd Eldredge, Paul Wylie, Nancy Kerrigan, Michelle Kwan, Tara Lipinski, Tim Goebel, and Sarah Hughes. A last-minute addition to this star-studded line-up was sixteen-year-old national competitor Joanna Glick, whose brother Jeremy was one of the heroes of the ill-fated United Flight 93, the last plane downed on September 11, 2001. Frank Carroll and Olympians Carol Heiss, Barbara Roles, and Ron Ludington contributed interviews and remembrances. Also on hand were Olympians Dick Button, Hayes Alan Jenkins, David Jenkins, and Peggy Fleming.[38]

The nationally televised evening was a compilation of skating, live singing, video clips, and commentary. "This group of skaters . . . [is] indeed the athletic descendants of all of those athletes of 1961," Dick Button said. It was a personally emotional evening for many skaters, as Scott Hamilton noted: "For me it was trying to let people know where [U.S. figure skating] came from, and what was done to help us. The evening . . . showed how far we have come after something horrible. We showed it's been done before, and it can be done again." After the event, family members, skaters, and VIP guests attended a reception at the Garden. There was a good representation of 1961 Team family members, but a number of families cancelled at the last minute because of the events of September 11th.[39]

A more lasting tribute to the 1961 World Team has been a series of inductions into the U.S. Figure Skating Hall of Fame. Early inductees were Maribel Vinson Owen in 1976, Harold Hartshorne in 1981, Walter S. Powell in 1993, and Maribel Vinson Owen again in 1994 with pair partner George E. B. Hill. A tribute to the 1961 Team coaches has been the induction of twenty of their former students into the U.S. Hall of Fame. In addition, the World Figure Skating Hall of Fame inducted Edi Scholdan in 1976 and Maribel Vinson Owen in 2002.[40]

These various recognitions culminated in a long-awaited announcement in September 2010 by U.S. Figure Skating. The entire 1961 U.S. World Team delegation, on the fiftieth anniversary of the tragedy, will be inducted into the U.S. Skating Hall of Fame during the 2011 U.S. Figure Skating Championships in Greensboro, North Carolina, in January 2011.

Besides memorializing the team, skaters of that era would love to know what really happened on the plane, because the crash was never satisfactorily explained. Lack of information left the door wide open for speculation. The official response of the USFSA officials at the time was that they themselves didn't know. "As to the cause of the crash, I do not know," Ken Kelley wrote a week after the crash. "There was, of course, a great deal of conjecture, rumor, argument, and some hysteria on the subject, both verbal and newspaper, but the facts developed so far do not seem at all conclusive, so far as I can see."[41]

Wayne Thomis, a World War II naval pilot and *Chicago Daily Tribune* aviation editor for twenty-five years, wrote a series of articles just weeks after the crash. Searching for clues, Sabena investigators theorized mechanical malfunction: a last-minute failure or jamming of the Boeing's flight control system, either in the wings or tail. However, no special inspections, replacement, or modification of parts had been recommended as a result of the crash, as Thomis noted:

> No operational changes in the flying or maintaining of the other Boeing 707 jet airliners now in use have come out of the investigations. These statements more than any other emphasize that no real clues to the cause of the accident have been uncovered. A resident Boeing engineer close to the inquiry said, "We haven't a single starting point." The investigators had recovered the mechanical screw-jacks and electric motors which operated the large horizontal stabilizer—the main focus of the investigation. Even after ground impact and subsequent fire, these still are in good working order.[42]

The most illuminating passage in Thomis's report was the condition of that era's black box. "Examination of the filmed tape of the flight recorder . . . disclosed that the autopilot was disconnected from the circuits and from all manual control of the plane approximately twenty minutes before the crash. If there were an electrical runaway, it could be stopped or reversed by seizing the elevator wheel on the pedestal. . . . Commander Louis Lambrechts and his colleague, Captain Jean Roy, were well trained in emergency procedures, both had flown Sabena's Boeing jets for more than a year, and both had taken written and flight examinations in how to prevent control runaways."[43]

Thomis's most sensational article raised the possibility of terrorist activity. He said investigators called the crash, "The Case of the Mad Boeing." He quoted Sabena technical experts and engineers who saw the drama unfold: "It was some of the wildest, most hair raising maneuvering of a giant airplane we ever saw," one eyewitness said. Another added: "It was as if the jet were being handled by a man who couldn't fly, or as if the crew were in a hand to hand struggle with jammed controls." From these eyewitnesses sprang one of Thomis's theories:

What were the crewmen in the Boeing's cockpit struggling against? A board of criminal inquiry is pursuing the possibility that someone aboard the airplane invaded the crew control area in the nose and physically interfered with the flight controls. FBI experts reportedly insisted upon the most exhaustive pathological examination of the bodies of the flight crew to determine whether they had been poisoned or shot.[44]

The USFSA discounted the *Chicago Daily Tribune* articles, but the stories struck a chord with skaters, as one noted: "That plane had been down in the Belgian Congo. I wouldn't be surprised if it was a terrorist thing that was hushed up by the government."[45]

Fifty years later, a wide variety of rumors continue to surface on the reasons for the crash—from ice on the wing to pilot error—but the most alarming are those that focus on a terrorist theory, based on the activities occurring in the former Belgian Congo at the time of the crash. However, there is no published documentation to verify or counteract any of these terrorist rumors, and terrorism remains conjecture.

The trouble in the Belgian Congo had begun the year before. After the Congolese rebelled against the Belgian government, they were finally granted independence on June 30, 1960. A coalition government was formed with thirty-five-year-old Prime Minister Patrice Lumumba and President Joseph Kasa-Vubu. In the beginning, Western governments had supported Lumumba but withdrew their support when Lumumba allied himself with the Kremlin, which sent massive military aid and a thousand Soviet military advisors to the Congo. Amid escalating violence, Europeans in the region fled. Sabena-owned Boeing 707s had made evacuation flights from the Congo for months. The Boeing 707 that crashed had just returned to passenger service after ferrying thousands of Europeans to Brussels.[46]

In September 1960, a coup deposed Lumumba, and he was put under house arrest. He escaped, was re-arrested in December, and was imprisoned with some of his colleagues. Reports surfaced on Sunday, February 12, that Lumumba had been killed. The new government under Kasa-Vubu confirmed the next day that Lumumba and two aides had escaped from prison and were killed by local tribesmen while they were on the run. Lumumba's supporters charged that they were the victims of a political assassination.[47]

The United Nations expressed its shock and promised full cooperation with an investigation. The Soviet Union denounced Lumumba's murder and requested an immediate withdrawal of the new government, the withdrawal of U.N. peace-keeping troops in the Congo, and the resignation of Secretary-General Dag Hammarskjold from the United Nations. President John F. Kennedy countered by confirming U.S. support for Hammarskjold, endorsing U.N. presence in the Congo, and affirming support for President Kasa-Vubu. Another cold war battle developed between the United States and the Soviet Union.[48]

On February 15, 1961, the two front-page stories were the crash of Sabena Flight 548 and riots at the United Nations in New York and embassies worldwide. Demonstrators broke through police lines and stormed Belgian embassies in Calcutta, Cairo, Moscow, Warsaw, Rome, and London; additional demonstrations occurred in Ghana, Paris, Chicago, Montreal, and Washington, D.C. When U.S. delegate Adlai Stevenson spoke at the United Nations, the proceedings were interrupted by a wild demonstration of screaming men and women. Because Belgian civilians were being arrested and beaten in the Congo, the U.N. encouraged any remaining Belgians and other foreign military and U.N. political advisers to evacuate.[49]

To this day, the Brussels Zaventem national airport has had only one crash: Sabena Flight 548. No further explanations have been given for the fatal accident. However, individuals have come forward with stories that support *Chicago Daily Tribune*'s Wayne Thomis's decades-old terrorist theory. Bill Wilkins, interviewed for this book, had lived with Ray Hadley one year. He came home early from college classes one day. "Ray was talking with some gentlemen dressed up in suits—they were from the FBI. They felt certain the plane had been taken down, because they had found a Russian machine gun in the cockpit."[50]

Most of the accident rumors came from Seattle, home of Boeing aircraft. "There were second and third party reports out of Boeing," David Mitchell recalled. "One story floating around was that there was a bullet in the pilot's head.... The rumors came out within months of the accident and then the story suddenly died—somebody put the lid on it." World pair champion Peter Kennedy, who worked at Boeing at the time of the crash, had had an insider's view of the investigation: "It never officially came out, but Boeing claimed the pilot was shot in the head, and that someone from the Belgian Congo took the plane down. This information came right down from the [Boeing] guys who went and checked out the crash, but the FBI didn't want them talking."[51]

It made sense that conspiracy theories would spring up in the Northwest because of its relationship to Boeing—but another terrorist story turned up separately. Palmer Hoyt, editor and publisher of the *Denver Post*, had personally known several American presidents, had been a houseguest in the White House, and numbered CIA among his acquaintances. "My mother said the Sabena cockpit was breached by the first aerial international terrorists and shot up," son Greg Hoyt said. "My mother told this story a number of times, and my father never refuted it." Another interviewee, speaking on conditions of confidentiality, also connected the unrest in the former Belgian Congo and the crash of Sabena Flight 548. But without access to investigation documents and forensic evidence, the mysterious crash of "the Mad Boeing" remains just that—a mystery.[52]

The crash, however, has not been forgotten in Belgium. Marie and Bob Pearce, who managed the Treadway Inn where the 1961 North American competitors stayed in Philadelphia, had a unique experience while living in Belgium in 1965. Before their daughters skated in an Antwerp exhibition, the president of the local club made an announcement. As Marie recalls, "he said he had been standing in the Brussels airport four years ago with bouquets of flowers for the U.S. Team. He witnessed the crash as he was waiting to hand out the roses to the girls. Now this was the first time that he had a chance to give American skaters flowers, and he gave bouquets of roses to my daughters." On February 10, 2001, the Belgians unveiled a stone monument on the site of the crash at Lemmekenstraat, Berg-Kampenhout. The Flemish inscription translates as: "Here, on February 15 1961, a B707 of SABENA went down. We commemorate the 73 victims."[53]

Other memorials of the 1961 Team exist in rinks across the country. Plaques are located at Iceland in Paramount, California, at Pickwick Arena in Burbank, California, at the Pepsi Coliseum in Indianapolis, at the Detroit Skating Club in Bloomfield Hills, at the Olympic Arena in Lake Placid, at The Skating Club of Boston, and two at the World Figure Skating Museum and Hall of Fame in Colorado Springs: the USFSA memorial plaque and one originally located in Allentown, Pennsylvania, on its way to the museum. The most iconic remembrance is the granite skating bench at the Broadmoor resort in Colorado Springs.[54]

But the prime memorial is the one carried in the hearts of those who personally knew the 1961 Team members, and those of later generations who owe a tremendous debt of gratitude to the 1961 Team. The U.S. 1961 World Figure Skating Memorial Fund, named in their honor, has helped generations of competitors represent U.S. figure skating impressively on the world stage.

CHAPTER 21

THE LEGACY

The determination to rebuild figure skating after the crash was strong; however, the emptiness lingered for years and the human impact on U.S. figure skating reverberates today. "For me it's like yesterday," said Pieter Kollen. "It's still as fresh in my mind now as it ever was." The news of the crash was "like the atomic bomb," and the anguish over the team's loss remains acute. "It stays with you these many years later. . . . It dashed our hopes for so many things," coach Sally Wells Van De Mark said. Coach Nancy Madden Leamy avoided The Skating Club of Boston for decades because it held too many memories. Men were equally affected. It took a long time for ice dancer David Mitchell to talk about the crash: "I get the chills and it still chokes me up . . . just remembering how I heard about the crash stops me cold."[1]

Emotions about the '61 Team hits friends when they least expect it, as Gary Clark explained: "I was sitting on the judges' stand, waiting to judge at Nationals one year. Suddenly, on the overhead screen, comes a montage of the '61 Team—all the people, their history, the wreckage. There was no warning that this was coming, and I started to cry—I just lost it. Then the lights come up, the skaters are on the ice, and my face is all red. I said, 'Wait! Give me a second to regroup.' I just couldn't shake it."[2]

There are reasons why the events of February 15 still haunt so many people. Figure skating was a small community in that era. Once skaters reached a certain level, they knew all the leading players, having interacted with them at summer centers or competed with them at the national level. *Skating*, which was published monthly from November to June, kept tabs on what American and Canadian skaters were doing. Skaters read issues from cover to cover, reread issues again and again, and kept a library of the magazines after retiring. *Skating* was prestigious; to be mentioned meant you had arrived.

Despite belonging to private clubs, skaters themselves were part of an open-door fraternity with no restrictions. After meeting at competitions or summer camps, they became pen pals. For the most part, everyone got along. Even intense rivals were good friends. This was because only other skaters understood the time, commitment, financial obligations, sacrifices, and joys derived from figure skating. The loneliness of discipline created a tight camaraderie among skaters across America.

After the crash, there were no counselors or crisis centers. Kids dealt with their sorrow on their own. Linda Landin's experience was similar to that of other young teenagers: "I tried to go to school and then I had to leave. I came home and just sat in the corner. . . . I didn't go to school for days. I just cried all the time. We all did. I didn't know how to handle it."[3]

Many skaters returned to the rinks, bonded with one another through their grief, and committed to rebuilding however they could, whether as competitors, coaches, or judges. For others, it was easier to leave skating behind all together. "It was so traumatic when everybody died," explained Diana Lapp Green, who had lived with Bill Swallender's family. "For years I was in shock. It was wild for all my friends to vanish in an instant. I [would] think about them and wish I could have a conversation with them."[4]

It wasn't just teenagers who fell apart. Skating veterans had lost their best friends, too. Dick Button recounted how the tragedy impacted him:

> I was woken out of a sound sleep at five in the morning. Priscilla Snow called me in a panic, in tears. I couldn't register what she was saying, and I kept saying, "Don't worry. It will be all right." She said, "No, no, no, you don't understand. They're all dead." At that moment, I came to. I hurriedly put an overcoat on to find the news. I walked down the street in my pajamas, with tears streaming down my face. I kept thinking, "They're all dead. They're all dead." It was such an enormous shock. It hit every aspect of my skating life. I had been raised with the older ones, like Harold Hartshorne and Edi Scholdan and Walter Powell, and then it was the new people I had been involved with, like Dudley Richards, and the young ones coming up. It was truly multi-generational for me.[5]

The tragedy was a peculiar experience for those who might have been on the 1961 Team. "I still can't believe it," Robert Brewer said. "I was really close with Maribel, Little Maribel, Laurence, and Dudley. I still have this feeling that I can call them up and talk to them. If one person dies, you realize it is bad and terrible; but when a whole family—one that you considered being part of—are now gone . . . I still can't accept it even today." For Brewer, his decision to leave the sport early has influenced his life in diverse ways. He never quits anything, as he explains: "The one thing in my life that I did quit was skating. It has always kind of burned in me. I could have been the World champion—Maribel could have taken me there—but I quit. On the other hand, if I hadn't of quit, I'd be dead—so where do I go with that? Still, because of the crash, I try to see everything through." Coach Peter

Dunfield, who almost joined the flight, was in free fall for a while. "When anybody loses that many close friends—a beloved fraternity—it was one of the great shocks of my life. At last I decided two years later, it wasn't going to wreck my life."[6]

For some, it took a lifetime to reconcile what had happened. Prospective 1961 Team member Vicky Fisher Binner recalls: "So much was left unfinished and unspoken. We were all fractured when they went down and had emotions that got stuffed. I had survivor's guilt. I turned inward and just tried to talk myself out of it; but in the end, it was healthier working on it. All of us have grown up with a shadow of grief that was so great. It's taken me fifty years to do it."[7]

Some youngsters couldn't pay their respects because their parents wouldn't let them attend the funerals, and they have never felt closure in losing their friends. Jennie Walsh Guzman attended funerals in Southern California; but through a mix-up she missed Rhode Michelson's service. It bothered Jennie so much that, when she was able to drive, seven years later, one of the first things she did was visit the cemetery to find Rhode's grave.[8]

Muriel LeMaire sheltered her daughters from everything. She didn't let them see a paper, a magazine, watch TV, or listen to the radio for months. However, it was difficult going to school. "The first thing I noticed was the flag at half mast, for my brother," said Dorinda, then eleven. "When I sat down at the lunch table, my friends got up and moved. I approached someone and asked, "Why won't you talk to me?" "We don't know what to say," they replied. "We don't want to upset you." Dorinda plaintively responded, "You could say hello." Diana, who was ten, was upset that her mother prevented her and Dorinda from attending the funeral:

> I was very close to Daddy and Dickie, and Mother was afraid I would fall apart in public. Her belief was that we "needed to rise above it." She never cried in front of us, and she knew I cried at the drop of a hat. She would have been very upset if I had cried at the funeral, so she probably did the right thing. We did go to a little memorial they had at the Day School, and she said, "Don't you dare cry." But how could you not? I remember welling up and trying to hold it in.[9]

Some families took Ritter Shumway's Memorial Service message to heart: "What should concern us, and what is of concern to God, is what happens to us who remain; for He has given us freedom to choose whether we go forward or go backward, whether we allow these experiences to make us finer, more useful people, or whether we allow them to crush us." Incorporating this message into their daily lives was an enormous challenge. Many family members valiantly tried and some succeeded; others withered away. In the days and years following the tragedy, every family had its own cross to bear.[10]

<hr/>

Seventeen children lost their fathers in the accident. Nine-month-old Bobby Dineen Jr. lost both parents. Dr. Joseph Dineen and his wife adopted their nephew. Now working in the film industry, Bobby showed up at the 40th Anniversary Tribute in New York City. At the reception, guests learned that Bobby didn't learn about his parents' deaths until he was older. Mary Dineen was forever haunted by the fact that she had given Bob and Pat the money for the airfare to Prague. She died in 1987 at age eighty-three.[11]

Widowed with five children, Rose Anne Ryan continued teaching at the Winter Club of Indianapolis. "It was difficult, but she was incredibly strong, and her family was always there helping out," Sally Schantz Urban said. Rose Anne also coached in Ottawa and Ontario, Canada, and in Watertown and Lake Placid, New York. She remarried and is now a real estate agent. The children are grown and have scattered throughout the East. The boys never skated but both girls did; Sheryl's son, Chris Nolan, has been a National pairs competitor.[12]

The crash of Flight 548 was the first in a series of calamities for the Hartshorne family; between 1961 and 1965, six family members died, claimed by a plane crash, falling from a cliff, in motorcycle accidents, or from cancer. Harold's death was particularly difficult for his teenage children. They lived with their Hatch grandparents or aunts and uncles until they were old enough to launch themselves. Son Dan had a checkered background in academics and joined the U.S. Army. After his military service, he graduated from Cornell and has worked in finance his whole career. Daughter Gail attended St. Johns in Annapolis, married, and raised a family. Daughter Daryl became a teacher and worked with learning-disabled children.[13]

Ruth Scholdan Harle, then eight, vividly remembered the morning of the crash. When she awoke, her nanny, Miriam, was upset, and the house was full of people crying, so she knew something bad had happened:

> A woman came in, sat down on my bed, and told me the plane had crashed and that Edi and Jimmy had died. I didn't know what to do or say because I didn't understand the words coming in. It took a while to process all of it. When I came out of my room, everybody made a big deal over me—so Father Harrington took me over to my godparents' home. They didn't know

what to do with me either, but several days later my mother arrived from Europe.[14]

Because Edi had had custody of the children, a court had to return custody of Ruth to her mother. After six months in Rhode Island, they moved to Austria. Edi would have been pleased that his baby girl grew up in his native country. As a bonus, she learned her father's tongue easily. "I grew up in the heart of the city and knew every square inch of Vienna—I loved it," she said. Ruth continued skating, but she soon hung up her skates because everyone had such high expectations of her, as Edi's daughter. In retrospect, however, she wishes she had made a different decision. "My father always wanted me to be a competitive skater, and if he had stayed alive I know I would have continued. I loved skating and it was very natural for me." At one point, Ruth envisioned building her own skating rink as a tribute to Edi. "I thought it would be a cool thing," she reflects, "but it turned out to be such a struggle." Ruth eventually returned to the United States, attended college, married, and has a daughter.[15]

In Europe Roberta gave birth to another son, Robert, and became a nurse in Austria, and then Rhode Island. Her life-long wanderlust inspired her to move to Nairobi, then to India. She lives part-time with her daughters in the States. Dixie graduated from college and taught skating in Dallas as she raised her family. Dixie and Ruth have remained avid skating fans and still skate occasionally. After Roberta whisked Ruth away from Colorado Springs in 1961, Ruth never returned. "It's not a burning desire," she said, "and maybe some things are best left to memory."[16]

Like the Scholdan girls, Dorinda and Diana LeMaire lost both their father and their brother. They grew up without skating; but years later Diana moved to Boston and U.S. champion John Petkevich encouraged her to take lessons. When she walked into The Skating Club of Boston, the woman at the desk said, "I have been waiting for this day ever since I saw your name. Your father was a member here, and I adored him. I was just waiting to meet you." Diana has grown closer to her father through his friends who have showered her with many stories. Diana has felt her father's presence her whole life. "I think he helped me get through some of my figure tests," she said, "by making sure the ice was very frosty so you couldn't really see the flat or change of the edge."[17]

After getting her mother's blessing to skate, Diana then asked her how she would feel if Diana began judging. "I had no interest in bringing up all the memories or having her ache any more than she had already suffered, but she said, 'No, it would be great,' so I had her support." Diana was pleased when judges across the country immediately recognized her name because of her father's legacy.[18]

Muriel LeMaire married Farison Jenkins and in 1999 passed away from colon cancer. "In the end she talked more about Dickie," Diana said. "It's so hard to replace a child." Diana credits her mother for instilling a positive outlook in her. "She used to say, 'At least you had them for ten years. Some people never had them at all.' She always had the silver lining, and I have always taken that with me. Out of the world's worst scenario, I will find something positive." Dickie was remembered at the Rye Country Day School with a Richard LeMaire Athletic Award and a Richard LeMaire Collection in the library, including his geology and mineralogy books. His grandmother had collages made from his geological rock collection and placed them in the family's Episcopal Church in Rye.[19]

———⊰⊱———

Sadly for five individuals, every other individual in their immediate families was killed in the crash. After the death of his wife and son, Alexander Campbell gave Roger's sweaters to other skaters to wear for figure tests and competitions. He also helped one skater with his expenses. Mr. Campbell had rarely come to the rink when his son was skating; and after the crash, he didn't stay in skating circles long. "We heard he had married a young woman and they went right through the [insurance] money in no time at all," Eleanor Curtis said. The last time anyone in skating saw him was in 1965; at the time he lived with his new wife on his boat in Marina Del Rey. He died in 1974 at age sixty-six.[20]

Myra Westerfeld had lived her entire life for her two daughters and was known to visit her daughters' gravesite often. She worked at Bryan & Scott Jewelers, the same downtown jewelry store where Sherri had worked. After the crash, Myra was dumbfounded to learn that Sherri had married a fellow employee at Bryan & Scott—Roberto Agnolini—in 1959. Sherri may have married her German friend so he could obtain his green card. None of her friends knew about this event, she retained her maiden name, and she continued to live with her family. Myra's constant companion after the crash was Sir Eric of Broadmoor, known as Seric, Sherri and Steffi's little black poodle, who was her last link to the girls. When he died, Myra collapsed, sobbing for days. The proprietors of the Evergreen Cemetery knew Myra well and took pity on her. Pet burials were not usually allowed, but a diamond-shaped marker in the Westerfeld family plot designated where Seric is buried. Myra passed away in 1984; when relatives acquired Myra's belongings, they found a box containing the reels of Stephanie's last filmed performances, but the containers had never been opened. "Her only solace in life was her memories of the girls and that eventually she would be with them," Eileen Seigh Honnen said. "That is what she focused on."[21]

Grammy Vinson remained a permanent fixture at The Skating Club of Boston. "She was remarkably resilient; and not long after the accident, she came to the rink and was very encouraging to everyone," Paul George said. The rink was the lifeline to her family. She attended every exhibition or gathering, and she always received lots of love and attention. In turn, many people visited her in her home and took take care of her; eventually club members moved her into a nursing home. Gertrude Vinson, age eighty-nine, passed away in 1969.[22]

Maribel Vinson Owen has no direct descendants, but her memory breathes fervently in the lives of her students, many of whom have become skating judges or coaches. "I learned how to teach from Maribel, and I can feel her spirit all around me at times," Nancy Madden Leamy said. But Maribel's students report feeling stung by The Skating Club of Boston's attitude toward her before and after the crash. "If you go there [The Skating Club of Boston], her pictures are plastered all over the place," Julie Graham Eavzan said. "It's ironic because she was turned down as a coach there for years. . . . [But now] they talk about how wonderful she was."[23]

Like Gertrude Vinson, Ray Hadley lost three loved ones and was despondent for the rest of his life. "After the crash, he became a very changed person," a skater commented. Ray turned to alcohol for solace. He was only forty, but he turned into an old man overnight—he lost weight, his skin turned yellow, his hair turned white, and his face became drained. Many skaters did not recognize him anymore, and teenage skaters were ill prepared to interact with this forlorn figure. "I couldn't find the words," one skater said. "You felt sorry for him because you could see his pain and anguish." Ray taught less after the insurance money came in. Linda had taken out insurance for the first time—double indemnity times three. He and Linda had dreamed of creating their own skating line, so Ray went to Japan and produced skating boots and skirts under the "Hadley and Hart" label. However, the line never really got off the ground, and the basement became a permanent warehouse for Hadley boots.[24]

Skater Bill Wilkins moved into Ray's home while attending college and slept in Ray Jr.'s attic bedroom. Ray had redone Ila Ray's room but no one was allowed to enter it. "The house ended up being a monument to the family," Bill said. He was initially drawn to Ray because he had planned to propose to Ila Ray when she returned from Prague, but he finally moved

out because of Ray's downward spiral. He was stunned to note that the basement was full of cases of beer, delivered by the semi-truckload. "He was going down the wrong path and there was nothing that anyone could do about
it." Ray's erratic behavior and inability to pull himself together led to a
quickening erosion of students and staff. "I was in the office and tried to
help but we became completely disappointed and didn't want to be around
him anymore," Arvilla Kauffman said. After Ray couldn't operate the studio,
a friend tried to run it, but by 1963 it had closed.[25]

Ray seemed to stabilize when, in December 1962, he married Lois
Kirner, a roller skater and ice dancer he had known for years, who had four
children of her own. However, marriage and a new family could not save
Ray from his demons. Five years after the crash, on February 19, 1966, Ray
passed away, just three days shy of his forty-fifth birthday. [26]

Helen Powell continued to skate after her husband's death. The St.
Louis SC hoped that Helen would buy the Winter Garden rink and put
Walter's name on it, but Helen had other ideas. The Powells had been
long-time patrons of the St. Louis Symphony and were close to St. Louis
SC President Katherine Wells, whose husband was president of the symphony. In need of a permanent home, the symphony had recently acquired a
1925-era vaudeville theatre, but it was badly in need of renovation.[27]

Helen Powell gave one million dollars to the symphony, which along
with a Ford Foundation challenge grant, provided the necessary funding.
The refurbished theatre opened in 1968 as the Powell Symphony Hall, its
restored 2,689-seat hall modeled after the royal chapel at Versailles. Violin-
ist Isaac Stern said Powell Hall ranked with Carnegie Hall in New York and
Symphony Hall in Boston. Listed in the National Register of Historic
Places, the elegant performance space is a long-lasting tribute to Walter
and the town he lived in for so many years. But the skating community
thought Walter would have made a different decision. "I think Walter is still
doing nip-ups because she endowed that symphony and she did not do that
much for the USFSA," coach Sally Haas Knoll said. "I imagine when they
meet up in heaven there may be a bit of a squabble." A million dollars could
have gone a long way in rebuilding figure skating after the crash.[28]

Helen continued to show up at skating events, accompanied by skater
"Jack Frost, who was about twenty-five years younger," according to a
friend. "We all knew why he married her, but he was very kind to her, so we
didn't care [about the reason] because he made her happy." Helen gradually
lost touch with her skating friends as the new couple moved about—Sun
Valley, Squaw Valley, Lake Tahoe, even Boston or Hawaii. Some thought
they had divorced, and some understood that Helen and Jack had never

married at all, suggesting it was purely an arrangement of convenience. She was used to being looked after, and he enjoyed their affluent lifestyle. But everyone agrees that Helen was devastated when Walter died, found someone to take care of her, and was very happy in her later years. And, sadly, Walter's money did not go to U.S. figure skating.[29]

Although the parents in two families—the Carriers and the Hickoxes—still had each other, they lost all of their children on February 15, 1961. With their flight insurance money, Floyd and Eleanor Carrier bought a hilltop home overlooking Forest Lawn, from which they could see the site of Dona Lee's grave. They commissioned a huge oil painting of their daughter to fill the space above their fireplace and Dona Lee's bedroom looked identical to her apartment bedroom—only bigger. Eleanor came to the rink often to talk about her daughter and brought a cake for the skaters on Dona Lee's birthday, but her eagerness to talk about the accident was off-putting. "She talked about the plane crash right in front of me and it was very upsetting," Joan Sherbloom Peterson recalled. Still, understanding the depth of her loss, the skaters tried to be as supportive as possible. Eleanor's primary concern was that Dona Lee be remembered. She donated numerous trophies in her daughter's name, including an enormous trophy for Los Angeles FSC gold medalists; the names of over 300 gold medalists are now engraved alongside Dona Lee's.[30]

Reverend Floyd Carrier also found it hard to accept his daughter's death and admitted that it was easier to comfort other people in their sorrow. He died in 1968. Eleanor often got up at 3 A.M.—the time she learned of the tragedy—and watched the USFSA films of her daughter. She passed away at age ninety-four on March 5, 1999.[31]

After her two children died, Elinor Hickox lived in the past. "They practically had a shrine in their house for years and wouldn't get rid of anything," a judge said. Elinor's hair turned white overnight, and she retreated into a shell. "She blamed herself because she wanted them to go so badly," coach Julie Barrett said. When Lute became a judge Ellie traveled with him, but she wouldn't go into the rink. Future USFSA President George Yonekura got her involved in the St. Moritz club by appointing her test chairman for the Judges Bureau. "She was the perfect person because of her skating background and because she could do it at home," he said. Elinor served as test chairman for a few years, also accompanying Lute to Inter-Club meetings. Elinor "took their picture everywhere and spoke about the kids," judge Joan Brader Burns said. After Lute stopped judging, he still returned to the rink annually to present the Hickox trophy at regionals. Elinor passed away on February 21, 1984, at age eighty-two, and Lute followed her three years later at age eighty-eight on December 3, 1987.[32]

Bill's girlfriend, Anne Frazier, married after her sophomore year at Smith to a diplomat also named Bill, who was six feet tall and had red hair—but there the similarities ended. They eventually divorced, and she returned home to California and taught group skating lessons in Berkeley. One student was future Olympic champion Kristi Yamaguchi, whom she taught for six years.[33]

Some families found it too painful to stay involved with the skating world. Vincent and Nathalie Kelley rarely visited The Skating Club of Boston after the accident that took Greg and Nathalie. "My father was devastated; and from that point on, wasn't himself," brother Stephen said. Ashland High School created a scholarship for Nathalie, and so did Sacred Heart in Newton in honor of Greg. Vincent Kelley died in 1975 at age seventy-five, followed by Nathalie two years later at age seventy-three. Stephen named one of his sons Gregory after his brother.[34]

Arthur Michelson had been president of the DeMorra Speed Skating Club; but after Rhode died, he lost all interest in going to the rink. Mike Michelson recalled: "I was fourteen and we lived quite a ways away, so the driving force—the person that would drive me to the rink for speed skating—that all dried up." In 1966, five years after the crash, Arthur Michelson died of a heart attack at age forty-nine. Marty Michelson passed away in 1990. Before Mike passed away in 2006, he expressed appreciation to the Memorial Fund for honoring the 1961 Team: "There are other people who have died and then you never hear about them. We will always hear about this crash. It was tragic that it happened, but it's good to see that something good has come out of it."[35]

The Ramsays regretted their decision to let Doug go to Prague at the last minute. Doug's skating had been the center of Jean Ramsay's world, and she dealt with her sorrow by sewing around the clock. "She could never get over his death, but I don't think anyone ever would, over a child," a sympathetic Detroit skater said. The parents divorced. In 1980, Jean Ramsay passed away. After the crash, the Detroit Skating Club renamed the skater's lounge the "Ramsay Lounge," displayed a five-foot black-and-white photograph of Doug in the rink, and created a Doug Ramsay Trophy—a large trophy featuring one of his bronzed boots. The Detroit Skating Club still honors his legacy at an annual award ceremony.[36]

Genevieve Swallender sold her home and her husband's ice studio seven months after the crash and moved in with her family in Minneapolis. By 1962 she had married her brother-in-law, Charles Simpson. Bill's sister, Madeleine, had died during childbirth in 1945, leaving Charles to raise the baby on his own. Gen was extremely ill after Bill died, and Charles stepped in and rescued her, as friend Christy Hansen White noted: "Gen once said 'He saved my life.' She couldn't have lived without Charles, but it's hard to lose your first love. She rarely talked about Bill, but when she did, she always said how devastated she was." Other than the occasional Ice Follies reunions, she left the skating world behind.[37]

Although some families felt uncomfortable in the skating world after the tragedy, the Kipp family embraced it. They were hit hard by the death of their youngest brother, but they kept Bill's spirit alive by going to regional shows and competitions, and watching every skating event on TV. "Bill believed that skating needed to have more visibility on TV and needed more publicity," sister-in-law Ruth said. "He would be happy to know his visions came to fruition." Bill's mother and all of his siblings have passed away, except for sister Timmy, now eighty-six, who still goes ballroom dancing—a fact that would have definitely pleased Bill. "I would like him to be remembered as he was—a happy, honest, and sincere person," she said.[38]

Dallas and Nellie Pierce always had difficulty talking about the accident, but it didn't prevent them from opening their home to skaters, just as they had when Larry was alive. A number of skaters lived with them and others visited often. In addition to continuing their de facto parenting of young skaters, they relied on their religious faith. Dallas wrote to Ritter: [We] take quite an active part in our church and receive just the help and strength through this connection to stand up under the cross we have to bear, but isn't it wonderful that we have the assurance that we will all be joined together again up there—Wonderful Peace of Mind. . . . [S]omeday I expect to see Larry again and I will expect to see you there too." Dallas died in 1986, followed by Nellie ten years later.[39]

Deane McMinn's brother Richard died in 1967. Three years later, so did their mother, Pearle. Deane's legacy was the success of the Arctic Blades FSC. Many of his protégées became national and world judges. His best friend, Bob McLeod, became the USFSA first vice president in 1973, and Deane's dance partner, Betty Sonnhalter, became the first USFSA woman officer when she was named third vice president in 1977. Beginning in 1962, the Arctic Blades FSC took home the Harned Trophy six times.[40]

Lefty and Alfreda Lord felt that everyone in the skating world—particularly the USFSA and The Skating Club of Boston—did all they could do to help them, but Alfreda was never again the same person. She struggled against depression, finding comfort in watching films of Bradley from Nationals and North Americans. The Lords continued to attend club functions and kept in touch with Bud Wilson until his death from cancer. A circle of Brad's friends kept in touch with Alfreda throughout her life. "I wanted her to know that I cared about her loss, and that I had suffered the loss of a friend," Aloise Samson Lurtsema said. "She appreciated hearing from people who knew Brad, and I think it helped to keep Brad alive." Lefty passed away in 1978 and Alfreda died in 1990. Bruce Lord named his older son Bradley.[41]

The year 1961 was the only time the USFSA had paid Dudley's way to Worlds; he had paid his own way on five other trips. The Richards family believed Dudley would have retired before the 1964 Olympics because he was in love with Little Maribel and was anxious to get back to his real estate business. "I think he was ready to retire soon, but he wanted to stay active in skating because he wanted to be on the USFSA committee," said sister Susan, who named one of her sons Dudley. "Despite the tragedy, a lot of good came because the Memorial Fund helps young skaters." Susan has a stinging memory from the time of the crash: "The Boston newspapers listed where he lived, and someone robbed his sixth floor apartment. That has always stuck in my mind because the elevator was broken and they had to carry the stuff down all those flights of stairs."[42]

Joan Sherbloom Peterson enjoyed her skating career, excelling in silver dance with Dave Turner. Being at the Polar Palace was therapeutic because it was like being with family. "When I was at the rink with everyone, it was like it didn't happen," she explained. "That way I didn't have to face the reality of it every day." The LAFSC provided free ice time for a year and her mother was grateful, "for it keeps her occupied so she won't miss Diane too much." The girls' father had trouble focusing on work, but his wife insisted, "You have to go on—you have another child." Joan felt that the children left behind were overlooked in this human tragedy. "Everybody was worried about the parents, but I couldn't talk to my parents because I didn't want to upset them. At school no one would talk to me, because they didn't know what to say. I ended up internalizing everything." Joan retired from skating in 1971, married, and had two sons. Tom Sherbloom died in August 1985, and Ruth Sherbloom passed away in December 1991.[43]

———•———

The landscape of ice rinks has changed dramatically in the last fifty years, and some of the skating centers frequented by members of the 1961 Team have vanished. The first casualty was the Polar Palace in Hollywood, where Diane Sherbloom, Dona Lee Carrier, and Roger Campbell had trained. In May 1963 there was an explosion at 2:30 A.M. "We lived behind the rink and we heard a boom," Jennie Walsh Guzman said. "People were yelling 'The back's on fire.' I ran down the street and found out it was the rink." Word spread quickly, and many skaters rushed to the scene to retrieve their skates from their lockers, but it was too late. "It was all made of wood, so it was a really hot, fast fire," Jennie recalled. "Mabel Fairbanks always had a box of donuts to bribe people to come to her Thursday morning session, so a bunch of us sat there eating donuts as we watched them put out the last embers at six o'clock in the morning. . . . It was like watching a death."[44]

Joan Sherbloom Peterson was one of the lucky ones who hadn't left her skates at the rink. Almost everything perished, but one special item survived, as Joan recalled:

> My father made the plaque honoring the 1961 Team. After it was cast, I took it to the Polar Palace that night [just days before the fire] and they hung the plaque in the club room. Over the next couple of days, the skaters sifted through the rubble and they came across this hunk. It was the plaque. It was the only thing that survived the fire. We were thrilled, but it had been damaged. When I returned it to be fixed, this guy noticed the names on the plaque. He said, "Is this your relative?" and I said, "It's my sister," and they did it for free. Originally the plaque was a goldish bronze, but to cover up some of the scars from the fire he darkened it.[45]

The plaque honoring Roger Campbell, Dona Lee Carrier, Deane McMinn, and Diane Sherbloom now hangs in the Pickwick Ice Arena in Burbank.[46]

Sutros, where Bill and Laurie Hickox trained in San Francisco, also burned to the ground. The old relic had been condemned in 1964 and vacated. Soon after, a fire engulfed the venerable edifice, reducing it to ruins. The Skating Club of San Francisco now claims two rinks as its home, Belmont Iceland and the Yerba Buena Ice Skating Center.[47]

Both of Doug Ramsay's skating homes are gone. The Detroit Skating Club on Seven Mile Road was sold in 1978, and the investors planned to

turn the former stable-turned-ice rink into a gymnastics center. Before re-
modeling began, however, vagrants set the place on fire. The memorial trophy and photograph of Doug Ramsay now are housed in the new DSC rink
in Bloomfield Hills, which has three ice surfaces. The Swallender Ice Studio on nearby Six Mile Road was sold to coach Don Stewart and renamed
the McNichols School of Skating but closed seven years later.[48]

The Seattle Civic Arena, the training home of the Hadley family, has
been condemned as structurally unsound. The club now skates at the
OlympicView Training Center in Mountlake Terrace. A construction company bought the Hadley and Hart Studio in 1963; recently the building was
demolished.[49]

The Winter Garden Ice Palace in St. Louis where Walter Powell had
skated was up for sale in the sixties. An investor turned the property into a
shopping center. The St. Louis SC moved several times and is now housed
in the Brentwood Ice Arena.[50]

The Broadmoor World Arena, site of the 1961 U.S. Championships,
closed its doors in 1994. The fifty-five-year-old rink was razed to make an
expansion of the golf course and new condominiums. The Broadmoor
Skating Club moved down the road to the new Colorado Springs World
Arena and an adjacent two-surface Ice Hall, built in 1995. The Professional
Skaters Association, in honor of its first president, Edi Scholdan, named its
annual awards "the Edi."[51]

A number of 1961 training centers still exist but lack the cachet they
had in the sixties. "After the crash, it was never quite the same at East Lansing; from then on it was never a big Mecca," Joanne Heckert Bachtel lamented. The old MSU rink is now the home of the ROTC. A new hockey
rink, the Munn Ice Arena, was built in 1974.[52]

From the outside, The Skating Club of Boston on Soldiers Field Road
looks the same. However, the 1961 tragedy diminished the club's spirit, and
it never regained the same prominence. The 1963 ladies champion Lorraine Hanlon and 1963 dance champion Sally Schantz were the last U.S. senior champions to represent the club.[53]

The Winter Club of Indianapolis, where Danny Ryan coached Larry
Pierce and Diane Sherbloom, still makes its home at the renamed Pepsi
Coliseum at the Indiana State Fairgrounds. A string of coaches, including
Red Bainbridge and Ron Ludington, came and went after the crash. Judy
Schwomeyer Sladky, whom Danny taught when she was small, became
five-time U.S. dance champion and four-time World medalist with Jim
Sladky. The current head coach at WCI is her sister Sandy Lamb, who be-
gan taking from Danny and Rose Anne in 1955.[54]

The Skating Club of New York (SCNY) has had several homes since the 1961 plane crash. Harold and Louise Hartshorne, Eddie LeMaire, and Bob and Pat Dineen skated at Iceland, but the rink was demolished when Madison Square Garden on West 50th Street and 8th Avenue was torn down to make way for the new Garden on 7th Avenue between 31st and 33rd Streets. The SCNY moved into new quarters at the Skyrink on 33rd Street and 10th Avenue, which opened in 1967. In 1995, the SCNY moved into the ice facilities on Pier 62 at Chelsea Piers.[55]

Frank Zamboni passed away in 1989, but the Zamboni family still owns the Iceland arena in Paramount, California, where Bill Kipp trained Rhode Michelson, Roger Campbell, and Dona Lee Carrier. After the crash, Arctic Blades was one of the most prominent clubs in the United States; but after declaring a bankruptcy in the nineties, the club moved to Lake Arrowhead.[56]

The Iceland rink in Berkeley, California, where Maribel Vinson Owen taught, and Little Maribel, Laurence, and Bill and Laurie Hickox trained, has temporarily closed. Local supporters formed "Save Berkeley Iceland"— a grassroots fundraising effort to bring the rink back to life.[57]

The Sun Valley rink, where Harold and Louise Hartshorne and Bill and Laurie Hickox skated during the summer, continues to be a popular tourist destination. Olympic silver medalist Linda Fratianne had been now head professional; and during the summers, the weekly ice shows have included Olympians Nancy Kerrigan, Brian Boitano, and Sasha Cohen.[58]

In Lake Placid, New York, the Olympic Arena has been renovated and continues to provide year-round training. The summer skating program, which included many 1961 Team coaches and skaters, is now in its seventy-fifth season. Lake Placid's rich history includes hosting the Olympic Winter Games for a second time in 1980 in a new rink built for those Games.[59]

One reason the preeminent skating centers in 1961 have lost their luster is the sheer number of rinks that now exist. Figure skaters had few choices fifty years ago. Southern California, which boasted more indoor rinks than other metropolitan areas, had six ice surfaces in 1960. Now there are more than two dozen. The proliferation of ice rinks across the nation in the last few decades has been spurred by the growth of hockey, but U.S. figure skating has also benefited from the availability of ice surfaces across the country. Any youngster in America who becomes interested in figure skating now has a greater opportunity to become a future champion.

The popularity and prominence of leading ice skating facilities varies primarily with the coaching staff. The natural talent and work ethic of a given skater has always been paramount, but the choice of a coach is also vital. A superb coach not only refines a skater's skills but has the instinct and the expertise to turn students into champions.

The loss of the 1961 Team was doubled by the loss of coaches. Skating lost its best-known coaches—Maribel Vinson Owen, Edi Scholdan, and Bill Swallender—and its most promising coaches—Bill Kipp, Danny Ryan, and Linda Hadley. Equally significant were the 1961 World Team competitors who might have coached the next generation. The vacuum prompted some competitive skaters, like Barbara Roles, Tim Brown, Jim Short, and Karen Howland, to move into coaching.[60]

A number of the top coaches in the past fifty years first gained prominence in the crucial period of rebuilding after the crash. Among the hundreds of coaches who have produced multiple champions over the years, Carlo Fassi, Ron Ludington, Frank Carroll, and John Nicks have been considered some of the most successful and influential. "We had lost our entire group of elite coaches . . . the cream of the crop," Ludington said, "but it opened doors for people like me and Carlo Fassi and John Nicks. Our careers blossomed."[61]

Carlo Fassi coached more Olympic champions than any other U.S. skating coach: Peggy Fleming in 1968, British champion John Curry in 1976, Dorothy Hamill in 1976, and British champion Robin Cousins in 1980. Fassi started at the Broadmoor, moved to Denver in 1969, returned to Colorado Springs, and ended his coaching career in Los Angeles. While coaching during the 1997 Worlds in Lausanne, Switzerland, Fassi died of a massive heart attack on March 21, 1997, at age sixty-seven and was immediately inducted into the World Figure Skating Hall of Fame. He had already been inducted into the U.S. Figure Skating Hall of Fame in 1994. "I owe him so much," Peggy Fleming said. "He was like your father, your mentor, your strength when you didn't feel you could do it. He always brought out the best in me, like no one else has ever done." Christa Fassi continues to teach in Los Angeles.[62]

Ron Ludington has coached skaters in nine Olympics and thirty-six Worlds. The highlight of his career was taking eight students to the 1984 Olympics. Starting in 1957 when he was a competitor, Ludington had been to forty World Championships in a row—except for 1961. "Oh yeah, it occurred to me that that could have been me," he said. His professional accolades include his induction into the U.S. Figure Skating Hall of Fame in 1993 and the World Figure Skating Hall of Fame in 1999. One of his most prized possessions is a photograph of Maribel Vinson Owen, prominently displayed in his office. "A lot of people looked at her and said she was too demanding, too difficult, and too rough on her skaters. But I know that if she hadn't been that way with me, I wouldn't be where I am today. I would love for Maribel to know how we're doing."[63]

Frank Carroll also turned to coaching because of Maribel Vinson Owen's strong influence on his life. After he retired from competitive skating in 1960, he joined Ice Follies, but Maribel encouraged him to quit and go to law school. "Now, remember," Maribel had told him, "this is your last year in the show . . . . And if you're not out of it, I'm going to call and have you fired!" Frank stayed in the show for more than four years, did a brief stint in movies, and then started teaching skating in Van Nuys, California. Since then he has coached Olympic medalists Linda Fratianne, Michelle Kwan, Timothy Goebel, and Olympic champion Evan Lysacek. Frank was inducted into the U.S. Figure Skating Hall of Fame in 1996 and the World Figure Skating Hall of Fame in 2007. Like Ludington, Frank wishes Maribel could see her legacy. When he coached Michelle Kwan he said, "I would hope that Maribel would be proud of the way Michelle skates, and I hope she'd be proud that there's a tradition from her, passed on to me, to my skaters. And I hope that they skate somewhat like she would envision them to skate if she were their teacher."[64]

John Nicks taught at Paramount's Iceland from 1961 to 1971. After taking his students to Canada for two summers, Nicks spent the summers of 1965 through 1968 at the Broadmoor at the invitation of Carlo Fassi, who had been a good friend ever since they met at the 1948 Olympics in St. Moritz. "He was a free spirit, and much more interesting than me," Nicks confessed. Nicks taught many champion skaters over the next five decades, including 2006 Olympic silver medalist Sasha Cohen, but his claim to fame was his pair teams: 1971-72 World bronze medalists JoJo Starbuck and Ken Shelley, 1979 World champions Tai Babilonia and Randy Gardner, and 1998 World silver medalists, Jenni Meno and Todd Sand.[65]

Even though he was inducted into the U.S. Figure Skating Hall of Fame in 1993 and the World Figure Skating Hall of Fame in 2000, Nicks, who replaced Bill Kipp at Iceland in Paramount, shrugs off questions about his place in history. "I never felt like I had arrived. In the ice skating business, you're a hero one year and a bum the next. I was always expecting to have two or three bad years, but I've been lucky to never really have those." Nicks is tied to the story of the 1961 Team in a unique way. He and Yvonne Littlefield eventually married. They first got to know each other when Nicks hired her to teach at an Ice Capades Chalet rink. "We never really think about the year '1961' in our relationship unless others bring it up," he explained. "I wouldn't be here if it wasn't for the crash, which was unhappy for so many people, but for me it provided opportunity. I have a bittersweet feeling about it."[66]

A bittersweet feeling also lingers for those skaters who could have been part of the 1961 World Team. One skater who narrowly missed the plane was Karen Howland Jones. After she retired from competitive skating, she began teaching and has coached scores of skaters across America for nearly fifty years.[67]

After a brief stint in Ice Capades, Barbara Roles Williams coached a number of champion skaters and taught in many skating centers, including Los Angeles, the Broadmoor, Las Vegas, and the University of Delaware. Because of the crash, she resolved to coach. "Retirement saved my life," she said. "I was grateful for being alive and I needed to give something back to skating."[68]

Lorraine Hanlon Comanor, who almost flew on the ill-fated flight, never considered quitting skating, but training for the 1962 season was difficult. After winning the 1963 U.S. title and competing through the 1964 season, she retired. "I can't say it was the aftereffects of the crash, but I didn't want to keep going," she said. Hanlon headed to Harvard, became a physician, and went into medical research. She thinks often of the many friends she lost. Ten years ago, she said: "I got 40 years that they didn't. They deserved some time when the pressure was off, some time just to take a stroll in the woods. I'm sure every one of those people would have done something good with those 40 years."[69]

Marilyn Meeker Durham recently celebrated her forty-eighth wedding anniversary. After her wedding in 1962, she went to Okinawa with her husband, had two children, and returned briefly to Indianapolis, where she taught skating. After winning the World dance professional championship with Ron Ludington, she left figure skating for good. Remembering the accident is easy because her birthday is February 16.[70]

After college, Jerry Fotheringill served in the army and had a career at the CIA, making numerous trips to NATO headquarters in Brussels. "I flew in many times and *always* upon approaching and landing I would look out my window and think about what had happened." Judianne Fotheringill married national skating judge Norman Fuller.[71]

Ron Joseph discontinued all his skating connections with the exception of 1986, when the USFSA invited all past national senior champions to Indianapolis for "Celebration . . . America On Ice!" His sister Vivian married and had a family; she also chose to leave the skating world behind.[72]

INDELIBLE TRACINGS

412

After a four-year stint as stars of the Ice Capades, Maria and Otto Jelinek returned to Canada. After the Communist downfall in 1989, Otto moved back to Prague. The Jelineks' childhood home is the current Austrian Embassy. "It's a historical palace and it's absolutely beautiful. They really fixed it up," Maria said. Otto and Maria had visited their home once before during the restless days after the 1961 crash. Their former maid was still there. She cried when she answered the door and showed them around. Much of their furniture was still there, including the monogrammed family plates. "They had known us from when we were little and were so excited," Maria said.[73]

Tim Brown taught skaters in Berkeley, including young Peggy Fleming and UC-Berkeley students. In sync with many Berkeley students, Tim grew his flattop into long hair and a full beard. A concert pianist who performed under the pseudonym of Jamie Catalpa, Tim taught music appreciation classes and choreographic workshops. Tim was aware that he followed the beat of his own drummer. He joked that many of the USFSA rules were actually the "Tim Brown Rules." After Tim did a split jump off the ice in 1961, the USFSA passed a rule that a skater must begin and end his program on the ice. Tim died in the late 1980s.[74]

U.S. figure skating was forever changed by the events of February 15, 1961. The heartache from that terrible disaster shadows figure skating to this day. But rather than crushing the spirit of the skaters left behind, those who came back to the rinks in the days and weeks following the tragedy did so to honor their friends. Skaters of today are directly connected to the 1961 Team through the Memorial Fund, which continues to financially support skaters as they compete in elite international competitions all over the world. Many young skaters are connected to the 1961 Team through the hundreds of coaches who were students of the six celebrated coaches. Their teaching styles have been passed down to new generations throughout the country.

Many great skaters came after the 1961 season, but those unique individuals on the 1961 Team could never be replaced. Russian novelist Anatoli Rybakov once wrote, "If there's no Pushkin in a library, I can replace it with a Tolstoy, but it would be Tolstoy and not Pushkin." And so it was with U.S. figure skating after the crash. As Ritter Shumway remarked, their death was " a loss which we all feel deeply beyond words that we can find to express, a loss from which our sport will be years in recovering, and a personal loss which will never be erased from our consciousness."[75]

Those who personally knew the 1961 Team members still feel the "big void," as 1962 World champion Donald Jackson described it. "All of my friends were wiped out," he said. "We were all good friends off the ice, and going on the ice we wished each other 'good luck.' Those people would have been all over the world teaching, and we would have been so close." Jim Short, who came out of retirement in 1962 to help U.S. figure skating, regularly placed ads in competitive programs with his motto—"Skate Because You Love It!" Skaters of that era didn't learn to skate so they could reap great financial rewards, because such rewards didn't exist. They skated because they loved getting on the ice and training with their friends.[76]

When the 1961 Team skaters, coaches, officials, and family members boarded Sabena Flight 548, there was nowhere else they would rather be. It was ironic that Diana LeMaire Squibb, twenty-five years later, found herself in the exact same position as her father. The USFSA asked Diana to be the team leader for the 1986 Junior Worlds in Sarajevo. She had a ten-year- old son, and she realized she would be doing exactly what her father had done. She sat several people down and told them what to tell her son if history repeated itself. She also wrote him a letter, explaining why she went, saying that if something happened to her he should not be sad because she died doing something she really wanted to do. "Please believe me," she wrote, "I really wanted to do this more than anything else in the whole wide world." As Ritter Shumway said decades ago, "We can find solace in knowing they were doing what they wanted to . . . [They were] the finest that our nation, our culture, our way of life can produce, not only as technicians of consummate skill in their chosen field, their beloved sport of figure skating, but also the finest in character, in lovable personality and in sportsmanship."[77]

The generation of Donald Jackson and Jim Short is also aging. As death takes them, more gently and one by one, their personal memories of 1961 will also go. Even for generations who don't have a personal memory of the extraordinary 1961 Team, they can step into that on-going legacy by emulating their spirit, their dedication, their passion, and the excellence with which they lived their lives.

A Zamboni can wipe a sheet of ice clean after the most intense patch, freestyle session, or competition. Evidence of lopsided figure eights, traveling spins, or cheated jumps can be permanently removed. But nothing can erase the indelible tracings created by every member of the 1961 U.S. World Figure Skating Team delegation. Their influence will forever impact U.S. figure skating.

NOTES

Unless otherwise noted, all letters are found in the files of the World Figure Skating Museum and Hall of Fame in Colorado Springs, Colorado, and are quoted by permission.

Introduction

[1] Louella Rehfield, telephone interview, August 31, 2004.

[2] Morry Stillwell, telephone interview, October 21, 2003.

[3] Pieter Kollen, telephone interview, July 29, 2003.

[4] Barlow Nelson, telephone interview, November 17, 2003.

[5] Bob Duffy, "Twists of Fate," *Boston Globe*, December 31, 2000, C1.

[6] Bob Duffy, "Shattered Dreams," *Boston Globe*, December 29, 2000, E16; Barbara Heilman, "Mother Set the Style," *Sports Illustrated*, February 13, 1961, 39-41.

[7] Kamon Simpson, "A Team That Went Down Together," *Times Union* (Albany, NY), February 18, 2001, A28.

[8] "18 U.S. Skaters among 73 Dead in a Jet Crash," *New York Times*, February 16, 1961, 1, 18.

[9] "Family Affair," *Time*, February 24, 1961, 13.

[10] Simpson, "A Team That Went Down Together."

[11] Paula Parrish, "Lost Generation of Athletes Lives On," *Rocky Mountain News*, March 19, 2001, 1C; Congressman Walter Rogers, letter to F. Ritter Shumway, March 20, 1961; "Sabena 707 Crash," *Aviation Week*, February 1961.

[12] Duffy, "Shattered Dreams;" F. Ritter Shumway, letter to USFSA Members and Clubs, February 23, 1961.

Chapter 1

[1] Lorin Caccamise O'Neil, telephone interview, February 4, 2005.

[2] Julia Whedon, *The Fine Art of Ice Skating: An Illustrated History and Portfolio of Stars* (New York: Harry N. Abrahams, 1988), 43, 62; James R. Hines, *Figure Skating: A History* (Urbana: University of Illinois Press/Colorado Springs: World Figure Skating Museum and Hall of Fame, 2006), 43; "Club History," www.pschs.org/Set_About_main_history.htm (accessed April 4, 2003); Doug Gelbert, "Figure Skating Hall of Fame," 2002, www.essortment.com/all/figureskatingh_rlzl.htm (accessed March 25, 2003); www.newhavenskatingclub.org (accessed June 7, 2010); Elaine Sonderegger, telephone interview, June 7, 2010; Benjamin T. Wright, "A Summary of The Skating Club of Boston," 2007, 1, www.scboston.org/about_history.php (accessed January 27, 2003).

[3] Hines, *Figure Skating*, 75, 313-19; "The Ladies Glorious 'Ice' Age," *Daily News* (New York City), January 26, 1998, 83; Whedon, *The Fine Art of Ice Skating*, 71-74.

[4] "Air Crash Last Chapter in Vinson-Owen Ice Saga," *Boston Globe*, February 15, 1961, 1, 36; Polly W. Baker, "A Family Tradition," *Skating*, June 1959, 10-11.

[5] 2001 State Farm U.S. Championships program, 61; Baker, "A Family Tradition," 10-11; Benjamin T. Wright, *Skating in America: The 75th Anniversary History of the United States Figure Skating*

Association (Colorado Springs: U.S. Figure Skating Association, 1996), 9; Laura Hilgers, Great Skates: *Sports Illustrated for Kids* (New York: Little, Brown and Company, 1996), 36.

[6] Hilgers, *Great Skates*, 36; Baker, "A Family Tradition," 10-11; Polly Blodgett Watson, telephone interview, October 14, 2003; Joan Tozzer Cave, telephone interview, October 30, 2007.

[7] Wright, *Skating in America*, 10-13, 16-17, 20.

[8] Benjamin T. Wright, "Maribel Vinson Owen," *Reader's Guide to Figure Skating's Hall of Fame* (Boston: United States Figure Skating Association, 1981), not paginated; Wright, *Skating in America*, ii.

[9] *Chronicle of the Olympics* (New York: DK Publishing, 2006), 17, 21, 25, 29, 33; Howard Bass, *The Love of Ice Skating and Speed Skating* (New York: Crescent Books, 1980), 67; "Historical Results," www.eskatefans.com/skatabase (accessed February 4, 2003); Wright, *Skating in America*, 9.

[10] "Historical Results"; Wright, *Skating in America*, 12.

[11] *Chronicle of the Olympics*, 41-42, 237; Bass, *The Love of Ice Skating*, 68.

[12] *Chronicle of the Olympics*, 49-51, 240-41; "Historical Results;" Joel B. Lieberman, "A Survey of the 1928 Olympics," *Skating*, April 1928, 5-8.

[13] Wright, *Skating in America*, 36; Maribel Y. Vinson, *Advanced Figure Skating* (New York: McGraw-Hill, 1940), 211.

[14] Frederick Goodridge, "Maribel Yerxa Vinson," *Skating*, February 1936, 15-16; Hilgers, *Great Skates*, 36-38; 2001 U.S. Championships program, 61.

[15] "Historical Results;" Wright, *Skating in America*, 40-43.

[16] *Chronicle of the Olympics*, 57; George M. Lattimer, *Official Report of III Olympic Winter Games, Lake Placid 1932* (Lake Placid, NY: III Olympic Winter Games Committee, 1932), 213.

[17] "The Olympics: 1932 and 1936," *Skating*, January 1960, 14; *Chronicle of the Olympics*, 244.

[18] "Historical Results;" "United States Gold Medalists," *Skating*, April 1949, 37; Vinson, *Advanced Figure Skating*, 270-73; Wright, *Skating in America*, 54.

[19] "Women Are Sportswriters Too: The Fractured Relationship between Reporters and Athletes," www.stwing.upenn.edu (accessed February 15, 2003); Vinson, *Advanced Figure Skating*, 273; Arthur Daley, "Maribel Vinson Owen," *The New York Times*, February 16, 1961, 40.

[20] Daley, "Maribel Vinson Owen," 40.

[21] "Historical Results;" Hilgers, *Great Skates*, 37; "The Olympics: 1932 and 1936," *Skating*, January 1960, 18.

[22] Patricia Shelley, *The Figure Skating Film: Its History and Contribution to the Motion Picture Industry* (M.A. thesis, Brigham Young University, 1980), iii; Raymond Straight and Leif Henie, *Queen of Ice, Queen of Shadows: The Unsuspected Life of Sonja Henie* (New York: Stein and Day, 1985), 76; Watson, interview.

[23] Joanna Niska Delaney, telephone interview, April 18, 2005; Hilgers, *Great Skates*, 36; Ardelle Kloss Sanderson, telephone interview, October 3, 2003; Daley, "Maribel Vinson Owen," 40.

[24] "Historical Results;" Vinson, *Advanced Figure Skating*, 265.

[25] Hilgers, *Great Skates*, 36-38; Wright, "Maribel Vinson Owen," *Reader's Guide*; "Local Skating Club Signs Pro Guy Owen," *Spokane Daily Chronicle*, September 25, 1951, 1; 2001 U.S. Championships program, 61; Sanderson, interview.

[26] "Air Crash Last Chapter," 36; "Champion Personals," *Skating*, November 1938, 15, 17; Vinson/Owen advertisement, *Skating*, November 1938, 35; Carolyn Welch Grimditch, letter to Patricia S. Bushman, November 20, 2005; "Book Reviews," *Skating*, November 1938, 24-25.

[27] Toni Sweet, "Robert Skrak," *St. Moritz ISC History, Oral History* (N.p.: privately published, 1991), copy in my possession; Barbara Ann Gingg Skerry, "Tracings from the Past," *Skating*, December 1944, 21; "Births," *Skating*, May 1940, 35.

[28] Toni Sweet, "Carolyn Welch Grimditch," *St. Mortiz ISC History*, 73; Toni Sweet, "Vonnie Marsh Dondero," *St. Mortiz ISC History*, 57; Mary L. Page, "Off-Ice Activities, *Skating*, March 1944, 22; Marcella May Willis Walker, telephone interview, July 24, 2004.

[29] Toni Sweet, "Jeanne Taylor Herst," *St. Mortiz ISC History*, 78; Toni Sweet, "Betty Jean Clark Moehnke," *St. Mortiz ISC History*, 91.

[30] Shirley Reflow Sherman, telephone interview, November 12, 2004; Joyce Brader Burns, telephone interview, October 29, 2003; Toni Sweet, "Constance B. Olson," *St. Mortiz ISC History*, 97.

[31] Vonnie Marsh Dondero, telephone interview, July 12, 2003; Toni Sweet, "Roy Cofer," *St. Mortiz ISC History*, 52; Toni Sweet, "Betty Jean Clark Moehnke," 92; Toni Sweet, "Beverly Licht Bloch," *St. Mortiz ISC History*, 36; Toni Sweet, "Aileen Kahre Arenson," *St. Mortiz ISC History*, 5.

[32] "Carnival Merry-Go-Round," *Skating*, April 1941; 36; Austin Holt, telephone interview, January 21, 2005.

[33] Holt, interview.

[34] "United States Championships," *Skating*, January 1942, 21; Mary Louise Premer, "Meet the United States Champions," *Skating*, March 1944, 18; Wright, *Skating in America*, i.

[35] Dondero, interview; "Births," *Skating*, October 1944, 12-13; "Attractions at Summer Seasons," *Skating*, May 1944, 12.

[36] Grimditch, letter to Bushman; Sweet, "Carolyn Welch Grimditch," 73.

[37] Wright, *Skating in America*, 101, i.

[38] *Chronicle of the Olympics*, 73.

[39] Dick Button, *Dick Button on Skates* (Englewood Cliffs, NJ: Prentice-Hall, 1955), 21-22; Dick Button, telephone interview, December 13, 2005; Wright, *Skating in America*, i, iv, vi; Doug Robinson, "It Only Figures That U.S. Excels," *Deseret News*, February 13, 1999, D1.

[40] Wright, *Skating in America*, 100.

[41] "U.S. Wins Three Olympic Contests," *Life*, February 1948, 32; "Dick and Barbara," *Newsweek*, February 16, 1948, 82; Wright, *Skating in America*, 105.

[42] "Dick and Barbara," 82.

[43] Hines, *Figure Skating*, 313; Watson, interview.

[44] Button, *Dick Button on Skates*, 25; Andra McLaughlin Kelly, telephone interview, September 26, 2005.

[45] Wright, *Skating in America*, 106; Watson, interview.

[46] "Air Crash Last Chapter," 36; "Spins through Professional Circles," *Skating*, November 1948, 34; Sweet, "Betty Jean Clark Moehnke," 91.

[47] Walker, interview; Ron Ludington, interviewed, Overland Park, KS, June 11, 2004.

[48] Walker, interview; "Spins through Professional Circles," *Skating*, December 1949, 42; Ginny Baxter Newman, telephone interview, August 30, 2004; "Warm Weather Skating Scoops," *Skating*, November 1950, 10.

[49] Roy Cofer, telephone interview, July 13, 2004; Wright, *Skating in America*, i; Professional Skaters Guild advertisement, *Skating*, November 1950, 47; Sandy Thomas, "The United States Championships," *Skating*, May 1953, 25.

[50] Robert Swenning, telephone interview, October 11, 2004.

[51] Grimditch, letter to Bushman; Ramona Allen McIntyre, telephone interview, July 22, 2004.

[52] Cofer, interview; Swenning, interview; Robin Greiner, telephone interview, September 27, 2004.

[53] "Tragedy Ends Her Sports Assignment," *Oakland Tribune*, February 15, 1961, 3; Kumfortites advertisement, *Skating*, November 1938, 41; Arnold Authentics advertisement, *Skating*, October 1941, 41; Knox Reeves Advertising check receipt, November 20, 1939, U.S. Figure Skating files.

[54] Wright, *Skating in America*, iv, vi; Maribel, Y. Vinson, "Figuring on Tenley," *Sports Illustrated*, February 7, 1955, 33.

[55] *Chronicle of the Olympics*, 81, 255; Theresa Weld Blanchard, "The Olympics: 1948 and 1952," *Skating*, February 1960, 33-34.

[56] "Andy Again," *Time*, March 3, 1952, 49; Blanchard, "The Olympics: 1948 and 1952," 4, 36; *Chronicle of the Olympics*, 255.

[57] "Spins through Professional Circles," *Skating*, November 1951, 28; "Michigan State College Ice Arena," *Skating*, February 1952, 25; "Deaths," *Skating*, June 1952, 27; "Deaths," *Skating*, January 1953, 28.

[58] Theresa W. Blanchard, "The 1952 World Championships," *Skating*, May 1952, 6-7; Theresa Weld Blanchard, "The Championships of the World," *Skating*, April 1953, 6, 11, 32.

[59] O'Neil, interview.

Chapter 2

[1] "Spins through Professional Circles," *Skating*, December 1954, 40.

[2] "Miss Vinson Honored," *Skating*, January 1935, 9; Barlow Nelson, telephone interview, November 17, 2003; Joyce Underwood Winship, telephone interview, October 1, 2003.

[3] Franklin Nelson, telephone interview, September 3, 2005; "Historical Results," www. eskatefans.skatabase (accessed September 30, 2003); "North American Figure Skating Championships," www.skate.org/can/comp/NorAm/FSC. html (accessed April 29, 2003); Polly W. Baker, "A Family Tradition," *Skating*, June 1959, 10-11.

[4] Ron Ludington, interviewed, Overland Park, KS, June 11, 2004; Paul George, interviewed, Portland, OR, January 13, 2005; Julie Graham Eavzan, telephone interview, April 20, 2005; Ronna Goldblatt Gladstone, telephone interview, April 25, 2010.

[5] "Spins through Professional Circles," *Skating*, November 1952, 34; Christie Allan-Piper, telephone interview, November 9, 2004; "Historical Results."

[6] Ann Pellegrino Bullock, telephone interview, October 18, 2004.

[7] Tom McGinnis, telephone interview, September 14, 2005.

[8] Allan-Piper, interview; Eavzan, interview; Frank Carroll, telephone interview, October 11, 2009.

[9] Carroll, interview; Allan-Piper, interview.

[10] Allan-Piper, interview; Don Bartleson, telephone interview, November 8, 2004.

[11] Allan-Piper, interview.

[12] Bill King, telephone interview, November 4, 2003; Allan-Piper, interview; Nancy Madden Leamy, telephone interview, May 19, 2005.

[13] Joanna Niska Delaney, telephone interview, April 18, 2005; Allan-Piper, interview; Gladstone, interview.

[14] Allan-Piper, interview; Eavzan, interview; "Spins through Professional Circles," *Skating*, December 1954, 40; "Spins through Professional Circles," *Skating*, January 1958, 42; Robert Brewer, interviewed, Phoenix, AZ, March 18, 2005.

[15] Frank Muckian, telephone interview, October 6, 2004; Gladstone, interview; Allan-Piper, interview; Eavzan, interview.

[16] Gladstone, interview; Eavzan, interview; Delaney, interview; Carroll, interview; Elizabeth George Busconi, telephone interview, May 5, 2005; George, interview.

[17] Barlow Nelson, interview; George, interview.

[18] George, interview; Delaney, interview; Gladstone, interview.

[19] Norvetta Tribby Pinch, telephone interview, March 12, 2005; Leamy, interview.

[20] Allan-Piper, interview.

[21] Delaney, interview; Leamy, interview; "U.S. Puts Best Skating Feet Forward," *Life*, January 23, 1956, 10; R. Gene Shelley's senior figures competition card, in my possession.

[22] Busconi, interview; Delaney, interview; George, interview.

[23] Allan-Piper, interview.

[24] Delaney, interview; Marcella May Willis Walker, telephone interview, July 24, 2004; Lorin Caccamise O'Neil, telephone interview, February 4, 2005.

[25] Austin Holt, telephone interview, January 21, 2005.

[26] Gerry Lane, telephone interview, November 17, 2004.

[27] Leamy, interview; Pieter Kollen, telephone interview, July 29, 2003; O'Neil, interview.

[28] Delaney, interview; Walter ("Red") Bainbridge, telephone interview, September 3, 2004.

[29] Leamy, interview.

[30] Christine Brennan, *Edge of Glory*, (New York: Penguin Books, 1999), 87-88; Carroll, interview; Eavzan, interview; Joyce Burden, telephone interview, August 22, 2004; Gladstone, interview.

[31] Newbold Black, telephone interview, November 3, 2003; Kollen, interview; Louella Rehfield, telephone interview, August 31, 2004.

[32] Nancy Ludington Graham, telephone interview, April 5, 2005; Allan-Piper, interview.

[33] Allan-Piper, interview; Eavzan, interview; Ludington, interview.

[34] Allan-Piper interview; Sidney Foster Arnold, interview, May 2, 2005; Barbara Babcock Kirby, telephone interview, November 8, 2004; Lane, interview.

[35] Leamy, interview; Eavzan, interview.

[36] George, interview; Muckian, interview; Rigney, interview; Nancy Graham, interview; Sheila Muldowny Stone, telephone interview, September 18, 2003.

[37] "Vinson-Owen House," *Winchester Historic Houses Tour*, pamphlet; Tom Downey and Gordon Hillman, "Hub Mourns Brilliant Owens Skating Clan," *Boston Daily Record*, February 16, 1961, 26; Leamy, interview; Busconi, interview; Muckian, interview.

[38] Peter Betts, telephone interview, February 7, 2005.

[39] George, interview; Eavzan, interview; Winship, interview.

[40] Nancy Graham, interview; Eavzan, interview; Dick Button, telephone interview, December 13, 2005.

[41] Ludington, interview.

[42] Maribel Y. Vinson, "Figuring on Tenley," *Sports Illustrated*, February 7, 1955, 28.

[43] Hugh Graham, interview; Catherine Machado Gray, telephone interview, December 2, 2004; Evelyn Muller Kramer, telephone interview, November 15, 2004.

[44] Hugh Graham, interview; George, interview; Brewer, interview; Gladstone, interview.

Chapter 3

[1] "Scholdan's Next Champion Hopes Perished in Tragic Jet Liner Crash," *Gazette Telegraph* (Colorado Springs), February 19, 1961, B5; Austin Holt, telephone interview, January 21, 2005; Fred Cheschier, telephone interview, June 4, 2005; Tommy Weinreich Allen, telephone interview, May 21, 2009.

[2] Roberta Jenks Scholdan, letter to Patricia S. Bushman, December 4, 2003; Ruth Scholdan Harle, telephone interview, October 9, 2007; Benjamin T. Wright, "Edi Scholdan," *Reader's Guide to Figure Skating's Hall of Fame* (Boston: United States Figure Skating Association, 1981).

[3] Roberta Scholdan, telephone interview, November 10, 2003; "Colorado Springs Skaters in Crash All National Leaders," *Free Press* (Colorado Springs), February 16, 1961, 1; Wright, "Edi Scholdan," *Reader's Guide.*

[4] "Victim of Brussels," *Boston Globe*, February 15, 1961, 15; Polly Blodgett Watson, telephone interview, October 14, 2003; Roberta Scholdan, interview; Edi Scholdan advertisement, *Skating*, January 1942, 41.

[5] Edi Scholdan Christmas greetings advertisement, *Skating*, December 1939, 37; "The Eastern Championships," *Skating*, March 1941, 29; "The Easterns," *Skating*, March 1942, 16.

[6] Edi Scholdan advertisement, January 1942, 41; Harle, interview; Edi Scholdan Christmas greetings advertisement, *Skating*, December 1941, 25; Louella Rehfield, telephone interview, August 31, 2004; Micki Asher Leiter, telephone interview, September 3, 2003; Andra McLaughlin Kelly, telephone interview, September 26, 2005; Sherry Dorsey Cook, telephone interview, May 9, 2005.

[7] Diane Lynne Betts, *The Broadmoor World Arena Pictorial History Book* (Colorado Springs: Broadmoor World Arena, 1988), 27.

[8] Elena Bertozzi-Villa, *Broadmoor Memories: The History of the Broadmoor* (Colorado Springs: Pictorial Histories Publishing Company, 1993), 12-63; Harry Shattuck, "The Broadmoor Tradition," *Houston Chronicle*, January 11, 1998, Travel Section, 1; Marsha Lopez, "Broadmoor: Skating's Mecca," *American Skating World*, July 1986, 14, 16.

[9] Lopez, "Broadmoor: Skating's Mecca," 14, 16; Bertozzi-Villa, *Broadmoor Memories*, 85-86; Shattuck, "The Broadmoor Tradition," 1; "Club History," www.broadmoorsc.com/history.aspx (accessed March 1, 2005).

[10] "Club History;" Michael DeBan, "William Thayer Tutt," *Rocky Mountain News*, March 21, 1999, 10C; Betts, *The Broadmoor World Arena*, 25.

[11] Broadmoor Skating Club advertisement, *Skating*, March 1943, 8; Skippy Baxter, telephone interview, September 19, 2007; Kelly, interview.

[12] Jeanie O'Brien Callahan, telephone interview, June 27, 2005; Broadmoor Skating Club advertisement, *Skating*, January 1945, 42; Helen Geekie Nightingale, telephone interview, November 18, 2004; Eileen Seigh Honnen, telephone interview, July 14, 2005.

[13] Kelly, interview; Christy Haigler Krall, interviewed Colorado Springs, May 9, 2003; Ardith Paul Hamilton, telephone interview, July 31, 2005; Connie Espander, telephone interview, September 7, 2005.

[14] Nightingale, interview; Holt, interview; Krall, interview.

[15] Kelly interview; Leiter, interview.

[16] Sheila Muldowny Stone, telephone interview, September 18, 2003; "Rockers and Counters," *Skating*, January 1938, 28; 1938 Nationals program; U.S.F.S.A. Figure Skating Nationals 1948 pro-

gram; Benjamin T. Wright, *Skating in America, The 75th Anniversary History of the United States Figure Skating Association*," (Colorado Springs: United States Figure Skating Association, 1996), xli; "Tracings from the Past," *Skating*, October 1944, 30; Leiter, interview.

[17] Harle, interview; "Births," *Skating*, October 1943, 26; Dixie Lee Burns Wilson, telephone interview, October 8, 2003; Nationals 1948 program.

[18] Scholdan, interview; Harle, interview; "Marriages," *Skating*, December 1946, 40.

[19] "Spins through Professional Circles," *Skating*, November 1947, 34; Harle, interview; "Historical Results," www.eskatefans.comskatabase/historical (accessed March 4, 2003); "1948 Olympic Try-Outs," *Skating*, February 1948, 6; "Pictures from the Clubs," *Skating*, May 1948, 24; Scholdan, letter to Bushman, December 4, 2003.

[20] Beth Sundene Graham, telephone interview, November 1, 2004; "Spins through Professional Circles," *Skating*, December 1948, 38; Betts, *The Broadmoor World Arena*, 3.

[21] Jan Serafine, telephone interview, May 12, 2005; Fran Haigler Ainsworth, telephone interview, August 2, 2003.

[22] Peter Kennedy, telephone interview, October 29, 2007; James R. Hines, *Figure Skating: A History* (Urbana: University of Illinois Press/Colorado Springs: World Figure Skating Museum and Hall of Fame, 2006), 317.

[23] Kennedy, interview.

[24] Marilyn Meeker Durham, telephone interview, July 30, 2003; Donna Merrill Schoon, telephone interview, September 23, 2005.

[25] Leiter, interview; Bill Boeck, telephone interview, November 6, 2003.

[26] Diana Lapp Green, telephone interview, April 28, 2005; Fred Chescheir, telephone interview, June 4, 2005; Pam Thatcher Marsh, telephone interview, May 24, 2005; Hamilton, interview; Cook, interview.

[27] Callahan, interview; Cook, interview.

[28] Kennedy, interview; Barlow Nelson, telephone interview, November 17, 2003; David Jenkins, telephone interview, November 30, 2005; Cindy Cheschier Walsh, telephone interview, May 8, 2007; Cook, interview; Callahan, interview.

[29] Patricia Firth Hansen, telephone interview, April 29, 2005; Loren Caccamise O'Neil, telephone interview, February 4, 2005; Krall, interview; Claralynn Lewis Barnes, telephone interview, August 22, 2005; Lynda Waldrop Lineberry, telephone interview, November 6, 2007.

[30] Edi Scholdan, "Individuality on Ice," *Skating*, January 1944, 7; Callahan, interview; Krall, interview.

[31] Callahan, interview; Hamilton, interview.

[32] Kelly, interview; Betts, *The Broadmoor World Arena*, 15; Greg Hoyt, telephone interview, July 12, 2005; Lineberry, interview; Espander, interview.

[33] Kelly, interview; Gladys H. Rankin, "Gym Classes Off-the-Ice," *Skating*, December 1945, 8-9; O'Neil, interview; Betts, *The Broadmoor World Arena*, 27.

[34] Kelly, interview.

[35] Betts, *The Broadmoor World Arena*, 29-32.

[36] Frances Dorsey Burke, telephone interview, June 7, 2005; Barnes, interview.

[37] Betts, *The Broadmoor World Arena*, 27; Kennedy, interview.

[38] Betts, *The Broadmoor World Arena*, 26, 30-31; Scholdan, interview; Leiter, interview; Carole Carlson Wolfswinkel, telephone interview, May 11, 1005; Burke, interview; Schoon, interview.

[39] Kelly, interview; Hamilton, interview; Debbie Might, telephone interview, June 2, 2010.

[40] "Around the Summer Circuit," *Skating*, November 1949, 7; "Sally Surveys Summer Centers," *Skating*, November 1954, 8; "Skimming around Summer Circles," *Skating*, November 1953, 15; "At the Summer Centers," *Skating*, November 1947, 14; Burke, interview.

[41] Allen, interview; "Rockers and Counters," *Skating*, January 1957, 36; "Circling the Summer Centers," *Skating*, November 1960, 10.

[42] Scholdan, interview; Allen, interview; Serafine, interview; Kay Servatius Ringsred, telephone interview, August 23, 2004; Hamilton, interview.

[43] Callahan, interview; David Jenkins, interview; Harle, interview.

[44] Helen Davidson Maxson, telephone interview, October 9, 2007; Cook, interview; Marsh, interview; Hansen, interview.

[45] Harle, interview.

[46] Honnen, interview; Debbie Kelley, "Thayer Tutt," *Gazette* (Colorado Springs), March 20, 2006, unpaginated clipping in my possession; "At the Summer Centers," *Skating*, November 1947, 14, 30; Richard Dwyer, telephone interview, May 28, 2005.

[47] "United States Olympic Team," *Skating*, November 1947, 7; "Around the Summer Circuit," *Skating*, November 1949, 7-8; "Historical Results."

[48] "Straw Hats and Ice Skates," *Skating*, November 1952, 6-7, 13; "Hayes Alan Jenkins," *Skating*, June 1953, 5; David Jenkins, interview.

[49] David Jenkins, interview; "Hayes Alan Jenkins," 5.

[50] David Jenkins, interview.

[51] Hayes Alan Jenkins, telephone interview, October 10, 2007.

[52] Honnen, interview; David Jenkins, interview; Rehfield, interview.

[53] Hayes Jenkins, interview.

[54] Theresa Weld Blanchard, "The Championships of the World," *Skating*, April 1953, 10, 34; Hines, *Figure Skating: A History*, 315; Hayes Jenkins, interview.

[55] Burke, interview; Cook, interview.

[56] David Jenkins, interview; Hoyt, interview.

[57] Burke, interview.

[58] "Tutt Terms Air Crash 'Horrible;' Lauds Scholdan," *Gazette-Telegraph*, February 15, 1961, 1.

[59] "Births," *Skating*, May 1953, 30; Betts, *The Broadmoor World Arena*, 27, 92; "Turned Professional" and "USFSA Judges List," *Skating*, February 1954, 25, 32; Barnes, interview.

[60] "Spins through Professional Circles," *Skating*, February 1955, 25; Barnes, interview; Ringsred, interview; Cook, interview; Hayes Jenkins, interview; Callahan, interview.

[61] Wilson, interview; Betts, *The Broadmoor World Arena*, 85-86.

[62] Wilson, interview; "Tutt Terms Air Crash 'Horrible,'" 1.

[63] "Meet the 1953 Champions," *Skating*, June 1953, 13-14; Wright, *Skating in America*, iv, vi; Hayes Jenkins, interview; Janet Gerhauser Allen Carpenter, telephone interview, November 29, 2004.

[64] "Men," *Skating*, April 1953, 34; Lee Meade, "Edi Scholdan Proved You Can't Knock Success," *Denver Post*, February 16, 1961, 62.

[65] Hoyt, interview; Wilson, interview.

[66] "Olimpiadi 1956," *Newsweek*, January 30, 1956, 59; Ezra Bowen and George Weller, "The 1956 Winter Olympics," *Sports Illustrated*, January 30, 1956, 26.

[67] "Tenley's Injury," *Skating*, April 1956, 22; "Ill-Omened Olympics," *Time*, January 30, 1956, 44.

[68] Theresa Weld Blanchard, "The Olympic Championships," *Skating*, April 1956, 23-24; Hayes Jenkins, interview.

[69] Blanchard, "The Olympic Championships," 23-30.

[70] Ibid.

[71] Ibid.

[72] Wright, *Skating in America*, 141.

[73] "The Olympics: 1956," *Skating*, March 1960, 11-12.

[74] *Chronicle of the Olympics* (New York: DK Publishing, 2006), 17, 21, 25, 29, 33; Howard Bass, *The Love of Ice Skating and Speed Skating* (New York: Crescent Books, 1980), 259-60.

[75] Theresa Weld Blanchard, "The Championships of the Worlds," *Skating*, May 1956, 7-10.

[76] "Mother, I Did It!" *Time*, February 27, 1956, 50.

[77] "World Champ at Last—and Carol Cries," *Life*, March 5, 1956, 141; "Trial by Snow," *Time*, March 7, 1960, 55.

[78] "Tragic Air Crash Claims Vinson-Owen Skate Team," *Oregonian* (Portland, OR), February 16, 1961, 4; Will Grimsley, "Crash Wipes Out Owen Family's Dream of Olympic Title," *Oregon Statesman* (Salem, OR), February 16, 1961, II, 9.

[79] "Mothers & Daughters," *Time*, March 26, 1956; Wright, *Skating in America*, 143-44.

[80] Hayes Jenkins, interview.

Chapter 4

[1] Walter S. Powell, "ISU Council Meeting," *Skating*, November 1956, 16.

[2] Hayes Alan Jenkins, telephone interview, October 10, 2007; Frances Dorsey Burke, telephone interview, June 7, 2005; Sidney Foster Arnold, telephone interview, May 2, 2005.

[3] Hayes Jenkins, interview; David Jenkins, "Outdoor Skating in Europe," *Skating*, June 1955, 19.

[4] Robert Swenning, telephone interview, October 11, 2004.

[5] Hayes Jenkins, interview; Scandinavian Airlines advertisement, *Skating*, January 1952, 4; Burke, interview.

[6] Powell, "ISU Council Meeting," 16; "World Events at the Broadmoor," *Skating*, May 1957, 24.

[7] Theresa Weld Blanchard and Edith E. Ray, "The Championships of the World," *Skating*, May 1957, 7, 24-25; "A Pair of Aces," *Time*, March 11, 1957, 74; Marsha Lopez, "Broadmoor: Skating's Mecca," *American Skating World*, July 1986, 14-15.

[8] Blanchard and Ray, "Championships," 7, 24-25, 38, 40; Lee Meade, "Edi Scholdan Proved You Can't Knock Success, *Denver Post*, February 16, 1961, 62; Nancy Ludington Graham, telephone interview, April 5, 2005.

[9] Harry A. Sims, "The United States Championships," *Skating*, May 1957, 16-18, 40, 42.

[10] "Harned Trophy," *Skating*, May 1957, 42; Benjamin E. Wright, *Skating in America: The 75th Anniversary History of the United States Figure Skating Association* (Colorado Springs: U.S. Figure Skating Association, 1996), vii.

[11] Wright, *Skating in America*, 50.

[12] Bradley Lord, "How I Got Interested in Skating" (unpublished school essay, Swampscott, MA, 1957), collection of Bruce Lord; Gerry Lane, telephone interview, November 17, 2004; Ron Ludington, interviewed, Overland Park, KS, June 11, 2004.

[13] "1961 World Team Meeting," U.S. Figure Skating files; Bruce Lord, telephone interview, May 4, 2005.

[14] Bruce Lord, interview; Bradley Lord, "How I Got Interested in Skating"; Norvetta Tribby Pinch, telephone interview, April 12, 2005.

[15] "Tests," *Skating*, November 1950, 40; Bruce Lord, interview.

[16] Benjamin T. Wright, "A Summary of The Skating Club of Boston," 2007, 1, www.scboston. org./about_history/php (accessed January 27, 2003); "Champions in Uniform," *Skating*, October 1943, 3.

[17] Nancy Meiss, telephone interview, April 7, 2005; Sue Blodgett Rigney, telephone interview, May 17, 2005.

[18] Frank Muckian, telephone interview, October 6, 2004.

[19] "The Eastern Championships," *Skating*, March 1951, 6; "Carnival Cavalcade," *Skating*, June 1951, 30; Bruce Lord, interview.

[20] Bradley Lord, "How I Got Interested in Skating."

[21] "Easterns," "The United States Championships," *Skating*, May 1953, 21, 27; Bradley Lord, "How I Got Interested in Skating"; "Rockers and Counters," *Skating*, November 1953, 27; "Rockers and Counters," *Skating*, June 1954, 31.

[22] Muckian, interview.

[23] Rikki Rendich Samuels, telephone interview, November 17, 2003; Bruce Lord, interview; Janet McConville, "An Inactive Member Is a Liability," *Skating*, November 1950, 16-17.

[24] "Easterns," *Skating*, April 1954, 11-12; "Men's Novice," *Skating*, May 1954, 28; Bradley Lord, "How I Got Interested in Skating."

[25] Bradley Lord, "Axel and Sit Spin," *Skating*, March 1954, 25; Bradley R. Lord, "Skate Because You Love To!" *Skating*, April 1954, 33.

[26] "Easterns," *Skating*, May 1955, 25; Bradley Lord, "How I Got Interested in Skating."

[27] "Easterns " and "The United States Championships," *Skating*, May 1956, 22, 38; Bradley Lord, "How I Got Interested in Skating."

[28] Nancy Madden Leamy, telephone interview, May 19, 2005; Gerry Lane, interview.

[29] Peter Betts, telephone interview, February 7, 2005; Ludington, interview.

[30] Ann Pellegrino Bullock, telephone interview, October 18, 2004; Joanna Niska Delaney, telephone interview, April 18, 2005; Christie Allan-Piper, telephone interview, November 9, 2004.

[31] Carol Heiss Jenkins, telephone interview, October 10, 2007; Nancy Heiss Jones, telephone interview, October 11, 2007; Frank Carroll, telephone interview, October 11, 2009.

[32] Bruce Heiss, telephone interview, July 19, 2005; Aloise Samson Lurtsema, telephone interview, August 29, 2005.

[33] Brenda Farmer Farkas, telephone interview, May 3, 2005; Arnold, interview; Lurtsema, interview; Joanne Heckert Bachtel, telephone interview, September 22, 2005.

[34] Jones, interview.

[35] Lurtsema, interview; Diana Lapp Green, telephone interview, April 28, 2005; "New Gold Medalists," *Skating*, November 1956, 10; Bruce Lord, interview; Roy F. Lord, "My Advice to Other Dads," *Skating*, January 1957, 28.

[36] Rigney, interview; Muckian, interview.

[37] "Eastern Championships," *Skating*, April 1957, 20; "Men's Junior," *Skating*, May 1957, 40; Bradley Lord, "How I Got Interested in Skating."

[38] "Swampscott Stunned by Tragic Death of Lord," *Daily Evening Item* (Lynn, MA) February 15, 1961, 8; 1957 Swampscott High School Yearbook, 30; Muckian, interview; Bruce Lord, interview.

[39] Bruce Lord, interview; "U.S. World Team," *Skating*, December 1957, 12.

[40] Marianne Beeler Bourke, telephone interview, June 1, 2004; Jimmy Stephens, telephone interview, September 9, 2004.

[41] Ray E. Hadley Sr., Obituary, *Register-Guard* (Eugene, OR), February 21, 1966; "Five Former Oregonians Aboard Doomed Airliner," *Oregonian* (Portland, OR), February 16, 1961, 1; Darrell Mathias, telephone interview, October 5, 2004.

[42] "Bette Bell: Social Security Death Index," www.sdsi.rootsancestry.com (accessed May 8, 2010); Lewis Hadley, telephone interview, February 9, 2010; "Two Skaters Once Lived in Eugene," *Register-Guard*, February 15, 1961, 1; "1961 World Team Meeting;" "Meet the Champions," *Skating*, June 1957, 27.

[43] Lavon Hart, telephone interview, October 9, 2007; Mathias, interview; Cindy Kauffman Marshall, telephone interview, November 5, 2003.

[44] Mathias, interview; "Marriages," *Skating*, November 1954, 30; "Obituary," *Register-Guard*, February 28, 1961, unpaginated clipping in my possession; Hart, interview; "Five Former Oregonians Aboard Doomed Airliner," 1; Harold Brown, telephone interview, October 15, 2004; Stephens, interview.

[45] Hart, interview; Arvilla Kauffman Christensen, telephone interview, October 6, 2003; Mathias, interview.

[46] Christensen, interview; Mathias, interview; Christine Cruickshank Tagas, telephone interview, October 27, 2003; Patricia Firth Hansen, telephone interview, April 29, 2005.

[47] Hansen , interview; Mathias, interview; Debbie Ganson Lane, telephone interview, November 15, 2004; Linda Adams Garl, telephone interview, February 8, 2005.

[48] Garl, interview; Nancy Moehring, telephone interview, March 3, 2005.

[49] Christensen, interview; Ron Kauffman, telephone interview, November 14, 2007.

[50] Mathias, interview; Marshall, interview.

[51] "Northwestern States," *Skating*, April 1953, 29; "Pacific Coast," *Skating*, May 1953, 38; "Northwestern States," *Skating*, April 1954, 42; "Northwestern States," *Skating*, April 1956, 42; "Pacific Coast," *Skating*, March 1956, 40.

[52] Hart, interview; Mathias, interview; Wilkins, interview.

[53] Allana Mittun Genchel, telephone interview, April 22, 2005; David Mitchell, telephone interview, September 20, 2004; Linda Landin, telephone interview, October 12, 2004; Bourke, interview; Marshall Campbell, telephone interview, April 18, 2005.

[54] Marshall, interview; Tagas, interview; Mitchell, interview.

[55] Bill Wilkins, telephone interview, November 4, 2004; Garl, interview.

[56] Wilkins, interview; Garl, interview.

[57] Tagas, interview; Bob Deuter, telephone interview, September 20, 2004; Carol Deuter Smith, telephone interview, September 20, 2004.

[58] Mitchell, interview; Lorna Dyer, telephone interview, November 4, 2003; Landin, interview; Bud Livesley, "Hadleys Achieve Olympic Goal 4 Years Ahead of Plan," *Seattle Times*, January 31, 1960, 27; Charlene Sharlock Hasha, telephone interview, October 14, 2007.

[59] Garl, interview; Marshall, interview; Deuter, interview.

[60] Garl, interview; Brown, interview; Landin, interview.

[61] Debbie Lane, interview; Garl, interview; Wilkins, interview.

[62] Garl, interview.

[63] Lane, interview; Marshall, interview; Christensen, interview.

[64] Marshall, interview; Garl, interview; Mathias, interview.

[65] Christensen, interview; Kauffman, interview.

[66] Ferne M. Bearse and Nancy Mitchell, "Meet the 1957 Champions," *Skating*, June 1957, 27; Wilkins, interview.

[67] Bearse and Mitchell, "Meet the 1957 Champions," 27; Landin, interview; Moehring, interview; Tagas, interview.

[68] Bearse and Mitchell, "Meet the 1957 Champions," 27; Christensen, interview; Mitchell, interview.

[69] Ice Parade photos and programs, collection of Linda Adams Garl; Tagas, interview.

[70] Sherry Dorsey Cook, telephone interview, May 9, 2005; Brown, interview; Wilkins, interview.

[71] "Pacific Coast Championships," *Skating*, April 1957, 22-23; Sims, "The United States Championships," 17, 40.

[72] Marshall, interview; Cynthia Kauffman, "Summer Trip," *The Skate Blade*, September 1961, copy in my possession.

[73] Ila Ray Hadley, "Are Skaters Crazy?" collection of Linda Adams Garl.

[74] "U.S. World Team," *Skating*, December 1957, 12.

Chapter 5

[1] "The Championships of the World," *Skating*, April 1958, 7.

[2] Ibid, 7-11; "Foreign Skaters to Train in U.S.," *Skating*, June 1957, 29.

[3] Glenn F. Ballard, "The United States Championships," *Skating*, May 1958, 7, 9; Ila Ray and Ray Hadley Jr. "Championnats Du Monde" postcards, collection of Linda Adams Garl.

[4] Ballard, "The United States Championships," 7-9, 40, 42.

[5] 1961 National Figure Skating Championships program; Susan Richards Abbe, telephone interview, August 29, 2003.

[6] Francis Lombardi, telephone interview, September 30, 2003; Abbe, interview; Fred Heller telephone interview, November 11, 2003; Catherine Machado Gray, telephone interview, December 2, 2004.

[7] "1961 World Team Meeting," U.S. Figure Skating files; Abbe, interview.

[8] Abbe, interview; Frances Shelton, "Meet the United States Champions: Dudley S. Richards," *Skating*, May 1951, 8; Pat Farrell Zeiser, telephone interview, June 1, 2004.

[9] Abbe, interview; Senator Edward M. Kennedy, telephone interview, November 27, 2005.

[10] U.S.F.S.A. Figure Skating Nationals 1949 program; E. Newbold Black IV, telephone interview, November 3, 2003; Abbe, interview; S. R. O'Haire, "The Easterns," *Skating*, March 1944, 25; "Rockers and Counters," *Skating*, May 1944, 23.

[11] Benjamin T. Wright, *Skating in America: The 75th Anniversary History of the United States Figure Skating Association* (Colorado Springs: U.S. Figure Skating Association, 1996), vi.; "U.S. Championships," *Skating*, November 1947, 23; Abbe, interview, unpaginated clipping in my possession.

[12] "Rockers and Counters," *Skating*, November 1947, 48; Kennedy, interview; Abbe, interview.

[13] "Rockers and Counters," *Skating*, January 1949, 25; Wright, *Skating in America*, iv; Heller, interview; Abbe, interview; Sheila Muldowny Stone, telephone interview, September 26, 2003; Kennedy, interview.

[14] "Junior Men," *Skating*, June 1949, 10; "Around the Summer Circuit," *Skating*, November 1949, 7; "Easterns," *Skating*, April 1950, 28; Marienne Tobriner, "The United States Championships," *Skating*, May 1950, 20, 22.

[15] Abbe, interview; Shelton, "Meet the United States Champions," 8.

[16] Abbe, interview; *Belmont Hill School Alumni Bulletin*, 25, no. 3 (October 1961), 51-52; Shelton, "Meet the United States Champions," 8; Gray, interview.

[17] Heller, interview; Kennedy, interview.

[18] Christie Allan-Piper, telephone interview, November 9, 2004; Joanne Scotvold Emanuelsen, telephone interview, July 13, 2004; Sidney Foster Arnold, telephone interview, May 2, 2005; Hugh Graham, telephone interview, November 17, 2003; Stone, interview.

[19] "Men's Championship," *Skating*, May 1951, 6.

[20] "The Eastern Championships," *Skating*, March 1951, 4, 6; Wright, *Skating in America*, 155.

[21] "Men," *Skating*, April 1951, 18; Shelton, "Meet the United States Champions," 8; Nellie Jensen, "The United States Championships," *Skating*, April 1951, 8-9.

[22] Bette Todd, "U.S. Olympic Tryouts," *Skating*, February 1952, 4-6; "Men's," *Skating*, May 1952, 32; Don Laws, telephone interview, November 1, 2004; Robert Swenning, telephone interview, October 12, 2004; Richard Dwyer, May 28, 2005; Stone, interview.

[23] Frank Muckian, telephone interview, October 6, 2004; "Senior Men," *Skating*, May 1952, 20.

[24] Abbe, interview; Stone, interview.

[25] John Nightingale, telephone interview, November 23, 2004; Gray, interview; Photo: Dudley Richards in Harvard sweater, *Skating*, November 1952, 6; Sonya Klopfer Dunfield, telephone interview, June 2, 2004; Evelyn Muller Kramer, telephone interview, November 15, 2004.

[26] Heller, interview; Dick Button, telephone interview, December 13, 2005; Abbe, interview.

[27] Theresa Weld Blanchard, "The Championships of the World," *Skating*, April 1953, 10, 34; "North American Championships," "The United States Championships," *Skating*, May 1953, 8-9, 24-25; Abbe, interview.

[28] Stone, interview.

[29] Anita Andres Rogerson, telephone interview, April 19, 2007; Allan-Piper, interview; "Easterns," *Skating*, April 1954, 12.

[30] Abbe, interview; "News about Skaters," *Skating*, November 1954, 29; "U.S. World Team," *Skating*, December 1953, 32; Rogerson, interview.

[31] Lombardi, interview; "Plane Crash in Brussels Hits Local Skating Ranks," *Daily Evening Item* (Lynn, MA), February 16, 1961, 8; "Meet the Champions," *Skating*, April 1961, 22; Abbe, interview.

[32] "News about Skaters," *Skating*, November 1954, 29; Abbe, interview.

[33] "Open Letter on Garmisch Rinks," *Skating*, December 1955, 24-25; Roy Blakey, telephone interview, September 2, 2003; Bill King, telephone interview, November 4, 2003.

[34] Blakey, interview.

[35] Franklin Nelson, telephone interview, September 3, 2005; Graham, interview.

[36] Gray, interview.

[37] "Open Letter on Garmisch Rinks," 24-25; Arnold, interview; Abbe, interview; *Belmont Alumni Bulletin*, 51-52.

[38] "Rockers and Counters," *Skating*, June 1957, 34.

[39] Abbe, interview; "Class of 1954," *1960 Harvard Alumni Bulletin*, 158; Rodger P. Nordblom, telephone interview, March 1, 2005.

[40] Allan-Piper, interview.

[41] "Births," *Skating*, May 1940, 35; "Meet the Champions," 22; "Tests," *Skating*, January 1949, 36.

[42] "Death Nips Promising Ice Careers," *Berkeley Daily Gazette*, February 14, 1961, 5; Maribel Y. Owen, "Children's Corner," *Skating*, January 1941, 17.

[43] "Pacific Coast," *Skating*, May 1950, 34; Polly W. Baker, "A Family Tradition," *Skating*, June 1959, 10-11; "Deaths," *Skating*, January 1953, 28.

[44] "Northern California," *Skating*, April 1954, 40; "Novice Ladies," *Skating*, May 1954, 28.

[45] "Changes in Position," *Skating*, December 1954, 40; Arnold, interview; Loren Caccamise O'Neil, telephone interview, February, 4, 2005.

[46] Arnold, interview; Chuck Foster, telephone interview, October 2, 2007.

[47] Arnold, interview; Foster, interview.

[48] "Easterns," *Skating*, May 1955, 27, 42; "The United States Championships," *Skating*, June 1955, 7, 36; Foster interview.

[49] "U.S. Olympic and World Teams," *Skating*, December 1955, 15; Annah McKaig Hall, "The United States Championships," *Skating*, May 1956, 19, 21.

[50] "U.S. World Team," *Skating*, December 1956, 10, 16; Foster, interview.

[51] Foster, interview; Nancy Madden Leamy, telephone interview, May 19, 2005.

[52] "Easterns," *Skating*, May 1955, 27; "Easterns," *Skating*, May 1956, 24; "Eastern Championships," *Skating*, April 1957, 20; Nancy Ludington Graham, telephone interview, April 5, 2005.

[53] "Meet the Champions," 22; Nancy Graham, interview; Allan-Piper, interview.

[54] Austin Holt, telephone interview, January 21, 2005; Allan-Piper, interview.

[55] Julie Graham Eavzan, telephone interview, April 20, 2004; Allan-Piper, interview.

[56] Gray, interview.

[57] Allan-Piper, interview.

[58] Joan Heiser Gruber, telephone interview, May 21, 2005.

[59] Leamy, interview.

[60] Joyce Burden, telephone interview, August 22, 2004; Leamy, interview; Arnold, interview.

[61] Nancy Graham, interview; Leamy, interview.

[62] 2001 State Farm U.S. Figure Skating Championships program; Leamy, interview.

[63] "Easterns," *Skating*, April 1958, 23; Joanna Niska Delaney, telephone interview, April 18, 2005.

[64] "Easterns," 22, 38; "Senior Pairs," *Skating*, May 1958, 8-9.

[65] "Tests," *Skating*, December 1958, 42; 1961 Nationals program.

Chapter 6

[1] Maribel Y. Owen and Dudley Richards cover photo, *Skating*, February 1959; Marian P. Condit, "The United States Championships," *Skating*, March 1959, 8.

[2] Condit, "The United States Championships," 32.

[3] Ibid., 32, 34, 36.

[4] Wanda Guntert, telephone interview, May 16, 2003.

[5] "The North American Championships," *Skating*, April 1959, 8.

[6] Doreen Denny-Routon, telephone interview, May 26, 2005; "Men," *Skating*, May 1959, 14.

[7] Ron Ludington, interviewed, Overland Park, KS, June 2, 2004; Benjamin T. Wright, *Chips*, 18, no. 7, 4.

[8] Stephen Kelley, interviewed, Quincy, MA, August 7, 2003; Wright, *Chips*, 4.

[9] "1961 World Team Meeting," January 29, 1961, U. S. Figure Skating files; Kelley, interview.

[10] Kelley, interview.

[11] Ibid; Ferne M. Bearse and Nancy Mitchell, "Meet the 1957 Champions," *Skating*, June 1957, 27; "Skating Star, Sister Die in Brussels Crash," *Villager*, February 16, 1961.

[12] Kelley, interview; Mary Lou Hunt, email interview, April 7, 2005.

[13] "Easterns," *Skating*, May 1955, 25, 27; "Skating Star, Sister Die in Brussels Crash;" Bearse and Mitchell, "Meet the 1957 Champions," 28; "The Summer Skating Circuit," *Skating*, November 1956, 10; "Tests," *Skating*, November 1956, 39.

[14] Ann Pellegrino Bullock, telephone interview, October 18, 2004; Joanna Niska Delaney, telephone interview, April 18, 2005; Ludington, interview.

[15] Sue Blodgett Rigney, telephone interview, May 17, 2005; Mary Batdorf Scotvold, telephone interview, May 25, 2004; Peter Betts, telephone interview, February 7, 2005.

[16] "Eastern Championships," *Skating*, April 1957, 20; Harry A. Sims, "The United States Championships," *Skating*, May 1957, 16, 42; "Rockers and Counters," *Skating*, November 1957, 26.

[17] "Easterns," *Skating*, April 1958, 22; Glenn F. Ballard, "The United States Championships," *Skating*, May 1958, 7, 40.

[18] Kelley, interview; Bearse and Mitchell, "Meet the 1957 Champions," 28; Benjamin T. Wright, telephone interview, April 22, 2010; Elizabeth George Busconi, telephone interview, May 4, 2005; "Meet the 1957 Champions," 28.

[19] Gary Visconti, interviewed, Long Beach, CA, September 14, 2004.

[20] Scotvold, interview.

[21] "The Summer Skating Story," *Skating*, November 1958, 8, 11, 42; Scotvold, interview.

[22] Rigney, interview.

[23] Condit, "The United States Championships," 9, 34.

[24] Betts, interview.

[25] "Meet the New Champions," *Skating*, June 1959, 11; Ronna Goldblatt Gladstone, telephone interview, April 25, 2010; Busconi, interview.

[26] Gerry Lane, telephone interview, November 17, 2004; Gregory Kelley and Bradley Lord cover photo, *Skating*, January 1958; Paul George, interviewed, Portland, OR, January 13, 2005; Rigney, interview; Christie Allan-Piper, telephone interview, November 9, 2004.

[27] Kelley, interview.

[28] Bullock, interview; George, interview; Wright, interview.

[29] "Crash Kills 2 Kelley Children," *Boston Traveler*, February 15, 1961, 12; "Gregory Kelley, Only 16, Held Many Titles," *Boston Globe*, February 15, 1961, 15; Kelley, interview; Allan-Piper, interview; Wright, *Chips*, 4.

[30] Kelley, interview.

[31] Rigney, interview; Tom McGinnis, telephone interview, September 14, 2004.

[32] "In Memoriam," *Aberjona* (1961 Winchester High School yearbook), 50.

[33] "Births," *Skating*, October 1944, 22; 2001 State Farm U.S. Championships program; Joyce Underwood Winship, telephone interview, October 1, 2003; Ludington, interview.

[34] Patricia Firth Hansen, telephone interview, April 29, 2005.

[35] "Northern California," *Skating*, April 1952, 32; "Pacific Coast," *Skating*, May 1952, 15; Laurence Owen, "Children's Corner," *Skating*, February 1953, 14.

[36] Robert Swenning, telephone interview, October 11, 2004.

[37] Joan Brader Burns, telephone interview, October 29, 2003; Toni Sweet, "Roy Cofer," *St. Moritz ISC History* (N.p.: Privately published, 1991), 51; Toni Sweet, "Betty Jean Clark Moehnke," *St. Moritz ISC History*, 9; Barbara Heilman, "Mother Set the Style," *Sports Illustrated*, February 13, 1961, 40.

[38] "Pacific Coast," *Skating*, May 1953, 42.

[39] Robin Greiner, telephone interview, September 27, 2004; "Easterns," *Skating*, May 1955, 27; Betts, interview; Swenning, interview.

[40] Julie Palmer Mayo, telephone interview, May 26, 2005.

[41] Ibid.; Georg N. Meyers, "The Sporting Thing," *Seattle Times*, January 27, 1960, 18.

[42] "The United States Championships," *Skating*, May 1956, 18, 21-22.

[43] Mayo, interview.

[44] "Easterns," *Skating*, April 1957, 20; Leah Grace Oathout, "Easterns," *Skating*, April 1958, 22-23.

[45] "The United States Championships," *Skating*, May 1958, 7, 9; E. Newbold Black IV, telephone interview, November 3, 2003.

[46] Oathout, "Easterns," 22; McGinnis, interview.

[47] Busconi, interview; Gladstone, interview, April 25, 2010.

[48] McGinnis, interview; Ludington, interview.

[49] Julie Graham-Eavzan, telephone interview, April 20, 2005; Delaney, interview, Rikki Rendich Samuels, telephone interview, November 17, 2003.

[50] Ludington, interview.

[51] Patty Gustafson Feeney, telephone interview, December 9, 2004; Bullock, interview; Lane, interview; Busconi, interview.

[52] Gladstone, interview.

[53] Joyce Burden, telephone interview, August 22, 2004.

[54] "Meet the New Champions," 10; "Owen Family, Champions All," *Boston Traveler*, February 15, 1961, 42; McGinnis, interview; Charles Roach, "Skate Team Tragedy Hits Denver Fireman," *Rocky Mountain News*, February 16, 1961, 16.

[55] Nancy Madden Leamy, telephone interview, May 19, 2005; Clinton Jonas, "Laurence as I Knew Her," *Winchester Star*, February 23, 1961, 7.

[56] Robert V. Leary, "All Winchester Hushed, Flags at Half Staff," *Boston Globe*, February 16, 1961, 21; Mayo, interview.

[57] Condit, "The United States Championships," 8, 23, 32; Dick Button, telephone interview, December 13, 2005.

[58] Christy Haigler Krall, interviewed Colorado Springs, May 9, 2003; Hansen, interview.

[59] "1961 World Team Meeting;" Diane Yeomans Robins, interviewed, Overland Park, KS, October 6, 2009; Kamon Simpson, "U.S. Skating Tragedy," *Gazette* (Colorado Springs), February 15, 2001, A10; Bobbie Parkinson, telephone interview, September 23, 2003.

[60] "1961 World Team Meeting;" Simpson, "U.S. Skating Tragedy, A10; Parkinson, interview.

[61] Stephanie Westerfeld, "Children's Corner," *Skating*, January 1949, 18.

[62] Parkinson, interview; Michelle Voepel, "Frozen in Time," *Kansas City Star*, March 4, 2001, C14; "Midwesterns," *Skating*, April 1950, 26; "New Gold Medalist," *Skating*, February 1951, 24.

[63] Eileen Seigh Honnen, telephone interview, July 14, 2005; "Midwesterns," *Skating*, April 1951, 23; "Senior Ladies," *Skating*, May 1952, 20; "U.S. Skaters for World Team," *Skating*, January 1953, 21; "Ladies' Senior," *Skating*, May 1953, 25.

[64] "Broadmoor Summer Dance Competition," *Skating*, November 1952, 37; Barlow Nelson, telephone interview, November 17, 2003; Sherry Dorsey Cook, telephone interview, May 9, 2005; Andra McLaughlin Kelly, telephone interview, September 26, 2005; Hugh Graham, telephone interview, November 17, 2003.

[65] Kelly, interview; Hansen, interview; Frances Dorsey Burke, telephone interview, June 7, 2005; "Straw Hats and Ice Skates," *Skating*, November 1952, 6; Hayes Alan Jenkins, telephone interview, October 10, 2007.

[66] Voepel, "Frozen in Time," C-14.

[67] Ann R. Walker, "Midwesterns," *Skating*, April 1950, 26; "Midwesterns," *Skating*, April 1952, 12; Roach, "Skate Team Tragedy," 16; Diana Lapp Green, telephone interview, April 28, 2005; Cook, interview.

[68] "Deaths," *Skating*, February 1952, 26; Diane Lynne Betts, *The Broadmoor World Arena Pictorial History Book* (Colorado Springs: Broadmoor World Arena, 1988), 89; Honnen, interview.

[69] Loren Caccamise O'Neil, telephone interview, February 4, 2005; Elena Bertozzi-Villa, *Broadmoor Memories: The History of the Broadmoor* (Colorado Springs: Pictorial Histories Publishing Company, 1993), 154, Honnen, interview.

[70] "Midwesterns," *Skating*, April 1953, 20-22; Honnen, interview; Stephanie Westerfeld, "This Is How I Do It," *Skating*, January 1954, 38.

[71] S. E. Cram, "The Midwestern Championships," *Skating*, April 1956, 10-11; "Novice Ladies," *Skating*, June 1955, 38; "The United States Championships," *Skating*, May 1956, 22.

[72] "Midwestern Championships," *Skating*, April 1957, 21; Pam Zekman, telephone interview, April 13, 2005; Patty Creed Smith, telephone interview, September, 28, 2004.

[73] "The United States Championships," *Skating*, May 1957, 18; "New Gold Medalists," *Skating*, November 1957, 16, 34; Sherri Westerfeld postcard, collection of Diane Yeomans Robins.

[74] "Midwesterns," *Skating*, April 1958, 23; O'Neil, interview; "The United States Championships," *Skating*, May 1958, 7, 9.

[75] Jeanie O'Brien Callahan, telephone interview, June 17, 2005.

[76] Carole Carlson Wolfswinkle, telephone interview; May 11, 2005; Green, interview; Pam Thatcher Marsh, telephone interview, May 24, 2005; Honnen, interview.

[77] Marsh, interview; Voepel, "Frozen in Time," C14; Esther Vance Piano Recital program, June 18, 1954, collection of Diane Yeomans Robins; Wilson, interview; Green, interview; Donna Abbott Baldwin, telephone interview May 21, 2004.

[78] Marsh, interview; Robins, interview; Cook, interview; Wilson, interview.

[79] "The Summer Skating Story," *Skating*, November 1958, 10; "Cups Today, Medals Tomorrow," *Sports Illustrated*, February 9, 1959, 32-33; Condit, "The United States Championships," 8, 20-21, 32.

Chapter 7

[1] Dorcas G. Griffin, "Three Summer Skating Seasons," *Skating*, November 1938, 3; Lake Placid advertisement, *Skating*, March 1950, inside front cover; Lake Placid advertisement, *Skating*, April 1956, back cover; Lake Placid advertisement, *Skating*, April 1957, 2; Lake Placid advertisement, *Skating*, April 1960, 4.

[2] Anne Batdorf Militano, telephone interview, May 25, 2004.

[3] "1961 World Team Meeting," January 29, 1961; Wilhelmina Kipp Gozzard, telephone interview, October 5, 2007; Bob Wittman, "When Darkness Fell over Olympic Ice," *Morning Call* (Allentown, PA), February 1992, unpaginated clipping in my possession.

[4] Gozzard, interview; Wittman, "When Darkness Fell Over Olympic Ice."

[5] "Tests," *Skating*, November 1948, 40; J. J. Bejshak, telephone interview, August 21, 2004; Theda Beck Bartynski, telephone interview, July 12, 2005.

[6] Jack Lapos, "Ace Tourney Skaters Coached by Local Native Practice Here," *Evening Chronicle* (Allentown, PA), February 2, 1961, 22; Bartynski, interview; "Lake Placid Summer Championships," *Skating*, November 1949, 34.

[7] Joseph P. Gibson Jr., "Easterns," *Skating*, April 1950, 27, 29; "Silver Dance," *Skating*, May 1950, 23; Bartynski, interview.

[8] 1950 *Comus*, Allentown High School yearbook), 120; "Rockers and Counters," *Skating*, June 1951, 20, 29; "Rockers and Counters," *Skating*, November 1952, 28.

[9] Wittman, "When Darkness Fell Over Olympic Ice;" "Gold Medalists," *Skating*, December 1952, 28.

[10] Joan Heiser Gruber, telephone interview, May 21, 2005; "Gold Dance," *Skating*, May 1953, 27; "Tests," *Skating*, November 1953, 38; "U.S. World Team," *Skating*, December 1953, 32; "Gold Dance," *Skating*, May 1954, 28.

[11] "Gold Medalists," *Skating*, December 1954, 6, 28; Joe McCarron, "Allentown Skater Sets Goal on 1956 Olympics," *Morning Call*, February 2, 1955, 24; Jack Lapos, "Bill Kipp, 3 Proteges Trained Here," *Evening Chronicle*, February 15, 1961, unpaginated clipping in my possession; Janet Roberts McLeod, telephone interview, July 11, 2003; Christie Allan-Piper, telephone interview, November 9, 2004; Sheila Muldowny Stone, telephone interview, September 18, 2003; Mary Lou Butler-Mitchell, telephone interview, April 2, 2005.

[12] Cynthia Hansen White, telephone interview, September 6, 2005; Gruber, interview; Peter Betts, telephone interview, February 7, 2005.

[13] McCarron, "Allentown Skater Sets Goal on 1956 Olympics," 24; Beth Sundene Graham, telephone interview, November 1, 2004; Evelyn Muller Kramer, telephone interview, November 15, 2004; Hugh Graham, telephone interview, November 17, 2003; Marilyn Grace Guilfoyle, telephone interview, May 24, 2004.

[14] Robin Greiner, telephone interview, September 27, 2004; "Middle Atlantics," *Skating*, April 1955, 40; "Easterns," *Skating*, May 1955, 25-27; "North Americans," *Skating*, May 1955, 7-9; "Gold Dance," *Skating*, June 1955, 38.

[15] Wittman, "When Darkness Fell over Olympic Ice;" Butler-Mitchell, interview; Bruce Hyland, telephone interview, January 24, 2005.

[16] Gozzard, interview.

[17] Ruth Ann Kipp, telephone interview, October 5, 2007.

[18] Irene Maguire Muehlbronner, telephone interview, October 15, 2004; Lapos, "Ace Tourney Skaters," 22.

[19] "Paramount Iceland," www.Zamboni.fr/story/IcelandPararmount.html (accessed January 27, 2003).

[20] Sharon McKenzie, telephone interview, May 16, 2005.

[21] Aileen Karhe Arenson, telephone interview, April 4, 2005.

[22] McKenzie, interview.

[23] McLeod, interview; Carol Galloway Goldrod, telephone interview, September 6, 2004; Maggie Hosford, telephone interview, October 24, 2003.

[24] Joyce Burden, telephone interview, August 22, 2004; Hosford, interview.

[25] Gruber, interview; Marie Pearce, interviewed, Overland Park, KS, April 14, 2005; Margie Ackles Jones, telephone interview, October 7, 2004.

[26] Lake Placid advertisement, *Skating*, June 1957, 2; "Season's Greetings from Jean Westwood," *Skating*, January 1958, 39; Mary Batdorf Scotvold, telephone interview, May 25, 2004; Gruber, interview; Sally Wells Van De Mark, telephone interview, August 27, 2004; Ray Chenson, telephone interview, September 3, 2004.

[27] "Bill Kipp Memorial," www.penguinfsc.com/Penguin2/pages/history_ BillKipp.htm (accessed April 13, 2006). Kipp, interview; Jean Westwood, telephone interview, July 13, 2004; Greiner, interview.

[28] Scotvold, interview; Gozzard, interview; Bob Munz, telephone interview, June 8, 2005; McKenzie, interview; Glenda Rhodes Pugh, telephone interview, September 25, 2007.

[29] Sarasue Gleis Essenprice, telephone interview, August 24, 2004; Walter Hypes, telephone interview, September 9, 2004.

[30] Jim Short, telephone interview, October 12, 2004; Anita Entrikin Miller, telephone interview, January 23, 2006; Essenprice interview.

[31] Short, interview; Van De Mark, interview; Miller, interview.

[32] Mike Michelson, telephone interview, July 1, 2003; Mike Mokler, telephone interview, November 15, 2009; Miller, interview.

[33] Michelson, interview; "Tests," *Skating*, May 1952, 38; "Tests," *Skating*, January, 1953, 38; "Tests," *Skating*, November 1954, 38; "Rhode Michelson was 'Headed for Olympics,'" *Los Angeles Examiner*, February 16, 1961, 3.

[34] Essenprice, interview; Westwood, interview; "Southern California Inter-Club," *Skating*, November 1956, 14; "Pacific Coast Championships," *Skating*, April 1957, 23; Gruber, interview.

[35] "Lake Placid Free Skating Championships," *Skating*, November 1957, 21.

[36] Hypes, interview; Goldrod, interview; Scotvold, interview; Barbara Roles Williams, telephone interview, September 25, 2003.

[37] Short, interview; Allan-Piper, interview.

[38] Jennie Walsh Guzman, telephone interview, September 9, 2003; Marlene Morris Van Dusen, telephone interview, June 27, 2005.

[39] "Pacific Coast," *Skating*, April 1958, 27; Marianne Beeler Bourke, telephone interview, June 1, 2004; Glenn F. Ballard, "The U.S. Championships," *Skating*, May 1958, 7, 42.

[40] Kramer, interview; Van De Mark, interview.

[41] "Meet the 1958 United States Champions," *Skating*, June 1958, 15; Austin Holt, telephone interview, January 21, 2005; Allan-Piper, interview.

[42] Patty Creed Smith, telephone interview, September 28, 2004; Allan-Piper, interview.

[43] Judianne Fotheringill Fuller, telephone interview; July 25, 2005; Don Bartleson, telephone interview, November 8, 2004; Betts, interview; Jerry Fotheringill, telephone interview, August 21,

2005; Barlow Nelson, telephone interview, November 17, 2003; Loren Caccamise O'Neil, telephone interview, February 4, 2005.

[44] Mary Miller Robicheaux, telephone interview, July 14, 2005; Munz, interview; Betts, interview.

[45] Allan-Piper, interview; Munz, interview.

[46] Munz, interview; "Lake Placid Free Skating Championships," *Skating*, November 1958,12.

[47] Michelson, interview; Pugh, interview.

[48] Michelson, interview; Hypes, interview; Goldrod, interview.

[49] Goldrod, interview; Burden, interview.

[50] Billy Chapel, telephone interview, September 10, 2003.

[51] Guzman, interview; Robicheaux, interview.

[52] Bejshak, interview; Robicheaux, interview; Miller, interview.

[53] Hypes, interview; Bartleson, interview.

[54] "Southwest Pacific," *Skating*, February 1959, 29; Marian P. Condit, "The United States Championships," *Skating*, March 1959, 8, 19, 32.

[55] Marilyn Meeker Durham, telephone interview, July 30, 2003.

[56] "1961 World Team Meeting," January 29, 1961; "Dies in Plane Crash," *Bridgeport Telegram*, February 16, 1961, 1; Rose Anne Paquette Ryan Wager, telephone interview, March 4, 2010; 1947 Fairfield Preparatory High School yearbook, 44.

[57] "Tests," *Skating*, February 1959, 36; "Air Victim's Ex-Partner Recalls Skating Career," *Washington Post*, February 16, 1961, A3; Duncan, interview; "1942-1949," www.usarsarollerskaters.org/19421949USARSANationalChampionships.html (accessed April 27, 2010).

[58] Duncan, interview.

[59] Ibid; "Easterns," *Skating*, April 1949, 26; "The United States Championships," *Skating*, June 1949, 10; "Lake Placid Summer Dance Championships," *Skating*, November 1949, 34.

[60] "Meet the United States Champions," *Skating*, June 1950, 7; Don Laws, telephone interview, November 1, 2004.

[61] Walter ("Red") Bainbridge, telephone interview, September 3, 2004.

[62] "Easterns," *Skating*, April 1950, 29; Marianne Tobriner, "The United States Championships," *Skating*, May 1950, 20, 23; Duncan, interview.

[63] Duncan, interview; "Grasshopper Plague Hits Lake Placid," *Skating*, November 1949, 14; White, interview; Slavka Kohout Button, telephone interview, May 13, 2005; Bainbridge, interview.

[64] John Nightingale, telephone interview, November 23, 2004; Hyland, interview; Gruber, interview.

[65] Helen Geekie Nightingale, telephone interview, November 23, 2004; Margaret Ann Graham Holt, telephone interview, November 16, 2003; "Meet the United States Champions," *Skating*, June 1950, 7; Westwood, interview; Laws, interview; "Lake Placid Summer Dance Championships," *Skating*, November 1950, 3.

[66] "Gold Dance," *Skating*, April 1951, 38; "North American Championships" *Skating*, May 1951, 19; "Carol Peters—Danny Ryan in National Dance Ice Feature," *Washington Daily Times*, March 28, 1953, unpaginated clipping in my possession; "Rockers and Counters," *Skating*, June 1951, 25.

[67] "The Boys and the Draft," *Skating*, June 1951, 11; "Meet the Champions," *Skating*, June 1953, 9; Duncan, interview; Ice Crystals of 1952, Baltimore Figure Skating Club program; John Nightingale, interview.

[68] Wright, *Skating in America*, 116, 126; Katherine Sackett, "Free Dancing," *Skating*, December 1951, 15; Duncan, interview; Bette Todd, "U.S. Olympic Try-Outs," *Skating*, February 1952, 5-6; "The United States Championships," *Skating*, May 1952, 5-6, 32.

[69] Michael McGean, telephone interview, October 12, 2004.

[70] "U.S. Skaters for World Team," *Skating*, January 1953, 21; "News of Competitors," *Skating*, December 1952, 7; Theresa Weld Blanchard, "The Championships of the World," *Skating*, April 1953, 10, 34.

[71] "North American Championships," *Skating*, May 1953, 7-9; "The United States Championships," *Skating*, May 1953, 24, 27; "Gold Medalists," *Skating*, December 1953, 24, 28, 48.

[72] "Meet the 1953 Champions," *Skating*, June 1953, 9-10; Duncan, interview; "Spins through Professional Circles," *Skating*, December 1953, 29, 33.

[73] Wager, interview; "Spins through Professional Circles," *Skating*, June 1955, 37; Pieter Kollen, telephone interview, July 29, 2003; Peter Dunfield, telephone interview, July 28, 2004; Bainbridge, interview; "Marriages," *Skating*, November 1955, 32.

[74] "Jet Crash Stills Dream of Indianapolis Skaters," *Indianapolis Star*, February 16, 1961, 24; White, interview.

[75] Van De Mark, interview; Sandy Schwomeyer Lamb, telephone interview, October 13 2003; Judy Schwomeyer Sladky, telephone interview, May 11, 2005.

[76] Durham, interview; Van De Mark, interview.

[77] Kollen, interview.

[78] Sally Schantz Urban, telephone interview, August 31, 2004; Kollen, interview; "Births," *Skating*, March 1956, 27; "Births," *Skating*, March 1957, 30; "Births," *Skating*, November 1958, 29; "Births," December 1959, 32; Nolan, interview; Wager, interview; Lamb interview.

[79] "Carnival Cavalcade," *Skating*, May 1958, 34; "Rockers and Counters," *Skating*, March 1959, 27; Wager, interview; Cobourg, Ontario, advertisement, *Skating*, April 1956, 3; Mount Royal, Quebec, advertisement, *Skating*, May 1958, 49.

[80] Bainbridge, interview; Michael Paikin, telephone interview, May 27, 2005; Munz, interview; Charles Fetter, telephone interview, September 14, 2004.

[81] Bainbridge, interview.

[82] Lamb, interview; Wager, interview.

[83] "Jet Crash Stills Dream," 24; Bette Todd, telephone interview, September 29, 2004.

[84] Van De Mark, interview; Karl Freed, telephone interview, October 9, 2007; Fetter, interview.

[85] Aloise Samson Lurtsema, telephone interview, August 29, 2005; Munz, interview.

[86] "1961 World Team Meeting"; Pierce funeral marker, Washington Park East, Indianapolis; Durham, interview.

[87] "Meet the Champions," *Skating*, April 1961, 23; Russell Pierce, telephone interview, September 26, 2004; "Dream of Honor Cruelly Crushed," *Indianapolis Times*, February 15, 1961, 3; Patty Williams Canary, October 12, 2004; 1955 *Riparian* (Broad Ripple High School yearbook); Dallas H. Pierce, letter to F. Ritter Shumway, August 13, 1961.

[88] "Tests," *Skating*, June 1955, 44; "Tests," *Skating*, March 1955, 40; "Tests," *Skating*, February 1957, 40; Henry Butler, "New Talent Enlivens Big Show," *Indianapolis Times*, January 20, 1955, 1, 3.

[89] Durham, interview.

[90] Ibid; "Tests," *Skating*, December 1954, 44.

[91] Durham, interview; Dick Mills, telephone interview, October 7, 2004.

[92] "Midwestern Championships," *Skating*, April 1957, 22; "Tests," *Skating*, April 1957, 40; Governor and Mrs. Harold W. Handley, Western Union telegram to Marilyn Meeker, February 4, 1957.

[93] "Midwesterns," *Skating*, April 1958, 42; "The United States Championships," *Skating*, May 1958, 8, 42.

[94] Durham, interview; Pierce, interview; Bainbridge, interview.

[95] Ken Ormsby, telephone interview, September 20, 2005; Julie Graham Eavzan, telephone interview, April 20, 2005; Munz, interview; Donna Lee Mitchell Zaleski, telephone interview, December 1, 2005.

[96] Paikin, interview.

[97] Munz, interview; Wager, interview.

[98] Durham, interview.

[99] "Meet the New Champions," *Skating*, April 1959, 36; Van De Mark, interview; Margie Jurmo Caton, telephone interview, November 3, 2004.

[100] Paikin, interview; Munz, interview.

[101] Fetter, interview.

[102] Kitty Teague Schaub, telephone interview, October 7, 2004; Pierce, interview; Van De Mark, interview; Durham, interview.

[103] Van De Mark, interview; Caton, interview.

[104] Kollen, interview.

[105] Fetter, interview; Van De Mark, interview.

[106] "Meet the New Champions," *Skating*, April 1959, 12; Pierce, interview.

[107] "Ends Basic," clipping from unidentified 1958 Indianapolis newspaper, (date incomplete); Durham, interview.

[108] Durham, interview.

[109] Condit, "The United States Championships," 8, 36.

[110] Durham, interview.

Chapter 8

[1] "On to Squaw Valley," *Newsweek*, February 9, 1959, 86, 88; "Track!" *Newsweek*, February 15, 1960, 59; Melvin Durslag, "The Great Winter Olympics Fight," *Saturday Evening Post*, February 22, 1958, 35.

[2] Durslag, "The Great Winter Olympics Fight," 73.

[3] Ibid.

[4] Ibid; "On to Squaw Valley!" 88.

[5] "Olympic Heaven," *Senior Scholastic*, February 3, 1960, 22; Durslag, "The Great Winter Olympics Fight," 73.

[6] Durslag, "The Great Winter Olympics Fight," 73-74; "Track!" 60.

[7] Durslag, "The Great Winter Olympics Fight," 73-74.

[8] Evan Hill, "California's Olympic Bonanza," *Saturday Evening Post*, February 13, 1960, 103-4.

[9] "14-Year Wait," *Seattle Times*, February 24, 1960, 15.

[10] Carol Heiss Jenkins, telephone interview, October 10, 2007.

[11] David Jenkins, telephone interview, November 30, 2005.

[12] Ibid.

[13] Ibid.

[14] Ibid.

[15] Nancy Rouillard Ludington Graham, telephone interview, April 5, 2005; Tom McGinnis, telephone interview, September 14, 2004.

[16] Wilhelmina Kipp Gozzard, telephone interview, October 5, 2007.

[17] "Tests," *Skating*, November 1959, 36; Joyce Butchart, telephone interview, September 13, 2003.

[18] "Easterns" and "Midwesterns," *Skating*, March 1960, 14, 17, 32; Bud Livesley, "Heiss Has New Challenger," *Seattle Times*, January 26, 1960, 12.

[19] Mary Miller Robicheaux, telephone interview, July 14, 2005.

[20] "Test Run for Olympics," *Skating*, December 1959, 13; 1960 Pacific Coast Championships program.

[21] Don Bartleson, telephone interview, November 8, 2004; Sandy Carson Gollihugh, telephone interview, September 10, 2004; Linda Adams Garl, telephone interview, February 8, 2005.

[22] Toni Sweet, "Howard Taylor," *St. Moritz ISC History* (N.p.: Privately published, 1991), 123; Garl, interview; Sondra Holmes Kovacovsky, telephone interview, February 23, 2005.

[23] Garl, interview.

[24] Bartleson, interview; Sweet, "Howard Taylor," 123; Garl, interview; Marshall Campbell, telephone interview, April 18, 2005; Gollihugh, interview.

[25] 1960 Pacific Coast Olympic Data Processing Results, collection of Linda Adams Garl; Allana Mittun Genchel, telephone interview, April 22, 2005.

[26] Howard Taylor, telephone interview, October 17, 2003; "Pacific Coast," *Skating*, February 1960, 18-19.

[27] Bud Livesley, "Dimpled Miss Heiss Back at Scene of First Triumph," *Seattle Times*, January 28, 1960, 31.

[28] Royal Brougham, "The Morning After," *Seattle Post-Intelligencer*, January 26, 1960, 18; Bud Livesley, "Ice-Skating Rules Call for Exacting Maneuvers," *Seattle Times*, January 25, 1960, 4.

[29] Phil Taylor, "U.S. Skate Tests Open Here Today," *Seattle Post-Intelligencer*, January 27, 1960, 18; Phil Taylor, "Figure Skate Draw Today," *Seattle Post-Intelligencer*, January 26, 1960, 19.

[30] Nancy Heiss Jones, telephone interview, October 11, 2007.

[31] Taylor, "Figure Skate Draw Today," 19; Bud Livesley, "Colorado Girl Will Bid for Olympic Spot," *Seattle Times*, January 26, 1960, 12.

[32] Lloyd L. Palmer, "The United States, Championships," *Skating*, March 1960, 7, 29; Taylor, "Figure Skate Draw Today," 19.

[33] Palmer, "The United States, Championships," 7, 29.

[34] Bill Prochnau, "Jenkins Seeks 4th U.S. Title Tonight," *Seattle Times*, January 30, 1960, 7; Taylor, "U.S. Skate Tests Open Here Today," 18; Palmer, "The United States Championships," 7-8, 29.

[35] Palmer, "The United States Championships," 8, 29; Bud Livesley, "Gay, Young Blade, 10, Skates Because of Mom's Broken 'Vow,'" *Seattle Times*, January 29, 1960, 14.

[36] Livesley, "Dimpled Miss Heiss Back at Scene of First Triumph," 31; Louella Rehfield, telephone interview, August 31, 2004; Palmer, "The United States Championships," 8, 29.

37 Palmer, "The United States Championships," 8-9, 29; Judianne Fotheringill Fuller, telephone interview, July 25, 2005; Karl Freed, telephone interview, October 9, 2007; Bud Livesley, "Hadleys Achieve Olympic Goal 4 Years Ahead of Plan," *Seattle Times*, January 31, 1960, 27.

38 Phil Taylor, "Carol Heiss Captures Fourth Skate Crown," *Seattle Post-Intelligencer*, January 30, 1960, 6; Palmer, "The United States, Championships," 8; Livesley, "Ice-Skating Rules Call for Exacting Maneuvers," 14.

39 Palmer, "The United States Championships," 8-9; Taylor, "Carol Heiss Captures Fourth Skate Crown," 6.

40 Phil Taylor, "From Hospital to Ice Glory," *Seattle Post-Intelligencer*, January 31, 2006, 21; Bud Livesley, "Seattle Girl Wins in Figure-Skating Meet," *Seattle Times*, January 31, 1960, 25; Palmer, "The United States Championships," 8, 30.

41 Palmer, "The United States Championships," 8-9, 29-30.

42 Bud Livesley, "U.S. Skating Meet Begins Wednesday," *Seattle Times*, January 24, 1960, 23; Bud Livesley, "Scholdan, Coach of Ice Champs, Picks Dave Jenkins," *Seattle Times*, January 27, 1960, 18.

43 Palmer, "The United States Championships," 9.

44 Ibid.

45 Robert Brewer, interviewed, Phoenix, AZ, March 18, 2005.

46 Bradley Lord, "How I Got Interested in Figure Skating."

47 Ibid.

48 Palmer, "The United States Championships," 7, 9.

49 Livesley, "Dimpled Miss Heiss Back at Scene of First Triumph," 31; Taylor, "From Hospital to Ice Glory," 21.

Chapter 9

1 Margie Jurmo Caton, telephone interview, November 3, 2004; Cynthia Hansen White, telephone interview, September 6, 2005.

2 "1961 World Team Meeting," January 29, 1961; Erik Swallender, telephone interview, October 12, 2005; Bill Swallender, telephone interview, September 3, 2005.

3 Dick Cullum, "Swallender Ready for National Title," unidentified Minneapolis newspaper clipping in my possession; "Swallender and Frances Johnson to Skating Meet," unidentified Minneapolis newspaper clipping in my possession; Edwin F. Washburn, "Meet the 1933 National Champions," *Skating*, May 1933, 6-7; William Swallender, "Impressions," *Skating*, May 1933, 16.

4 Bill Swallender, interview; Virginia Baxter Newman, telephone interview, August 30, 2004; White, interview; "Skating Club Teacher Didn't Plan to Be Pro," unidentified Detroit newspaper clipping in my possession.

5 Jane Bucher Jones, "A History of Ice Skating in Kansas City;" "New Club Brings Famous Figure to KC," 4, undated clipping from unidentified 1935 Kansas City paper in my possession; "Ice Show Draws 4,500," undated clipping from unidentified 1936 Kansas City paper in my possession.

6 Erik Swallender, interview; Ice Follies of 1939 program, Madison Square Garden, New York, November 29-December 3, 1938, 12.

7 Erik Swallender, interview; Jones, interview; "Rockers and Counters," *Skating*, May 1938, 9-11; Swallender Christmas greetings advertisement, *Skating*, December 1938, 37; "Rockers and Counters," *Skating*, March 1939, 36; "Shipstad Is 'Heartbroken,'" *San Francisco Examiner*, February 16, 1961, IV2; Newman, interview; Diane Lynne Betts, *The Broadmoor World Arena Pictorial History Book*

(Colorado Springs: Broadmoor World Arena, 1988), 92; "Spins through Professional Circles," *Skating*, October 1941, 2.

[8] Beth Sundene Graham, telephone interview, November 1, 2004.

[9] Nancy Meiss, interviewed, Overland Park, KS, April 7, 2005; Norma Sahlin, telephone interview, September 10, 2004; Diana Lapp Green, telephone interview, April 28, 2005.

[10] Newman, interview; Mary Lou Butler-Mitchell, telephone interview, April 2, 2005; Sahlin, interview; Bill Martin, telephone interview, August 24, 2005; Maxine Ceramin Rayner, telephone interview, August 22, 2005.

[11] "Spirals through the Summer," *Skating*, October 1943, 17; Walter ("Red") Bainbridge, telephone interview, September 3, 2004; Mrs. J. Donald Baxter, "Let Your Skater Play," *Skating*, October 1944, 8; Newman, interview.

[12] "Births," *Skating*, October 1943, 26; Sahlin, interview.

[13] "Spin through Professional Circles," *Skating*, November 1947, 34; Newman, interview.

[14] E. Newbold Black IV, telephone interview, November 3, 2005; Irene Maguire Muehlbronner, telephone interview, October 15, 2004; Joyce Komperda, telephone interview, December 13, 2007.

[15] Bill Swallender, interview; White, interview.

[16] White, interview; Bill Swallender, interview.

[17] Bill Swallender, interview; Joan Heiser Gruber, telephone interview, May 21, 2005; White, interview.

[18] "Check-up on Today's Competitors," *Skating*, November 1948, 9; Newman, interview.

[19] "Historical Results," www.eskatefans/skatabase/historical (accessed September 30, 2003); Newman, interview; "Spins through Professional Circles," *Skating*, November 1950, 35; Bill Swallender, interview.

[20] "They Built Their Rinks Recently," *Skating*, April 1950, 13; Louise Samson, telephone interview, September 1, 2005; Martin, interview; Brenda Farmer Farkas, telephone interview, May 3, 2005.

[21] Aloise Samson Lurtsema, telephone interview, August 29, 2005.

[22] Samson, interview; Gruber, interview; Patty Creed Smith, telephone interview, September 28, 2004.

[23] White, interview.

[24] Newman, interview; Caton, interview.

[25] Pieter Kollen, telephone interview, July 29, 2003.

[26] "Births," *Skating*, May 1953, 30; Bill Swallender, interview; "The Studio Schools," *Skating*, February 1955, 10-11; Newman, interview.

[27] Ken Williams, "Year-Round Drills Aid Ice Skaters," *Detroit News*, 1958, unpaginated and undated clipping in my possession; Rayner, interview; Ann Seror Barr, telephone interview, July 25, 2004.

[28] Bill Swallender, interview; Martin, interview.

[29] Williams, "Year-Round Drills Aid Ice Skaters;" Bill Swallender, interview; Bruce Heiss, telephone interview, July 19, 2005.

[30] Ann Pellegrino Bullock, telephone interview, October 18, 2004; Bill Swallender, interview.

[31] Bill Swallender, interview.

[32] Green, interview.

[33] Bill Swallender, interview.

[34] H. H. Barcus, "He Will Skate Solo," undated clipping from unidentified Detroit newspaper in my possession; Ken Williams, "Skater, 14, Nears Top," *Detroit News*, April 25, 1959, 11; Gary Clark, telephone interview, May 24, 2005.

[35] "1961 World Team Meeting;" "Fate Put Detroit Boy on Doomed Jet," *Detroit Free Press*, February 16, 1961, 2; Williams, "Year-Round Drills;" Smith, interview.

[36] Molly Okuley, "Skater Doug Ramsay Only 10, Is Future Olympic Champ," *Detroit Times*, March 29, 1955, 13; George Puscas, "City Mourns a Star, Coach; Nation a Sport," *Detroit Free Press*, February 16, 1961, 35; Barcus, "He Will Skate Solo;" Caton, interview.

[37] Smith, interview; "Midwesterns," *Skating*, April 1955, 25; "Members Do Bit to Aid DSC Show," unidentified Detroit newspaper clipping in my possession.

[38] Gary Visconti, telephone interview, September 16, 2004.

[39] Ibid.

[40] Eleanor Breitmeyer, "Detroit Club Mourns Its Finest Star," *Detroit News*, February 15, 1961, 19A; Barnas, "Wood's Tale Begins and Ends on the Ice," *Detroit Free Press*, April 3, 1998; www.freep.com/sports/othersports/qwood3 (accessed January 27, 2003).

[41] Smith, interview; Lurtsema, interview; Rayner, interview.

[42] Lurtsema, interview.

[43] Visconti, interview; David Mitchell, telephone interview, September 20, 2004; Sally Wells Van De Mark, telephone interview, August 27, 2004; Green, interview.

[44] Barr, interview; Green, interview; Rayner, interview.

[45] Janet Harley Browning, telephone interview, September 6, 2005; S. E. Cram, "The Midwestern Championships," *Skating*, April 1956, 10-11.

[46] "Midwestern Championships," *Skating*, April 1957, 22, 42; "Men's Novice," *Skating*, May 1957, 42.

[47] Bill Swallender, interview; "Senior Men," *Skating*, April 1958, 24; Glenn F. Ballard, "The United States Championships," *Skating*, May 1958, 7, 40.

[48] Heiss, interview; Eleanor Breitmeyer, "Who Said Skating Season's Over?" *Detroit News*, 1958, undated clipping in my possession; "The Summer Skating Story," *Skating*, November 1958, 11, 35; Okuley, "Skater Doug Ramsay Only 10, Is Future Olympic Champ," 13.

[49] Visconti, interview.

[50] Joanne Heckert Bachtel, telephone interview, September 22, 2005.

[51] Marian P. Condit, "The United States Championships," *Skating*, March 1959, 9, 20, 34.

[52] "Skimming around Summer Circles," *Skating*, November 1953, 17; Ron Pfenning, telephone interview, May 27, 2005; Clark, interview.

[53] Heiss, interview; Coco Gram Sheehan, telephone interview, October 10, 2007; Bachtel, interview; Donald Jackson, telephone interview, October 11, 2007.

[54] Lurtsema, interview; Maud Dubos, telephone interview, August 22, 2005.

[55] Clark, interview; Pfenning, interview; Sheehan, interview.

[56] Jan Serafine, telephone interview, May 12, 2005; Sheehan, interview; Visconti, interview; Lurtsema, interview.

[57] Clark, interview; Lurtsema, interview; Bachtel, interview.

[58] Bachtel, interview; Bill Swallender, interview; Anne Batdorf Militano, telephone interview, May 25, 2004 .

[59] Bachtel, interview; Carol Heiss Jenkins, telephone interview, October 10, 2007.

[60] Lurtsema, interview; Visconti, interview; Martin, interview.

[61] Williams, "Skater, 14, Nears the Top," 11; Visconti, interview.

[62] Williams, "Skater, 14, Nears the Top," 11.

[63] Mrs. Lloyd L. Palmer, "The United States Championships," *Skating*, March 1960, 7-8, 29; Mrs. Lloyd L. Palmer, "Meet the New Champions," *Skating*, April 1960, 22.

[64] Williams, "Year-Round Drills;" "Rockers and Counters," *Skating*, May 1960, 30.

[65] Joseph Dineen, telephone interview, October 19, 2004.

[66] Dineen, interview; Joseph Gorsky, telephone interview, January 20, 2005; "Tests," *Skating*, February 1956, 28; Marilyn Grace Guilfoyle, telephone interview, May 24, 2004.

[67] "1961 World Team Meeting;" Mary Santilli Miloscia, email interview, April 29, 2005.

[68] Miloscia, email interview.

[69] "Rockers and Counters," *Skating*, June 1956, 35; R. David Owen, telephone interview, September 28, 2005.

[70] "Middle Atlantics," April 1956, 36; Emily Van Voorhis and Ethel W. Badger, "Easterns," *Skating*, May 1956, 38, 40; "U.S. Championships," *Skating*, May 1956, 20.

[71] Guilfoyle, interview; Palmer, "Meet the U.S. Dance Champions," 23; Liz Herman McLoughlin, telephone interview, May 18, 2004.

[72] Owen, interview; "David Schwartzer," www.ssdi.rootsweb.ancestry.com/cgi-bin/ssdi/cgi (accessed May 12, 2010); "Tests," *Skating*, June 1954, 36; Ron Ludington, interviewed Overland Park, KS, June 11, 2004; Nancy Ludington Graham, telephone interview, April 5, 2005.

[73] Smith, interview.

[74] Jean Westwood, telephone interview, July 13, 2004.

[75] Eleanor Banneck Curtis, telephone interview, October 7, 2003; Janet Roberts McLeod, telephone interview, July 11, 2003; Charlie Rizzo, telephone interview, May 19, 2004.

[76] "Pacific Coast Championships," *Skating*, April 1957, 22; "Silver Dance," *Skating*, May 1957, 42.

[77] "Meet the U.S. Dance Champions," *Skating*, May 1960, 23; Guilfoyle, interview.

[78] Rizzo, interview; Owen, interview; Dottie Otto Halama, telephone interview, April 9, 2004; Gruber, interview.

[79] "Middle Atlantics," *Skating*, March 1958, 34; "Easterns," *Skating*, April 1958, 38; "Silver Dance," *Skating*, May 1958, 42.

[80] "Deaths," *Skating*, June 1958, 32; "Marriages," *Skating*, November 1958, 30; Owen, interview; Guilfoyle, interview.

[81] Sonya Klopfer Dunfield, telephone interview, June 2, 2004; Rizzo, interview.

[82] Dunfield, interview; "North Atlantic States," *Skating*, February 1959, 32; Condit, "The United States Championships," 8, 23, 36.

[83] Christie Allan-Piper, telephone interview, November 9, 2004; Bob Munz, telephone interview, June 8, 2005; Guilfoyle, interview.

[84] Guilfoyle, interview.

[85] Rizzo, interview.

[86] Guilfoyle, interview; Palmer, "The United States Championships," 8, 30.

[87] Don Bartleson, telephone interview, November 8, 2004; Hank Hickox, telephone interview, August 30, 2005.

[88] Hickox, interview; Elinor H. Hickox, Obituary, *Berkeley Daily Gazette*, February 25, 1984, unpaginated newspaper clipping in my possession.

[89] "Hickoxes' Father Worked in Yuba County," *Sacramento Bee*, February 16, 1961, D1; Lute H. Hickox, Obituary, *Oakland Tribune*, December 5, 1987, B1; Elinor Hickox, Obituary; Hickox, interview; Julie Marcus Barrett, telephone interview, June 4, 2005; Jean Frazier Fahmie, interview in Dublin, CA, October 24, 2007.

[90] Hickox, interview; Cathy Stevenson, email interview, May 24, 2003; "1961 World Team Meeting;" Hickox, interview.

[91] Hickox, interview; Nancy Hickox Hileick, telephone interview, August 31, 2005.

[92] Hickox, interview; Terry Hansen, "Death Nips Promising Ice Careers," *Berkeley Daily Gazette*, February 15, 1961, 5; Barrett, interview.

[93] Barrett, interview; "Tests," *Skating*, December 1951, 44; "Northern California," *Skating*, April 1953, 30; "Pacific Coast," *Skating*, May 1953, 38, 42; "Spins through Professional Circles," *Skating*, December 1954, 40.

[94] "Pacific Coast," *Skating*, May 1955, 26; "Pacific Coast," *Skating*, March 1956, 40; "Novice Men," *Skating*, May 1956, 21-22; "Pacific Coast Championships," *Skating*, April 1957, 23; "Men's Novice," *Skating*, May 1957, 29, 42.

[95] "Tests," *Skating*, November 1952, 41; "Pacific Coast," *Skating*, March 1956, 40; "California State" and "Pacific Coast," *Skating*, April 1958, 27, 36; "Men's Novice," *Skating*, May 1958, 42.

[96] Ferne Bearse, "Fabulous Sutro's," *Skating*, November 1957, 9.

[97] "Harry A. Sims, "The United States Championships," *Skating*, May 1957, 18; Bearse, "Fabulous Sutro's," 9; Michaela Randolph, telephone interview, April 29, 2005; Monnier, interview.

[98] Randolph, interview; Bill Wilkins, telephone interview, November 2004; Monnier, interview; Bearse, "Fabulous Sutros," 9.

[99] "A Versatile Pair," *Skating*, February 1959, 32; "Pacific Coast" and "Junior Pairs," *Skating*, March 1959, 19-20, 34.

[100] Robert Swenning, telephone interview, October 12, 2004.

[101] Gene Turner, telephone interview, July 28, 2003.

[102] Barrett, interview.

[103] Sandy Carson Gollihugh, telephone interview, September 10, 2004; "Meet the New Champions," *Skating*, April 1960, 22; Loren Caccamise O'Neil, telephone interview, February 4, 2005; Monnier, interview.

[104] Palmer, "Meet the New Champions," 22; Anne Frazier, telephone interview, November 2, 2007; Lorna Dyer, telephone interview, November 4, 2003.

[105] Barrett, interview; Palmer, "Meet the New Champions," 22.

[106] Jessica Gaynor, telephone interview, August 30, 2004; Hileick, interview; Frazier, interview.

[107] Barrett, interview; Bartleson, interview; Karen Howland Jones, September 11, 2003.

[108] Dyer, interview; Marshall Campbell, telephone interview, April 18, 2005.

[109] 1960 Berkeley High School yearbook.

[110] Hickox, interview; Frazier, interview; Ramona Allen McIntyre, telephone interview, July 22, 2004.

[111] 1960 Gleaner, Garfield Junior High School yearbook; DeeDee DeRoche Cross, letter to Patricia S. Bushman, December 11, 2005; Robin Greiner, telephone interview, September 27, 2004; Monnier, interview.

[112] Frazier, interview.

[113] "Pacific Coast," *Skating*, February 60, 19; 1960 Berkeley High School yearbook.

[114] Palmer, "Meet the New Champions," 22; Frazier, interview; "In Memoriam," Air Force Academy funeral program, February 27, 1961.

[115] Palmer, "The United States Championships," 7, 29.

[116] George Yonekura, telephone interview, October 16, 2003.

Chapter 10

[1] "Squawk Valley," *Time*, February 8, 1960, 49.

[2] Ibid.

[3] *The Chronicle of the Olympics* (New York: DK Publishing, 2006), 264; "Squawk Valley," 49; "Track," *Newsweek*, February 15, 1960, 59; Edith E. Ray, "The Olympics: 1960," *Skating*, April 1960, 10; "Olympic Heaven," *Senior Scholastic*, February 3, 1960, 22.

[4] "Squawk Valley," 49; "Track," 59; Robert Swenning, telephone interview, October 12, 2005; Evan Hill, "California's Olympic Bonanza," *Saturday Evening Post*, February 13, 1960, 26; "Cortina d'Ampezzo," *Chronicle of the Olympics*, 89.

[5] Arthur G. Lentz, *United States 1960 Olympic Book* (New York: United States Olympic Association, 1961), 46; "Track," 60.

[6] Carol Heiss Jenkins, telephone interview, October 10, 2007; *Red and Black* (Winchester High School newspaper), March 23, 1961, 4.

[7] "Olympic Heaven," 22; Robert Rubin, *VIII Olympic Winter Games: Final Report* (N.p.: California Olympic Committee: 1961), 58-59; Carol Jenkins, interview.

[8] Ila Ray Hadley, "The 1960 Olympics," school essay, collection of Linda Adams Garl; Barbara Roles Williams, telephone interview, September 25, 2003.

[9] Linda Hadley, postcard to Adams family, February 7, 1960, collection of Linda Adams Garl.

[10] Ila Ray Hadley, "The 1960 Olympics"; Ray, "The Olympics: 1960," 10; "Olympic Heaven," 22; Rubin, *VIII Olympic Winter Games: Final Report*, 55.

[11] Ila Ray Hadley, "The 1960 Olympics;" "Olympic Heaven," 22.

[12] "Track," 61; "Canada Pair Win Games Skate Title, Hadleys 11th," *Seattle Post-Intelligencer*, February 20, 1960, 6; Georg N. Meyers, "Oh That Nina! If Only She Could Skate," *Seattle Times*, February 20, 1950, 6.

[13] Ray, "The Olympics: 1960," 10-12, 40; Lentz, *United States 1960 Olympic Book*, 200; Maria Jelinek, telephone interview, October 3, 2007.

[14] Ray, "The Olympics: 1960," 10-11, 40; Meyers, "Oh that Nina!" 6; "'Just Goofed,' Says Ila Ray," *Seattle Post-Intelligencer*, February 20, 1960, 6; Bruce Hyland, telephone interview, January 24, 2005; Carol Jenkins, interview.

[15] Ted Smits, "Carol Heiss Wins," *Seattle Post-Intelligencer*, February 24, 1960, 20; Ray, "The Olympics: 1960," 13.

[16] Ray, "The Olympics: 1960," 12, 14; Lentz, *United States 1960 Olympic Book*, 201.

[17] Georg N. Meyers, "The Sporting Thing," *Seattle Times*, February 24, 1960, 14; Curley Grieve, "Maribel Had a Way—and You Couldn't Forget Her," *San Francisco Examiner*, February 16, 1961, IV2; Joan Brader Burns, telephone interview, October 29, 2003; Swenning, interview; Ray, "The Olympics: 1960," 14.

[18] Carol Jenkins, interview; "Some Golden Oldies," *People Weekly*, February 24, 1992, 78-79.

[19] Paul Preuss, "Laurence Was Top U.S. Hope," *Detroit News*, February 15, 1961, C1.

[20] Bill Prochnau, "Concentration," *Seattle Times*, January 31, 1960, 7.

[21] Ray, "The Olympics: 1960," 14-15, 40; Burt Sims, "Jenkins Flashes to Skating Crown," *Seattle Post-Intelligencer*, February 27, 1960, 6; Lentz, *United States 1960 Olympic Book*, 206; David Jenkins, telephone interview, November 30, 2005.

[22] Ray, "The Olympics: 1960," 40; Grieve, "Maribel Had a Way," IV–2.

[23] Lentz, *United States 1960 Olympic Book*, 200.

[24] Anthony J. Yudis, "A Dynasty of Skaters Comes to End," *Boston Globe*, February 16, 1961, 20.

[25] *Red and Black*, 4; Hadley, "The 1960 Olympics."

[26] *The Chronicle of the Olympics*, 264; Hadley, "The 1960 Olympics."

[27] David Jenkins, interview.

[28] Robert Brewer, interviewed, Phoenix, AZ, March 18, 2005.

[29] Edith E. Ray, "The Championships of the World," *Skating*, May 1960, 7, 11.

[30] Ibid; "A Family Affair," 2001 State Farm U.S. Figure Skating Championships program, 66; Ron Vincent, telephone interview, May 20, 2005.

[31] Ray, "The Championships of the World," 7-8.

[32] Ibid, 8, 10.

[33] Ibid.

[34] Ibid; Nancy Ludington Graham, telephone interview, April 5, 2005.

[35] Ray, "The Championships of the World," 8-10; Marilyn Meeker Durham, telephone interview, July 30, 2003.

[36] George Sherwood, "Things We Will Remember about the Worlds," *Skating*, May 1960, 11-12.

[37] Loren Caccamise O'Neil, telephone interview, February 4, 2005; Walter Hypes, telephone interview, September 9, 2004; Yvonne Littlefield Nicks, telephone interview, November 15, 2004; Sarasue Gleis Essenprice, telephone interview, August 24, 2004.

[38] "1961 World Team Meeting," January 29, 1961; "Alexander Campbell," www.ssdirootsweb.ancestry.com/cgi-bin/ssdi.cgi (accessed May 12, 2010); Edward Adler, "He Loses His Wife and Son," *Los Angeles Examiner*, February 16, 1961, 14; "Five Former Oregonians Aboard Doomed Airliner," *Oregonian*, February 16, 1961, 1; Nicks, interview.

[39] "Tests," *Skating*, June 1956, 41; "Five Former Oregonians Aboard Doomed Airliner," 1; Ralph Clark, "Skate Stars of Valley Die," *Valley Times Today*, February 15, 1961, 2; Hypes, interview; O'Neil, interview; "Pacific Coast," and "California State," *Skating*, April 1958, 27, 36.

[40] "Southwest Pacific," *Skating*, February 1959, 29; "Pacific Coast," and "Rockers and Counters," *Skating*, March 1959, 20, 28.

[41] "Silver Dance," *Skating*, March 1959, 36.

[42] Joan Sherbloom Peterson, telephone interview, July 22, 2003; "Tests," *Skating*, December 1959, 42.

[43] Roger Berry, telephone interview, June 3, 2005; Adler, "He Loses His Wife and Son," 14; Nicks, interview.

[44] Billy Chapel, telephone interview, September 10, 2003; Berry, interview.

[45] Ray Chenson, telephone interview, September 3, 2004; Jennie Walsh Guzman, telephone interview, September 9, 2003.

[46] Margie Ackles Jones, telephone interview, October 7, 2004; Chapel, interview; Essenprice, interview, Don Bartleson, telephone interview, November 8, 2004.

[47] Hypes, interview; O'Neil, interview.

[48] Nicks, interview; Eleanor Banneck Curtis, telephone interview, October 7, 2003; Bartleson, interview.

[49] Pam Milligan McDonald, telephone interview, April 27, 2005; "Skater's Mother Had Premonition," *Los Angeles Herald & Express*, February 15, 1961, A5; "USFSA Executive Committee Meeting," *Skating*, December 1957, 11.

[50] 1961 Nationals program; Anita Entrikin Miller, telephone interview, February 2006; Sylvia Clay Stoddard, telephone interview, April 26, 2007.

[51] "Rockers and Counters," *Skating*, May 1959, 30; "Southern California Inter-Club Competition," *Skating*, November 1959, 12; Nicks, interview.

[52] Nicks, interview; "Pacific Coast," and "Southwest Pacific," *Skating*, February 1960, 19, 25.

[53] "Gold Dance," *Skating*, March 1960, 9, 30; Nicks, interview; "Dance," *Skating*, May 1960, 10; "Tests," *Skating*, June 1960, 46.

[54] Nicks, interview; Curtis, interview; Sandy Carson Gollihugh, telephone interview, September 10, 2004.

[55] Clark, "Skate Stars of Valley Die," 2; Sharon McKenzie, telephone interview, May 16, 2005.

[56] Mary Ellen Young, telephone interview, July 20, 2004; Franklin S. Nelson, telephone interview, September 3, 2005; Helen Geekie Nightingale, telephone interview, November 18, 2004; "Walter S. Powell Was with Shoe Firm," *St. Louis Post-Dispatch*, February 15, 1961, 3A.

[57] Helen Nightingale, interview; "Walter S. Powell Was with Shoe Firm," 3A; "W. S. Powell among Air Crash Victims," *St. Louis Globe-Democrat*, February 16, 1961, 1.

[58] Winter Olympic Ice Follies program, St. Louis Skating Club, March 27-28, 1935.

[59] 2006 State Farm U.S. Figure Skating Championships program, 81; "Rockers and Counters," *Skating*, December 1944, 28; Sally Haas Knoll, telephone interview, May 12, 2004; Evelyn Robson, telephone interview, November 1, 2004; Shirley Reflow Sherman, telephone interview, November 29, 2004.

[60] Robson, interview; Bill Boeck, telephone interview, November 6, 2003; 2006 State Farm Nationals program, 82; Helen Nightingale, interview; Knoll, interview.

[61] Benjamin T. Wright, *Skating in America: The 75th Anniversary History of the United States Figure Skating Association* (Colorado Springs: U.S. Figure Skating Association, 1996), xvii-xviii, 96; Walter Powell, "USFSA Executive Committee Meeting," *Skating*, December 1944, 15.

[62] Austin Holt, telephone interview, January 21, 2005; Dick Button, telephone interview, December 13, 2005; "Skating Boss Checks Up," undated clipping from unidentified 1943 St. Paul newspaper in my possession.

[63] Walter S. Powell, "1947 Congress of the ISU," *Skating*, November 1947, 18.

[64] Helen Nightingale, interview; Powell, "1947 Congress of the ISU," 18-19.

[65] Powell, "1947 Congress of the ISU," 19; "Rockers and Counters," *Skating*, January 1949, 24; "Sally Surveys Summer Centers," *Skating*, November 1954, 8.

[66] "Marriages," *Skating*, February 1952, 26; Sherman, interview; Helen Nightingale, interview.

[67] "W. S. Powell among Air Crash Victims," 1; "Olympic Appointments," *Skating*, April 1954, 36; Walter S. Powell, "The 1960 Winter Olympic Games," *Skating*, January 1957, 30.

[68] Sheila Muldowny Stone, telephone interview, September 26, 2003; Theresa Weld Blanchard, "The Olympic Championships," *Skating*, April 1956, 23.

[69] Walter S. Powell, "Figure Skating in the Soviet Union," *Skating*, February 1956, 5-6; Knoll, interview.

[70] Michael McGean, telephone interview, October 12, 2004; Janet Gerhauser Allen Carpenter, telephone interview, November 29, 2004; John Nightingale, telephone interview, November 23, 2004; Nancy Graham, interview; Nelson, interview; Carol Jenkins, interview.

[71] Nancy Graham, interview; Claralynn Lewis Barnes, telephone interview, August 22, 2005; Margaret Ann Graham Reed Holt, telephone interview, November 16, 2003.

[72] "Walter Powell," Benjamin T. Wright, *Chips*, Vol. 18, No. 7, 8; Nightingale, interview.

[73] Brewer, interview; Paul, interview.

[74] Walter S. Powell, "ISU Council Meeting," *Skating*, November 1960, 23; Knoll, interview; Helen Nightingale, interview.

[75] Boeck, interview; Helen Nightingale, interview; Young, interview; Knoll, interview.

[76] Wright, *Chips*, 7; Powell, "ISU Council Meeting," 23.

Chapter 11

[1] "News about Competitors," *Skating*, May 1960, 12-13.

[2] Hayes Alan Jenkins, telephone interview, October 10, 2007; "News about Competitors," 13; Robert Brewer, interviewed, Phoenix, AZ, March 18, 2005.

[3] "News about Competitors," 12.

[4] Ibid; Julie Palmer Mayo, telephone interview, May 26, 2005.

[5] Joan Sherbloom Peterson, telephone interview, September 24, 2003.

[6] Henry M. Beatty, "The New USFSA President," *Skating*, November 1952, 12-13.

[7] "Rockers and Counters," *Skating*, May 1953, 31.

[8] Dottie Otto Halama, telephone interview, April 9, 2004; Sonya Klopfer Dunfield, telephone interview, June 6, 2004.

[9] Marilyn Grace Guilfoyle, telephone interview, May 24, 2004; "Births," *Skating*, November 1960, 33.

[10] Guilfoyle, interview; Joseph Dineen, telephone interview, October 19, 2004.

[11] Ibid.

[12] R. David Owen, telephone interview, September 28, 2005; Charlie Rizzo, telephone interview, May 19, 2004.

[13] Liz Herman McLoughlin, telephone interview, May 19, 2004; Rizzo, interview.

[14] "News about Competitors," 13; "Skating Star Is Son of Plumbing Contractor," undated 1960 clipping from unidentified Indianapolis paper in my possession ; *Skating*, November 1960, 8-9.

[15] Pieter Kollen, telephone interview, July 29, 2003; Munz, interview; Sally Schantz Urban, telephone interview, November 7, 2004; Christie Allan-Piper, telephone interview, November 9, 2004; Marilyn Meeker Durham, telephone interview, July 30, 2003.

[16] Sandy Schwomeyer Lamb, telephone interview, October 13, 2003; Kollen, interview; "Lake Placid Summer Dance Championships," *Skating*, November 1960, 16.

[17] Bruce Lord, telephone interview, May 4, 2005; Susan Austin, Randy Gardner, and Roy Blakey, "Richard Dwyer," www.proskaters.org/foundation/richarddwyer.asp (accessed on May 17, 2010).

[18] Richard Dwyer, telephone interview, May 28, 2005.

[19] Frank Muckian, telephone interview, October 6, 2004; Joanne Heckert Bachtel, telephone interview, September 22, 2005.

[20] Jan Serafine, telephone interview, May 12, 2005; Bachtel, interview.

[21] Sally Wells Van De Mark, telephone interview, August 27, 2004.

[22] Dwyer, interview; Connie Espander, telephone interview, September 7, 2005; Christy Haigler Krall, interviewed, Colorado Springs, May 9, 2003.

[23] Donna Merrill Schoon, telephone interview, September 23, 2005; Gregory Hoyt, telephone interview, July 12, 2005; Ardith Paul Hamilton, telephone interview, July 31, 2005; "News about Skaters," *Skating*, December 1959, 8; Krall, interview.

[24] Pam Thatcher Marsh, telephone interview, May 24, 1005; Phil Cagnoni, telephone interview, October 15, 2007; Skip Mullins, telephone interview, September 25, 2005.

[25] Mechelle Voepel, "Frozen in Time," *Kansas City Star*, March 3, 2001, C15; Hamilton, interview; Krall, interview.

[26] Diana Lapp Green, telephone interview, April 28, 2005; Roberto Agnolini, telephone interview, February 9, 2005; Voepel, "Frozen in Time," C1, 14-15; Mullins, interview.

[27] "Rockers and Counters," *Skating*, November 1960, 10, 35.

[28] Walter S. Powell, "ISU Council Meetings," *Skating*, November 1960, 23.

[29] Henry Jelinek Jr. and Ann Pinchot, *On Thin Ice* (New York: Signet, 1965), 27-28, 33.

[30] Ibid., 34-45, 65-70, 94.

[31] Ibid., 117-18.

[32] Ibid., 118.

[33] Ballard Sunset Ice Arena 1958 summer session information sheet in my possession; Linda Landin, telephone interview, October 12, 2004; Bill Wilkins, telephone interview, November 4, 2004.

[34] Pat Pawelak-Kort, letter to Patricia S. Bushman, March 21, 2005; 1961 Glacier, Ingraham High School yearbook, 75; Landin, interview; Bob Deuter, telephone interview, September 20, 2004; Linda Adams Garl, telephone interview, February 8, 2005.

[35] Garl, interview; Wilkins, interview.

[36] Moehring, interview; Garl, interview.

[37] "Circling the Summer Centers" and "Tests," *Skating*, November 1960, 12, 35.

[38] Anne Frazier, telephone interview, November 2, 2007.

[39] Ibid; "Tests," *Skating*. February 6, 1961.

[40] Ibid.

[41] "Circling the Summer Centers, 12; Mary Miller Robicheaux, telephone interview, July 14, 2005.

[42] Carol Lee Galloway Goldrod, telephone interview, September 6, 2004; Sarasue Gleis Essenprice, telephone interview, August 24, 2004.

[43] "Downey Ice Skater Plane Crash Victim," *Downey Live Wire*, February 16, 1961, 1; "Rockers and Counters," *Skating*, November 1960, 28.

[44] "News about Skaters," *Skating*, November 1960, 18; Barbara Roles Williams, telephone interview, September 25, 2003.

[45] Mary Batdorf Scotvold, telephone interview, May 24, 2004; Tom McGinnis, telephone interview, September 14, 2004.

[46] McGinnis, interview.

[47] Allan-Piper, interview; "Owen Family, Champions All," *Boston Traveler*, February 15, 1961, 42; "Meet the Champions," *Skating*, April 1961, 20.

[48] Tom Murray, "An Empty Desk Tells Their Star Is Dead...," *Boston Traveler*, February 15, 1961, 29; "News about Skaters," *Skating*, November 1960, 18.

[49] Ibid.

[50] Rodger Nordblom, telephone interview, March 1, 2005.

[51] Ibid; Elizabeth George Busconi, telephone interview, May 4, 2005; Bill McSwenny, "Fatal Brussels Tragedy Felt in Boston," *Boston Daily Record*, February 16, 1961, 39.

[52] Allan-Piper, interview; Ronna Goldblatt Gladstone, telephone interview, April 25, 2010; Williams, interview; "Class of 1954," Harvard Alumni Report, 1960, 158; Nancy Ludington Graham, telephone interview, April 5, 2005.

[53] Julie Graham-Eavzan, telephone interview, April 20, 2005; McGinnis, interview; Allan-Piper, interview; Nancy Madden Leamy, telephone interview; May 19, 2005; Georg N. Meyers, "Larry Is a Lady," *Seattle Times*, January 27, 1960, 18.

[54] Louis and Marijane Stong, telephone interview, January 11, 2006.

[55] Maribel Vinson Owen, *The Fun of Figure Skating* (New York: Harper and Row, 1960).

[56] Busconi, interview.

[57] "New Gold Medalists," *Skating*, November 1960, 8-9.

[58] "Brown a Choreographer," clipping from unidentified San Francisco Bay area paper, May 2, 1961; "Tests," *Skating*, December 1950, 44; "News of Competitors," *Skating*, December 1952, 7.

[59] Michelle Monnier, telephone interview, September 8, 2003; Williams, interview.

[60] "News about Skaters," *Skating*, December 1956, 11; Monnier, interview; Jean Fahmie, telephone interview, October 24, 2007.

[61] Tim Brown, "This Is How I Do It," *Skating*, May 1953, 28; Loren Caccamise O'Neil, telephone interview, February 4, 2005; Krall, interview.

[62] O'Neil, interview; David Jenkins, telephone interview, November 30, 2005.

[63] Brewer, interview.

[64] "Bad Heart Saved Life of Brown," *Oregon Statesman*, February 16, 1961, II9.

Chapter 12

[1] Spencer E. Cram, letter to Selection & Executive Committee, March 17, 1960; Daryl Hartshorne, telephone interview, November 26, 2004.

[2] Spencer E. Cram, letter to Selections Committee, September 8, 1960; Spencer E. Cram, letter to Kendall Kelley, October 10, 1960; "USFSA Officials for 1961 Championships," *Skating*, December 1960, 18; "Glass Firm Executive among Crash Victims," *Evening Star*, February 15, 1961, A8; Bob Duffy, "Twists of Fate," *Boston Globe*, December 31, 2000, C1.

[3] Spencer E. Cram letter to Kendall Kelley, November 19, 1960; James Koch, letter to Kendall Kelley, December 9, 1960; Barbara Drake Holland, interviewed, Overland Park, KS, May 16, 2009; Theresa Weld Blanchard, letter to Kendall Kelley, February 22, 1961.

[4] Ritter Shumway, letter to Kendall Kelley, November 21, 1960; Kendall Kelley, letter to John Shoemaker, December 20, 1960.

[5] Cram to Kelley, November 19, 1960; Spencer E. Cram, letter to Selections Committee, November 23, 1960; Spencer E. Cram, letter to Kendall Kelley, November 29, 1960.

[6] Diana LeMaire Squibb, interviewed, Manchester-by-the-Sea, MA, August 7, 2003.

[7] Kendall Kelley, letter to "Potential U.S. World Team Members," November 15, 1960.

[8] Kendall Kelley, letter to Virginia Bremer, January 29, 1961.

[9] Theresa Weld Blanchard and Edith E. Ray, "The Championships of the World," *Skating*, May 1957, 9.

[10] Barbara Roles Williams, telephone interview, September 25, 2003; Mary Miller Robicheaux, telephone interview, July 14, 2005.

[11] "1961 World Team Meeting," January 29, 1961; *1934 El Eco* (Narbonne High School yearbook), Long Beach, CA; "Judges as People," *Skating*, April 1957, 34; "Deane E. McMinn," *Skating*, April 1961, 16.

[12] "Judges as People," 34; Janet McLeod, telephone interview, July 11, 2003; ABFSC Memorial Plaque.

[13] "Tests," *Skating*, November 1950, 39; "Pacific Coast Championships" and "California State," *Skating*, May 1950, 34, 35; "California State," *Skating*, March 1951, 28; "Pacific Coast," *Skating*, April 1951, 25; "Southern California Inter-Club," *Skating*, November 1952, 36; "Southern California Inter-Club," *Skating*, November 1953, 34.

[14] "Judges as People," 34; "USFSA Judges List," *Skating*, February 1952, 28; "USFSA Judges List," *Skating*, June 1953, 34; "Ladies' Senior," *Skating*, May 1957, 18.

[15] Joyce Burden, telephone interview, August 22, 2004; McLeod, interview; "Judges as People," 34; *Skating*, November 1960, 12, 29.

[16] Burden, interview; Margaret Hosford, telephone interview, October 24, 2003; Pam Milligan McDonald, telephone interview, April 27, 2005.

[17] Williams, interview; Sarasue Gleis Essenprice, telephone interview, August 24, 2004.

[18] Sandy Carson Gollihugh, telephone interview, September 10, 2004; Sondra Holmes Kovacovsky, telephone interview, February 23, 2005; Jim Short, telephone interview, October 7, 2004.

[19] Short, interview.

[20] Walter Hypes, telephone interview, September 9, 2004; Burden, interview.

[21] Deane E. McMinn, "The Value of Inter-Club Associations," *Skating*, November 1954, 22; 1954 National Figure Skating Championships program; Benjamin T. Wright, *Skating in America: The 75th Anniversary History of the United States Figure Skating Association*," (Colorado Springs: U.S. Figure Skating Association, 1996), xxx, xxxiii.

[22] Deane E. McMinn, "The Low Test Figures Are the Foundation," *Skating*, November 1957, 11.

[23] J.J. Bejshak, telephone interview, August 21, 2004; "USFSA Executive Committee Meeting," *Skating*, December 1959, 17.

[24] Deane E. McMinn, "The Club Competition Fund," *Skating*, December 1958, 22.

[25] "Rockers and Counters," *Skating*, November 1954, 27.

[26] Ben Wade, telephone interview, July 11, 2003; Hosford, interview.

[27] Eleanor Banneck Curtis, telephone interview, October 7, 2003.

[28] "USFSA Judges List," *Skating*, February 1958, 40; "USFSA Executive Committee Meeting," 13, 17-18; "The United States Championships," *Skating*, March 1960, 9, 30.

[29] McLeod, interview; Hosford, interview.

[30] "Rockers and Counters," *Skating*, December 1960, 26; Pearle Sutherland, letter to Ritter Shumway, March 26, 1961.

[31] Diana LeMaire Squibb, interviewed Manchester-by-the-Sea, MA, August 7, 2003.

[32] Ibid; Shirley Reflow Sherman, telephone interview, November 29, 2004; "Rockers and Counters," *Skating*, January 1938, 32; LeMaire and Reynolds advertisement, *Skating*, December 1937, 39.

[33] Sherman, interview; Trinity School Alumni Bulletin, Spring 1960, 1; Wendy Howard, "Edward LeMaire: My Ancestor," May 9, 1997, 1, school essay, copy in my possession; "Fifth Former Goes to Cleveland Meet," *Trinity Times*, February 14, 1940.

[34] Ardelle Kloss Sanderson, telephone interview, October 3, 2003; Robert Swenning, telephone interview, October 11, 2004.

[35] Wendy Howard, "Eddie LeMaire," 2; E. Newbold Black IV, telephone interview, November 8, 2003; Trinity School Alumni Bulletin, 1; Anne Gerli, telephone interview, November 17, 2003.

[36] Gerli, interview; "Edward LeMaire," *Chips*, 18, no. 7, March 28, 1961, 6-7.

[37] Squibb, interview; www.usarsarollerskaters.org/1942-1949USARSANationalChampionships (accessed April 27, 2010).

[38] Barbara Lutz, letter to Patricia S. Bushman, October 19, 2004; *Trinity Times*, May 20, 1942, 2-3.

[39] "73 Killed in Jet Crash; 18 Are Yank Ice Stars," *Daily News* (NYC), February 16, 1961, 8; Squibb, interview.

[40] Squibb, interview.

[41] Trinity School Alumni Bulletin, 1; "Champions in Uniform," *Skating*, October 1943, 3; Squibb, interview; Wendy Howard, "Edward LeMaire," 2-3.

[42] Edward LeMaire and Muriel Maria Gerli marriage certificate, Corpus Christi, Texas; Squibb, interview; Swenning, interview; Wendy Howard, "Edward LeMaire," 3.

[43] Squibb, interview; Trinity School Alumni Bulletin, 1.

[44] Squibb, interview; Dorinda Howard, telephone interview, May 2, 2010; "Canvassing the Champions," *Skating*, March 1955, 9; "Canvassing the Champions," *Skating*, January, 1955, 10.

[45] Patty LeMaire advertisement, *Skating*, January 1955, 37; Squibb, interview; "USFSA Executive Committee Meeting," *Skating*, December 1955, 36; Black, interview.

[46] Black, interview.

[47] Dorinda Howard, interview; Black, interview.

[48] Squibb, interview.

[49] Ibid; Carol Heiss Jenkins, telephone interview, October 10, 2007.

[50] Black, interview; Lucy Curley Brennan, telephone interview. September, 15, 2004.

[51] Thomas Hartshorne, interviewed, Brooklyn, NY, August 12, 2003.

[52] Ibid.

[53] Ibid; David W. Dunlap, "Fixing Monument to Mother-in-Law; Sara Delano Roosevelt Ruled Home of Franklin and Eleanor," *New York Times*, March 18, 2003, unpaginated copy.

[54] Harry Hartshorne, telephone interview, October 7, 2003.

[55] Thomas Hartshorne, interview.

[56] Ibid; Harry Hartshorne, interview.

[57] Thomas Hartshorne, interview; Harry Hartshorne, interview; Gail Hartshorne, telephone interview, February 28, 2005.

[58] Harry Hartshorne, interview; Thomas Hartshorne, interview.

[59] Harry Hartshorne, interview.

[60] Ibid.

[61] Ibid; Marietta Chapin Hartshorne headstone, Greenwood Cemetery, Brooklyn, NY.

[62] Harry Hartshorne, interview; "Harold Hartshorne," *Skating*, April 1961, 16.

[63] Thomas Hartshorne, interview; "U.S. Skaters Die, Crash Kills 73," *Newark Evening News*, February 15, 1961, 1, 5.

[64] The Skating Club of New York Sixth Annual Carnival program, 1939, 7, 19, 31; Marjorie Parker Smith, telephone interview, May 12, 2004.

[65] Smith, interview.

[66] Anne Gerli, telephone interview, November 17, 2003; Harry Hartshorne, interview; Daryl Hartshorne, telephone interview, November 26, 2004; Gail Hartshorne, interview.

[67] Harry Hartshorne, interview; Smith, interview; Harold G. Storke, "The 1936 National Championships," *Skating*, March 1936, 16.

[68] Smith, interview; "Sandy Macdonald," *Skating*, November 1949, 30-31.

[69] "The 1944 United States Championships," March 1944, 7; Irene Maguire Muehlbronner, telephone interview, October 15, 2004.

[70] Gail Hartshorne, interview; Dan Hartshorne, telephone interview, November 16, 2004.

[71] Harry Hartshorne, interview.

[72] Ibid; "Engagements," *Skating*, April 1942, 38; "Births," *Skating*, October 1943, 26.

[73] Dan Hartshorne, interview.

[74] Ibid; Wright, *Skating in America*, xxix, xli; Dan Hartshorne, interview; Gail Hartshorne, interview; "USFSA Annual Meeting," *Skating*, June 1953, 21.

[75] Marcella May Willis, telephone interview, July 24, 2004; Harold Hartshorne, "U.S.F.S.A. Dance Conference," *Skating*, November 1938, 27; "Veterans Dance" and "Tests," *Skating*, April 1950, 29, 46; "Lake Placid Summer Dance Championships," *Skating*, November 1952, 37; "Easterns," *Skating*, May 1953, 20-22; *Skating*, June 1954, 22; "Easterns," *Skating*, March 1959, 23.

[76] "Skimming around Summer Circles," *Skating*, November 1953, 15; "USFSA Executive Committee Meeting," *Skating*, December 1953, 15; Gerli, interview.

[77] "Marriages," *Skating*, December 1953, 29; Louisa Heyer Hartshorne headstone, Greenwood Cemetery, Brooklyn, NY; Smith, interview; Gerli, interview.

[78] Smith, interview; "Easterns," *Skating*, March 1946, 14; Louisa Hartshorne headstone; Muehlbronner, interview; Daryl Hartshorne, interview; Dan Hartshorne, interview.

[79] Harry Hartshorne, interview; Gerli, interview; Gail Hartshorne, interview.

[80] Daryl Hartshorne, interview; Gail Hartshorne, interview.

[81] Dan Hartshorne, interview.

[82] Daryl Hartshorne, interview; Gail Hartshorne, interview.

[83] Daryl Hartshorne, interview; Gail Hartshorne, interview.

[84] Gail Hartshorne, interview; Dan Hartshorne, interview.

[85] Dan Hartshorne, interview; Brennan, interview.

[86] "Veterans Dance," *Skating*, April 1954, 12; Michael McGean, telephone interview, October 12, 2004; Dan Hartshorne, interview; Daryl Hartshorne, interview.

[87] Daryl Hartshorne, interview; Dan Hartshorne, interview.

[88] Harry Hartshorne, interview.

[89] Linda Charbonneau Agneta, telephone interview, August 18, 2005.

[90] Hosford, interview.

[91] Floyd and Eleanor Carrier headstones, Forest Lawn Cemetery, Los Angeles; "1961 World Team Meeting;" Tests," *Skating*, December 1952, 46.

[92] "Tests," *Skating*, June 1955, 44; Mary Lou Butler-Mitchell, telephone interview, April 2, 2005.

[93] Butler-Mitchell, interview; Hosford, interview.

[94] "Junior Ladies," *Skating*, April 1958, 23; "Tests," *Skating*, April 1957, 40; Butler-Mitchell, interview.

[95] "R.I.T. Summer Dance Competition," *Skating*, November 1957, 18; Marilyn Grace Guilfoyle, telephone interview, May 24, 2004; Butler-Mitchell, interview; Jennie Walsh Guzman, telephone interview, September 9, 2003.

[96] RPI Ice Carnival program; Ray Chenson, telephone interview, September 3, 2004; Aileen Kahre Arenson, telephone interview, April 4, 2005; Guzman, interview.

[97] Carole MacSween Beazer, telephone interview, September 23, 2005; "Tests," *Skating*, February 1959, 38.

[98] "Southwest Pacific," *Skating*, February 1959, 29; "Pacific Coast," *Skating*, March 1959, 20.

[99] "Southern California Inter-Club," *Skating*, November 1959, 12.

[100] "Pacific Coast" and "Southwest Pacific," *Skating*, February 1960, 19, 25; *Skating*, November 1960, 8-9, 35.

[101] Dona Lee Carrier photograph, new gold medalist, *Skating*, December 1960, 7; Butler-Mitchell, interview; Don Bartleson, telephone interview, November 8, 2004; Essenprice, interview; Beazer, interview; Hosford, interview; Jones, interview.

[102] Yvonne Littlefield Nicks, telephone interview, November 15, 2004.

[103] Ibid.

[104] Joan Sherbloom Peterson, telephone interview, July 22, 2003; Robicheaux, interview; Curtis, interview.

[105] Robicheaux, interview; Essenprice, interview.

[106] Essenprice, interview; Sylvia Clay Stoddard, interview, April 26, 2007; "Tests," *Skating*, March 1961, 38.

[107] Dan Tompkins, "Only Valentine Left to Dona's Parents," *Los Angeles Examiner*, February 16, 1961, 3; "Southland Victims Prominent in Skating," *Los Angeles Times*, February 16, 1961, 15; Peterson, interview.

[108] Ralph Clark, "Skate Stars of Valley Die," *Valley Times Today*, February 15, 1961, 2; Guzman, interview.

[109] "Los Angeles FSC Competition," *Skating*, November 1960, 29; Nicks, interview.

[110] Hadley & Hart brochure (copy in my possession); Debbie Ganson Lane, telephone interview, November 14, 2005; Cynthia Kauffman Marshall, telephone interview, November 5, 2003; Ronald Kauffman, telephone interview, November 4, 2007; Linda Adams Garl, telephone interview, February 8, 2005.

[111] Hadley & Hart brochure; Nancy Moehring, telephone interview, March 3, 2005; Linda Landin, telephone interview, October 12, 2004.

[112] Lane, interview; Darrell Mathias, telephone interview, October 5, 2004; Moehring, interview; Arvilla Kauffman, telephone interview, October 6, 2003.

[113] Judianne Fotheringill Fuller, telephone interview, July 23, 2005; Janet Harley Browning, telephone interview, September 6, 2005.

[114] Kendall Kelley, "Potential U.S. World Team Members/Letter No. 2," December 21, 1960; www.sabena.com/EN/Historique_FR.htm (accessed on April 22, 2005).

[115] "Meet the 1958 United States Champions," *Skating*, June 1958, 14; Barbara Roles Williams, telephone interview, September 25, 2003.

[116] Cover, *Skating*, December 1960; "Marriages," *Skating*, February 1961, 27.

Chapter 13

[1] Diana LeMaire Squibb, interviewed, Manchester-by-the-Sea, MA, August 7, 2003.

[2] "Births," *Skating*, November 1947, 40; Squibb, interview; David Pinkham, telephone interview, January 8, 2010.

[3] Dorinda LeMaire Howard, telephone interview, May 2, 2010; Squibb, interview; Pinkham, interview.

[4] Howard, interview; Squibb, interview; "Richard O. LeMaire," *Chips*, 18, no. 7, 7.

[5] Pinkham, interview; Squibb, interview; Howard, interview.

[6] Squibb, interview; "Richard LeMaire Award," Rye Country Day School, Rye, NY; Howard, interview.

[7] Squibb, interview; "Richard LeMaire Collection," Rye Country Day School; Howard, interview.

[8] Howard, interview; Squibb, interview.

[9] Squibb, interview; Howard, interview.

[10] Squibb, interview; "Colorado Springs Skaters All National Leaders," *Free Press* (Colorado Springs), February 16, 1961, 1.

[11] Roberta Scholdan, letter to Patricia S. Bushman, December 4, 2003; Fred Cheschier, telephone interview, June 4, 2005; Jeanie O'Brien Callahan, telephone interview, June 27, 2005.

[12] Callahan, interview; Cheschier, interview.

[13] Ruth Scholdan Harle, telephone interview, October 9, 2007; Cheschier, interview.

[14] Christy Haigler Krall, interviewed Colorado Springs, May 9, 2003; Cheschier, interview.

[15] Cheschier, interview.

[16] Ibid; Harle, interview.

[17] Diane Lynne Betts, *The Broadmoor World Arena Pictorial History Book* (Colorado Springs: Broadmoor World Arena, 1988), 15; Phil Cagnoni, telephone interview, October 15, 2007.

[18] Cheschier, interview.

[19] Ibid; Scholdan, interview; Dixie Lee Burns Wilson, telephone interview, October 8, 2003; "Tutt Terms Air Crash 'Horrible,' Lauds Scholdan," *Gazette Telegraph* (Colorado Springs), February 15, 1961, 1.

[20] Cheschier, interview; Harle, interview; Wilson, interview; Callahan, interview.

[21] Harle, interview.

[22] Ibid.

[23] Connie Espander, telephone interview, September 7, 2005; Wilson, interview; Andra McLaughlin Kelly, telephone interview, September 26, 2005.

[24] Cheschier, interview; Wilson, interview.

[25] Harle, interview; Wilson, interview; Cheschier, interview; "Tutt Terms Air Crash 'Horrible,'" 1.

[26] "News about Skaters," *Skating*, November 1960, 18; Bill Hickox, letters to Anne Frazier, July 10, September 3 and 11, October 12 and 30, 1960, photocopies in my possession.

[27] Anne Frazier, telephone interview, November 2, 2007; George Yonekura, telephone interview, October 16, 2003.

[28] Bill Hickox, letter to Anne Frazier, November 27, 1960; "Central Pacific," *Skating*, February 1961, 30; "Pacific Coast," *Skating*, March 1961, 19; "Hickox Duo Is 'Adopted' Favorite in Nationals," *Gazette Telegraph*, January 20, 1961, 8; "Five Famed Berkeley Skaters Perish in Flaming Wreck," *Oakland Tribune*, February 15, 1961, 3.

[29] Bill Hickox, letters to Anne Frazier, December 27, 1960, January 5, 1961.

[30] Espander, interview; Bill Hickox, letters to Anne Frazier, January 8 and 9, 1961; Terry Hansen, "Death Nips Promising Ice Careers," *Berkeley Daily Gazette*, February 14, 1961, 1; Frazier, interview.

[31] Marilyn Meeker Durham, telephone interview, July 31, 2003.

[32] Ibid.

[33] "City Skater, Coach among 72 Jet Dead," *Indianapolis News*, February 15 1961, 1; Durham, interview.

[34] Durham, interview.

[35] "News about Competitors," *Skating*, May 1960, 18; Durham, interview.

[36] Joan Sherbloom Peterson, telephone interview, July 22, 2003; "Meet the Champions," *Skating*, April 1961, 23; 1961 Southwest Pacific program.

[37] "1961 World Team Meeting," U.S. Figure Skating files.

[38] Peterson, interview; "Ice Sculpture," *Life*, May 12, 1947, 94-96.

[39] Peterson, interview; Ted Thackery, Jr., "Skaters Here Mourn Stars; Six from L.A. Lose Lives," *Los Angeles Examiner*, February 16, 1961, 1.

[40] Ray Chenson, telephone interview, September 3, 2004; Peterson, interview; "Southern California Inter-Club Competition," *Skating*, November 1957, 22.

[41] Chenson, interview; "Pacific Coast" and "California State," *Skating*, April 1958, 27, 36.

[42] Chenson, interview; Peterson, interview.

[43] "Tests," *Skating*, February 1958, 38; "Tests," *Skating*, November 1958, 36; Chenson, interview.

[44] Loren Caccamise O'Neil, telephone interview, February 4, 2005.

[45] "Southwest Pacific," *Skating*, February 1959, 29; "Pacific Coast," *Skating*, March 1959, 20; "Rockers and Counters," *Skating*, March 1959, 28.

[46] "The United States Championships," *Skating*, March 1959, 36.

[47] Peterson, interview.

[48] Sarasue Gleis Essenprice, telephone interview, August 24, 2004; "Meet the Champions," *Skating*, April 1961, 23; Yvonne Littlefield Nicks, telephone interview, November 15, 2004; Eleanor Banneck Curtis, telephone interview, October 7, 2003.

[49] "Pacific Coast," *Skating*, February 1960, 19, 25; "Meet the Champions," 23; Peterson, interview.

[50] Peterson, interview; Margie Ackles Jones, telephone interview, October 9, 2004.

[51] "Palms Girl Victim of Air Crash," *Venice Evening Vanguard* (Venice, CA), February 15, 1961, 1; "6 Area Rink Stars Died in Air Tragedy," *Citizen-News* (Hollywood, CA), February 15, 1961, 1; Peterson, interview; "1961 World Team Meeting."

[52] Durham, interview; "Father Says Diane Always Practiced," *Los Angeles Examiner*, February 16, 1961, 14; "Diane Sherbloom 'Imported,'" January 1961 clipping from unidentified Indianapolis newspaper in my possession.

[53] Sally Wells Van De Mark, telephone interview, August 27, 2004; Bette Todd, telephone interview, September 29, 2004.

[54] Ardith Paul Hamilton, telephone interview, July 31, 2005.

[55] "Midwesterns," *Skating*, March 1961, 17; Vicky Fisher Binner, telephone interview, February 27, 2009.

[56] "Midwesterns," 17.

[57] "Easterns," *Skating*, March 1961, 16-17; Jean Westwood, telephone interview, July 13, 2004.

[58] Dottie Otto Halama, telephone interview, April 9, 2005; Charlie Rizzo, telephone interview, May 19, 2004.

[59] "Southwest Pacific," *Skating*, February 1961, 28; "Pacific Coast," *Skating*, March 1961, 19.

[60] "Victims from Southland Prominent in Ice Skating," *Los Angeles Times*, February 15, 1961, 2; Ralph Clark, "Skate Stars of Valley Die," *Valley Times Today* (San Fernando Valley, CA) February 15, 1961, 2.

[61] Marlene Morris Van Dusen, telephone interview, June 27, 2005.

[62] Val Rodriguez, telephone interview, November 4, 2004; Ralph Bernstein, "Tragedy Wipes Out Owen Family," *Los Angeles Herald Express*, February 15, 1961, B11; "Harbor Girl Skater Also Plane Victim," *San Pedro News Pilot* (CA), February 16, 1961, 1.

[63] Jennie Walsh Guzman, telephone interview, September 9, 2003.

[64] Mary Miller Robicheaux, telephone interview, July 14, 2005.

[65] "Fate Put Detroit Boy on Doomed Jet," *Detroit Free Press*, February 16, 1961, 2; Ken Williams, "Skater, 14, Nears Top," *Detroit News*, April 25, 1959, 11; John McManis, "Biggest Thrill, Then Death for Detroiter," *Detroit News*, February 15, 1961, 10A.

[66] Hamilton, interview; *The Villager*, February 16, 1961, clipping missing headline and page, in my possession.

[67] "All But 2 of Victims Skated Here in '60," *Seattle Times*, February 16, 1961, Sports, 26; Lee Meade, "Stapleton Luncheon Joke Grim Omen for Skaters' Trip," *Denver Post*, February 15, 1961, 3; Harle, interview.

[68] Frazier, interview.

[69] Stephen Kelley, interviewed, Quincy, Massachusetts, August 7, 2003; Christie Allan-Piper, telephone interview, November 9, 2004; "B.U. to Hold Service for Bradley Lord," *Daily Evening Item* (Lynn, MA), February 24, 1961, 2.

[70] Tom McGinnis, telephone interview, September 14, 2004; Gerry Lane, telephone interview, November 17, 2004.

[71] Patty Gustafson Feeney, telephone interview, December 9, 2004; Will Grimsley, "Crash Wipes Out Owen Family's Dream of Olympic Title," *Oregon Statesman* (Salem, OR), February 16, 1961, Sec. II, 9; "Owen Family, Champions All," *Boston Traveler*, February 15, 1961, 42.

[72] *1961 Aberjona* (Winchester High School yearbook), 41, 50-51, 53.

[73] "Owen Memorial Service at B.U.," *Winchester Star*, March 2, 1961, 2; Allan-Piper, interview.

[74] McGinnis, interview; Susan Richards Abbe, telephone interview, August 29, 2003; Ron Ludington, interviewed, Overland Park, KS, June 2, 2003.

[75] "Tell Love for Dead Skaters," *Los Angeles Herald & Express*, February 16, 1961, A20; Ronna Goldblatt Gladstone, telephone interview, April 22, 2010.

[76] "Town Mourns 'First Family of Figure Skating,'" *St. Louis Post-Dispatch*, February 17, 1961, 3D; Ludington, interview; Gladstone, interview.

[77] Linda Adams Garl, telephone interview, February 8, 2005; Rolf Stromberg, "Friends Here Mourn Hadleys' Death," *Seattle Post-Intelligencer*, February 16, 1961, 16; Linda Landin, telephone interview. October 12, 2004.

[78] Pat Pawelak-Kort, letter to Patricia S. Bushman, March 21, 2005; Stan Freed, "Brother, Sister, Top Ice Skaters," *Seattle Post-Intelligencer*, undated clipping in my possession; Darrell Mathias, telephone interview, October 5, 2004; Garl, interview.

[79] Bill Wilkins, telephone interview, November 4, 2004; Landin, interview.

[80] Charlene Cruickshank Tagas, telephone interview, October 27, 2003; Carol Deuter Smith, telephone interview, September 20, 2004.

[81] Mathias, interview.

[82] Curley Grieve, "Maribel Had a Way—and You Couldn't Forget Her," *San Francisco Examiner*, February 16, 1961, Sec. IV–2.

[83] Bill McSwenny, "Fatal Brussels Tragedy Felt in Boston," *Boston Daily Record*, February 16, 1961, 39.

Chapter 14

[1] Dick Mittman, *Indianapolis Times*, January 1961 (clipping missing headline and page number, in my possession); Marilyn Meeker Durham, telephone interview, July 30, 2003.

[2] Pieter Kollen, telephone interview, July 29, 2003; Sally Wells Van De Mark, telephone interview, August 27, 2004; Bette Todd, telephone interview, September 29, 2004.

[3] William R. Haigler, "The 1961 United States Championships," *Skating*, April 1961, 7; Marsha Lopez, "Broadmoor: Skating's Mecca," *American Skating World*, July 1986, 14; "Arena Enlarged," *Gazette Telegraph* (Colorado Springs), January 29, 1961, 2; Harry Shattuck, "The Broadmoor Tradition," *Houston Chronicle*, January 11, 1998, Travel section, 1.

[4] "National Figure Skating Set for Broadmoor," *Gazette Telegraph*, January 15, 1961, E6; Loy Holman, "National Figures at World Arena," *Gazette Telegraph*, January 22, 1961, 4.

[5] Loy Holman, "Novice Skaters Start National Test," *Gazette Telegraph*, January 24, 1961, 16; Benjamin T. Wright, *Skating in America: The 75th Anniversary History of the United States Figure Skating Association* (Colorado Springs: U.S. Figure Skating Association, 1996), vii.

[6] Holman, "Novice Skaters Start National Test," 16; "National Figure Skate Meet Opens in Broadmoor Arena," *Rocky Mountain News* (Denver, CO), January 24, 1961, 56.

[7] "Kennedy Sworn in as 35th President," *Gazette Telegraph*, January 20, 1961, 1; Anne Frazier, telephone interview, November 2, 2007; Fred Heller, telephone interview, November 11, 2003.

[8] F. Ritter Shumway, "A Tribute to Howard D. Herbert," *Skating*, March 1961, 7; Haigler, "The 1961 United States Championships," 7.

[9] Haigler, "The 1961 United States Championships," 7.

[10] "1961 National Figure Skating Championships" advertisement, *Gazette Telegraph*, January 28, 1961, 11; "Cream of Skaters Arrive," *Gazette Telegraph*, January 22, 1961, 4.

[11] Dick Button, telephone interview, December 2005.

[12] Haigler, "The 1961 United States Championships," 7; E. Newbold Black IV, telephone interview, November 3, 2003.

[13] Haigler, "The 1961 United States Championships," 7.

[14] Ibid; Billy Chapel, telephone interview, September 10, 2003; Gary Visconti, interviewed, Long Beach, CA, September 16, 2004.

[15] Elizabeth George Busconi, telephone interview, May 5, 2005; Gary Clark, telephone interview, May 24, 2005; Paul George, interviewed, Portland, OR, January 13, 2005.

[16] Black, interview; Haigler, "The 1961 United States Championships," 8-9; Dick Tucker, "12-Year-Old Boston Girl Wins Skate Title," *Rocky Mountain News,* January 27, 1961, 62; Vicky Fisher Binner, telephone interview, February 27, 2009.

[17] Haigler, "The United States Championhips," 8, 34.

[18] Ibid; "1961 U.S. Figure Skating Championships," *CBS Sports Spectacular,* January 29, 1961 (in private collection).

[19] Loy Holman, "Even Competition Starts Nationals," *Gazette Telegraph,* January 26, 1961, 15; Janet Harley Browning, telephone interview, September 6, 2005.

[20] Browning, interview.

[21] United Press International, "Skating Title Meet Taken from Prague," Davos, Switzerland, January 25, 1961, unidentified newspaper clipping in my possession; "Skate Group Threatens to Skip Prague," *Denver Post,* February 26, 2010, 53.

[22] Haigler, "The 1961 United States Championships," 8.

[23] Roger Berry, telephone interview, June 3, 2005; Tommy Litz, telephone interview, July 20, 2005.

[24] Robert Brewer, interviewed, Phoenix, AZ, March 18, 2005.

[25] Brewer, interview.

[26] Visconti, interview; Walter Hypes, telephone interview, September 9, 2004.

[27] "1961 U.S. Figure Skating Championships," *CBS Sports Spectacular,* January 29, 1961.

[28] Ibid.

[29] Ibid.

[30] "Hickox Duo Is 'Adopted' Favorite in Nationals," *Gazette Telegraph,* January 20, 1961, 4; Terry Hansen, "Death Nips Promising Ice Careers," *Berkeley Daily Gazette* (CA), February 14, 1961, 5; Hickox performance, 1961 Nationals, in private collection.

[31] "1961 U.S. Figure Skating Championships," *CBS Sports Spectacular,* January 29, 1961.

[32] Ibid.

[33] Ibid; Visconti, interview.

[34] Judianne Fotheringill Fuller, telephone interview, July 25, 2005.

[35] Browning, interview.

[36] Haigler, "The 1961 United States Championships," 9.

[37] Ibid., 8; Julie Barrett, telephone interview, June 4, 2005; Frazier, interview.

[38] Jerry Fotheringill, telephone interview, August 21, 2005; Fuller, interview.

[39] Browning, interview.

[40] Pam Zekman, telephone interview, April 13, 2005; "1961 U.S. Figure Skating Championships," *CBS Sports Spectacular,* January 29, 1961.

[41] Ibid.

[42] Ibid.; Scott Allen, telephone interview, September 1, 2010; David Mitchell, telephone interview, September 20, 2004.

[43] Karen Howland Jones, telephone interview, September 11, 2003.

[44] Dick Tucker, "Laurence Owen, Monty Hoyt Top National Skate Fields," *Rocky Mountain News,* January 28, 1961, 44; "Steffi Bids for Ladies Title in National Figure Skating," *Gazette Telegraph,* January 27, 1961, 8; Ardith Paul Hamilton, telephone interview, July 31, 2005.

[45] 1961 National Figure Skating Championships program; Loy Holman, "Men's National Title Up for Grabs Tonight," *Gazette Telegraph*, January 28, 1961, 10.

[46] "1961 North American Figure Skating Championships," in private collection; "1961 U.S. Figure Skating Championships," *CBS Sports Spectacular*, January 29, 1961.

[47] Ibid; Greg Hoyt, telephone interview, July 12, 2005; Holman, "Men's National Title," 10.

[48] *CBS Sports Spectacular*, January 29, 1961.

[49] Ibid.

[50] Ibid.

[51] Ibid.

[52] Hamilton, interview; Litz, telephone interview; Visconti, interview.

[53] Binner, interview.

[54] Haigler, "The 1961 United States Championships," 8; Hamilton, interview.

[55] Haigler, "The 1961 United States Championships," 9; Binner, interview.

[56] "1961 U.S. Figure Skating Championships," *CBS Sports Spectacular*, January 29, 1961.

[57] "Laurence Owen," *Chips*, 18, no. 7, 2; "1961 U.S. Figure Skating Championships," *CBS Sports Spectacular*, January 29, 1961.

[58] Visconti, interview; Irene Maguire Muehlbronner, telephone interview, October 15, 2004.

[59] Jones, interview.

[60] Visconti, interview.

[61] "Steffi Bids for Ladies Title in National Figure Skating," 8; "World's Test Set for Prague," *Gazette Telegraph*, January 28, 1961, 10.

[62] Kollen, interview.

[63] "Ladies' Junior," *Skating*, April 1961, 9; Michelle Monnier, telephone interview, September 8, 2003.

[64] Litz, interview.

[65] "1961 U.S. Figure Skating Championships," *CBS Sports Spectacular*, January 29, 1961.

[66] Ibid.

[67] Hoyt, interview; Kollen, interview; Van De Mark, interview; Monnier, interview.

[68] "1961 U.S. Figure Skating Championships," *CBS Sports Spectacular*, January 29, 1961.

[69] Bruce Heiss, telephone interview, July 19, 2005.

[70] Kollen, interview.

[71] "1961 U.S. Figure Skating Championships," *CBS Sports Spectacular*, January 29, 1961.

[72] Ibid; Kollen, interview.

[73] Stephen Kelley, telephone interview, August 7, 2003; "Men's National Title Up for Grabs Tonight," 10; Loy Holman, "Compulsory Figures Start National Skating," *Gazette Telegraph*, January 25, 1961, 16; Lee Meade, "Colorado Skaters Battle East Sweep," *Denver Post*, January 28, 1961, 7.

[74] "1961 U.S. Figure Skating Championships," *CBS Sports Spectacular*, January 29, 1961; Busconi, interview.

[75] "1961 U.S. Figure Skating Championships," *CBS Sports Spectacular*, January 29, 1961.

[76] Ibid; Peter Betts, telephone interview, February 7, 2005.

[77] "Dance Favorites," *Gazette Telegraph*, January 23, 1961, 13.

[78] Visconti, interview; Van De Mark, interview.

[79] "Bradley Lord Takes National Men's Title," *Gazette Telegraph*, January 29, 1961, 12.

[80] Irma Staro Magee, telephone interview, March 31, 2005; Margaret Hosford, telephone interview, October 24, 2003.

[81] "1961 U.S. Figure Skating Championships," *CBS Sports Spectacular,* January 29, 1961.

[82] "1961 North American Championships" video, World Figure Skating Museum & Hall of Fame; "1961 U.S. Figure Skating Championships," *CBS Sports Spectacular,* January 29, 1961.

[83] Marilyn Grace Guilfoyle, telephone interview, May 24, 2004.

[84] Haigler, "The United States Championships," 36; Betts, interview.

[85] "Receive Radix Trophy," *Indianapolis Times,* January 30, 1961, 11; "1961 U.S. Figure Skating Championships," *CBS Sports Spectacular,* January 29, 1961.

[86] Ron Ludington, interviewed, Overland Park, KS, June 11, 2004.

[87] Haigler, "The United States Championships," 9; Heiss interview.

[88] "1961 U.S. Figure Skating Championships," *CBS Sports Spectacular,* January 29, 1961; Bruce Lord, telephone interview, May 4, 2005.

[89] Loy Holman, "Between the Lines," *Gazette Telegraph,* January 29, 1961, 5; Phil Taylor, "From Hospital to Ice Glory," *Seattle Post-Intelligencer,* January 31, 1960, 21; Roger Williams, "U.S. Team Tragedy Hits Close to Home," *San Francisco News-Call Bulletin,* February 16, 1961, 26.

[90] Eddie Shipstad III, telephone interview, September 12, 2004.

[91] Brewer, interview.

[92] Loy Holman, "Between the Lines," *Gazette Telegraph,* January 29, 1961, 5.

[93] "1961 U.S. Figure Skating Championships," CBS Sports Spectacular, January 29, 1961.

[94] Ibid.

[95] Bob Duffy, "Shattered Dreams," *Boston Globe,* December 29, 2000, E17; Barbara Roles Williams, telephone interview, September 25, 2003.

[96] Haigler, "The United States Championships," 36; Tim Horgan, "Bright Boston Skating Future Ends in Crash," *Boston Traveler,* February 15, 1961, 35.

[97] "Bradley Lord," *Chips,* 18, no. 7, 2.

[98] "Meet the Champions," April 1961, 22; Bill McSwenny, "Fatal Brussels Tragedy Felt in Boston," *Boston Daily Record,* February 16, 1961, 39; George, interview.

[99] Joanne Heckert Bachtel, telephone interview, September 6, 2005.

[100] Haigler, "The United States Championships," 8-9.

[101] Ron Pfenning, telephone interview, May 27, 2005.

[102] Peter Dunfield, telephone interview, July 28, 2004; Brewer, interview.

[103] Sonya Kloper Dunfield, telephone interview, June 2, 2004; Hugh Graham, telephone interview, November 17, 2003.

[104] Peter Dunfield, interview.

Chapter 15

[1] Robert Brewer, interviewed, Phoenix, AZ, March 18, 2005; Kendall Kelley, letter to Virginia Bremer, January 29, 1961; "1961 World Team Meeting," U.S. Figure Skating files.

[2] "1961 World Team Meeting," January 29, 1961; Kelley, letter to Bremer; Kendall Kelley, "Letter No. 2" to Potential U.S. World Team Members," December 21, 1960.

[3] Bob Bowie, "Improve Style, Button Tells Skaters," *Denver Post,* January 27, 1961, 39; "1961 National Skating Championships," *CBS Sports Spectacular,* January 29, 1961, in private collection.

[4] Pieter Kollen, telephone interview, July 29, 2003; Joan Sherbloom Peterson, telephone interview, July 22, 2003.

[5] Lee Meade, "Stapleton Luncheon Joke Grim Omen for Skaters' Trip," *Denver Post*, February 15, 1961, 1.

[6] Hank Hickox, telephone interview, August 30, 2005; Anne Frazier, telephone interview, November 2, 2007; Mrs. Lute Hickox, letter to Kendall Kelley, January 31, 1961.

[7] Kendall Kelley, letter to Deane McMinn, January 23, 1961; Kelley, "Letter No. 2, December 21, 1960"; Nancy Moehring, telephone interview, March 7, 2005; Ron Kauffman, telephone interview, November 14, 2007.

[8] "Two Pass Up Jet Trip and Save Lives," *Chicago Daily Tribune*, February 16, 1961, 8; Peter Dunfield, telephone interview, July 28, 2004; Ron Joseph, telephone interview, October 3, 2003.

[9] "U.S. World Team," *Skating*, March 1961, 10.

[10] Theda Beck Bartynski, telephone interview, July 12, 2005; "Ace Tourney Skaters Coached by Local Native Practice Here," *Evening Chronicle* (Allentown, PA), February 2, 1961, 22; "North American Figure Skating Championships to Be in Ardmore Saturday, *Main Line Times* (Ardmore, PA), February 9, 1961, 22; Jack Lapos, "Billy Kipp Personified Optimism," *Evening Chronicle*, undated clipping in my possession.

[11] "Laurence Owen Was Due to Skate Here," *Washington Post*, February 16, 1961, D1; "Miss Owen Was Set for Show Here," *Newark Evening News*, February 15, 1961, 1.

[12] "Swampscott Stunned by Death of Lord," *Daily Evening Item* (Lynn, MA), February 15, 1961, 1, 8; Bruce Lord, telephone interview, May 4, 2005.

[13] Deane McMinn, letter to Kendall Kelley, January 30, 1960.

[14] Karen Howland Jones, telephone interview, September 11, 2003.

[15] Gerty Desjardins Verbiwski, telephone interview, May 10, 2005; "Comments on the 1961 Canadians," *Skating*, April 1961, 13.

[16] Verbiwski interview; Maria Jelinek, telephone interview, October 3, 2007.

[17] Kendall Kelley, letter to G. Hasler, January 23, 1961; USFSA correspondence, December 1960.

[18] Kendall Kelley, letter to Czech Figure Skating Section, January 24, 1961.

[19] Kendall Kelley, letter to G. Hasler, January 27, 1961.

[20] Deane McMinn, letter to Kendall Kelley, February 2, 1961.

[21] Hickox, letter to Kelley, January 31, 1961; Janet Harley Browning, telephone interview, September 6, 2005; Judianne Fotheringill Fuller, telephone interview, July 23, 2005.

[22] "Detroit Boy and Noted Coach on Skaters' Flight as 'Subs,'" *Detroit News*, February 15, 1961, 19A; Cathy Ramsay, telephone interview, June 17, 2009; Gary Visconti, interviewed, Long Beach, CA, September 16, 2004; Maxine Ceramin Rayner, telephone interview, August 22, 2005; Ginny Baxter Newman, telephone interview, August 30, 2004; Bill Swallender, telephone interview, September 3, 2005.

[23] "Hadleys Had Won Success," *Register-Guard* (Eugene, OR), February 15, 1961, B 2-4; Jimmy Stephens, telephone interview, September 9, 2004; Peter Dunfield, interview.

[24] Joseph Dineen, telephone interview, October 19, 2004; Marilyn Grace Guilfoyle, telephone interview, May 24, 2004.

[25] Jane Vaughn Sullivan, telephone interview, December 7, 2004; "Five Famed Berkeley Skaters Perish in Flaming Wreck," *Oakland Tribune*, February 15, 1961, 3.

26 Carol Heiss, "Skating Abroad on 44 Pounds;" David Jenkins, "Skating Abroad on 44 Pounds," n.d.; Bill Hickox, letter to Anne Frazier, February 6, 1961, in private collection.

27 "Harvard Cited Richards with Special Major 'H,'" *Boston Traveler*, February 15, 1961, D35.

28 "Air Crash Last Chapter in Vinson-Owen Ice Saga," *Boston Globe*, February 15, 1961, 36; Lorin Caccamise O'Neil, telephone interview, February 4, 2005; Ron Kauffman, interview; Cynthia Kauffman Marshall, telephone interview, November 5, 2003; Fran Haigler Ainsworth, telephone interview, August 2, 2003; Eleanor Banneck Curtis, telephone interview, October 7, 2003; Ruth Ann Kipp, telephone interview, October 5, 2007; Mary Ellen Young, telephone interview, July 20, 2004.

29 Rayner, interview; Visconti, interview; Maud Dubos, telephone interview, August 22, 2005; George Puscas, "City Mourns a Star, Coach; Nation a Sport," *Detroit Free Press*, February 16, 1961, 33.

30 Joyce Underwood Winship, telephone interview, October 1, 2003.

31 Ron Ludington, interviewed, Overland Park, KS, June 11, 2004; Jean Westwood, telephone interview, July 13, 2004.

32 "Detroit Boy and Noted Coach," 9A; "Fate Put Detroit Boy on Doomed Jet," *Detroit Free Press*, February 16, 1961, 2.

33 Meade, "Stapleton Luncheon Joke," 3.

34 Ibid.

35 "Dream of Honor Cruelly Crushed," *Indianapolis Times*, February 15, 1961, 3; "Births," *Skating*, May, 1961, 31; Kollen, interview; Sheryl Ryan Nolan, telephone interview, August 21, 2005.

36 Sherbloom and Pierce photo, *Philadelphia Inquirer*, February 11, 1961, 20; "Skate Champs Open Drills Here," *Philadelphia Inquirer*, February 10, 1961, 28.

37 Moehring, interview; George Gross, "Skaters' Death Stuns Tely . . . ," *Telegram* (St. John's, Newfoundland), February 16, 1961, unpaginated clipping with partial headline in my possession; "Skaters Here Mourn Stars; Six from L.A. Lose Lives," *Los Angeles Examiner*, February 16, 1961, 2.

38 Sally Wells Van De Mark, telephone interview, August 27, 2004; Kollen, interview; Carol Ann Peters Duncan, telephone interview, September 5, 2003; E. Newbold Black IV, telephone interview, November 3, 2003; Lucy Curley Brennan, telephone interview, September 15, 2004.

39 Bradley Black, telephone interview, May 13, 2005; Dick Button, telephone interview, December 2005.

40 Ron Vincent, telephone interview, May 20, 2005; Shirra Kenworthy, telephone interview, October 13, 2005.

41 Wendy Griner Ballantyne, telephone interview, October 10, 2005; Barbara Heilman, "Mother Set the Style," *Sports Illustrated*, February 13, 1961, 39-41.

42 Gross, "Skaters' Death"; Ralph Bernstein, "Tragedy Wipes Out Owen Family," *Los Angeles Herald & Express*, February 15, 1961, B6; "Philadelphia Cheered Flashing Skates at the Arena," *Philadelphia Inquirer*, February 16, 1961, 3.

43 Floyd C. Carrier, letter to Dona Lee Carrier, January 27, 1961.

44 Virginia Thompson Brookshill, telephone interview, September 21, 2005; Bruce Hyland, telephone interview, January 24, 2005.

45 Westwood, interview.

46 Ballantyne, interview.

47 1961 North American Championships program, copy in my possession.

48 Ibid; "Jackson-Lord Battle Feature of North American Tourney," *Gazette Telegraph* (Colorado Springs), February 10, 1961, 15; Bernstein, "Tragedy Wipes Out Owen Family," B-6; "Men's," *Skating*, April 1961, 34.

[49] Ibid; "Southland Victims Prominent in Skating," *Los Angeles Times*, February 16, 1961, 15.

[50] Mayer Brandschain, "Laurence Owen Gains Slight Lead over Miss Griner in Figure Skating," *Philadelphia Inquirer*, February 12, 1961, Sec. 2–3; Suzanne Davis King, "The North American Championships," *Skating*, April 1961, 10.

[51] Vincent, interview; Hyland, interview; George Gross, "Jackson Wins Singles Handily," *Telegram*, February 13, 1961.

[52] "Miss Owen Lone U.S. Skate Winner," *Denver Post*, February 13, 1961, 38; "Laurence Owen Wins Figure Skating Crown," *Rocky Mountain News* (Denver), February 13, 1961, 58; King, "The North American Championships, 10; Jelinek, interview; Hyland, interview, "Richards' Death Saddens Friend, Ted Kennedy," *Boston Traveler*, February 15, 1961, 29.

[53] 1961 North American program; Brookshill, interview; "Philadelphia Cheered," 1.

[54] King, "The North American Championships," 10.

[55] Paulette Doan Ormsby, telephone interview, September 20, 2005; King, "The North American Championships," 10-11.

[56] King, "The North American Championships," 10-11; Brookshill, interview.

[57] Ralph Clark, "Skate Stars of Valley Die," *Valley Times Today* (Los Angeles), February 15, 1961, 1; "Dance," *Skating*, April 1961, 34.

[58] Gross, "Skaters' Death"; Sally Schantz Urban, telephone interview, November 7, 2004; "Southland Families Mourn Plane Dead," *Los Angeles Mirror*, February 15, 1961, 4; *Los Angeles FSC News Bulletin* 2, no. 5 (February 1961).

[59] Joan Heiser Gruber, telephone interview, May 21, 2005.

[60] King, "The North American Championships," 11.

[61] Ibid; Ballantyne, interview.

[62] Gross, "Skaters' Death"; "Arena Saw Laurence Triumph," *Boston Traveler*, February 15, 1961, 12; Ralph Bernstein, "Champs Last Week—Mourned Today," *Pittsburgh Post-Gazette*, 33.

[63] 1961 North Americans telecast; Brookshill, interview; Debbi Wilkes, *Ice Time* (Scarborough, Ontario: Prentice Hall Canada, 1994), 19.

[64] Mayer Brandschain, "Miss Owen Only U.S. Skate Victor," *Philadelphia Inquirer*, February 13, 1961, 27; "Family Tragedy," *Newark Evening News*, February 15, 1961, 4.

[65] "Owen Family, Champions All," *Boston Traveler*, February 15, 1961, 42.

[66] Bernstein, "Champs Last Week—Mourned Today," 33; Kenworthy, interview; Jones, interview.

[67] Peter Betts, telephone interview, February 7, 2005; Don Jackson, telephone interview, October 11, 2007; Gross, "Skaters' Death"; Ballantyne, interview.

[68] Ballantyne, interview.

[69] Jelinek, interview; Brandschain, "Miss Owen Only U.S. Skate Victor," 24; Vincent, interview.

[70] King, "The North American Championships," 32.

[71] Ibid; Gross, "Skaters' Death."

[72] Gross, "Skaters' Death"; Jelinek, interview; "Disa and Data," *Telegram*, February 12, 1961, unpaginated clipping in my possession.

[73] King, "The North American Championships," 32; Gross, "Skaters' Death."

[74] King, "The North American Championships," 32.

[75] Vincent, interview; Gross, "Skaters' Death."

[76] King, "The North American Championships," 32; Stephen Kelley, interview, August 7, 2003.

[77] Vincent, interview; Verbiwski, interview.

[78] Verbiwski, interview; Brad Black, interview.

[79] Brookshill, interview; Gross, "Skaters' Death."

[80] Frank Muckian, telephone interview, October 6, 2004; Rikki Rendich Samuels, telephone interview, November 17, 2003; Brookshill, interview; Ormsby, interview.

[81] Betts, interview.

[82] Ibid.

[83] Bob Duffy, "Twists of Fate," *Boston Globe*, December 31, 2000, C14-15.

[84] Jay Weiner, "Plane Crash in 1961 Changed Course of Skating," *Star Tribune* (Minneapolis), April 4, 1998, 8C; Button, interview; "Owen Skating Family Wiped Out in Crash," *Evening Star* (Washington D.C.), February 15, 1961, D4.

[85] Gary Clark, telephone interview, May 25, 2004; Bob Pearce, telephone interview, July 12, 2005.

[86] "Fate Put Detroit Boy on Doomed Jet," 2; Kendall Kelley, Personal memo, Chronology of Events, February 1961.

[87] Bucky Yardume, "Traveler Writer Last to Interview Owens," *Boston Traveler*, February 15, 1961, 35; "Owen Family, Champions All," 1, 42.

[88] Tom Downey and Gordon Hillman, "Hub Mourns Brilliant Owens Skating Clan," *Daily Record* (Boston), February 16, 1961, 3; "Air Crash Last Chapter in Vinson-Owen Ice Saga," *Boston Globe*, February 15, 1961, 36.

[89] Swallender, interview; Norma Sahlin, telephone interview, September 10, 2004.

[90] Daryl Hartshorne, telephone interview, November 26, 2004.

[91] Ice Chips Date Kept Bud Wilson from Fatal Trip," *Boston Globe*, February 15, 1961, 19; Winship, interview.

[92] Norton, "The Legacy," 17.

[93] Greg Hoyt, telephone interview, July 12, 2005; "Two Pass Up Jet Trip and Save Lives," *Chicago Daily Tribune*, February 16, 1961, 8; Joseph, interview.

[94] Duffy, "Twists of Fate," C15; Lorraine Hanlon Comanor, telephone interview, February 1, 2010.

[95] Hyland, interview; Westwood, interview.

[96] "Shaker Couple Avoided Flight," *Cleveland Press*, February 15, 1961, 4.

[97] Ballantyne, interview; Jackson, interview.

[98] Daryl Hartshorne, interview; Harry Hartshorne, telephone interview, October 7, 2003; Dan Hartshorne, telephone interview, November 16, 2004.

[99] Daryl Hartshorne, interview; Gail Hartshorne, telephone interview, February 28, 2005.

[100] Kendall, Chronology of Events; Jones, telephone interview.

[101] Jones, interview; Marie Pearce, interviewed, Overland Park, KS, April 14, 2005.

[102] Verbiwski, interview; Jackson, interview.

[103] Diana LeMaire Squibb, interviewed, Manchester-by-the-Sea, MA, August 7, 2003; Dorinda LeMaire Howard, telephone interview, May 2, 2010.

[104] "Ice Follies' Stars Weep over News," *Los Angeles Mirror*, February 15, 1961, Sports sec., 4; Jackson, interview; Bob Duffy, "Shattered Dreams," *Boston Globe*, December 29, 2000, E17.

[105] Elizabeth George Busconi, telephone interview, May 5, 2005; Peterson, interview.

[106] "Tutt Terms Air Crash 'Horrible;' Lauds Scholdan," *Gazette-Telegraph*, February 15, 1961, 1; "Springs Mourns 8 Area Victims of Air Tragedy," *Rocky Mountain News*, February 16, 1961, 7; Cindy Chescheir Walsh, interviewed, Colorado Springs, May 8, 2007.

[107] Kelley, Letter No. 2; Peterson, interview; "Maribel Vinson Owen: She Loved Life, and Lived It," *Newark Evening News*, February 15, 1961, 53.

[108] Heilman, "Mother Set the Style," 39-41; Paul George, interviewed, Portland, OR, January 13, 2005.

[109] Hyland interview; Vincent, interview.

[110] Ormsby, interview.

[111] Jelinek, interview.

[112] David Mitchell, telephone interview, September 20, 2004; Hyland, interview.

[113] Brad Black, flight itinerary, L. G. Masson Travel, Ltd., St. Catharines, Ontario; "Trip Saddened by Crash," unidentified Canadian newspaper in my possession; Debbi Wilkes, telephone interview, December 2, 2005.

[114] Sally Haas Knoll, telephone interview, May 12, 2004; Kendall Kelley, letter to Elden R. Sternberg, April 26, 1961; Western Union telegram, Ritter Shumway to Deane McMinn, February 14, 1961.

[115] Scott Allen, telephone interview, December 8, 2005.

[116] Coco Gram Shean, telephone interview, October 10, 2007.

[117] Guilfoyle, interview; Marilyn Meeker Durham, telephone interview, July 31, 2003; Arvilla Kauffman Christensen, telephone interview, October 6, 2003; Rose Anne Ryan Wager, telephone interview, March 4, 2010; Jennie Walsh Guzman, telephone interview, September 9, 2003.

[118] "L.A. Kin Mourn Death of 7," *Los Angeles Herald & Express*, February 15, 1961, 5; "Southland Victims Prominent in Skating," 15; Sharon McKenzie, telephone interview, May 16, 2005; Curtis, interview.

[119] Lord, interview; "Swampscott Stunned by Death of Lord," 8.

[120] "Five Berkeleyans among 73 Victims of Jet Crash," *Berkeley Daily Gazette*, February 15, 1961, 1; Hickox, interview; Julie Marcus Barrett, telephone interview, June 4, 2005.

[121] Dan Tompkins, "Only Valentine Left to Dona's Parents," *Los Angeles Examiner*, February 16, 1961, 3; "Father of Victim," *Los Angeles Times*, February 16, 1961, 2; Cathy Ramsay, telephone interview, June 17, 2009.

[122] Susan Richards Abbe, telephone interview, August 29, 2003.

[123] Mike Michelson, telephone interview, July 1, 2003; Mary Miller Robicheaux, telephone interview, July 14, 2005.

[124] Wager, interview; "Fate's Hand in Crash of Sabena," *Indianapolis News*, February 18, 1961, 13; Donna Lee Mitchell Zaleski, interviewed December 1, 2005.

[125] Brewer, interview; George E. Van, "Fund for Skaters Becomes Memorial," March 1961, unidentified Detroit clipping in my possession; Linda Landin, telephone interview, October 12, 2004; Fred Baker, "Area Skating Fans 'Shocked' by Plane Deaths," *Denver Post*, February 16, 1961, 3; "Mother of Two Crash Victims 'Holding Up Well,'" *Gazette-Telegraph*, February 15, 1961, unpaginated clipping in my possession.

[126] Norton, "The Legacy," 17.

[127] Anne Gram Gerli, telephone interview, November 17, 2003; Squibb, interview.

[128] Simpson, "U.S. Skating Tragedy," A10; Royal Brougham, "Ice Skaters Rated First," *Seattle Post-Intelligencer*, January 27, 1960, 18.

[129] Simpson, "U.S. Skating Tragedy," A10.

[130] Kollen, interview.

[131] "Gayety and Fear Rode with Airliner to Doom," *Hartford Courant* (CT), February 16, 1961, 11.

[132] Mary Neiswender, "Wilmington Girl Skater Air Victim," *Press-Telegram* (Long Beach, CA), February 15, 1961, A8; Durham, interview.

[133] Frazier, interview.

Chapter 16

[1] "Jet Crash Kills 73, U.S. Skaters Die," *Detroit Free Press*, February 15, 1961, 1; "Skaters' Jet Fell in 3rd Bid to Land," *Detroit Free Press*, February 16, 1961, 1-2; Kamon Simpson, "U.S. Skating Tragedy," *Gazette* (Colorado Springs, CO), February 15, 2001, A10.

[2] "Radio Silence before Sabena Crash Probed," *Minneapolis Star*, February 16, 1961, 11; Simpson, "U.S. Skating Tragedy," A10.

[3] "Jet Crash Kills 73," *Minneapolis Star*, February 15, 1961, 4A; "Radio Silence before Sabena Crash Probed," 11.

[4] "Family Affairs," *Time*, February 24, 1961, 13; Simpson, "U.S. Skating Tragedy," A10; "Radio Silence before Sabena Crash Probed," 11.

[5] Bob Duffy, "Shattered Dreams," *Boston Globe*, December 29, 2000, E16; "Radio Silence before Sabena Crash Probed," 11; "Plane Crash in Brussels Hits Local Skating Ranks," *Daily Evening Item* (Lynn, MA), February 15, 1961, 8.

[6] "Family Affairs," 13; Simpson, "U.S. Skating Tragedy," A10; Wellington Long, "U.S. Skaters among 73 Dead in Belgium Crash," *Rocky Mountain News*, (Denver, CO), February 16, 1961, 1.

[7] "Family Affairs," 13; Long, "U.S. Skaters among 73 Dead in Belgium Crash," 12; "Jet Crash Kills 73," 4A; "Plane Circled Brussels Airport, Then 'Fell in a Series of Spins,'" *New York Times*, February 16, 1961, 18; "Sunny Day Turns 'Dark' As Giant Plane Crashes," *Oregonian* (Salem, OR), February 16, 1961, 1.

[8] Harry Gilroy, "73 Dead, 49 Americans, in First 707 Disaster," *Seattle Post-Intelligencer*, February 16, 1961, 3; Long, "U.S. Skaters among 73 Dead in Belgium Crash," 1; Simpson, "U.S. Skating Tragedy," A10.

[9] Simpson, "U.S. Skating Tragedy," 2A; "Sunny Day Turns 'Dark' As Giant Plane Crashes," 1; "Skaters' Jet Fell in 3rd Bid to Land," 1-2; "Plane Circled Brussels Airport," 18.

[10] "Jet's Strange Antics Stir Crash Probe," *Chicago Daily Tribune*, February 16, 1961, 2; "49 Americans among 73 Dead in Brussels," *St. Louis Post-Dispatch*, February 15, 1961, 5; "Entire U.S. Figure Skating Team Killed in Plane Crash; Eight Are from Springs," *Gazette Telegraph* (Colorado Springs, CO), February 15, 1961, 8; Gordon Simpson, "Owen Girls, Mother, with U.S. Team," *Boston Herald*, February 16, 1961, 3; Kendall Kelley, letter to Ritter Shumway, February 19, 1961; Simpson, "U.S. Skating Tragedy," A10.

[11] "Jet Crash Kills 73," 1A.

[12] Duffy, "Shattered Dreams," E17.

[13] "City Shocked As Young Ice Skaters Perish in Flaming Plane Crash," *Daily Evening Item*, February 16, 1961, 3.

[14] Long, "U.S. Skaters among 73 Dead in Belgium Crash," 12; "U.S. Figure Skating Team Killed in Jet Airliner Crash," *Register-Guard* (Eugene, OR), February 15, 1961, 1; "Belgian Air Crash

Kills 73, Including U.S. Skate Team," *Sacramento Bee*, February 15, 1961, 1; "Jet Crash Kills 73," 1A, 4A.

[15] "Family Affairs," 13.

[16] "49 Americans among 73 Dead in Brussels," 1.

[17] Duffy, "Shattered Dreams," E16; "49 Americans among 73 Dead in Brussels," 1.

[18] "Priest Saw a Flash, Then Jet Nose-Dived," *Boston Globe*, February 15, 1961, 19.

[19] "The Bright Hope Killed," *Newsweek*, February 27, 1961, 34; "Priest Saw a Flash, Then Jet Nose-Dived," 19; "Watchers Sense Tragedy before Jet Liner Crashed," *Seattle Times*, February 15, 1961, 4.

[20] "Officials Begin Probing Belgian Air Crash," *Oregonian*, February 17, 1961, 3; "Jet's Strange Antics Stir Crash Probe," 1-2; "Plane Circled Brussels Airport," 18.

[21] "Jet Plane Victims Had a Warning," *San Francisco Chronicle*, February 16, 1961, 1, 8; "Skaters' Jet Fell in 3rd Bid to Land," 2; "73 Died in Crash; 7 from L.A. Area," *Citizen-News* (Hollywood, CA), February 15, 1961, 2; "Priest Saw a Flash," 19.

[22] "Plane Circled Brussels Airport," 18; Simpson, "U.S. Skating Tragedy," 1; "U.S. Skate Stars Killed in Belgian Plane Crash," *Oregonian*, February 16, 1961, 1; "38 Victims of Crash Identified at Brussels," *Boston Herald*, February 17, 1961, 29; "2 Detroiters Killed in Crash Fatal to 72," *Detroit News*, February 15, 1961, 2A; "Jet Liner Crash," *San Francisco Chronicle*, February 15, 1961, 5; "City Skater, Coach among 72 Jet Dead," *Indianapolis News*, February 15, 1961, 1.

[23] Duffy, "Shattered Dreams," E17.

[24] "Jet Crash Kills 73, U.S. Skaters Die," 1; "18 Top U.S. Skaters Die As Jet Crash Kills 73," *Newark Evening News*, February 15, 1961, 4; George Sibera, "Jet Flight Tape Found in Wreck," *Citizen-News*, February 16, 1961, 2; "Radio Silence before Sabena Crash Probed," 11; "Sabena 707 Crash," *Aviation Week*, February 20, 1961; "Five Berkeleyans among 73 Victims of Jet Crash," *Berkeley Daily Gazette*, February 15, 1961, 2.

[25] Gilroy, "73 Dead, 49 Americans, in First 707 Disaster," 1, 3; Sibera, "Jet Flight Tape Found in Wreck," 2.

[26] Long, "U.S. Skaters among 73 Dead in Belgium Crash," 12; Sibera, "Jet Flight Tape Found in Wreck," 2.

[27] Duffy, "Shattered Dreams," E17.

[28] "Jet Crash Kills 73," 1A, 4A; "Jet Plane Victims Had a Warning," 8; Gilroy, "73 Dead, 49 Americans, in First 707 Disaster," 3; "King Baudouin, Queen Console Wife of Plane Victim," *Boston Globe*, February 15, 1961, 11; Long, "U.S. Skaters among 73 Dead in Belgium Crash," 12.

[29] "Officials Begin Probing Belgian Air Crash," 3; Long, "U.S. Skaters among 73 Dead in Belgium Crash," 12.

[30] "18 U.S. Skaters among 73 Dead in a Jet Crash," *New York Times*, February 16, 1961, 1, 18.

[31] "Canadian Team on Other Plane, Flies to Prague," *Boston Globe*, February 15, 1961, 11.

[32] Paulette Doan Ormsby, telephone interview, September 20, 2005; Maria Jelinek, telephone interview, October 3, 2007.

[33] Gerty Desjardins Verbiwski, telephone interview, May 10, 2005; Debbi Wilkes, telephone interview, December 9, 2005.

[34] Marie Vichova Millikan, telephone interview, September 25, 2007.

[35] Wilkes, interview.

[36] Don Jackson, telephone interview, October 11, 2007; Shirra Kenworthy, telephone interview, October 13, 2005; J. D. Mitchell, telephone interview, November 16, 2005.

[37] "List of Casualties in Belgian Crash," *New York Times*, February 16, 1961, 18; "18 Top U.S. Skaters Die as Jet Crash Kills 73," 4; Kelley to Shumway, February 19, 1961.

[38] "List of Casualties in Belgian Crash," 18; "Radio Silence before Sabena Crash Probed," 11.

[39] "Texans on Flight," *Kansas City Star*, February 16, 1961, 2; Griff Singer, "Vacation Plans for Three Had Gone Awry from First," *Dallas Morning News*, February 16, 1961, 8.

[40] "Air Victim Was to Join Husband," *Times-Picayune* (New Orleans), February 16, 1961, 1; "Drexel Hill Wife Was on Way to Army Husband," *Philadelphia Inquirer*, February 16, 1961, 3; "Pittsburgh GI Aboard Belgian Jet," *Pittsburgh Post-Gazette*, February 16, 1961, 1, 22; "Hoosier, Bride Die in Disaster," *Indianapolis Star*, February, 16, 1961, 24.

[41] "Sketches of Passengers Killed in Sabena Crash," *New York Times*, February 16, 1961, 19; "73 Killed in Jet Crash," *Daily News* (New York City), February 16, 1961, 2; "Westport Man Is Killed in Brussels Air Crash," *Bridgeport (CT) Post*, February 15, 1961, 1, 5; "Laconia Firm's Vice Pres. Kellett One of Victims," *Boston Globe*, February 16, 1961, 21; "Glass Firm Executive among Crash Victims," *Evening Star* (D.C.), February 15, 1961, A8; "2 New Jerseyans Killed on Plane," *Newark Evening News*, February 15, 1961, 1, 5; Barbara Bundschu,"73 Die on 'Joyous Trip' to Europe," *Independent* (Long Beach, CA), February 16, 1961, A3.

[42] "Dr. Soria Traveling to Meet in Spain," *Lansing State Journal*, February 15, 1961, 1-2; "F. C. Medina, Bank Cashier Dies in Crash," *Chicago Daily Tribune*, February 16, 1961, 8; "Priest Was on Way to Ski Vacation," *Seattle Times*, February 15, 1961, 1; "18 U.S. Skating Stars among 73 Victims of Crash at Brussels," *Globe and Mail* (Toronto), undated and unpaginated clipping in my possession.

[43] "Kennedy in Tribute to Victims of Crash," *New York Times*, February 16, 1961, 18.

[44] Dean Rusk, telegram to Ritter Shumway, February 15, 1961.

[45] Ritter Shumway press release, February 15, 1961.

[46] Diana LeMaire Squibb, telephone interview, August 7, 2003.

[47] Wanda Guntert, telephone interview, May 16, 2003; Mike Michelson, telephone interview, July 1, 2003; Simpson, "Owen Girls, Mother, with U.S. Team," 3; Terry Hansen, "Death Nips Promising Ice Careers," *Berkeley Daily Gazette*, February 15, 1961, 1, 5; Anne Frazier, telephone interview, November 2, 2007.

[48] Wilhelmina Kipp Gozzard, telephone interview, October 5, 2007.

[49] Bill Swallender, telephone interview, September 3, 2005; Fran Haigler Ainsworth, telephone interview, August 2, 2003.

[50] Joseph Dineen, telephone interview, October 19, 2004; Joan Sherbloom Peterson, telephone interview, July 22, 2003.

[51] "L.A. Kin Mourn Death of 7," *Los Angeles Herald & Express*, February 15, 1961, 5; "Only Valentine Left to Dona's Parents," *Los Angeles Examiner*, February 16, 1961, 3.

[52] Joe Jarvis, "Skater's Kin Grief-Stricken," *Indianapolis News*, February 16, 1961, 17.

[53] Dan Hartshorne, telephone interview, November 16, 2004; Harold Hartshorne Jr., telephone interview, April 9, 2007.

[54] Sally Haas Knoll, telephone interview, May 12, 2004; Robert Browning, "Three of Seattle Skating Family Perish," *Seattle Post-Intelligencer*, February 16, 1961, 3; "Father Wishes He'd Been with Skaters," undated and unidentified Seattle clipping in my possession.

[55] "Air Crash Last Chapter in Vinson-Owen Ice Saga," *Boston Globe*, February 15, 1961, 36; "Mrs. Vinson Bravely Hears Family Dead," *Boston Globe*, February 16, 1961, 21.

[56] Stephen Kelley, telephone interview, August 7, 2003; Jarvis, "Skater's Kin Grief-Stricken," 17.

[57] "Fate Kept Brown off Death Plane," *Sacramento Bee*, February 16, 1961, D1; "Bad Heart Saved Life of Brown," *Oregon Statesman*, February 16, 1961, II–9.

[58] Susan Richards Abbe, telephone interview, August 29, 2003; Fred Heller, telephone interview, November 11, 2003; Roberta Scholdan, telephone interview, November 10, 2003.

[59] "Will Take 4 Years to Build Team," *Boston Globe*, February 16, 1961, 19; Tom Downey and Gordon Hillman, "Hub Mourns Brilliant Owens Skating Clan," *Boston Daily Record*, February 16, 1961, 26; "Never to Skate Again," *Life*, February 24, 1961, 22.

[60] Janet Harley Browning, telephone interview, September 6, 2005; Wendy Griner Ballantyne, telephone interview, October 10, 2005; Paulette Ormsby, interview.

[61] Tom McGinnis, telephone interview, September 14, 2004; "New Prep Ice Coach Dies at 29," *Boston Globe*, February 16, 1961, 17.

[62] Richard Hurt, "Ice Follies Cast Tearful," *Boston Globe*, February 16, 1961, Sports sec., 19; "Shipstad Is Heartbroken," *San Francisco Examiner*, February 16, 1961, IV–2.

[63] Hurt, "Ice Follies Cast Tearful," 19; Susan Blodgett Rigney, telephone interview, May 17, 2005; Dwyer, interview.

[64] Bob Deuter, telephone interview, September 20, 2004; "Sullivan Voices AFA's Grief over Death of Skaters," *Gazette-Telegraph*, February 15, 1961.

[65] Tom Murray, "An Empty Desk Tells Their Star Is Dead," *Boston Traveler*, February 15, 1961, 29.

[66] "Telegraphic Poll Among Nations Began," *Seattle Daily Times*, February 15, 1961, Sports, 26; "U.S. Urges Title Meet to Go On," *New York Times*, February 17, 1961, 33.

[67] "U.S. Urges Title Meet to Go On," 33.

[68] "Telegraphic Poll among Nations Began," Sports sec., 26; "ISU Asks to Halt Ice Meet," *St. Louis Post-Dispatch*, February 16, 1961, unpaginated clipping in my possession.

[69] "World Ice Skate Test Cancelled," *San Francisco Chronicle*, February 16, 1961, 41; "Shocked at Crash, Official Urges Meet Cancellation," *Seattle Post-Intelligencer*, February 16, 1961, 3; "World Ice Meet Off; Czechs May Protest," *Seattle Daily Times*, February 16, 1961, 30.

[70] "Skating Cancellation May Be Reconsidered," *Boston Herald*, February 17, 1961, 63; "ISU Urged Not to Cancel Tourney," *Minneapolis Morning Tribune*, 44, undated clipping in my possession; Ballantyne, interview; Bradley Black, telephone interview, May 13, 2005.

[71] Doreen Denny-Routon, telephone interview, May 26, 2005; Christa Fassi, telephone interview, October 13, 2007.

[72] Bruce Heiss, telephone interview, July 19, 2005; Lorraine Hanlon Comanor, telephone interview, February 1, 2010.

[73] Wilkes, interview; Ballantyne, interview.

[74] Millikan, interview; "Reconsider Cancellation, ISU Asked," *San Diego Union*, February 17, 1961, A40.

[75] "World Figure Skating Tourney Is Still 'No Go,'" *Rocky Mountain News*, February 18, 1961, 55; Millikan, interview.

[76] Paulette Doan Ormsby, interview; Denny-Routon, interview, Peter Burrows, telephone interview, May 19, 2005; Karol Divin, email interview, June 13, 2010.

[77] Millikan, interview; Denny-Routon, interview; Jelinek, interview.

[78] "World Figure-Skating Meet Is Cancelled as Result of Plane Crash," *New York Times*, February 17, 1961, 33; "U.S. Group Urges Title Meet to Go On," *New York Times*, February 16, 1961, 18.

[79] ISU Council Member photo, *Skating*, November 1956, 16; "Walter S. Powell," *Skating*, April 1961, 15.

[80] Nigel Stephens, *CFSA Newsletter*, March 1961; Ritter Shumway letter to E.R.S. (Dick) McLaughlin, February 27, 1961.

[81] Kendall Kelley, letter to Ritter Shumway, February 19, 1961.

[82] Heller, interview; "Bodies of Plane Victims May Be Returned Home," *Daily Evening Item*, February 16, 1961, 3; Kelley to Shumway, February 19, 1961.

[83] Kelley to Shumway, February 19, 1961.

[84] "Family Affairs," 13; Kelley to Shumway, February 19, 1961; "Sabena Jet Crash Probe Blackout," undated and unidentified Indianapolis paper, in my possession.

[85] Kelley to Shumway, February 19, 1961; Jean Westwood, telephone interview, July 13, 2004.

[86] *Minneapolis Star*, February 16, 1961, 11; "18 U.S. Skaters among 73 Dead in a Jet Crash," 18; "707 Has First Passenger Loss in Crash," *Seattle Times*, February 15, 1961, 4; "Belgian Jet Crash Kills 73; "Recorder Found in Debris of Jet in Which 73 Died," *St. Louis Post-Dispatch*, February 16, 1961, 4E.

[87] "Only 46 Dead in Belgium Air Crash Can Be Identified," "Jet Crash Probe," both from undated and unidentified Boston newspaper clippings in my possession, not paginated.

[88] "Sabena Had Earlier Snag," unidentified Boston newspaper clipping in my possession; "Tragic Air Dead Wait Identity," *Boston American*, February 16, 1961, 3.

[89] Duffy, "Shattered Dreams," E17; "Recorder Found in Debris of Jet in Which 73 Died," 4; Simpson, "U.S. Skating Tragedy," A10; Sean Overton, interviewed, Overland Park, KS, November 18, 2008; www.aviation-safety.net/database/record; www.skystef.be/B707/OO-SJB.htm (accessed on April 5, 2003).

[90] P. Nottet, "Report of the Inquiry Related to the Accident Occurred to Aircraft OO-SJB at Berg on 15th February 1961," Ministry of Communications, Kingdom of Belgium, 10, 31-32.

[91] Ibid., 31-32.

[92] Jay Weiner, "Plane Crash in 1961 Changed Course of Skating," *Star Tribune* (Minneapolis), April 4, 1998, 8C.

[93] "U.S. Skating Team Killed in Jet Crash," *San Diego Union*, February 16, 1961, 1; Long, "U.S. Skaters among 73 Dead in Belgium Crash," 1; "Family Affairs," 13.

[94] "707 Has First Passenger Loss in Crash," *Seattle Times*, February 15, 1961, 4; "Other Milestones in Airline History," *USA Today*, March 23, 2007, D2.

[95] www.brusselsairport.be/en/about-airport/about-history (accessed on April 22, 2005); "18 U.S. Skaters among 73 Dead in a Jet Crash," 18; "Jet's Strange Antics Stir Crash Probe," 1-2.

[96] "Inevitable Accidents," *Oregonian*, February 16, 1961, 24.

[97] "Brussels Plane Crash Is Fifth involving Teams," *Sacramento Bee*, February 15, 1961, D1.

[98] http://news.bbc.co.uk/onthisday/hi/dates/stories/february/6; "All World Mourns Tragedy of Skaters," *Boston Herald*, February 16, 1961, 33.

[99] www.lib.calpoly.edu/universityarchives/history/1960crash (accessed on April 23, 2005); "Brussels Plane Crash Is Fifth involving Teams," D1.

[100] "Toll of Athletes High in Planes," *New York Times*, February 16, 1961, 18; "List Air Disasters involving Athletes," *San Francisco News-Call Bulletin*, February 16, 1961, 26; Roger Williams, "U.S. Team Tragedy Hits Close to Home," *San Francisco News-Call Bulletin*, February 16, 1961, 26.

[101] Williams, "U.S. Team Tragedy Hits Close to Home," 26.

[102] Mary Miller Robicheaux, telephone interview, July 14, 2005; Sheryl Ryan Nolan, telephone interview, August 21, 2005; Louise Samson, telephone interview, September 1, 2005; Dwyer, interview.

103 Henry Machirella, "Lost—Our Galaxy of Ice Stars," *Daily News* (NYC), February 16, 1961, 8.

Chapter 17

1 "Bodies of Plane Victims May Be Returned Home," *Daily Evening Item* (Lynn, MA), February 16, 1961, 3; Joe Jarvis, "Skaters' Kin Grief-Stricken," *Indianapolis News*, February 16, 1961, 17; "Only 46 Bodies in Jet Identified," *Rocky Mountain News* (Denver, CO), February 17, 1961, 18.

2 "Only 38 Identified in Belgian Crash," *Seattle Post-Intelligencer*, February 17, 1961, 32; Maggie Hosford, telephone interview, October 24, 2003; Kendall Kelley, letter to Ritter Shumway, February 19, 1961.

3 Kelley to Shumway, February 19, 1961; "Bodies of Five Springs Skaters Are Identified," *Gazette Telegraph* (Colorado Springs), February 23, 1961, 1; Fred Heller, telephone interview, November 11, 2003; Theresa Weld Blanchard, letter to Kendall Kelley, February 22, 1961; Kendall Kelley, "Chronology of Events," personal memo, March 1, 1961.

4 "Jet Victim's Survivors Await Word on Bodies," *Denver Post*, February 16, 1961, 1; "Volpe Orders Flag Tribute to U.S. Skaters," *Boston Globe*, February 17, 1961, 3.

5 Richard Dwyer, telephone interview, May 28, 2005; "Walter S. Powell," *Skating*, April 1961, 15; "Walter S. Powell Obituary," *St. Louis Globe-Democrat*, February 18, 1961, 5.

6 Remarks at Dudley Richards's service, February 18, 1961, Barrington, RI; Susan Richards Abbe, telephone interview, August 29, 2003.

7 Donna Logan, "Chapel Filled as Tribute Paid to Victims of Air Crash," *Gazette Telegraph*, February 19, 1961, A1, A8.

8 Ritter Shumway, letter to Senator Kenneth B. Keating, February 1961.

9 Bruce Lord, telephone interview, May 4, 2005; Stephen Kelley, interview in Quincy, MA, August 7, 2003.

10 Shumway to Keating, February 1961.

11 Diana LeMaire Squibb, telephone interview, August 7, 2003.

12 "Skating Team Identification Is Completed," *Daily Evening Item* (Lynn, MA), February 23, 1961, 3; Gerry Lane, telephone interview, November 17, 2004.

13 Ritter Shumway, letter to Henry Beatty, March 6, 1961; Kendall Kelley, letter to Peter DeMaerel, March 18, 1961.

14 Hartshorne family, letter to Ritter Shumway, February 24, 1961; Blanchard, letter to Kelley, February 22, 1961; Ritter Shumway's remarks at Hartshorne service, May 24, 1961, New York City; Dan Hartshorne, telephone interview, November 16, 2004; Harold and Louisa Hartshorne marker, Green-Wood Cemetery, Brooklyn, New York.

15 "Kipp Obituary," *Morning Call* (Allentown, PA), February 27, 1961, 6; Wilhelmina Kipp Gozzard, telephone interview, October 5, 2007.

16 "Memorial Service for the Owens Saturday," *Winchester Star* (MA), February 23, 1961, 1, 8; "Services for the Owens Held Saturday at Epiphany Church," *Winchester Star*, March 2, 1961, 2; Franklin Nelson, telephone interview, September 3, 2005.

17 Christie Allan-Piper, telephone interview, November 9, 2004; Gertrude Vinson, letter to Ritter Shumway, March 12, 1961; Owen marker, Mount Auburn Cemetery, Cambridge, MA.

18 "Memorial Rites Set for Ice Skaters," clipping from unidentified San Francisco area paper in my possession; "Chuck Foster, telephone interview, October 2, 2007.

19 "Magazine's Hex Hits Again As Skater Dies," *Los Angeles Mirror*, February 15, 1961, 7.

[20] "Memorial Service for Rye Victims of Plane Crash," *Rye Chronicle* (NY), February 23, 1961, 1; Edward and Richard LeMaire markers, Greenwood Union Cemetery, Rye, NY; "Obituary: Edward LeMaire Funeral," *Rye Chronicle*, March 2, 1961, 4.

[21] Patricia Schumacher, telephone interview, November 28, 2007; Charlie Rizzo, telephone interview, May 19, 2004; Robert and Patricia Dineen marker, Calvary Cemetery, Queens, NY.

[22] Hickox service, undated clipping from unidentified San Francisco area paper; Julie Barrett, telephone interview, June 4, 2005; Hank Hickox, telephone interview, August 30, 2005; "Memorial Services Held for Skaters Bill and Laurie," *Falcon News*, Colorado Springs, March 3, 1961; William and Laurie Hickox markers, Sunset View Cemetery, El Cerrito, CA.

[23] Sylvia Clay Stoddard, www.squareone.org/PolarPalace (accessed on May 2, 2006); Janet McLeod, letter to Patricia S. Bushman, July 14, 2003; Deane E. McMinn marker, Green Hills Memorial Park, San Pedro, CA.

[24] Rhode Lee Michelson funeral program, copy in my possession; Sylvia Clay Stoddard, telephone interview; April 26, 2007; Ted Thackery Jr., "Skaters Here Mourn Stars; Six from L.A. Lose Lives," *Los Angeles Examiner*, February 16, 1961, 1.

[25] Gary Visconti, interview in Long Beach, CA, September 16, 2004; "Services Set for Skater in Plane Crash," undated clipping from unidentified Detroit newspaper in my possession; George E. Van, "Fund for Skaters Becomes Memorial," March 1, 1961, undated clipping from unidentified Detroit newspaper in my possession; Gary Clark, telephone interview, May 24, 2005; Doug Ramsay marker, White Chapel Memorial Cemetery, Troy, MI.

[26] "Rites for Four Skaters Will Be Held Wednesday," *Rocky Mountain News*, February 26, 1961, 1; Ardith Paul Hamilton, telephone interview, July 31, 2005; Kelly, letter to Shumway, February 19, 1961; Edi and Jimmy Scholdan markers, Evergreen Cemetery, Colorado Springs.

[27] "Rites for Four Skaters Will Be Held Wednesday," 1; Hamilton, interview; Connie Espander, telephone interview, September 7, 2005; Westerfeld marker, Evergreen Cemetery, Colorado Springs.

[28] Kelley, interview; Tom McGinnis, telephone interview, September 14, 2004; "Services Held Wednesday for Plane Victims," *The Villager* (Newton, MA), March 1961; Kelley family marker, St. Joseph's Cemetery, West Roxbury, MA.

[29] "B.U. to Hold Service for Bradley Lord," *Daily Evening Item*, February 24, 1961, 2; "Owen Memorial Service at B.U.," *Winchester Star*, March 2, 1961, 2; "A Family Affair," 2001 State Farm U.S. Figure Skating Championships program, 66.

[30] "Swampscott Stunned by Tragic Death of Lord," *Daily Evening Item*, February 15, 1961, 8; "Bradley Lord Funeral on Wednesday," *Daily Evening Item*, February 25, 1961, 1; "World Skating Stars at Service for Bradley Lord at Swampscott," *Daily Evening Item*, March 2, 1961, 1-2.

[31] "Rites Set for City Skaters Who Died in Air Crash," *Indianapolis Star*, February 28, 1961, 19; Louise Mounts, letter to Ritter Shumway, April 10, 1961.

[32] "Rites Set for City Skaters Who Died in Air Crash," 19; Sally Wells Van De Mark, telephone interview, July 28, 2004.

[33] "Carl W. Swallender," *Minneapolis Morning Tribune*, March 1, 1961, 14; Bill Swallender, telephone interview, September 3, 2005; Carl William Swallender marker, Sunset Memorial Park Cemetery, Minneapolis.

[34] "Funeral Notices: Hadley," *Register-Guard* (Eugene, OR), February 28, 1961, unpaginated clipping in my possession; Edmund Bold, letter to Virginia Bremer, March 6, 1961.

[35] Dona Lee Carrier funeral program, copy in my possession; Stoddard, interview; Sarasue Gleis Essenprice, telephone interview, August 24, 2004; Hosford, interview.

[36] Dona Lee Carrier marker, Forest Lawn Cemetery, Glendale, CA.

[37] Sherbloom funeral program, copy in my possession; Joan Sherbloom Peterson, telephone interview, July 22, 2003; Diane Sherbloom marker, Holy Cross Cemetery, Culver City, CA.

[38] Bold to Bremer, March 6, 1961; Arvilla Kauffman Christensen, telephone interview, October 6, 2003; Nancy Moehring, telephone interview, March 2005.

[39] Long Beach memorial service program, copy in my possession; Joyce Burden, telephone interview, August 22, 2005.

[40] Joanne Funakoshi McLaren, telephone interview, September 7, 2004; Stoddard, interview.

[41] Roger Campbell marker, Big Hill Cemetery, Providence, KY.

[42] Visconti, interview; Ron Vincent, telephone interview, May 20, 2005; Andra McLaughlin Kelly, telephone interview, September 26, 2005; Kay Servatius Ringsred, telephone interview, August 23, 2004; Lord, interview.

[43] Ritter Shumway, letter to Otto Westerfeld, March 1, 1961; Ritter Shumway, letter to Gertrude Vinson, February 27, 1961.

[44] Dallas and Nellie Pierce, letter to Ritter Shumway, April 30, 1961.

[45] Walter Rogers, letter to Ritter Shumway, March 20, 1961; Walter Rogers Obituary, *New York Times*, June 9, 2001.

[46] Ritter Shumway, letter to Congressman Walter Rogers.

[47] Ibid; www.emergency-management.net/avi_acc_1959_1969.htm (accessed August 20, 2007).

[48] Ritter Shumway, form letter with separate addresses; see, e.g. Al Campbell, April 21, 1961; "1961 Governing Council Meeting Report," 22; Ritter Shumway, USFSA Memorial Service, May, 6, 1961, 2-4; "Colonel Harold Grey Storke" obituary, *Skating*, June 1961, 24; Blanchard to Kelley, February 22, 1961.

[49] Ritter Shumway, USFSA Memorial Service, May 6, 1961, 2-4.

[50] Ritter Shumway, letter to Floyd and Eleanor Carrier, June 16, 1961; Ritter Shumway, form letter with separate addresses; see, e.g,, Al Campbell, March 8, 1962; Gertrude Vinson, letter to Ritter Shumway, March 18, 1962; Gertrude Vinson, letter to Ritter Shumway, May 15, 1962.

[51] Gertrude C. Vinson, letter to Ritter Shumway, June 24, 1961.

[52] "Skaters Who Died Honored in Vienna," March 1, 1961, unpaginated clipping from unidentified newspaper.

[53] Shumway, form letter with separate addresses; see, e.g., Al Campbell, November 10, 1961.

[54] Muriel LeMaire, letter to Ritter Shumway, November 15, 1961; Lute and Elinor Hickox, letter to Ritter Shumway, December 13, 1961.

[55] Elmer Kipp, letter to Ritter Shumway, October 24, 1961; Ritter Shumway, letter to Floyd Carrier, July 5, 1961.

[56] Tom and Ruth Sherbloom letter to Ritter Shumway, October 11, 1961; Ritter Shumway, letter to Ruth Sherbloom, February 14, 1962.

[57] Bill Haigler, letter to Lute and Elinor Hickox, October 27, 1961.

[58] Ed Minkoof, letter to Ritter Shumway, February 16, 1961; Ritter Shumway, letter to Ed Bold, February 27, 1961.

[59] Dallas H. Pierce, letter to F. Ritter Shumway, August 13, 1961; Byron V. Richards, Jr. to Ritter Shumway correspondence, March 19, 1961.

[60] Ritter Shumway, USFSA Memorial Service, May 6, 1961, 4.

Chapter 18

[1] "U.S. Group Urges Title Meet to Go On," *New York Times*, February 16, 1961, 18.

[2] Prentis Rogers, "1994 Goodwill Games," *Atlanta Journal Constitution*, August 5, 1994, D12; Marshall Campbell, telephone interview, April 18, 2005.

[3] Christie Allan-Piper, telephone interview, November 19, 2004; Joyce Underwood Winship, telephone interview, October 1, 2003; Gerry Lane, telephone interview, November 17, 2004.

[4] "Father Says Diane Always Practiced," *Los Angeles Examiner*, February 16, 1961, 14; Nelson F. Waters, letter to Fred C. LeFevre, March 6, 1961.

[5] Mrs. Etienne Noir, "In Memoriam," February 1961.

[6] Dick Button, telephone interview, December 5, 2005.

[7] 1961 Ice Chips program, *Ice Chips*, 18, no. 7, March 1961; John F. Kennedy Address, 1961 Memorial Benefit, March 1961, World Figure Skating Museum files.

[8] Virginia Thompson Brookshill, telephone interview, September 21, 2005; Debbi Wilkes, telephone interview, December 9, 2005; Wendy Griner Ballantyne, telephone interview, October 10, 2005; Donald Jackson, telephone interview, October 11, 2007.

[9] Sonya Klopfer Dunfield, telephone interview, June 2, 2004; "The Summer Skating Survey," *Skating*, November 1961, 10.

[10] Patti Gustafson Feeney, telephone interview, December 9, 2004.

[11] Hugh Fullerton Jr., "America's Hopes Are Dim in Skating," *Gazette-Telegraph* (Colorado Springs), February 16, 1961, 25; Aileen Kahre Ahrenson, telephone interview, April 4, 2005.

[12] John Wheeler, "Sacramento Skater Missed Trip—Heart Condition," *San Francisco Examiner*, February 16, 1961, IV–2; Bruce Heiss, telephone interview, July 19, 2005; Nancy Heiss Jones, telephone interview, October 11, 2007; Robert Brewer, interviewed, Phoenix, AZ, March 18, 2005.

[13] "Broadmoor Official 'Crushed' by Tragedy," *Denver Post*, February 15, 1961, 3; Ardith Paul Hamilton, telephone interview, July 31, 2005; Christa Fassi, telephone interview, October 13, 2007.

[14] Fassi, interview; Christy Haigler Krall, interviewed, Colorado Springs, CO, May 9, 2003.

[15] Fassi, interview; Greg Hoyt, telephone interview, July 12, 2005.

[16] Judianne Fotheringill Fuller, telephone interview, July 25, 2005.

[17] Donna Merrill Schoon, telephone interview, September 23, 2005; Krall, interview; Debbie Might, telephone interview, June 2, 2010.

[18] Krall, interview; Doreen Denny-Routon, telephone interview, May 26, 2005.

[19] Helen Davidson Maxson, telephone interview, October 9, 2007.

[20] Coco Gram Shean, telephone interview, October 10, 2007; Joanne Heckert Bachtel, telephone interview, September 22, 2005; Jim Browning, telephone interview, October 15, 2007.

[21] Jean Westwood, telephone interview, July 13, 2004; John Nicks, telephone interview, June 15, 2005.

[22] "The Skater's Exchange," *Skating*, March 1961, 40; John Nicks, interview.

[23] John Nicks, interview; Marlene Morris Van Dusen, telephone interview, June 27, 2005; Mary Miller Robicheaux, telephone interview, July 14, 2005.

[24] Barbara Roles Williams, telephone interview, September 25, 2003.

[25] Peter Betts, telephone interview, February 7, 2005; Bud Collins, "Mrs. Pursely Titlist," *Boston Herald*, February 4, 1962, 17.

[26] Jim Short, telephone interview, October 7, 2004.

[27] Bob Munz, telephone interview, June 8, 2005; Pieter Kollen, telephone interview, July 29, 2003; Ron Ludington, interviewed, Overland Park, KS, June 11, 2004.

[28] Cynthia Kauffman Marshall, telephone interview, November 5, 2003; Arvilla Kauffman Christensen, telephone interview, October 6, 2003.

[29] Kollen, interview.

[30] Marilyn Meeker Durham, telephone interview, July 30, 2003; Dallas and Nellie Pierce, letter to Ritter Shumway, September 28, 1961; "Lake Placid Summer Dance Championships," *Skating*, November 1961, 9; Stan Urban, telephone interview, August 31, 2004.

[31] Durham, interview; Campbell, interview.

[32] Julie Graham Eavzan, telephone interview, April 20, 2005.

[33] Aileen Kahre Arenson, telephone interview, April 4, 2005.

[34] "Pacific Coast," *Skating*, March 1962, 21-22; Yvonne Littlefield Nicks, telephone interview, November 15, 2005; Betts, interview; Eleanor Carrier, letter to Ritter Shumway, January 12, 1962.

[35] Darrell Mathias, telephone interview, October 5, 2004; "Pacific Coast," 22.

[36] Bill Wilkins, telephone interview, November 4, 2004; Joan Sherbloom Peterson, telephone interview, July 22, 2003; Betts, interview.

[37] Westwood, interview; Betts, interview; Peggy Fleming, *The Long Program* (New York: Pocket Books, 1999), 35.

[38] "Skating Area Due for Split," January 29, 1961, 2B; "Midwesterns," *Skating*, March 1962, 22-23.

[39] Durham, interview.

[40] "Midwesterns," 23; Durham, interview.

[41] Durham, interview.

[42] Ibid; Marshall Campbell, telephone interview, April 18, 2005.

[43] "Easterns," *Skating*, March 1962, 16, 21.

[44] Evelyn L. Carroll, Robert Claflin and Dorothy H. Albert, "The United States Championships," *Skating*, April 1962, 7; Bud Collins, "U.S. Skaters Start U.S. Meet Today, *Boston Herald*, February 1, 1962, 34.

[45] Carroll, Claflin, Albert, "The United States Championships," 7; Lorna Dyer, telephone interview, November 14, 2003; Fuller, interview.

[46] Louella Rehfield, telephone interview, August 31, 2004; Roy and Alfreda Lord, letter to Ritter Shumway, March 16, 1962; Krall, interview; Peter Dunfield, telephone interview, July 28, 2004.

[47] Carroll, Claflin, and Albert, "The United States Championships," 10; National Figure Skating Championships program, Boston, 1962.

[48] Carroll, Claflin, and Albert, "The United States Championships," 7; "Silver Dance," *Skating*, March 1962, 19.

[49] Carroll, Claflin, and Albert, "The United States Championships," 7; Betts, interview; "Novice Ladies," *Skating*, March 1962, 18; "Novice Men," *Skating*, March 1962, 18.

[50] "Junior Pairs," *Skating*, March 1962, 18; Elizabeth George Busconi, telephone interview, May 5, 2005; Bachtel, interview.

[51] Bud Collins, "Hoyt Skating Champion," *Boston Herald*, February 4, 1962, 61; "Junior Ladies," *Skating*, March 1962, 17; Hoyt, interview.

[52] Carroll, Claflin, and Albert, "The United States Championships," 9; Bud Livesley, "Gay, Young Blade, 10, Skates Because of Mom's Broken 'Vow,'" *Seattle Times*, January 29, 1960, 14; Short, interview.

[53] Gretchen Merrill Gay, "A Personal Viewpoint," *Skating*, April 1962, 11; Pam Zekman, telephone interview, April 13, 2005; Eavzan, interview.

[54] Carroll, Claflin, and Albert, "The United States Championships," 8; Gary Visconti, interviewed, Long Beach, CA, September 16, 2004.

[55] Winship, interview; *Skating*, January 1962, cover; John Powers, "No Routine Event," *Boston Globe*, January 17, 2001, E8.

[56] Karen Howland Jones, telephone interview, September 11, 2003.

[57] Bud Collins, "Skaters Start U.S. Meet Today," *Boston Herald*, February 1, 1962, 34; Bud Collins, "Watertown Pair Captures Junior Skating Crown," *Boston Herald*, February 3, 1962, 13.

[58] Peter Dunfield, interview.

[59] Williams, interview.

[60] Peter Dunfield, interview.

[61] "Ladies' Senior," *Skating*, March 1962, 17; Bud Collins, "Mrs. Pursely Titlist," 17.

[62] "Dance Championship," *Skating*, March 1962, 18; Betts, interview.

[63] "Dance Championship," 18; Kollen, interview; Dyer, interview.

[64] "Dance Championship," 18; R. David Owen, telephone interview, September 28, 2005; Campbell, interview.

[65] "Dance Championship," 18; Arenson, interview; Eavzan, interview.

[66] Kollen, interview; Carroll, Claflin, and Albert, "The United States Championships," 8-9; Fuller, interview; Fotheringill, interview.

[67] "Pairs," *Skating*, March 1962, 18; Ron Joseph, telephone interview, October 3, 2003; Peter Dunfield, interview.

[68] "Pairs," 18; Janet Harley Browning, telephone interview, September 6, 2005; Jim Browning, interview.

[69] Zekman, interview.

[70] "Bedell H. Harned Trophy," *Skating*, March 1962, 19; Gay, "A Personal Viewpoint," 11.

[71] "1962 U.S. World Team Plans," *Skating*, March 1962, 19.

[72] Freda Alexander, "Skating's First Lady," *Skating*, November 1963, 2-4.

[73] Yvonne Littlefield Nicks, interview.

[74] Edward Adler, "He Loses His Wife and Son," *Los Angeles Examiner*, February 16, 1961, 14; Button, interview.

[75] "1962 U.S. World Team Plans," 19; Ritter Shumway, letter to USFSA Executive Committee, October 18, 1961; Ritter Shumway, letter to Vincent Kelley, January 2, 1962; Gerty Desjardins Verbiwski, telephone interview, May 10, 2005.

[76] Scott Allen, telephone interview, September 1, 2010; Wilkes, interview.

[77] Fuller, interview; Marie Vichova Millikan, telephone interview, September 25, 2007.

[78] Donna Mitchell Zaleski, telephone interview, December 1, 2005; J.D. Mitchell, telephone interview, November 16, 2005; Ballantyne, interview.

[79] Millikan, interview; Jane Vaughn Sullivan, "The Worlds Day by Day," *Skating*, May 1962, 7.

[80] "Pairs," *Skating*, May 1962, 8; Fotheringill, interview; Fuller, interview.

[81] Sullivan, "The Worlds Day by Day," 7-8; Millikan, interview.

[82] Sullivan, "The Worlds Day by Day," 7; Millikan, interview.

[83] Sullivan, "The Worlds Day by Day," 8; Millikan, interview; Hoyt, interview.

[84] George Gross, *Donald Jackson: King of Blades* (Toronto: Queen City Publishing, 1977), 107; Sullivan, "The Worlds Day by Day," 9.

[85] Millikan, interview; Sullivan, "The Worlds Day by Day," 9.

[86] "Men," *Skating*, May 1962, 9.

[87] Ibid; Millikan, interview; Jackson, interview.

[88] Bill McLaughlin, telephone interview, November 27, 2005; Sullivan, "The Worlds Day by Day," 10.

[89] McLaughlin, interview; Jackson, interview; Virginia Thompson Brookshill, telephone interview, September 21, 2005.

[90] "Dance," *Skating*, May 1962, 10; Betts, interview.

[91] Sullivan, "The Worlds Day by Day," 10-12.

[92] Ibid, 11; Ballantyne, interview.

[93] "Results," *Skating*, May 1962, 8-12; Sullivan, "The Worlds Day by Day," 12.

[94] Zaleski, interview; Kollen, interview; Sullivan, *Skating*, "The Worlds Day by Day," 12.

[95] Ann-Margreth Frei Hall, telephone interview, July 8, 2005.

Chapter 19

[1] "Ladies' Senior," *Skating*, April 1963, 22; Karen Howland Jones, telephone interview, September 11, 2003.

[2] "Senior Pairs," *Skating*, April 1963, 22.

[3] Betty Sonnhalter and Janet McLeod, "The 1963 United States Championships," *Skating*, April 1963, 11-12; Tom Litz, telephone interview, July 20, 2005; Gregory Hoyt, telephone interview, July 12, 2005.

[4] Sonnhalter and McLeod, "The 1963 United States Championships," 12; Stan Urban, telephone interview, November 17, 2004.

[5] "Bedell H. Harned Trophy," *Skating*, April 1963, 24.

[6] "The 1963 North American Championships," *Skating*, April 1963, 8.

[7] John Noel, "Arctic Cold Chills World Championships," *Skating*, May 1963, 6; Litz, interview.

[8] "Pairs," *Skating*, May 1963, 11; Debbi Wilkes, telephone interview, December 2, 2005.

[9] Noel, "Arctic Cold Chills World Championships," 6, 10; Hoyt, interview; Litz, interview.

[10] "Dance," *Skating*, May 1963, 11; Peter Betts, telephone interview, February 7, 2005.

[11] "Ladies," *Skating*, May 1963, 10; Wendy Griner Ballantyne, telephone interview, October 10, 2005.

[12] Jones, interview.

[13] Charles A. Demore, "Youngsters Revive U.S. Hopes," *Skating*, March 1964, 4; "Today with Women," *Cleveland Press*, January 11, 1964, 22.

[14] Urban, interview; Patti Gustafson Feeney, telephone interview, December 9, 2004.

[15] Barbara Roles Williams, telephone interview, September 25, 2003; Demore, "Youngsters Revive U.S. Hopes," 5.

[16] John Nicks, telephone interview, June 15, 2005; Jane Artale, "Teen-Age Skaters Hoping to Waltz into 1964 Winter Olympic Games," *Plain Dealer* (Cleveland, OH), January 7, 1964, 30; Marjorie Alge, "Skating Debutante Is at Home on Ice or Dance Floor," *Cleveland Press*, January 11, 1964, 22.

[17] Demore, "Youngsters Revive U.S. Hopes," 5-6.

[18] Ibid; Thomas Place, "West Coast Girl, 15, Is Ice Queen," *Plain Dealer,* January 12, 1964, C7.

[19] Peggy Fleming Jenkins, telephone interview, May 24, 2010; Place, "West Coast Girl, 15, Is Ice Queen," C1, C7; Betts, interview.

[20] "Ladies' Senior," *Skating,* March 1964, 32; Christy Haigler Krall, interviewed, Colorado Springs, CO, May 19, 2005; Williams, interview.

[21] Demore, "Youngsters Revive U.S. Hopes," 7, 32; Harry McClelland, "Whiz Kid on Skates Best Bet in Olympics," *Cleveland Press,* January 13, 1964, D2; Litz, interview.

[22] Thomas Place, "Cleveland Pair Near Skate Lead," *Plain Dealer,* January 11, 1964, 26; Gary Visconti, interviewed, Long Beach, CA, September 16, 2004.

[23] "Dance," *Skating,* March 1964, 34; Darlene Dyer Gilbert, telephone interview, July 23, 2003.

[24] Demore, "Youngsters Revive U.S. Hopes," 6; Feeney, interview; Pieter Kollen, telephone interview, July 29, 2003.

[25] "Senior Pairs," *Skating,* March 1964, 32; Peter Dunfield, telephone interview, July 28, 2004; Ron Joseph, telephone interview, October 3, 2003.

[26] Joseph, interview.

[27] "Scorecard," *Sports Illustrated,* October 28, 1963, 13; "ABC on Thick Ice," *Broadcasting & Cable,* April 21, 1997, 37.

[28] E. Newbold Black IV, telephone interview, November 3, 2003.

[29] Cynthia Kauffman Marshall, telephone interview, November 5, 2003; John Powers, "Pushed to the Rink," *Boston Globe,* December 30, 2003, G1.

[30] *The Chronicle of the Olympics* (New York: DK Publishing, 1996), 107; John Noel, "Olympic Drama," *Skating,* April 1964, 4.

[31] Noel, "Olympic Drama," 6-7.

[32] Ibid; Ron Kauffman, telephone interview, November 14, 2007.

[33] Noel, "Olympic Drama," 7; Joseph, interview.

[34] Noel, "Olympic Drama," 8-10.

[35] Ibid., 9-10.

[36] Ibid., 10; Ballantyne, interview.

[37] James Bell, "A Flash of Fire on the Ice," *Sports Illustrated,* January 27, 1964, 52; Noel, "Olympic Drama," 11.

[38] Noel, "Olympic Drama," 11, 32.

[39] "Avalanche at Innsbruck," *Time,* February 14, 1964, 62; Noel, "Olympic Drama," 11, 32.

[40] Noel, "Olympic Drama," 32, 34.

[41] Freimut Stein, ed., *The IXth Olympic Winter Games at Innsbruck 1964* (Lausanne, Switzerland: International Olympic Committee, 1965), 149; Noel, "Olympic Drama," 32, 34; Scott Allen, telephone interview, September 1, 2010.

[42] Noel, "Olympic Drama," 34; Litz, interview.

[43] *The Chronicle of the Olympics,* 268-69; "For the Record," *Sports Illustrated,* February 17, 1964, 65; Dunfield, interview.

[44] Andre Laguerre, "The Russians Take Over at Cortina," *Sports Illustrated,* February 6, 1956, 20.

[45] *U. S. Olympic Book* (United States Olympic Committee, 1961), 34.

[46] Powers, "Pushed to the Rink," G1; Williams, interview.

[47] Ardelle Kloss Sanderson, telephone interview, October 3, 2003; Dunfield, interview.

[48] Dunfield, interview.

[49] Vicky Fisher Binner, telephone interview, October 1, 2007.

[50] Kauffman, interview; Anne Frazier, telephone interview, November 2, 2007; Paul George, interviewed, Portland, OR, January 13, 2005; Dunfield, interview.

[51] David Jenkins, telephone interview, November 30, 2005.

[52] John Noel, "TV Brings Skating to Millions," *Skating*, May 1964, 4-5.

[53] Ibid., 6-7; "World Championships," *Skating*, April 1964, 13.

[54] Ronay Titus, "World Highlights," *Skating*, May 1964, 20-21; Noel, "TV Brings Skating to Millions," 33-34.

[55] Noel, "TV Brings Skating to Millions," 32.

[56] Joseph, interview; Dunfield, interview.

[57] "Professionals," *Skating*, January 1965, 12; "Winning and Losing and Rewinning the Silver," *International Figure Skating*, September 10, 1999, 21; Wilkes, interview; Joseph, interview.

[58] Wilkes, interview; "Winning and Losing and Rewinning the Silver," 21; Joseph, interview.

[59] "Deaths," *Skating*, November 1964, 50; "Deaths," *Skating*, January 1965, 32.

[60] Dwight Chapin, "Skating's Darkest Day," *San Francisco Chronicle*, February 15, 2002, C4.

[61] Barbara La Fontaine, "There Is a Doctor on the Ice," *Sports Illustrated*, February 8, 1965, 29.

[62] Frank P. Muckian, "Quality Hits New High," *Skating*, April 1965, 30-34; Peter A. Pender, "U.S. Recovers Three Trophies," *Skating*, April 1965, 14-17.

[63] Dick Button, "1965 World Championships," *Skating*, May 1965, 24-31.

[64] "Peggy Fleming: A Little Girl for a Tough Sport," *Sports Illustrated*, February 7, 1966, 15; Joanne Heckert Bachtel, telephone interview, September 22, 2005.

[65] "Newsmakers," *Skating*, November 1965, 11; George Gross, "High-Altitude Triumph for a Tough Little Miss," *Sports Illustrated*, March 7, 1966, 58; Christa Fassi, telephone interview, October 13, 2007.

[66] Krall, interview.

[67] Fassi, interview; Peggy Fleming, *The Long Program* (New York: Pocket Books, 1999), 54-55; Bob Paul, telephone interview, November 15, 2004.

[68] Joseph, interview.

[69] *Skating*, April 1966, 44.

[70] "Peggy at 17," *Newsweek*, March 14, 1966, 56; "Delicacy at Davos," *Time*, March 11, 1966, 70.

[71] Gross, "High-Altitude Triumph for a Tough Little Miss," 58-59; *Sports Illustrated*, May 2, 1966, cover; "Peggy Fleming: A Little Girl for a Tough Sport," 15.

[72] Gross, "High-Altitude Triumph for a Tough Little Miss," 58-59.

[73] "Delicacy at Davos," 70.

[74] Dennis Sveum, telephone interview, September 23, 2003; "A Paris Fling for a Teen Queen," *Sports Illustrated*, May 2, 1966, 32; "Some Golden Oldies," *People*, February 24, 1992, 78; Fleming, *The Long Program*. 59.

[75] Ann Udell, "In Berkeley California USA," *Skating*, April 1966, 40-45.

[76] Bob Ottum, "Crystal and Steel on the Ice," *Sports Illustrated*, March 13, 1967, 24; "Peggy Fleming: A Little Girl for a Tough Sport," 15; "Growing Up & Staying There," *Time*, March 10, 1967, 76; "Elegance on Ice," *Newsweek*, March 13, 1967, 88.

[77] Ottum, "Crystal and Steel on the Ice," 27; "Elegance on Ice," 88; "Virtuoso Performance from a 'Pure Ballerina,'" *Life*, February 23, 1968, 52C.

[78] Ottum, "Crystal and Steel on the Ice," 24; "The Other Americans: Keen Blades and Cautious Hopes," *Sports Illustrated*, February 5, 1968, 30.

[79] Fleming, *The Long Program*, 62; "Going for Sixes," *Time*, February 2, 1968, 45.

[80] "The Other Americans: Keen Blades and Cautious Hopes," 30; "U.S. Olympic Outlook: Good TV, Few Winners," *U.S. News & World Report*, February 5, 1968, 12.

[81] *Chronicle of the Olympics*, 273; Bob Ottum, "The Perils of Peggy and a Great Silver Raid," *Sports Illustrated*, February 19, 1968, 18; "Olympic Mettle," *Time*, February 19, 1968, 84.

[82] "Olympic Mettle," 84; "Strictly 24-Carat," *Time*, February 16 1968, 57; Helene Elliott, "The Gold Standard," *Times Union* (Albany, NY), February 8, 2002, C1; "Some Golden Oldies," 78.

[83] "Strictly 24-Carat," 57; "Olympic Results," www.eskatefans.com/skatabase/olyladies1960 (accessed April 1, 2003).

[84] Bud Greenspan, "10 Greatest Winter Olympians," www.media.gm.com/events/olympics/25 _greatest (accessed February 14, 2003).

[85] "The Gold Medal Favorites," *Sports Illustrated*, February 5, 1968, 26; "Climax at Grenoble," *Newsweek*, February 26, 1968, 83; www.eskatefans. com/ skatabase/olypairs1950 (accessed April 1, 2003).

[86] "Climax at Grenoble," 83; Tim Wood, telephone interview, June 4, 2009.

[87] www.eskatefans.com/skatabase/olymen1960 (accessed April 1, 2003); Visconti, interview.

[88] David Jenkins, telephone interview, November 30, 2005.

[89] "Medal Winners of the Grenoble Winter Games," *Sports Illustrated*, February 26, 1968, 18; Paul, interview.

[90] Carl Steward, "Radiant Queen of the Ice Artists," www.sports. insidebayarea.com/top50 (accessed April 14, 2003).

[91] Bill Colson, "Honoring the Best," *Sports Illustrated*, November 29, 1999; Carol Heiss Jenkins, telephone interview, October 10, 2007.

Chapter 20

[1] www.eskatefans/skatabase/historical (accessed April 1, 2010).

[2] Sarasue Gleis Essenprice, telephone interview, August 24, 2004.

[3] Mary Bartdorf Scotvold, telephone interview, May 25, 2004.

[4] Ibid.

[5] Richard Dwyer, telephone interview, May 28, 2005; Lorin Caccamise O'Neil, telephone interview, February 4, 2005.

[6] Andree Anderson Jacoby Oseid, telephone interview, September 7, 2004.

[7] Slavka Kohout Button, telephone interview, May 13, 2005.

[8] Ron Joseph, telephone interview, October 3, 2003.

[9] Ken Shelley, telephone interview, November 1, 2008; Joseph, interview.

[10] "Winter Warm-Up," *Sports Illustrated*, October 28, 1963, 13.

[11] Peter Betts, telephone interview, February 7, 2005.

[12] "World Team Memorial Fund," *Skating*, June 1961, 23; Ritter Shumway, letter to USFSA Member Clubs and USFSA Executive Committee Members, February 23, 1961; Wissahickon SC, letter to Ritter Shumway, March 1, 1961.

[13] Henry M. Beatty, "The 1961 U.S. World Figure Skating Team Memorial Fund," December 1961.

[14] Ritter Shumway, "The Report of the President," October 18, 1961; Button, interview; Henry Beatty, "Report of the 1961 Memorial Fund Committee, April 7, 1962.

[15] "Meet the New USFSA President: F. Ritter Shumway," *Skating*, November 1961, 14; Trudi Marrapodi, "A Tribute to F. Ritter Shumway," www. petershumway.org/nti/nti06893.htm (accessed May 24, 2005); "Memorial," *Princeton Alumni Weekly*, September 16, 1992; Mary Lou Butler-Mitchell, telephone interview, April 2, 2005; Wolfgang Saxon, "Frank Shumway: Manufacturer, Sportsman, and Philanthropist, 85," *New York Times*, March 19, 1992, D23.

[16] "Meet the New USFSA President," 15; Marrapodi, "A Tribute to F. Ritter Shumway."

[17] "Meet the New USFSA President," 14-15; Marrapodi, "A Tribute to F. Ritter Shumway."

[18] Marrapodi, "A Tribute to F. Ritter Shumway"; Butler-Mitchell, interview.

[19] Oseid, interview.

[20] Marrapodi, "A Tribute to F. Ritter Shumway;" Butler-Mitchell, interview.

[21] Valerie Powell, telephone interview, June 22, 2010.

[22] "Hall of Fame," www.worldskatingmuseum.org/Museum_HoF_inductees (accessed April 22, 2005); 2009 PSA Membership & Resource Directory, 12; Saxon, "Frank Shumway"; Peter Dunfield, telephone interview, July 28, 2004; Sandy Schwomeyer Lamb, telephone interview, October 13, 2003.

[23] Powell, interview.

[24] Jan Serafine, telephone interview, May 12, 2005; Leslie Gianelli, telephone interview, June 22, 2010.

[25] "February Is Memorial Fund Month," *Skating*, December 2007, 39.

[26] Dwyer, interview; John Nicks, telephone interview, June 18, 2005; Serafine, interview.

[27] Joyce Underwood Winship, telephone interview, October 1, 2003.

[28] Bette Todd, telephone interview, September 27, 2004; Lamb, interview.

[29] Christie Allan-Piper, telephone interview, November 9, 2004; Barbara Wagner, telephone interview, July 20, 2005; Sundae Bafo Lebel, telephone interview, May 9, 2005.

[30] Debbie Ganson Lane, telephone interview, November 15, 2004; "Rockers and Counters," *Skating*, June 1961, 26, 29; "Rockers and Counters," *Skating*, May 1961, 28.

[31] "1961 Governing Council Report," 5; "USFSA Annual Meeting," *Skating*, June 1961, 20; "Rockers and Counters," *Skating*, June 1961, 28; "Rockers and Counters," *Skating*, November 1961, 29; "Pacific Coast Trophies," 1963 Pacific Coast program, 18.

[32] "Vinson-Owen Memorial Scholarship Fund/Radcliffe College" letter; "A Fitting Memorial," *Winchester (MA) Star*, March 2, 1961, 6; John Vellante, "Winchester Hall of Fame to Induct 8," *Boston Globe*, March 28, 1993, Northwest Weekly, 13.

[33] "On Top of the World," *Maclean's*, March 22, 1993, 44; Christine Brennan, "Boitano 'Not Assuming Anything' at Trials," *Washington Post*, January 5, 1994, C2.

[34] John Powers, "U.S. Skaters Falling," *Boston Globe*, March 27, 1994, Sports section, 55; John Powers, "Return to Glory for the U.S.," *Boston Globe*, March 25, 1996, Sports section, 58.

[35] "Celebration . . . America On Ice!" program, 4; Susan Dresel Caudill, "An Evening to Remember," *Skating*, December 1986, 23-24.

[36] "Remembering Flight 548," *Boston Globe*, December 31, 2000, Sports, C15.

[37] Charles Fetter, telephone interview, September 14, 2004.

[38] www.allyourtv.com/moviespecials/a/moviesspecialsabcsportspresentskating (accessed January 27, 2003).

[39] Amy Rosewater, "A Skating Tribute Remembers Those Lost," October 9, 2001, www.iskater.com (accessed February 3, 2003); "Glick's Sister Gives Tribute a Personal Tone," October 5, 2001, www.espn.go.com/skating/news/2001/1005 (accessed February 14, 2003).

[40] www.worldskatingmuseum.org/Museum_HoF_inductees (accessed April 22, 2005).

[41] Kendall Kelley, letter to John F. Groden, April 11, 1961.

[42] Wayne Thomis, "Belgian Jet's Debris Void of Clew to Crash," *Chicago Daily Tribune*, March 29, 1961, 1.

[43] Ibid.

[44] Wayne Thomis, "2 Theories Rise in Bizarre Case of 'Mad Boeing,'" *Chicago Daily Tribune*, March 28, 1961, 1.

[45] Ibid; Sally Wells Van De Mark, telephone interview, July 28, 2004.

[46] Robert Craig Johnson, "Heart of Darkness: The Tragedy of the Congo, 1960-67," www.worldatwar.net/chandelle (accessed November 4, 2004).

[47] "Congo's Week of Agonizing History: A Day-by-Day Capsule Summary," *Minneapolis Morning Tribune*, February 19, 1961, 4A.

[48] "New Crisis in Congo," *St. Louis Post-Dispatch*, February 19, 1961, 2; "Congo's Week of Agonizing History," 4A.

[49] "Congo's Week of Agonizing History," 4A; "Details of Riots in Cairo," *St. Louis Post-Dispatch*, February 15, 1961, 1; "Congo Area Soldiers Beat 25 Belgians," *San Diego Union*, February 16, 1961, A2.

[50] "History," www.brusselsairport.be/en/about-airport/airport-history (accessed November 7, 2004); Bill Wilkins, telephone interview, November 4, 2004.

[51] David Mitchell, telephone interview, September 20, 2004; Linda Landin, telephone interview, October 12, 2004; Peter Kennedy, telephone interview, October 10, 2007.

[52] Gregory Hoyt, telephone interview, July 12, 2005.

[53] Marie Pearce, interviewed, Overland Park, KS, April 12, 2005; Moehring, interview.

[54] Christine Davies, telephone interview, October 30, 2009.

Chapter 21

[1] Pieter Kollen, telephone interview, July 29, 2003; Andra McLaughlin Kelly, September 26, 2005; Eleanor Banneck Curtis, telephone interview, August 7, 2003; Sally Wells Van De Mark, telephone interview, July 28, 2004; Nancy Madden Leamy, telephone interview, May 19, 2005; David Mitchell, telephone interview, September 20, 2004.

[2] Gary Clark, telephone interview, May 24, 2005.

[3] Linda Landin, telephone interview, October 12, 2004.

[4] Diana Lapp Green, telephone interview, April 28, 2005.

[5] Dick Button, telephone interview, December 2005.

[6] Robert Brewer, interviewed, Phoenix, AZ, March 18, 2005; Peter Dunfield, telephone interview, July 28, 2004.

[7] Vicky Fisher Binner, telephone interview, October 1, 2007.

[8] Jennie Walsh Guzman, telephone interview, September 9, 2003.

[9] Diana LeMaire Squibb, telephone interview, August 7, 2003; Dorinda LeMaire Howard, telephone interview, May 2, 2010.

[10] F. Ritter Shumway, Memorial Service, May 6, 1961, 2-4.

[11] Marilyn Grace Guilfoyle, telephone interview, May 24, 2007; Joan Sherbloom Peterson, telephone interview, July 22, 2004; Mechelle Voepel, "Skaters' Tribute Coincides with New York's Own Tribulations," October 6, 2001, www.kcstar.com (accessed October 16, 2002); Joseph Dineen, telephone interview, October 19, 2004.

[12] Sally Schantz Urban, telephone interview, November 7, 2004; Sheryl Ryan Nolan, telephone interview, August 21, 2005.

[13] Tom Hartshorne, interviewed, Brooklyn, NY, August 12, 2003; Dan Hartshorne, telephone interview, November 16, 2004; Gail Hartshorne Haggard, telephone interview, February 28, 2005; Daryl Hartshorne, telephone interview, February 28, 2005.

[14] Ruth Scholdan Harle, telephone interview, October 9, 2007.

[15] Jeanie O'Brien Callahan, telephone interview, June 17, 2005; Harle, interview.

[16] Harle, interview; Dixie Lee Burns Wilson, telephone interview, October 8, 2003.

[17] Squibb, interview.

[18] Ibid.

[19] Muriel LeMaire Gerli headstone, Greenwood Union Cemetery, Rye; Squibb, interview; Rye Country Day School, letter to Patricia Bushman, September 15, 2003.

[20] Roger Berry, telephone interview, June 3, 2005; Iain Kite, telephone interview, May 28, 2005; Curtis, interview; www.ssdi.rootsweb.ancestry.com.

[21] Wilson, interview, October 8, 2003; Roberto Agnolini, telephone interview, February 9, 2005; Mechelle Voepel, "Frozen in Time," *Kansas City Star*, March 4, 2001, C15; Westerfeld headstone, Evergreen Cemetery, Colorado Springs; Eileen Seigh Honnen, telephone interview, July 14, 2005.

[22] Paul George, interviewed, Portland, OR, January 15, 2005; Joyce Winship, telephone interview, October 1, 2003; Owen marker, Mount Auburn Cemetery, Cambridge, MA.

[23] Leamy, interview; Julie Graham Eavzan, telephone interview, April 20, 2005.

[24] Bob Deuter, telephone interview, September 20, 2004; Darrell Mathias, telephone interview, October 5, 2004; Nancy Moehring, telephone interview, March 3, 2005; Harold Brown, telephone interview, October 15, 2004; Lorna Dyer, telephone interview, November 4, 2003; Landin, interview; Charlene Cruickshank Tagas, telephone interview, October 27, 2003; Bill Wilkins, telephone interview, November 4, 2004.

[25] Wilkins, interview; Arvilla Kauffman Christenson, telephone interview, October 6, 2003; Moehring, interview.

[26] Moehring, interview; Morry Stillwell, telephone interview, 2003; "Ray E. Hadley Sr. Obituary," *Register-Guard* (Salem, OR), February 21, 1966, unpaginated clipping in my possession.

[27] Sally Hass Knoll, telephone interview, May 12, 2004; Helen Geekie Nightingale, telephone interview, November 18, 2004; Katie Wells Wheeler, telephone interview, December 1, 2004; Katherine Gladny Wells, *Symphony and Song: The St. Louis Orchestra, The First Hundred Years, 1880–1980* (St Louis: Countryman Press, 1980), 103, 212.

[28] Wells, *Symphony and Song*, 103; "Powell Symphony Hall," www.slso.org/0203powell/psh (accessed November 6, 2003) ; Knoll, interview.

[29] Shirley Reflow Sherman, telephone interview, November 29, 2004; Knoll, interview; Mary Ellen Young, telephone interview, July 20, 2004; November 18, 2004; Nancy Meiss, interviewed, Overland Park, KS, April 7, 2005.

[30] Curtis, interview; Guzman, interview; Peterson, interview; my observations at Pickwick ice rink, July 6, 2004.

[31] Peterson, interview; Carrier headstones, Forest Lawn Cemetery; Kamon Simpson, "U.S. Skating Tragedy," *The Gazette* (Colorado Springs), February 15, 2001, A11.

[32] Roberta Allen McIntyre, telephone interview, July 22, 2004; Roy Cofer, telephone interview, July 13, 2004; George Yonekura, telephone interview, October 16, 2003; Joan Brader Burns, telephone interview, October 29, 2003; "Elinor H. Hickox Obituary," *Berkeley Daily Gazette*, February 25, 1984; "Lute Hickox Obituary," *Oakland Tribune*, December 5, 1987, B11.

[33] Anne Frazier, telephone interview, November 2, 2007.

[34] Joyce Underwood Winship, telephone interview, October 1, 2003; Stephen Kelley, interviewed, Quincy, MA, August 7, 2003; Kelley headstones, West Roxbury, MA.

[35] Mike Michelson, telephone interview, July 1, 2003; www.ssdi.rootsweb.ancestry.com.cgi-bin-ssdi.cgi (accessed April 15, 2010).

[36] Aloise Samson Lurtsema, telephone interview, August 29, 2005; Ramsay headstones, White Chapel Memorial Cemetery, Troy, MI; Ann Seror Barr, telephone interview, July 25, 2004.

[37] Bill Swallender, telephone interview, September 3, 2005; Erik Swallender, telephone interview, October 12, 2005; Cynthia Hansen White, telephone interview, September 6, 2005.

[38] Ruth Ann Kipp, telephone interview, October 5, 2007; Wilhelmina Kipp Gozzard, telephone interview, October 5, 2007.

[39] Kollen, interview; Van De Mark, interview; Dallas H. Pierce, letter to F. Ritter Shumway, November 27, 1961; Larry Pierce marker, Washington Park East Mausoleum, Indianapolis; Marilyn Meeker Durham, telephone interview, July 31, 2003.

[40] McMinn headstones, Green Hills Memorial Park, Rancho Palos Verdes, California; Benjamin T. Wright, *Skating in America: The 75th Anniversary History of the United States Figure Skating Association* (Colorado Springs: U.S. Figure Skating Association, 1996), vii, xvii-xviii.

[41] Bruce Lord, telephone interview, May 4, 2005; Lurtsema, interview; Swampscott Cemetery.

[42] Susan Richards Abbe, telephone interview, August 29, 2003.

[43] Peterson, interview; Ruth Sherbloom, letter to Ritter Shumway, June 23, 1961.

[44] Guzman, interview.

[45] Peterson, interview.

[46] My observations at Pickwick ice rink.

[47] Michelle Monnier, telephone interview, September 8, 2003; "Club Ice Program," www.scfs.org/scfsc_clubice (accessed April 14, 2010).

[48] Bill Martin, telephone interview, August 24, 2005; Gary Visconti, telephone interview, September 16, 2004.

[49] My observations at Seattle Civic Arena; Moehring, interview.

[50] Bill Boeck, "St. Louis SC History," www.stlouisskatingclub.org (accessed April 4, 2009).

[51] Harry Shattuck, "The Broadmoor Tradition," *Houston Chronicle*, January 11, 1998, Travel, 1; World Arena Ice Hall, telephone interview, May 2, 2006; "2008 Edi Awards," *PS Magazine*, March/April 2008, 11.

[52] Joanne Heckert Bachtel, telephone interview, September 22, 2005, "About the Munn," www.munnicearena.com (accessed February 3, 2008).

[53] Barbara Babcock Kirby, telephone interview, November 8, 2004; Wright, *Skating in America*, i, iii.

[54] Darlene Dyer Gilbert, telephone interview, July 23, 2003; Sandy Schwomeyer Lamb, telephone interview, October 12, 2003.

[55] "History," www.thescny.org (accessed October 4, 2007).

[56] www.arcticbladesfsc.org (accessed September 1, 2007).

[57] "History Timeline," www.saveberkeleyiceland.org (accessed September 10, 2007).

[58] www.sunvalley.com (accessed May 1, 2007).

[59] "Inside the House of Miracles," *Flame*, Summer 2008, 8.

[60] Dick Button, telephone interview, December 8, 2005.

[61] John Powers, "Pushed to the Rink," *Boston Globe*, December 30, 2000, G9.

[62] Jere Longman, "Carlo Fassi, Skating Coach, Is Dead at 67," *New York Times*, March 21, 1997, B9; www.worldskatingmuseum.org/Museum_HOF_inductees; Christa Fassi, telephone interview, October 13, 2007.

[63] "Skating Director Named to Hall of Fame," May 18, 2000, www.udel.edu (accessed April 15, 2003); Bob Duffy, "Twists of Fate," *Boston Globe*, December 31, 2000, C15; Martin Frank, "UD Coach Sparked Skating Revival," *News Journal*, February 14, 2001, www.delawareonline.com (accessed February 14, 2003); www. worldskatingmuseum.org/Museum_HOF_inductees; *American Skating World*, October 1982.

[64] Helene Elliott, "Shock Absorber," *Los Angeles Times*, January 6, 2002, www.sunspot.net (accessed February 15, 2003); www.worldskatingmuseum .org/ Museum_HOF_inductees; Christine Brennan, *Edge of Glory*, 87-88; Paula Parrish, "Lost Generation of Athletes Lives On," *Rocky Mountain News*, March 19, 2001, Sports, C1.

[65] John Nicks, telephone interview, June 18, 2005.

[66] Ibid.

[67] Karen Howland, telephone interview, September 11, 2003.

[68] Duffy, "Twists of Fate," C15.

[69] Ibid.

[70] Durham, interview.

[71] Jerry Fotheringill, telephone interview, August 21, 2005.

[72] Ron Joseph, telephone interview, October 13, 2003.

[73] Maria Jelinek, telephone interview, October 3, 2007.

[74] Peggy Fleming, *The Long Program* (New York: Pocket Books, 1999), 33-34; Sam Singer, telephone interview, October 23, 2003; Jean Frazier Fahmie, interviewed, Dublin, CA, October 24, 2007; Barbara Roles Williams, telephone interview, September 25, 2003.

[75] Anatoli Rybakov, *Children of the Arbat*, translated by Deti Arbata (Boston: Little, Brown and Company, 1988), 267; Shumway, Memorial Service.

[76] Donald Jackson, telephone interview, October 11, 2007; 1971 Southwest Pacific program.

[77] Squibb, interview; Shumway, Memorial Service.

INDEX